Handbook of Research on Consumer Behavior Change and Data Analytics in the Socio-Digital Era

Pantea Keikhosrokiani
School of Computer Sciences, Universiti Sains Malaysia, Malaysia

A volume in the Advances in Marketing, Customer Relationship Management, and E-Services (AMCRMES) Book Series

IGI Global
PUBLISHER of TIMELY KNOWLEDGE

Published in the United States of America by
IGI Global
Business Science Reference (an imprint of IGI Global)
701 E. Chocolate Avenue
Hershey PA, USA 17033
Tel: 717-533-8845
Fax: 717-533-8661
E-mail: cust@igi-global.com
Web site: http://www.igi-global.com

Library of Congress Cataloging-in-Publication Data

Names: Keikhosrokiani, Pantea, DATE- editor.
Title: Handbook of research on consumer behavior change and data analytics in the socio-digital era / Pantea Keikhosrokiani.
Description: Hershey, PA : Business Science Reference, [2022] | Includes bibliographical references and index. | Summary: "This book focuses on concepts, theories, and analytical techniques to track consumer behavior change for the sake of better decision making among businesses, covering various techniques such as opinion mining, behavioral and social media analytics using machine learning, deep learning, ensemble learning, and emotional intelligence"-- Provided by publisher.
Identifiers: LCCN 2022001858 (print) | LCCN 2022001859 (ebook) | ISBN 9781668441688 (hardcover) | ISBN 9781668441701 (ebook)
Subjects: LCSH: Consumer behavior. | Content analysis (Communication)--Data processing. | Social media--Data processing. | Data mining.
Classification: LCC HF5415.32 .C663 2022 (print) | LCC HF5415.32 (ebook) | DDC 658.8/342--dc23/eng/20220114
LC record available at https://lccn.loc.gov/2022001858
LC ebook record available at https://lccn.loc.gov/2022001859

This book is published in the IGI Global book series Advances in Marketing, Customer Relationship Management, and E-Services (AMCRMES) (ISSN: 2327-5502; eISSN: 2327-5529)

British Cataloguing in Publication Data
A Cataloguing in Publication record for this book is available from the British Library.

All work contributed to this book is new, previously-unpublished material. The views expressed in this book are those of the authors, but not necessarily of the publisher.

For electronic access to this publication, please contact: eresources@igi-global.com.

Advances in Marketing, Customer Relationship Management, and E-Services (AMCRMES) Book Series

Eldon Y. Li
National Chengchi University, Taiwan & California Polytechnic State University, USA

ISSN:2327-5502
EISSN:2327-5529

Mission

Business processes, services, and communications are important factors in the management of good customer relationship, which is the foundation of any well organized business. Technology continues to play a vital role in the organization and automation of business processes for marketing, sales, and customer service. These features aid in the attraction of new clients and maintaining existing relationships.

The Advances in Marketing, Customer Relationship Management, and E-Services (AMCRMES) Book Series addresses success factors for customer relationship management, marketing, and electronic services and its performance outcomes. This collection of reference source covers aspects of consumer behavior and marketing business strategies aiming towards researchers, scholars, and practitioners in the fields of marketing management.

Coverage

- Customer Retention
- CRM in financial services
- Social Networking and Marketing
- Relationship Marketing
- Web Mining and Marketing
- CRM strategies
- Database marketing
- Cases on CRM Implementation
- Cases on Electronic Services
- B2B marketing

IGI Global is currently accepting manuscripts for publication within this series. To submit a proposal for a volume in this series, please contact our Acquisition Editors at Acquisitions@igi-global.com or visit: http://www.igi-global.com/publish/.

The Advances in Marketing, Customer Relationship Management, and E-Services (AMCRMES) Book Series (ISSN 2327-5502) is published by IGI Global, 701 E. Chocolate Avenue, Hershey, PA 17033-1240, USA, www.igi-global.com. This series is composed of titles available for purchase individually; each title is edited to be contextually exclusive from any other title within the series. For pricing and ordering information please visit http://www.igi-global.com/book-series/advances-marketing-customer-relationship-management/37150. Postmaster: Send all address changes to above address.

Titles in this Series

For a list of additional titles in this series, please visit: www.igi-global.com/book-series

Critical Perspectives on Diversity, Equity, and Inclusion in Marketing
Ayantunji Gbadamosi (University of East London, UK)
Business Science Reference • © 2022 • 325pp • H/C (ISBN: 9781668435908) • US $215.00

Disruptive Innovation and Emerging Technologies for Business Excellence in the Service Sector
Vipin Nadda (University of Sunderland, London, UK) Pankaj Tyagi (Chandigarh University, India) Malini Singh (Amity University, India) and Priyanka Tyagi (Chandigarh University, India)
Business Science Reference • © 2022 • 285pp • H/C (ISBN: 9781799891949) • US $225.00

Cases on Academic Program Redesign for Greater Racial and Social Justice
Ebony Cain-Sanschagrin (Pepperdine University, USA) Robert A. Filback (University of Southern California, USA) and Jenifer Crawford (University of Southern California, USA)
Information Science Reference • © 2022 • 361pp • H/C (ISBN: 9781799884637) • US $195.00

Adoption and Implementation of AI in Customer Relationship Management
Surabhi Singh (IMS Ghaziabad, India)
Business Science Reference • © 2022 • 272pp • H/C (ISBN: 9781799879596) • US $215.00

Handbook of Research on IoT, Digital Transformation, and the Future of Global Marketing
Hatem El-Gohary (College of Business and Economics, Qatar University, Qatar) David Edwards (Birmingham City University, UK) and Mohamed Slim Ben Mimoun (Qatar University, Qatar)
Business Science Reference • © 2021 • 471pp • H/C (ISBN: 9781799871927) • US $295.00

Management and Marketing for Improved Competitiveness and Performance in the Healthcare Sector
José Duarte Santos (Polytechnic Institute of Gaya, Portugal) and Inês Veiga Pereira (ISCAP, Polytechnic Institute of Porto, Portugal)
Business Science Reference • © 2021 • 355pp • H/C (ISBN: 9781799872634) • US $225.00

Advanced Digital Marketing Strategies in a Data-Driven Era
Jose Ramon Saura (Rey Juan Carlos University, Spain)
Business Science Reference • © 2021 • 342pp • H/C (ISBN: 9781799880035) • US $225.00

IGI Global
PUBLISHER of TIMELY KNOWLEDGE

701 East Chocolate Avenue, Hershey, PA 17033, USA
Tel: 717-533-8845 x100 • Fax: 717-533-8661
E-Mail: cust@igi-global.com • www.igi-global.com

List of Contributors

Table of Contents

Detailed Table of Contents

This chapter intends to probe into the predictability of consumer behavior classification (CBC) in online virtual stores under the trend of electronic commerce (e-commerce) and provide better consumer services (CS) for online shopping. First, the recurrent neural network (RNN) is expatiated and improved; thereupon, the bidirectional long short-term memory (BiLSTM) algorithm is designed and applied to the CBC; then, the support vector machine (SVM) and naive bayes classifier (NBC) are cited, and a CBC prediction model based on multi-class machine learning (ML) algorithms is implemented. Further, the proposed model is compared with other models from the perspectives of precision, accuracy, F1, and recall; the results signify that the proposed CBC prediction model has presented a 93.95% accuracy, which is at least 4.19% higher than that of other literature algorithms; besides, the performance analysis of network data transmission synchronization reveals that the proposed algorithm outperforms other algorithms with an overall transmission throughput around 1.

The goal of "serving all" is similar to "serving none." Marketers are constantly looking for ways to refine the way they segment markets. Segmentation involves diving markets into smaller portions (segments) of consumers with similar needs for a given good or service. This chapter explores the application of various algorithms and analytical techniques that are used to segment markets. These techniques include regression, cross-tabulation, hierarchical clustering, and k-means clustering performed through

study of companies using big data.

Section 2
Theories, Conceptual Frameworks, and Modelling to Predict Consumer Behavior Change in the Socio-Digital Era

The chapter builds on previous research and offers an updated theoretical model to determine the relationships among social media technologies, customer experience flow, customer relationship management, brand loyalty, word of mouth, firm performance, and customer engagement across a set of moderators in pandemic time. In line with the literature, customer engagement serves as a mediator that fully translates the effects of social media technology, customer flow experience, and customer relationship management into positive levels of brand loyalty, word of mouth, and firm performance. However, all of the relationships conceptualized in the model are hypothesized to be moderated by COVID-19 developments and perceptions.

During the COVID-19 pandemic, the electronic commerce industry hit a phenomenal change. Many retail locations had to close, and customers were forced to place orders from home. Online retailers had a challenge in the supply of products on time due to unpredictable demand. Goods sold out at an alarming rate, supply diminished, and conveyance periods diminished. Online business stores slowly began to acquire new and expanded interest from the consumers. The purpose of this chapter is to investigate the effect of e-tail factors such as quality of information on the online store, price of product/service, user-friendly website design, privacy/security control, online customer service, and post purchase delivery service on Malaysian-based consumers purchase decision. This research is based on primary samples collected from 154 Malaysian residents online. The results indicate that there is a significant effect of e-tail factors on Malaysian-based consumers' purchase behavior, which transforms web traffic into actual purchase behavior.

This study aims to ascertain the factors responsible for the behavior change of consumers in Nigeria towards the use of online shopping as impacted by the COVID-19 pandemic. For this reason, two quantitative studies were conducted to find user behavior towards using online shopping before and during the COVID-19 pandemic. Questionnaire was used as the research instrument and an online survey was conducted in which 82 respondents in Nigeria participated for both studies. Both studies develop hypotheses through the integration of technology acceptance models, unified theory of acceptance and use of technology, and theory of planned behavior. The results of the study before and during COVID-19 pandemic are compared accordingly. Based on the findings of this study, recommendations were proffered in relation to the results of the various hypothesized factors. Lastly, the study gave suggestions for subsequent research.

This chapter deals with the issue of consumer behavior change by taking the case of a digital service such as m-banking and supports the arguments with suitable data analytics. To fulfill this objective, it utilizes the two indicators of awareness and perceived value as the determinants of consumer behavior. The chapter intends to throw light on the relationship between awareness, perceived value, and usage of m-banking, and also helps to find out how the interaction of age affects this relationship. For this purpose, a sample of 524 m-banking users was utilized from the state of Punjab in India. Further, the generated data is analyzed using linear regression and moderated regression analysis. The findings reveal important implications for the banks and other researchers in terms of awareness and perceived value and also depict how the behavior of consumers can change as per their age in this socio-digital era.

For the time being, people are becoming habitual on social media and digital marketing. This has changed the behaviour of the consumer and the strategies in which companies run their business. Social-media and digital marketing offer significant opportunities to organizations through lower costs, improved brand awareness, and increased sales. This chapter tries to highlight the impact of social media and digital marketing on consumer behaviour from the collective discussion from several experts and researchers. This chapter offers a significant and timely contribution to both researchers and practitioners in the form of challenges and opportunities where the authors highlight different factors that affect the consumer behaviour as well as strategies adopted by the companies to attract the consumers.

Section 3
Case Studies and Reviews on Consumer Behavior Change in the Socio-Digital Era

Preface

The emergence of new technologies within the industrial revolution has transformed businesses to a new socio-digital era. In this new era, businesses are concerned with collecting data on customer needs, behaviors, and preferences for driving effective customer engagement and product development, as well as for crucial decision making. However, the ever-shifting behaviors of consumers provide many challenges for businesses to pinpoint the wants and needs of their audience.

Handbook of Research on Consumer Behavior Change and Data Analytics in the Socio-Digital Era focuses on the concepts, theories, and analytical techniques to track consumer behavior change. It provides multidisciplinary research and practice focusing on social and behavioral analytics to track consumer behavior shifts and improve decision making among businesses. It covers a wide range of topics such as behavioral analytics, consumer behavior change, consumer behavior prediction, consumer sentiment analysis, customer recommendation model, customer segmentation model, digital social customer relationship management, emotional intelligence, mobile banking, online purchase decision making, and panic buying.

Consumer behavior is the study of the interrelationships that exist between individual consumers, groups, or organizations as they select, acquire, use, and dispose of ideas, commodities, and services to meet their wants and requirements. A diversity of factors inspires consumer behavior and change their decision for any product (Khan et al., 2022; Taghikhah et al., 2021). In order to enhance consumer behavior change, its determinants need to be discovered instantly. This book includes theoretical and conceptual frameworks to predict the effective factors or determinants of changing consumer behavior. Figure 1 proposes a framework for the consumer behavior change and data analytics in socio-digital era. As shown in the Figure, PEPSCA includes the main important determinants of changing consumer behavior. PEPSCA stands for the factors such as (1) personal, (2) economic, (3) social, (4) psychological, (5) cultural, and (6) advertisement which change consumer behavior. The first determinant of consumer behavior change orthe first item of PEPSCA is personal factor (Gbadamosi, 2019). Personal characteristics such as age, gender, occupation, education, lifestyle, childhood experience, personality, goals, self-concept, life cycle stages, political and world views are the factors that are unique to each customer and have a significant impact on their purchasing decisions (Rehman et al., 2017). Economic factor is the second element of PEPSCA which is related to personal income, family income, liquid asset, consumer credit, future income expectations, savings, the level of standard of living, and other economic factors. The third element of PEPSCA is related to psychological factors (Keikhosrokiani et al., 2018; Keikhosrokiani et al., 2020; Keikhosrokiani et al., 2019) that include attitude, trust, perception, intention, involvement, motivation, beliefs, learning, etc. Social factors are considered as another important determinants of consumer behavior change (Li et al., 2022; P. Wang et al., 2022) or the fourth element of PEPSCA. Social factors consist of social class, social group, opinion leader, social status, and the role in society. Cultural factors are the fifth element of PEPSCA which deals with family culture, culture in the society, subculture, religion, nationality, consumer needs, and preferences (Nainggolan et al., 2022). Finally, advertisement has a significant impact on changing consumer behavior by attracting their attention, arousing their interest, and instilling a desire to purchase products (Y. Wang et al., 2022).

Figure 1. A framework for consumer behavior change and data analytics in socio-digital era

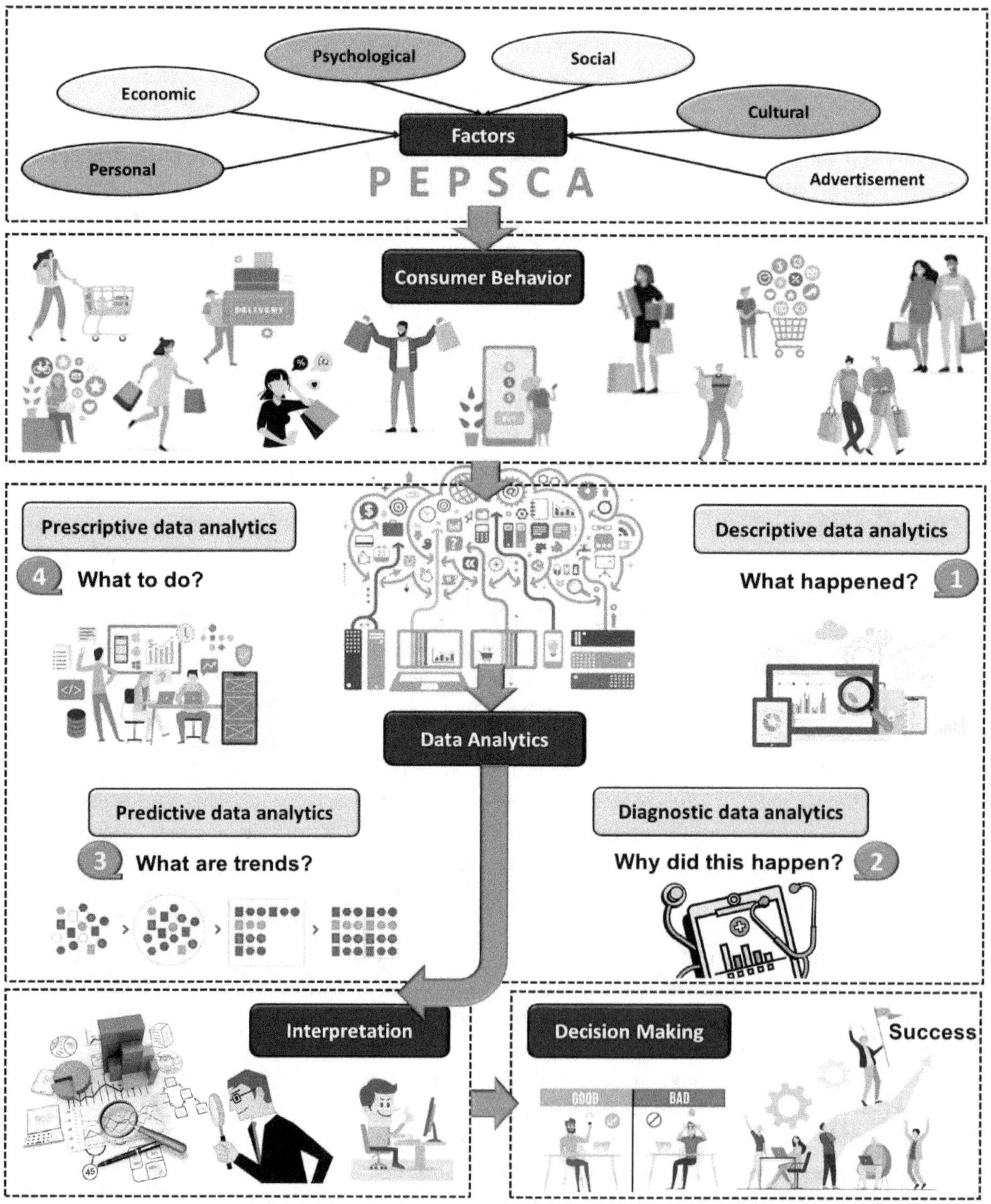

Consumer behavior is always changing, making it difficult for organizations to determine their target market's demands and requirements. Furthermore, handling big consumer data, which is coming to organizations from various sources, with diverse types, on different times is very challenging. In order to track, analyze, classify, and predict consumer behavior change for better decision making in the organizations, analytical techniques are valuable. For this reason, this book mainly focuses on various analytical methods and cases studies to shed a light on consumers' behavior change. As illustrated in Figure 1, different analytical methods are required for various purposes as follows:

1. Descriptive analytics can analyze the consumer historical data to better understand "what happened" that a consumer behavior has changed based on various determinants such as time, age, gender, culture, etc. It is the most basic type of analytics, describing or summarizing current data using existing business intelligence tools. Decision-makers gain a comprehensive perspective of performance and trends on which to build corporate strategy by utilizing a variety of historical data and benchmarking. Different classical techniques such as numerical and categorical data descriptive statistics, testing normality, assumption of homogeneity, correlations univariate and multivariate statistical inference, and bootstrapping for parameter estimates are used for descriptive analytics. Furthermore, some text mining techniques (Keikhosrokiani & Pourya Asl, 2022) such word frequency, sentiment analysis (Al Mamun et al., 2022; Fasha et al., 2022), topic modelling (Asri et al., 2022), term vs. document frequency, word relationships, etc. can be used for descriptive analysis of consumers' historical data. Finally, some unsupervised learning methods such as K-means Clustering, Hierarchical Clustering and Principal Component Analysis can be used for descriptive analytics.
2. The second analytical method which can be used for analyzing consumer behavior change is diagnostic data analytics which focuses on "why did consumer behavior changed". Businesses employ this type of analytics to gain a comprehensive understanding of a specific situation, assuming they have adequate data at their disposal. Diagnostic analytics aids in the detection of anomalies and the establishment of casual relationships in data (Abdelrahman & Keikhosrokiani, 2020; Ridzuan & Wan Zainon, 2022). Some concepts such as hypothesis testing, diagnostic regression analysis, and the difference between correlation and causation needs to be understand before we dive into diagnostic analytics. Diagnostic analytics is the key to understand why did consumers behavior change to assist the organizations that collect customer data. These findings may be utilized to enhance products and user experience (UX), reposition brand message, and assure product-audience fit. Diagnostic analytics uses a number of methodologies to give insights into the underlying causes of trends. One of the techniques for diagnostics analytics is data drilling into a dataset, which can offer more specific information about which components of the data are causing the observed trends. For example, data analysts may delve into national sales data to discover whether certain areas, consumers, or retail channels are to blame for greater sales growth. Another technique for diagnostic analytics is data mining, which is the process of searching through enormous amounts of data for patterns and correlations. For example, data mining might indicate the most prevalent causes of an increase in insurance claims. Mining data can be done manually or automatically using data mining techniques. Correlation analysis investigates how strongly distinct variables are connected to one other. On warmer days, for example, customers may buy more ice cream and chilled beverage.

3. Predictive data analytics (Taghikhah et al., 2021; Teoh Yi Zhe & Keikhosrokiani, 2021) is the third analytical method utilized for analyzing consumer behavior change which answers the question of "what are trends in consumer behavior change". Predictive methodologies employ knowledge, which is often derived from previous or historical data, to forecast the future or unknown occurrences. For instance, predictive analytics aids in identifying the most profitable segments based on previous customer behavior within each segment. This data is used by marketing managers to allocate resources to the most profitable segments. A wide range of approaches are considered in predictive analytics such as time series forecasting, linear regression, multilevel modeling, simulation methods such as discrete event simulation and agent-based modeling; classification methods such as logistic regression and decision trees; and artificial intelligence methods such as artificial neural networks and Bayesian networks. In general, machine learning, deep learning, time series, machine learning interpretation, feature engineering, and resampling methods are fallen into the category of predictive analytics.
4. The fourth methodological aspect for analyzing consumer behavior change it prescriptive analytics (Akturk et al., 2021). Prescriptive analytics tries to answer the question "what to do to create a worthy customer experience in the future". It can provide the degrees of insights related to consumer behavior change. Businesses can use the information that their clients provided, acquire insights into what it means about their future behavior, and then act to reap large profits. Prescriptive methodologies not only forecast the future, but also attempt to shape the future by optimizing the targeted business objective while balancing constraints. Analytic techniques that fall into this category include optimization techniques such as linear programming, goal programming, integer/mixed-integer programming, and search algorithms; artificial intelligence optimization techniques such as genetic algorithms and swarm algorithms; and multi-criteria decision models such as analytic hierarchy process, analytic network, process, multi-attribute utility and value theories, and value analysis. Prescriptive analytics makes a highly tailored consumer experience feasible with localized data on consumption behaviors and customer trends. It can assist marketers to identify which strategic decisions to make to yield outcomes. Finally, it can reduce the business risk and assist them to improve decision making.

After the using analytical techniques, the interpretation of the findings is necessary to be aligned with business goal and process. Interpreting the findings entails determining if what businesses discovered confirms or contradicts the conclusions of earlier research in the business goals and objectives. Interpretation assists businesses in categorizing, manipulating, and summarizing information to answer crucial issues. Interpreting the findings is about seeing whether what businesses found fulfill their needs, answer their questions, and direct them to the better decision making. The final step of the proposed framework is making decision based on the analyzed data. The business decision-making process is a step-by-step procedure that allows experts to solve problems by analyzing facts, examining options, and then choosing a course of action. This stated method also allows for a final evaluation to determine whether the choice was correct.

The present book is an interdisciplinary project that engages various disciplines such as computer sciences, data sciences, marketing, management, and business studies. Covering topics such as consumer sentiment analysis, emotional intelligence, and online purchase decision making, this premier reference source is a timely resource for students and educators of higher education, researchers, academicians, and libraries. In academia, the publication will benefit researchers, lecturers, and students by providing them with new insights into different fields such as behavioral analytics, digital marketing, digital transformation, consumer behavior change, decision making, and data science. Furthermore, the book is beneficial for business executives, entrepreneurs, data analysts, marketers, advertisers, government officials, social media professionals by offering them new techniques and methods to consumer behavior change using analytical techniques.

Although his book covers various concepts, theories, and analytical techniques to address consumer behavior change in the current world, tracking consumer behavior change in metaverse and their adoption of metaverse remains a challenge which requires to be discussed as the future direction of this book. The term "metaverse" refers to three-dimensional virtual, augmented, or mixed reality environments in which consumers may behave, explore, and interact with others differently. Although there is already a connection between digital commerce and video games, the metaverse takes shopping to the next level by offering virtual goods and services, opening new income channels for businesses, and allowing marketers to engage with new generations of customers. The advent of metaverses will have a profound influence on consumer behavior, from how individuals make decisions and create brand connections to how they experience a sense of self and well-being. Therefore, it is necessary to investigate metaverse themes such as customer behavior in virtual reality (VR), augmented reality (AR), and mixed reality (MR).

ORGANIZATION OF THE BOOK

The book is organized into three main sections and 16 chapters. A brief description of each of the chapters follows:

Section 1: Data Analytics and Consumer Behavior Change in Socio-Digital Era

Chapter 1 aims to investigate the predictability of Consumer Behavior Classification (CBC) in online virtual stores and give improved Consumer Services (CS) for online shopping. The Recurrent Neural Network (RNN) is first expanded and improved; then, the Bidirectional Long Short-Term Memory (BiLSTM) algorithm is designed and applied to the CBC; finally, the Support Vector Machine (SVM) and Naive Bayes Classifier (NBC) are mentioned, and a CBC prediction model based on multi-class Machine Learning (ML) algorithms is implemented. In addition, the suggested model is evaluated and compared with other literature algorithms in terms of Precision, Accuracy, F1, and Recall.

Chapter 2 explores the application of various algorithms and analytical techniques that are used to segment markets. Regression, cross-tabulation, hierarchical clustering, and K-Means clustering are some of the approaches used in this chapter, and they're all implemented with analytical tools such as R-Studio and MS Excel. The findings show how the statistics may help the firms to better understand their consumers and target certain customer personas with tailored campaigns and offers.

Chapter 3 aims to analyze consumer sentiment in the evolution of panic buying. For which the authors identified the trend themes and some important influencers during the contingency. The results depicts that the President of Taiwan and Australia's Prime Minister had the greatest levels of positive emotion, according to the data. During the pandemic, WHO was the most prominent account with the most unfavorable opinion. Cleaning and disinfection items are the dataset with the most favorable sentiment when it comes to trending topics. The face mask data set received the most negative sentiment and is the most polarized trending topic. The least polarized trending subject was health foods, vitamins, and food supplements.

Chapter 4 introduces a new criterion known as Aspect Relevancy in the process of ranking aspects. The study also incorporates Multi-criteria decision-making (MCDM) to recognize vital aspects retrieved from the consumers reviews of products and services. In ranking the selected aspects, the Subjective Technique for Order of Preference by Similarity to Ideal Solution (TOPSIS) is employed. The experimental results using Bing Liu and SemEval 2016 Task 5 datasets have demonstrated positive outcome of the proposed approach when compared with two baseline approaches in terms of NDCG@k ranking measure.

Chapter 5 presents the core time series and machine learning models to analyze and process consumer behavior data, in order to convert raw data into useful and informative analyses, predictions and forecasts. It accomplishes this by introducing, explaining, using, and analyzing the outcomes of ARIMA models, regression analysis, artificial neural network models, machine learning decision trees, bootstrap approaches, and many other techniques. To ensure replicability and serve as a hands-on handbook, each approach is shown using the R programming language, and the R code is supplied within the text.

Chapter 6 aims to explore the use of historical sales and behavioral data analytics to construct a recommendation model. The combination of the Recency, Frequency, and Monetary (RFM) analysis approach with the k-means clustering algorithm is offered as a process model. The Association Rule theory and the Apriori algorithm are used to complete the shopping basket analysis and propose items based on the results, while RFM analysis is used to categorize client levels within the organization. This research provided a real-world business transformation case study that can assist organizations to modify their business models accordingly and increase their revenues.

Chapter 7 is a ground-breaking and informative volume that connects new possibilities and techniques with existing academic consumer research. Furthermore, the aspects of Big Data and the framework of Consumer Data Analysis are discussed in this chapter. Finally, this chapter also includes a case study of a company that is utilizing Big Data.

Section 2: Theories, Conceptual Frameworks, and Modelling to Predict Consumer Behavior Change in Socio-Digital Era

Chapter 8 is prepared based on previous research by providing an updated theoretical model for determining the relationships between social media technologies, customer experience flow, customer relationship management, brand loyalty, word of mouth, firm performance, and customer engagement across a set of moderators in pandemic time. Customer engagement, according to the literature, functions as a mediator, completely translating the impacts of social media technology, customer flow experience, and customer relationship management into favorable levels of brand loyalty, word of mouth, and firm performance. However, all of the relationships conceptualized in the model are hypothesized to be moderated by COVID-19 developments and perceptions.

Chapter 9 aims to find the impact of e-tail factors such as Quality of information on the online store, Price of Product/Service, User-friendly Website Design, Privacy/Security control, Online Customer Service and Post Purchase Delivery Service on Malaysian-based Consumers Purchase Decision. This study is based on primary data acquired online from 154 Malaysian citizens. The findings show that e-tail characteristics have a considerable impact on Malaysian customers' buying behavior, converting online traffic into real purchase activity.

Chapter 10 intends to identify the elements that have influenced consumer behavior in Nigeria toward online buying as a result of the Covid-19 epidemic. For this reason, two quantitative studies were conducted to find user behavior towards using online shopping before and during Covid-19 pandemic. The research tool was a questionnaire, and data was collected online from 82 respondents in Nigeria for both investigations. Both research employ a combination of technological acceptance models, the unified theory of acceptance and use of technology, and theory of planned behavior to construct hypotheses. The study's findings are compared for the survey conducted before and after the Covid-19 pandemic.

Chapter 11 deals with the issue of consumer behavior change by taking the case of a digital service such as m-banking and supports the arguments with suitable data analytics. It uses the two measures of awareness and perceived value as predictors of customer behavior to achieve this goal. The purpose of this chapter is to shed light on the link between m-banking awareness, perceived value, and usage, as well as to determine how the interplay of age influences this relationship. A sample of 524 m-banking users from the Indian state of Punjab was used for this study. In addition, linear regression and moderated regression analysis are used to examine the collected data.

Chapter 12 tries to highlight on the impact of social-media and digital marketing on consumer behavior from the collective discussion from several experts and researchers. This chapter offers a significant and timely contribution to both researchers and practitioners in the form of challenges and opportunities where the different factors that affect consumer behavior as well as strategies adopted by the companies to attract the consumers are highlighted.

Section 3: Case Studies and Reviews on Consumer Behavior Change in Socio-Digital Era

Chapter 13 presents a qualitative and quantitative analysis on the comparison of social media audience, social posts and engagement over Instagram, Facebook and Twitter for the main five lingerie brands In Spain during the week prior to Valentine's Day. The results show that a direct relationship between audience growth and posting frequency could not be confirmed but both factors may affect on engagement and content. Indeed, it was demonstrated that giveaways and influencer collaborations as well as carousel and photos received better feedback on average for Instagram and Facebook and GIFs for Twitter.

Chapter 14 discusses the challenge to the higher education sector during the coronavirus pandemic. It examines higher education students' changing communication practices and shopping habits during the coronavirus pandemic. The chapter outlines research needs, emphasizing the impact on developing nations, the psychological impact of transition, and the critical role of management in the coronavirus pandemic. During the coronavirus epidemic, two case studies detail the experiences of undergraduate students of computer science in digital communication and buying behavior. A correspondence analysis was used on a small sample of undergraduate university students to uncover the most critical elements influencing their shopping decisions during the epidemic.

Chapter 15 provides an in-depth discussion of the disruptive nature of reselling technologies. The collaborative consumption movement, a popular emerging trend, encourages consumers to live in a more collective, sharing economy. In addition, the disruptive nature of the reselling technologies, particularly as they impact the fashion industry, prompting an explosion of vintage/second-hand retailing are discussed.

Chapter 16 discusses the evolution of consumer behavior from utilitarian consumption to hedonic consumption. By considering utilitarian consumption and hedonic consumption approaches, this chapter evaluates the latest point of consumer behavior in the socio-digital age that represents the 21st century.

Finally, I would like to thank the contributors and reviewers for their high-quality intellectual work to publish this book.

Pantea Keikhosrokiani
School of Computer Sciences, Universiti Sains Malaysia, Malaysia

REFERENCES

Abdelrahman, O., & Keikhosrokiani, P. (2020). Assembly Line Anomaly Detection and Root Cause Analysis Using Machine Learning. *IEEE Access: Practical Innovations, Open Solutions*, *8*, 189661–189672. doi:10.1109/ACCESS.2020.3029826

Akturk, M. S., Ketzenberg, M., & Yıldız, B. (2021). Managing consumer returns with technology-enabled countermeasures. *Omega*, *102*, 102337. doi:10.1016/j.omega.2020.102337

Al Mamun, M. H., Keikhosrokiani, P., Asl, M. P., Anuar, N. A. N., Hadi, N. H. A., & Humida, T. (2022). Sentiment Analysis of the Harry Potter Series Using a Lexicon-Based Approach. In P. Keikhosrokiani & M. Pourya Asl (Eds.), *Handbook of Research on Opinion Mining and Text Analytics on Literary Works and Social Media* (pp. 263–291). IGI Global. doi:10.4018/978-1-7998-9594-7.ch011

Asri, M. A. Z. B. M., Keikhosrokiani, P., & Asl, M. P. (2022). Opinion Mining Using Topic Modeling: A Case Study of Firoozeh Dumas's Funny in Farsi in Goodreads. Advances on Intelligent Informatics and Computing.

Fasha, E. F. B. K., Keikhosrokiani, P., & Asl, M. P. (2022). Opinion Mining Using Sentiment Analysis: A Case Study of Readers' Response on Long Litt Woon's The Way Through the Woods in Goodreads. Advances on Intelligent Informatics and Computing.

Gbadamosi, A. (2019). A Conceptual Overview of Consumer Behavior in the Contemporary Developing Nations. In A. Gbadamosi (Ed.), *Exploring the Dynamics of Consumerism in Developing Nations* (pp. 1–30). IGI Global. doi:10.4018/978-1-5225-7906-9.ch001

Keikhosrokiani, P., Mustaffa, N., & Zakaria, N. (2018). Success factors in developing iHeart as a patient-centric healthcare system: A multi-group analysis. *Telematics and Informatics*, *35*(4), 753–775. doi:10.1016/j.tele.2017.11.006

Keikhosrokiani, P., Mustaffa, N., Zakaria, N., & Abdullah, R. (2020). Assessment of a medical information system: The mediating role of use and user satisfaction on the success of human interaction with the mobile healthcare system (iHeart). *Cognition Technology and Work*, *22*(2), 281–305. doi:10.100710111-019-00565-4

Keikhosrokiani, P., Mustaffa, N., Zakaria, N., & Baharudin, A. S. (2019). User Behavioral Intention Toward Using Mobile Healthcare System. In Consumer-Driven Technologies in Healthcare: Breakthroughs in Research and Practice (pp. 429-444). IGI Global. doi:10.4018/978-1-5225-6198-9.ch022

Keikhosrokiani, P., & Pourya Asl, M. (Eds.). (2022). *Handbook of Research on Opinion Mining and Text Analytics on Literary Works and Social Media*. IGI Global. doi:10.4018/978-1-7998-9594-7

Khan, S., Tomar, S., Fatima, M., & Khan, M. Z. (2022). Impact of artificial intelligent and industry 4.0 based products on consumer behaviour characteristics: A meta-analysis-based review. *Sustainable Operations and Computers, 3*, 218-225.

Li, S., Kallas, Z., & Rahmani, D. (2022). Did the COVID-19 lockdown affect consumers' sustainable behaviour in food purchasing and consumption in China? *Food Control*, *132*, 108352. doi:10.1016/j.foodcont.2021.108352

Nainggolan, S., Kernalis, E., & Carolin, D. Z. (2022). Analysis of Factors Affecting the Behavior of Coffee Shop Consumers in Jambi City. *Randwick International of Social Science Journal*, *3*(1), 53–60. doi:10.47175/rissj.v3i1.369

Rehman, F., Bin Md Yusoff, R., Bin Mohamed Zabri, S., & Binti Ismail, F. (2017). Determinants of personal factors in influencing the buying behavior of consumers in sales promotion: A case of fashion industry. *Young Consumers*, *18*(4), 408–424. doi:10.1108/YC-06-2017-00705

Ridzuan, F., & Wan Zainon, W. M. N. (2022). Diagnostic analysis for outlier detection in big data analytics. *Procedia Computer Science*, *197*, 685–692. doi:10.1016/j.procs.2021.12.189

Taghikhah, F., Voinov, A., Shukla, N., & Filatova, T. (2021). Shifts in consumer behavior towards organic products: Theory-driven data analytics. *Journal of Retailing and Consumer Services*, *61*, 102516. doi:10.1016/j.jretconser.2021.102516

Teoh Yi Zhe, I., & Keikhosrokiani, P. (2021). Knowledge workers mental workload prediction using optimised ELANFIS. *Applied Intelligence*, *51*(4), 2406–2430. doi:10.100710489-020-01928-5

Wang, P., Fang, D., & Cao, G. (2022). How social learning affects customer behavior under the implementation of TOU in the electricity retailing market. *Energy Economics*, *106*, 105836. doi:10.1016/j.eneco.2022.105836

Wang, Y., Wang, T., Mu, W., & Sun, Y. (2022). What is the glamor of black-and-white? The effect of color design on evaluations of luxury brand ads. *Journal of Consumer Behaviour*. doi:10.1002/cb.2030

Section 1

Data Analytics and Consumer Behavior Change in the Socio-Digital Era

Chapter 1
Consumer Behavior Classification in Online Virtual Stores Using Emotional Intelligence

Zhihan Lv
Uppsala University, Sweden

Lv Haibin
Ministry of Natural Resources, North Sea Bureau, China

ABSTRACT

This chapter intends to probe into the predictability of consumer behavior classification (CBC) in online virtual stores under the trend of electronic commerce (e-commerce) and provide better consumer services (CS) for online shopping. First, the recurrent neural network (RNN) is expatiated and improved; thereupon, the bidirectional long short-term memory (BiLSTM) algorithm is designed and applied to the CBC; then, the support vector machine (SVM) and naive bayes classifier (NBC) are cited, and a CBC prediction model based on multi-class machine learning (ML) algorithms is implemented. Further, the proposed model is compared with other models from the perspectives of precision, accuracy, F1, and recall; the results signify that the proposed CBC prediction model has presented a 93.95% accuracy, which is at least 4.19% higher than that of other literature algorithms; besides, the performance analysis of network data transmission synchronization reveals that the proposed algorithm outperforms other algorithms with an overall transmission throughput around 1.

DOI: 10.4018/978-1-6684-4168-8.ch001

INTRODUCTION

The widespread adoption of Internet technology has allowed more diversified consumption choices for consumers by creating a new consumer Consumption Pattern (CP) that couples the traditional offline spending mode with online purchases. In particular, Electronic-Commerce (E-commerce) has become one of the mainstream CP. Data statistics show that as of December 2018, Chinese netizens have passed 820 million, with 70% of them having at least one-time Online Shopping Experience (OSE). Thanks to e-commerce platforms, people can easily shop over the Internet after busy work, which greatly reduces people's consumption time cost (Lombart et al., 2020; Wu et al., 2019). Meanwhile, as the Fifth Generation (5G) mobile network and the big data analysis technology continues to be extended, more targeted services can be provided through Consumer Behavior (CB) Classification (CBC) that has become the focus of scientific research and commercial applications.

With the increasing rise of e-commerce, consumer browsing history-based big data acquisition is widely used in User Behavior Analytics (UBA), Emotion Analytics (EA), Marketing Analytics (MA), and Internal Operation Management (IOM), or more specifically, consumer content recommendation, accurate advertising, and Risk Control (RC) (Dzardanova et al., 2018). Internet companies, operators, and banks have strong demand for fine operation, especially, such Internet companies as Tmall, 360buy, and TikTok depend highly on Data Analytics (DA) system support to customize user recommendations. By effectively analyzing the CB data using big data analysis technology, merchandisers can recommend targeted commodities and services to users while ensuring a high User Experience (UE) and safety in shopping, payment, and other scenes (Park et al., 2018). The effective application of big data analysis and Artificial Intelligence (AI) technologies improves the operation efficiency and service quality of e-commerce enterprises, as well as UE in commodity purchase and order payment. As one of the AI algorithms, Machine Learning (ML) has been applied in many fields, such as Data Mining (DM), Text Classification (TC), and medical diagnosis. It has become the mainstream DM and Data Classification (DC) prediction method.

When consumers browse the online goods in virtual stores on e-commerce platforms, a series of CB data is acquired, which are then stored in the background servers of the e-commerce websites. For many Internet enterprises, an effective mechanism to mine voluminous CB data can provide targeted quality services to boost their market share. For example, issuing platform or merchant coupons, building commodity personalized recommendation systems, and pushing messages according to users' browsing data and purchase behaviors are effective CB DM methods to improve UE (Chang et al., 2019; Basalamah et al., 2020). Deep Learning (DL) algorithm is designed to autonomously extract the multi-level features from the massive amounts of raw data in an unsupervised state, and it can well abstract the overall picture of a user's information and provide effective support for further accurate and rapid analysis of interests, consumption habits, and other personalized information in CB (Paolanti et al., 2019). These new CB analysis methods can provide data decision-making basis for product sales and operation of online virtual stores, improve user stickiness and transaction rate of commercial applications, but also help to optimize product design, measure and improve online UE, and improve product competitiveness, which is of great significance to Internet enterprises.

To sum up, under the vigorous development of e-commerce today, providing a better UE in the virtual Internet space is of great practical value to social and economic development. Innovatively, the CB sequence is statistically analyzed from the time dimension; by introducing and improving the Recurrent Neural Network (RNN), the Bidirectional Long Short-Term Memory (BiLSTM) algorithm is designed and applied to the CBC. At the same time, Support Vector Machine (SVM) and Naive Bayes Classifier (NBC) are introduced. Finally, a CBC prediction model based on the fusion multi-class ML algorithms is implemented, and its performance is evaluated through case analysis, providing empirical guidance for CBC intellectualization in online virtual stores.

RECENT RELATED WORK

Research Status of CBC

Consumer reviews in e-commerce systems are often deemed as a key index for UE, consumer feelings, and Purchase Intention (PI), which express their interests, emotions, and opinions on specific commodities and services. At the same time, a personalized recommendation system also greatly regulates CB. Many scholars in related fields have studied CBC. For example, Jhala et al. (2018) introduced a unique CB prediction model based on prospect theory and found that the proposed model systematically incorporated realistic CB, including irrationality, and accurately classified and predicted CB. Zhang and Zhong (2019) proposed a review analysis method for an emotional similarity mining-oriented e-commerce system to explore users' similarity and trust. Then, an entity sentiment word was proposed to extract similarity features of the mining method. The experimental results showed that emotional similarity analysis was an effective method to discover user trust and classify CB in e-commerce systems (Zhang & Zhong, 2019). Wang et al. (2020) suggested a personalized recommendation system for e-commerce products based on learning clustering representation for the voluminous user data, which could effectively classify CB and provide consumers with high-quality services. Finally, the system performance was validated (Wang et al., 2020). Wang et al. (2021) constructed a distributed power user consumption feature recognition method based on federated learning, in which three weighted average strategies were used to jointly train the Artificial Neural Networks (ANN) to connect smart meter data with consumers' social demographic characteristics.

Application and Development Trend of ML

As one of the AI algorithms, ML has seen broad applications and abundant studies. Ping et al. (2019) introduced two ML methods to evaluate Driving Behavior (DB) and Fuel Economy (FC) using Naturalistic Driving Data (NDD). The experiments proved that the proposed method could effectively identify the relationship between DB and FC from both macro and micro levels and could effectively predict vehicle DB (Ping et al., 2019). Xu et al. (2019) proposed detailed methods rooted in Remote Sensing (RS), ML, and computer vision, and combined Convolutional Neural Networks (CNN) with subtle earth observation data from scientists' expertise utilizing the existing data. Gui et al. (2019) designed a normalized model based on the Random Forest (RF) and Long Short-Term Memory (LSTM) algorithms to classify and predict Flight Delay (FD). The results implied that the proposed RF-based model could obtain higher prediction accuracy [Binary Classification (BC) is 90.2%] and overcome the overfitting (Gui et al., 2019). Lv et al. (2020) constructed a context-perceivable datastream-based cognition-oriented calculation model by optimizing the Decision Tree (DT) in ML. The results suggested that the application of the proposed model algorithm could provide more accurate and stable CBC outcomes and were of great significance for CB operational analysis and individualized Customer Service (CS) provision (Lv et al., 2020). Kanagaraj et al. (2021) established an enhanced multi-class normalized Optimal Clustering Algorithm (OCA), which was used for data object grouping and classification. The results summarized the demand for Energy Consumption (EC) in different regions of India and also proved the excellent performance of the designed model (Kanagaraj et al., 2021).

The research points out that although scholars in relevant fields have comprehensively studied CBC, there are still many defects in combining CBC ad prediction with ML algorithm. Particularly, the exploration of CBC is worthy of further discussion to improve the quality of goods in online virtual stores, make consumers enjoy higher service quality, and increase their PI. Therefore, this paper improves the ML algorithm and applies it to the CBC, which is of high value to the development of Internet enterprises in the field of e-commerce.

IMPLEMENTATION AND ANALYSIS AND PREDICTION (A&P) OF CBC MODEL BASED ON ML

Demand Analysis of CBC Prediction

With the accelerated socio-economic progression, the online virtual store consumption market has been burgeoning. Moreover, under the ongoing global COVID-19 pandemic, virtual shopping centers, such as community group purchases and online pharmacies are gradually popularizing among all age groups. Nowadays, even an administrative district as small as a village can provide enough online transaction resources and platforms (Altarteer & Charissis, 2019). Therefore, the effective classification and prediction of CB have become the pivot of many research and commercial enterprises.

The CBC is mainly driven by data. Usually, the main data factors are selected from miscellaneous data information, such as consumers, goods, and consumption behavior, and the selected user data information are trained by the ML algorithm to predict the possibility of PI on specific commodities (Alcañiz et al., 2019; Schein & Rauschnabel, 2021). The CB-based prediction method is one of the important ways to accurately recommend and improve the purchase rate in the field of e-commerce.

Generally, the A&P problem of CB can be abstracted as a BC problem. It is assumed that the data set is composed of n (x_1,y_1), (x_2,y_2), …, (x_n,y_n) samples, in which $x_i = (x_{i1}, x_{i2}, \ldots, x_{im})$ indicates the ith sample with the feature $_m$, and y_i represents the sample category label, which is either 0 or 1: 1 refers to a positive label (purchased), while 0 stands for a negative label (not purchased). Features are extracted through data learning and artificial construction methods and are used to train the model.

Meanwhile, in the online virtual store, the recommendation system learns the offline consumer-commodity interaction data set within one month, trains the proposed prediction model, and, based on the training network parameters, constructs the probability prediction algorithm. After training, the recommendation system predicts the PI probability for the subset of online commodities and recommends corresponding times to consumers according to the results. The commodity recommendation system requires high prediction accuracy and short offline training time; a protracted training time might miss the best purchasing time point of consumers; on the other hand, inappropriate timing recommendation could arouse resentment for consumers against specific products, thereby reducing the potential purchase rate of goods. Therefore, real-time CB analysis and classification are essential for building a CBC model.

Analysis of Classification Algorithm in ML

Today, with the alteration of CP from complete offline to online+offline modes, the application of AI algorithms, especially, ML is becoming more popular. Besides, consumers' online browsing behaviors are usually accompanied by a generation of huge amounts of data. Thus, well-classified CB data can ensure the preferable goods presentation to consumers with high accuracy and timeliness, thus boosting the possibility of consumer PI (Golestan et al., 2018). Therefore, it is particularly important to effectively classify the CB data in online virtual stores.

The CB data in online virtual stores and other Internet spaces are usually stored in the form of logs that include CB log, behavior event log, and commodity category log, which are then be used for CB analysis. The specific data processing flow is shown in Figure 1.

As depicted in Figure 1, the processing of user-commodity interaction data in an online virtual store mainly includes the following five links. Firstly, the interaction log is extracted from the user-commodity interaction system to prepare data related to CB A&P. Secondly, the generated data are preprocessed through data cleaning, missing values filling in, and outliers and redundancy removal, thereby ensuring data uniqueness; then, the time-division data set is generated; specifically, the missing values are filled in with the average, and the specific data preprocessing process is shown in Figure 2. Thirdly, the sample data are described in the form of charts and other forms, and Random Sampling (RS) is conducted according to the unbalanced distribution of CBC. Fourthly, feature processing and extraction are carried out; the raw data are randomly split as the test set and the training set, the shallow features are extracted manually, the feature dimensions are expanded, and then the features are normalized by the ML algorithm in AI. Fifthly, a prediction model is created and then evaluated through experimental design.

To efficiently extract the features of massive amounts of CB data, this section introduces the ML algorithm in AI. Commonly used ML algorithms vary greatly, including DT (Pizzi et al., 2019), NBC (Schnack et al., 2021), SVM (Guo et al., 2019), RF (Wedel et al., 2020), and ANN (Shabani et al., 2018) algorithms, which can independently analyze data features. Here, SVM, NBC, and ANN algorithms are integrated for CBC of Internet virtual stores to accurately predict purchase behavior and offer consumers personalized recommendations.

The standard SVM mathematical model can be solved through Convex Quadratic Programming (CQO), during which hard interval maximization learning is used to obtain the linear classification machine (Y. Wang et al., 2018). When the model is trained with inseparable non-linear data, the input space can be mapped to the feature space by the kernel function, while soft interval maximization is used to implicitly learn the linear SVM in the high-dimensional feature space. The linearly separable Optimal Classification Hyperplane (OCH) is shown in Figure 3.

In Figure 3, a separable linear sample set $T = \{(x_1,y_1),\ldots,(x_n,y_n)\}$ is given, in which (x_i,y_i) refers to sample points, $x_i \in R^n$, $y_i \in \{+1,-1\}$, $i=1,2,\ldots,n$. Circles and asteroids stand for two sets of training samples, discretely. Since infinite interfaces can be generated to correctly distinguish the two sample groups, it is necessary to find the method that can correctly classify the sample under the minimum empirical risk; meanwhile, this method can also obtain the largest interval for OCH by minimizing the real risks. The primary principle of a linearly separable SVM is to find the optimal hyperplane by maximizing the classification interval under a unique solution (C. Wang et al., 2018). In Figure 3, H is the OCH; H1 and H2 specify the planes with the sample points (support vectors) closest to the Classification Hyperplane (CH); H is parallel to both H1 and H2 who are distanced by a classification interval. The CH function of linearly separable SVM reads:

$$w \bullet x + b = 0 \tag{1}$$

In Eq. (1), w means the normal hyperplane vector, and b is the offset. The following conditions shall be met for accurate sample classification with a maximum interval:

$$y_i(w \bullet x + b) \geq 1 \tag{2}$$

Figure 1. Schematic diagram of user-commodity interaction data processing flow

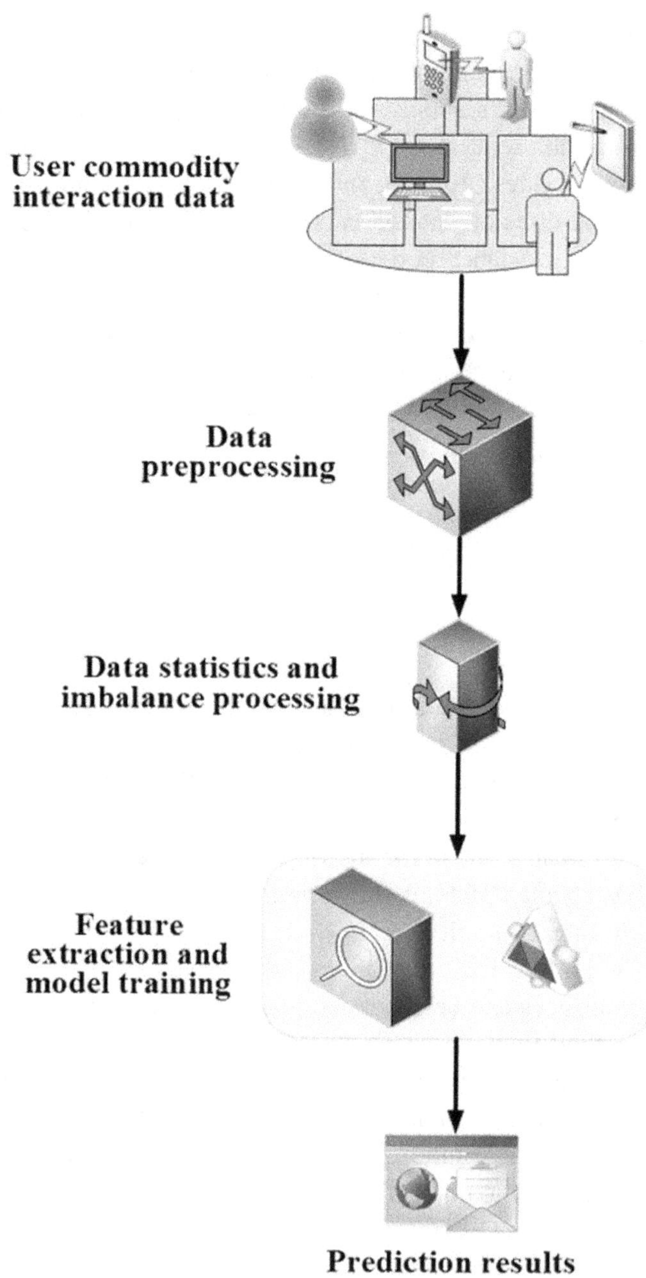

Figure 2. CB Data Preprocessing (DPP)

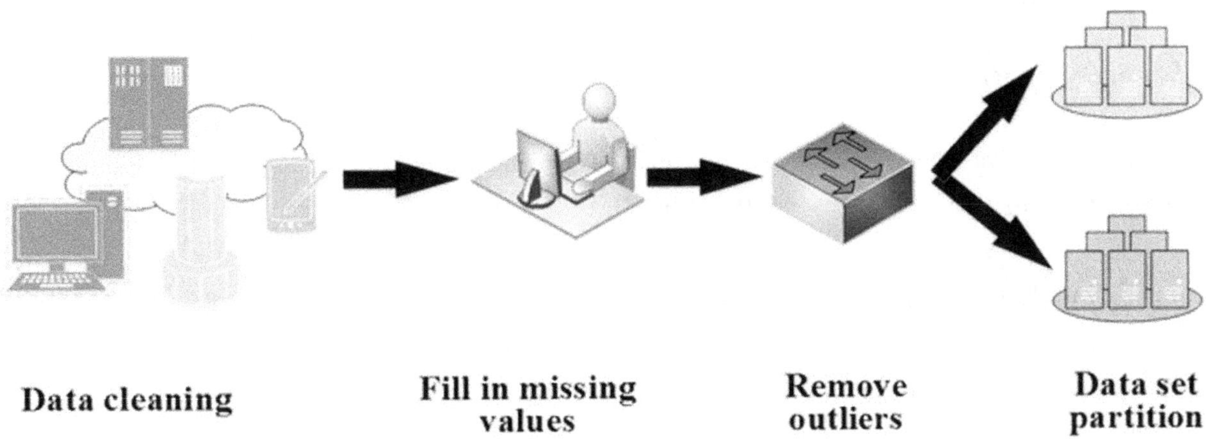

Figure 3. Hyperplane of linear separable optimal classification in SVM

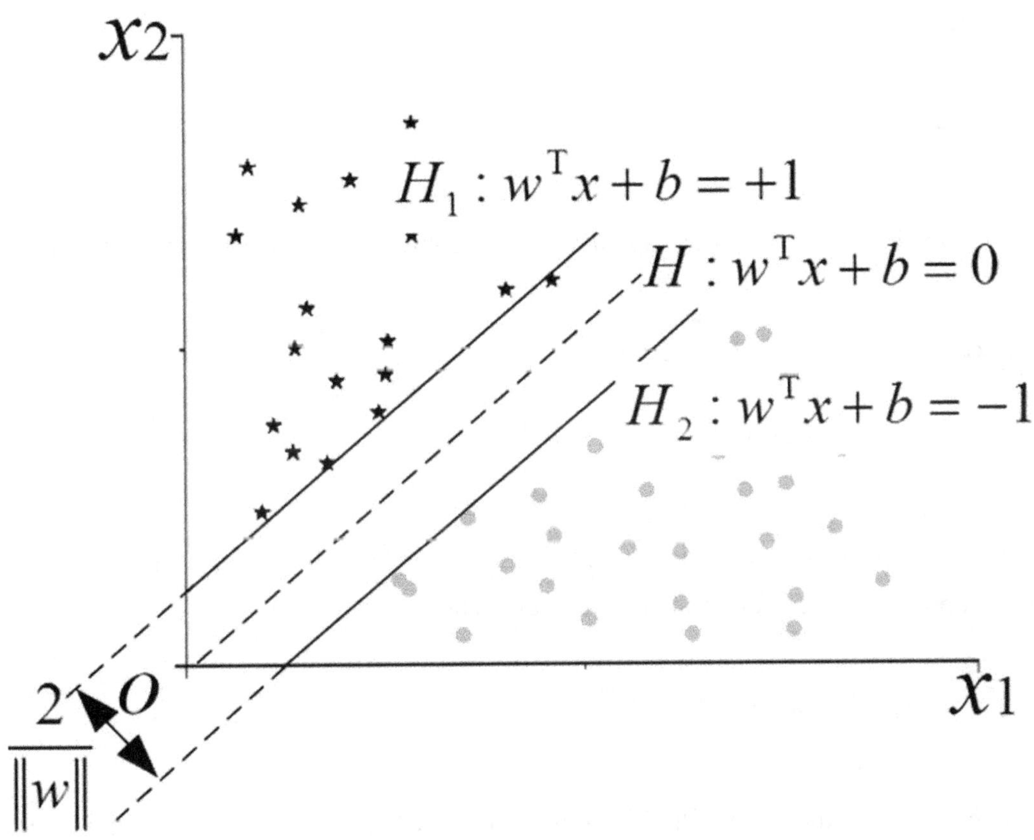

According to Eq. (2), the classification interval is 2/H. The solution of optimal hyperplane problem for training sample set T can be expressed as Eq. (3):

$$\min_{a,b} \frac{\|w\|^2}{2} \quad \text{s.t.} \quad y_i(w \cdot x + b) \geq 1, i = 1, 2, \cdots, n \tag{3}$$

Eq. (3) is equivalent to Quadratic Programming (QP) and solved by Lagrange duality optimization, and the Lagrange function is introduced as Eq. (4):

$$L(w,b,\alpha) = \frac{\|w\|^2}{2} - \sum_{i=1}^{n} \alpha_i \left[y_i(w \cdot x + b) - 1 \right] \quad \text{s.t.} \quad \alpha_i \geq 1, i = 1, 2, \cdots, n \tag{4}$$

α_i represents the Lagrange Multiplier (LM). The partial derivative of Eq. (4) is obtained according to the extreme value conditions:

$$\frac{\partial L}{\partial b} = 0 \rightarrow \sum_{i=1}^{n} y_i \alpha_i = 0 \qquad \frac{\partial L}{\partial w} = 0 \rightarrow w = \sum_{i=1}^{n} y_i \alpha_i x_i \tag{5}$$

Eq. (5) is substituted into Eq. (4) to obtain the dual problem about the original problem:

$$\min_{\alpha} \frac{1}{2} \sum_{i=1}^{n} \sum_{j=1}^{n} y_i y_j \alpha_i \alpha_j (x_i \cdot x_j) - \sum_{i=1}^{n} \alpha_i \quad \text{s.t.} \quad \sum_{i=1}^{n} y_i \alpha_i = 0, \alpha_i y_i \geq 0, i = 1, 2, \cdots, n \tag{6}$$

Then, Eq. (6) is solved to obtain the optimal solution $\alpha^* = (\alpha_1^*, \cdots, \alpha_n^*)^{\mathrm{T}}$, $w*$ and $b*$ are calculated, and then the optimal classification function is obtained as Eq. (7):

$$f(x) = \operatorname{sgn}\left[\sum_{i=1}^{n} \alpha_i^* y_i (x_i \cdot x) + b* \right] \tag{7}$$

As shown in Eq. (7), the OCH of SVM is only determined by the training sample points (x_i, y_i) with $\alpha_i^* > 0$, which are just set upon the interval boundary. Generally, the sample points $x_i \in R^n$ corresponding to $\alpha_i^* > 0$ are called support vectors. The feature extraction of CB data based on SVM is further analyzed.

Given a training set $\left\{(x_i, y_i)_{i=1}^{l}, (x_j)_{j=l+1}^{l+u}\right\}$ with both labeled and unlabeled data. $g=(V,E)$ represents a graph, where V indicates the set of nodes, and E denotes the edge set. The Weight Matrix (WM) W of graph g is symmetric, which can be expressed as Eq. (8):

$$W_{ij} = \begin{cases} w(e) = w_{ij} = 0 \quad \text{if} \quad e = (x_i, x_j) \in E \\ 0 \qquad\qquad\qquad \text{otherwise} \end{cases} \tag{8}$$

In Eq. (8), the weight $w(e)=w_{ij}=w_{ji}$ of edge $e=(x_i,x_j)$ refers to the node similarity of x_i,x_j and is solved based on the K-Nearest Neighbor (KNN) graph. Each KNN vertex only connects to its k nearest neighbors with a specific distance, such as the Euclidean distance. Noticeably, the neighboring relationship of vertexes is single-directional; thus, even if x_i is the k-nearest neighbor of x_j, x_j might not be the k-nearest neighbor of x_i; yet, given each case, the two vertexes will be connected with an edge, and the corresponding weight can be determined by the radial basis kernel function:

$$W_{ij} = \exp\left(-\frac{\left\|x_i - x_j\right\|^2}{2\sigma^2}\right) \tag{9}$$

σ the kernel parameter, which is used to control the speed of weight reduction. When, $x_i=x_j$, $w_{ij}=1$; when $\|x_i-x_j\|$ approaches infinity, $w_{ij}=0$.

NBC can calculate the problem occurrence probability under the assumption that the effects of different feature attributes from the sample on the classification results are independent of each other; it only needs a small amount of data for prediction, with a simple implementation, and fast classification, and missing value insensitivity.

Given data set D, there are K possible category labels $Y=\{C_1,C_2,\ldots,C_k\}$; X refers to the set of samples to be classified, in which there are d attributes, recorded as $X=\{x_1,x_2,\ldots,x_d\}$; The construction process is as follows:

First, the a priori probability of category C_i in the dataset is estimated:

$$P(Y = C_i) = \frac{D_{C_i}}{D} \tag{10}$$

In Eq. (10), D_{C_i} refers to the set composed of the C_i-th class sample in the data set.

Second, the Conditional Probability (CP) of the jth feature in the category C_i is estimated for the dataset. The CP of discrete data is calculated by Eq. (11):

$$P(x_j \mid C_i) = \frac{D_{C_i,x_j}}{D_{C_i}} \tag{11}$$

Continuous data are assumed to follow the normal distribution, and the calculation of CP reads:

$$P(x_j \mid C_i) = \frac{1}{\sqrt{2\pi}\sigma_{C_i,j}} \exp\left(-\frac{\left(x_j - \mu_{C_i,j}\right)^2}{2\sigma_{C_i,j}^{\ 2}} \right) \tag{12}$$

In Eq. (12), D_{C_i,x_j} refers to the set of samples whose values are x_i on the attribute j in D_{C_i}; $\mu_{C_i,j}$ and $\sigma_{C_i,j}$ respectively refers to the μ and σ^2 of the C_i-the class samples on the attribute j.

Third, according to the conditional independence assumption, Eq. (13) can be concluded:

$$P(C_i)P(x_j \mid C_i) = P(C_i)\prod_{i=1,j=1}^{k,d} P(x_j \mid C_i) \tag{13}$$

Then, Eq. (14) is deduced from the Bayesian theorem:

$$P(C_i \mid X) = \frac{P(C_i)P(X \mid C_i)}{P(X)} \tag{14}$$

The first step for CB prediction and classification is to understand the research objectives and the overall situation of CB data. Basic features of CB data include consumer Identity Document (ID), commodity category ID, commodity ID, behavior category, and timestamp of behavior occurrence. Here, the basic features of the consumer purchase probability are analyzed and predicted, and the impact is summarized for different features on CB to improve the classification accuracy.

RNN in ANN can process sequence data. Specifically, it inputs data sequence and performs recursion along the sequence evolution direction, thereby connecting all nodes (cyclic units) in a chain. The standard RNN recursive execution is expressed as in Eq. (15):

$$h_t = H\left(W\left[h_{t-1}, x_t\right] + b\right) \tag{15}$$

In Eq. (15), h_t means the generation of hidden layer output, H can be a nonlinear function, such as a simple Tanh function, or a series of complex transformations; W refers to weight. In RNN, in addition to x_t, the hidden layer input at time t also includes the output h_{t-1} of the hidden layer at the previous time. In this way, the information (h_{t-1}) of other data in front of the t-th piece of CB data in the sentence can be used to process and predict the CB.

The classification label C of CB data by RNN is as follows:

$$C = \begin{cases} Y_0 = 0, & \text{Consumers will not buy} \\ Y_1 = 1, & \text{Consumers will buy} \end{cases} \tag{16}$$

First, after the sequence is divided into levels according to the number of different behaviors, the behavior sequence of a level is *X*, as shown in Eq. (17):

$$X = \begin{bmatrix} x_{11} & x_{12} & \cdots & x_{1n} \\ x_{21} & x_{22} & \cdots & x_{2n} \\ \vdots & \vdots & \ddots & \vdots \\ x_{m1} & x_{m2} & \cdots & x_{mn} \end{bmatrix} \tag{17}$$

In Eq. (17), *n* refers to the CB sequence length, the time range is between 0 and 24 hours, and integers are chosen to represent behaviors. Every behavior is filled to the point in time, and other hour points are set to 0; then, the sequence length is 24×1. *m* refers to the total input behavior records. The hidden layer is initialized at time t_1, namely, $h^{(0)}=0$. The input, hidden, and output layers' parameters *U, W,* and *V* are randomly initialized, and Eq. (18) is used for calculation:

$$h^{(t)} = f(Ux_t + Wh_{t-1} + b) \tag{18}$$

In Eq. (18), *f*() refers to the Activation Function (AF) of RNN. Here, the Tanh function can introduce nonlinear factors into neurons. *b* denotes the bias of the model linear relationship, and the bias is initialized as 1. Only the output of the last behavior is transformed to obtain a separate output. Afterward, the SoftMax function is used to obtain the Score to classify CB:

$$Score = Soft\max(Wh_t + c) \tag{19}$$

In Eq. (19), *c* is the value calculated from the state of the last hidden layer. $L^{(t+1)}$ refers to the ultimate RNN loss and can measure the gap of output $O^{(t+1)}$ and training results $Y^{(t+1)}$ and evaluate the model predictability. The cross-entropy function is selected for RNN loss calculation, as shown in Eq. (2):

$$L_t = -\hat{y}_t^T \log(y_t) \tag{20}$$

In Eq. (20), y_t stands for the true result of the sequence, and $\hat{y}_t$ indicates the model prediction output result.

Still, the standard RNN also has two deficiencies in CB prediction. Firstly, under a lengthy gradient transmission, the long-distance dependence will be difficult to capture in the sequence; secondly, gradient disappearance or gradient explosion will be caused given long-sequence data. There is a widely used improved version of standard RNN, namely, the LSTM (Aldayel et al., 2020), but both the standard RNN and LSTM can only extract the historical information from the CB data sequence, while they cannot acquire the future information which is a must in the complex CB for correct sequence labeling. Accordingly, the periodicity of historical sequence data of CB is analyzed from two dimensions: forward and backward, and, thus, the Bidirectional LSTM (BiLSTM) is introduced. Figure 4 illustrates the framework of the BiLSTM algorithm applied to the classification and prediction of CB.

Figure 4. The framework of the BiLSTM algorithm applied to CBC and prediction

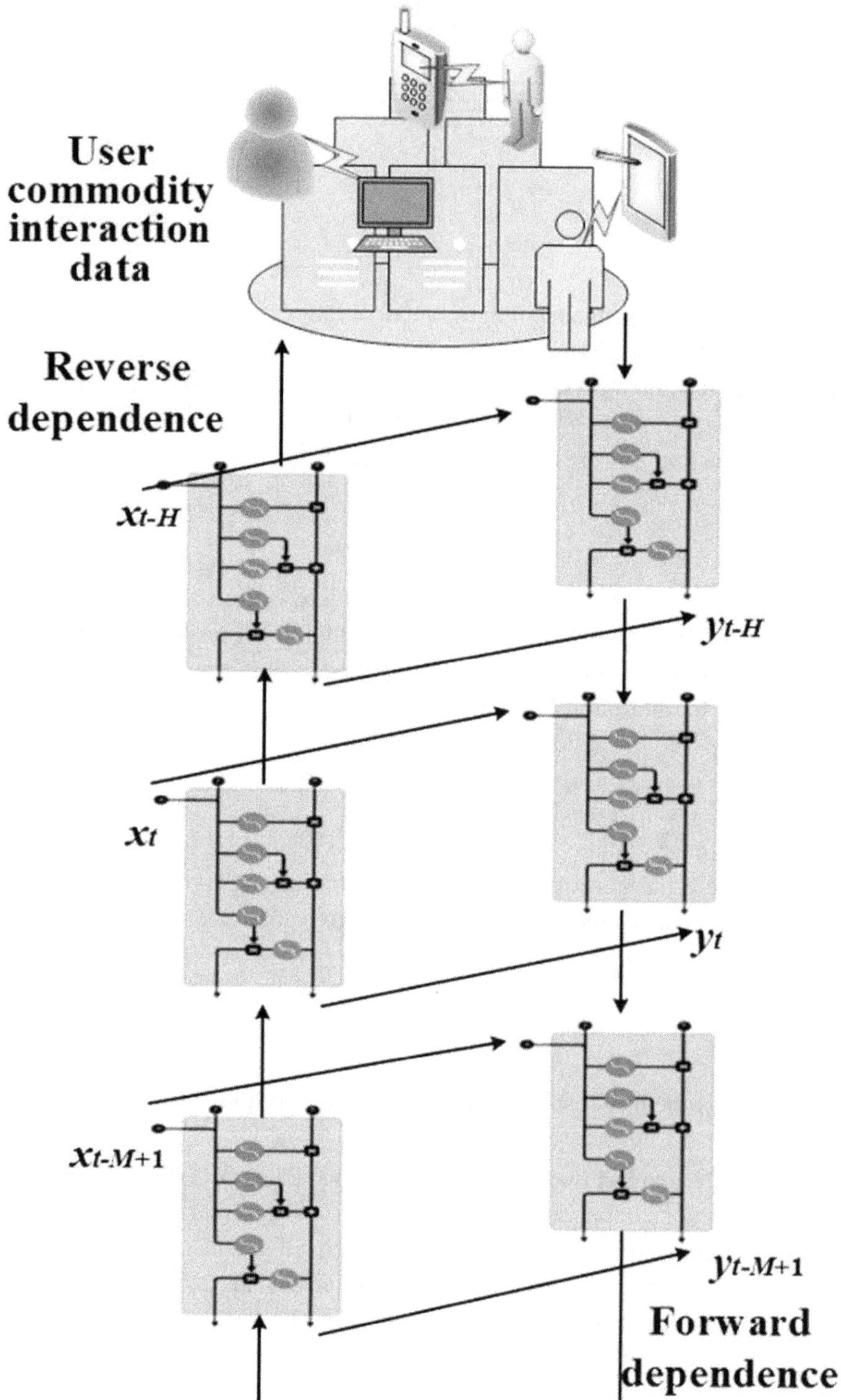

As shown in Figure 4, BiLSTM employs two LSTMs in the hidden layer to model the sequence from front to back (forward) and from back to front (backward), respectively, and then connect their outputs. The RNN calculation reads:

$$h_t^l = H\left(W^l \cdot \left[h_{t-1}^l, x_t\right] + b^l\right) \tag{21}$$

The RNN backward calculation reads:

$$h_t^r = H\left(W^r \cdot \left[h_{t-1}^r, x_t\right] + b^r\right) h_t = \left[h_t^l : h_t^r\right] \tag{22}$$

The $h_t = \left[h_t^l : h_t^r\right]$ of time t means the splice of two vectors the h_t^l and h_t^r. BiLSTM replaces the cycle unit in BiRNN with LSTM structure so that the advantages of BiRNN and LSTM can be integrated to classify and identify CB identification and classification.

Construction and Analysis of ML-Based CBC Prediction Model

In the online virtual store, in terms of consumers' interest in commodities, CB can be sorted in the order of clicking, appreciating, adding to the shopping cart, and buying, and the operational sequence and opportunities on consumer goods also affect the purchase decision. In many cases, when consumers peruse several pieces of product information within the same category, the previous browsing behavior is believed to have an impact on the following CB. This section statistically researches the CB data sequences under the time dimensional perspective and takes consumer ID, commodity category ID, and commodity ID as keywords to count CB into behavior sequence based on time sequence; the improved RNN, namely BiLSTM algorithm, is applied to the CBC; meanwhile, the SVM and NBC are cited; then, a CBC prediction model based on the combination of multi-class ML algorithms is implemented. The specific framework of the proposed model is shown in Figure 5.

Specifically, the proposed CBC prediction model ignores the interspersed selection behavior of consumers between different commodities and takes only the time point of the first-time behavior on a commodity as the starting point; then, the operation behaviors of the commodity are counted, and the behavior time attribute is changed to the 24-hour system.

Then, three ML methods are applied to analyze the CB sequence and other features. Firstly, the CB time sequence is analyzed by the proposed BiLSTM algorithm; each input record in the dataset is an n+1 array; the output is the PI probability, which is in the [-1,1] range. Secondly, the obtained PI probability is supplemented into other feature sets to input into the fusion model of NBC and SVM; afterward, the final PI probability is gained through fusion model training, which is used as the final judgment results, expressed by 0 and 1.

The data set in the NBC +SVM combination model has two possible classification labels, $Y=\{C_1,C_2\}$, which are several different CB, including whether they will buy or not. X represents the sample set. The preliminary classification score of the BiLSTM model is taken as one attribute feature of the sample set to be classified. There are d+1 attributes altogether. The (d+1)-th attribute expresses the BiLSTM classification result, that is $x_{d+1}=y_l$. The model input data set is labeled as X, as shown in Eq. (23):

Figure 5. The framework of CBC prediction model based on multi-class ML algorithm

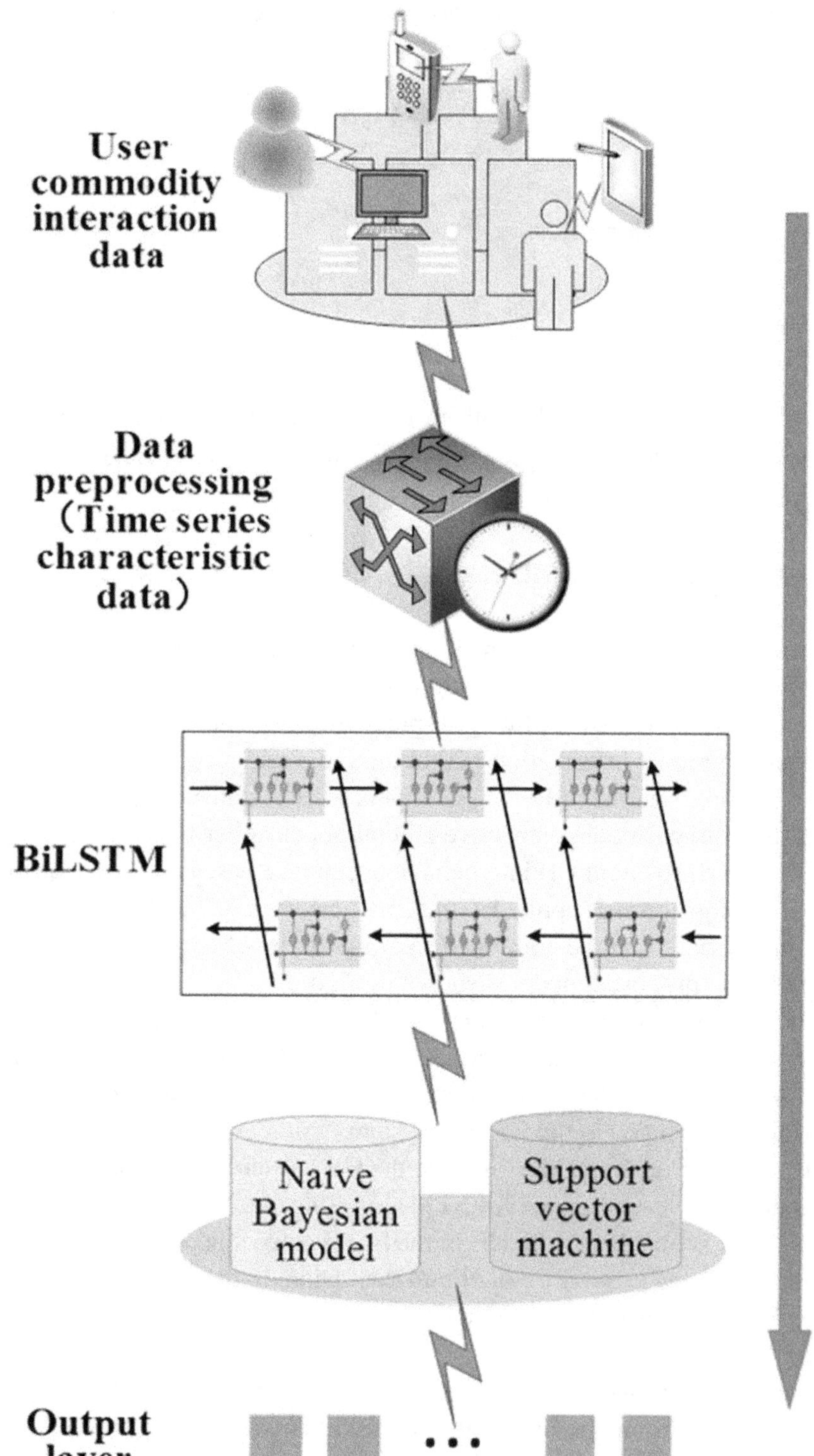

$$X = \begin{bmatrix} x_{11} & x_{12} & \cdots & x_{1d} & y_1 \\ x_{21} & x_{22} & \cdots & x_{2d} & y_2 \\ \vdots & \vdots & \ddots & \vdots & \vdots \\ x_{m1} & x_{m2} & \cdots & x_{md} & y_m \end{bmatrix} \tag{23}$$

Firstly, the a priori probability estimation for category C reads:

$$P(Y = C_i) = \frac{D_{C_i}}{D}(i = 1,\cdots,k) \tag{24}$$

In Eq. (24), D_{C_i} refers to the subset of samples belonging to category C in dataset D.

Secondly, the CP of the jth feature in the category C_i is estimated for dataset D. The CP is calculated by Eq. (25):

$$P(x_j \mid C_i) = \frac{D_{C_i,x_j}}{D_{C_i}}(i = 1,\cdots,k, j = 1,\cdots,d+1) \tag{25}$$

Thirdly, according to the conditional independence assumption, Eq. (26) can be obtained:

$$P(C_i)P(x_j \mid C_i) = P(C_i)\prod_{i=1,j=1}^{k,d} P(x_j \mid C_i), \quad i = 1,\cdots,k, j = 1,\cdots,d+1 \tag{26}$$

Fourthly, finally, the classifier equation combining NBC and SVM is deduced as follows:

$$h_{kd} = \arg\max_{C_i \in Y} P(C_i \mid X) = \arg\max_{C_i \in Y} P(C_i)\prod_{i=1,j=1}^{k,d} P(x_j \mid C_i) \tag{27}$$

After the classification by the above algorithms, the output is the classification label corresponding to the maximum probability, that is, the output result of the proposed model is 0 or 1. An output result 0 means that consumers will not purchase the commodity next; an output result 1 suggests that a purchasing CB will occur next. At the end of the training, each record shall be kept, and the probability with the training result 1 shall be used to visualize the model performance test in the next stage.

The training is optimized through the Weighted Cross-Entropy (WCE)-based cost function. $z_n(x,\theta)$ refers to the unnormalized logarithm probability of the nth category of CB data under a given network parameter θ; then the SoftMax function is defined as Eq. (28):

$$p_k(x,\theta) = \frac{\exp\{z_k(x,\theta)\}}{\sum_{n'}^{N} \exp\{z_{k'}(x,\theta)\}} \tag{28}$$

In Eq. (28), N denotes the total CB categories. During the test phase, the maximum of Eq. (28) is labeled as the nth category, namely, $n^*=\arg\max\{P_n(x,\theta)\}$. Generally, it is necessary to sum the CB data loss in each input mini-batch, $p_n(x_i,\theta)$ symbolizes the prediction probability of the nth CB category, namely, the probability after logarithmic normalization, which is abbreviated as p_{in}. Therefore, the model training attempts to decide the optimal network parameter θ^* by diminishing the WCE-based loss function $\ell(x,\theta)$, which can be expressed as Eq. (29):

$$\theta^* = \min_{\theta} \ell(x,\theta) \tag{29}$$

The specific step flow of ANN in the CBC prediction model is shown in Figure 6.

Figure 6. Algorithm flowchart of CBC prediction model based on multi-class ML algorithm

start
Input: training set $\{(x_1,y_1),(x_2,y_2),\ldots,(x_n,y_n)\}$, the maximum number of iterations n, initial learning rate η, number of neurons in the hidden layer and output layer m_1,m_2 respectively
Output: CBC prediction model
For i=1 **to** n
Calculate the residual δ^L between the predicted value and the real value
$$\delta^L \leftarrow \frac{\partial}{\partial Z^L_{z_i}}\frac{1}{2}\left|y-h(x)\right| = -\left(y_i - a_i^L\right) f'\left(z_i^L\right)$$
Calculate the hidden layer residual δ^l
$$\delta^l \leftarrow \left(\left(w^{(l)}\right)^T \delta^{(l+1)}\right)\cdot f'\left(z^{(l)}\right)$$
Calculate the partial derivative and update △ W ', 4b
$$\nabla_{w^{(l)}} J(w,b) \leftarrow a^{(l)}\delta^{(l+1)}$$
$$\nabla_{b^{(l)}} J(w,b) \leftarrow \delta^{(l+1)}$$
The weight parameters m and N are updated by the gradient descent method
$$w^l \leftarrow w^l - \eta \nabla_{w^{(l)}} J(w,b)$$
$$b^l \leftarrow b^l - \eta \nabla_{b^{(l)}} J(w,b)$$
Adjust learning rate η
$$init\_lr \times \left(1 - \frac{epoch}{\max\_epoch}\right)^{power}$$
end for
end

Case Analysis

This section verifies the performance of the proposed CBC prediction model based on the combined multi-class ML algorithms; the simulation generation of the model is empirically studied by MATLAB. The experimental data set is chosen from the desensitized Taobao CB data officially provided by Alibaba cloud Tianchi, including data of Taobao from January 17, 2020, to February 17, 2020; the raw data set includes 987,857 consumers, 4,163,789 commodities, 9,439 commodity categories, and over 100 million behaviors. Firstly, after statistics and visual analysis, the raw data are preprocessed to remove the duplicated and default values. Then, the behavior sequence of each consumer is counted for a specific commodity. Finally, the data are subgrouped with an 8:2 (training/test set) ratio.

The case analysis compares the proposed combination classification method based on the multi-class ML algorithm and the single model algorithm from the latest literature, including LSTM (Yolcu et al., 2020), CNN (Aslam et al., 2020), RNN (Argyris et al., 2020), SVM (Yang et al., 2020), and NBC (Côté-Allard et al., 2019). The comparative analysis is conducted from the perspectives of Packet Loss Rate (PLR), access collision rate, access time, transmission throughput, and reception throughput, respectively. Firstly, the following hyperparameters of the proposed model algorithm should be set: the number of iterations is 60, and the batch size is 128. Then, the prediction accuracy of the proposed method is comparatively analyzed. The simulation experimental hardware and software environments are as follows. Software environment: the Linux 64bit Operating System (OS), Python 3.6.1, and Pycharm developmental platform; hardware: Intel Core i7- 7700@4. 2GHz 8-Core CPU, Kingston DDR4 2400MHZ 16G Memory, NVIDIA GeForce GPU 1060 8G.

RESULTS AND DISCUSSIONS

Comparative Analysis of Classification and Prediction of Each Model Algorithm

This section validates the prediction performance of the proposed CBC prediction model based on the combination of multi-class ML algorithms through comparative analysis with LSTM, CNN, RNN, SVM, and NBC from Accuracy, Precision, Recall, F1 value, and AUC, respectively, as evinced in Figs. 7 and 8, while the training duration is shown in Figure 9.

Figure 7 compares the proposed system model with other state-of-art algorithms in terms of Accuracy, Precision, Recall, and F1 value reflects that the recognition accuracy of the proposed model comes to 93.95%, which is at least 4.19% higher than those of other model algorithms; more in-depth analysis indicates that the Precision, Recall, and F1 value of the proposed model algorithm are 90.31%, 81.52%, and 77.27% respectively, which are at least 3.26% higher than those of other algorithms. Thus, compared with the latest model algorithms in related fields, the proposed multi-class ML algorithm-based CBC prediction model has better accuracy.

Figure 8 outlines the AUC of different algorithms in the training set and test set, separately; the comparative analysis of other literature algorithms and the proposed model has proved that the AUC of the proposed model reaches 96.51% and 90.44% in the training set and test set, respectively, which outperforms the remaining algorithms by at least 2.56% in terms of accuracy. Clearly, the proposed algorithm based on BiLSTM, NBC, and SVM algorithm outperforms any single model algorithm. Hence, the proposed algorithm solves the degradation problem of deep-layered ANN and ensures the parameter training and updating for the deep ANN.

Figure 9 depicts the training duration of each algorithm. Apparently, with the increase of iterations, the training and test duration first decrease and then stabilize (convergence). The proposed model algorithm stabilize at 53.98s and 19.09s during training and test, respectively; that is, the prediction time of the proposed model algorithm has been significantly reduced over other algorithms. Probably, it is because the proposed fusion algorithm of BiLSTM with NBC and SVM proposed accelerates the model convergence and training process. Therefore, the proposed fusion algorithm in the CBC prediction model can achieve a higher prediction effect in a shorter time.

Figure 7. Influence curve of behavior sequence length on recognition accuracy under different algorithms (a. Accuracy; b. Precision; c. Recall; d. F1 value)

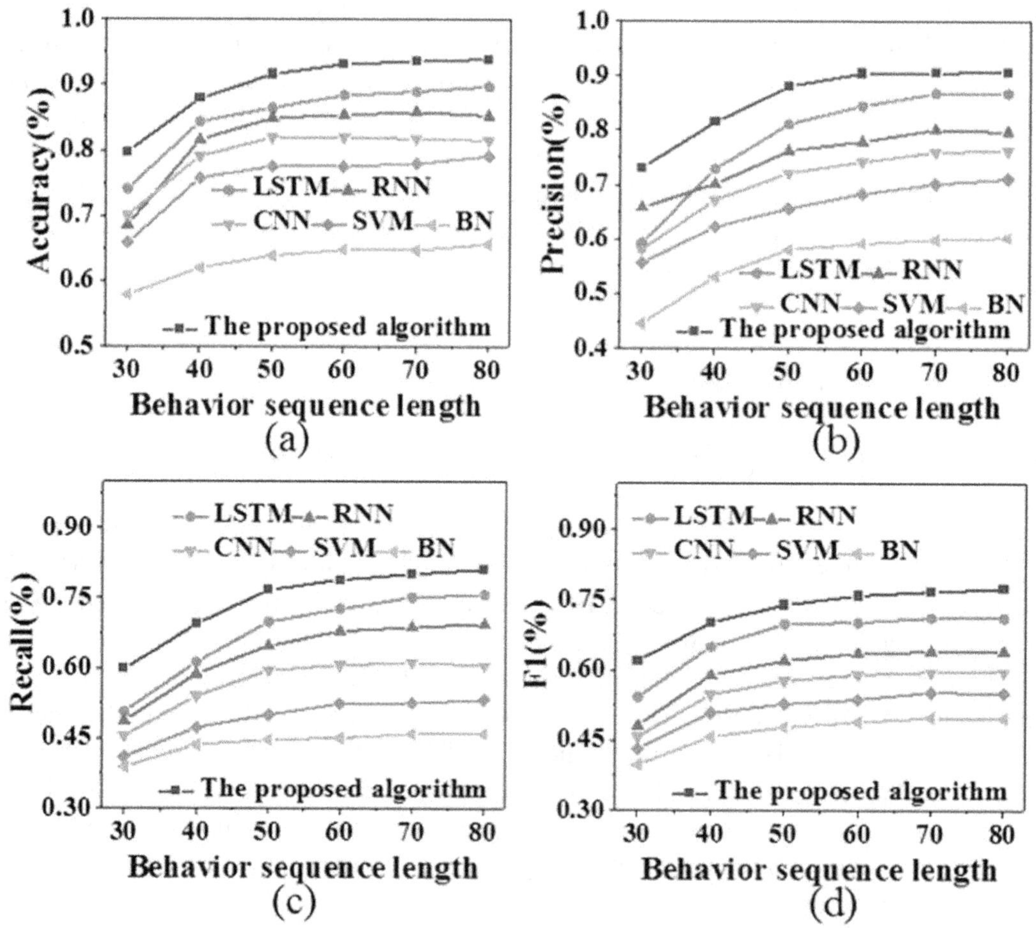

Figure 8. Variation of AUC under different algorithms with the increase of behavior sequence length (a. Training set; b. Test set)

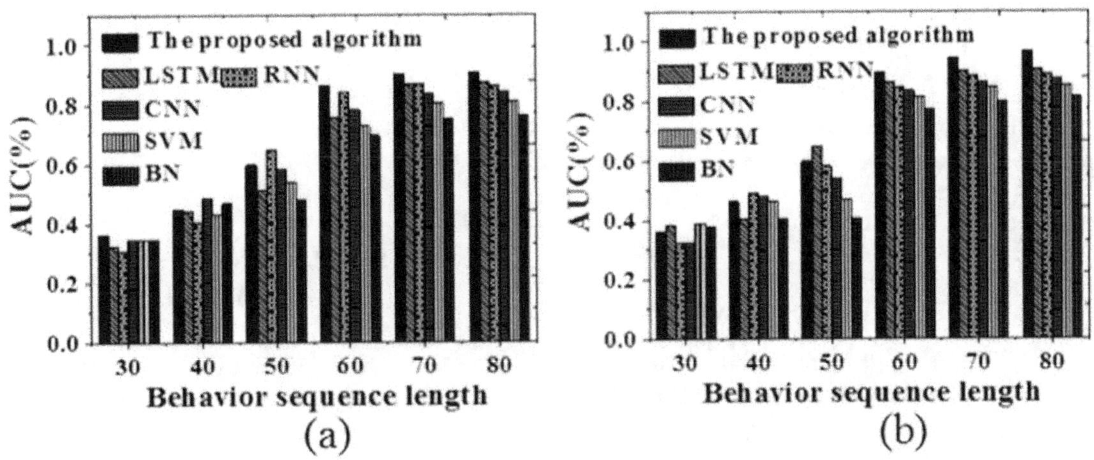

Figure 9. Comparison curve of time required for CBC and recognition under different algorithms with the increase of iterations (a. Training duration; b. Test duration)

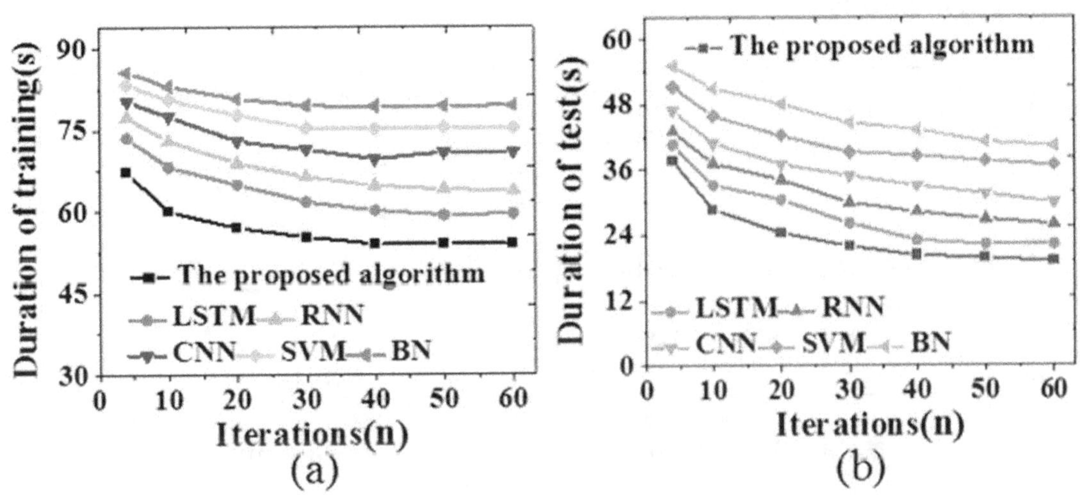

Data Transmission Synchronization Performance Under Different Model Algorithms

This section evaluates the performance of the proposed multi-class ML algorithm-based CB prediction model through comparative analysis with LSTM, CNN, RNN, SVM, and NBC from the perspectives of transmission throughput, reception throughput, and data transmission synchronization performance. The results are shown in Figs. 10 and 11.

Figure 10. Throughput curve with the increase of behavior sequence length under different algorithms (a. Reception throughput; b. Transmission throughput)

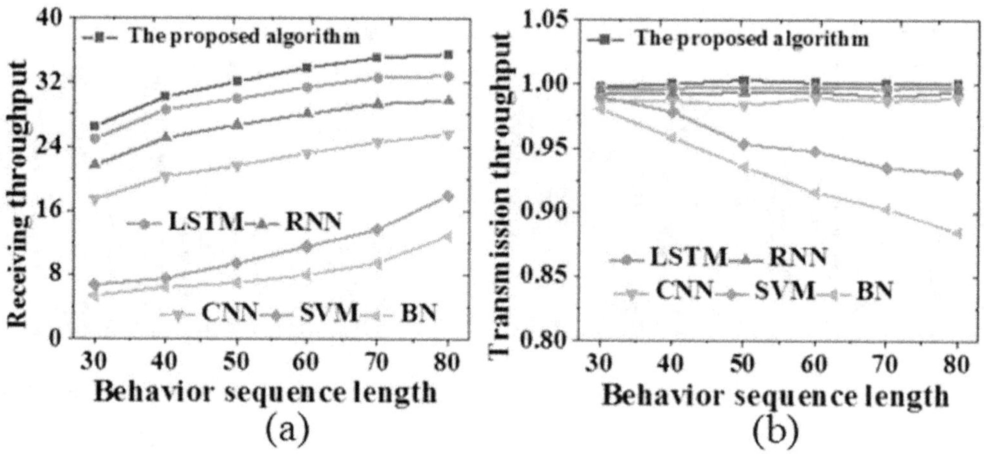

Figure 11. Comparison and analysis of transmission performance of each algorithm under different data amounts (a. Data average delivery rate (ADR), b. Data average leakage rate (ALR), c. Data average delay (AD), and d. Data PLR)

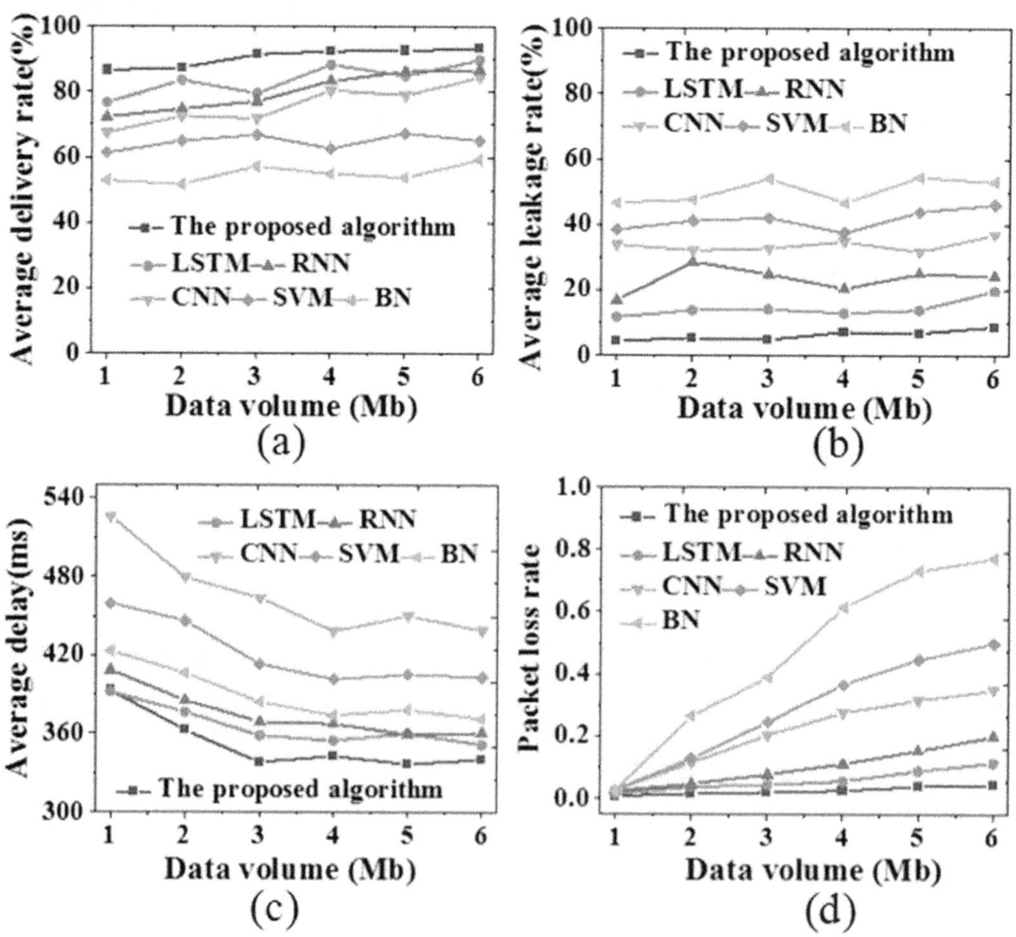

Figure 10 implies that the throughput increases with the behavior sequence length under different algorithms. Figure 10a signifies the reception throughput, of which the proposed fusion algorithm is the highest, followed by the single BiLSTM, and NBC is the lowest. Reception throughput refers to the number of packets received from its neighbors, and if it is higher, the model can obtain more neighborhood information, thereby meeting the requirements of CBC prediction. By comparison, transmission throughput indicates how many packets can be sent; given security requirements, the transmission throughput should be about one Packet Per Frame (PPF) to ensure that the location and speed of each type of CB can be broadcasted. The results show that, except SVM and NBC algorithms, other algorithms have almost the same transmission throughput (reaching approximately 1), and that of the proposed algorithm is closest to 1 (Figure 10b). Therefore, compared with other algorithms, the fusion algorithm in the proposed CBC prediction model can adaptively change the communication range, lead to less interference, and increase the network throughput.

Lastly, the network data transmission performance is studied for each algorithm, the results show that when the transmitted data amounts rise continuously, the ADR of network data presents an upward trend, and the data Delivery Rate (DR) of the proposed model is no less than 80% (Figure 11a); the data ALR has shown no obvious change, and the data Leakage Rate (LR) of the proposed model does not exceed 10% (Figure 11b); in terms of AD, the AD decreases as the amount of transmitted data grow, and the AD of the proposed model finally stabilizes at about 350ms (Figure 11c); in terms of PLR, ResNet algorithm has a high PLR, which may attribute to Packet Loss (PL) and hidden terminal. The proposed model shows the smallest PLR, below10%; this is probably because of the data equalization processing (Figure 11d). Therefore, from the perspective of different transmission data volume, the proposed model of CBC prediction based on a multi-class ML algorithm have presented a significantly higher ADR and the lowest ALR; meanwhile, it has a low delay and good network security transmission performance.

CONCLUSION

Today, with the vigorous expansion of the Internet and information technology, the market share of e-commerce is hiking. The CBC prediction shows great application potential for online virtual stores to provide better services. This paper introduces the multi-class ML algorithms into the CBC for online stores and implements a CBC prediction model based on the fusion multi-class ML algorithms. Case analysis reveals that the accuracy of the proposed CBC prediction is 93.95%; the network data transmission performance is excellent, which supplies an empirical basis for the CB digital and intelligent analysis in the field of e-commerce. However, there are also some deficiencies. First, the follow-up study will attempt to integrate consumers' interspersed behavior between different categories of goods to form a multi-dimensional behavioral time sequence to predict consumer PI and study the tentacle of the subtle association of different goods on CB; second, there is a need to further improve the information dimension of consumers and commodity categories, combine the two types of data to analyze CB sequences, and explore the behavior sequence law of different consumers in different commodity categories; this is of substantial meaning to the intelligent classification of virtual goods in online stores and the provision of high-quality services in the future e-commerce system.

REFERENCES

Alcañiz, M., Bigné, E., & Guixeres, J. (2019). Virtual reality in marketing: A Framework, review, and research agenda. *Frontiers in Psychology*, *10*, 1530. doi:10.3389/fpsyg.2019.01530 PMID:31333548

Aldayel, M., Ykhlef, M., & Al-Nafjan, A. (2020). Deep learning for EEG-based preference classification in neuromarketing. *Applied Sciences (Basel, Switzerland)*, *10*(4), 1525. doi:10.3390/app10041525

Altarteer, S., & Charissis, V. (2019). Technology acceptance model for 3D virtual reality system in luxury brands online stores. *IEEE Access: Practical Innovations, Open Solutions*, *7*, 64053–64062. doi:10.1109/ACCESS.2019.2916353

Argyris, Y. A., Wang, Z., Kim, Y., & Yin, Z. (2020). The effects of visual congruence on increasing consumers' brand engagement: An empirical investigation of influencer marketing on Instagram using deep-learning algorithms for automatic image classification. *Computers in Human Behavior*, *112*, 106443. doi:10.1016/j.chb.2020.106443

Aslam, Z., Javaid, N., Ahmad, A., Ahmed, A., & Gulfam, S. M. (2020). A combined deep learning and ensemble learning methodology to avoid electricity theft in smart grids. *Energies*, *13*(21), 5599. doi:10.3390/en13215599

Basalamah, J., Syahnur, M. H., Ashoer, M., & Bahari, A. F. (2020). Consumer behavior in online transportation services: A systematic review of business strategies. *Ilomata International Journal of Management*, *1*(3), 134–144. doi:10.52728/ijjm.v1i3.135

Chang, C. W., Yeh, S. C., Li, M., & Yao, E. (2019). The introduction of a novel virtual reality training system for gynecology learning and its user experience research. *IEEE Access: Practical Innovations, Open Solutions*, *7*, 43637–43653. doi:10.1109/ACCESS.2019.2905143

Côté-Allard, U., Fall, C. L., Drouin, A., Campeau-Lecours, A., Gosselin, C., Glette, K., Laviolette, F., & Gosselin, B. (2019). Deep learning for electromyographic hand gesture signal classification using transfer learning. *IEEE Transactions on Neural Systems and Rehabilitation Engineering*, *27*(4), 760–771. doi:10.1109/TNSRE.2019.2896269 PMID:30714928

Dzardanova, E., Kasapakis, V., & Gavalas, D. (2018). On the effect of social context in virtual reality: An examination of the determinants of human behavior in shared immersive virtual environments. *IEEE Consumer Electronics Magazine*, *7*(4), 44–52. doi:10.1109/MCE.2018.2816204

Golestan, S., Mahmoudi-Nejad, A., & Moradi, H. (2018). A framework for easier designs: Augmented intelligence in serious games for Cognitive Development. *IEEE Consumer Electronics Magazine*, *8*(1), 19–24. doi:10.1109/MCE.2018.2867970

Gui, G., Liu, F., Sun, J., Yang, J., Zhou, Z., & Zhao, D. (2019). Flight delay prediction based on aviation big data and machine learning. *IEEE Transactions on Vehicular Technology*, *69*(1), 140–150. doi:10.1109/TVT.2019.2954094

Guo, B., Liu, Y., Ouyang, Y., Zheng, V. W., Zhang, D., & Yu, Z. (2019). Harnessing the power of the general public for crowdsourced business intelligence: A survey. *IEEE Access: Practical Innovations, Open Solutions*, *7*, 26606–26630. doi:10.1109/ACCESS.2019.2901027

Jhala, K., Natarajan, B., & Pahwa, A. (2018). Prospect theory-based active consumer behavior under variable electricity pricing. *IEEE Transactions on Smart Grid*, *10*(3), 2809–2819. doi:10.1109/TSG.2018.2810819

Kanagaraj, R., Rajkumar, N., & Srinivasan, K. (2021). Multiclass normalized clustering and classification model for electricity consumption data analysis in machine learning techniques. *Journal of Ambient Intelligence and Humanized Computing*, *12*(5), 5093–5103. doi:10.100712652-020-01960-w

Lombart, C., Millan, E., Normand, J.-M., Verhulst, A., Labbé-Pinlon, B., & Moreau, G. (2020). Effects of physical, non-immersive virtual, and immersive virtual store environments on consumers' perceptions and purchase behavior. *Computers in Human Behavior*, *110*, 106374. doi:10.1016/j.chb.2020.106374

Lv, Z., Qiao, L., & Singh, A. K. (2020). Advanced machine learning on cognitive computing for human behavior analysis. *IEEE Transactions on Computational Social Systems*, *8*(5), 1194–1202. doi:10.1109/TCSS.2020.3011158

Paolanti, M., Romeo, L., Martini, M., Mancini, A., Frontoni, E., & Zingaretti, P. (2019). Robotic retail surveying by deep learning visual and textual data. *Robotics and Autonomous Systems*, *118*, 179–188. doi:10.1016/j.robot.2019.01.021

Park, M., Im, H., & Kim, D. Y. (2018). Feasibility and user experience of virtual reality fashion stores. *Fashion and Textiles*, *5*(1), 1–17. doi:10.118640691-018-0149-x

Ping, P., Qin, W., Xu, Y., Miyajima, C., & Takeda, K. (2019). Impact of driver behavior on fuel consumption: Classification, evaluation and prediction using machine learning. *IEEE Access: Practical Innovations, Open Solutions*, *7*, 78515–78532. doi:10.1109/ACCESS.2019.2920489

Pizzi, G., Scarpi, D., Pichierri, M., & Vannucci, V. (2019). Virtual reality, real reactions?: Comparing consumers' perceptions and shopping orientation across physical and virtual-reality retail stores. *Computers in Human Behavior*, *96*, 1–12. doi:10.1016/j.chb.2019.02.008

Schein, K., & Rauschnabel, P. (2021). Augmented reality in manufacturing: Exploring workers' perceptions of barriers. *IEEE Transactions on Engineering Management*, 1–14. doi:10.1109/TEM.2021.3093833

Schnack, A., Wright, M. J., & Holdershaw, J. L. (2021). Does the locomotion technique matter in an immersive virtual store environment? – Comparing motion-tracked walking and instant teleportation. *Journal of Retailing and Consumer Services*, *58*, 102266. doi:10.1016/j.jretconser.2020.102266

Shabani, N., Munir, A., & Hassan, A. (2018). E-marketing via augmented reality: A case study in the tourism and hospitality industry. *IEEE Potentials*, *38*(1), 43–47. doi:10.1109/MPOT.2018.2850598

Wang, C., Han, D., Liu, Q., & Luo, S. (2018). A deep learning approach for credit scoring of peer-to-peer lending using attention mechanism LSTM. *IEEE Access: Practical Innovations, Open Solutions*, *7*, 2161–2168. doi:10.1109/ACCESS.2018.2887138

Wang, K., Zhang, T., Xue, T., Lu, Y., & Na, S.-G. (2020). E-commerce personalized recommendation analysis by deeply-learned clustering. *Journal of Visual Communication and Image Representation*, *71*, 102735. doi:10.1016/j.jvcir.2019.102735

Wang, Y., Bennani, I. L., Liu, X., Sun, M., & Zhou, Y. (2021). Electricity consumer characteristics identification: A federated learning approach. *IEEE Transactions on Smart Grid*, *12*(4), 3637–3647. doi:10.1109/TSG.2021.3066577

Wang, Y., Chen, Q., Gan, D., Yang, J., Kirschen, D. S., & Kang, C. (2018). Deep learning-based socio-demographic information identification from Smart Meter Data. *IEEE Transactions on Smart Grid*, *10*(3), 2593–2602. doi:10.1109/TSG.2018.2805723

Wedel, M., Bigné, E., & Zhang, J. (2020). Virtual and augmented reality: Advancing research in consumer marketing. *International Journal of Research in Marketing*, *37*(3), 443–465. doi:10.1016/j.ijresmar.2020.04.004

Wu, J., Lu, F., Zhang, J., Yang, J., & Xing, L. (2019). Choice of distribution channels for experience products using virtual reality. *IEEE Access: Practical Innovations, Open Solutions*, *7*, 85319–85326. doi:10.1109/ACCESS.2019.2920308

Xu, Y., Du, B., Zhang, L., Cerra, D., Pato, M., Carmona, E., Prasad, S., Yokoya, N., Hansch, R., & Le Saux, B. (2019). Advanced multi-sensor optical remote sensing for urban land use and land cover classification: Outcome of the 2018 IEEE GRSS data fusion contest. *IEEE Journal of Selected Topics in Applied Earth Observations and Remote Sensing*, *12*(6), 1709–1724. doi:10.1109/JSTARS.2019.2911113

Yang, D., Gao, X., Kong, L., Pang, Y., & Zhou, B. (2020). An event-driven convolutional neural architecture for non-intrusive load monitoring of residential appliance. *IEEE Transactions on Consumer Electronics*, *66*(2), 173–182. doi:10.1109/TCE.2020.2977964

Yolcu, G., Oztel, I., Kazan, S., Oz, C., & Bunyak, F. (2020). Deep learning-based face analysis system for monitoring customer interest. *Journal of Ambient Intelligence and Humanized Computing*, *11*(1), 237–248. doi:10.100712652-019-01310-5

Zhang, S., & Zhong, H. (2019). Mining users' trust from e-commerce reviews based on sentiment similarity analysis. *IEEE Access: Practical Innovations, Open Solutions*, *7*, 13523–13535. doi:10.1109/ACCESS.2019.2893601

Chapter 2
Segmenting the Retail Customers:
A Multi-Model Approach of Clustering in Machine Learning

Mansurali Anifa
PSG College of Technology, India

Mary Jeyanthi P.
Jaipuria Institute of Management, India

Dieu Hack-Polay
Crandall University, Canada

Ali B. Mahmoud
https://orcid.org/0000-0002-3790-1107
St John's University, USA & London South Bank University, UK & Brunel University London, UK

Nicholas Grigoriou
Monash University, Australia

ABSTRACT

The goal of "serving all" is similar to "serving none." Marketers are constantly looking for ways to refine the way they segment markets. Segmentation involves diving markets into smaller portions (segments) of consumers with similar needs for a given good or service. This chapter explores the application of various algorithms and analytical techniques that are used to segment markets. These techniques include regression, cross-tabulation, hierarchical clustering, and k-means clustering performed through analytical tools such as R-Studio and MS Excel. The analyses drew upon the "customer data" dataset, which contained eight variables: age, income, marital status, ownership status, household size, family total sales, and family total visit. The findings demonstrate how such statistics could help the businesses understand the customers and target the specific customer with unique campaigns and offerings.

DOI: 10.4018/978-1-6684-4168-8.ch002

INTRODUCTION

Segmentation is an integral part of marketing strategy. Accurate segmentation leads to better use of organisational resources and improves financial outcomes for a market-driven organisation. Kotler, Keller, Brady, Goodman and Hansen (2019) assert there is no single way to segment a market. A marketer must try different segmentation variables, in combination or alone. Catering to consumers' different needs and preferences with a unique value proposition is mandatory for any market-driven organisation (Day, 2012).

Given the array of competing products found in most retail markets, segmentation helps marketers formulate and implement relevant strategies to promote, distribute, position, and price their goods and services. Organisations follow two major segmentation strategies: concentration and multi-segment strategies (Chinwendu, 2018). An organization will focus its marketing efforts on only one market segment using the concentration strategy. In the multi-segment strategy, a company focuses its marketing efforts on two or more market segments (Dibb & Simkin, 2016). Thus, companies are creating different marketing mixes for a different segment, and it is, therefore, necessary to define the segment and its characteristics. Market segmentation uses geographic, demographic, psychographic, and behavioural variables. The dataset considered in this study for the segmentation comprises marital status, age, income, marital status, owner status, family category, family value, household size. The data-driven approach using consumer data is explicitly critical for any business to succeed in its markets (Camilleri, 2020).

This tutorial study aims to demonstrate how retailers can improve the accuracy of market segmentation through the use of clustering techniques via machine learning. We use demographic variables acquired from Kaggle.

In machine learning, segmentation has been conducted using clustering techniques, an unsupervised learning method with known X, i.e. demographic variables, and an unknown Y— the segments to be concluded. Four segments are identified comprising consumer persona, which the company needs to know to devise the unique marketing strategies in terms of offers and offerings. Grouping customers into segments will help marketers understand their own customers' characteristics and competitors' customers. Further, segmentation addresses the homogeneity and heterogeneity of customers' groups to help maximise the potential for a given good or service. Out of the various techniques available, our research has taken two a priori techniques, such as Pivoting and regression-based segmentation and two Post Hoc portioning based clustering methods, such as hierarchical and K –Means clustering.

Background

Though there are several ways to segment the market, a market-driven organisation chooses the segmentation strategy that is best suited for its goods and services. Markets are imperfect such that the customers are heterogeneous, and thus the marketing stimuli that consumers respond to have to be different too. Segmentation is the means for aligning consumer needs and organizational marketing strategy (Nasir, Keserel, Surgit, & Nalbant, 2021; Serrano-Malebrán & Arenas-Gaitán, 2021). Since its formal introduction in the 1950s, its use for better customer understanding, product improvement, and marketing strategy have grown significantly (Christopher, Payne, & Ballantyne, 2013). Marketing research has again highlighted the importance of understanding what customers want and profiling them based on the segmentation of the market into defined groups who can then be targeted with a marketing strategy (Cohen & Ramaswamy, 1998; McKinsey, 2014).

The rising disruptive power of artificial intelligence technology has changed the phase of marketing segmentation. For instance, customer segmentation through internet reviews and ratings may aid companies to develop more informed marketing strategies and optimising marketing expenditures (Ahani, Nilashi, Ibrahim, Sanzogni, & Weaven, 2019). However, due to their scale, many dimensions, and characteristics of online customer data, typical market segmentation methodologies are inadequate for social data analysis (Arunachalam & Kumar, 2018; Naeem, Jamal, Diaz-Martinez, Butt, Montesano, Tariq, De-la-Hoz-Franco, & De-La-Hoz-Valdiris, 2022).

Born from computer science, machine learning techniques can aid in the development of successful hybrid algorithms that address the data-related issues inherent in online reviews (Naeem et al., 2022). Defined as "the study of methods and algorithms designed to learn the underlying patterns in data and make predictions based on these patterns" (Dzyabura & Yoganarasimhan, 2018, p. 255), machine learning assists marketers in general and retailers specifically in that it addresses non-causal inference problems (e.g. if an increase in X will cause a change Y), relying instead on out of sample predictive accuracy (Dzyabura & Yoganarasimhan, 2018). Such accuracy is evidence of computer science's greater involvement in marketing research (Hair & Sarstedt, 2021), conducted with minimal human involvement (Cui, Wong, & Lui, 2006). Accordingly, at its core, machine learning is a powerful tool that market-driven organisations use to gain new insights into consumer behaviour and to improve the performance of marketing operations (Cui et al., 2006). Accurate segmentation is based on such performance metrics (Valanarasu, Sindagi, Hacihaliloglu, & Patel, 2020). Indeed, the true power of machine learning lies in its ability to discover "interesting," nonobvious patterns or knowledge hidden in a database that can improve the bottom line (Cui et al., 2006).

Big data analytics is a primary driver of the fourth industrial revolution (Industry 4.0) and one of its foundations (Hack-Polay, Mahmoud, Ikafa et al., 2022; Lasi, Fettke, Kemper, Feld, & Hoffmann, 2014; Liao, Deschamps, Loures, & Ramos, 2017; Mahmoud, 2021; Mahmoud, Tehseen, & Fuxman, 2020; Zhou, Taigang, & Lifeng, 2015). Business analytics is increasingly being employed to derive business insights from internet reviews of products and services submitted by a diverse array of organisations and businesses (Arunachalam & Kumar, 2018; Aydiner, Tatoglu, Bayraktar, Zaim, & Delen, 2019; Delen & Ram, 2018; Yin & Fernandez, 2020). Other machine learning methods have also benefited from this trend and expanded their applications. Yet, big data presents a formidable challenge to market-driven organisations (Ma & Sun, 2020).

METHODOLOGY

Segmentation Process

While market segmentation has evolved into a critical marketing strategy for many organisations, it is not always the optimal marketing strategy to follow (Weinstein, 2013). Prior to devoting time and resources to market segmentation study, it is critical to grasp the consequences of market penetration (Davila, 2000; Dolnicar, Grün, & Leisch, 2018a).

The critical conclusion is that the organisation must commit to a long-term segmentation plan. Segmentation of the market is a marriage, not a date (Dolnicar et al., 2018a). Commitment to market segmentation is inextricably linked to the organisation's desire and capacity to make significant changes (Dolnicar et al., 2018a; McDonald, Christopher, & Bass, 2003) and investments. As Cahill (2012) contends, segmenting a market is not a cost-free exercise. There are expenditures associated with conducting research, conducting surveys and focus groups, creating numerous packages, as well as creating multiple promotions and communication messages (Cahill, 2012; Dolnicar et al., 2018a). Cahill (2012) advises against segmenting until the anticipated improvement in sales is sufficient to warrant executing a segmentation strategy. Cahill (2012) notes that one of the truisms of segmentation strategy is that employing the scheme must be more lucrative than marketing without it, net of the cost of establishing and implementing the plan. Changes that may be necessary include the production of new goods, the modification of current products, adjustments to the product's price and distribution channels, as well as all contacts with the market (Deepak & Jeyakumar, 2019; Dolnicar et al., 2018a; Schilling & Hill, 1998). In turn, these changes are likely to affect the organisation's internal structure, which may need to be altered in light of addressing a number of distinct market groups (Dolnicar et al., 2018a). Croft (1994) suggests that companies organise around market segments rather than goods to maximise the benefits of market segmentation. Strategic business units responsible for segments provide an organisational structure that is facilitative to constantly emphasising market segments' demands and dynamics (Dolnicar et al., 2018a). There are significant consequences for such a long-term organisational commitment; thus, it must be decided at the highest executive level to look into the possibility of a market segmentation strategy (Wheelen, Hunger, Hoffman, & Bamford, 2017). This choice then must be communicated and reinforced at all levels within the organisation and throughout each unit (Dolnicar et al., 2018a).

The market segmentation process is typically motivated by an organisation's desire to better serve a segment of the market and thus gain a competitive advantage (Foedermayr & Diamantopoulos, 2008; Venter, Wright, & Dibb, 2015). After committing to researching the benefits of segmentation strategies, the organisation must contribute significantly to market segmentation evaluation. That is important to segmentation. Knock-out factors (see Dolnicar, Grün, & Leisch, 2018b; Karlsson, 2015) are used to ascertain whether market segments identified through market segmentation analysis meet the criteria for segment attractiveness assessment. Data-driven market segmentation is typically founded on empirical facts (Hajibaba, Grün, & Dolnicar, 2020). The phrase "segmentation criteria" refers to the characteristics of the data utilised to segment markets (Schlager & Christen, 2022). Typically, the segmentation variable is a single attribute of the sampled customers.

Exploratory data analysis cleans and, if required, pre-processes the data following data collection (Kohli & Gupta, 2021). Additionally, this level of inquiry provides suggestions on the best appropriate methodology for identifying significant market segments (Schlager & Christen, 2022). On a more technical level, data exploration assists in (1) identifying the variables' measurement levels, (2) investigating the variables' univariate distributions, and (3) assessing the dependence structures between variables (Dolnicar, Grün, & Leisch, 2018c).

The data exploration stage results illuminate the appropriateness of various segmentation techniques for obtaining market segments (Raiter, 2021). Additionally, data may need pre-processing and preparation prior to being utilised as input for various segmentation methods (Dolnicar et al., 2018c). Numerous segmentation techniques are derived from the discipline of cluster analysis and are used to generate market categories. If this is the case, market segments may be compared to clusters. As Hennig and Liao (2013) assert, finding an appropriate clustering technique entails aligning the resultant clustering's data analytic characteristics to the researcher's context-dependent needs. It is critical to investigate market segmentation options resulting from a variety of clustering techniques as well as to comprehend how various algorithms impose structure on the extracted segments (Dolnicar, Grün, & Leisch, 2018d). In their study, segmenting consumers in food and grocery retail, Narasimham and Gupta (2016) discussed the importance of demographics, pricing, and other variables. In an attempt to learn more about wine, aesthetics, and ephemerality, Hall (2016) utilised clustering analysis to create four customer clusters for the consumption of luxury wine brands, which complemented an existing framework of aesthetics and ontology.

The next phase is profiling and describing segments. Profiling segments entails learning about the market segments identified during the extraction stage (Dolnicar, 2018). Profiling is only necessary when using data-driven market segmentation. If, for example, age is employed as the segmentation variable, the resultant segments are unambiguously age groups (Dolnicar, Grün, & Leisch, 2018e). Further, additional information about segment members is used to characterise market segments. If committing to a target segment is analogous to marriage, then profiling and describing market segments is analogous to going on several dates to get to know the potential spouse to give the marriage the best potential to succeed. Once the target market segments have been selected and the marketing mix has developed, market segmentation analysis, as a strategic process, becomes subject to ongoing periodic evaluation and monitoring (Dolnicar, Grün, & Leisch, 2018f).

Clustering Methods

Green, Frank and Robinson (1967) recorded the significance of clustering analysis to match the prospective test markets by analysing the large basket of consumer characteristics. Moreover, the research in that cluster analysis done on the pre-selection of test markets reduces the variability among the markets selected for the test. McCurley Hortman, Allaway, Barry Mason and Rasp (1990) used a priori segmentation to categorise the shoppers based on the reason for shopping trips made to discount image stores and non-discount image stores. Kevin, Nigel and Mark (2002) demonstrated the analysis of variables related to psychographic characteristics of shopping orientation and web purchase intentions using K-means clustering and rough clustering approaches. They confirmed the significance of clustering techniques in helping marketers to reach the right consumers. Shindler, Wong and Meyerson (2011) confirmed in their research that K- Means clustering is the best technique for clustering when the dataset is large.

Brida, Disegna and Osti (2012) guided the use of the Silhouette Index (Rousseeuw, 1987) as a selection criterion to determine the K for both hierarchical and non-hierarchical techniques for effective partitioning. Gnanaraj, Kumar and Monica (2014), in their attempt to study K-Means algorithms, discuss the partitional clustering algorithms that created various partitions and conclude that the k-Means algorithm is one of the most popular partitional clustering algorithms. They further argue that the K-Means algorithm is a centroid-based algorithm in which each data point is placed in precisely one of the K non-overlapping clusters selected before the algorithm is run.

Chen, Agrawal and Kumara (2015) employed hierarchical and non-hierarchical clustering algorithms on the transactional data of the retail market and found that the heterogeneity of the shopping behaviours among the clusters can be used to target the customers and develop better promotional plans. Sajana, Rani and Narayana (2016), in their study, stated that, in *partitioned based clustering*, all data points are taken as a single cluster in the beginning. These data points are then separated into clusters by iteratively positioning these objects between the clusters. Some of the partitioning algorithms are K-Means, K-Medoids, and K-Modes

This chapter offers practical examples of how marketers can understand the consumer demographics and patterns using exploratory data analysis, develop the customer segments of a retail store using multiple analytical approaches and identify the consumer profiles and personas based on the segments arrived at using multi models.

Conceptualization

The chapter presents an unsupervised learning algorithm working on unlabeled data to discover the clusters (i.e. segments), which is unknown before the study. This approach is suitable for dealing with customer profiles characterised by demographic variables (see Table 1). The dataset "Customer's Data – Retail store" consisting of 796 data points was used in the study. It is secondary data gathered from Kaggle to uncover the data segments, consisting of demographic characteristics such as marital status, age, income, marital status, owner status, family category, family value, and household size. Data in its raw form was not suited for the analytics research method planned in the study, and it went through the processing steps such as missing value handling, converting categorical into a binary or numeric variable as and when it required and most importantly, the scaling process to standardise the data of various units into a standardised form. The random sampling technique was adopted in the study as the machine learning algorithms sample the data points randomly to select data points for clustering and building models. Processed data points had been fed into the algorithmic process, such as K- Means Clustering and Hierarchical clustering methods, which are post hoc methods of segmentation analytics. The study also attempted to create segments using a priori segmentation methods such as cross-tabulation (using Pivot)- a descriptive method of segmentation and regression-based segmentation, a predictive-based technique. The number of clusters has arrived based on the elbow method (see Thorndike, 1953). Statistical tools such as R and Excel have been used to arrive at the segments in the study. Visualisation software Tableau has been used for the final phase of the research was to create an ideal customer profile of the segments by describing the characteristics of cluster members.

The chapter's ultimate goal is to offer a tutorial showing how to segment customers using various methods, which will assist marketers in determining the segment's profile and the most efficient method of targeting the segments. Figure 1 shows the elements discussed in this chapter.

Table 1. Data overview - demographics characteristics

Demographics Characteristics of Retail Customers		
Data Point – Variable	**Data Type**	**Data Description**
Marital Status	VARCHAR	Marital status of Family head
Age	INT	Age of the Family head
Income	INT	Income range of the Family head
Owner Status	VARCHAR	If the Family head owns a house
Family Category	VARCHAR	Family category: With/Without kids
Family Value	INT	Total Sales Potential of a Family
Household Size	INT	Number of people in the Customer's Family

Source. National Center for Education Statistics, 1998-2007

Figure 1. Chapter framework; Source: Authors' work.

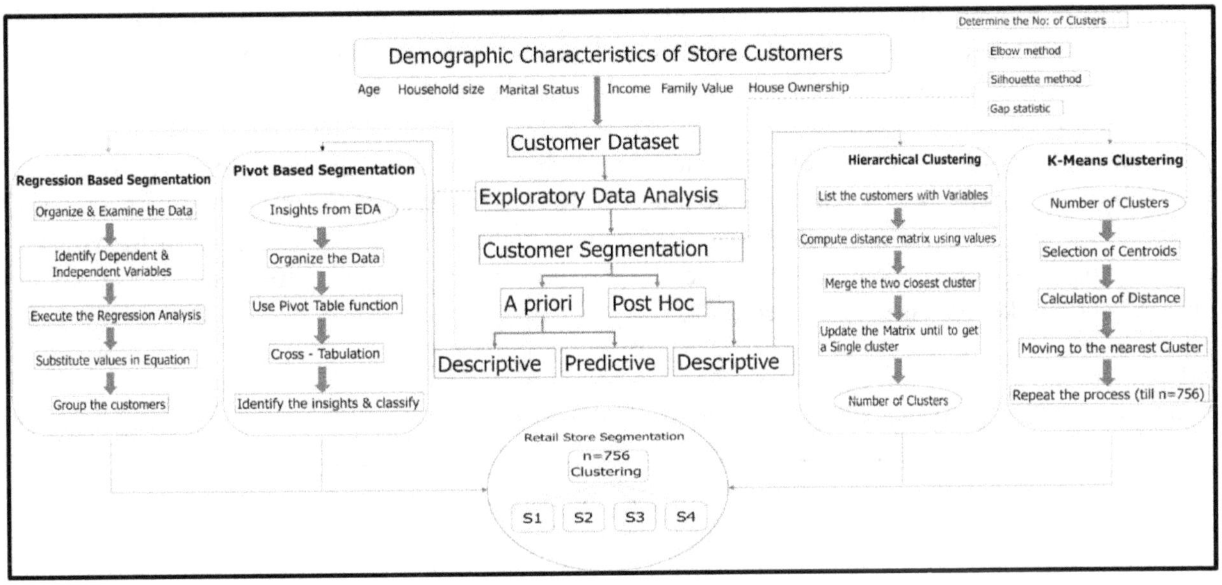

ANALYSIS AND DISCUSSION

Exploratory Data Analysis – EDA

In an attempt to understand and explore the consumer characteristics, exploratory data analysis has been done on the dataset with the help of visualisation techniques using Tableau (see Figure 2).

Figure 2. Consumer demographics; Source: Authors' work.

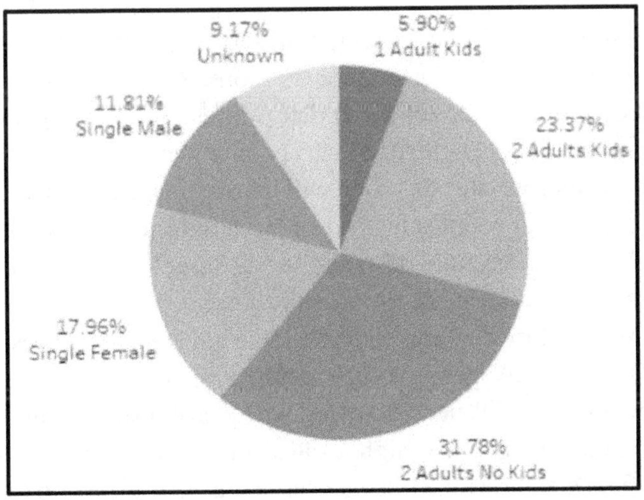

Single persons constituted 29% of total customers, whereas adults without kids were 32%. Six per cent of customers are single parents. Only 30% of family has kids in the customer database. Couple customers are high, and we could also see that 32% of customers are couples without kids who may have a chance to spend more. So, the store can use this insight into tailoring marketing communications and increasing sales.

Figure 3 shows 40 and 50-year-old customers who earned a very high income (cumulative) compared with other age groups. This would provide a chance for retailers and marketers to tap that market to increase revenue. Furthermore, it can be assumed that the higher income group would have high disposable income, which could explain why retailers would target the age group of 40-50 and devise product offering and marketing campaigns accordingly.

Figure 3. Income across age groups; Source: Authors' work.

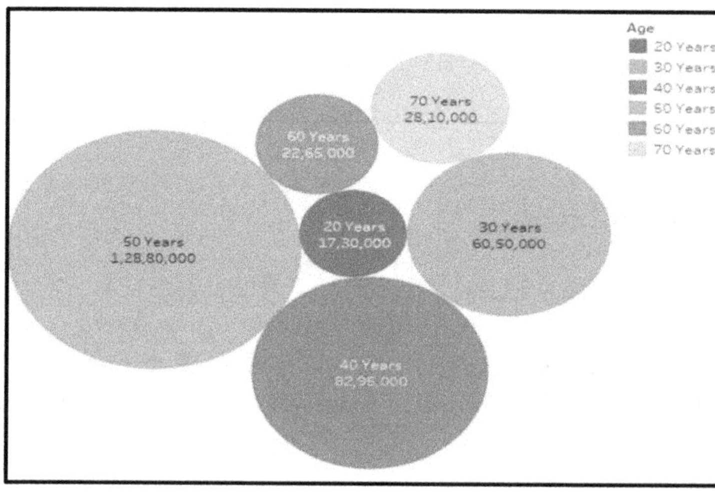

Figure 4 explains the store's total sales arranged in terms of age and household size. Households with 1 or 2 members were the top demand group for the store. People of 50 years old contributed a high quota. Compact families can be a reason for these data values. So, our target customers can be people 40 -50 years old with a compact household size—4.6 people per household, according to PRB (2021). Focusing on products for the appropriate age group will increase sales. Thus, marketing communications campaigns could target singles and couples instead of large families, as that procedure would probably boost sales. Marketing campaigns specially designed for the target group will increase customer loyalty, which improves the customers' wallet share towards the store.

Figure 5 shows the linkage of ownership status and marital status in terms of Total Sales. Predominantly owners had more tendency to spend on their purchases, and that segment must be captured well to increase the sales in the long term. When compared with marital status, couples contribute a lot to the overall sales. Thus, couple customers led to higher sales compared to single ones. Retailers can use this insight to segment customers and target the relevant segments. Couples who owned a house contributed more to the overall sales and might be targeted by customised and individualised messages of discounts and coupons for buying regularly, which could help earn their trust and increase future sales.

Figure 4. Sales vs age & household size; Source: Authors' work.

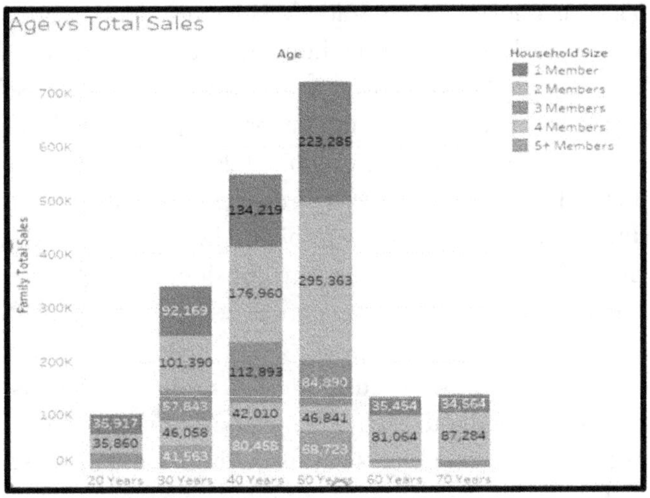

Figure 5. Marital status vs ownership (sales); Source: Authors' work.

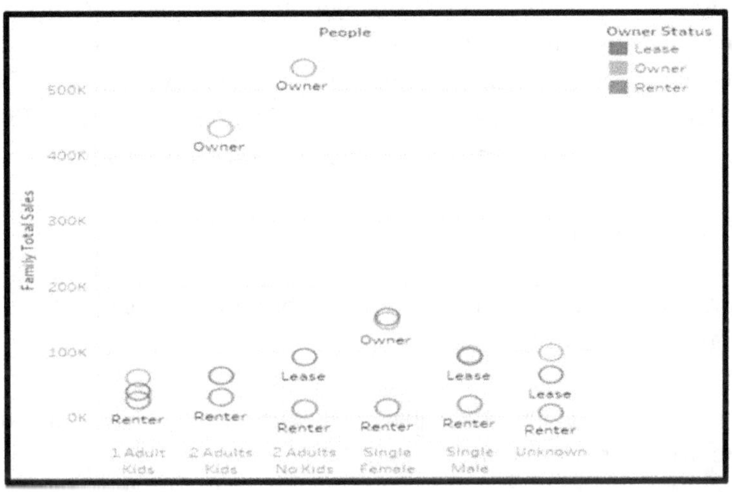

Clustering

Segmentation, also known as clustering, is a critical component of data mining and machine learning to classify unlabeled data. The aim is to develop the customer segments of the retail store using multiple analytical approaches. Data points are partitioned into groups, and objects in each group are kept in the cluster related to each other. Objects (customers) are grouped based on attribute closeness. In post hoc segmentation, finding out the optimum number of clusters (segments) is a critical step conducted through multiple methods such as *elbow* (e.g. Bholowalia & Kumar, 2014), *silhouette* (e.g. Zeeshan, Jun, & Zahida, 2020) and *gap statistic* (e.g. Yang, Lee, Choi, & Joo, 2020) techniques. Elbow refers to the use of "a square of the distance between the sample points in each cluster and the centroid of the cluster to give a series of K values" (Yuan & Yang, 2019, p. 228). Gap statistic is an algorithm put forward by

Tibshirani, Walther and Hastie (2001) to "determine the number of clusters of data sets with unknown classification numbers. The basic idea of Gap Statistic is to introduce reference measurements, which can be obtained by the Monte Carlo sampling method (Xiao & Yu, 2007) and to calculate the sum of the squares of the Euclidean distance between two measurements in each class." (Yuan & Yang, 2019, p. 230). Whilst the Silhouette algorithm offers a technique for interpreting and validating the consistency of data clusters' consistency, it generates a concise graphical depiction of the degree to which each object has been categorised properly (Rousseeuw, 1987). The data points will be grouped based on the distance calculation in the clustering process. Since each variable in the dataset is of different units, it should not be processed in a raw format. If the actual data units are considered for the analysis, variables with high numeric values dominate in this process. Thus, the data need to be scaled so that every variable will be in a standardised form.

Hierarchical clustering is an algorithm used to cluster similar objects as groups. The individuals within the same group are closely similar to each other. Dendrograms are very commonly used tools for visualising the segment and cluster of the objects in this method. Here the observations from the dataset are grouped into clusters. Eventually, objects that are close together are merged into groups until all the data are merged into a single cluster. There are two approaches to hierarchical clustering: the "from the bottom up" approach, grouping small clusters into larger ones, or "from the top down", splitting significant clusters into small ones. These are called agglomerative and divisive clustering. Hierarchical clustering, the divisive algorithm, uses Ward's (1963) method to create the clusters with the following sequential steps which are used to calculate the similarity between two clusters: Other methods that are used to calculate similarity through the distance in hierarchical clustering are MIN, MAX, Group Average and Distance Between Centroids. The working mechanism of Hierarchical clustering is as follows

- Compute the proximity matrix
- Let each data point be a cluster
- Combine or merge the two closest clusters, and the proximity matrix gets updated
- Until only a single cluster remains

Ward's method calculates the sum of the square of the distances of the point from the other clusters and allocates the point to the smallest or nearest cluster.

$$sim(C1,C2) = \text{å} (dist(P1, P2))^2/|C1|*|C2|$$

The difference between the heights of tree branches indicates the level of difference from one cluster to another. The longer the lines, the greater the difference. Thus, this method merges the closest data points and separates the furthest ones effectively. The code we used to create segments using hierarchical clustering is attached in the appendix.

K-means algorithm is an iterative algorithm that attempts to partition the dataset into 'K' predefined distinct non-overlapping subgroups (clusters) where each data point belongs to only one group. K – Means algorithm will execute based on the K –value, any number can be given to K, but the optimum number of K can be found using multiple methods such as Elbow Methods, Silhouette Index and Gap – Statistic method with the appropriate package and function in the R. Codes for the respective methods are attached in the appendix. The working mechanism of K-Means clustering is as follows

- Step one: Initialise cluster centres
- Step two: Assignment of observations to the cluster centres which are closest
- Step three: Revision of cluster centres using the mean of observations assigned
- Step four: Repetition of step 2 and step 3 until convergence is achieved

The K factor is selected using the Gap, Silhouette, and elbow methods. K will determine the optimum number of clusters required to categorise our customer base. Here the selected value for K is '4', found to be an optimal number of clusters to arrive at the segment based on all three methods. The closest centroid will capture the new observation into its cluster. This is based on the Euclidean distance between the object and the centroid. The kth clusters update the centroid by calculating the new mean values of the observations in the dataset. The kth cluster's centroid has a length that contains all variables for customers in the kth cluster, denoted as "p". R-software uses '10' as the default value of maximum iterations. Through the iterative minimisation of the total sum of the square, maximum iteration is achieved, and thus the assignment stops wavering. Thus, with the help of the k-means clustering method, segmentation using clustering has been done. The code we used to create segments using K-Means clustering is attached in the appendix.

Cross- Tabulation (Pivoting)

Segmentation needs not to be conducted with complex methods and algorithms. Segmentation can be achieved through cross tabulating the data. Cross tabulation is often used to check the relationship of the variables in the data, which may not be readily apparent. It is usually used categorical data, classified into mutually exclusive groups. For analysing market research survey responses, cross-tabulation is needed the most. Tools like SPSS, Excel, R, and Tableau can be used to cross-tabulate the data. In this study, Excel was used to pivot the data values

Regression Approach

Linear regression is a statistical model that analyses the relationship between a dependent variable (known as y) and one or more independent variables and their interactions (often called x or explanatory variables). In this study, total sales are the dependent variable, while household size, age, total family visits, and owner status are independent variables.

Family Total Sales= a +Household Size*b+ Age*c+ Total Visits*d + Owner Status*e

where 'a' denotes intercept and 'b,' 'c,' 'd' and 'e' represent slopes

Family Sales = 940.18 + Household size*166.8 +(-9.3) *Age + Total Visits*16.25 + Ownership Status*477

Clusters were derived based on predicted sales figures (average). The code used for executing the regression appears in the appendix.

Hierarchical Clustering

Agglomerative hierarchical clustering analysis was performed (see Figure 6 and Figure 7) using the "hclust()" method from the Cluster package in R. At each iteration, the similar clusters merge with other clusters until one cluster or K clusters) are formed., Here we chose four clusters (k=4), meaning customers are grouped into four clusters, and a personalised marketing strategy can be formulated.

Figure 6. Cluster dendrogram – hierarchical clustering; Source: Authors' work.

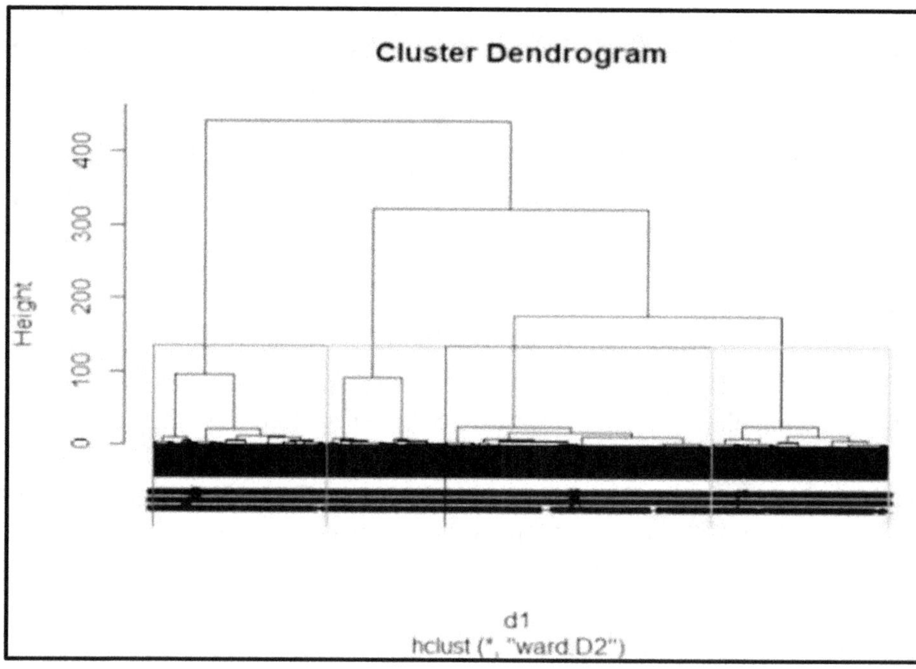

K- Means Clustering

As Figure 8 shows, the first cluster (red) represents the customers with a high income, but their expenditure (sales) is deficient. In this segment, the expenditure reduces as the income increases. The second cluster (green) represents the premium customers of the store. They have a high income, and their yearly expenditure is also high. Cluster three (blue) comprises meagre income and low annual expenditure customers. This segment has meagre potential profitability. The fourth cluster (purple) represents the store's core loyal customers. They have low annual income, but their annual expenditure is high.

Multimodel Clustering

To develop the consumer profiles and personas based on the segments arrived at using multi models. Clustering assists in making careful decisions only when the relevant variables are understood. Profiling our customers will enable companies to specifically target their customers with the appropriate products and services based on segmentation variables like age, income, household size, marital status, etc.

Figure 7. Cluster plot – hierarchical clustering; Source: Authors' work.

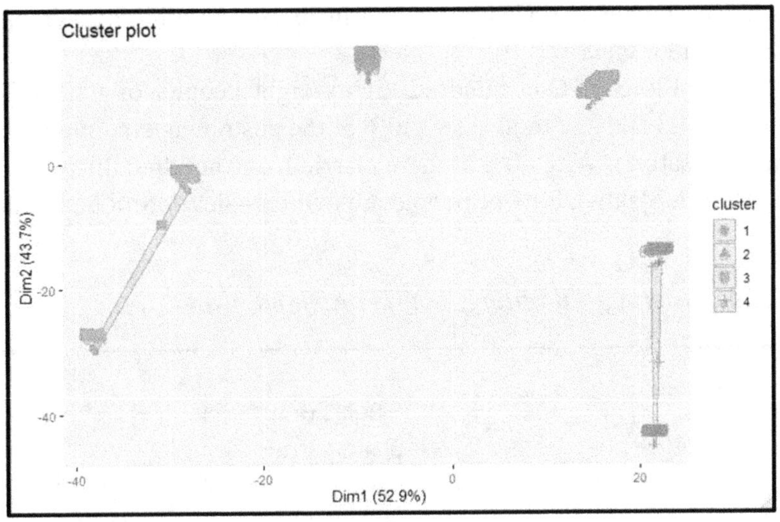

Figure 8. Cluster plot – K- Means clustering; Source: Authors' work.

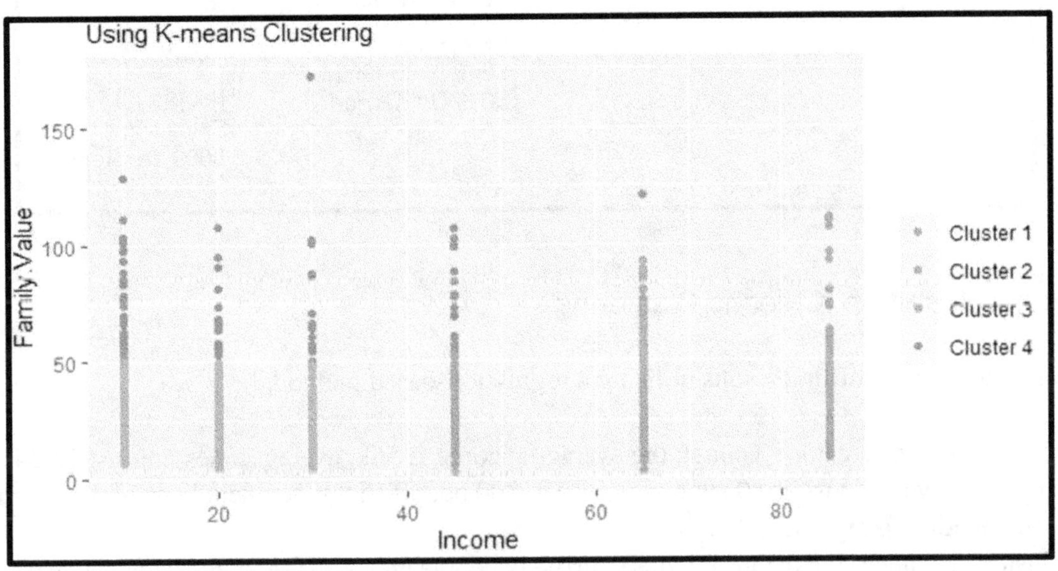

Profiling – Based on Hierarchical Clustering

Figure 9 shows the profiling results utilising a regression-based method.

- Cluster 1 (Sales Boosters): People with high income contribute 5.5 lakhs of rupees, i.e. 28% of overall store sales. One hundred ninety-three people come under this group. 50% of the customer are married in this group.

- Cluster 2 (Golden Eggs): The group with the highest sales (7.2 lakhs). Two hundred eighty-five customers with 50% unmarried. Customers are primarily with high income. Thus, focusing on them can generate more sales.
- Cluster 3 (Budding Florets): One hundred eighty-eight people, of which 50% possess leased homes. It generates 4.3 lakhs in total sales. 50% of the customers are unmarried.
- Cluster 4 (Traffic Creators): With 50% of them married, one hundred thirty people contribute least to the overall sales (2.7 lakhs). 80% of people are owners—low-profit generators.

Figure 9. Hierarchical clustering— profiling; Source: Authors' work

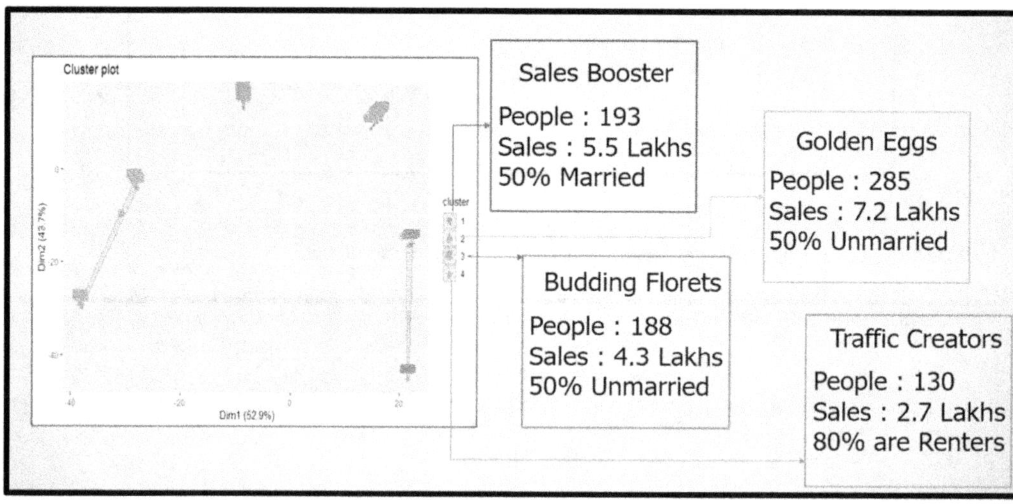

Profiling – Based on K-Means Clustering

Figure 10 shows the profiling results utilising a regression-based method.

- Cluster 1 (Sales creator): Though the average income is 56k, average sales are just 1,934. In this group, the average visit is 80 per customer. So, 300 people in this segment have high potential, but their spending is significantly low.
- Cluster 2 (Golden Eggs): One hundred thirty-six people are in this segment. They have the highest income average of 75k. Average sales are 3,089, with 60 average visits per customer. Less average visits and more sales, customers in this segment are comfortable buying from the store, but there is enough disposable income to spend.
- Cluster 3 (Traffic Creator): People with the lowest Average Income of 17k with Average sales of 2,326. Two hundred sixty-nine people in this segment can be tagged as middle-class customers who frequently visit the store (93 average visits per customer)
- Cluster 4: Loyalist group consists of 91 customers with 3,816 as average sales & only 54 average visits per customer. The average income is 23k

Figure 10. K-Means clustering — profiling; Source: Authors' work

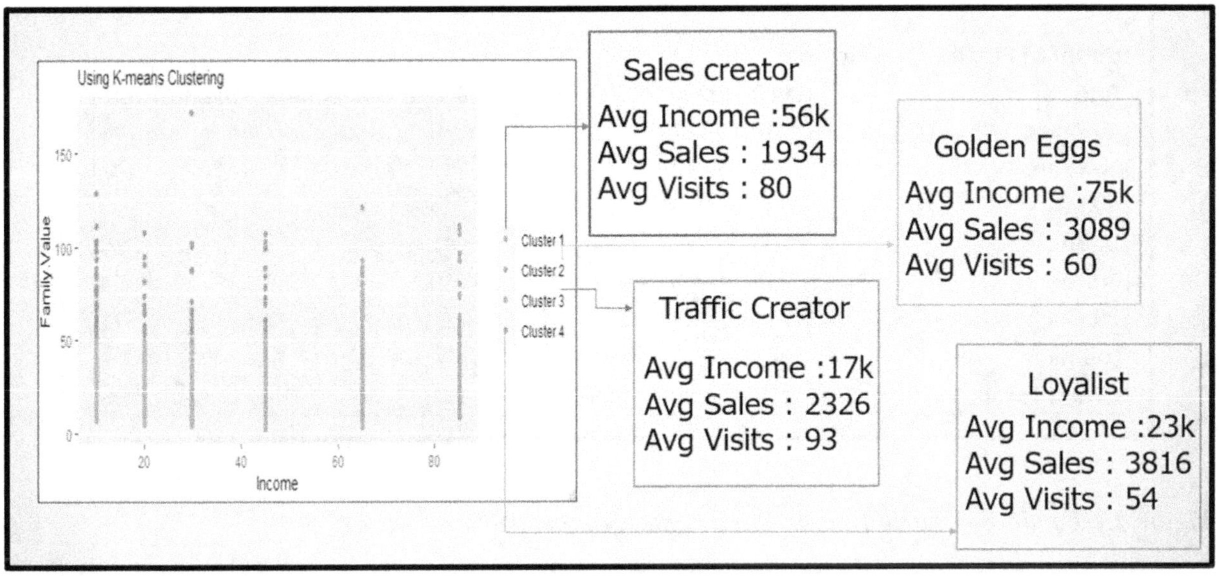

Profiling – Based on the Pivot approach

Figure 11 shows the total families cross-tabulated by Age and Income. Golden Eggs (Green Segment) is the segment with high disposable income. We can target them to sell premium goods and look out for cross-selling opportunities. Tortoise (Blue Segment) & Young Bloomers (Orange) have meagre income and may influence future sales. So, use them as Traffic creators.

In Figure 12, we cross-tabulated marital status and income. Golden Eggs (Green Segment) has a family and higher income than others. Lone warriors (Orange Segment) has a single population and high disposable income. Both segments have high potential to target. Figure 13 shows that Old & Economic (Blue Segment) has the lowest sales compared with other segments. We can stock products which single people would love to buy and increase sales. Proud Singles (Yellow Segment) has the second-largest sales record. Their age ranges from 30 to 50.

Figure 11. Age vs. household composition (saleswise); Source: Authors' work

Sum of Family Total Sales	Column Labels							
Row Labels	1 Adult Kids	2 Adults Kids	2 Adults No Kids	Single Female	Single Male	Unknown	(blank)	Grand Total
20 Years	11289.18	23261.52	29213.17	25241.25	6100.53	4575.39		99681.04
30 Years	38996.72	113195.46	78181.85	43392.46	54133.38	11124.09		339023.96
40 Years	30043.32	212856.24	145654.99	89769.37	41056.76	27159.36		546540.04
50 Years	36377.34	162250.8	259372.98	89622.39	63916.66	107561.7		719101.87
60 Years	1188.03	14834.32	55183.59	29877.53	18409.89	13046.74		132540.1
70 Years	7823.79	7042.05	67505.6	33948.46	19173.13	1220.62		136713.65
(blank)								
Grand Total	**125718.38**	**533440.39**	**635112.18**	**311851.46**	**202790.35**	**164687.9**		**1973600.66**

Figure 12. Families—age and income; Source: Authors' work

Count of Family	Income							
Age	10000	20000	30000	45000	65000	85000	(blank)	Grand Total
20 Years	10	7	5	13	9	2		46
30 Years	30	13	15	34	37	13		142
40 Years	43	23	18	38	44	27		193
50 Years	58	31	24	51	81	40		285
60 Years	17	5	6	16	9	6		59
70 Years	14	11	8	20	11	7		71
(blank)								
Grand Total	172	90	76	172	191	95		796

Figure 13. Families— marital status and income; Source: Authors' work

Count of Family Total Sales	Income							
A	10000	20000	30000	45000	65000	85000	(blank)	Grand Total
1 Adult Kids	11	6	7	14	8	1		47
2 Adults Kids	49	21	11	39	38	28		186
2 Adults No Kids	51	29	20	57	60	36		253
Single Female	30	21	25	26	28	13		143
Single Male	20	9	12	29	15	9		94
Unknown	11	4	1	7	42	8		73
(blank)								
Grand Total	172.00	90.00	76.00	172.00	191.00	95.00		796.00

Profiling – Regression-Based Approach

Figure 14 shows the profiling results utilising a regression-based method.

- Cluster 1— Occasional Buyers: The Average sales of customers in this segment are 1,302. Customers have averagely visited 37 times throughout the year. Since the average visits are significantly less, the sales are less in this segment. More than 50% of the customers in this segment are unmarried. The average household size is 1.69 per family.
- Cluster 2— Budding Fans: The Average Total sales are 2,512. The average total number of visits is 71. 50% of the customers in this segment are Married. The average number of members in the household are 2.4 in this segment. As the average household size increases, the total sales will also increase exponentially.

- Cluster 3—Store Evangelist: Customers in this segment have average total sales of 4,174. The average household size is 2.5. A family has, on average, visited the store 130 times throughout the year. As per our regression equation, total sales will increase with increasing visits.
- Cluster 4— Premium Buyers: The premium customers of the store are categorised in this segment. Each customer has an average sales of 5,108. On average, each household has three members in its family. Each family has averagely visited the store about 247 times. Thus, the higher the visits, the higher the sales, as proved with our regression analysis.

Figure 14. Families— regression output; Source: Authors' work

```
Call:
lm(formula = Family.Total.Sales ~ Household.Size + Age + Family.Total.Visit +
    Owner.Status, data = check)

Residuals:
    Min      1Q  Median      3Q     Max
-5337.0  -894.1  -287.1   569.3  9181.9

Coefficients:
                    Estimate Std. Error t value Pr(>|t|)
(Intercept)         940.1898   236.5128   3.975 7.68e-05 ***
Household.Size      166.8802    46.9049   3.558 0.000396 ***
Age                  -9.2987     4.2926  -2.166 0.030591 *
Family.Total.Visit   16.2595     0.7984  20.365  < 2e-16 ***
Owner.StatusOwner   477.8351   125.9082   3.795 0.000159 ***
Owner.StatusRenter  -65.8428   254.8672  -0.258 0.796210
---
Signif. codes:  0 '***' 0.001 '**' 0.01 '*' 0.05 '.' 0.1 ' ' 1

Residual standard error: 1480 on 790 degrees of freedom
Multiple R-squared:  0.3618,    Adjusted R-squared:  0.3578
F-statistic: 89.58 on 5 and 790 DF,  p-value: < 2.2e-16
```

Profiling – Consolidated

The demographic segments (the output of segmentation analytics methods) are named considering the value of characteristics listed in each segment cluster. Two a-priori methods, such as cross-tabulation (descriptive), regression (predictive) based methods and two post-hoc methods, such as hierarchical clustering and k-means algorithm, were employed to create four segments out of demographic characteristics. Consolidated profiles of the segments arrived, along with the key inferences, are tabulated below (Table 2).

CONCLUSION

To conclude, the study has attempted to do customer segmentation for the retail store using various Segmentation analytic methods. Dataset has been initially explored with the visualization techniques using Tableau. Unsupervised machine learning techniques such as K-Means Clustering and Hierarchical clustering have been employed to group the customers into segments. Also, segments have been derived using the Apriori approach, such as pivot and regression modelling. As a result, the study has categorised 796 customers into four Segments. This helps retail stores marketers target customer groups through personalized marketing communications and offerings, thus increasing their loyalty to the store and increasing revenue. The limitation of this study is that only the demographic characteristics of the customer profile have been considered. In addition to future replications, the use of the survey, consumer preference and choices can be considered in selecting the products and performing a conjoint analysis to segment the customers more accurately.

Table 2. Customer segmentation— profiles

	Synchronous E-Learning	Asynchronous E-Learning
When	• Discussing less complex issues. • Getting acquainted. • Planning tasks.	• Reflecting on complex issues. • When synchronous classes cannot be attended due to illness, work, family or other commitments.
Why	• Students become more committed and motivated due to getting a quick response.	• Students have more time to reflect as quick response is not immediately expected.
How	• In addition to face-to-face class, various synchronous means were used, including video conferencing, instant messaging, and conversation (chat).	• Various asynchronous means such as e-mail, discussion boards, and blogs are used.
Online	Synchronous means: • Virtual Classroom. • Video/teleconferencing. • Conversation (chat) rooms/instant messaging.	Asynchronous means: • Web-based teaching/ computer-based teaching. • Threaded discussion groups. • Recorded live events. • Online documents/ e-mail/global announcement.
Offline	Synchronous means: • Face to face classroom. • Hands-on laboratory practices. • Field trips, fieldwork.	Asynchronous means: • Bound books/ learning resources. • Videos/Echo360/Lectopia. • Audiotapes.
Examples	• Students work in groups and can use instant messaging to get to know each other, exchange ideas, and plan tasks. • A teacher who wants to present concepts from the literature in a simplified way might give an online lecture by video conferencing.	• Students expected to reflect individually on course topics may be asked to maintain a blog. • Students are expected to share reflections regarding course topics and critically assess their peers' ideas. They may be asked to participate in online discussions on a discussion board.

Source: Authors' work

ACKNOWLEDGMENT

This research received no specific grant from any funding agency in the public, commercial, or not-for-profit sectors.

REFERENCES

Ahani, A., Nilashi, M., Ibrahim, O., Sanzogni, L., & Weaven, S. (2019). Market segmentation and travel choice prediction in Spa hotels through TripAdvisor's online reviews. *International Journal of Hospitality Management*, *80*, 52–77. doi:10.1016/j.ijhm.2019.01.003

Arunachalam, D., & Kumar, N. (2018). Benefit-based consumer segmentation and performance evaluation of clustering approaches: An evidence of data-driven decision-making. *Expert Systems with Applications*, *111*, 11–34. doi:10.1016/j.eswa.2018.03.007

Aydiner, A. S., Tatoglu, E., Bayraktar, E., Zaim, S., & Delen, D. (2019). Business analytics and firm performance: The mediating role of business process performance. *Journal of Business Research*, *96*, 228–237. doi:10.1016/j.jbusres.2018.11.028

Bholowalia, P., & Kumar, A. (2014). EBK-means: A clustering technique based on elbow method and k-means in WSN. *International Journal of Computers and Applications*, *105*(9).

Brida, J. G., Disegna, M., & Osti, L. (2012). Segmenting visitors of cultural events by motivation: A sequential non-linear clustering analysis of Italian Christmas Market visitors. *Expert Systems with Applications*, *39*(13), 11349–11356. doi:10.1016/j.eswa.2012.03.041

Cahill, D. (2012). Lifestyle market segmentation. The Haworth Press.

Camilleri, M. A. (2020). The use of data-driven technologies for customer-centric marketing. *International Journal of Big Data Management*, *1*(1), 50–63. doi:10.1504/IJBDM.2020.106876

Chen, C.-B., Agrawal, D., & Kumara, S. (2015). *Retail analytics: Market segmentation through transaction data*. Academic Press.

Chinwendu, O. D. (2018). An Exploratory Analysis of Market Segmentation and Young Mobile Phone Consumers in Nigeria. *International Journal of Marketing Research Innovation*, *2*(2), 30–37. doi:10.46281/ijmri.v2i2.223

Christopher, M., Payne, A., & Ballantyne, D. (2013). *Relationship marketing*. Routledge. doi:10.4324/9780080516042

Cohen, S. H., & Ramaswamy, V. (1998). Latent segmentation models. *Marketing Research*, *10*(2), 14.

Croft, M. J. (1994). *Market segmentation: A step-by-step guide to profitable new business*. Cengage Learning Emea.

Cui, G., Wong, M. L., & Lui, H.-K. (2006). Machine Learning for Direct Marketing Response Models: Bayesian Networks with Evolutionary Programming. *Management Science*, *52*(4), 597–612. doi:10.1287/mnsc.1060.0514

Davila, T. (2000). An empirical study on the drivers of management control systems' design in new product development. *Accounting, Organizations and Society*, *25*(4), 383–409. doi:10.1016/S0361-3682(99)00034-3

Day, G. S. (2012). *The Market Driven Organization: Attracting And Keeping Valuable Customers*. Simon & Schuster UK. https://books.google.co.uk/books?id=8xZiORNX3hIC

Deepak, R. K. A., & Jeyakumar, S. (2019). *Marketing management*. Educreation Publishing.

Delen, D., & Ram, S. (2018). Research challenges and opportunities in business analytics. *Journal of Business Analytics*, *1*(1), 2–12. doi:10.1080/2573234X.2018.1507324

Dibb, S., & Simkin, L. (2016). Market segmentation and segment strategy. *Marketing theory: A student text, 251279.*

Dolnicar, S. (2018). Understanding and Satisfying Consumer Needs: Segmentation, Targeting and Positioning. The SAGE Handbook of Tourism Management: Applications of Theories And Concepts to Tourism, 257.

Dolnicar, S., Grün, B., & Leisch, F. (2018a). Market Segmentation. In *Market Segmentation Analysis* (pp. 3–9). Springer. doi:10.1007/978-981-10-8818-6_1

Dolnicar, S., Grün, B., & Leisch, F. (2018b). Step 2: Specifying the Ideal Target Segment. In S. Dolnicar, B. Grün, & F. Leisch (Eds.), *Market Segmentation Analysis* (pp. 31–37). Springer Singapore. doi:10.1007/978-981-10-8818-6_4

Dolnicar, S., Grün, B., & Leisch, F. (2018c). Step 4: Exploring Data. In S. Dolnicar, B. Grün, & F. Leisch (Eds.), *Market Segmentation Analysis: Understanding It, Doing It, and Making It Useful* (pp. 57–73). Springer Singapore. doi:10.1007/978-981-10-8818-6_6

Dolnicar, S., Grün, B., & Leisch, F. (2018d). Step 5: Extracting Segments. In S. Dolnicar, B. Grün, & F. Leisch (Eds.), *Market Segmentation Analysis: Understanding It, Doing It, and Making It Useful* (pp. 75–181). Springer Singapore. doi:10.1007/978-981-10-8818-6_7

Dolnicar, S., Grün, B., & Leisch, F. (2018e). Step 6: Profiling Segments. In S. Dolnicar, B. Grün, & F. Leisch (Eds.), *Market Segmentation Analysis: Understanding It, Doing It, and Making It Useful* (pp. 183–197). Springer Singapore. doi:10.1007/978-981-10-8818-6_8

Dolnicar, S., Grün, B., & Leisch, F. (2018f). Step 10: Evaluation and Monitoring. In S. Dolnicar, B. Grün, & F. Leisch (Eds.), *Market Segmentation Analysis: Understanding It, Doing It, and Making It Useful* (pp. 255–267). Springer Singapore., doi:10.1007/978-981-10-8818-6_12

Dzyabura, D., & Yoganarasimhan, H. (2018). Machine learning and marketing. In N. Mizik & D. M. Hanssens (Eds.), *Handbook of Marketing Analytics* (pp. 255–279). Edward Elgar Publishing. doi:10.4337/9781784716752.00023

Foedermayr, E. K., & Diamantopoulos, A. (2008). Market Segmentation in Practice: Review of Empirical Studies, Methodological Assessment, and Agenda for Future Research. *Journal of Strategic Marketing, 16*(3), 223–265. doi:10.1080/09652540802117140

Gnanaraj, T. N., Kumar, K. R., & Monica, N. (2014). Survey on mining clusters using new k-mean algorithm from structured and unstructured data. *Int. J. Adv. Comput. Sci. Technol, 3*(2).

Green, P. E., Frank, R. E., & Robinson, P. J. (1967). Cluster Analysis in Test Market Selection. *Management Science, 13*(8), B387–B400. doi:10.1287/mnsc.13.8.B387

Grewal, D., & Levy, M. (2020). *Loose Leaf for M: Marketing*. McGraw-Hill Education. https://books.google.co.uk/books?id=OIj9yAEACAAJ

Hack-Polay, D., Mahmoud, A. B., Ikafa, I., Rahman, M., Kordowicz, M., & Verde, J. M. (2022). Steering resilience in nursing practice: Examining the impact of digital innovations and enhanced emotional training on nurse competencies. *Technovation, 102549*. Advance online publication. doi:10.1016/j.technovation.2022.102549

Hair, J. F. Jr, & Sarstedt, M. (2021). Data, measurement, and causal inferences in machine learning: Opportunities and challenges for marketing. *Journal of Marketing Theory and Practice*, *29*(1), 65–77. doi:10.1080/10696679.2020.1860683

Hajibaba, H., Grün, B., & Dolnicar, S. (2020). Improving the stability of market segmentation analysis. *International Journal of Contemporary Hospitality Management*, *32*(4), 1393–1411. doi:10.1108/IJCHM-02-2019-0137

Hall, D. (2016). Exploring wine knowledge, aesthetics and ephemerality: Clustering consumers. *International Journal of Wine Business Research*, *28*(2), 134–153. doi:10.1108/IJWBR-09-2015-0044

Hennig, C., & Liao, T. F. (2013). How to find an appropriate clustering for mixed-type variables with application to socio-economic stratification. *Journal of the Royal Statistical Society: Series C (Applied Statistics), 62*(3), 309-369. doi:10.1111/j.1467-9876.2012.01066.x

Karlsson, L. (2015). *The impact of checklists on organisational target segment selection*. Academic Press.

Kevin, E. V., Nigel, K. L. P., & Mark, R. B. (2002). Cluster Analysis of Marketing Data Examining On-line Shopping Orientation: A Comparison of K-Means and Rough Clustering Approaches. In A. A. Hussein, S. N. Charles, & S. Ruhul (Eds.), *Heuristic and Optimization for Knowledge Discovery* (pp. 208–225). IGI Global. doi:10.4018/978-1-930708-26-6.ch011

Kohli, A., & Gupta, N. (2021). *Big Data Analytics: An Overview*. Academic Press.

Kotler, P., Keller, K., Brady, M., Goodman, M., & Hansen, T. (2019). *Marketing Management* (4th European Edition). Pearson. https://books.google.co.uk/books?id=_-2hDwAAQBAJ

Lasi, H., Fettke, P., Kemper, H.-G., Feld, T., & Hoffmann, M. (2014). Industry 4.0. *Business & Information Systems Engineering*, *6*(4), 239–242. doi:10.100712599-014-0334-4

Liao, Y., Deschamps, F., Loures, E. F. R., & Ramos, L. F. P. (2017). Past, present and future of Industry 4.0 - a systematic literature review and research agenda proposal. *International Journal of Production Research*, *55*(12), 3609–3629. doi:10.1080/00207543.2017.1308576

Ma, L., & Sun, B. (2020). Machine learning and AI in marketing – Connecting computing power to human insights. *International Journal of Research in Marketing*, *37*(3), 481–504. doi:10.1016/j.ijresmar.2020.04.005

Mahmoud, A. B. (2021). Like a Cog in a Machine. In C. Machado & J. P. Davim (Eds.), *Advances in Intelligent, Flexible, and Lean Management and Engineering* (pp. 1–20). IGI Global. doi:10.4018/978-1-7998-5768-6.ch001

Mahmoud, A. B., Tehseen, S., & Fuxman, L. (2020). The Dark Side of Artificial Intelligence in Retail Innovation. In E. Pantano (Ed.), *Retail Futures* (1st ed., pp. 165–180). Emerald Publishing Limited. doi:10.1108/978-1-83867-663-620201019

Malhotra, S. (2022). Embrace the Data Analytics Chase: A Journey from Basics to Business. In K. Chaudhary & M. Alam (Eds.), *Big Data Analytics* (pp. 1–17). CRC Press. doi:10.1201/9781003175711-1

McCurley Hortman, S., Allaway, A. W., Barry Mason, J., & Rasp, J. (1990). Multi-segment analysis of supermarket patronage. *Journal of Business Research, 21*(3), 209–223. doi:10.1016/0148-2963(90)90029-D

McDonald, M., Christopher, M., & Bass, M. (2003). Market segmentation. In M. McDonald, M. Christopher, & M. Bass (Eds.), *Marketing: a complete guide* (pp. 41–65). Macmillan Education UK. doi:10.1007/978-1-4039-3741-4_3

McKinsey. (2014). *Big Data, Analytics, and the Future of Marketing & Sales*. Createspace Independent Pub. https://books.google.co.uk/books?id=u-XRoQEACAAJ

Naeem, M., Jamal, T., Diaz-Martinez, J., Butt, S. A., Montesano, N., Tariq, M. I., De-la-Hoz-Franco, E., & De-La-Hoz-Valdiris, E. (2022). Trends and future perspective challenges in big data. In *Advances in Intelligent Data Analysis and Applications* (pp. 309–325). Springer. doi:10.1007/978-981-16-5036-9_30

Narasimham, N. V., & Gupta, M. K. (2016). Segmenting Consumers in Food and Grocery Retail. *Indian Journal of Marketing*, *46*(4), 24–38. doi:10.17010/ijom/2016/v46/i4/90527

Nasir, V. A., Keserel, A. C., Surgit, O. E., & Nalbant, M. (2021). Segmenting consumers based on social media advertising perceptions: How does purchase intention differ across segments? *Telematics and Informatics*, *64*, 101687. doi:10.1016/j.tele.2021.101687

PRB. (2021). *International Data*. Population Reference Bureau. Retrieved 2022 from https://www.prb.org/international/indicator/hh-size-av/map/country/

Proctor, T. (2021). *Absolute Essentials of Strategic Marketing*. Routledge.

Raiter, O. (2021). Segmentation of Bank Consumers for Artificial Intelligence Marketing. *International Journal of Contemporary Financial Issues*, *1*(1), 39–54.

Rousseeuw, P. J. (1987). Silhouettes: A graphical aid to the interpretation and validation of cluster analysis. *Journal of Computational and Applied Mathematics*, *20*, 53–65. doi:10.1016/0377-0427(87)90125-7

Sajana, T., Rani, C. M. S., & Narayana, K. V. (2016). A survey on clustering techniques for big data mining. *Indian Journal of Science and Technology*, *9*(3), 1–12. doi:10.17485/ijst/2016/v9i3/75971

Schilling, M. A., & Hill, C. W. L. (1998). Managing the new product development process: Strategic imperatives. *The Academy of Management Perspectives*, *12*(3), 67–81. doi:10.5465/ame.1998.1109051

Schlager, T., & Christen, M. (2022). Market Segmentation. In C. Homburg, M. Klarmann, & A. Vomberg (Eds.), Handbook of Market Research (pp. 939-967). Springer International Publishing. doi:10.1007/978-3-319-57413-4_29

Serrano-Malebrán, J., & Arenas-Gaitán, J. (2021). When does personalization work on social media? a posteriori segmentation of consumers. *Multimedia Tools and Applications*, *80*(30), 36509–36528. doi:10.100711042-021-11303-2

Shindler, M., Wong, A., & Meyerson, A. (2011). *Fast and Accurate k-means For Large Datasets*. Academic Press.

Thorndike, R. L. (1953). Who belongs in the family? *Psychometrika, 18*(4), 267–276. doi:10.1007/BF02289263

Tibshirani, R., Walther, G., & Hastie, T. (2001). Estimating the number of clusters in a data set via the gap statistic. *Journal of the Royal Statistical Society: Series B (Statistical Methodology), 63*(2), 411-423. doi:10.1111/1467-9868.00293

Valanarasu, J. M. J., Sindagi, V. A., Hacihaliloglu, I., & Patel, V. M. (2020). KiU-Net: Towards Accurate Segmentation of Biomedical Images Using Over-Complete Representations. Medical Image Computing and Computer Assisted Intervention, MICCAI 2020.

van der Aalst, W. (2016). *Process Mining*. Springer. doi:10.1007/978-3-662-49851-4

Venter, P., Wright, A., & Dibb, S. (2015). Performing market segmentation: A performative perspective. *Journal of Marketing Management, 31*(1-2), 62–83. doi:10.1080/0267257X.2014.980437

Ward, J. H. Jr. (1963). Hierarchical Grouping to Optimize an Objective Function. *Journal of the American Statistical Association, 58*(301), 236–244. doi:10.1080/01621459.1963.10500845

Weinstein, A. (2013). *Handbook of market segmentation: Strategic targeting for business and technology firms*. Routledge. doi:10.4324/9780203862483

Wheelen, T. L., Hunger, J. D., Hoffman, A. N., & Bamford, C. E. (2017). *Strategic management and business policy* (Vol. 55). Pearson.

Xiao, Y., & Yu, J. (2007). *Gap statistic and K-means algorithm. Chinese Academic Conference on Classification Technology and Application*, Zhengzhou, China.

Yang, J., Lee, J.-Y., Choi, M., & Joo, Y. (2020). A New Approach to Determine the Optimal Number of Clusters Based on the Gap Statistic. Machine Learning for Networking.

Yin, J., & Fernandez, V. (2020). *A systematic review on business analytics*. doi:10.3926/jiem.3030

Yuan, C., & Yang, H. (2019). Research on K-Value Selection Method of K-Means Clustering Algorithm. *J, 2*(2), 226-235. doi:10.3390/j2020016

Zeeshan, A., Jun, L., & Zahida, L. (2020). Discovering Knowledge by Comparing Silhouettes Using K-Means Clustering for Customer Segmentation. *International Journal of Knowledge Management, 16*(3), 70–88. doi:10.4018/IJKM.2020070105

Zhou, K., Taigang, L., & Lifeng, Z. (2015). Industry 4.0: Towards future industrial opportunities and challenges. *2015 12th International Conference on Fuzzy Systems and Knowledge Discovery (FSKD).*

KEY TERMS AND DEFINITIONS

Cluster Analysis: Is a statistical technique for data analysis. It operates by classifying objects into groups, or clusters, based on their degree of association. *Clustering* is an unsupervised learning approach, which means that prior to running the model, marketers have no idea how many clusters exist in the data.

Market Segmentation: The practice of dividing the market into distinct segments of customers with distinct requirements, desires, or characteristics—who may benefit from goods or services tailored specifically to them (Grewal & Levy, 2020).

Marketing Analytics: Is a systematic process through which marketing business challenges are addressed via the use of data, statistics, mathematics, and technological innovation. Modelling and computer software is used to make marketing decisions.

Marketing Strategy: Is a plan of action in order to achieve a major or overall marketing aim (Proctor, 2021).

Silhouette Algorithm: Offers a technique for interpreting and validating the consistency of data clusters—it generates a concise graphical depiction of the degree to which each object has been categorised properly (Rousseeuw, 1987).

APPENDIX

Hierarchical Clustering

```
hc1 <- agnes(df, method = "ward")
pltree(hc1, cex=0.7, hang =-2, main = "Dendogram using AGNES function")
#plotting dendogram with 4 borders
plot(hc2, cex=0.7)
rect.hclust(hc2, k=4, border = 2:5)
fviz_cluster(list(data=d1, cluster=sub_group))
```

Optimum Number of Clusters- Calculation – Elbow Method

```
library(purrr)
set.seed(123)
# function to calculate total intra-cluster sum of square
iss <- function(k) {
  kmeans(customer_data[,3:5],k,iter.max=100,nstart=100,algorithm="Lloyd")$tot.
withinss
}
k.values <- 1:10
iss_values <- map_dbl(k.values, iss)
plot(k.values, iss_values,
     type="b", pch = 19, frame = FALSE,
     xlab="Number of clusters K",
     ylab="Total intra-clusters sum of squares")
```

Optimum Number of Clusters- Calculation – Silhouette Method

```
library(NbClust)
library(factoextra)
fviz_nbclust(customer_data[,3:5], kmeans, method = "silhouette")
set.seed(125)
stat_gap <- clusGap(customer_data[,3:5], FUN = kmeans, nstart = 25,
                    K.max = 10, B = 50)
fviz_gap_stat(stat_gap)
```

Optimum Number of Clusters- Calculation – Gap Statistic

```
set.seed(125)
stat_gap <- clusGap(customer_data[,3:5], FUN = kmeans, nstart = 25, K.max =
10, B = 50) fviz_gap_stat(stat_gap)
```

K – Means Clustering:

```
k4<kmeans(customer_data[,3:5],4,iter.max=100,nstart=50,algorithm="Lloyd") k4
pcclust=prcomp(customer_data[,3:5],scale=FALSE) #principal component analysis
summary(pcclust)
pcclust$rotation[,1:2]
ggplot(customer_data, aes(x =Income, y = Family.Value)) + geom_point(stat =
"identity", aes(color = as.factor(k4$cluster))) +
 scale_color_discrete(name=" ", breaks=c("1", "2", "3", "4"), labels=c("Cluster
1", "Cluster 2", "Cluster 3", "Cluster 4")) +
 ggtitle("Segments of Customers", subtitle = "Using K-means Clustering")
```

Regression:

```
linearMod <- lm(Family.Total.Sales ~ Household.Size + Age +Family.Total.Visit
+ Owner.Status, data=check)
print(linearMod)
summary(linearMod)
```

Chapter 3
Panic Station:
Consumer Sentiment Analysis of the Evolving Panic Buying During the COVID-19 Pandemic

J. Patricia Muñoz-Chávez
Technological University of the Metropolitan Area of the Valley of Mexico, Mexico

Rigoberto García-Contreras
Autonomous University of Mexico State, Mexico

David Valle-Cruz
Autonomous University of Mexico State, Mexico

ABSTRACT

The COVID-19 pandemic led to changes in consumer behavior, where social commerce played a relevant role. Through the theory of protection motivation as a theoretical basis, this chapter´s purpose is the analysis of consumer sentiment in the evolution of panic buying for which the authors identified the trend themes and some important influencers during the contingency. The results show that the leaders with the highest positive sentiment levels were the President of Taiwan and the Prime Minister of Australia. WHO was the influential account with the most negative sentiment during the pandemic. Relative to trending topics, the dataset with the highest positive sentiment is related to cleaning and disinfection products. The face mask data set had the highest negative sentiment and is the trending topic with the highest polarity. The trending topic on health foods, vitamins, and food supplements had the lowest polarity.

DOI: 10.4018/978-1-6684-4168-8.ch003

INTRODUCTION

Technological advances have transformed the structures of various organizations, facilitating the way firms communicate with their audiences. The impact of social networks has generated a virtual world based on communities and platforms (Sann & Lai, 2020; Tuncer, 2021), where users create, share and exchange opinions, emotions, and experiences (Liao et al., 2021). By reviewing and rating products, services, and brands, Internet users generate data that constitute a valuable source of information for companies and business decision-makers (Kauffmann et al., 2019). E-commerce has emerged as a new mechanism in the digital economy age.

In this regard, e-commerce is one of the most widely used digital tools today. Not only because the incursion into the digital ecosystem has become a global necessity, but also because of the solution, it has represented different problems such as the pandemic caused by COVID-19, where many consumers prefer online shopping as a more convenient and secure method (Hasiloglu & Kaya, 2021). As part of this transformation, a new e-commerce paradigm emerged, called social commerce or s-commerce (Qalati et al., 2021). The first hint of the implementation of s-commerce emerged in 2005 on Yahoo! when users of that platform issued opinions and ratings about products and shopping experiences, providing textual reviews (Liao et al., 2021). Nowadays, s-commerce represents an exchanging system of products or services through social networks. S-commerce is a combination of commercial and social activities, as it connects sellers and consumers through websites and social platforms like Twitter, Facebook, YouTube, and Tik-Tok (Abed, 2020).

Numerous online social networking platforms represent an opportunity to immerse oneself in the new socio-digital era due to their great popularity and ease of use in personal and business terms. Before purchasing any product or service, consumers are accustomed to seeking evaluations online, transforming and empowering the "word of mouth" (WOM) to "electronic word of mouth" (e-WOM). According to Zhou et al. (2019), approximately 83.5% of online shoppers value the opinions of other consumers. In turn, companies can leverage this information to expand their knowledge of consumer behavior and have elements to formulate marketing strategies that contribute to organizational growth and competitive advantage (Lin et al., 2020; Sann & Lai, 2020).

Due to such information being generally unstructured and its manual processing would be a complex task (Jain et al., 2021), in recent years, sentiment analysis or opinion mining constitutes an efficient technique, by extracting, classifying, and analyzing content in Big Data; sentiment analysis has become an increasingly useful tool for processing consumer attitudes and emotions in online reviews (Chaturvedi et al., 2018). In this regard, consumer sentiment analysis allows processing large amounts of data to extract and detect polarity (positivity, neutrality, and negativity) in product reviews (Do et al., 2019)which can help Internet users to make purchasing decisions and also to rationalize them, as well as companies to a better understanding of consumer behavior, identifying problems, experiences, satisfaction, trust, and position in front of their competitors. All this could provide valuable information to improve the service (Jain et al., 2021).

Consumer sentiment analysis can be done at three levels: document, sentence, and aspect (Liu & Zhang, 2012). This paper will analyze consumer polarity towards highly demanded products during the SARS-CoV-2 pandemic, and to achieve this, the authors will identify emerging trending topics related to product purchases. Each dataset (trending topic) will be analyzed using a lexicon approach to capture positivity, neutrality, and negativity levels during the pandemic.

Studies have been carried out from different approaches such as service failures (Sann & Lai, 2020), popularity and convenience products (Greco & Polli, 2020). In this context, because consumer behavior is dynamic and generally responds to the influence of cultural, personal, psychological and social factors, as well as in response to unpredictable crisis events, generating panic buying, that is, purchases in large quantities of a certain product motivated by fear (Yuen et al., 2022), it is interesting to analyze consumer polarity regarding panic purchases since social media posts tend to influence other consumers who tend to imitate others (Zheng et al., 2021). Panic buying often occurs in the face of natural disasters, such as hurricanes and storms; pandemics, such as that generated by COVID-19; bans or shortages, such as prohibition, where consumers tend to store staples, essential products, or others that they tend to buy for fear of their prices rising or shortages (Prentice et al., 2020; Su, 2010; Yoon et al., 2018).

The COVID-19 pandemic sparked panic purchases in more than 90 countries (Arafat et al., 2021), which in many cases generated that vulnerable groups did not have access to the necessary satisfiers (David et al., 2021). For example, there was unusual demand for disinfectants, masks, food, and toilet paper first, followed by drugs, vitamins, and oxygen tanks, negatively impacting consumer welfare, prices, and the supply chain (Ivanov, 2020; Li et al., 2021). These emerging topics are used for our data collection, identifying trending topics related to these products.

The theoretical premise that this study adopts is the protection motivation theory (PMT) (Rogers, 1975), which refers to the responses to health-related threats, and explains people's motivation for self-protection (Mccullock & Perrault, 2020; X. Wang et al., 2021). The PMT proposes two cognitive processes characterized, first, by a threat and then a response assessment. In this regard, the evaluation of the threat posed by the COVID-19 pandemic, followed by the evaluation of the comments and opinions posted on Twitter about the products that should be purchased to deal with the pandemic.

In brief, the chapter focuses on the analysis of consumer sentiment in the evolution of the COVID-19 pandemic, which significantly modified shopping habits by closing businesses or limiting their hours, as well as limiting the percentage of people who could enter shopping centers to make purchases (Figliozzi & Unnikrishnan, 2021). The study will provide information that may be useful for a better understanding of consumer behavior and the effects of panic purchases, giving elements for better coping in future events. The research is guided by three questions:

RQ1: What products are the most purchased by consumers during the Covid-19 pandemic?
RQ2: What are the trending topics related to the products most purchased by consumers during the Covid-19 pandemic?
RQ3: What is the polarity of customers towards the products most purchased during the Covid-19 Pandemic?

The rest of this chapter is as follows: Section two introduces the literature review related to panic buying in natural disasters or pandemics, social commerce, panic buying during the Covid-19 pandemic, and sentiment analysis. The method based on multimodal sentiment analysis is explained in Section Three. Analysis results are presented in Section Four. Finally, conclusions and future research are provided in Section Five.

BACKGROUND

Natural Disasters and Panic Buying

It is common to observe changes in collective behavior when severe events happen and trigger anxiety and uncertainty in society. These changes are often considered irrational and have their roots in diverse emotional reactions to sudden events that represent a potential threat (Gao & Liu, 2017). For instance: nuclear disasters, terrorist attacks, earthquakes, pandemics, hurricanes, snowfalls, wildfires, economic crises, product shortages, among other natural and human disasters (Gao & Liu, 2015; Prentice et al., 2020; Wang et al., 2019).

A frequent reaction in critical situations is the panic of consumers (Naeem, 2021). In this regard, panic buying is defined as erratic human behavior, which is observed in a sudden and unusual increase in the purchase (impulsive or planned) of one or more essential goods and is triggered by some adversity and impacts on the balance between supply and demand (Arafat et al., 2021; Loxton et al., 2020).

As previously mentioned, this kind of behavior is frequent in critical events, aiming to prevent shortages, ensuring the accumulation of goods and products for survival, and even reducing fear and uncertainty in the face of the crisis. Food, medicines, medical supplies, and fuel are the most sought-after items during these periods (Anastasiadou et al., 2020; Loxton et al., 2020). Disasters that lead to panic buying can have either a human cause (e.g., terrorist attacks, cyber-attacks, environmental disasters, or wars) or a natural cause (e.g., earthquakes, hurricanes, tornadoes, wildfires, and floods). Although man-made disasters have catastrophic consequences for humankind (Chernobyl nuclear accident), according to Larson and Shin (2018), there is an increased concern of people for natural disasters; therefore, researchers have inquired into how consumers react during these kinds of disasters. Following the above, the authors have identified studies on panic and consumption behaviors during hurricanes and storms (Kemp et al., 2012; Larson & Shin, 2018; Sneath et al., 2009); earthquakes (Ballantine et al., 2014; Hori & Iwamoto, 2014); previous pandemic disease outbreaks (Ching, 2018; Wilson et al., 2015); and the ongoing SARS-COV-2 outbreak (Anastasiadou et al., 2020; Prentice et al., 2020). Some related studies identified during the literature review are listed below (Table 1).

In this sense, social commerce plays a relevant role since Naeem & Ozuem (2021) stand out. The information and comments issued on social networks (often with erroneous data or rumors) influence the rational decision-making of consumers and therefore motivate panic buying.

Social Commerce and Panic Buying during the COVID-19 Pandemic

Since the arrival of the COVID-19 pandemic, various changes have been identified in consumer behavior and the forms of response to the crisis (Chopdar et al., 2022). Currently, social networks are part of people's daily lives and have even become indispensable. During the pandemic, these were the prime source of information for citizens (Wu et al., 2022). In this sense, social networks have played a preponderant role, since social communities based on the Internet along with the desire of Internet users to belong to these communities have generated an increase in social commerce, since opinions and recommendations from other users have a greater influence on the purchase intentions of consumers, even above the information and advertising provided by the company itself, since they are usually more credible (Sohn & Kim, 2020). S-commerce represents an exchange of detailed information, shopping experiences, consumption, and evaluations in real time between consumers, which provides a sense of cooperation that promotes trust and perceived value, thus influencing the purchase decision (Liu et al., 2019; Liu et al., 2021).

Although e-commerce personalizes shopping experiences and offers superior features to enhance the efficiency of companies, s-commerce creates collaborative experiences and social interactions that generate a sense of community in which it is a creator of value and it can even be said that he participates in marketing and selling (Molinillo et al., 2021). In this way, social commerce is a combination of e-commerce and social networks. Therefore, it offers an innovative and cooperative way of marketing through social networks, for its potential value of influencing the intentions of Internet users to buy goods or services (P. Liu et al., 2021); Wang et al., 2019). Since purchases, evaluations and reviews of consumers in the social network are automatically added and are seen by friends of the same network (Sohn & Kim, 2020).

Table 1. Natural disasters and panic buying

Natural Disaster	Event	Study Features	Authors
Hurricanes and storms	Katrina (2005)	• Quantitative. • 427 individuals (sample). • Stress, depression, impulsive and compulsive buying.	(Sneath et al., 2009)
	Issac (2012)	• Quantitative. • 318 individuals (sample). • Negative emotions and consumption.	(Kemp et al., 2012)
	Matthew (2016)	• Quantitative. • 231 individuals (sample). • Fear, shopping convenience and shopping behavior.	(Larson & Shin, 2018)
Earthquakes	Christchurch, New Zealand (2010)	• Qualitative. • 10 individuals (sample). • Consumers modified their shopping behavior (survival essentials).	(Ballantine et al., 2014)
	Tohoku, Japan (2011)	• Quantitative. • Data panel set. • Increase in daily expenditure due to panic buying of sustenance and goods.	(Hori & Iwamoto, 2014)
Outbreak pandemic diseases	H5N1 (1997)	• Documentary. • Panic buying of antiviral drugs and tonics to reduce fear of infection.	(Ching, 2018)
	H1N1 (2009)	• Quantitative. • Agent-based models. • The relationship between pandemic trajectories and the relationship to social responses.	(Wilson et al., 2015)
	SARS-COV-2 (2019-present)	• Qualitative. • Two case studies. • Changes in consumer behavior due to fear caused by the spread of the coronavirus.	(Anastasiadou et al., 2020)
	SARS-COV-2 (2019-present)	• Opinion mining. • Twitter • The relationship between pandemic countermeasures and side effects such as panic buying.	(Prentice et al., 2020)

Source Authors' Own Elaboration.

In this context, e-WOM is generated through s-commerce, which has a driving force in consumer purchasing decisions considering that allows positive or negative statements to be disseminated to anyone worldwide (Bu et al., 2021). Therefore, interactions on social networks and the opinions of celebrities or health representatives can generate anxiety in consumers and induce them to make panic purchases. It is where PTM is related to consumer fear appeals. It suggests the motivation to protect against physical, psychological, or social threat(Rogers, 1975), represented by the COVID-19 pandemic. It led consumers to assess threats and address how opinions on social media influenced their responsiveness and led them to encourage shopping behaviors to reduce harmful effects in health and well-being (Good & Hyman, 2020).

It is important to note that not all the infodemic is reliable since studies showed that erroneous information was spread on social networks (Adekoya & Fasae, 2021). This misinformation and rumors went viral and socially validated, which generated panic purchases in many countries; for example, the images on social networks of empty shelves in grocery stores and long lines of people struggling to buy goods to satisfy life necessities (Naeem & Ozuem, 2021). It confirms that the fears raised stemming from the spread of the COVID-19 virus prompted a coping process that led to motivation for protection (Milne et al., 2000). For example, panic buying toilet paper and hand sanitizers (Mao, 2020). In this context, Taylor (2021) refers that toilet paper is a means of escaping disgust stimuli, and for this and other reasons became a target of panic buying for people frightened of contracting COVID-19; in addition, selfish over-purchasing occurred, motivated by certain personality traits.

RELATED WORK

Research has helped understand consumer buying behavior in the face of panic arising from the COVID-19 pandemic. Tan et al. (2021), examined the influences of elements of planned behavior on panic shopping and how perceived probability can be affected by online news, thereby finding that neither checking online news nor monitoring perceived behavior has a significant influence on panic buying. Keane & Neal (2021) analyzed buying behavior in 54 countries and developed an econometric panic buying model, using Google search data on relevant keywords and government policy announcements findings. The results showed that blocking policies drove panic buying. Thus they found significant heterogeneity in intensity and at the time of decision making.

(Kassas & Nayga (2021) investigated the main factors that correlate with the perceived importance and timing of panic shopping decisions. The authors found heterogeneities in the correlation based on demographic and behavioral characteristics and highlighted the association with the need for control, the belief in doing the smart thing, and reducing grocery store visits. Naeem & Ozuem (2021) investigated misinformation and rumors shared on social media turned into psychological, physical, and social threats that led to panic buying. Barnes et al. (2021) used text analysis and data models of Twitter users in Italy to understand panic buying during the pandemic. Their findings showed that anxiety driving a lack of perceived control, moderated by effective government announcements, and a lack of perceived control leading to purchasing, negatively moderated by utilitarian qualities.

In addition, among the contributions on consumer behavior and panic purchases in light of the COVID-19 pandemic, Islam et al. (2021) showed that external stimuli such as limited quantity scarcity and limited time scarcity significantly increase emotional arousal in consumers and lead them to make more impulsive and obsessive purchases. Lins & Aquino (2020) found that men buy more by panic than women. Naeem (2021) points out that uncertainties, buying as persuasion, product unavailability proof, authorities' communication, global logic, and expert opinion on social media favored consumer panic buying during the pandemic.

Information and Influencer Opinion on Twitter and Panic Buying

New media and electronic devices have connected the whole world, and social networks are the bridge for the global connectivity of their users. By 2021, there were more than three billion users on social networks, and their importance has increased since the confinement by Covid-19, changing the way people work, communicate, consume and entertain themselves (Naeem, 2021). Specifically, Twitter has enabled users to reflect their emotions and express their opinions on specific topics. Twitter also provides data about helpful posts for academic research purposes on all sorts of current issues (Leung et al., 2021).

During the Covid-19 pandemic stage, as well as in previous outbreaks (SARS and Avian Flu), people relied on alternative ways, such as social networks (Twitter), to keep informed about daily news related to the virus (Billore & Anisimova, 2021). However, during the pandemic, social media has also been a source of misinformation, rumors, and fake news that turned viral and presented a psychological, physical, and social threat. Rumors during the pandemic caused panic buying. As a result, there was an unusual demand for disinfectants, masks, food and toilet paper, medicines, vitamins, and oxygen tanks (Chenarides et al., 2021; Naeem, 2021).

It led people to take actions such as panic buying around the world, leaving supermarket shelves empty, and creating a potential social problem (Billore & Anisimova, 2021; Naeem & Ozuem, 2021; Shahi et al., 2021).

On the other hand, Twitter has become an essential tool for world and opinion leaders to communicate quickly and direct information about Covid-19 and related issues. This information could influence the views and behavior of citizens (Rufai & Bunce, 2020). Likewise, in the face of uncertainty and insecurity, the profiles and information shared (tweets) on these influential accounts influence consumer decision-making, both negatively and positively. In this regard, studies by Naeem (2021) and Naeem & Ozuem (2021) indicate that people consider information posted by experts, opinion leaders, and authorities on their Twitter profile. This information can modify society's panic consumption behaviors (e.g., a person who buys plenty of paracetamol boxes because a pharmaceutical manager posted on his Twitter that it is effective against some symptoms of Covid-19). Therefore, the general information posted on Twitter (tweets); and the one posted by opinion leaders provide valuable data to analyze the trajectory and evolution of panic buying during the Covid-19 pandemic.

In this way, the social construction, derived from the interpretation of the trending topics and the tweets broadcast, motivate changes in consumer behavior, such as panic purchases. For this reason, the people who express these opinions and evaluations have a great social responsibility, since when they create, share, respond and consume information on social networks, they even involuntarily participate in social commerce.

METHODS

Currently, sentiment analysis is an area of artificial intelligence that allows the identification of patterns or characteristics in large data sets. Among its benefits is its usefulness for governments and organizations in decision-making (Chau et al., 2021; Valle-Cruz et al., 2021).

To study the consumer sentiment analysis, the authors identified the trending topics and some popular influencers during the COVID-19 pandemic, although. Data analyzed consisted of tweets contained in some trending topics that emerged during the period of uncertainty and panic caused by COVID-19. Tweets from some influencers who posted information during the pandemic were also downloaded. The twitteR library (of the R language) was used to download the tweets. twitteR is an R package which provides access to the Twitter API. Most functionality of the API is supported, with a bias towards API calls that are more useful in data analysis as opposed to daily interaction (Gentry, 2016). In this research, sentiment analysis consisted of only of tweets in English and polarity detection. Data analysis consisted of six steps described below (See Figure 1).

Step 1: The authors identified in the literature vital trending topics related to the products most purchased during the COVID-19 pandemic. The top products purchased during the pandemic period also appeared as trending topics on Twitter. Among the most important were toilet paper, which generated controversy and panic at the beginning of the pandemic. Sanitizers and disinfectants to clean surfaces exposed to the virus. Medicines to prevent infection or recovery from the disease. Healthy foods to strengthen the immune system. As well as masks, useful to prevent the spread of the virus.

Step 2. The authors identified some important influencers and selected those who own a Twitter account. Then, the authors chose Twitter account with posts just in English. In this regard, our sentiment analysis is only for the English language. These tweets were added to the sentiment analysis to enrich the understanding of the study phenomenon.

Step 3: Tweets were downloaded for each trending topic and influencer with the *TwitteR Library*; just Donald Trump's tweets it was by Kaggle. Since Donald Trump's Twitter account was were shut down, the @realdonaldtrump dataset was downloaded from https://www.kaggle.com/, an online community of data scientists and machine learning professionals. Trending topics related to products most purchased and influencers during the COVID-19 pandemic are presented in Table 2. Table 2 also shows the number of tweets downloaded for the sentiment analysis.

Step 4: The authors developed a content analysis of each data set through word clouds to identify the main topics in each data set. At this level, the authors used the tool https://wordart.com/ to make the word clouds. To achieve this, characters or symbols that had no meaning in English were excluded. The word cloud shows the frequency of most used words in each dataset to identify which topics are most recurrent in each trending topic or influencer.

Step 5: The authors calculated the magnitude of positive and negative sentiments for each Tweet (with SenticNet (Cambria et al., 2020)) and the resulting polarity as the sum of the absolute values of positive and negative sentiments:

$$polarity = |\text{å}\,positive\ sentiments| + |\text{å}\,negative\ sentiments|$$

Table 2. Analyzed data sets about consumer during the COVID-19 pandemic

Twitter account or trending topic		Tweets
Prime Minister of Jamaica	@AndrewHolnessJM	2015
President of Sri Lanka	@GotabayaR	2000
President of Taiwan	@iingwe	257
Prime Minister of Canada	@JustinTrudeau	286
Prime Minister of Singapore	@leehsienloong	2574
Prime Minister of the Commonwealth of The Bahamas	@minnis_dr	156
South Korean President	@Plaid_Moon	1121
President of the Republic of Uzbekistan	@president_uz	2613
President of the US	@realdonaldtrump	1657
Prime Minister of Australia	@ScottMorrisonMP	257
World Human Organization	@WHO	308
Influencers' total tweets		**13244**
Cleaners, disinfectants, and sanitizers	#cleaners, #disinfectants, and #sanitizers	272
Medicines	#cure, #drugs, #medicine, and #pharmaceutical	20438
Facemasks	#facemask, #mask, and #maskup	24019
Vitamins and food	#healthfood, #supplement and #vitamin	2320
Toilet paper	#toiletpaper, #toiletroll, and #toilettissue	183
Trending topics' total tweets		**47232**
Total tweets		**60476**

Source: Own elaboration

Step 6: Finally, to understand and compare the polarity of customers towards the products most purchased during the COVID-19 pandemic, the authors calculated the mean of positive and negative sentiments, as well as the polarity mean of each data set.

RESULTS

This section presents the results of the content analysis with word clouds, as well as the sentiment analysis showing the polarity of consumers and influencers.

Content Analysis of Tweets and Influencers Profiles

Each influencer had different content in his or her speech on Twitter. It depended on the context and the political situation in their country. However, the pandemic was a recurring theme in each nation, the biggest concern of the world's leaders was vaccination against COVID-19.

Figure 1. Consumer Sentiment analysis process
Source: Own elaboration

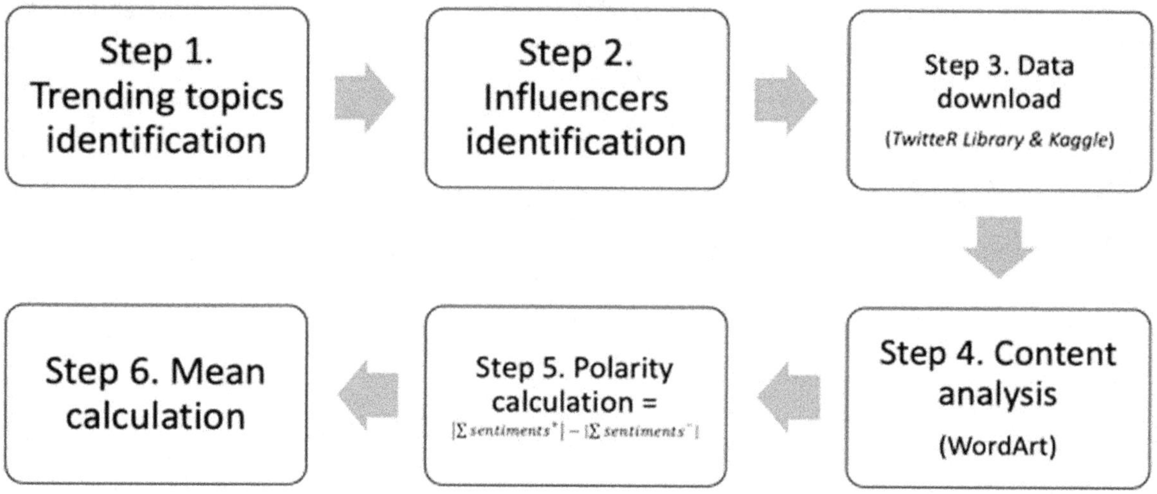

In the tweets of the Prime Minister of Jamaica, there is a sharp concern for vaccination against COVID-19. The President of Sri Lanka shows a speech of promises addressed to the people. These publications are oriented towards combating COVID-19. Similarly, the President of Taiwan shows concern for vaccination against COVID-19 with a speech of promises during the pandemic. However, Australia is a reference (on Twitter) for the Taiwanese government. The Prime Minister of Canada shows concern for two critical issues. First, vaccination, and second, climate change. However, much of his postings are in French. The Prime Minister of Singapore shows a discourse similar to the previous leaders, with promises on the fight against COVID-19.

For the Prime Minister of the Commonwealth of The Bahamas, the vaccination process against COVID is the central topic on Twitter; when the South Korean President shows a speech of promises with a great concern towards nuclear energy. The President of the Republic of Uzbekistan does not share a big topic beyond his meetings or political commitments. For the period of analysis, Donald Trump was the incumbent President of the USA. However, the most significant issues identified during the analysis period were related to his political campaign, although there is evidence of some publications related to the new coronavirus. Unlike the presidents of Uzbekistan and the US, the Prime Minister of Australia shows concern for combating the pandemic through vaccines. Finally, the WHO shows great interest in the vaccination process to combat COVID-19, led by its president, Dr. Tedros Adhanom Ghebreyesus (See Figure 2).

Content Analysis of Trending Topics

When the pandemic started, one of the most consumed products was toilet paper; this was one of the main trending topics in social networks. The high demand for this product led to shortages, which generated some supply problems at the beginning of 2020. Several posts of the pandemic are centered on toilet paper, shortage, tissue. (See Figure 3).

Figure 2. Influencers' word clouds
Source: Own elaboration

Figure 3. Toilet paper trending topic
Source: Own elaboration

Cleaners have been among the most requested products during the pandemic. These products are used at work and home for disinfection, especially on floors and different types of commonly used accessories (See Figure 4).

Figure 4. Cleaners, disinfectants, and sanitizers trending topics
Source: Own elaboration

Another product widely used during the pandemic has been medications or pharmaceuticals to prevent and treat the symptoms of the disease caused by the SARS-CoV-2 virus. However, one of the problems with vaccines and medicament is that they are not available to those most in need. In addition, the development of new drugs is still under research (See Figure 5).

Facemask is one of the most used products during the pandemic, including to combat the new variant: Omicron. The requirement in this data set is to wear masks to prevent infection (see Figure 6).

Healthy food was another relevant issue during the pandemic, since good nutrition made it possible to resist the onslaught of the disease. Meanwhile, poor nutrition favored the development of chronic degenerative diseases that caused more deaths worldwide (See Figure 7).

Sentiment Analysis and Polarity

Table 3 shows the results of the sentiment analysis and the average polarity of each data set. According to our results, the leaders with the highest levels of positive sentiment were the President of Taiwan and the Prime Minister of Australia. The WHO was the influential account with the highest negative sentiment during the pandemic, as well as the account with the highest polarity. The President of the Republic of Uzbekistan is the influencer with the lowest polarity level.

Related to the trending topics, the dataset with the highest positive sentiment has to do with cleaning and disinfecting products. The facemask dataset shows the highest negative sentiment, and it is also the trending topic with the highest polarity. The trending topic with the lowest polarity is healthy food, vitamins, and food supplements shows.

Figure 5. Medicines trending topic
Source: Own elaboration

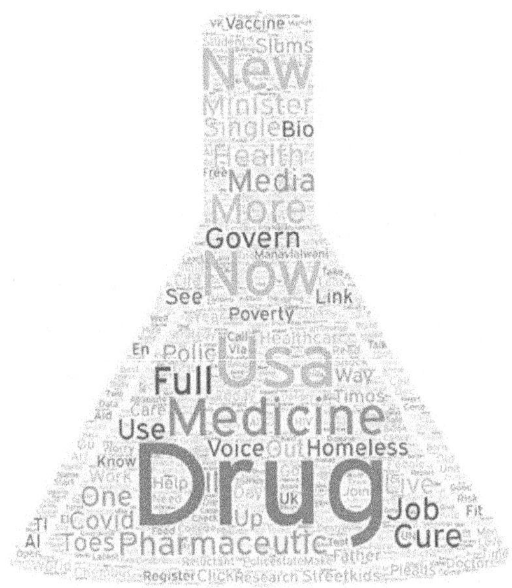

Figure 6. Facemask trending topic
Source: Own elaboration

As can be seen, the use of facemasks and the perception about their helpfulness to prevent contagions is a topic with higher polarity and controversy compared to food supplements and vitamins. The second trending topic with the highest polarity is toilet paper; it was one of the first topics during the pandemic, and panic purchases of this product caused controversy and disputes among consumers. Finally, according to our findings, on average, the influencers analyzed show a higher polarity than the trending topics.

Figure 7. Vitamins and food trending topics
Source: Own elaboration

Table 3. Positive and negative sentiments and polarity of each data set

Data set	Positive	Negative	Polarity
@AndrewHolnessJM	0.58	0.41	0.99
@GotabayaR	0.51	0.34	0.85
@iingwe	0.62	0.41	1.03
@JustinTrudeau	0.57	0.40	0.98
@leehsienloong	0.58	0.33	0.92
@minnis_drs	0.61	0.37	0.98
@Plaid_Moon	0.59	0.45	1.04
@president_u	0.46	0.29	0.76
@realdonaldtrump	0.52	0.42	0.94
@ScottMorrisonMP	0.62	0.41	1.03
@WHO	0.61	0.48	1.10
Mean	**0.57**	**0.39**	**0.96**
#cleaners	0.56	0.31	0.87
#cure	0.47	0.38	0.84
#facemask	0.48	0.42	0.90
#healthfood	0.34	0.27	0.61
#toiletpaper	0.50	0.37	0.87
Mean	**0.47**	**0.35**	**0.82**

Source: Own elaboration

SOLUTIONS AND RECOMMENDATIONS

The COVID-19 pandemic represented a threat to health, tranquility, and in general, to the well-being of human beings, which motivated self-protection as established by the PTM. In conjunction with the increase in the use of social networks derived from the confinement and uncertainty, generated a pattern of marketing and panic purchases among consumers (Arafat et al., 2021; Islam et al., 2021; Lahath et al., 2021).

Some solutions and recommendations are described below to reduce the effects in future emerging events:

1. Use social networks to provide more information to the population and counteract the fake news that accelerates the population's panic of the population in the face of emerging situations. The publication of information must be clear, sufficient, and virialized as much as possible, relying on solid arguments and support.
2. Engage the government to carry out awareness campaigns and supply the necessary products to counteract the emerging situation and avoid the population going to shopping centers and cause shortages.
3. Implement a notorious campaign of free courses taught by the public sector, civil organizations, or companies to make the population aware of the importance of not falling into panic and making compulsive buying. With this, generate a responsible, supportive, and analytical consumption behavior to take care of people's income and not affect the supply chain.
4. Shopping centers must implement a maximum number of items purchased per person to guarantee stocks, for which they must reinforce their security area to avoid riots and rioters. The entrance of the people will be gradual and taking care of the entry and stay times to avoid saturation of clients within the establishment.
5. Responsible schools, nursing homes, hospitals, cultural centers, and mass media will generate an exhaustive campaign of information and awareness to face the emerging situation by mitigating panic buying.

FUTURE RESEARCH DIRECTIONS

Currently, there have been developments in data analysis that make it possible to identify trends or behaviors through efficient methods. This research presents timely contributions to consumer panic behavior in the COVID-19 pandemic through data analysis on social media, specifically on Twitter.

Future research may focus on investigating consumer behavior on other social platforms such as Facebook, which would provide further evidence and validity to the findings. Also, future research could use different methods and tweets in languages other than English to diversify data sources.

CONCLUSION

S-commerce is a compound of commercial and social activities where sellers and consumers interact through social platforms. This digital tool increased due to the confinement that the COVID-19 pandemic implied. Which affected the commercial dynamics worldwide, modifying the behavior of the consumer, who, being exposed to the influence of social networks and trending topics, created panic in the consumer and led him to irrational behavior when making purchases to store certain products such as disinfectants, masks, toilet paper, vitamins and healthy foods, which is consistent with previous research (Billore & Anisimova, 2021; Li et al., 2021).

This study contributes to knowledge about consumer behavior in emerging times, specifically during the COVID-19 pandemic and panic purchases motivated by opinions or comments on social networks, specifically on Twitter, since users and influencers by creating and sharing information on social networks participate in social commerce, voluntarily or involuntarily influencing the purchase decision.

This chapter sheds light on the issues of judgment about the most purchased products during the pandemic, the trend issues handled by some influencers, and, through sentiment analysis, the authors identified the magnitude of positive and negative feelings, as well as the polarity of consumers towards the most purchased products during the pandemic. Likewise, some recommendations were presented that, although they are not a panacea, are intended to help by providing elements to planners and decision-makers to increase people's awareness and mitigate panic buying.

With this, the authors seek to contribute information that may be useful in better understanding consumer behavior in times of panic and provide elements for better coping in future events.

REFERENCES

Abed, S. S. (2020). Social commerce adoption using TOE framework: An empirical investigation of Saudi Arabian SMEs. *International Journal of Information Management*, *53*, 102118. doi:10.1016/j.ijinfomgt.2020.102118

Adekoya, C. O., & Fasae, J. K. (2021). *Social media and the spread of COVID-19 infodemic*. Global Knowledge, Memory and Communication. doi:10.1108/GKMC-11-2020-0165

Anastasiadou, E., Chrissos Anestis, M., Karantza, I., & Vlachakis, S. (2020). The coronavirus' effects on consumer behavior and supermarket activities: Insights from Greece and Sweden. *The International Journal of Sociology and Social Policy*, *40*(9–10), 893–907. doi:10.1108/IJSSP-07-2020-0275

Arafat, S. M. Y., Yuen, K. F., Menon, V., Shoib, S., & Ahmad, A. R. (2021). Panic Buying in Bangladesh: An Exploration of Media Reports. *Frontiers in Psychiatry*, *11*, 628393. Advance online publication. doi:10.3389/fpsyt.2020.628393 PMID:33536953

Ballantine, P. W., Zafar, S., & Parsons, A. G. (2014). Changes in retail shopping behaviour in the aftermath of an earthquake. *International Review of Retail, Distribution and Consumer Research*, *24*(1), 1–13. doi:10.1080/09593969.2013.821419

Barnes, S. J., Diaz, M., & Arnaboldi, M. (2021). Understanding panic buying during COVID-19: A text analytics approach. *Expert Systems with Applications*, *169*, 114360. doi:10.1016/j.eswa.2020.114360

Billore, S., & Anisimova, T. (2021). Panic buying research: A systematic literature review and future research agenda. *International Journal of Consumer Studies*, *45*(4), 777–804. doi:10.1111/ijcs.12669

Bu, Y., Thaichon, P., & Parkinson, J. (2021). Igniting the Flame with Electronic Word-of-mouth in Digital Marketing. *Developing Digital Marketing*, 181–190. doi:10.1108/978-1-80071-348-220211010

Cambria, E., Li, Y., Xing, F. Z., Poria, S., & Kwok, K. (2020). SenticNet 6: Ensemble Application of Symbolic and Subsymbolic AI for Sentiment Analysis. *International Conference on Information and Knowledge Management, Proceedings*, 105–114. 10.1145/3340531.3412003

Chaturvedi, I., Cambria, E., Welsch, R. E., & Herrera, F. (2018). Distinguishing between facts and opinions for sentiment analysis: Survey and challenges. *Information Fusion*, *44*, 65–77. doi:10.1016/j.inffus.2017.12.006

Chau, A. L., Valle-Cruz, D., & Sandoval-Almazán, R. (2021). Sentiment Analysis in Crisis Situations for Better Connected Government: Case of Mexico Earthquake in 2017. In Web 2.0 and Cloud Technologies for Implementing Connected Government (pp. 162–181). IGI Global. doi:10.4018/978-1-7998-4570-6.ch008

Chenarides, L., Grebitus, C., Lusk, J. L., & Printezis, I. (2021). Food consumption behavior during the COVID-19 pandemic. *Agribusiness*, *37*(1), 44–81. doi:10.1002/agr.21679 PMID:33362340

Ching, F. (2018). *Bird Flu, SARS and Beyond. In 130 Years of Medicine in Hong Kong*. Springer. doi:10.1007/978-981-10-6316-9

Chopdar, P. K., Paul, J., & Prodanova, J. (2022). Mobile shoppers' response to Covid-19 phobia, pessimism and smartphone addiction: Does social influence matter? *Technological Forecasting and Social Change*, *174*, 121249. doi:10.1016/j.techfore.2021.121249

David, J., Visvalingam, S., & Norberg, M. M. (2021). Why did all the toilet paper disappear? Distinguishing between panic buying and hoarding during COVID-19. *Psychiatry Research*, *303*, 114062. doi:10.1016/j.psychres.2021.114062 PMID:34175712

Do, H. H., Prasad, P. W. C., Maag, A., & Alsadoon, A. (2019). Deep Learning for Aspect-Based Sentiment Analysis: A Comparative Review. *Expert Systems with Applications*, *118*, 272–299. doi:10.1016/j.eswa.2018.10.003

Figliozzi, M., & Unnikrishnan, A. (2021). Home-deliveries before-during COVID-19 lockdown: Accessibility, environmental justice, equity, and policy implications. *Transportation Research Part D, Transport and Environment*, *93*, 102760. doi:10.1016/j.trd.2021.102760 PMID:33649701

Gao, C., & Liu, J. (2015). Uncovering spatiotemporal characteristics of human online behaviors during extreme events. *PLoS One*, *10*(10), 1–14. doi:10.1371/journal.pone.0138673 PMID:26492043

Gao, C., & Liu, J. (2017). Network-Based Modeling for Characterizing Human Collective Behaviors During Extreme Events. *IEEE Transactions on Systems, Man, and Cybernetics. Systems*, *47*(1), 171–183. doi:10.1109/TSMC.2016.2608658

Gentry, J. (2016). Package 'twitteR.' *Cran*, 1–32. http://lists.hexdump.org/listinfo.cgi/twitter-users-hexdump.org

Good, M. C., & Hyman, M. R. (2020). Protection motivation theory and brick-and-mortar sales-people. *International Journal of Retail & Distribution Management*, *48*(8), 865–879. doi:10.1108/IJRDM-05-2019-0155

Greco, F., & Polli, A. (2020). Emotional Text Mining: Customer profiling in brand management. *International Journal of Information Management*, *51*, 101934. doi:10.1016/j.ijinfomgt.2019.04.007

Hasiloglu, M., & Kaya, O. (2021). An analysis of price, service and commission rate decisions in online sales made through E-commerce platforms. *Computers & Industrial Engineering*, *162*, 107688. doi:10.1016/j.cie.2021.107688

Hori, M., & Iwamoto, K. (2014). The Run on Daily Foods and Goods After the 2011 Tohoku Earthquake. *Journal of Political Economy*, *40*(1), 69–113. doi:10.2753/JES2329-194X400103

Islam, T., Pitafi, A. H., Arya, V., Wang, Y., Akhtar, N., Mubarik, S., & Xiaobei, L. (2021). Panic buying in the COVID-19 pandemic: A multi-country examination. *Journal of Retailing and Consumer Services*, *59*, 102357. doi:10.1016/j.jretconser.2020.102357

Ivanov, D. (2020). Predicting the impacts of epidemic outbreaks on global supply chains: A simulation-based analysis on the coronavirus outbreak (COVID-19/SARS-CoV-2) case. *Transportation Research Part E, Logistics and Transportation Review*, *136*, 101922. doi:10.1016/j.tre.2020.101922 PMID:32288597

Jain, P. K., Pamula, R., & Srivastava, G. (2021). A systematic literature review on machine learning applications for consumer sentiment analysis using online reviews. *Computer Science Review*, *41*, 100413. doi:10.1016/j.cosrev.2021.100413

Kassas, B., & Nayga, R. M. Jr. (2021). Understanding the importance and timing of panic buying among U.S. Households during the COVID-19 pandemic. *Food Quality and Preference*, *93*, 104240. doi:10.1016/j.foodqual.2021.104240

Kauffmann, E., Peral, J., Gil, D., Ferrández, A., Sellers, R., & Mora, H. (2019). A framework for big data analytics in commercial social networks: A case study on sentiment analysis and fake review detection for marketing decision-making. *Industrial Marketing Management*, *90*, 523–537. doi:10.1016/j.indmarman.2019.08.003

Keane, M., & Neal, T. (2021). Consumer panic in the COVID-19 pandemic. *Journal of Econometrics*, *220*(1), 86–105. doi:10.1016/j.jeconom.2020.07.045 PMID:32863535

Kemp, E., Kennett-hensel, P. A., & Williams, K. H. (2012). *The Calm before the Storm : Examining Emotion Regulation Consumption in the Face of an Impending Disaster*. doi:10.1002/mar

Lahath, A., Omar, N. A., Ali, M. H., Tseng, M. L., & Yazid, Z. (2021). Exploring food waste during the COVID-19 pandemic among Malaysian consumers: The effect of social media, neuroticism, and impulse buying on food waste. *Sustainable Production and Consumption*, *28*, 519–531. doi:10.1016/j.spc.2021.06.008 PMID:34722847

Larson, L. R. L., & Shin, H. (2018). Fear During Natural Disaster: Its Impact on Perceptions of Shopping Convenience and Shopping Behavior. *Services Marketing Quarterly*, *39*(4), 293–309. doi:10.1080/15332969.2018.1514795

Leung, J., Chung, J. Y. C., Tisdale, C., Chiu, V., Lim, C. C. W., & Chan, G. (2021). Anxiety and Panic Buying Behaviour during COVID-19 Pandemic—A Qualitative Analysis of Toilet Paper Hoarding Contents on Twitter. *International Journal of Environmental Research and Public Health*, *18*(3), 1127. Advance online publication. doi:10.3390/ijerph18031127 PMID:33514049

Li, X., Zhou, Y., Wong, Y. D., Wang, X., & Yuen, K. F. (2021). What influences panic buying behaviour? A model based on dual-system theory and stimulus-organism-response framework. *International Journal of Disaster Risk Reduction*, *64*, 102484. doi:10.1016/j.ijdrr.2021.102484

Liao, S. H., Widowati, R., & Hsieh, Y. C. (2021). Investigating online social media users' behaviors for social commerce recommendations. *Technology in Society*, *66*, 101655. doi:10.1016/j.techsoc.2021.101655

Lin, H. C. K., Wang, T. H., Lin, G. C., Cheng, S. C., Chen, H. R., & Huang, Y. M. (2020). Applying sentiment analysis to automatically classify consumer comments concerning marketing 4Cs aspects. *Applied Soft Computing*, *97*, 106755. doi:10.1016/j.asoc.2020.106755

Lins, S., & Aquino, S. (2020). Development and initial psychometric properties of a panic buying scale during COVID-19 pandemic. *Heliyon*, *6*(9), e04746. doi:10.1016/j.heliyon.2020.e04746 PMID:32895636

Liu, B., & Zhang, L. (2012). A survey of opinion mining and sentiment analysis. In Mining text data (pp. 415–463). Springer. 3 doi:10.1007/978-1-4614-3223-4_13

Liu, C., Bao, Z., & Zheng, C. (2019). Exploring consumers' purchase intention in social commerce: An empirical study based on trust, argument quality, and social presence. *Asia Pacific Journal of Marketing and Logistics*, *31*(2), 378–397. doi:10.1108/APJML-05-2018-0170

Liu, P., Li, M., Dai, D., & Guo, L. (2021). The effects of social commerce environmental characteristics on customers' purchase intentions: The chain mediating effect of customer-to-customer interaction and customer-perceived value. *Electronic Commerce Research and Applications*, *48*, 101073. doi:10.1016/j.elerap.2021.101073

Loxton, M., Truskett, R., Scarf, B., Sindone, L., Baldry, G., & Zhao, Y. (2020). Consumer Behaviour during Crises: Preliminary Research on How Coronavirus Has Manifested Consumer Panic Buying, Herd Mentality, Changing Discretionary Spending and the Role of the Media in Influencing Behaviour. *Journal of Risk and Financial Management*, *13*(8), 166. Advance online publication. doi:10.3390/jrfm13080166

Mao, F. (2020). *Coronavirus panic: why are people stockpiling toilet paper?* BBC News. https://www.bbc.co.uk/news/world-australia-51731422

Mccullock, S. P., & Perrault, E. K. (2020). Exploring the Effects of Source Credibility and Message Framing on STI Screening Intentions: An Application of Prospect and Protection Motivation Theory. *Journal of Health Communication*, *25*(1), 1–11. doi:10.1080/10810730.2019.1692262 PMID:31724913

Milne, S., Sheeran, P., & Orbell, S. (2000). Prediction and intervention in health-related behavior: A meta-analytic review of protection motivation theory. *Journal of Applied Social Psychology*, *30*(1), 106–143. doi:10.1111/j.1559-1816.2000.tb02308.x

Molinillo, S., Aguilar-Illescas, R., Anaya-Sánchez, R., & Liébana-Cabanillas, F. (2021). Social commerce website design, perceived value and loyalty behavior intentions: The moderating roles of gender, age and frequency of use. *Journal of Retailing and Consumer Services*, *63*, 102404. Advance online publication. doi:10.1016/j.jretconser.2020.102404

Naeem, M. (2021). Do social media platforms develop consumer panic buying during the fear of Covid-19 pandemic. *Journal of Retailing and Consumer Services*, *58*, 102226. doi:10.1016/j.jretconser.2020.102226

Naeem, M., & Ozuem, W. (2021). Understanding misinformation and rumors that generated panic buying as a social practice during COVID-19 pandemic: Evidence from Twitter, YouTube and focus group interviews. *Information Technology & People*. Advance online publication. doi:10.1108/ITP-01-2021-0061

Prentice, C., Chen, J., & Stantic, B. (2020). Timed intervention in COVID-19 and panic buying. *Journal of Retailing and Consumer Services*, *57*, 102203. doi:10.1016/j.jretconser.2020.102203

Qalati, S. A., Yuan, L. W., Khan, M. A. S., & Anwar, F. (2021). A mediated model on the adoption of social media and SMEs' performance in developing countries. *Technology in Society*, *64*, 101513. doi:10.1016/j.techsoc.2020.101513

Rogers, R. W. (1975). A Protection Motivation Theory of Fear Appeals and Attitude Change1. *The Journal of Psychology*, *91*(1), 93–114. doi:10.1080/00223980.1975.9915803 PMID:28136248

Rufai, S. R., & Bunce, C. (2020). World leaders' usage of Twitter in response to the COVID-19 pandemic: A content analysis. *Journal of Public Health*, *42*(3), 510–516. doi:10.1093/pubmed/fdaa049 PMID:32309854

Sann, R., & Lai, P. C. (2020). Understanding homophily of service failure within the hotel guest cycle: Applying NLP-aspect-based sentiment analysis to the hospitality industry. *International Journal of Hospitality Management*, *91*, 102678. doi:10.1016/j.ijhm.2020.102678

Shahi, G. K., Dirkson, A., & Majchrzak, T. A. (2021). An exploratory study of COVID-19 misinformation on Twitter. *Online Social Networks and Media*, *22*, 100104. doi:10.1016/j.osnem.2020.100104 PMID:33623836

Sneath, J. Z., Lacey, R., & Kennett-Hensel, P. A. (2009). Coping with a natural disaster : Losses, emotions, and impulsive and compulsive buying. *Marketing Letters*, *20*(1), 45–60. doi:10.100711002-008-9049-y

Sohn, J. W., & Kim, J. K. (2020). Factors that influence purchase intentions in social commerce. *Technology in Society*, *63*, 101365. doi:10.1016/j.techsoc.2020.101365

Su, X. (2010). Intertemporal pricing and consumer stockpiling. *Operations Research, 58*(4-part-2), 1133–1147. doi:10.1287/opre.1090.0797

Tan, K. L., Sia, J. K. M., & Tang, D. K. H. (2021). To verify or not to verify: Using partial least squares to predict effect of online news on panic buying during pandemic. *Asia Pacific Journal of Marketing and Logistics*. Advance online publication. doi:10.1108/APJML-02-2021-0125

Taylor, S. (2021). Understanding and managing pandemic-related panic buying. *Journal of Anxiety Disorders*, *78*, 102364. doi:10.1016/j.janxdis.2021.102364 PMID:33517219

Tuncer, I. (2021). The relationship between IT affordance, flow experience, trust, and social commerce intention: An exploration using the S-O-R paradigm. *Technology in Society*, *65*, 101567. doi:10.1016/j.techsoc.2021.101567

Valle-Cruz, D., Fernandez-Cortez, V., López-Chau, A., & Sandoval-Almazán, R. (2021). Does Twitter Affect Stock Market Decisions? Financial Sentiment Analysis During Pandemics: A Comparative Study of the H1N1 and the COVID-19 Periods. *Cognitive Computation, 14*(1), 372-387. doi:10.1007/s12559-021-09819-8

Wang, X., Wong, Y. D., Qi, G., & Yuen, K. F. (2021). Contactless channel for shopping and delivery in the context of social distancing in response to COVID-19 pandemic. *Electronic Commerce Research and Applications*, *48*, 101075. doi:10.1016/j.elerap.2021.101075

Wang, Z., Liu, X., & Zhang, S. (2019). A New Decision Method for Public Opinion Crisis with the Intervention of Risk Perception of the Public. *Complexity*, *9527218*, 1–14. Advance online publication. doi:10.1155/2019/9527218

Wilson, J. M., Fast, S. M., Gonza, M. C., & Markuzon, N. (2015). Modelling the propagation of social response during a disease outbreak. *Journal of the Royal Society, Interface*, *12*(104), 20141105. doi:10.1098/rsif.2014.1105 PMID:25589575

Wu, G., Deng, X., & Liu, B. (2022). Managing urban citizens' panic levels and preventive behaviours during COVID-19 with pandemic information released by social media. *Cities (London, England)*, *120*, 103490. doi:10.1016/j.cities.2021.103490 PMID:34642529

Yoon, J., Narasimhan, R., & Kim, M. K. (2018). Retailer's sourcing strategy under consumer stockpiling in anticipation of supply disruptions. *International Journal of Production Research*, *56*(10), 3615–3635. doi:10.1080/00207543.2017.1401748

Yuen, K. F., Tan, L. S., Wong, Y. D., & Wang, X. (2022). Social determinants of panic buying behaviour amidst COVID-19 pandemic: The role of perceived scarcity and anticipated regret. *Journal of Retailing and Consumer Services*, *66*, 102948. doi:10.1016/j.jretconser.2022.102948

Zheng, R., Shou, B., & Yang, J. (2021). Supply disruption management under consumer panic buying and social learning effects. *Omega*, *101*, 102238. doi:10.1016/j.omega.2020.102238

Zhou, Q., Xu, Z., & Yen, N. Y. (2019). User sentiment analysis based on social network information and its application in consumer reconstruction intention. *Computers in Human Behavior*, *100*, 177–183. doi:10.1016/j.chb.2018.07.006

ADDITIONAL READING

Al-Garadi, M. A., Khan, M. S., Varathan, K. D., Mujtaba, G., & Al-Kabsi, A. M. (2016). Using online social networks to track a pandemic: A systematic review. *Journal of Biomedical Informatics, 62*, 1–11. doi:10.1016/j.jbi.2016.05.005 PMID:27224846

Arafat, S. Y., Kar, S. K., Marthoenis, M., Sharma, P., Apu, E. H., & Kabir, R. (2020). Psychological underpinning of panic buying during pandemic (COVID-19). *Psychiatry Research, 289*, 113061. doi:10.1016/j.psychres.2020.113061

Arafat, S. Y., Kar, S. K., Menon, V., Kaliamoorthy, C., Mukherjee, S., Alradie-Mohamed, A., Sharma, P., Marthoenis, M., & Kabir, R. (2020). Panic buying: An insight from the content analysis of media reports during COVID-19 pandemic. *Neurology, Psychiatry & Brain Research, 37*, 100–103. doi:10.1016/j.npbr.2020.07.002 PMID:32834528

Leung, J., Chung, J. Y. C., Tisdale, C., Chiu, V., Lim, C. C., & Chan, G. (2021). Anxiety and panic buying behaviour during COVID-19 pandemic—A qualitative analysis of toilet paper hoarding contents on Twitter. *International Journal of Environmental Research and Public Health, 18*(3), 1127. doi:10.3390/ijerph18031127 PMID:33514049

Mourad, A., Srour, A., Harmanani, H., Jenainati, C., & Arafeh, M. (2020). Critical impact of social networks infodemic on defeating coronavirus COVID-19 pandemic: Twitter-based study and research directions. *IEEE eTransactions on Network and Service Management, 17*(4), 2145–2155. doi:10.1109/TNSM.2020.3031034

Valle-Cruz, D., Fernandez-Cortez, V., & Gil-Garcia, J. R. (2021). From E-budgeting to smart budgeting: Exploring the potential of artificial intelligence in government decision-making for resource allocation. *Government Information Quarterly, 101644*. Advance online publication. doi:10.1016/j.giq.2021.101644

Valle-Cruz, D., Fernandez-Cortez, V., López-Chau, A., & Sandoval-Almazán, R. (2021). Does twitter affect stock market decisions? financial sentiment analysis during pandemics: A comparative study of the h1n1 and the covid-19 periods. *Cognitive Computation*, 1–16. doi:10.100712559-021-09819-8 PMID:33520006

Varshney, A., Kapoor, Y., Thukral, A., Sharma, R., & Bedi, P. (2022). Performing Sentiment Analysis on Twitter Data Using Deep Learning Models: A Comparative Study. In *Advances in Data and Information Sciences* (pp. 371–381). Springer. doi:10.1007/978-981-16-5689-7_33

KEY TERMS AND DEFINITIONS

E-WOM: Positive or negative information received or issued by Internet users about products, services, or brands.

Panic: Emotional state of a group in a situation of uncertainty that significantly affects the behavior of human beings.

Panic Buying: Consumer behavior that arises as a response to crisis situations, where customers purchase and store large quantities of products to avoid future threat.

Polarity: Emotional or sentiment level from negative to positive towards an event.

S-Commerce: Type of electronic commerce that, through social networks, voluntarily or involuntarily helps to motivate sales, by combining commercial and social activities.

Sentiment Analysis: Artificial intelligence technique that detects emotions and sentiments in social media.

Study of Consumer Behavior: It is to analyze what consumers buy, why they buy it, where, why, when, what use they give even after the purchase.

Chapter 4
Product Aspect Ranking Using Multi-Criteria Decision Making

Saif A. Ahmad Alrababah
Department of Information Systems, Al alBayt University, Jordan

Keng Hoon Gan
School of Computer Sciences, Universiti Sains Malaysia, Malaysia

Tien-Ping Tan
School of Computer Sciences, Universiti Sains Malaysia, Malaysia

Mohammed N. Al-Kabi
Department of Information Technology, Al-Buraimi University College, Oman

ABSTRACT

Online product reviews often mention several aspects of the product. Reviews with multiple aspects are sometimes problematic because some of the aspects mentioned are of little or no relevance to either consumers or providers. Hence, it is important to identify relevant aspects of a product by ranking them in the order of their importance. With that, this chapter introduces a new criterion known as Aspect Relevancy in the process of ranking aspects. The study also incorporates multi-criteria decision-making (MCDM) to recognize vital aspects retrieved from the consumers reviews of products and services. In ranking the selected aspects, the subjective technique for order of preference by similarity to ideal solution (TOPSIS) is employed. The experimental results using Bing Liu and SemEval 2016 Task 5 datasets have demonstrated positive outcome of the proposed approach when compared with two baseline approaches in terms of NDCG@k ranking measure.

DOI: 10.4018/978-1-6684-4168-8.ch004

INTRODUCTION

Google, YouTube, Facebook, and Twitter, among others, have become services of social networking and Online news which also provide vital information for its users. Research have exposed how people's behaviors can be considerably affected by the services they receive from social media. When a certain product or service receives a sizeable number of positive comments and reviews, this could directly lead to a considerable increase in the sales of that product or service. On the other hand, negative reviews could lead to the collapse of business institutions and even governments. A good instance can be found in the toppling of some regimes in some Middle Eastern countries (Zha et al., 2014). To this end, several political parties hold social media reviews and comments in high esteem. Production firms study and filter reviews of their products on social media to determine the situation of their products and services. On the part of consumers, they use comments and reviews from the social media to guide them in acquiring good products and services and boycotting the bad ones. Furthermore, social media reviews are an essential way of determining the degree of people's beliefs and satisfaction levels, or the opinions of people about a certain government. Tourists and travelers are not left behind in the acquisition of opinion and information using social media. For example, a site known as TripAdvisor (tripadvisor.com) is visited by intending tourists and travelers to help them in the choice of suitable accommodation (e.g., hotels and motels), restaurants, and places to visit. By following reviews on the site, the travelers know which hotels, motels, and restaurants to patronize during their visit.

The different aspects of reviews of products are different in terms of degrees of relevance. In aspect-based sentiment analysis, it is not unusual to realize that certain aspects have more effects on the final decisions of probable customers (Rana & Cheah, 2016). It is therefore important to recognize the very essential aspects to not only consumers but also to firms for the following reasons: (1) Whenever consumers are faced with the dilemma of choosing one product among many, the very essential aspects will help them in proper decision making (Rana & Cheah, 2016). (2) The very essential aspects will assist production firms in producing better products and services, and also in developing better techniques of marketing their products (Quan & Ren, 2014). The need of automatic recognition of important aspects becomes crucial considering the large quantity of reviews retrieved, which is not easy to be sorted out into relevant aspects manually.

Aspect ranking can be defined as the process of giving higher recognition to aspects of products which are more relevant. Such ranking can be carried out by sorting out the ratings of aspects which have been reviewed online. From the feedbacks of ratings in reviews, prioritization of aspects can be determined. Two underlying assumptions can be drawn from previous research concerning products aspect. The first is that the more consumers talk about a certain product aspect in online reviews, the more important it is. The second assumption is that essential product aspects attract different standpoints and sentiments in online reviews. Using probabilistic approaches, these two assumptions are further examined to prioritize the extracted aspects (Zha et al., 2014). Some scholars argue against this point that detecting the presence of product aspect alone using sentiments have its limitations. This is because product aspects which are unimportant can also be included.

Although both assumptions mentioned in previous paragraph do play essential roles in the process of prioritizing aspects, but it may not be able to cover some aspects which are contextually important such as the durability of batteries in a smartphone, for instance. This process of recognizing the aspects can be referred to as identification of domain dependent entities (Quan & Ren, 2014). Therefore, it is essential to include additional criterion that takes into the consideration of domain, which is known as aspect relevancy thereafter in this chapter. This criterion will take into account the relationship between domain products and aspects that have been retrieved.

In order to recognize the importance of aspects in a domain, relevance criteria for various aspects need to be investigated in detailed. Thus, this study focuses on the method for prioritizing aspects by using all available criteria of retrieved aspects into consideration. With that, Multi-Criteria-Decision-Making (MCDM) is deemed as suitable method because of its efficiency in analyzing several criteria simultaneously. MCDM can also evaluate the relevance of each criterion by analyzing the participated alternatives. The main idea of this work is to sort numerous criteria that are active in the products aspects using ranking process, giving more priority to more vital aspects going by the criteria. As far as we know, we have not come across past works that have attempted to utilize MCDM approach in tackling the issue of ranking of product aspects as a problem of decision making. Difference from the preliminary conference version (Alrababah et al., 2016b), this chapter advances its methods in the following ways: (1) the issue of product aspect ranking is analyzed and discussed in detail. (2) more domains have been evaluated extensively. (3) the proposed approach in this chapter has been analyzed using new measurements of evaluation (NDCG).

BACKGROUND

Related Approaches in Aspect Ranking

In the study of identification of opinion targets, it is important to note that some products have several aspects, for example, the iPhone 3GS has over 300 aspects as report by (Zha et al., 2014). Due to the differences of aspects in terms of their relevance given by customers, this makes sorting them out manually is very difficult and inefficient. In the area of aspect ranking, different methods have been suggested to solve the issues associated with aspect ranking (see Table 1).

Table 1. Related approaches on aspect ranking

Study	Ranking criteria	Approach
Hu and Liu (2004a)	Frequent-based	Extracted aspects based on the frequency of their appearances in the customer reviews
Snyder and Barzilay (2005)	Opinion-based	Proposed a ranking approach by combining ranking models for extracted aspects by modelling the dependencies among assigned ranks
Wang et al. (2010)	Opinion-based	Latent aspect rating analysis model based on analysing opinions about specific aspects in all reviews to discover the latent rating on each aspect that forming the overall aspect's rate
Eirinaki et al. (2012)	Opinion-based	Ranked the aspects based on the number of opinion words (adjectives) associated the noun to which it is the closest
Sobitha Ahila & Shunmuganathan (2015)	Opinion-based	Naive Bayes classifier & aspect ranking algorithm to analyse the pros and cons of individual aspects based on the opinions in customer reviews
Zha et al. (2014)	Frequent-based Opinion-based	Probabilistic aspects ranking approach to rank the frequent aspects based on combined weights

The works conducted by previous research in terms of aspects ranking are posed as the problem of search. In order to rank the results of web searches in the earlier days, search engines relied on the frequency of occurrence of words and expressions. A similar idea was used on the extracted aspects where the previous methods prioritized them based on the number of times they appeared in customer posts (reviews) (Hu & Liu, 2004a). In Eirinaki et al. (2012), it prioritized aspects based on how often adjectives (opinion words) are used in association to its closest noun; in that case, for every adjective used, the score of the noun receives an additional value of one. These two previous approaches are limited by the outcomes as several aspects from reviews which are actually irrelevant to the domain product were retrieved. Snyder and Barzilay (2005) presented an algorithm which adopts different ranking models for different aspects by modelling the dependencies that exist between assigned ranks. Such dependencies are obtained through relations of agreement, trying to establish if the consumers of certain products are comfortable with all aspects (parts) of the product; or if the rates of satisfaction vary as shown by customers concerning similar aspects. This work suggested attaching an integer of 1 to *k* to every aspect in their methodology to show the different levels of dissatisfaction in the viewpoints regarding other aspects (Zha et al., 2014).

In Wang et al. (2010), a latent aspect rating analysis model was proposed to combine the weights of all aspects from latent's ratings. The weights are then used for the overall relevance when producing the general rating. The focus of this work was also on the study of the measurement of different levels of opinions on the aspect, and the evaluation of the patterns of ratings by reviewers, not solely according to aspect ranking. In another work by Pham et al. (2015), authors introduced the use of a model known as the Least Squares model. This model used both specific aspect ratings and the total ratings of the reviews in order to rate product aspects from various client review.

Sobitha and Shunmuganathan (2015) introduced a new ranking approach which was based on probabilities using Naïve Bayes (NB) classifier. This method is used to further ranked aspects based on either an aspect belongs to Pros or Cons categories. A similar work is seen in the research by Zha et al. (2014). In this work, ranking of aspects was also based on probability algorithm, where the basic aspects are identified from consumer reviews gathered. Two criteria were employed: 1) The main aspects of reviews are usually part of the overall consumer reviews. 2) The frequency of points of view about certain aspects mentioned in consumer reviews greatly affects the general point of view about that product. In process of collecting and analyzing reviews, this work used a shallow dependency parser to identify nouns from the Pros and Cons reviews. Using the most common nouns extracted from the Pros and Cons reviews, a vocabulary is formed. After that, a sentiment classifier based on MPQA lexicon (Wilson et al., 2005) was employed to retrieve sentiment terms in both the Pros and Cons classes of reviews to evaluate the viewpoints of customers on different aspects. Finally, an algorithm was developed by using a unified probabilistic model to analyze the frequency of an aspect and the influence of customers' opinion about the aspects of a product. Although this work included sentiment viewpoints in its aspect ranking method, nevertheless, the relationship that exists between candidate aspects and product domain still has not been addressed.

Moreover, the work from Hu and Liu (2004b) found that by using nouns to obtain aspects will result in aspects which are non-domain related as the presence of several nouns that share no significance with the domain product in consumer reviews. Hence, in this chapter, our interest on aspect ranking shall focus on the selection of important aspects with respect to a particular domain. As far as we know, this research pioneers the investigation of the concept of product aspect ranking in relation to the problem of decision making, with the aim to establish the more relevant product aspects using both MCDM and sentiment analysis.

Product Aspect Ranking Criteria

Before an aspect can be ranked, there must be a collection of aspects obtained from the opinionated source. Hence, the gathering of aspects from consumer reviews is the first step of the ranking process of product aspects (Zha et al., 2014). This step involves the selection of probable targets from the opinions in consumer reviews. The opinions could come from different services ranging from medicine to childcare, to dentistry, or surgical pet care, to housekeeping, or even transportation. The form of opinions could be about different aspects of a particular product, for instance, a Huawei smartphone, and its different aspects ranges from screen size, battery life, screen resolution, wireless charging, and so on (Quan & Ren, 2014).

After possible aspects or targets have been identified, the second step involves the process of identifying the relevant ones. The following three criteria are the commonly used approach in the process of selecting products aspect within consumer reviews.

- Frequency-based criterion: A general assumption is that the more aspect of a product is mentioned in online reviews, the more important they are to both consumers and products/services providers. (Hu & Liu, 2004a),(Hu & Liu, 2004b; Shamim et al., 2014) This criterion is in line with the manual inspection or reading of product reviews when one wants to check out the opinion of a product. A frequently appeared aspect would be seen more often by a consumer; hence it has higher potential to draw the attention of a consumer and influence the decision of purchasing.
- Opinion-based criterion: When shortlisting aspect from review, the subjective nature of the discussions is valuable as it provides a reasonable picture of consumer's feelings about a particular product. It is not unusual to find sentiment, emotions, viewpoints etc. which will go a long way in affecting the choices of potential consumers. As such, whether an aspect contains an opinion plays an important role in the aspect selection process. (Eirinaki et al., 2012), (Pisal et al., 2011; Yan et al., 2014, 2015).
- Aspect relevancy criterion: This criterion expresses the need for selected aspects to be related to the context of consumer reviews (for instance, hotels, camera, cars, and so on). This is in line with the idea that every domain's product will have specific aspects representing it. (Quan & Ren, 2014), (Balahur & Montoyo, 2008; Chen et al., 2013, 2014). Nevertheless, since review text is subjective in nature, it will be common to find additional aspects from the words of consumers. The challenge is to determine whether a newly discovered aspect is related to a domain or not.

Using each of these criteria, selected aspects will be listed as guidance to enable consumers make better purchases, and also for producers of products and services to improve on in their business. The aspects in each list will differ from one another in terms of relevance, for the purpose of decision making. Therefore, it is important to use a scoring measure or selection criteria to prioritize the selected aspects based on their importance.

Selection of MCDM Approach

Selecting a suitable MCDM technique can be regarded as a challenge (Zavadskas & Turskis, 2011) as no particular MCDM technique can singly handle all problems of decision making (Kornyshova & Salinesi, 2007). The researches that have employed MCDM approach in the past have presented that the outcomes of the researches differ with the use of different MCDM techniques on the same decision-making problem (Dragisa et al., 2013). However, guidelines have been provided by the previous researches to assist intending researchers in choosing a suitable MCDM approach (Kornyshova & Salinesi, 2007; Roy & Słowiński, 2013). On the other hand, it is possible to record more success by applying more than one MCDM approach to a particular decision-making problem (Velasquez & Hester, 2013; Zavadskas & Turskis, 2011). This simply means that in the course of the research, emphasis should not be on the choice of the MCDM approach to be used but rather, more emphasis should be placed on adequate structuring of the decision problem by utilising appropriate evaluative criteria, criteria weights and participated alternatives.

In the next section, a framework for product aspect ranking in line with the above observations is proposed. The presented criteria will be taken into consideration during the ranking of aspects: 1) Frequent product aspects 2) Opinionated product aspects, and 3) Aspect relevancy. The ranking tasks itself is modelled as a problem of MCDM, with the prioritization of product aspects presented as an activity of ranking alternative product aspects according to the criteria.

PRODUCT ASPECT RANKING FRAMEWORK

The design of our proposed product aspect ranking framework is presented in Figure 1. SThe framework is divided into two phases, i.e., aspect extraction and aspect ranking.

Aspect extraction: This phase employs the methods of extraction of products aspect as presented in our earlier research study (Alrababah et al., 2016a), where it retrieve the candidate product aspects from the reviews of consumers based on three extraction criteria.

Aspect ranking: This phase uses MCDM to prioritize the retrieved aspects based on the criteria.

Phase One: Product Aspect Extraction

In this phase, candidate aspects will be extracted. Three stages of candidate aspects extraction are conducted based on the criteria mentioned in the previous section.

Frequent Aspect Extraction

At this stage, first, consumer reviews are tagged using the Stanford POS Tagger (http://nlp.stanford.edu) to obtain the part of speech for each term in a sentence (Abulaish et al., 2009). For this research, noun phrases (NN) are viewed as the candidate product aspects. After identifying the nouns, text preprocessing is performed to the selected nouns to get rid of unimportant characters, including the hyphen (-), for instance, 'auto-focus'. Besides, stop word deletion is performed by utilizing Stop Word list (http://www3.nd.edu/~mcdonald/Word_Lists.html). The purpose of the stop word elimination in this part of the process is to remove irrelevant product aspects. Follow, it is also essential in reducing the variety of forms of one word together in one base form to avoid duplication. For instance, 'cameras→camera', 'qualities→quality'. This is achieved through lemmatization to normalize different forms of nouns.

The outcome of this stage is a list of all the terms selected as candidate aspects as $N= \{n_1,n_2,\ldots,n_m\}$. For every $n \in N$, a frequency f_n is obtained. N is then sorted in increasing order based on the frequency of recurrence. The final list contains noun words that have received much attention, that is being mentioned at least twice in the customer reviews, thus: $N= \{(n_1,f_{n1}),(n_2,f_{n2}),\ldots,(n_m,f_{nm})\}$, where $f_n>1$.

Figure 1. The product aspect ranking framework with MCDM weighting.

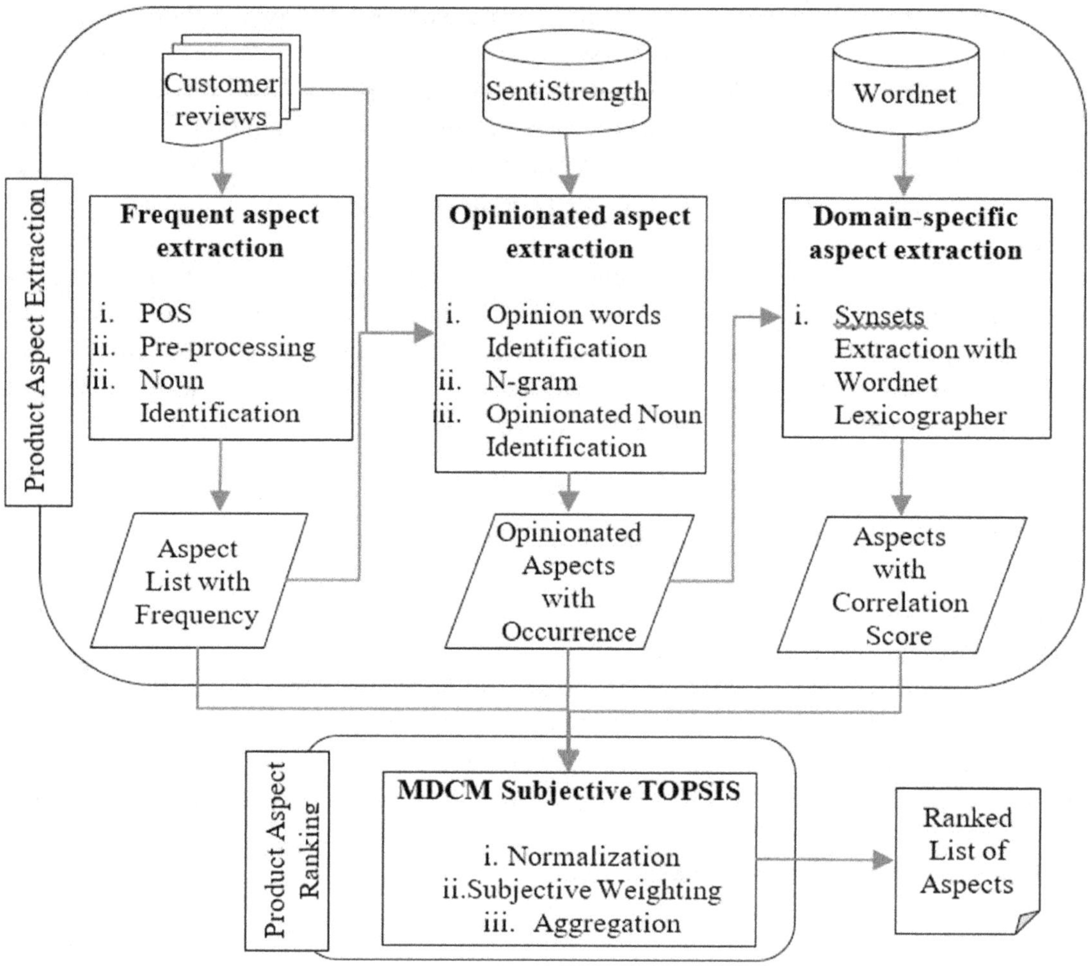

Opinionated Aspect Extraction

At this stage, consumer reviews are first cleaned using basic pre-processing steps like punctuation removal, tokenisation, lower casing and stop word elimination. Contrary to the previous stage which begin the process of aspects selection by identifying the nouns in consumer reviews, this stage will first identify the opinion word in all the reviews, followed by the available nouns accompanying the opinion words. This is referred to as the candidate opinionated aspects.

To select the opinion words in customer reviews, we use the sentiment lexicon, SentiStrength (Thelwall et al., 2010), that has been developed from different linguistic resources like Bing Liu and MPQA lexicons (Novielli et al., 2015). The selection of candidate opinionated aspects is achieved by N-gram analysis. This study performs trigram analysis for text located at two sides of the opinion word (forward and backward) to identify the candidate product aspects (nouns). This process is performed on every opinion word in the review. After locating a candidate aspect from the opinion word, we increase a numerical score referred to as the aspect score, *as*, for every aspect by 1. We then repeat this step until the final opinion word in the review has been treated. This process is then applied to the entire collection of consumer reviews, to reach a list of candidate opinionated aspects (OA). OA is denoted as follows,

$OA = \{(n_1,as_1), (n_2,as_2), \ldots, (n_m,as_m)\}$, $n_i \in N$ and $as_i > 0$.

Domain Specific Aspect Extraction

At this stage, Wordnet lexicographer files are utilised to evaluate the association between the domain product word (e.g., camera, phone) and all the opinionated aspects from the previous stage. The lexicographer files contain categories of WordNet synsets depending on syntactic classifications of noun, adjective, verb, or adverb. For this task, the noun lexicographer file is used. First, the domain(s) of the product name is located from the lexicographer files, followed by n estimation of the correlation between the domain term of the product and opinionated aspects. The correlation between the domain product term (P) and individual aspects (A) is calculated as follows.

$$C(A,P) = \frac{|A(synsets) \cap P(synsets)|}{|A(synsets)|} \quad (1)$$

The closeness between a particular aspect and product is shown by values of $C(A,P)$, taking the ranges of the values between 0 and 1. The outcome of this stage is the list of candidate product aspects and will passed to the next phase for aspect ranking.

Phase Two: Product Aspect Ranking

In determining the relevant product aspects from consumer reviews, each extraction criterion presented in phase one has its own strength. In this phase, our aim is to investigate if relevant aspects can improvise when all the criteria are considered collectively and not individually. For this purpose, MCDM technique is adopted in the context of product aspect ranking. MCDM has recorded significant success in its application to various domains, and this serves as a basis to introduce its use for product aspect ranking as shown in Figure 2.

TOPSIS Method

In the recent past, the variety of MCDM approaches have grown considerably with only very little differences among some of them, but enough to make each variety worthy to stand as an independent aspect of research (Velasquez & Hester, 2013). These reasons have influenced the choice of TOPSIS as the MCDM approach to be examined in this study because it is more readily applicable in a variety of disciplines, and more reasonable (Aloini et al., 2014). Therefore, to investigate the multi-criteria product aspect ranking in this chapter, TOPSIS has been chosen as the instrument of analysis.

MCDM problems are marked as a decision matrix of D^K, where $k=1, 2, \ldots, K$, for every decision-maker as illustrated in Figure 3, where A_i stands for the alternative and X_j is the criteria. The notation X^k_{ij} represents the performance score of alternative A_i according to criteria X_j which is signified by decision maker k.

Figure 2. High level diagram of product aspect ranking using MCDM

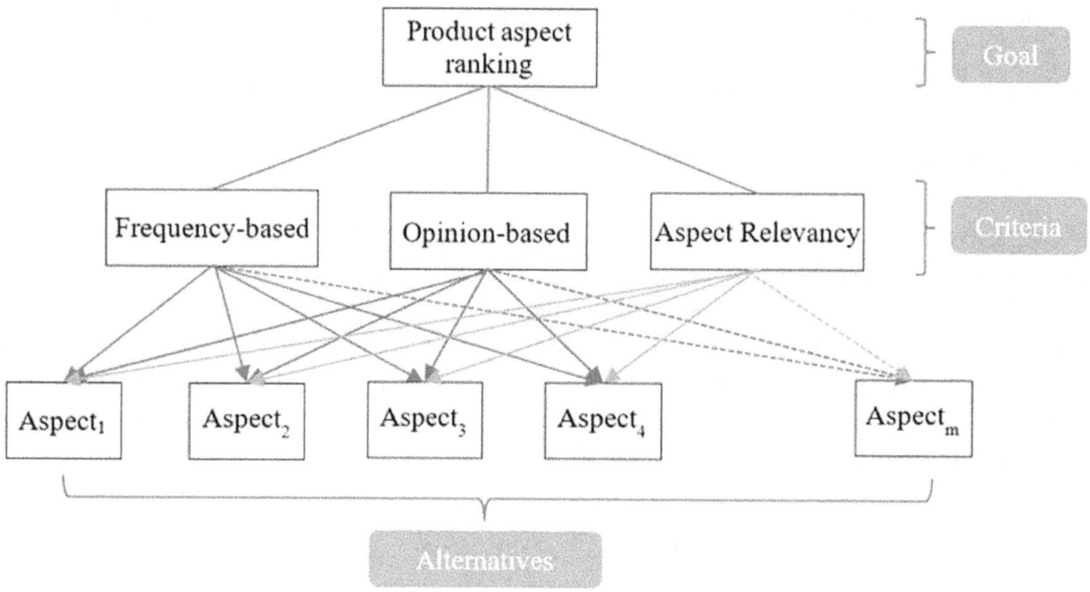

Furthermore, the reasons why TOPSIS was chosen among the many varieties of MCDM approach, is due to the fact that it possesses the least quality of rank reversal, unlike other MCDM approaches. Also, the number of criteria does not affect the number of steps of its procedure; the steps remain the same. Its simplicity of application is also another factor why it is more preferred over other MCDM techniques (Shih et al., 2007). In conducting the ranking process of aspects using TOPSIS, the shortest distance to the positive ideal solution and the largest distance from the negative solution is considered, where a positive ideal solution refers to the most preferred values of the criteria in the decision matrix, while the negative solution is made up of the least preferred values (Bai et al., 2014) . The following steps make up the TOPSIS procedure.

Figure 3. MCDM decision matrix

$$
D^k = \begin{array}{c} \\ A_1 \\ A_2 \\ \vdots \\ A_3 \\ \vdots \\ A_m \end{array}
\begin{array}{c}
\begin{array}{ccccccc} X_1 & X_2 & \cdots & X_j & \cdots & X_n \end{array} \\
\begin{bmatrix}
x^k_{11} & x^k_{12} & \cdots & x^k_{1i} & \cdots & x^k_{1n} \\
x^k_{21} & x^k_{22} & \cdots & x^k_{2i} & \cdots & x^k_{2n} \\
\vdots & \vdots & & \vdots & & \vdots \\
x^k_{i1} & x^k_{i2} & \cdots & x^k_{ij} & \cdots & x^k_{in} \\
\vdots & \vdots & & \vdots & & \vdots \\
x^k_{m1} & x^k_{m2} & \cdots & x^k_{mi} & \cdots & x^k_{mn}
\end{bmatrix}
\end{array}
$$

1. The decision matrix D^K is constructed for every *k* decision-maker as illustrated in Figure 3. The information is generally gotten in advance by a decision group or team (Shih et al., 2007b).
2. Decision matrix normalisation: For aspects to be comparable, it is important to normalise the performance scores of the aspects. The normalised scores range from [0, 1]. Equation 2 shows the vector normalisation method of TOPSIS (Dragisa et al., 2013). It is, however, possible to utilise other normalisation procedures in TOPSIS, for instance, linear normalisation and non-monotonic normalisation, particularly in the fuzzy extensions of TOPSIS (Shih et al., 2007b).

$$r_{ij} = \frac{x_{ij}}{\sqrt{\sum_{i=1}^{m} x_{ij}^2}} \tag{2}$$

3. Weights *W* is assigned to every criterion to indicate its relative importance. In classical TOPSIS, it has been stated that the weighting of criterion is the only subjective step (Cui et al., 2011; Olson, 2004; Wang & Lee, 2009), where the decision marker produces a weight w_j for each criterion j=1,2,…,n and $\sum_{j=1}^{n} w_j = 1$.
4. Establish the ideal positive response and the negative response A_i^+ and A_i^- respectively as follows.

$$A_i^+ = \{r_1^+, r_2^+, \ldots, r_n^+\} = (\max r_{ij}^+ \mid j \in J) \tag{3}$$

$$A_i^- = \{r_1^-, r_2^-, \ldots, r_n^-\} = (\min r_{ij}^- \mid j \in J) \tag{4}$$

5. Compute the separation measures for each alternative from A_i^+ and A_i^- individually. Euclidean distance measure used in TOPSIS are as follows.

$$S_i^+ = \sqrt{\sum_{j=1}^{n} w_j (r_i^+ - r_{ij})^2} \tag{5}$$

$$S_i^- = \sqrt{\sum_{j=1}^{n} w_j (r_i^- - r_{ij})^2} \tag{6}$$

for each alternative *i, i=1, 2, … m*

6. Calculate the relative closeness for each alternative to the positive ideal solution as follows.

$$C_i^* = S_i^- / (S_i^+ + S_i^-) \tag{7}$$

7. Ranking the alternatives in descending order based on the value of C_i^*

Product Aspect Ranking using TOPSIS

MCDM method deal with the assessment of a set of alternatives against numerous decision criteria. Thus, for any MCDM problem, the following stages should be observed.

1. Identifying the relevant evaluative criteria
2. Determining the participated alternatives in the decision-making problem
3. Assigning weights for all criteria, where the criterion weight indicates the relative importance of the criterion in the decision-making process
4. Processing the numeric values criteria weights and the quantitate performance of the alternatives on the criteria and aggregating these values to rank the alternatives in descending order

In this work, product aspect ranking is posed as MCDM problem. The evaluative criteria, and the alternatives are listed as follows.

1. **Evaluative criteria**:
    a. **Frequent aspect:** the raw frequency of each extracted candidate aspect, denoted as *Freq(A)*
    b. **Opinionated aspect**: the score of each candidate aspect which indicates to the number of times an aspect is opinionated in the reviews, denoted as Opinionated Score of Aspect, *OS(A)*
    c. **Aspect relevancy**: the correlation score of aspect *A* to a specific domain product, which is indicated by the number of synsets that shared between the domain product name (like 'camera') and the aspect (like 'battery') using the lexicographer files in WordNet, this criterion is denoted as *C(A,P)*
2. **Alternatives:** the product aspects that have frequently been discussed in the customer reviews are most likely to be important product aspects (Zha et al., 2014). Accordingly, all the extracted product aspects based on the frequent aspect criterion are the candidate product aspects that to be assessed against the extraction criteria.

As the first step in TOPSIS is to construct the Decision matrix D^k, if there is a K decision makers in a group of decision-making for a specific problem, then there should be K decision matrices which contain the evaluation the decision makers regarding each alternative (Shih et al., 2007). However, in our case, we have only one decision matrix, and the decision makers are all the customers who discussed the product aspects with sentiments in their reviews. Based on their feedback the important product aspects will be defined. The structure of our matrix is shown in Table 2, where X_{i1}, X_{i2}, and X_{i3} indicate to the aspect performance rating with respect to the extraction criteria *Freq(A)*, *OS(A)*, and *C(A,P)* respectively.

3. **Criteria weights**: Assigning the weights to the criteria is a critical step in TOPSIS, where the process is more subjective and based on the decision maker judgements. Generally, in aspect extraction process we are looking for the most important aspects that have been mentioned in customer reviews. Many studies indicated that if an aspect is discussed by many customers, then it is most likely to be an important product aspect (Ghorashi et al., 2012; Hu & Liu, 2004b; Yan et al.,

2015; Yu et al., 2011; Zha et al., 2014). Accordingly, in this approach, we experimentally assign the highest weight to the frequency of the candidate aspect (i.e., *freq*(*A*)). The second criterion in our approach (i.e., *OS*(*A*)) has been assigned a second higher importance, because this criterion is correlated with the aspect frequency criterion. In other words, if a product aspect is opinionated by many customers in the reviews, then it is an indicator to the importance of this aspect (Eirinaki et al., 2012). The last criterion in our decision matrix (*C*(*A*,*P*)) is given the least weight. Totally, the weights w_j that have been experimentally assigned to the criteria, j=1,2,…,n are

$$freq(A)=\alpha,\ OS(A)=\beta,\ \text{and}\ C(A,P)=\gamma,\ \text{where}\ \alpha>\beta>\gamma\ \text{and}\ \sum_{j=1}^{n} w_j = 1.$$

Table 2 The structure of decision matrix D^k for aspect ranking

Candidate Aspects	Extraction Criteria		
	Freq(A)	*OS(A)*	*C(A,P)*
Aspect $_1$	X_{11}	X_{12}	X_{13}
Aspect $_2$	X_{21}	X_{22}	X_{23}
….	….	….	….
Aspect $_i$	X_{i1}	X_{i2}	X_{i3}
….	….	….	….
Aspect $_m$	X_{m1}	X_{m2}	X_{m3}

The remaining steps of the TOPSIS procedure that have been discussed in the previous section are applied in our work to get a ranked list of candidate product aspects based on three extraction criteria. At this stage, we also apply grouping for synonyms of candidate aspects in which the customers may use different words for the same aspect. For instance, the words "*photo*", *picture*", and "*image*" refer to the same aspect in digital camera reviews. Therefore, we relatively exploit the approach of Liu et al. (2005) which is based on WordNet synsets. Furthermore, the brand name of the product has been filtered out from the ranked list of aspects as it is not an important aspect for the potential customer. For example, if the final ranked list of aspects for the digital camera "Nikon Coolpix 4300" includes the candidate aspect "Nikon", then this aspect will be discarded.

Finally, once we get the ranked list of aspects using TOPSIS, a threshold setting has been identified to select the most representative product aspects for a given domain product.

EVALUATIONS AND DISCUSSIONS

For the evaluation, two benchmark datasets of customer reviews are used. First dataset is the four electronic products that have been introduced by Bing Liu (Hu & Liu, 2004b), and the second dataset is SemEval 2016 Task 5 dataset of Laptop reviews (Pontiki et al., 2016). These two benchmarks' datasets with different sizes have been selected to investigate the ability of the proposed approach to prioritise the domain relevant aspects that are more frequent and opinionated instead of identifying only more frequent aspects. The original laptop reviews contain about 2375 sentences. Among these sentences, we focused on the sentences that have opinions, as the subjective information is the focus of sentiment analysis. Accordingly, the total number of opinionated sentences in Laptop reviews is 2039.

The effectiveness of the proposed product aspects ranking using TOPSIS has been examined using *Normalised Discounted Cumulative Gain* at top-*k* (*NDCG@k*), which is considered an important measure for ranking quality compared to many ranking measures (Järvelin & Kekäläinen, 2002; Wang et al., 2013). The importance of the NDCG ranking measure comes from its ability to handle multiple levels of relevance judgements by using a graded relevance as a measure of usefulness, whereas other ranking measures like Mean Average Precision (MAP) can only handle cases with binary relevance ("*relevant*" or "*irrelevant*") (Liu et al., 2007) where the measure of *NDCG* accumulated at a particular rank *k* is defined as:

$$NDCG@k = \frac{1}{Z}\sum_{i=1}^{k}\frac{2^{t(i)}-1}{\log(1+i)} \quad (8)$$

where $t(i)$ indicates the relative importance of the candidate product aspect at position i, and Z is a normalisation term that has been derived from the perfect ranking at the top-k aspects.

To determine the importance of the aspect, we have relatively adopted the evaluation approach introduced in the research study of (Zha et al., 2014). The evaluation approach for the aspect importance is based on human judgements by inviting three annotators to judge the importance of each aspect using three levels of importance as shown in Table 3 The annotators should read all the customer reviews in the two data sets and then judge the importance of the aspects. However, this process is time-consuming for the annotators and extremely difficult. To address this problem, we collected the top-k aspects that have been resulted from all the ranking criteria that have been discussed previously as the importance of these aspects will be determined using NDCG@k. Then a random sample of the 100 reviews sentences from each data set that discussed the collected aspects is provided to the annotators to determine the importance levels of the aspects.

Table 3 Importance levels of product aspects

Importance level	Score
Unimportant	1
Ordinary	2
Important	3

Moreover, to support the decisions of the annotators in determining the importance level of the aspects, the relevance judgements of the 100 review sentences from the two data sets, which have been attached with the benchmark datasets of customer reviews that we used in this research, are presented to the annotators. Furthermore, two files are presented to the annotators: 1) the occurrences of the aspects in all customer reviews 2) the number of times that each aspect is discussed positively or negatively in all reviews. It has been acknowledged that the frequent, as well as the opinionated aspects, are more likely to be relevant product aspects (Eirinaki et al., 2012; Zha et al., 2014). Lastly, the relative importance of the aspects is computed by averaging the annotators' ratings for each aspect.

The results of our proposed approach of product aspect ranking have been compared with the following methods:

1. **Frequency-based ranking**, which ranks the candidate product aspects based on their occurrences in the customers' reviews. This approach is similar to the approach of (Hu & Liu, 2004b).
2. **Opinion-based ranking**, where the aspects are ranked based on the number of times that each aspect is opinionated in the reviews, which is relatively similar to the approach in (Eirinaki et al., 2012).
3. **Domain specific-based ranking**. In this method, the candidate aspects are ranked based on the number of shared synsets between each aspect and the domain product name using lexicographer files in WordNet. This method is introduced in (Alrababah et al., 2016a).

Table 4 presents the results of product aspect ranking based on the above approaches in addition to our proposed ranking approach using subjective TOPSIS. The top 15 aspects are shown for the product "Digital camera1: Nikon". From this table, following observations are made.

The brand name of the product (Nikon) is considered a representative aspect of the frequency-based and opinion-based methods, as it has been mentioned in the customer reviews frequently and it was close to opinion words in some cases like the following customer review statement: "*Overall the Nikon 4300 is a very dependable…*". In the proposed approach, the name of the product has been eliminated from the candidate product aspects as it does not consider as a genuine product aspect in addition that it is not a functional aspect that could be used in comparison process like other functional aspects like "*zoom*", "*flash*".

The other methods considered synonym words are different aspects, which provides redundant information for the customers, also it affects negatively on the ranked list of aspects by preventing more important aspects to appear in advanced ranked positions. For instance, in the domain-specific ranking approach, the words "*picture*" and "*photo*" are considered different aspects. However, in our approach, by grouping the synonyms, new aspects are introduced to the customer in top ranked positions which provide more information about the product.

From Table 4, the results of our proposed approach of ranking the product aspects using subjective TOPSIS are more reasonable than other approaches, as the presented aspects are more relevant to the domain of camera and represent comparative aspects that assist the probable customers to make a wise purchasing decision. Considering all the extraction criteria jointly ranked the frequent, opinionated, and relevant aspects to the domain at top positions which are better than to adapt only one extraction criterion to identify the most important aspects. For instance, the candidate product aspect "*lens*" has been ranked at lower positions in the frequency-based approach, but in Subjective TOPSIS its ranking position was enhanced because of considering the aspect relevancy criterion, which considers this aspect as most relevant to the product name. Also, the two candidate aspects "*travel*" and "*result*" have been identified as important aspects of the opinion-based approach, which is difficult to consider as genuine product aspect. Conversely, they have not appeared in the ranking result of the Subjective TOPSIS.

Table 4. Top 15 aspects ranked by four methods for Nikon Coolpix 4300

#	Frequent	Opinionated	Domain Specific	Subjective TOPSIS
1	camera	camera	camera	camera
2	picture	picture	lens	picture
3	quality	feature	autofocus	feature
4	feature	Nikon	auto	mode
5	mode	setting	photo	battery
6	battery	photo	closeup	setting
7	shot	produce	pixel	manual
8	Nikon	image	telephoto	size
9	setting	manual	cable	lens
10	scene	**result**	setting	price
11	image	**travel**	lens	software
12	manual	accessory	picture	zoom
13	size	quality	battery	autofocus
14	**lens**	battery	design	control
15	price	shot	video	flash

Furthermore, Table 5 presents the top-15 product aspects that have been extracted from the Semeval 2016 Task 5 dataset of laptop reviews based on all the extraction approaches and the proposed approach of Subjective TOPSIS.

The domain specific approach identified the main components of the laptop as aspects of an electronic device such as "webcam" and "hardware". On the other hand, important product aspects like "price" and "quality" are obtained from frequent-based and opinionated-based approaches with different ranking positions. The importance of subjective TOPSIS approach is to prioritise important product aspects by considering all the extraction criteria jointly. For instance, the product aspect "screen" has been identified in all extraction approaches with different ranking positions. As such, in subjective TOPSIS this product aspect scored a high-rank position because of the higher weight of the frequent-based criterion. On the other hand, the product aspect "battery" is not listed as one of the top 15 product aspects of a laptop based on the opinionated-based approach, but it has frequently been discussed in the customer reviews. Accordingly, Subjective TOPSIS has an advantage in prioritising this aspect in a high ranked position as an important aspect. To sum up, considering all the extraction criteria simultaneously is more appropriate to identify those frequent, opinionated, and domain relevant aspects.

Figure 4-6 show the comparison between the proposed ranking approach using Subjective TOPSIS and the other ranking criteria of the product aspects in terms of NDCG@5, NDCG@10, and NDCG@15 respectively. From the experiments, it is clear that the proposed approach of ranking the aspects on average significantly outperformed the frequency-based, opinionated-based, and aspect relevancy ranking methods in terms of NDCG@5 by over 5.5%, 13.68%, and 27.36% respectively. In terms of NDCG@5 frequency-based approach, it outperformed the TOPSIS approach only in the product of "*Digital camera2: Canon G3*" because the competition was between candidate aspects "A" and "B" at rank position 5. In the frequency-based approach, they have the same co-occurrence scores, and thus they have been

Table 5. Top 15 aspects ranked by four methods for laptop reviews of SemEval-2016

#	Frequent	Opinionated	Domain Specific	Subjective TOPSIS
1	laptop	laptop	laptop	laptop
2	battery	product	keyboard	screen
3	screen	price	internet	product
4	product	screen	graphic	price
5	price	MacBook	wifi	battery
6	Toshiba	machine	photo	keyboard
7	keyboard	keyboard	hardware	MacBook
8	window	quality	webcam	window
9	MacBook	window	ethernet	machine
10	machine	**feature**	equipment	quality
11	quality	**light**	mousepad	money
12	drive	Toshiba	burner	feature
13	money	money	depot	drive
14	**apple**	apple	mike	apple
15	feature	display	screen	display

ranked alphabetically, but in the TOPSIS approach, the second criterion of opinionated aspects makes the difference in which the aspect "B" is opinionated much more than "A" and its performance rating is better in this criterion so that in TOPSIS the candidate aspect "B" is ranked before "A". Finally, the relevance judgement for "A" was higher than "B" which caused the frequency-based approach to outperform the TOPSIS approach. The proposed work improved the ranking of the aspects over the three methods in terms on NDCG@10 by more than 11.18%, 14.7%, and 31.48% respectively, while in terms of NDCG@15 by over 12.52%, 12.46%, and 26.84% respectively.

Figure 4. Performance of aspect ranking in terms of NDCG@5

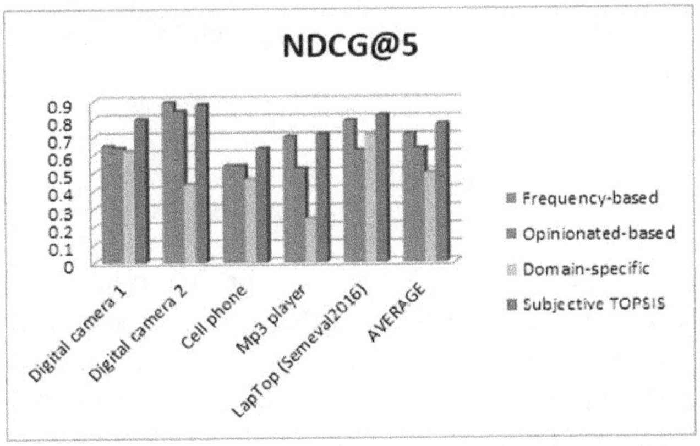

Figure 5. Performance of aspect ranking in terms of NDCG@10

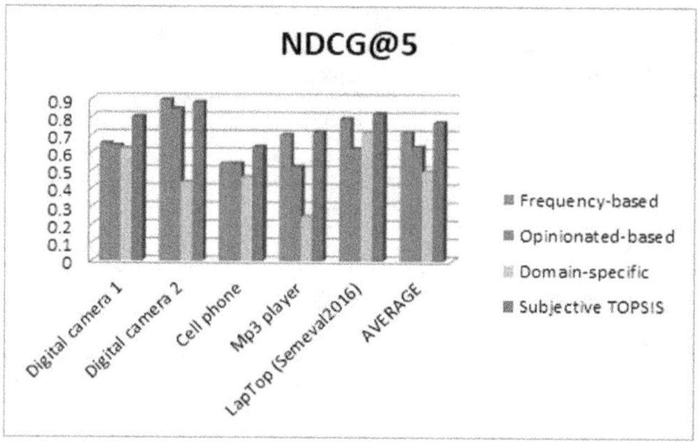

Figure 6. Performance of aspect ranking in terms of NDCG@15

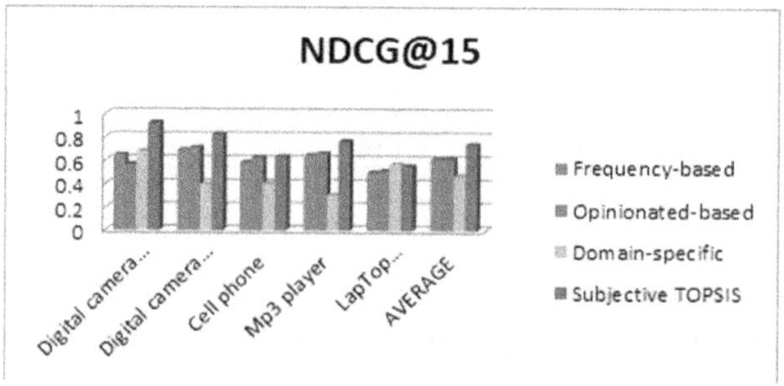

In a nutshell, we can consider that the proposed work has realised the objective of this research in identifying relevant product aspects by exploiting all the three aspect extraction criteria simultaneously using MCDM approach. Each of the three criteria considers one dimension for extracting the product reviews. The frequency-based method uses the number of occurrences of an aspect in the customer reviews; the opinion-based method is based on the number of times that the aspect is opinionated, whereas the domain-specific method identified the product aspects only based on its correlation to the domain product term. Our approach considers all these criteria collectively to identify the most representative aspects for a specific product.

CONCLUSION

Overall, this chapter presents a product aspect ranking approach to identify the most important product aspects from customer reviews. The outcome of the work can be applied to support a purchasing decision of the probable customers as well as to assist the decision makers in businesses to enhance the marketing strategies and the production plans for their products. Specifically, the proposed ranking approach has demonstrated the possibility that identification process of the product aspect can be posed as a decision-making problem in which several criteria are involved in the aspect identification process. The research has validated the approach by using MCDM to identify the most important aspects in the customer reviews, whereby TOPSIS was used to rank the extracted product aspects based on three extraction criteria to identify the most important aspects.

This work can be extended by conducting a comparative research of ranking product aspects using other MCDM approaches like VIKOR, COPRAS, etc with more criteria related to aspects. These methods could be used and evaluated to discover the similarities and differences among these methods and the ranking results obtained, in addition to considering their applicability in prioritising the most important product aspects.

REFERENCES

Abulaish, M. J., Doja, M. N., & Ahmad, T. (2009). Feature and opinion mining for customer review summarization. Lecture Notes in Computer Science, 5909, 219–224. doi:10.1007/978-3-642-11164-8_35

Aloini, D., Dulmin, R., & Mininno, V. (2014). A peer IF-TOPSIS based decision support system for packaging machine selection. *Expert Systems with Applications*, *41*(5), 2157–2165. doi:10.1016/j.eswa.2013.09.014

Alrababah, S., Gan, K., & Tan, T.-P. (2016). Domain-independent approach for mining opinionated product features using WordNet lexicographer files. *Journal of Information Science*, 1–17. doi:10.1177/0165551510000000

Alrababah, S., Gan, K., & Tan, T.-P. (2017). Comparative Analysis of MCDM Methods for Product Aspect Ranking: TOPSIS and VIKOR. *Proceedings of International Conference on Information and Communication Systems, ICICS 2017*. 10.1109/IACS.2017.7921949

Bai, C., Dhavale, D., & Sarkis, J. (2014). Integrating Fuzzy C-Means and TOPSIS for performance evaluation: An application and comparative analysis. *Expert Systems with Applications*, *41*(9), 4186–4196. doi:10.1016/j.eswa.2013.12.037

Balahur, A., & Montoyo, A. (2008). A feature dependent method for opinion mining and classification. *Proceedings on the International Conference on Natural Language Processing and Knowledge Engineering*, 1–7. 10.1109/NLPKE.2008.4906796

Chen, Z., Mukherjee, A., Hsu, M., & Castellanos, M. (2013). Exploiting Domain Knowledge in Aspect Extraction. In *Proceedings of the 2013 Conference on Empirical Methods in Natural Language Processing* (pp. 1655–1667). Association for Computational Linguistics.

Chen, Z., Mukherjee, A., & Liu, B. (2014). Aspect Extraction with Automated Prior Knowledge Learning. In *Proceedings of the 52nd Annual Meeting of the Association for Computational Linguistics (*Volume 1*: Long Papers)* (pp. 347–358). Association for Computational Linguistics. 10.3115/v1/P14-1033

Cui, Z. X., Yoo, H. K., Choi, J. Y., & Youn, H. Y. (2011). Multi-criteria group decision making with fuzzy logic and entropy based weighting. *Proceedings of the 5th International Confernece on Ubiquitous Information Management and Communication - ICUIMC '11*, 1. 10.1145/1968613.1968706

Dragisa, S., Bojan, D., & Mira, D. (2013). Comparative analysis of some prominent MCDM methods: A case of ranking Serbian banks. *Serbian Journal of Management*, *8*(2), 213–241. doi:10.5937jm8-3774

Eirinaki, M., Pisal, S., & Singh, J. (2012). Feature-based opinion mining and ranking. *Journal of Computer and System Sciences, 78*(4), 1175–1184. doi:10.1016/j.jcss.2011.10.007

Ghorashi, S. H., Ibrahim, R., Noekhah, S., & Dastjerdi, N. S. (2012). A Frequent Pattern Mining Algorithm for Feature Extraction of Customer Reviews. *International Journal of Computer Science Issues, 9*(4), 29–35.

Hu, M., & Liu, B. (2004a). Mining and summarizing customer reviews. *Proceedings of the 2004 ACM SIGKDD International Conference on Knowledge Discovery and Data Mining KDD 04, 4*, 168. 10.1145/1014052.1014073

Hu, M., & Liu, B. (2004b). Mining Opinion Features in Customer Reviews. *Proceedings of the 19th National Conference on Artifical Intelligence, 4*, 755–760. 10.1145/1014052.1014073

Järvelin, K., & Kekäläinen, J. (2002). Cumulated gain-based evaluation of IR techniques. *ACM Transactions on Information Systems, 20*(4), 422–446. doi:10.1145/582415.582418

Kornyshova, E., & Salinesi, C. (2007). MCDM techniques selection approaches: State of the art. *Proceedings of the 2007 IEEE Symposium on Computational Intelligence in Multicriteria Decision Making, MCDM 2007*, 22–29. 10.1109/MCDM.2007.369412

Liu, B., Hu, M., & Cheng, J. (2005). Opinion Observer: Analyzing and Comparing Opinions. *Proceedings of the 14th International Conference on World Wide Web - WWW '05*, 342. 10.1145/1060745.1060797

Liu, T., Xu, J., Qin, T., Xiong, W., & Li, H. (2007). LETOR: Benchmark Dataset for Research on Learning to Rank for Information Retrieval. *Proceedings of the SIGIR 2007 Workshop Learning to Rank for Information Retrieval, 3*(49), 3–10. 10.1561/1500000016

Novielli, N., Calefato, F., & Lanubile, F. (2015). The Challenges of Sentiment Detection in the Social Programmer Ecosystem. In *Proceedings of the 7th International Workshop on Social Software Engineering (SSE 2015)*. Association for Computing Machinery. 10.1145/2804381.2804387

Olson, D. L. (2004). Comparison of weights in TOPSIS models. *Mathematical and Computer Modelling, 40*(7–8), 721–727. doi:10.1016/j.mcm.2004.10.003

Pham, D. H., Le, A. C., & Le, T. K. C. (2015). A least square based model for rating aspects and identifying important aspects on review text data. *Proceedings of 2015 2nd National Foundation for Science and Technology Development Conference on Information and Computer Science*, 265–270. 10.1109/NICS.2015.7302204

Pisal, S., Singh, J., & Eirinaki, M. (2011). AskUs: An Opinion Search Engine. *2011 IEEE 11th International Conference on Data Mining Workshops*, 1243–1246. 10.1109/ICDMW.2011.24

Pontiki, M., & Pavlopoulos, J. (2014). SemEval-2014 Task 4: Aspect Based Sentiment Analysis. *Proceedings of the 8th International Workshop on Semantic Evaluation,* 27–35. 10.15520/ajcsit.v4i8.9

Quan, C., & Ren, F. (2014). Unsupervised product feature extraction for feature-oriented opinion determination. *Information Sciences, 272*, 16–28. doi:10.1016/j.ins.2014.02.063

Rana, T. A., & Cheah, Y.-N. (2016). Aspect extraction in sentiment analysis: Comparative analysis and survey. *Artificial Intelligence Review*, *46*(4), 459–483. Advance online publication. doi:10.100710462-016-9472-z

Roy, B., & Słowiński, R. (2013). Questions guiding the choice of a multicriteria decision aiding method. *EURO Journal on Decision Processes*, *1*(1-2), 69–97. doi:10.100740070-013-0004-7

Shamim, A., Balakrishnan, V., Tahir, M., & Shiraz, M. (2014). Critical Product Features' Identification Using an Opinion Analyzer. *TheScientificWorldJournal*, *2014*, 1–9. doi:10.1155/2014/340583 PMID:25506612

Shih, H.-S., Shyur, H.-J., & Lee, E. S. (2007). An extension of TOPSIS for group decision making. *Mathematical and Computer Modelling*, *45*(7–8), 801–813. doi:10.1016/j.mcm.2006.03.023

Snyder, B., & Barzilay, R. (2005). Multiple Aspect Ranking using the Good Grief Algorithm. *Human Language Technologies 2007: The Conference of the North American Chapter of the Association for Computational Linguistics; Proceedings of the Main Conference*, 300–307.

Sobitha Ahila, S., & Shunmuganathan, K. L. (2015). Multi agent-based aspect ranking review summarization for customer guidance. *Journal of Engineering and Applied Sciences (Asian Research Publishing Network)*, *10*(9), 4090–4096.

Velasquez, M., & Hester, P. T. (2013). An Analysis of Multi-Criteria Decision-Making Methods. *International Journal of Operations Research*, *10*(2), 56–66.

Wang, D., Zhu, S., & Li, T. (2013). SumView: A Web-based engine for summarizing product reviews and customer opinions. *Expert Systems with Applications*, *40*(1), 27–33. doi:10.1016/j.eswa.2012.05.070

Wang, H., Lu, Y., & Zhai, C. (2010). Latent aspect rating analysis on review text data. *Proceedings of the 16th ACM SIGKDD International Conference on Knowledge Discovery and Data Mining - KDD '10*, 783. 10.1145/1835804.1835903

Wang, J. H., & Lee, C. C. (2011). Unsupervised opinion phrase extraction and rating in Chinese blog posts. *Proceedings - 2011 IEEE International Conference on Privacy, Security, Risk and Trust and IEEE International Conference on Social Computing, PASSAT/SocialCom 2011*, 820–823. 10.1109/INFCOM.2011.5935305

Wilson, T., Wiebe, J., & Hoffmann, P. (2005). Recognizing contextual polarity in phrase-level sentiment analysis. *Proceedings of the Conference on Human Language Technology and Empirical Methods in Natural Language Processing - HLT '05*, 347–354. 10.3115/1220575.1220619

Yan, Z., Xing, M., Zhang, D., & Ma, B. (2015). EXPRS: An Extended PageRank Method for Product Feature Extraction from Online Consumer Reviews. *Information & Management*, *52*(7), 850–858. doi:10.1016/j.im.2015.02.002

Yan, Z., Xing, M., Zhang, D., Ma, B., & Wang, T. (2014). A Context-Dependent Sentiment Analysis of Online Product Reviews based on Dependency Relationships. *Proceedings of International Conference on Information Systems*, 1–14.

Yu, J., Zha, Z.-J., Wang, M., & Chua, T.-S. (2011). Aspect Ranking: Identifying Important Product Aspects from Online Consumer Reviews. *Computational Linguistics*, 1496–1505. https://dl.acm.org/doi/10.5555/2002472.2002654

Zavadskas, E. K., & Turskis, Z. (2011). Multiple criteria decision making (MCDM) methods in economics: An overview. *Technological and Economic Development of Economy*, *17*(2), 397–427. doi:10.3846/20294913.2011.593291

Zha, Z., Yu, J., & Tang, J. (2014). Product aspect ranking and its applications. *IEEE Transactions on Knowledge and Data Engineering*, *26*(5), 1211–1224. doi:10.1109/TKDE.2013.136

Chapter 5
Machine Learning and Time Series Models for Consumer Behavior Prediction in the Data Analytics Paradigm

Javier Sánchez García
https://orcid.org/0000-0002-5907-0340
University of Almería, Spain

ABSTRACT

In the big data paradigm, everyday consumers produce an infinite amount of data with their decisions. These data are available to companies, researchers, and institutions, and it is crucial for them to process it correctly in order to understand consumer behavior. This chapter presents the core time series and machine learning models to analyze and process consumer behavior data in order to convert raw data into useful and informative analyses, predictions, and forecasts. To do that, it introduces, explains, applies, and analyzes the results of ARIMA models, regression analysis, artificial neural networks models, machine learning decision trees, bootstrap methods, and much more. Every technique is illustrated through the R programming language, and the R code is provided through the text in order to ensure replicability and serve as a hands-on manual.

INTRODUCTION

The world generates billions of data every day. Much of this data relates to consumption, as there are 7.9 billion of people in the world who are considered as consumers. These consumers make decisions every day, leading to a footprint of consumption patterns. However, the majority of these data are non-informative without the proper treatment.

DOI: 10.4018/978-1-6684-4168-8.ch005

Companies need to adjust their production and supply decisions to the effective demand in order to minimize loses, governments need to adjust taxes to consumption in order to be non-distortionary, public and private institutions need to know consumption patterns to recommend actions to governments. Thus, there are many agents in the society interested in knowing how consumption behaves.

In order to achieve that, it is required to convert uninformative datasets in consumer behavior information. Statistical, econometrical and machine-learning models provide a solution to that. They take raw data, and through a set of steps, convert it in consumption behavior information.

This book chapter presents the main methods to model consumption behavior and convert data into predictions. For that purpose, it presents statistical, econometrical and machine-learning models and applies them to two datasets of sales and consumption, one of time series, and other of cross-sectional data. All the applications are made with the R programming language, and code for replication is provided throughout the entire chapter.

The rest of the chapter organizes as follows. Section 2 provides a revision of the state-of-the-art literature. Section 3 exposes the methods, applies them and analyzes the results. Finally, section 4 concludes.

LITERATURE REVIEW

The literature of consumer behavior prediction and analysis with machine learning and time series methods is a very rich field of research. Researchers try to develop new models or variations of existing models to adapt them to the circumstances of specific markets.

One example of this is the work from Yukseltan et al. (2021). Yukseltan et al. (2021) argue that supply conditions of natural gas differ from those of petroleum or coal, generating expensive infrastructures and difficulties in storage. In order to achieve that, suppliers require take-or-pay contracts for quantities of natural gas supply. These conditions make very important to forecast the gas demand in order to minimize risks. To achieve that, the authors propose a modulated expansion in Fourier series including comfortable temperatures as a regressor.

Hu et al. (2022) argue that including tourism-generated online review data related to tourism destinations highly increases the performance of tourism demand prediction models. Specifically, mixed data sampling (MIDAS) models, which include high frequency data of tourism review data in addition to traditional variables, outperform any other alternative. Zang and Chiu (2021) study how the epidemic outbreak affected consumer behavior in China by comparing how consumers behave before and after the COVID-19 pandemic by employing consumer's confidence and other indices). In a similar fashion, Rathnayaka et al. (2022) study consumer's demand patterns in ten Asian countries, revealing important dissimilarities between countries in their consumption patterns.

In the field of big data and machine learning techniques, Tian et al. (2021) and Li et al (2020) outline the importance of including big data of search engines, review platforms and social media, among other sources, to tourism consumption forecasting. As their studies reveal, including these kinds of data, and if possible, from multiple sources, highly improves predictions of tourism consumption behavior in comparison with traditional models. Li et al. (2021) compare four machine learning based feature selection methods in order to optimize the selection of variables to include in time series forecasting models. Their results show that machine learning feature selection increases the performance of ARMAX models without feature selection. Finally, Andariesta and Wasesa (2022) compare Artificial Neural Network (ANN), Support Vector Regression (SVR) and Random Forest (RF) machine learning models fed with multisource big data to predict international tourist arrivals. Their results indicate that RF models are the most accurate.

METHODS AND RESULTS

Microeconomic Determinants of Consumer Behavior

The demand of a consumer for a good or service (interchangeable hereon) is directly related to its price. Very frequently, this relationship is negative, and, indeed, it is for normal goods, which will be the focus of this analysis. Therefore, when people think about changes in the consumer demand for a good, they usually think about the good's price changes. Following this reasoning generates a demand function of a good *X* that mathematically can be represented as follows

$$Q_x = Q_x(P_x)$$

Where Q_x stands for the quantity demanded of the good *X*, and P_x for its price. As aforementioned, this relationship is normally negative in nature, except for inferior goods, where the Giffin's Paradox applies. Figure 1 represents that negative relationship between prices and quantities demanded, known as the inverse demand function.

Although the reasoning behind the inverse demand function is economically correct, it is also incomplete. This is because not only the price of a good affects its demand, but a big list of additional factors govern consumer behavior. Changes in the utility perceived by the consumer of a good (U_x), changes in the income of the consumers (Y), changes in the prices of substitute or complementary goods ($P_{y,z}$), taxes (T) and other factors determine the demand function. If the good becomes obsolete in comparison with competitors, the demand for it will decrease. Similarly, even if the price of the good declines, if the income of a group of consumers gets higher, the demand for it can increase. If a complementary good gets more expensive, consumers may consider removing the good of their consumption basket. A tax increase decreases the demand for the good as a price increase, and so on. Therefore, a more complete demand function will be

$$Q_x = Q_x(P_x, U_x, Y, P_{y,z}, T)$$

Moreover, when the price of a good declines, the demand for other a priori unrelated goods modifies in two ways. Firstly, as that good becomes cheaper than before, and goods are known to have decreased marginal utility (meaning by this that at a certain amount of quantity demanded, increasing the demand for that good will give less and less utility, this is, there normally exists a limit for the quantity demanded for most goods), the consumer will substitute the now cheaper good for others that are more expensive in comparison in his/her consumption basket. Economists call this the substitution effect. Secondly, when the price of a good diminishes, the purchasing power of a consumer increases, as he/she has more money available to buy any other good. This is the income effect.

Because of this, it is easy to see that it is very difficult, impossible sometimes, to capture all the factors that shock and shape the demand function for a good. Therefore, analytical models that capture every factor affecting the consumption path of a good are very hard to write and very costly to estimate in computational terms. Fortunately, there exist techniques that allow predicting consumption behavior with much fewer restrictions and computational costs. These methods, rooted in machine learning and time series analysis, operate by capturing the behavior and regularities of the data to get predictions. Thus, it all starts with data.

Figure 1. Inverse demand function.

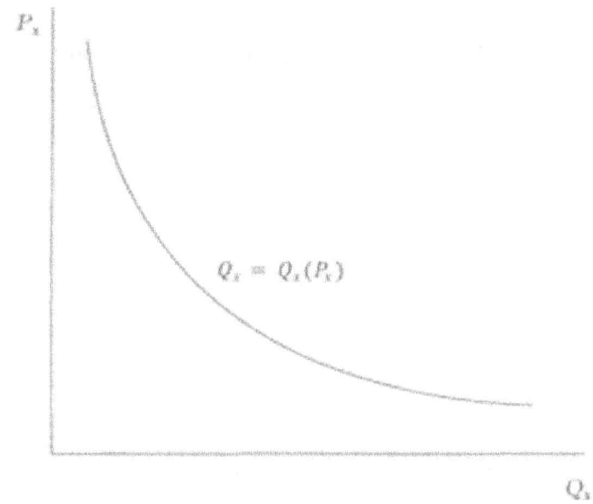

PRESENTATION AND DESCRIPTIVE ANALYSIS OF THE CONSUMPTION AND SALES DATASETS

This chapter employs two datasets. First, a univariate (with only one variable) quarterly dataset of iPhone sales from 2007 to 2016. The data unit is millions of USD. It is available free at ry. Second, a multivariate (with two or more variables) dataset available in Gretl, the Gnu Regression, Econometrics and Time-series Library, available free at http://gretl.sourceforge.net/. The dataset is called broiler.gdt, and contains data about per capita broiler chicken consumption in the US from 1950 to 2001, and other related variables. Alternatively, the reader can download both datasets clean at https://data.world/jsg608/consumer-behavior.

To carry out analysis of these datasets, the chapter will employ the statistical computing programming language R. The recommendation to the reader is to employ it for simplicity, but any other statistical package or analytics oriented programming language with machine learning capabilities will do. Through the rest of the chapter, the text in italics will be R code.

The first step is to load the datasets. This is done by the following commands.

```
library(readxl)
iphone_unit_sales_univariate <- read_excel("Path",
                                            col_types = c("date", "numeric",
"numeric"))
View(iphone_unit_sales_univariate)
library(readxl)
```

```
chickendata_multivariate <- read_excel("Path",
                                        col_types = c("numeric", "numeric",
"numeric" "numeric", "numeric", "numeric", "numeric", "numeric", "numeric",
"numeric", "numeric", "numeric"))
View(chickendata_multivariate)
```

After loading the datasets, some descriptive and graphical analysis is necessary to get a good grasp of the data. The following code will generate Figure 2 and 3, respectively.

```
st(chickendata_multivariate)
plot(iphone_unit_sales_univariate$Category,iphone_unit_sales_univariate$iPhone,
type = "l", col = "red", xlab="Time", ylab="Iphone Sales (million USD)",
pch=19, cex=1.1)
```

Figure 2. Summary statistics of the chicken consumption data.

sumtable {vtable} Summary Statistics

Summary Statistics

Variable	N	Mean	Std. Dev.	Min	Pctl. 25	Pctl. 75	Max
obs	52	1975.5	15.155	1950	1962.75	1988.25	2001
Q	52	31.238	11.986	14.3	20.975	39.925	53.9
Y	52	14850.346	4918.372	7863	9831	19599.75	23692
PCHICK	52	90.99	38.674	47.4	53.925	126.75	168
PBEEF	52	76.163	43.399	26.7	34.4	113.9	160.5
PCOR	52	81.115	28.682	44.8	53.9	101.275	158.5
PF	40	3044812.025	2754690.61	53151	1139428	5161726.75	9525909
CPI	52	77.102	51.482	24.1	30.5	119.725	177.1
QPRODA	51	11460293.941	8040556.474	2628500	5133104	15710044.5	30495171
POP	52	213660.242	48280.383	196.56	185826.25	245601.25	286362
MEATEX	42	454.881	534.46	44	76.5	646	1737
TIME	52	66.5	15.155	41	53.75	79.25	92

Figure 2 shows some insights about the chicken data. The mean per capita boneless chicken consumption is of 31.24 pounds during the period from 1950 to 2001 in the USA. Additionally, the price of beef (PBEEF), a substitute good (another kind of meat), varies more than the price of chicken (PCHICK), this is, is more volatile, as its standard deviation is 43.399 against 38.764. On the other hand, the price of corn (PCOR), a complementary good, is the least volatile with a standard deviation of 28.682, and is the highest on average among the three, with a mean value of 81.115.

Figure 3 gives intuition about some relevant aspects for constructing machine learning and time series analysis models to predict the consumption behavior of iPhones. First, the data shows symptoms of high seasonality since 2012. This means that iPhone sales vary depending on the period of the year. This tendency aggravates with the pass of the years. The models have to capture this component in order to predict correctly the behavior of consumption. Second, the sales seem to grow over time. In the same manner that seasonality, a deterministic trend should incorporate this component to our model, augmenting its forecasting power, otherwise the forecasts will be biased. Another technique available to the reader is to deseasonalize and detrend the data. However, these techniques do not allow for ignoring seasonality and trends in prediction models because it may still be present in another form (IMF, 1996).

Figure 3. Time series plot of the IPhone sales data.

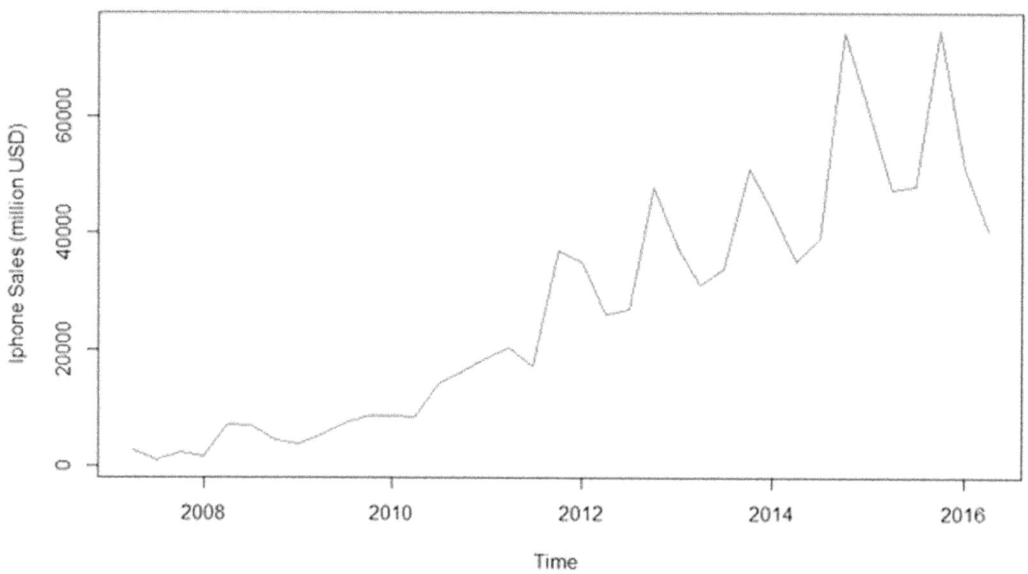

PERIODICITY, STATIONARITY AND SEASONALITY ANALYSIS

Most companies are interested in how the consumption of their products will evolve in future periods. This implies working with time series data. When working with time series data, it is important to note that data are compiled, stored, and reported in various frequencies. For example, the Gross Domestic Product (GDP) of a country is reported for each month (monthly frequency), quarter (quarterly frequency), and year (annual frequency). This is, the interval between observations are months, quarters, and years, respectively.

The periodicity of the data refers directly to the compilation of the data. Thus, the time series of the GDP can be available with a quarterly frequency via mathematical transformations, however, if the original data are compiled weekly, then the data have a weekly periodicity.

Let the reader suppose that the dataset of the Iphone sales are reported monthly, instead of quarterly. Then, at a first glance, figure 3 should not differ. However, although this is not obvious, this has important implications for the prediction models, and require a different treatment. This is directly related to the concept of seasonality introduced at the end of epigraph 2. The seasonal component of a prediction model will not be the same if the data is in a monthly or a quarterly periodicity.

Many economic sectors have seasonal consumption patterns. The retail sector sales increase exponentially in Christmas. Ice-creams sales are much higher during summer. Seasonality of the data refers to that existence of variations that happen regularly in certain periods of the time series, under a complete year. The variations are regular, predictable, and repetitive, and forecasting models have to include this or their variance will be too high. Sometimes the weather causes these variations, such as the ice-cream sales example, and therefore are easy to infer and include in the prediction model. Sometimes it is not that easy. Other times, seasonal variations are present even in deseasonalized data. Finally, as pointed by Enders (2008) the estimation of the seasonal parameters is optimally done jointly with the rest of the coefficients of a model.

Formally, consider the variable Iphone sales of the Iphone sales dataset as y_t and the seasonal trend as s. Then, the seasonal trend will appear at periods s,$2s$,$3s$, and so on. This is, taking into account that s=4 for quarterly data, then the seasonal trend will appear at periods 4,8,12, this is, at each quarter. Thus, a lineal model, which captures this seasonal trend, is

$$y_t = \alpha_4 y_{t-4} + \varepsilon_t$$

Where ε_t is an error term that captures all those things that affect Iphone sales other than the seasonal component of the time series. This model is what is called autoregressive (AR) model, as the variable is regressed on its own lagged values, and is a powerful technique to forecast consumption and sales, among other relevant time series indicators. The coefficient α_4 will therefore incorporate the seasonal tendency to our forecasting model. Here is where the periodicity and seasonality of the data interconne, as if the data had a trimestral instead of quarterly periodicity, the correct model to capture seasonality would be

$$y_t = \alpha_3 y_{t-3} + \varepsilon_t$$

Being α_4 the parameter capturing seasonality in the prediction model.

Seasonality also interacts with the sample size of the data with which the researcher feeds a model. For example, when working with seasonally adjusted data of an important trusted international organization or agency, if the modeller selects only a subset of the full sample, even when the data is seasonally adjusted, seasonality may still be present. Therefore, larger sample sizes are always preferred. This is not only true for seasonality, but in general. When sample sizes grow, the estimators employed to estimate the theoretical models proposed in paper are more robust, and therefore converge better to their true value. Not only that, but when applying a contrast of hypothesis, the bigger the sample size, the more degrees of freedom, this is, the quantity of numbers in the calculation of a statistic of interest that can change. This means better statistics. For example, let the reader think that a structural change, this is, a change in the nature of the process governing iPhone sales has happened in 2011, for example, due to informational leaks. It is possible to contrast this formally in a prediction model by employing a statistic, which will be, indeed, more powerful the more degrees of freedom it has, or putting it differently, the bigger the sample size employed.

Nevertheless, not only seasonality is a fundamental concept when starting to work with consumption behavior prediction models. Sometimes, not only a point prediction is of interest, but statistical moments such as the mean or the variance of consumption or sales are required. As the researcher can only observe realizations of consumption in one period, the only way that she can approach these moments if for long enough time samples of stationary processes. Stationary processes are those that have a constant variance and mean over time.

Let the reader recall figure 3. It is obvious that the mean and the variance of iPhone sales are quite different in the period ranging from 2008 to 2010 than in the period ranging from 2014 to 2016. Consequently, the series is not stationary. Fortunately, the researcher can transform the series to get stationary sales. In the case of the mean, by first differencing or integrating the series from itself, such as

$$\Delta y_t = y_t - y_{t\text{-}1}$$

Where Δy_t is the first differenced series that equals the rate of growth of iPhone sales. In the case of the variance, applying natural logarithms usually makes the series stationary. However, the modeller may not be interested in transforming the original series, as she is interested in levels predictions and not rate of changes of consumption behavior. Then, she can recur to techniques such as adding a deterministic or stochastic (drift) time trends to the model for capturing the change in the mean.

TIME SERIES ANALYSIS PREDICTION OF CONSUMPTION BEHAVIOR AND SALES

As aforementioned, time series techniques allow for consumer behavior prediction without further information but consumption or sales data. This means operating in a univariate setting.

The first model, to estimate is the seasonal model presented in equation 1. This will be model 1, which captures the seasonal component of the time series. After the estimation the model will look like this

$$\hat{y}_t = \hat{\alpha}_4 y_{t-4} + \hat{\varepsilon}_t$$

Where the hat indicates an estimated parameter and $\hat{\varepsilon}_t$ are called the residuals. The residuals are everything that the parameter $\hat{\alpha}_4$ does not capture from the variable $\hat{y}_t$. The following R code estimates model 1, presented in Table 1

```
iphone_ts <- ts(data = iphone_unit_sales_univariate$iPhone, start = c(2007,
1), frequency = 4)
iphone_ts
ars4 <- arima(iphone_unit_sales_univariate$iPhone, seasonal = list(order =
c(1, 0, 0)))
 install.packages("texreg")
 library(texreg)
 screenreg(ars4)
```

As table 1 shows, the parameter $\hat{\alpha}_4 = 0.93$ is statistically significant at a p-value of 0.001 and therefore the seasonal component is relevant to the model. As the reader will see, this is an AR(0,0,0)$(1,0,0)_4$ model, where the term $(1,0,0)_4$ means the model has a quarterly autoregressive term. Let the reader check the forecasts with this model in Figure 4.

```
install.packages("forecast")
library(forecast); library(tidyverse); library(dplyr)
forecast (ars4, h=4) %>%
   autoplot() +
  theme_classic() +
  ylab("Iphone sales (million dollars)") + xlab("")
```

Table 1. Model 1.

Alpha4	0.93 *** (0.05)
intercept	27568.82 * (10863.54)
AIC	794.00
BIC	798.83
Log Likelihood	-394.00
Num. obs.	37
*** $p < 0.001$; ** $p < 0.01$; * $p < 0.05$	

Figure 4. Four quarter ahead forecast of the $AR(0,0,0)(1,0,0)_4$ model.

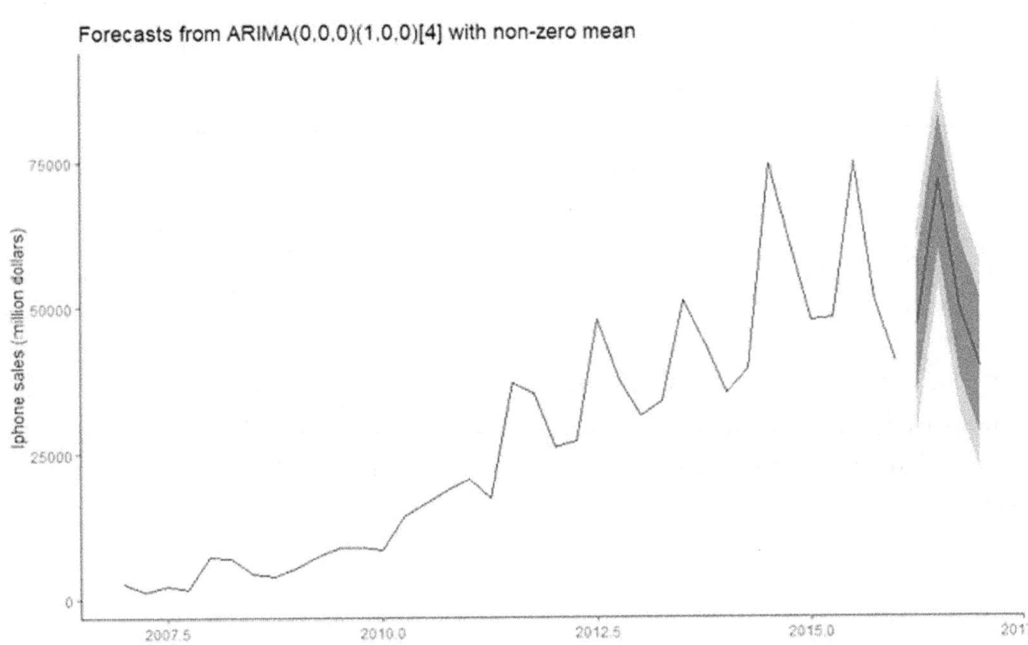

Figure 4 shows how the model's forecasts capture the seasonal trend of the time series and reproduce it. This seasonal trend is a cyclical pattern in which Iphone sales boom at the last quarter, the Christmas quarter, such as introduced before. Consumers tend to buy much more Iphones in Christmas, and to gift

Iphones to their family and friends. In the next quarter, the first of the following year, the consumption behavior is to buy still many Iphones compared to the second and third quarter, but the consumption path starts to decline from there and peaks down in the second and third quarter of the year.

However, this object will be of little interest when forecasting future Iphone sales, as it only incorporates the seasonal component, but does not capture the recurrent component of the time series. This task requires, at least, amplifying the model with the following expression, name it model 2.

$$y_t = \alpha_1 y_{t-1} + \alpha_4 y_{t-4} + \varepsilon_t$$

This is the AR$(1,0,0)(1,0,0)_4$ model. It is an autoregressive model that incorporates an AR(1) (α_1) term and an AR$(1)_4$ (α_4) seasonal term. Estimating this model means that Iphone sales depend on their latest value, and an autoregressive seasonal term.

```
ar1s4 <- arima(iphone_ts, order=c(1,0,0), seasonal=list(order = c(1,0,0)))
screenreg(ar1s4)
```

Table 2. Model 2.

Alpha1	0.76 *** (0.09)
Alpha4	0.87 *** (0.07)
intercept	24468.90 (19403.90)
AIC	762.09
BIC	768.53
Log Likelihood	-377.05
Num. obs.	37
*** p < 0.001; ** p < 0.01; * p < 0.05	

As shown in Table 2 has lower AIC and BIC values and bigger Log Likelihood, then, it has better statistical properties. Furthermore, the parameter $\hat{\alpha}_1 = 0.76$ is statistically significant at a p-value of 0.001. Thus, including an autoregressive term significantly improves the model. Let the reader check the forecasts of this model

```
forecast(ar1s4, h=4) %>%
  autoplot() +
  theme_classic() +
  ylab("Iphone sales (million dollars)") + xlab("Time")
```

Figure 5 shows tinier variations of point forecasts and confidence intervals, although nothing substantially different from Figure 4.

The reader may, at this point, figure out that model 2 is still missing a crucial aspect. Although, model 2 incorporates the seasonal trend, it omits the time trend of the series. This leads to bad forecasts. Now, recall that the modeller has two options here: integrating the series for a rate of growth forecast or including a deterministic time trend to keep the series in levels. Let the reader check model 3.

```
trend <- seq_along(iphone_ts)
ar1s4t <- Arima(iphone_ts, order=c(1,0,0), seasonal=list(order = c(1,0,0)),
xreg=trend)
screenreg(ar1s4t)
forecast(ar1s4t, xreg = length(iphone_ts) + 1:4) %>%
  autoplot() +
  theme_classic() +
  ylab("Iphone sales (million dollars)") + xlab("Time")
```

Figure 5. Four quarter ahead forecast of the AR(1,0,0)(1,0,0)$_4$ model.

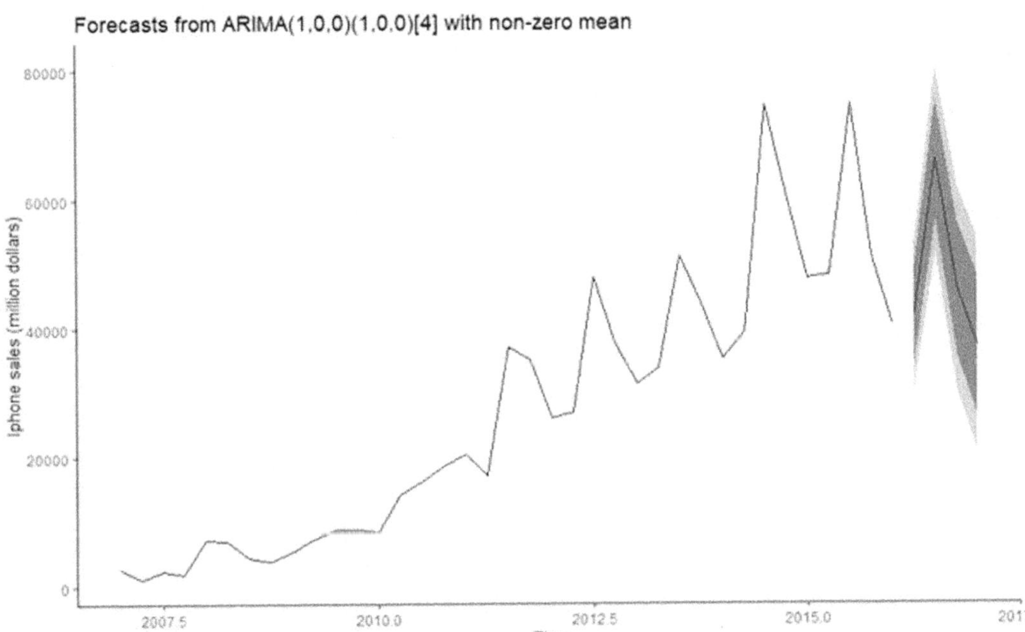

$y_t = \alpha_1 y_t\text{-}1 + \alpha_4 y_t\text{-}4 + \beta_{1t} + \varepsilon_t$

Now the coefficient β_1 captures the linear time trend which let the reader see the properties of model 3 (See Table 3).

Table 3 shows some important information about the sales prediction model. First, the inclusion of the deterministic time trend improves the model, as $\widehat{\beta}_1$ is statistically significant at any usual value and the AIC, BIC and Log Likelihood of the model improve. Moreover, including β_{1t} in the model makes $\widehat{\alpha}_1$ reducing from .76 in model 2 to .49 in model 3. This means that $\widehat{\alpha}_1$ in model 2 was suffering from omitted variable bias, and therefore was inflated as it incorporated part of the missing deterministic time trend.

Figure 6 shows significant differences in comparison with previous sales forecasts. The volume of sales is now appreciable higher than in previous models, in concordance with the time trend.

Table 3. Model 3.

trend	1482.16 *** (352.77)
Alpha1	0.49 ** (0.15)
Alpha4	0.82 *** (0.09)
intercept	1611.09 (9578.38)
AIC	757.73
BIC	765.79
Log Likelihood	-373.87
Num. obs.	37
*** p < 0.001; ** p < 0.01; * p < 0.05	

Figure 6. Four quarter ahead forecast of the $AR(1,0,0)(1,0,0)_4$ model with a deterministic time trend.

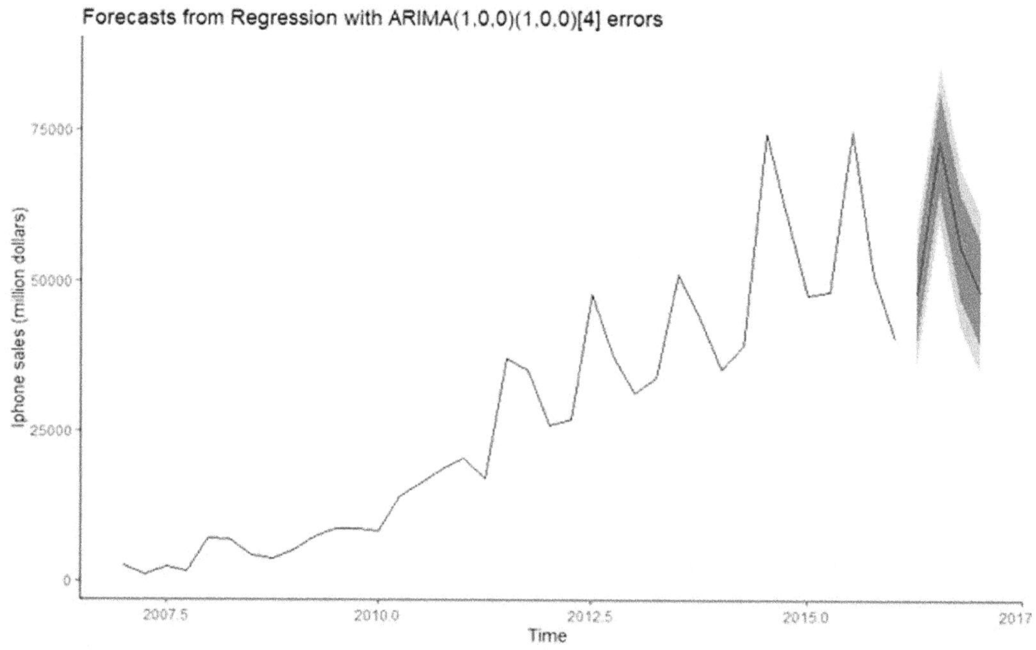

There is still one component missing to get the full picture here. Consumption behavior models can also depend on all the factors omitted by the model until now, this is, error past values. Incorporating this to the consumption behavior model can significantly improve sales predictions. Consider model 4

$$y_t = \alpha_1 y_{t-1} + \alpha_4 y_{t-4} + \beta_{1t} + \varepsilon_t + \theta_1 \varepsilon_{t-1}$$

Model 4 incorporates a parameter θ_1 that gathers the effect of the one-quarter lag of the omitted variables of the model; this is, the error term. This is called a moving average of order 1 model MA(1). Table 4 shows the results of model 4.

```
arma1s4 <- Arima(iphone_ts, order=c(1,0,1), seasonal=list(order = c(1,0,0)))
screenreg(arma1s4)
```

Table 4. Model 4.

Theta1	-0.15 (0.25)
Trend	1482.16 *** (352.77)
Alpha1	0.82 *** (0.12)
Alpha4	0.87 *** (0.07)
Intercept	23602.34 (20579.71)
AIC	763.77
BIC	771.83
Log Likelihood	-376.89
Num. obs.	37
*** p < 0.001; ** p < 0.01; * p < 0.05	

Table 4, however, shows that the inclusion of the MA(1) does not improve the forecasting model, but the contrary. The parameter $\hat{\theta}_1 = -0.15$ is not statistically significant, and the AIC and BIC criteria and the Log Likelihood exhibit worse results in comparison with model 3.

Now, the modeller has all the factors of the full AutoRegressive Integrating Moving Average model (ARIMA) model of order $(p,d,q)(p_s,d_s,q_s)$, where p is the order of autoregressive lags, d is the order of differentiation, and q is the order of differencing, and (p_s,d_s,q_s) are the seasonal equivalence. Mathematically, lags extend in the following way

$$y_t = \alpha_1 y_{t-1} + \alpha_2 y_{t-2} + \ldots + \alpha_p y_{t-p} + + \varepsilon_t + \theta_1 \varepsilon_{t-1} + \theta_2 \varepsilon_{t-2} + \ldots + \theta_q \varepsilon_{t-q}$$

Or equivalently

$$y_t = \sum_{i=1}^{p} \alpha_i y_{t-i} + \sum_{i=0}^{q} \theta_i \varepsilon_{t-i}$$

However, which is the best model to fit? In practice, the modeller has to try to fit the best model by estimating the statistically significant parameters and comparing the best results for the AIC and BIC criteria. This makes consumption behavior prediction an art besides a science. Nevertheless, R provides a technique in order to make the life of the researcher much easier.

The auto.arima() function in R is based in the Hyndman-Khandakar algorithm (Hyndman and Khandakar, 2008). It automatically fits the best ARIMA model for the time series of interest. According to Hyndman and Athanasopoulos (2018), the algorithm goes as follows

1. Determine the order of difference $0 \leq d \leq 2$ by repeating KPSS tests.
2. Select the lag values p,q by the minimum of the AICc criteria after step 1. The algorithm applies a stepwise search across the model space.
    a. Five models are fitted initially.
        i. ARIMA(0,d,0)
        ii. ARIMA(2,d,2)
        iii. ARIMA(1,d,0)
        iv. ARIMA(0,d,1)
        v. ARIMA(0,d,0) without constant term if $d \leq 1$.
    b. Every model includes a constant term except for d=2.
    c. The best fit, with the tiniest AICc, of step a. is considered the current model.
    d. Consider the following variations
        i. Modify =p,q from c. by ± 1.
        ii. Include/exclude the constant term from c.
        iii. The current model becomes the new best model considered so far.
    e. Iterate step 2.d until reaching the optimum.

Where the AICc criteria is the AIC criteria corrected for preventing overparametrizing. The results of auto.arima applied to the Iphone sales dataset is shown in model 5 (See Table 5).

```
 autoarimas4 <- auto.arima(iphone_ts)
screenreg(autoarimas4)
forecast(autoarimas4) %>%
  autoplot() +
  theme_classic() +
  ylab("Iphone sales (million dollars)") + xlab("Time")
```

Surprisingly, the best fit is an ARIMA(0,0,1)$(0,1,0)_4$ model with drift, which includes a moving average component, seasonal differencing and a seasonal quarterly moving average term. Reaching this result by hand would be, at the least, costly. Let the reader see model 5 forecasts.

Table 5. Model 5.

Ma1	0.62 *** (0.14)
drift	1527.28 *** (394.88)
AIC	670.66
BIC	675.15
Log Likelihood	-332.33
Num. obs.	33
*** p < 0.001; ** p < 0.01; * p < 0.05	

Figure 7 shows much more realistic forecasts in comparison with the previous ones. This is the first time that the forecasts are higher than the previous years, in concordance with the trend of the series. If IPhone sales have been increasing with time all over the series, it is realistic to expect that they will keep doing it.

Figure 7. Forecasts of the ARIMA(0,0,1)(0,1,0)$_4$ model with drift selected by the auto.arima algorithm.

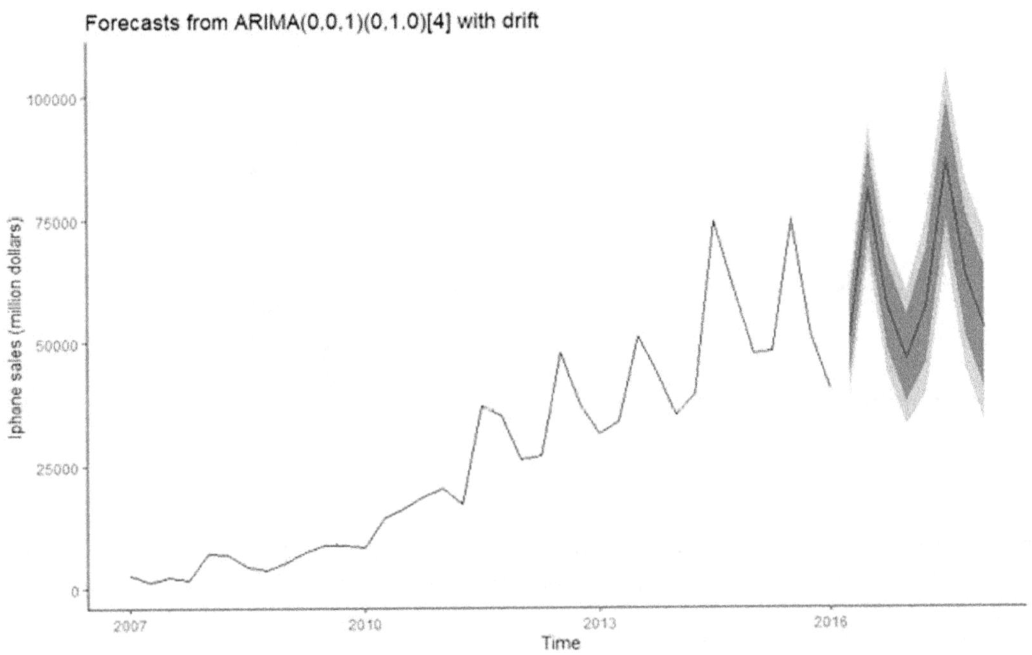

However, as in previous years this growth is small, the new sales cycles are not much higher than the previous ones.

How can the modeller know if these forecasts are good from the statistical point of view? This is the last part of the task. To know it, the modeller must check if the residuals of the model are similar to a white noise process, this is, if they are stationary.

```
checkresiduals(autoarimas4) %>%
  theme_classic()
```

The first plot of Figure 8 shows residuals that oscillate around a constant mean value of 0, and with a constant variance, although there are periods of different variability, specially from 2011. As mentioned before, the variance can be more constant if the series is log transformed.

The second plot shows that autocorrelations between the lagged values of the residuals are not statistically significant, as no value is beyond the confidence interval threshold (the blue dotted lines). The third plot shows the distribution of the residuals. The interpretation here is not easy, and a more formal test would give clearer results. The residuals are weakly stationary, and therefore the forecasting model is operative.

Figure 8. Plots of the residuals of model 5.

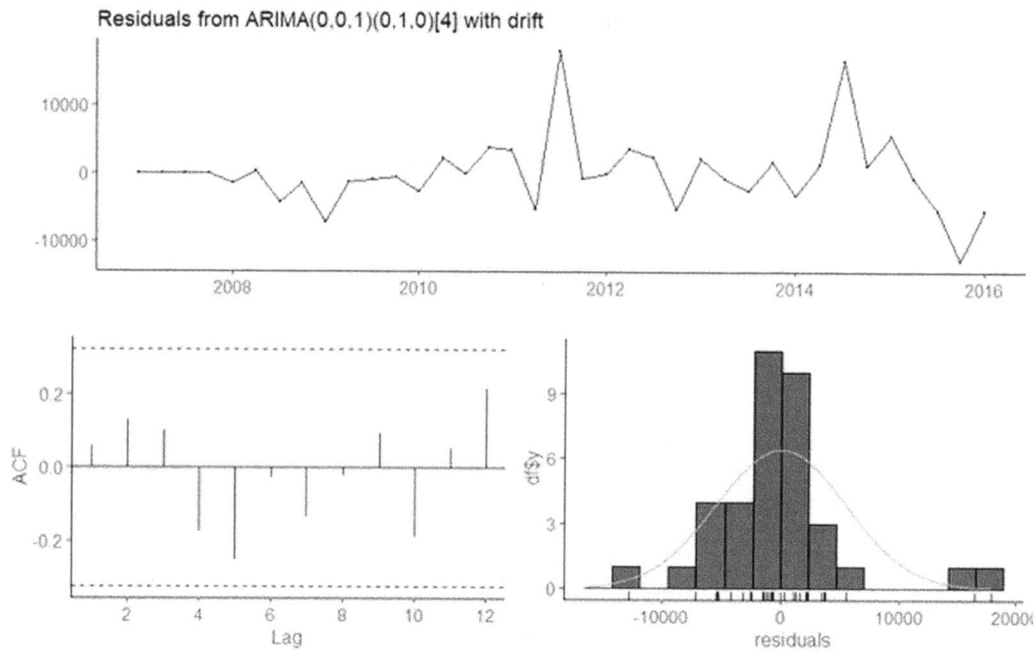

There are other time series models that are of interest for consumption behavior analysis, such as volatility models that extend the scope of this book (see Enders (2008); Sanchez and Cruz (2020)).

MACHINE LEARNING PREDICTION OF CONSUMPTION AND SALES BEHAVIOR

Until now, the modeler has only considered a univariate setting, where she only had one dataset, Iphone sales, and wanted to predict future paths of Iphone consumption. Therefore, she observed regularities in the data, such as seasonality and a trend, and designed a forecasting model that captured those components.

However, consider now a different setting. Suppose that the modeler is a worker in a chicken production company and has the set of variables listed in Table 6.

Now, the modeler is interested in predicting the consumption behavior of chicken (Y_t) based on a set of variables that potentially have an impact on it ($X_1, X_2, \ldots, X_9$). In the machine learning literature, this kind of methods are called supervised machine learning methods, as the variables X "supervise" the training of the model to estimate the best values of Y.

Table 6. Broiler chicken dataset.

Q = Y_t	Per capita chicken consumption in pounds boneless equivalent (USDA)
Y =X_1	Per capita real disposable income, chained, 1996=100
PCHICK = X_2	Consumer price index for whole fresh chicken, 1982-84=10(BLS)
PBEEF = X_3	Consumer price index for beef, 1982-84 = 100 (BLS)
PCOR = X_4	Producer price index for corn, 1982 = 100 (BLS)
PF = X_5	National price index for broiler feed, scaled to 1982-1984 = 100 (USDA)
CPI = X_6	Consumer price Index, 1982-84 = 100 (BLS)
QPRODA = X_7	Aggregate production of young chickens, pounds (USDA)
POP = X_8	U.S. population on July 1, residents plus armed forces (PLS)
MEATEX = X_9	Exports for beef, veal and pork, pounds (USDA
TIME = t	Time index, 1910=1
Periodicity	Year
Sample size	1950-2001

Mathematically, this generates a relationship of the form

$$Y_t = f(X_t) + \varepsilon_t$$

Where ε_t is the error term that captures the factors that influence Y_t and the set of explanatory variables $X_1, X_2, \ldots, X_9$ do not capture.

To make the model operative $f(X_t)$ must have a functional form. One of the most studied ones is the linear relationship, which assumes that $f(X_t)$ is linear. Mathematically

$$Y_t = \beta_0 + \beta_! X_! + \beta_2 X_2 + \ldots + \beta_9 X_9 + \varepsilon_t = \beta_0 + \sum_{i=1}^{9} X_i \beta_i + \varepsilon_t$$

Which configures the linear regression model. This model assumes that whatever the form of the variables (squared, cubic, logarithmic, etc.), the model is linear in the parameters of interest $\beta_{i=1,\ldots,9}$. These parameters determine the effect of the explanatory variables, $X_{i=1,\ldots,9}$ on the explained variable of interest Y.

The linear regression model bases its forecasts on the effects of important variables, such as the consumer's price of beef or chicken, over the variable of interest, in this case, chicken consumption. It then lets the door open to simulate consumer behavior scenarios depending on the evolution of the price of supplementary or complementary goods, income, etc. Thus, it is a much closer approach to approximating a demand function for chicken than the ARIMA approach. This is not overall better or worse, but a different approximation that has, in comparison with univariate methods, its own strengths and weaknesses. It serves different purposes in the consumption behavior-forecasting toolkit in comparison with univariate forecasting, such as scenario based consumption behavior.

However, the $\beta_{i=1,\ldots,9}$ parameters are unknown, and, the only approximation here is to estimate them from a dataset. One of the most, if not the most, employed estimators is the ordinary least squares estimator (OLS). The ordinary least square estimator selects the $\widehat{\beta}_{i=1,\ldots,9}$ that minimizes the Sum of the Squared Errors (SSE). Mathematically,

$$\widehat{\beta}_{ols} = \min_{\beta_0,\beta} \sum_{t=1}^{T} \left(y_t - \beta_0 - \sum_{t=1}^{T} X_{i,t}\beta_i \right)^2$$

Or

$$\widehat{\beta}_{ols} = (X'X)^{-1} X'y$$

After feeding the model with the chicken data and finding the best $\widehat{\beta}_{i=1,\ldots,9}$ by OLS, the model learns how to predict $\widehat{Y}$ from new data. To do this in R, execute the following code

```
sjt.lm(mlmodel1, file="mlmodel1.doc")
tab_model(mlmodel1, file= "mlmodel1.doc")
plot_model(mlmodel1, file= "mlmodel1")
```

Table 7 and Figure 9 show the OLS estimates of the linear regression model. Here, the R^2 and adjusted R^2 statistic, that range from zero to one, indicate how well the predictors X explain the predicted variable Y. Although a value of 0.99 indicates an exceptional fit (that appear a lot in time series regression), a value being that high also can show signs of statistical problems with the errors terms or the input variables, such as autocorrelation or multicollinearity.

The first problem violates the assumptions about the errors that are, following Hyndman and Khandakar (2008), the following:

1. The errors have zero mean. Violating this biases the forecasts.
2. The errors are not autocorrelated. Violating this makes forecasts inefficient.
3. The errors are not correlated with the predictor variables. Violating his makes necessary considering more variables to incorporate to the model.
4. Having normally distributed errors with constant variance. Violating this complicates a little bit the results.

Table 7. Ordinate least squares estimation of the linear regression model.

	Q		
Predictors	***Estimates***	***CI***	***p***
(Intercept)	5.93	-3.95 – 15.81	0.229
Y	0.00	-0.00 – 0.00	0.605
PCHICK	-0.03	-0.07 – 0.02	0.193
PBEEF	0.06	0.03 – 0.08	**<0.001**
PCOR	-0.01	-0.02 – -0.00	**0.007**
PF	0.00	-0.00 – 0.00	0.798
CPI	-0.06	-0.10 – -0.02	**0.007**
QPRODA	0.00	0.00 – 0.00	**<0.001**
POP	-0.00	-0.00 – 0.00	0.527
MEATEX	-0.01	-0.01 – -0.01	**<0.001**
TIME	0.11	-0.21 – 0.43	0.492
Observations	52		
R^2 / R^2 adjusted	0.999 / 0.999		

The reader can check the residuals of the model using the following code:

```
checkresiduals(mlmodel1)
```

There are clear symptoms of autocorrelations in these residuals. First, the correlogram of Figure 10 shows statistically significant lag correlations. Second, the Breusch-Godfrey test for serial correlation of order up to 14 drops an LM statistic value of 32.217 and a p-value of 0.0003, rejecting the null hypothesis of no serial autocorrelation. Therefore, the Breusch-Godfrey test concludes autocorrelation by far. Furthermore, the plot of the residuals in Figure 10 shows residuals that are not stationary in mean or in variance.

Despite this, the regression does not seem to be spurious, at least economically speaking. Figure 9 shows that income has a direct positive impact per capita chicken consumption. The price of chicken has a direct negative impact on per capita chicken consumption, such as the inverse demand function states. The price of beef, a supplementary good, has a direct positive effect over per capita chicken consumption. Beef that is more expensive means more consumption of chicken.

The price of corn has a negative effect over per capita chicken consumption. If corn, a complementary good, is more expensive, the costs of producing chicken will be higher, and therefore its demand will decrease. The Consumers Price Index has a negative effect over chicken consumption. Logically, everything being more expensive means less demand of everything, including chicken. More population means less per capita consumption of chicken by definition, as per capita consumption of chicken has population in the denominator. Finally, per capita chicken consumption increases with time.

However, the relationship of other variables do not make much sense. First, the price of broiler feed increasing chicken consumption. If chicken is more expensive to produce, then chicken should be more expensive and the demand for it decrease. On the other hand, more exports of beef, veal and pork means more demand for a supplementary good. The relationship here is tricky and not clear.

Figure 9. OLS estimates of the linear regression model.

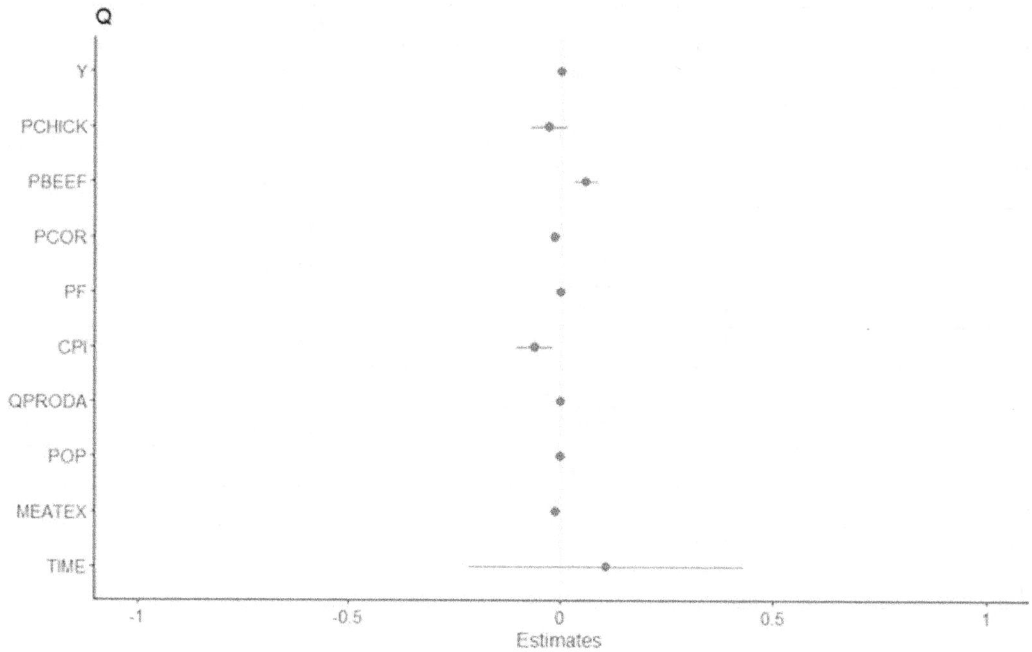

Nevertheless, only the coefficients for the price of beef, the price of corn, the Consumers Price Index, the production of chicken and the exports of other meat are statistically significant. Autocorrelation plays a big role here, as it specially affects statistical inference by inflating *t* statistics. As Figure 10 shows, there is statistical evidence of autocorrelation in the residuals of the model in lags between 5 and 10 of the Auto Correlation Function. This has an intimate relationship with the plot above the ACF in Figure 10. In that figure, it is easy to see that residuals are not stationary, and they are far from being white noise, therefore statistical inference is misleading. The following codes can be used to try regression model again with log-differentiated stationary data.

```
Q2 <- diff(log(Q), differences = 1)
Y2 <- diff(log(Y), differences = 1)
PCHICK2 <- diff(log(PCHICK), differences = 1)
PBEEF2 <- diff(log(PBEEF), differences = 1)
PCOR2 <- diff(log(PCOR), differences = 1)
PF2 <- diff(log(PF), differences = 1)
CPI2 <- diff(log(CPI), differences = 1)
QPRODA2 <- diff(log(QPRODA), differences = 1)
POP2 <- diff(log(POP), differences = 1)
MEATEX2 <- diff(log(MEATEX), DIFFERENCES = 1)
chickendatastationaryfinal <- as.data.frame(cbind(Q2, Y2, PCHICK2, PBEEF2,
PCOR2, PF2, CPI2,QPRODA2, POP2, MEATEX2))
tab_model(mlmodel2, file= "mlmodel2.doc")
plot_model(mlmodel2, file= "mlmodel2")
```

Figure 10. Residual plots of the linear regression model.

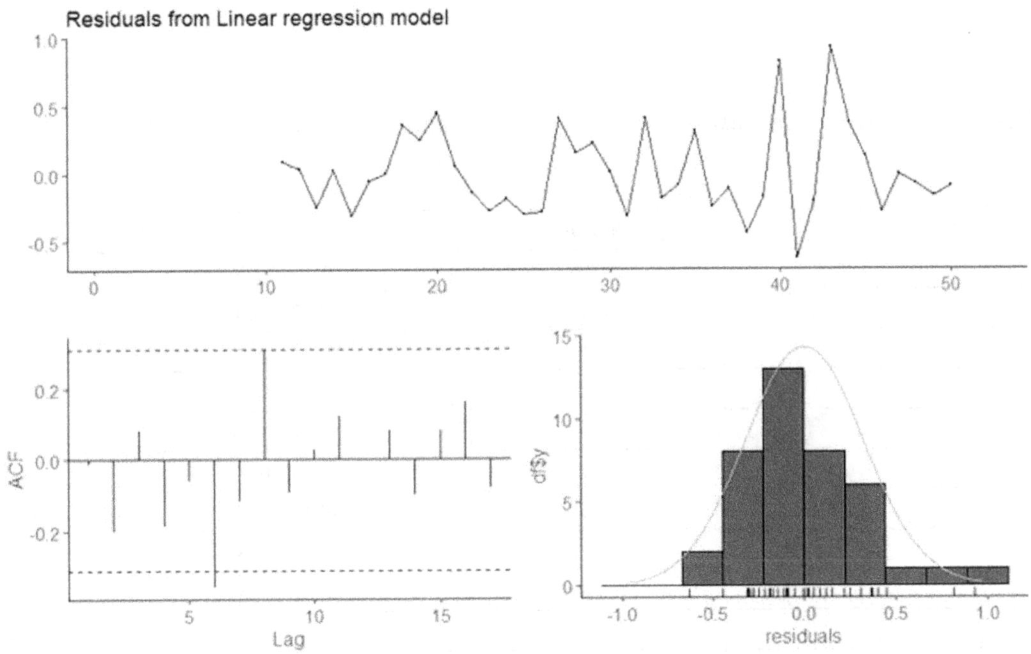

The picture drawn by Table 8 and Figure 11 varies substantially from the previous machine learning model. Now, only the intercept, the price of corn and the production of chicken are statistically significant at a 5% of significance, and the income, the price of beef, and the exports of beef, veal and pork are significant at a 10% level of statistical significance. Every coefficient has the expected sign, higher corn price means less consumption of chicken (through more expensive chicken and the inverse demand relationship), more production of chicken means higher consumption of chicken. Higher income means more consumption of chicken, while higher beef prices, a complementary good, also means a higher consumption of chicken. More exports of other meat means less chicken consumption.

Residuals from Figure 11 are mean and variance stationary taking into account the scale of the Y-axis (they gravitate towards 0 and vary at a level of 0.01 or 0.02), and the correlogram of the ACF shows no autocorrelation. The R^2 and adjusted R^2 show more reasonable values of 88.4% and 84.8% now.

The log differentiation of data is a solution for autocorrelation. In the case of multicollinearity, there is not such a straightforward method. The solution is to employ alternative estimators that introduce some bias but solve the problem. The most famous ones are the ridge and lasso estimators.

$$\widehat{\beta}_{ridge} = \left(X'X + kI_p\right)^{-1} X'y$$

$$\widehat{\beta}_{lasso} = \min_{\beta_0,\beta} \sum_{t=1}^{T} \left(y_t - \beta_0 - \sum_{t=1}^{T} X_{i,t}\beta_i \right)^2$$

Subject to

$$\sum_{i=1}^{p} |\beta_i| \le k$$

Table 8. Ordinate least squares estimation of the linear regression model with stationary data.

	Q		
Predictors	***Estimates***	***CI***	***P***
(Intercept)	-0.02	-0.03 – -0.00	**0.024**
Y	0.24	-0.02 – 0.51	0.072
PCHICK	-0.03	-0.12 – 0.05	0.413
PBEEF	0.08	-0.01 – 0.16	0.069
PCOR	-0.03	-0.05 – -0.01	**0.011**
PF	0.00	-0.00 – 0.00	0.514
CPI	0.03	-0.14 – 0.20	0.724
QPRODA	0.73	0.58 – 0.88	**<0.001**
POP	0.00	-0.00 – 0.00	0.537
MEATEX	-0.02	-0.04 – 0.00	0.051
Observations	51		
R^2 / R^2 adjusted	0.884 / 0.848		

Figure 11. Residual plots of the linear regression model with stationary data.

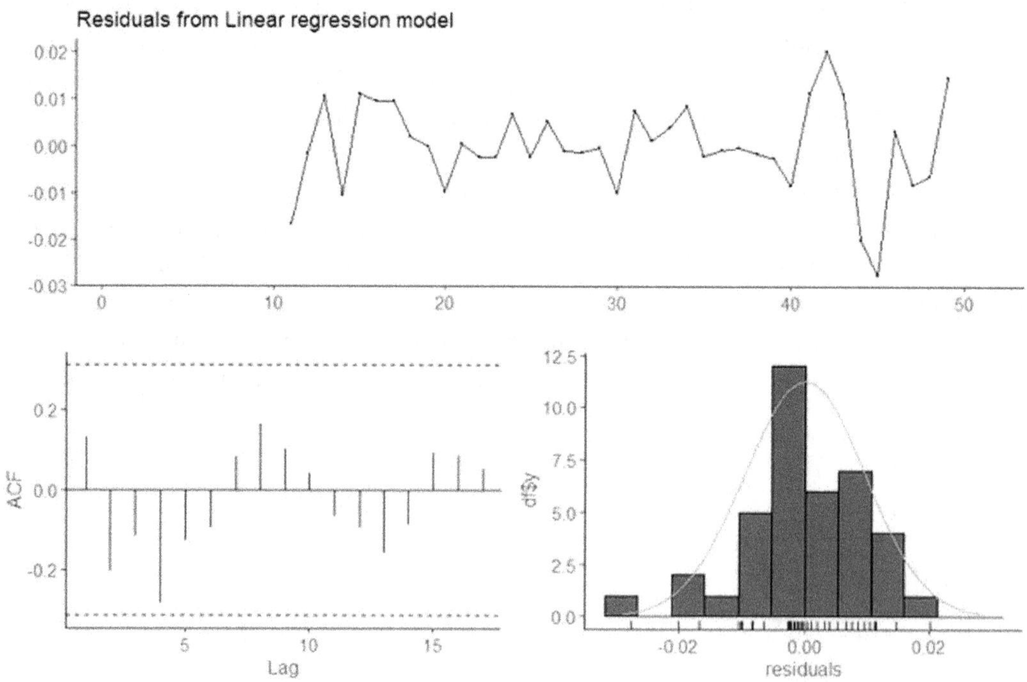

Where I_p is the *pxp* identity matrix and $k>0$ has an arbitrary small value, that the modeller selects discretionary. Other estimators such as the Generalized Method of Moments (GMM) are available at, for example, Woolridge (2010); Arellano (2003); Griliches et al. (1983).

The second machine learning regression model is now suitable for forecasting. Taking advantage of the presence of multiple variables, this model is able to produce scenario forecasting, answering to questions such as, how much will chicken consumption decrease if the price of beef increases in some expected quantity? How much will it increase if chicken production increases at some desired level?

Figure 12. Scenario based predictions made by the second regression model.

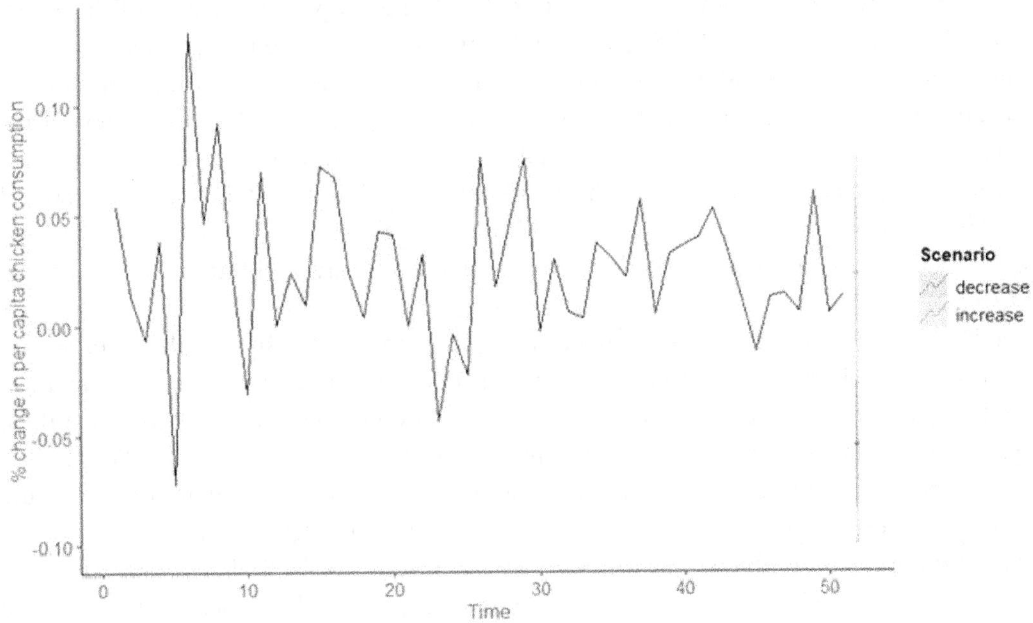

The following codes chunk can be executed to reproduce Figure 12.

```
forecast(mlmodel3)
h <- 1
newdata <- data.frame(
  Y = c(0), PCHICK = c(0),  PBEEF = c(0.5),  PCOR = c(0),  PF = c(0), CPI =
c(0), QPRODA = c(0),  POP = c(0),  MEATEX = c(0))
fcast.increase <- forecast(mlmodel3, newdata = newdata)
newdata2 <- data.frame(
  Y = c(0),  PCHICK = c(0), PBEEF = c(-0.5), PCOR = c(0),  PF = c(0), CPI =
c(0),  QPRODA = c(0),  POP = c(0), MEATEX = c(0))
fcast.decrease <- forecast(mlmodel3, newdata = newdata2)
as.ts(chickendata_stationary)
autoplot(as.ts(chickendata_stationary$Q, chickendata_stationary$obs)) +
  ylab("% change in per capita chicken consumption") +
```

```
autolayer(fcast.increase, PI = TRUE, series = "increase") +
autolayer(fcast.decrease, PI = TRUE, series = "decrease") +
guides(colour = guide_legend(title = "Scenario"))
```

Figure 12 shows forecasts of two scenarios, one in which the logarithmic rate of growth of the price of beef increases by 0.5, and one in which it decreases by 0.5. The modeler has to remind here that the data was log-differentiated in order to make it stationary. The shaded areas are confidence intervals that complement point forecasts.

The forecasts of Figure 12 are *ceteris paribus* increases and decreases of the price of beef, this is, holding every other variable constant. However, the machine learning regression model has a multivariate nature, so the study of combined scenarios is possible. For example, an increase of the income of the population added to the variation of the price will determine another scenario, and so on.

The linear regression model allows for consumption scenario based forecasting by assuming that the parameters are interrelated via a clear and interpretable linear relationship. However, there are nonlinear methods that capture nonlinearities in the data that the linear regression model cannot, at the expense of formulating a clear and interpretable stochastic relationship. These methods are interesting for forecasting irregular consumption and sales paths, and combine well with interpretable linear methods for a bigger picture. One of the most employed by far in the machine learning literature are Artificial Neural Networks (ANN).

Artificial neural networks are mathematical models that mirror the brain cells layer structure. Explanatory or input variables situate on a left layer, there are one or more hidden layers of relationships in between, where the output of these layers are weighted linear combinations of the inputs of the previous layers Hyndman and Althanasopoulos (2018).. Thus, various layers of processing take action, and the final layer is a nonlinear function, such as the sigmoid one, that gives the final nonlinear output. The ANN minimizes a cost function, for example, the SSE, by selecting the optimal weights.

One of the main ANN in time series frameworks are NNARs or Neural Network Autorregresions. These employ lagged values of the, in this case, the per capita chicken consumption time series for predicting future behavior. The NNAR(p,k) model has p lags and k nodes in a hidden layer (see, for example, Hyndman and Althanasopoulos (2018)). Figure 13 shows the forecasts done by this model. The blue lines are confidence intervals done by simulation. The following code reproduces Figure 13.

```
fitnnetwork <- nnetar(ts_chicken)
autoplot(forecast(fitnnetwork, h=10, PI = TRUE))
```

As Figure 13 shows, ANNs, although much less interpretable, they capture better irregularities and cyclicality in the data, as they are nonlinear models. Although confidence intervals by statistical inference are not possible, generating hundreds or thousands future sample paths of the NNAR(p,k) model and averaging them allows for inferring the distribution of the predictions.

Another crucial family of nonlinear models are machine-learning decision trees. These models approximate the true relationships between the variables, and allow for interpretability and nonlinearity at the same time. They employ decision regions known as terminal nodes or leaves, in an upside down manner (it starts at the upper part and the terminal nodes are at the end of the tree). The moments where the input space splits are internal nodes (James et al., 2013). The goal, again, is to minimize the SSE in the different classification regions of the tree.

Figure 13. Forecasts from the neural network autorregresive model.

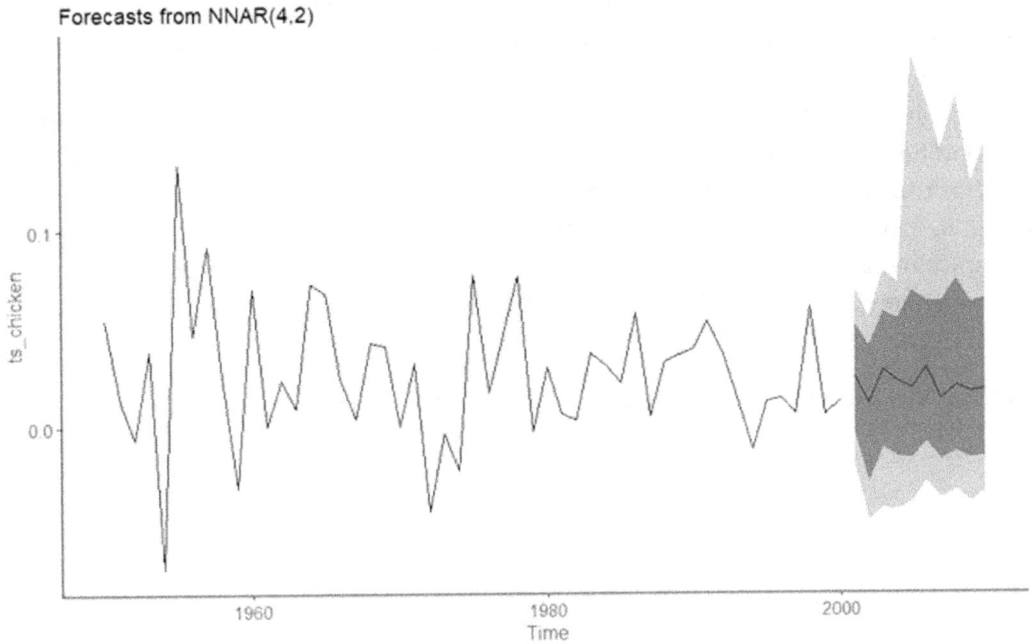

Figure 14 shows a decision tree model of the chicken consumption data. The name the variables with bigger or smaller symbols and numbers are the leaves, this is, the decision rules. The following code reproduces Figure 14.

```
tree1 <- rpart(Q ~ Y + PBEEF + PCOR + QPRODA + MEATEX, data = chickendata_sta-
tionary, method = "anova")
plot(tree1)
text(tree1)
summary(tree1)
```

Considering that the data is log differentiated, the tree splits the predictions in two parts at the beginning. If the rate of growth of the production of chicken is bigger than $e^{0.07387}$=1.08, then the predicted consumption rate of chicken is 1.08. If it is smaller than this quantity, then it goes to the left side of the tree. From here, it splits again. If the rate of growth of QPRODA is smaller than $e^{0.0406}$=1.04. then it goes to the left, and vice versa. At the left, if the rate of growth of QPRODA is again smaller than $e^{0.009881}$=1.01, it goes to the left, with a predicted rate of growth of chicken consumption of $e^{0.02275}$=1.02, if not, it goes to the right, with a prediction of $e^{0.006558}$=1.01.

If at the terminal node of QPRODA < $e^{0.0406}$=1.04 it went to the right, then the new decision rule would be the price of corn. If the rate of growth of the price of corn is bigger or equal than $e^{0.0488}$=1.05, then the predicted rate of growth of the per capita chicken consumption is equal to $e^{0.01996}$=1.02. If it is smaller, then it is 1.04. This makes economic sense as lower prices of corn mean lower prices of chicken, and therefore more consumption of it by the inverse demand relationship. The summary(tree1) command provides a lot of extra information about the tree. For example, the most important variable for the model is QPRODA with a value of 70, against a value of 13 for PBEEF, a value of 8 for income, a value of 8 for PCOR, and a value of two for MEATEX.

Nonlinear machine learning techniques, as the regression model, have well-of-fit criteria. Although the main goal is to get the minimum SSE, there are specific criteria for each model, such as the number of hidden layers in an ANN. In the same manner, in the machine learning literature there are advanced models, such as Support Vector Machines (SVM), and other problems, such as classification scenarios, that are relevant for consumption behavior analysis. The reader is referred to James et al. (2013) for an introduction, and to Friedman et al. (2001) for a technical course in these topics, as well as to other important topics in machine learning modelling, such as bias and variance considerations, model complexity and parsimony, AIC and BIC criteria, overfitting, and others.

Figure 14. Machine learning tree of the per capita chicken consumption dataset.

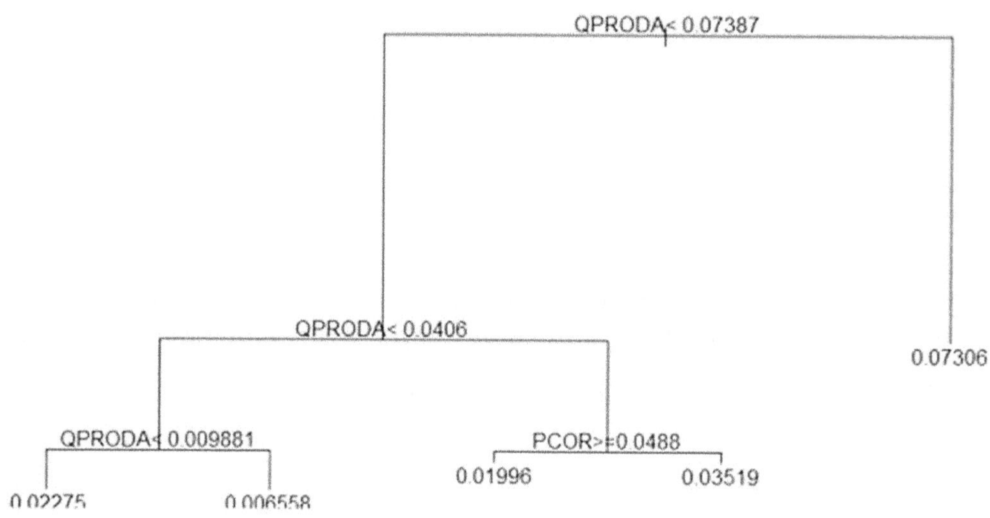

RESAMPLING METHODS AND PREDICTION PERFORMANCE

Machine learning methods employ data and algorithms to create models that predict new outcomes when fed with new data. However, they may behave well for a dataset, but not predict well new data, a concept known as overfitting. To overcome this, very frequently cross-validation is used.

One of the most employed cross-validation techniques is Leave-One-Out Cross-Validation (LOOCV).

LOOCV splits the dataset employed to feed the model in two parts. It feeds the model with all the observations of the variables but the first one, and then employs that one left observation to test the forecasting properties of it. Then, it reproduces the process for the second observation, and so on and so forth. For each iteration, it calculates a SSE, such that at the end of the procedure there are *n* SSEs. Then, it averages the SSEs to get an approximation of the out-of-sample SSE of the model.

$$LOOCV = \frac{1}{n}\sum_{i=1}^{n} SSE_i$$

There are various extensions of cross-validation to use depending on the situation (see James and others (2013); Refaeilzadeh et al. (2009); Berrar (2019)).

Bootstrapping is a resample technique proposed by Efron (1992). It allows to simulate the distribution of an estimator, and therefore calculate standard deviations, confidence, and prediction intervals, and so on, in situations where statistical inference cannot, such as in the case of ANNs.

Suppose a dataset with n observations of k random variables. Then, selecting randomly n observations give a bootstrap iteration B_1. Iterating this procedure with replacement, gives $B_1, B_2, \ldots, B_i$ bootstrapped datasets. Repeating this procedure for a large i, gives an estimate of the distribution of the data, which behaves better the larger the i. Then, a modeller can calculate the standard distribution of parameter of interest such as an estimator, and then calculate its standard deviation, from where to construct prediction intervals and so on. For mathematical and statistical expositions of the Bootstrap see, for example, Horowitz (2001); Hesterberg (2011); Wehrens et al. (2000).

CONCLUSION

Consumer behavior prediction is a rich field in which statistical, econometrical and machine-learning models are constantly being applied, modified and amplified depending on the market. Indeed, there is not an optimal model for each situation, but a set of tools, which may be better or worse depending on the sector of consumption, the type of data, the variables available, and so on and so forth. This leads to this field being an art besides a science, where the knowledge and experience of the researcher plays a crucial role at the moment of selecting a model, modify and amplify it, and finally, apply it to the data. This way, the reader can think of the modeler as a mechanic and of models as tools, which can be selected depending on the needs of the mechanic to fix a certain part of the car. Therefore, as in many other fields, the trajectory and experience of the modeler plays a crucial role.

Another important matter to remember is that multiplicity is always better than unicity in consumer behavior prediction. This means that there is always better to run various models and compare how they perform that running only one model. The decisions taken after comparison are always better informed and closer to full information than the results extracted from one individual model.

In this book chapter, the reader can find the tools to get a good grasp in the field of consumer behavior prediction. However, this is only the start of the journey, as the field is constantly evolving, and a continuous actualization is required in order to stay at the frontier of knowledge.

ACKNOWLEDGMENT

The author thanks the Mediterranean Center for research in Economics and Sustainable Development (CIMEDES) for all the support given.

REFERENCES

Andariesta, D. T., & Wasesa, M. (2022). Machine learning models for predicting international tourist arrivals in Indonesia during the COVID-19 pandemic: A multisource Internet data approach. *Journal of Tourism Futures*. doi:10.1108/JTF-10-2021-0239

Arellano, M. (2003). *Panel data econometrics*. Oxford University Press. doi:10.1093/0199245282.001.0001

Berrar, D. (2019). Cross-Validation. In S. Ranganathan, M. Gribskov, K. Nakai, & C. Schönbach (Eds.), *Encyclopedia of Bioinformatics and Computational Biology* (pp. 542–545). Academic Press. doi:10.1016/B978-0-12-809633-8.20349-X

Chakrabarty, S., Chopin, M., & Darrat, A. (1998). Predicting future buyer behavior with consumers' confidence and sentiment indexes. *Marketing Letters*, *9*(4), 349–360. doi:10.1023/A:1008089400754

Efron, B. (1992). Bootstrap methods: another look at the jackknife. In *Breakthroughs in statistics* (pp. 569–593). Springer. doi:10.1007/978-1-4612-4380-9_41

Enders, W. (2008). *Applied econometric time series*. John Wiley & Sons.

Friedman, J., Hastie, T., & Tibshirani, R. (2001). *The elements of statistical learning*. Springer.

Griliches, Z., Heckman, J. J., Intriligator, M. D., Engle, R. F., Leamer, E. E., & McFadden, D. (Eds.). (1983). *Handbook of econometrics*. Elsevier.

Hesterberg, T. (2011). Bootstrap. *Wiley Interdisciplinary Reviews: Computational Statistics*, *3*(6), 497–526. doi:10.1002/wics.182

Horowitz, J. L. (2001). The bootstrap. In J. Heckman & E. Leamer (Eds.), *Handbook of Econometrics* (Vol. 5, pp. 3159–3228). Elsevier., doi:10.1016/S1573-4412(01)05005-X

Hu, M., Li, H., Song, H., Li, X., & Law, R. (2022). Tourism demand forecasting using tourist-generated online review data. *Tourism Management*, *90*(104490). Advance online publication. doi:10.1016/j.tourman.2022.104490

Hyndman, R. J., & Athanasopoulos, G. (2018). *Forecasting: principles and practice*. Otexts.

Hyndman, R. J., & Khandakar, Y. (2008). Automatic time series forecasting: The forecast package for R. *Journal of Statistical Software*, *27*(1), 1–22. doi:10.18637/jss.v027.i03 PMID:19777145

International Monetary Fund. (1996). *Guide to the Data Dissemination Standards, Module 1: The Special Data Dissemination Standard*. IMF.

James, G., Witten, D., Hastie, T., & Tibshirani, R. (2013). *An introduction to statistical learning*. Springer. doi:10.1007/978-1-4614-7138-7

Li, H., Hu, M., & Li, G. (2020). Forecasting tourism demand with multisource big data. *Annals of Tourism Research*, *83*(102912). Advance online publication. doi:10.1016/j.annals.2020.102912

Li, X., Li, H., Pan, B., & Law, R. (2021). Machine learning in internet search query selection for tourism forecasting. *Journal of Travel Research*, *60*(6), 1213–1231. doi:10.1177/0047287520934871

Rathnayaka, S. D., Selvanathan, E. A., & Selvanathan, S. (2022). Modelling the consumption patterns in the Asian countries. *Economic Analysis and Policy*, *74*, 277–296. doi:10.1016/j.eap.2022.02.004

Refaeilzadeh, P., Tang, L., & Liu, H. (2009). Cross-validation. Encyclopedia of Database Systems, 5, 532-538. doi:10.1007/978-0-387-39940-9_565

Sánchez García, J., & Cruz Rambaud, S. (2020). A GARCH approach to model short-term interest rates: Evidence from Spanish economy. *International Journal of Finance & Economics*. Advance online publication. doi:10.1002/ijfe.2234

Struhl, S. (2017). *Artificial intelligence marketing and predicting consumer choice: an overview of tools and techniques*. Kogan Page.

Tian, F., Yang, Y., Mao, Z., & Tang, W. (2021). Forecasting daily attraction demand using big data from search engines and social media. *International Journal of Contemporary Hospitality Management*, *33*(6), 1950–1976. doi:10.1108/IJCHM-06-2020-0631

Wehrens, R., Putter, H., & Buydens, L. M. (2000). The bootstrap: A tutorial. *Chemometrics and Intelligent Laboratory Systems*, *54*(1), 35–52. doi:10.1016/S0169-7439(00)00102-7

Wooldridge, J. M. (2010). *Econometric analysis of cross section and panel data*. MIT Press.

Yukseltan, E., Yucekaya, A., Bilge, A. H., & Aktunc, E. A. (2021). Forecasting models for daily natural gas consumption considering periodic variations and demand segregation. *Socio-Economic Planning Sciences*, *74*(100937). Advance online publication. doi:10.1016/j.seps.2020.100937

Zhang, S., & Chiu, J. L. (2021). The impact of epidemic outbreak on Chinese consumers spending behavior. *New Normal and New Rules in International Trade, Economics and Marketing*, 349-363.

Chapter 6
An RFM Model Using K-Means Clustering to Improve Customer Segmentation and Product Recommendation

Zhao Xian
https://orcid.org/0000-0003-1794-6233
School of Computer Sciences, Universiti Sains Malaysia, Malaysia

Pantea Keikhosrokiani
https://orcid.org/0000-0003-4705-2732
School of Computer Sciences, Universiti Sains Malaysia, Malaysia

Chew XinYing
School of Computer Sciences, Universiti Sains Malaysia, Malaysia

Zuoyong Li
College of Computer and Control Engineering, Minjiang University, China

ABSTRACT

The COVID-19 pandemic instigated thousands of companies' closures and affected offline retail shops. Thus, online B2C business models enable traditional offline stores to boost their sales. This study aims to explore the use of historical sales and behavioral data analytics to construct a recommendation model. A process model is proposed, which is the combination of recency, frequency, and monetary (RFM) analysis method and the k-means clustering algorithm. RFM analysis is used to segment customer levels in the company while the association rule theory and the apriori algorithm are utilized for completing the shopping basket analysis and recommending products based on the results. The proposed recommendation model provides a good marketing mix to improve sales and market responsiveness. In addition, it recommends specific products to new customers as well as specific groups of target customers. This study offered a practical business transformation case that can assist companies in a similar situation to transform their business model and improve their profits.

DOI: 10.4018/978-1-6684-4168-8.ch006

INTRODUCTION

Advances in computing have allowed faster deployment and better optimization of machine learning (ML), which has the potential to be applied in all types of industries today (Abdelrahman & Keikhosrokiani, 2020; Keikhosrokiani, 2022; Keikhosrokiani & Asl, 2022; Teoh Yi Zhe & Keikhosrokiani, 2021). In the e-business world, online shopping has already become a popular shopping trading methods in more and more countries. The advanced algorithms used in recommender system and customer value management will make more customer-oriented marketing strategy, which improve customer satisfaction and corporate profits at the same time. Improved recommendation and prediction models, which are based on user behavior analysis (UBA), have greatly benefited the retail industry. However, many traditional offline stores don't have time or chance to transform their business model to online stores or combination model due to the sudden COVID-19 pandemic.

Data mining is the most effective way to analyze customer purchase behavior, and it can discover hidden useful information from massive online transaction data (Ngai et al., 2009; Pantea Keikhosrokiani, 2021; Shaw et al., 2001). A start-up e-commerce company can utilize data mining techniques to find customers' favorites commodities, such as books, music records, clothes, electronic equipment or foods from the historical shopping data. In addition, this is also conducive to the company's optimization inventory to avoid the backlog of goods. Conversely, hot goods can also be explicitly increased to maximize sales, avoid insufficient inventory, thereby reducing sales stagnation due to outstanding stocks. Therefore, a start-up cosmetics e-commerce company must establish and implement a system to predict sales and product recommendation. Conversely, it is also possible to add popular items or similar items to maximize sales and avoid running out of stock, thus reducing sales stagnation due to product out-of-stock (Sarwar et al., 2000). Therefore, a start-up cosmetics e-commerce company must implement a system to forecast sales and product recommendations.

Traditional offline shops usually face three problems: (1) limited market, (2) long sale cycle, and (3) complex and time-consuming sale process due to the current market situation affected by COVID-19 pandemic. In addition, they generally face two types of customers. One is general public consumer that their purchase decision usually involves two or three decision makers such as themselves, their family, or their friends. As a result, the total time for a purchase decision is usually very short. Another is the big customer in which their B2B sales cycles involve a complex set of factors involving multiple stakeholders, purchasing process decision makers, professional purchasing teams, experts from different positions or fields who have more specialized and process-oriented operations. For the big customer group, many business negotiations would be carried out and therefore, it is not surprising that decision times are usually longer up to several months. Longer sales cycles pose a company's cash flow which establishes a huge challenge that many companies must face, but maybe it is critical for a company seeking to transformation.

In compared to the e-commerce industry, more traditional industries are gradually paying attention to the importance of customer segmentation. For example, in the telecommunications industry, which is a data-intensive field, communication customers will continue to generate a lot of data. Therefore, customer segmentation is one of the most important applications in data mining in the telecommunications industry. Customer segmentation methods divides customers into different groups according to customer properties. The customer's similarities with more similarities will be segmented in the same group whereas the customers in different groups have the many difference (Qiu et al., 2020). Then, based on customers' characteristics, it is more likely to explore whether elder customers prefer to call, young customers prefer data traffic to watch videos, play games, etc.

This chapter aims to track the historical purchase behavior of the customers. In line with this, this study utilizes a RFM model and K-means algorithm to conduct customer segmentation and value analysis for finding the possible maximum sales strategies and then recommending suitable products to target customers. Based on statistical results and indicators, companies in the retail industry can design a variety of sales and marketing strategies, such as promotional activities, seasonal discounts, or floating sales, and making coupons which play a maximum efficiency to increase sales and improve customer retention.

Therefore, in this research, we developed a customer segmentation model and a product recommendation system using machine high performance learning algorithms to help the traditional offline stores transform their business model. The following part of this paper is organized as follows: Section 2 describes related works, Section 3 presents the methodology used in this chapter including the proposed data science life cycle and process model, Section 4 discusses the results, and Section 5 wrapped up the study by conclusions and future directions.

RELATED WORKS

Group-specific marketing is common and much needed from the traditional mass marketing perspective. Customer segmentation is a part of various activities under the Customer Relationship Management (CRM) value chain (Ngai et al., 2009; Shaw et al., 2001). Moreover, product recommendation is considered an essential topic in big data and machine learning (Sarwar et al., 2000). Therefore, we reviewed the existing studies and introduced the most relevant technologies and methods for customer segmentation and product recommendation in this section.

Customer Segmentation

At present, marketing strategies are widely used. The modern marketing approach promote the use of CRM as part of an organization's business strategy to improve customer service satisfaction (Ngai et al., 2009). Establishing of long-term relationships with customers is a recent marketing strategy which is very profitable. Understanding the true value of the customer can be used as the starting point for relationship management, as marketing strategies are deployed based on target customers and final profits (Kim et al., 2006). Therefore, it is strategic to provide customers with a business strategy to provide refinement of customers. Recency, Frequency, and Monetary (RFM) model was first proposed by Hughes of the American Database Institute in 1994 (RobJackson et al., 1994), which is a popular tool for customer value analysis, and it is used for customer segmentation and consumption behavior analysis. This method can segment customers based on present customer behavior characteristics. A study done by Hosseini et al., (2010) proposed a new procedure based on expanded RFM model which introduces one additional parameter as W. Thus, R, F, M and W were used in k-means clustering technique to classify customer product loyalty under B2B concept (Hosseini et al., 2010). In another study by Wu & Chou, (2011), a soft clustering method was developed which uses a latent mixed-class membership clustering approach to classify online customers based on customer purchase data across categories (Wu & Chou, 2011). Moreover, they proposed a technique based on the Latent Dirichlet Allocation (LDA) model to create the customer segments. Based on the RFM method, the Customer Value Matrix (CVM) was developed for the retail environment of small businesses (Marcus, 1998). This method was used by Boston Consulting Group's (BCG) Growth-Share, which is very easy to understand. Wei et al., (2012) proposed an extended RFM model, namely LRFM (Length RFM) by using self-organizing maps (SOM) technique for children's dental clinic in Taiwan. Dursun & Caber, (2016) explored profiling the profitable hotel customers from a five-star hotel at Antalya by using the content of CRM, RFM analysis, and k-means algorithm.

Product Recommendation

Due to the rapid increase of shared content on the internet as well as millions of users surfing the Internet looking for various products, items or information, recommender systems have become an essential part in almost all e-commerce applications and social media platforms. Recommender systems aim to understand users' preferences and recommend items of interest to users, including a movie to watch, a restaurant to dine in, music to listen to, a job to apply for, etc. Despite the advantage of access to a significant amount of online data, users are led to frustration when they are looking for some desirable information and they faced the problem of information overload. Another example of information overload is where millions of users, who participate in various social media applications, share texts, pictures, or videos of their daily activities, while others can review and respond to these posts based on their interests. With the help of recommender systems, users will not be overwhelmed by the huge number of options available on the Internet. Indeed, these enormous choices can be filtered out into a small number of personalized items, saving users' time and effort.

The recommendation system is based on algorithms and developed to predict the ratings of an item that the user has not purchased even reviewed through historical sales data. Then the system will recommend other similar items to the user (Adomavicius & Tuzhilin, 2005). There are mainly four common methods to conduct a recommendation system, (1) Content-Based Filtering, (2) Collaborative Filtering, (3) Hybrid Recommendation Systems, and (4) Association Rules (Kim et al., 2006; RobJackson et al., 1994). The above methods or models are the mainstream method used by the online shopping platform, where they have generated good recommendation results. Deep learning technology has powerful feature extraction and learning capabilities in recent years. Its rapid emergence and development have contributed to the rapid progress of artificial intelligence technology, which has been widely used in the fields of speech recognition processing, Computer Vision (CV), Natural Language Processing (NLP), and other fields with great success. Studies have shown that applying deep learning methods to recommender systems can achieve very good recommendation results. Currently, combining deep learning with recommendation techniques is a popular research direction in the development of recommendation systems. Deep learning-based recommender methods have received widespread attention and have been successfully applied to real applications such as Youtube, Jingdong, etc. The main principle is based on the traditional content-based recommendation method and collaborative filtering recommendation. The powerful data processing ability of deep learning technology is used to integrate the user and item feature learning, and item recommendation process into a unified recommendation model. However, there are some long-term existence and serious issues, such as the "Cold Start Problem" (Lika et al., 2014) and "Shilling Attack" (Marcus, 1998), which need to be addressed urgently. The cold start problem refers to recommendations for novel users or new items whereas the shilling attack is related to the use of forged user-generated content data such as user ratings and reviews by attackers to manipulate recommendation ranking (Wang et al., 2016). These two important issues need to be considered in future recommendation systems. Many studies have continuously improved the recommender system to make up for shortboards through deep learning, knowledge maps, social media, interests or hobbies, and other auxiliary information. But in this study, we pay more attention to provide an online transformation case for traditional stores and developing appropriate marketing strategies.

METHODOLOGY

This study utilized a dataset related to the cosmetics e-commerce platform which was collected from October 2019 to February 2020. We have divided the attributes included in the dataset into two categories: (1) One type of attribute is numeric attribute, including "time", "product_id", category_id", price", "user_id" and user_session". The attribute "time" is numeric attribute to describe detail behavior time. The attribute "product_id" refers to the ID of each product. The attribute "category_id" refers to the ID of a category of product. The attributes such as "price", "user_id", and "user_session" refer to the price of each product, ID of each user, and users' session number, respectively. (2) Another type of attribute is categories attribute, which contains "event_type", "category" and "brand". The attribute "event _type" record users' specific behavior, for example, whether the user viewed a product, added a product to the shopping cart, or purchased the product. The attribute "category" refers to product category, such as book, clothes etc. The attribute "brand" describes the brand name of product. Table 1 shows the description of the dataset attributes.

Table 1. Description of attributes

Attribute	Category	Description
time	Numeric	Time of behavior happened
event_type	Categorical	Type of Customer behaviors: view; cart; purchase
product_id	Numeric	ID of product
category_id	Numeric	Category ID of a product
category	Categorical	Category of a product
brand	Categorical	Brand name
price	Numeric	Price of a product
user_id	Numeric	User ID
user_session	Numeric	Users' session ID

Figure 1 displays the percentage of different behaviors and conversion rate of purchase calculated according to counts of different behavior. The figure illustrates that the number of viewing the products is 4 million, the number of adding products to the shopping cart is 2.3 million, and the number of purchases is 510k, so the purchase rate is 12.67% from October 2019 to February 2020. "cart" is a type of user behavior between "view" and "purchase" which determines user have the purchase intentions. Figure 1 shows the conversion rate from "view" to "purchase" is only 57.55%, which is relatively high in e-Commerce domain. The results depict that some users prefer to adding their favorite products before purchasing. In another word, it shows that most of the users who browse the page more times use the shopping cart function. The number of purchases accounted for 22.02% (Counts of purchase/Counts of cart) of the used shopping cart indicates that the stage from viewing to adding products to the shopping cart is the key link in index improvement and there is a large lifting space in this process. Therefore, we need to develop more interesting sales strategies to attract customers and increase sales.

Figure 1. Conversion rate in the sale process

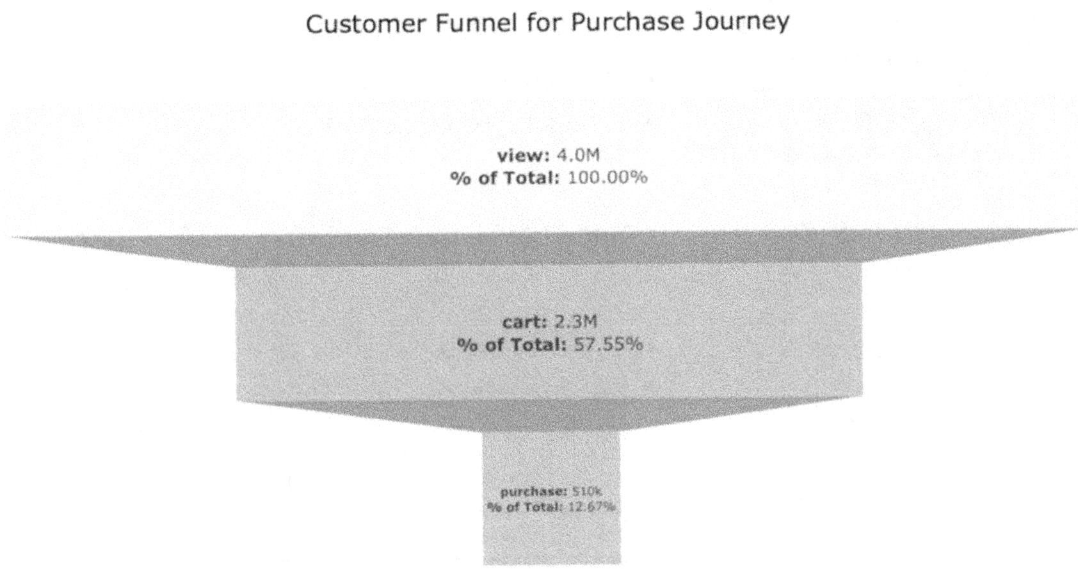

Proposed Data Science Lifecycle

In this research, we used data science life cycle to address the problem and achieve the objectives of this study, as shown in Figure 2. The data science life cycle includes five critical phases of understanding data, data preprocessing, modeling, evaluation, and developing the sales marketing strategies which are explained in detail in the following sections.

Data Preprocessing

In order to have high quality data analysis and construct the model successfully, we need to complete many preparation tasks for making the dataset suitable for machine learning algorithms. In this research, these processes include removing incomplete or duplicate instances and feature engineering as follows: (1) Removing incomplete instances. For instance, we found a lot of missing values, which will affect the performance of machine learning. We need to remove them in the preprocessing stage. Thus, the training dataset contains non-duplicated transactions (within the same session, only keep one record for a particular product in the cart) with the new features. (2) Extract additional attributes. The existing attributes cannot meet our analytical needs, but they contain other important information. Thus, for overcoming this problem, we extracted some new attributes into the dataset for analyzing and modeling purposes (Table 2).

Figure 2. Proposed data science life cycle

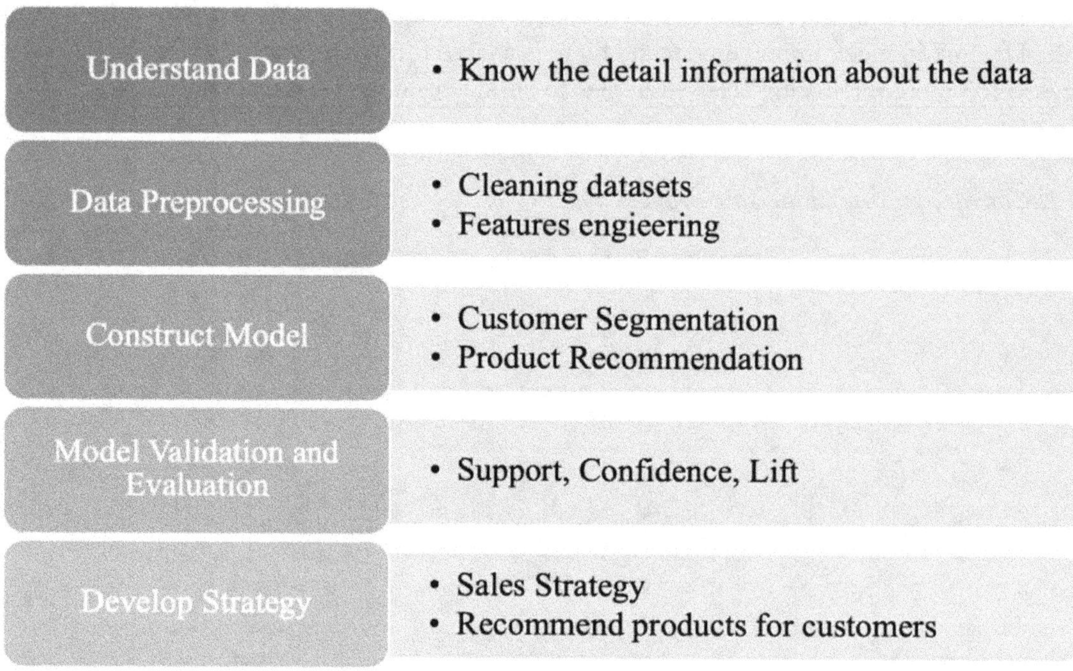

Table 2. Extracted attributes in feature engineering

Extracted Attributes	Description
timezone	Identify time zone
date	year/month/day
time	Specific time, for example, 01:10:24
hours	24 hours a day, the hour when behaviors occurred.
weekday	"0 ~ 6": From Monday to Sunday
weeknum	"week_1", "week_2"...based on the research period

As shown in Figure 3, there are usually two peaks in a day which happen around 10:00 am to 14:00 pm and from 18:00 pm to 20:00 pm. It is important to understand the viewing conditions of all-day shoppers to formulate a timely business strategy. We can target campaigns (especially conversion campaigns) to run specifically targeting highly converting hours and provide targeted products for specific level customers to improve the company's overall interests.

Constructing Proposed Model

The model construction phase was divided into three parts: (1) The first part is to develop a customer segmentation model and identify customer value based on the RFM method and k-means clustering to achieve the goal of customer segmentation. (2) The second part is to develop shopping basket based on association rules and Apriori algorithm and analyze the results from to get the association information of frequently purchased items. The last part is to develop good strategies or decisions through combination between customer segmentation and recommendation. In e-commerce domain, systems development combined sales strategies based on shopping basket analysis to enhance customer shopping interests further and increase economic benefits (Zhao & Keikhosrokiani, 2022).

Figure 3. Number of customers by hours

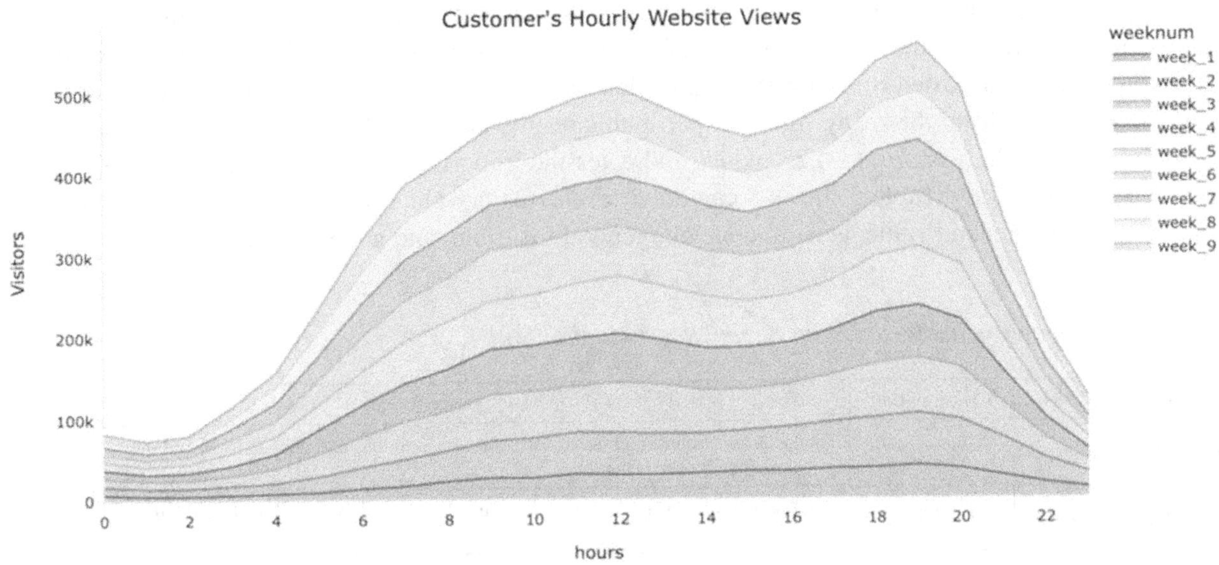

RFM Model of Customer Segmentation

The most powerful and simplest model to implement CRM may be RFM model – Recency (R), Frequency (F), and Monetary (M) value (Cheng & Chen, 2009). According to Bult & Wansbeek, (1995), who defined RFM as: (1) R: the period since the last purchase. The lower value corresponds to the customer's repeat purchase with a higher probability. (2) F: consumption frequency, which is the number of purchases made within a certain period. (3) M: consumption amount during a certain period, which is regarded as important indicators to analyze and segment customers. The higher value indicates that the company should focus more on that customer. Because the higher the total purchase amount of a customer over time, the more value the customer creates for the company (Blattberg et al., 2008). In RFM analysis, customers are sorted and grouped by the sum score of Recency score, the Frequency sore and Monetary score in descending order.

The RFM score is defined as the follows:

$$\text{RFM score} = \text{recency} \times \text{weight}_R + \text{frequency} \times \text{weight}_F + \text{monetary} \times \text{weight}_M, \quad (1)$$

where weights need to be discussed according to a particular problem or research objectives and determined by experts. The higher RFM scores represent the higher customer value.

RFM segmentation is an effective way to segment or identify customer that require special treatment (Allegue et al., 2020). In this research, we construct a customer segmentation model on customers with the purchase records. Tsai & Chiu, (2004) proposed that the sum of the weight of each RFM measure should be equal to 1. In various academic papers or industries, the weights of recency, frequency, and monetary need to be determined by experts' opinions based on specific research objectives or actual business goals. Because it would not be fair to average the R, F and M scores of each customer for different industries to obtain RFM segments based only on their purchase or engagement behavior. Average weights at all the time will cause significant errors, so depending on the nature of real business, we can scientifically increase or decrease the weight of RFM variable to arrive at a final score. In the research, it is crucial for this part to determine three weight values, and the final weight value for recency, frequency, and monetary are from the many times' experiments results and expert's opinions. We set $weight_R$ to 0.4, $weight_F$ to 0.35, $weight_M$ to 0.25, which indicates the importance of three parameters, recency > frequency > monetary. Table 3 shows 8 customer levels, major value, major develop, major maintain, major retention, general value, general develop, general maintain, and general retention.

Table 3. Customer value level (Zhao & Keikhosrokiani, 2022)

Customer Level	Classification	Description
Major Value	$R\uparrow F\uparrow M$	The last time of consumption is close, the consumption frequency is high, and the consumption amount is high.
Major Develop	$R\uparrow F\downarrow M$	The last time of consumption is close, the consumption frequency is low, and the consumption amount is high.
Major Maintain	$R\downarrow F\uparrow M$	The last consumption time was long, the consumption frequency was high, and the consumption amount was high.
Major Retention	$R\downarrow F\downarrow M$	The last consumption time was long, the consumption frequency was low, and the consumption amount was high.
General Value	$R\uparrow F\uparrow M^{-}$	The last time of consumption is close, the consumption frequency is high, and the consumption amount is low.
General Develop	$R\uparrow F\downarrow M\downarrow$	The last time of consumption is close, the consumption frequency is low, and the consumption amount is low.
General Maintain	$R\downarrow F\uparrow M\downarrow$	The last consumption time is long, the consumption frequency is high, and the consumption amount is low.
General Retention	$R\downarrow F\downarrow M\downarrow$	The last consumption time was long, the consumption frequency was low, and the consumption amount was low.

K-Means Clustering Algorithm

The k-means algorithm is a kind of clustering algorithm (Li & Wu, 2012). Clustering is sometimes called unsupervised classification because it can automatically form clusters of similar things as classification without predefined classes. K-means is an algorithm that can find k clusters for a given dataset. The number of clusters k is user-defined. Each cluster is described by a single point known as the centroid, which means it is at the center of all the points in the cluster (Harrington, 2012). The k-means algorithm process is as follows: The first step is to assign k centroids to points randomly. Next, each point in the dataset is assigned to a cluster. The assignment is done by finding the closest centroid and assigning the point to that cluster. After this step, the centroids are all updated by taking the mean value of all the points in that cluster. The following is the pseudo-code:

In this research, we decided to use Squared Error Distortion to assess which number of clusters is the most appropriate. The detail processes are:

Given a data point **v** *and a set of points* **X**,
define the distance from **v** *to* **X**

$d(v,X)$

as the (Euclidian) distance from **v** *to the closest point from* **X**.
Given a set of n data points $V=\{v_1,\dots,v_n\}$ *and a set of k points* **X**,
define the ***Squared Error Distortion***

$$d(\boldsymbol{V},\boldsymbol{X}) = \sum d(v_i,\boldsymbol{X})^2 / n \qquad (1 \le i \le n).$$

Then we set a wide number range of clusters and consider the size of the square error and the number of clusters to select the number of clusters with relatively small square error.

Product Recommendation

Association rule, a traditional data mining method, is the rule-based machine learning method that can find interesting relations between variables in large datasets. Agrawal et al., (1993) believe that association rules can fast-mine relations between products from historical transaction data in supermarkets. We all know the classic example, a rule {Beer} → {Diapers} means that a customer will buy diapers after buying beer, in another word, customer will buy beer and diapers together. Such interesting relationships and information can be discovered between various products, which are useful for both e-commerce and traditional stores in determining promotional pricing and combination sales strategies (Cheng & Chen, 2009; Wang et al., 2016; Zhao & Keikhosrokiani, 2022; Zhou et al., 2018).

We generally define the transactions set as $D=\{T_1,T_2,\dots,T_n\}$, items set as $I=\{i_1,i_2,\dots,i_m\}$, and each transaction is an item set. An association rule can be denoted as an implied form of $X \rightarrow Y$, $Y \in I$, and $X \cap Y = \varnothing$ (Chen et al., 2017). The following equation (Eq. (2)-(6)) can express the theory in more detail. In the equation, the P(X) and P(Y) refer to the probability of the appearance of itemsets X and Y in D, respectively. And $P(X \cup Y)$ is the probability of the appearance of item sets X and Y in D.

$$\text{Support}(X) = P(X) \tag{2}$$

$$\text{Support}(Y) = P(Y) \tag{3}$$

$$Support(X \rightarrow Y) = Support(X \cup Y) = P(X \cup Y) \tag{4}$$

$$Confidence(X \to Y) = \frac{Support(X \cup Y)}{Support(X)} \tag{5}$$

$$Lift(X \to Y) = \frac{Confidence(X \to Y)}{Support(Y)} = \frac{Support(X \cup Y)}{Support(X) \times Support(Y)} \tag{6}$$

Association rule mining algorithms are the core works of association rule mining research, and many efficient associations rule mining algorithms have been proposed so far. The most famous association rule discovery method is the Apriori algorithm proposed. Apriori is a seminal algorithm for discovering frequent item-sets using candidate generation (Agarwal & Srikant, 1994). Mining association rules within a historical transaction dataset is an important application and function in e-commerce domain. It can find the relationship between different items from the dataset. This algorithm is also often applied to decision support area. Association rule mining proceeds based on two main steps. The first step is to find all itemsets in the transaction database that are greater than or equal to the minimum support specified by the user. And the second step is to use the frequent item sets to generate the required association rules, which are traded off according to the minimum confidence level set by the user. Finally, we can get the strong association rules (Kannan & Bhaskaran, 2009; Yan et al., 2017). The main idea of the Apriori algorithm for obtaining frequent itemsets is a hierarchical search and iterative approach that makes the use of the prior knowledge of infrequent item sets. To explore the set of all frequent (K+1) itemsets, it generates the set of candidates (K+1) itemsets by concatenating the set of all frequent K itemsets with itself. It proceeds as follows: (1) the first step is to select the length K = 1, scan the database, and search for all individual itemsets that have a minimum support; (2) then the step size increases according to the frequent itemsets and the new itemsets are recomputed and generate a real frequent itemset; (3) the final step is to repeat the above one step to search for all K+1 itemsets based on the result of the previous search until no new itemsets can be found and the algorithm is terminated (Yan et al., 2017).

In the business domain, we will be able to capture user preferences through association rules using Apriori knowledge. After identifying user preferences, we are able to develop effective product recommendations based on this. We can then recommend products to our customers to get better sales. Because the association rules can generate precise recommendations with confidence values of 76.92% (Fatoni et al., 2018), which is relatively satisfactory confidence. The design process model for customer segmentation and product recommendation through user behavior analysis are proposed in this study (Figure 4). The proposed model utilizes a combination of k-means and RFM methods for customer segmentation and uses the Apriori algorithm to create a basket analysis for the product recommendation model.

Develop Strategy and Implementation

Based on the literature review, many studies have mentioned that precision marketing can improve the overall profitability of a store. Thus, we combined the results of the customer segmentation and product recommendation model, then developed business strategies for different business goals. In the overall model constructing process, we used Jupyter Notebook and PyCharm as the main tools. Moreover, multiple libraries are utilized, including Pandas, NumPy, Matplotlib, Scikit-learn, etc.

Figure 4. The proposed design process model.

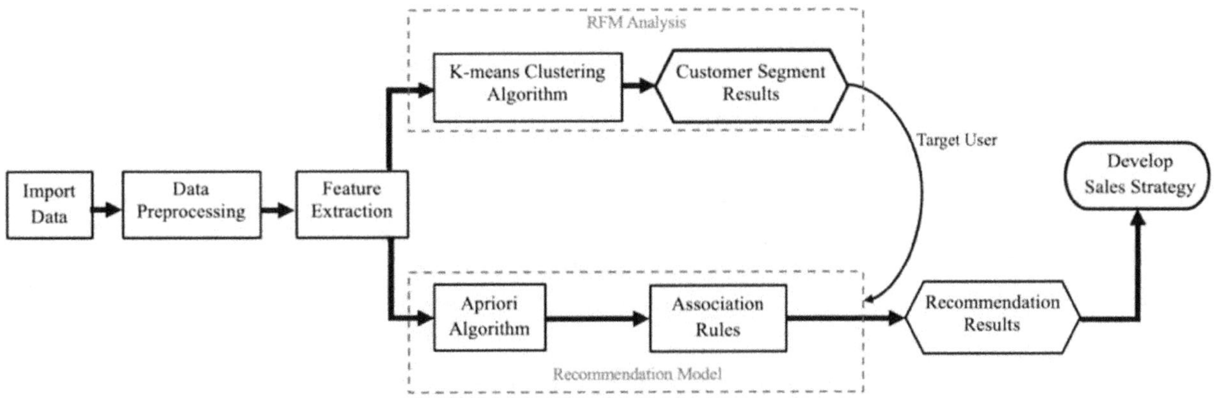

RESULTS AND DISCUSSION

Customer Segmentation

In this part, we use RFM analysis and k-means clustering algorithm to process the data anlytics. We use the "purchase" data of October 2019 to February 2020 for the proposed model. We transferred the "time" which is deal date time to date as the format "%Y%m%d". There were 908776 rows after removing duplicate or incomplete data.

First, we started the initial exploration of the cleaned data and got some results as shown in Figure 5. The results show: (1) The number of customers soared in November 2019 and the end of January 2020, and there was a big drop in customer numbers on New Year's Eve; (2) Sales increased from 0.95 million dollars in October 2019 to 1.3 million dollars in November 2019, droped to 0.85 million dollars in December 2019, and then remained around 1 million dollars/month in the following two months; (3) For the average spends per customer, it didn't change much over the five continuous months. Then we grouped the data by "user_id" and calculated each customer's Recency (how many months had been passed since the customer's last purchase until February 29, 2020), Frequency (how often had a customer purchased from October 2019 to Feb 2020), and Monetary Value (how much did the customer spend from October 2019 to February 2020). Therefore, we could get the results as shown in Table 4.

Traditionally, in RFM models, each customer is assigned a score for each RFM factor. These scores are then combined and used for segmentation. Inspired by Cho et al., (2012), we decided to do RFM analysis by k-means clustering. After calculating each customer's recency, frequency, and monetary, the distributions are visualized as shown in Figure 6. The first step was finding the optimal number of clusters based on the Elbow Method. We use recency, frequency, and monetary as clustering variables. The squared error in different numbers of clusters is shown in Figure 7. The squared error is relatively very low when the number of clusters is equal to 4, and too many clusters are not conducive to the refinement management of real marketing. Therefore, we set 4 customer levels as shown in Table 5 that are "New Customers", "At-Risk Customers", "Potential Loyal Customers" and "Loyal Customers", respectively.

The initial examination of the RFM data is shown in Figure 6 which revealed: (1) The number difference in customer distribution was small along the recency curve; (2) Most of the customers made purchases fewer than 10 times; (3) Most of the customers spent less than 100 dollars.

Figure 5. Exploration for RFM analysis

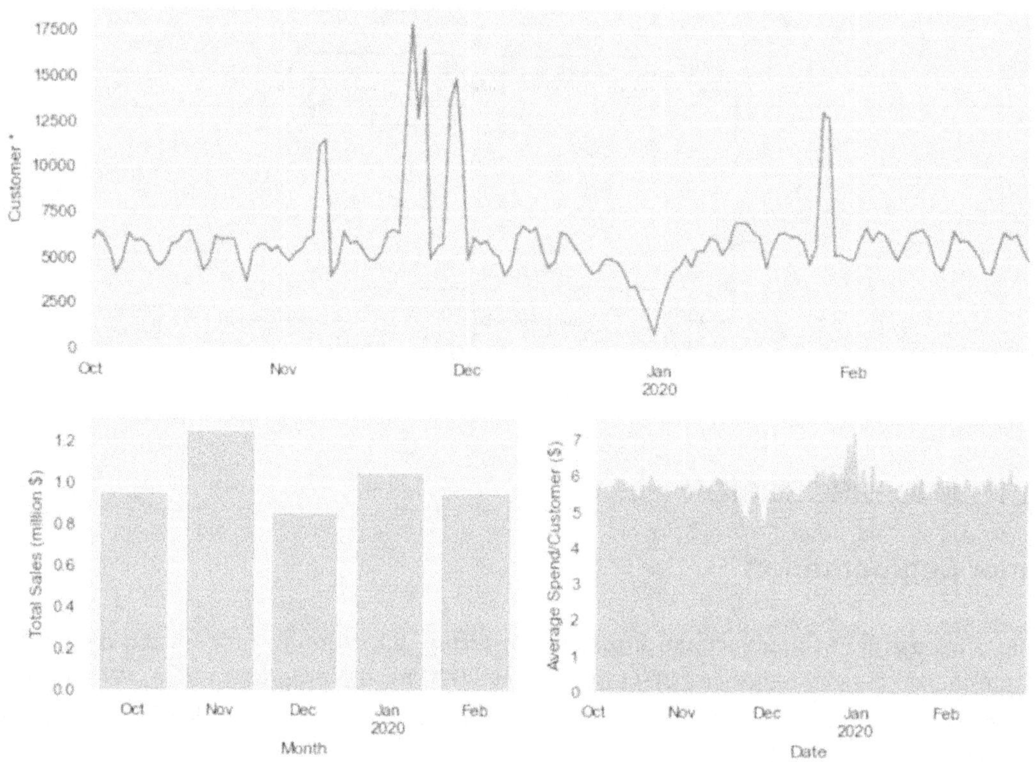

Table 4. Example of the calculated value for R, F, M

No.	user_id	Recency	Frequency	Monetary
0	9794320.0	3	2	7.72
1	10079204.0	3	2	25.81
2	10280338.0	0	19	63.29

Figure 6. Visualization of the distribution for "recency", "frequency", "monetary"

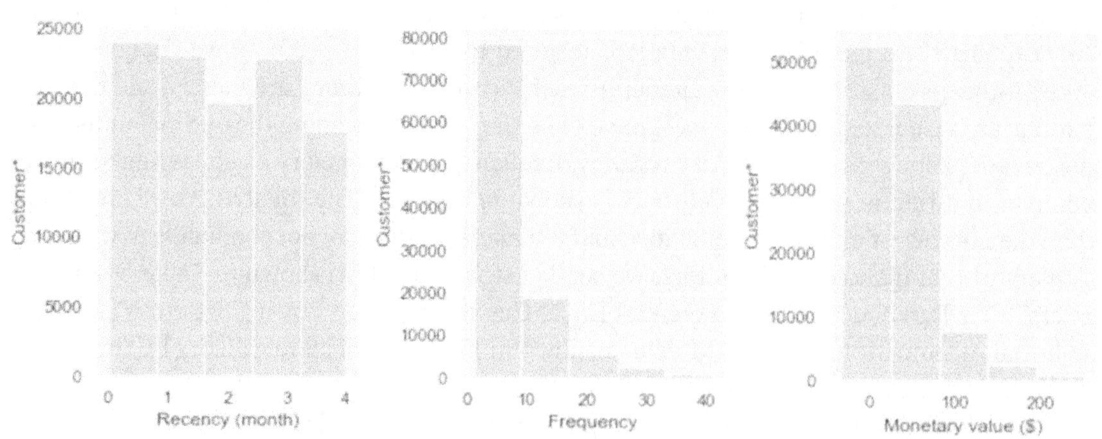

Figure 7. Optimal number of clusters

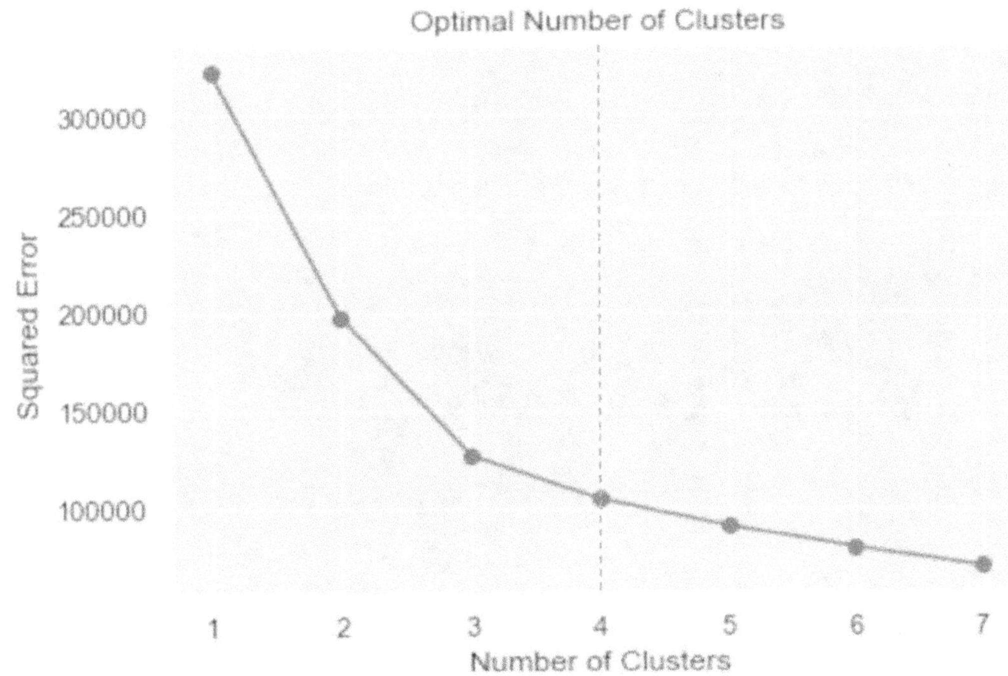

Table 5 depicts the cluster number and the symbols used for the customers' levels in which cluster 0 indicates new customers, cluster 1 at-risk customers, cluster 2 potential loyal customers, and cluster 3 shows loyal customers.

Table 5. Cluster number and the symbol of customer level

Cluster No.	Symbol	Group
Cluster 0	0	New Customers
Cluster 1	1	At-Risk Customers
Cluster 2	2	Potential Loyal Customers
Cluster 3	3	Loyal Customers

Figures 8 and 9 illustrate the result of RFM analysis combined with k-means clustering. Figure 8 depicts the results based on the value of recency, frequency and monetary for each customer levels whereas Figure 9 provides recommender systems with the characteristics of different customer levels as the basis for precision marketing. This information helps us to provide a more comprehensive overview of our customer groups and it is essential for developing reliable and highly implementable sales strategies at a later stage, such as promotional pricing, offering trial products and vouchers to customers, etc. It also can offer the segmentation level of a specific group of customers (Figure 10).

Figure 8. Visualization of four clusters based on "Recency", "Frequency", "Monetary" value

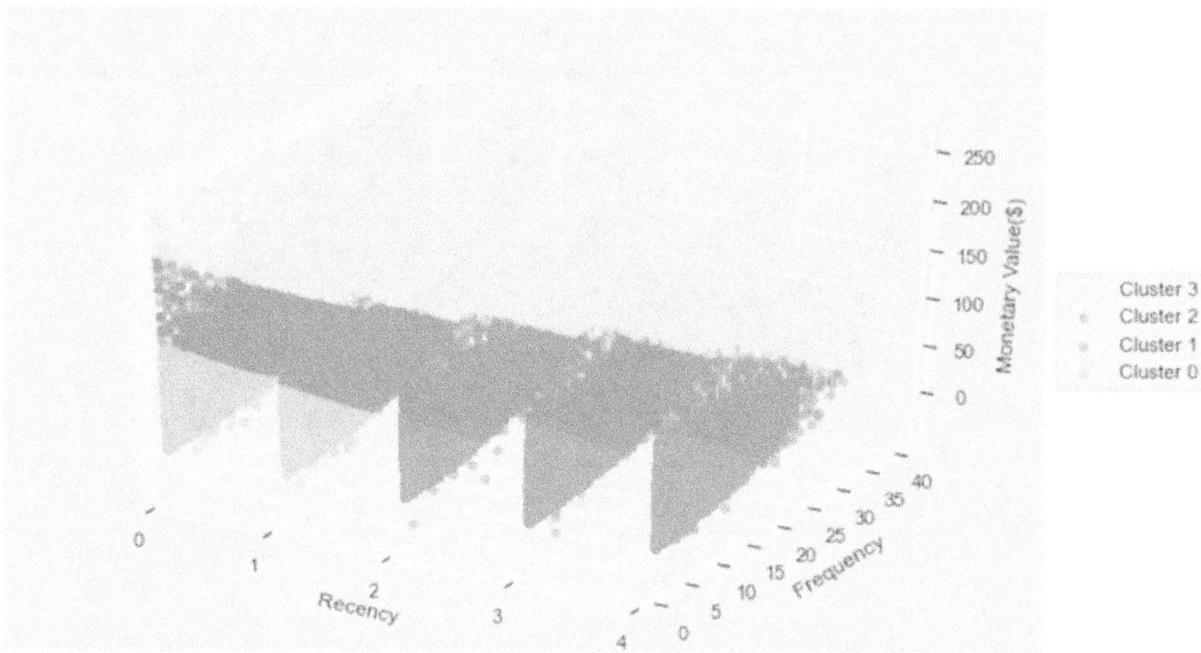

Figure 9. Visualization of four clusters based on customer details

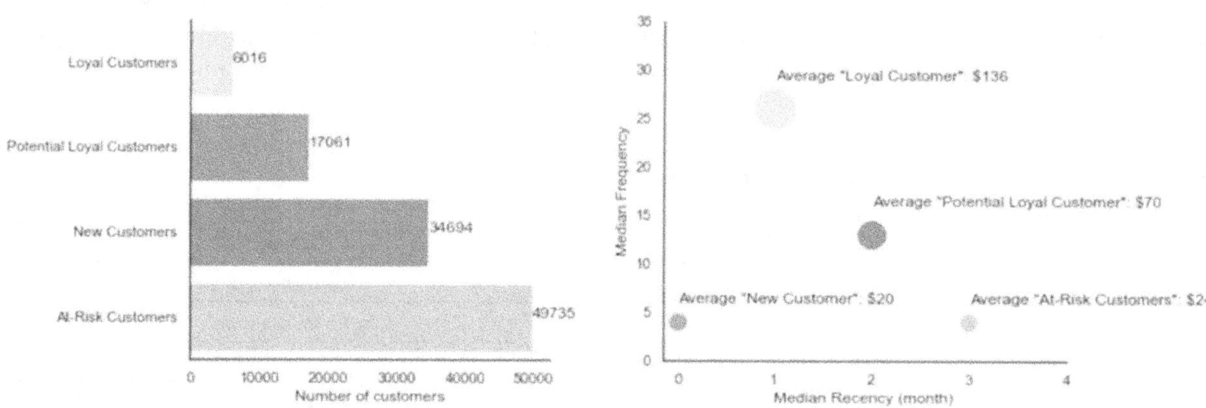

As shown in Figure 9, the number of "Loyal Customers" is the least, but average money spent was the highest, more than half of the other customer group. "Potential Loyal Customers" refers to making high spending power but haven't come back to buy favorite products for a while. This group of the customers is very important to the company, and if the sales strategy is applied properly, it is more likely to develop them into loyal customers. Therefore, we need to take the form of contacts or visits to survey the reasons for the low repurchase rate, thereby increasing the retention rate. Furthermore, we need to distribute online reminder messages and investigate the reasons why they haven't browsed or repurchased for a long time. These strategies can assist us to increase customer's retention rate.

Figure 10. Segmentation level of a customer

```
In [16]:

# Determite the type for a targeted customer
user_id = input('Please enter its user_id of the targeted customer:')
user_segment = df_RFM2[df_RFM2['user_id'] == float(user_id)]
print('The segment type of Customer "user_id":  ', set(user_segment['segments']))

Please enter its user_id of the targeted customer:10079204.0
The segment type of Customer "user_id":   {'At-Risk'}
```

The typical characteristic for "Potential Loyal Customers" is that the consumption amount is not high enough, but they also have a relatively high consumption capacity. We can recommend higher-priced products of the same category for them while introducing other good functions of new products and providing free trials to increase customer interest. For "At-Risk Customers", we need to send messages about some new products and appropriately give them vouchers to stimulate the purchase of products or recommend them to purchase accessories at a lower price to improve their experience. At the same time, we must notice that they have not placed an order for a long time, and some customers may belong to customer churn. For "New Customers", we must provide high-quality products and services to meet their needs while giving them vouchers to stimulate consumption, making them like and visit our store more. Figure 10 shows the codes for the segmentation level of a customer.

Product Recommendation Model

Our product recommendation model is based on market basket analysis, which is one of the key techniques used by large retailers to discover associations between products. Market basket analysis requires the use of a dataset that includes user IDs, purchase IDs, and product IDs, all of which are associated by each user ID. It was then developed based on the process shown in Figure 4.

For mining frequent itemsets and discovering association rules, we use the Apriori algorithm and Arules library. In our research, we set the minimum support value to 0.001 and the minimum confidence value to 0.1 based on the characteristics of stores and exploratory experimental results, and sort the rules by decreasing lift (Figure 11).

From the marketing perspective, the support and confidence are generally the main points of attention. To get maximum marketing response means more customers will buy other products recommended by the system with a high probability. For example, for product 5848909, if we want to get the highest marketing response rate, we need to think about what products are most likely to be purchased. The higher confidence we have, the more likely the item on the right will be purchased. Figure 12 shows the steps and results to get the highest marketing response sorted by confidence. In addition, it depicts that we should recommend product 5833330 as the first product.

From the perspective of maximizing sales, Figure 13 illustrates we should focus on the lift, because the bigger the lift, the better value will be gained. Hence, product 5906122 should be recommended to customers as the first product because its lift value is the largest (around 13). This indicates that the relationship between products 5848909 and 5906122 is stronger than the other products. It also shows that the relationship between products 5848909 and 5906122 is stronger than the other products. In other words, customers are most likely to buy product 5906122 after purchasing product 5848909.

Figure 11. Result of association rules

```
In [32]: # Complementary Products are recommended through the shopping basket
         # lift > 1 and then sort the Top n.
         Complements = result[result['lift'] > 1].sort_values(by='lift', ascending=False).head(10)
         print(Complements)

                    lhs                               rhs   support  \
667  (5584840, 5584836)  ==>           (5584844, 5584838)  0.001239
664  (5584844, 5584838)  ==>           (5584840, 5584836)  0.001239
668  (5584836, 5584838)  ==>           (5584840, 5584844)  0.001239
663  (5584840, 5584844)  ==>           (5584836, 5584838)  0.001239
695  (5875320, 5875319)  ==>           (5875321, 5875318)  0.001239
696  (5875321, 5875318)  ==>           (5875320, 5875319)  0.001239
693  (5875320, 5875321)  ==>           (5875318, 5875319)  0.001239
698  (5875318, 5875319)  ==>           (5875320, 5875321)  0.001239
670           (5584838)  ==>  (5584840, 5584844, 5584836)  0.001239
562           (5584838)  ==>           (5584840, 5584844)  0.001371

     confidence        lift
667    0.800000  452.120000
664    0.700000  452.120000
668    0.636364  435.928375
663    0.848485  435.928375
695    0.700000  405.748718
696    0.717949  405.748718
693    0.700000  395.605000
698    0.700000  395.605000
670    0.491228  382.920750
562    0.543860  372.560340
```

Figure 12. Recommend from a marketing perspective

```
In [33]: # Goal: Get the highest marketing response rate, take product 5848909 as an example
         purchase_good = result[result['lhs'] == frozenset({5848909})]

         # Sort by Confidence
         purchase_good.sort_values(by='confidence', ascending=False)

Out[33]:
```

	lhs		rhs	support	confidence	lift
498	(5848909)	==>	(5833330)	0.001106	0.208333	8.023140
234	(5848909)	==>	(5906122)	0.001062	0.200000	13.618072

Figure 13. Recommend from the perspective of maximizing sales

```
In [34]: # Goal: Maximize Sales
         purchase_good.sort_values(by='lift', ascending=False)

Out[34]:
```

	lhs		rhs	support	confidence	lift
234	(5848909)	==>	(5906122)	0.001062	0.200000	13.618072
498	(5848909)	==>	(5833330)	0.001106	0.208333	8.023140

There are often new customers on e-commerce platforms who have never purchased a product before, and we cannot analyze their preferences through their transaction data. In order to recommend products to these new customers, we can use a combination of recommendations for sales success rate. For example, if we want to recommend product 5906122 to a customer, using the right-hand rule, it is best to find the high frequency set that appears together with product 1005203 and recommend it together (Figure 14). Thus, it shows that we should recommend product 5906114, 5906121, 5833323, 5906119, 5906108, 5833334, 5833335, 5848909, 5833325, 5833326, and 5833330 to new customers together.

Figure 14. Products recommendation for new customers

```
In [35]: # The user does not have consumption, recommending a product for him/her
         # If recommend product 5906122, how should you develop a sales strategy?
         # The right-hand rule should be used here, because it is directly recommended product without consumption or spending.
         purchase_good = result[result['rhs'] == frozenset({5906122})].sort_values(by='confidence', ascending=False)

         # Sort by Confidence or Lift, because directly according to the data box selected by the right hand rule, confidence ar
         print(purchase_good)

               lhs              rhs   support  confidence       lift
         526  (5906114)  ==>  (5906122)  0.001504    0.576271  39.238513
         278  (5906121)  ==>  (5906122)  0.001150    0.565217  38.485856
         143  (5833323)  ==>  (5906122)  0.002389    0.375000  25.533886
         523  (5906119)  ==>  (5906122)  0.002256    0.280220  19.080266
         25   (5906108)  ==>  (5906122)  0.001106    0.277778  18.913989
         237  (5833334)  ==>  (5906122)  0.001814    0.210256  14.316435
         521  (5833335)  ==>  (5906122)  0.002875    0.205047  13.961746
         234  (5848909)  ==>  (5906122)  0.001062    0.200000  13.618072
         519  (5833325)  ==>  (5906122)  0.002123    0.148148  10.087461
         199  (5833326)  ==>  (5906122)  0.001858    0.124260   8.460932
         469  (5833330)  ==>  (5906122)  0.002964    0.114140   7.771813
```

For a specific customer from one target group, the recommended products were sorted by lift value of association rules. Figure 15 shows the process of selecting the specific customer and the interaction with the model, which recommends products by using the customer's purchase history included in the frequent item set and association rules. For example, the recommendation model can recommend the product (product ID: 5843546) for the user (user ID: 567580675) who purchased the product 5843545 based on association rules with the lift value greater than 2. We also can combine the characteristic of the target customer, based on result of customer segmentation, to offer vouchers to them for a few categories of products.

Figure 15. Recommendation example for one specific customer from targeted customer group

```
In [41]: # Screening users who need prediction
         df_basket['lhs'] = df_basket['product_id'].apply(lambda x: frozenset({int(x)}))
         baskets_user = pd.merge(df_basket, result, how='inner', on='lhs')
         all_users = list(baskets_user['user_id'])
         print('\n Total number of users:  ', len(all_users))
         small = input('Please enter the interval starting point of the user you want to view (an integer between 0-114617): ')
         big = input('Please enter the interval end point of the user you want to view (an integer between 1-114617): ')
         print('The user ID list in the user interval you selected is as follows: \n', set(all_users[int(small):int(big)]))
         user_id = input('Please enter the user ID you want to predict: ')
         user_data = baskets_user[baskets_user['user_id'] == int(user_id)]
         print('The list of purchased goods is as follows: \n', set(list(user_data['product_id'])))
         first_product = input('Please enter the product ID you want to buy: ')

         # Recommendation Process
         recommend_product_data = result[result['lhs'] == frozenset({int(first_product)})].sort_values(by='lift', ascending=Fals
         print('According to your 'lift' indicator, the result is as follows: \n', recommend_product_data)
         recommend_product_list = list(recommend_product_data['rhs'])
         recommend_product_list = [list(item)[0] for item in recommend_product_list]
         print('According to your purchase situation, the items recommended for you according to the priority order are: \n', re

          Total number of users:   114617
         Please enter the interval starting point of the user you want to view (an integer between 0-114617): 150
         Please enter the interval end point of the user you want to view (an integer between 1-114617): 200
         The user ID list in the user interval you selected is as follows:
          {464302593, 567580675, 565042441, 354650380, 434682133, 571350433, 387237026, 591555107, 473429668, 589311394, 53633
         4374, 572215207, 585807267, 572464809, 434898865, 394640308, 510669236, 523841847, 569504059, 592042559, 551065727, 5
         81379903, 436456899, 518099907, 589720775, 475078606, 307427791, 515020110, 563137234, 592776658, 587802325, 45409480
         6, 470171861, 575168216, 568808409, 583152214, 585748191, 562364771, 519060453, 583193706, 587858667, 457731440, 4234
         33076, 580525301, 582994167, 592455419, 583804412, 581907325, 492551807}
         Please enter the user ID you want to predict: 567580675
         The list of purchased goods is as follows:
          {4600, 4554, 5687151, 5843545, 5773361, 5809912, 5677465, 5814046}
         Please enter the product ID you want to buy: 5843545
         According to your 'lift' indicator, the result is as follows:
                    lhs              rhs   support  confidence        lift
         198  (5843545)  ==>  (5843546)  0.001371    0.322917  112.305449
         According to your purchase situation, the items recommended for you according to the priority order are:
          [5843546]
```

CONCLUSION AND FUTURE WORKS

This research proposed a novel data science life cycle and developed a customer segmentation model with RFM analysis, k-means clustering, and product recommendation through user behavior analytics. For this reason, we studied the important parts and processes of traditional store business transformation. Firstly, we used customer segmentation through the RFM method and k-means clustering. Comparing our previous research (Zhao & Keikhosrokiani, 2022), we combined two methods mentioned above in this research rather than only using RFM analysis. In addition, we set a more suitable number of customer groups to eight levels rather than by default. Finally, we got clear customer levels from the results, establishing the first important base for the business transition from a traditional store to an e-commerce company. In the recommendation system, we got strong association rules of historical products purchased by customers to analyze the transaction datasets. The overall system can display how online shopping platform recommends products to customers according to different business requirements, especially it can provide recommendations for a special customer from a targeted customer group by combining the customer segmentation results. This is very beneficial for deploying precision marketing and has very good scalability to add other supporting modules in further works. This research is also useful for an e-commerce company to improve its inventory management level.

Although the existing customer segmentation and recommendation model can recommend suitable products, we always believe that there is still a lot to do to get better performance. For instance, two important issues of "Clod Start" (Lika et al., 2014) and "Shilling Attack Detection" (Zhou et al., 2018) need to be solved urgently in recommender system. Hence, the future studies can focus on these limitations and improve the overall performance of the recommender system. Another future work can be to develop an expert system based on specific domain knowledge or rules, and then assist the customer's value and behavioral preference.

ACKNOWLEDGMENT

The authors are thankful to the School of Computer Sciences, Universiti Sains Malaysia (USM) for the unlimited support.

REFERENCES

Abdelrahman, O., & Keikhosrokiani, P. (2020). Assembly Line Anomaly Detection and Root Cause Analysis Using Machine Learning. *IEEE Access: Practical Innovations, Open Solutions*, *8*, 189661–189672. doi:10.1109/ACCESS.2020.3029826

Adomavicius, G., & Tuzhilin, A. (2005). Toward the next generation of recommender systems: A survey of the state-of-the-art and possible extensions. *Transactions on Knowledge and Data Engineering*, *17*(6), 734–749. doi:10.1109/TKDE.2005.99

Agarwal, R., & Srikant, R. (1994). Fast Algorithms For Mining Association Rules In Datamining. *The Proceeding of the 20th International Conference on Very Large Data Bases*, 487–499.

Agrawal, R., Imielinski, T., & Swami, A. (1993). Mining Association in Large Databases. *Proceedings of the 1993 ACM SIGMOD International Conference on Management of Data - SIGMOD '93*, 207–216. 10.1145/170035.170072

Allegue, S., Abdellatif, T., & Bannour, K. (2020). RFMC: A spending-category segmentation. *Proceedings of the Workshop on Enabling Technologies: Infrastructure for Collaborative Enterprises, WETICE*, 165–170. 10.1109/WETICE49692.2020.00040

Blattberg, R. C., Kim, B.-D., & Neslin, S. A. (2008). *Database Marketing: Analyzing and Managing Customers*. Springer. doi:10.1007/978-0-387-72579-6

Bult, J., & Wansbeek, T. (1995). Optimal Selection for Direct Mail. *Marketing Science*, *14*(4), 378–394. doi:10.1287/mksc.14.4.378

Chen, Q., Zhang, M., & Zhao, X. (2017). Analysing customer behaviour in mobile app usage. *Industrial Management & Data Systems*, *117*(2), 425–438. doi:10.1108/IMDS-04-2016-0141

Cheng, C.-H., & Chen, Y.-S. (2009). Classifying the segmentation of customer value via RFM model and RS theory. *Expert Systems with Applications*, *36*(3, Part 1), 4176–4184. doi:10.1016/j.eswa.2008.04.003

Cho, Y. S., Moon, S. C., Noh, S. C., & Ryu, K. H. (2012). Implementation of personalized recommendation system using k-means clustering of item category based on RFM. *2012 IEEE 6th International Conference on Management of Innovation and Technology, ICMIT 2012*, 378–383. 10.1109/ICMIT.2012.6225835

Dursun, A., & Caber, M. (2016). Using data mining techniques for profiling profitable hotel customers: An application of RFM analysis. *Tourism Management Perspectives*, *18*, 153–160. doi:10.1016/j.tmp.2016.03.001

Fatoni, C. S., Utami, E., & Wibowo, F. W. (2018). Online Store Product Recommendation System Uses Apriori Method. *Journal of Physics: Conference Series*, *1140*(1), 012034. Advance online publication. doi:10.1088/1742-6596/1140/1/012034

Harrington, P. (2012). *Machine Learning in Action*. Manning Publications Co.

Hosseini, S. M. S., Maleki, A., & Gholamian, M. R. (2010). Cluster analysis using data mining approach to develop CRM methodology to assess the customer loyalty. *Expert Systems with Applications*, *37*(7), 5259–5264. doi:10.1016/j.eswa.2009.12.070

Jackson, Wang, & Schultz. (1994). *Strategic database marketing*. Academic Press.

Kannan, S., & Bhaskaran, R. (2009). Association Rule Pruning based on Interestingness Measures with Clustering. *International Journal of Computer Science Issues*, *6*(1), 35–43.

Keikhosrokiani, P. (2021). Predicating Smartphone Users' Behaviour Towards a Location-Aware IoMT-Based Information System: An Empirical Study. *International Journal of E-Adoption*, *13*(2), 52–77. doi:10.4018/IJEA.2021070104

Keikhosrokiani, P. (2022). *Big Data Analytics for Healthcare: Datasets, Techniques, Life Cycles, Management, and Applications*. Elsevier Science. https://books.google.com.my/books?id=WbJYEAAAQBAJ

Keikhosrokiani, P., & Asl, M. P. (Eds.). (2022). *Handbook of Research on Opinion Mining and Text Analytics on Literary Works and Social Media* (1st ed.). IGI Global. doi:10.4018/978-1-7998-9594-7

Kim, S.-Y., Jung, T.-S., Suh, E.-H., & Hwang, H.-S. (2006). Customer segmentation and strategy development based on customer lifetime value: A case study. *Expert Systems with Applications*, *31*(1), 101–107. doi:10.1016/j.eswa.2005.09.004

Li, Y., & Wu, H. (2012). A Clustering Method Based on K-Means Algorithm. *Physics Procedia*, *25*, 1104–1109. doi:10.1016/j.phpro.2012.03.206

Lika, B., Kolomvatsos, K., & Hadjiefthymiades, S. (2014). Facing the cold start problem in recommender systems. *Expert Systems with Applications*, *41*(4), 2065–2073. doi:10.1016/j.eswa.2013.09.005

Marcus, C. (1998). A practical yet meaningful approach to customer segmentation. *Journal of Consumer Marketing*, *15*(5), 494–504. doi:10.1108/07363769810235974

Ngai, E. W. T., Xiu, L., & Chau, D. C. K. (2009). Application of data mining techniques in customer relationship management: A literature review and classification. *Expert Systems with Applications*, *36*(2), 2592–2602. doi:10.1016/j.eswa.2008.02.021

Qiu, Y., Chen, P., Lin, Z., Yang, Y., Zeng, L., & Fan, Y. (2020). Clustering Analysis for Silent Telecom Customers Based on K-means++. *Proceedings of 2020 IEEE 4th Information Technology, Networking, Electronic and Automation Control Conference, ITNEC 2020, Itnec*, 1023–1027. 10.1109/ITNEC48623.2020.9084976

Sarwar, B., Karypis, G., Konstan, J., & Riedl, J. (2000). Analysis of recommendation algorithms for e-commerce. *Proceedings of the 2nd ACM Conference on Electronic Commerce*, 158–167. 10.1145/352871.352887

Shaw, M. J., Subramaniam, C., Tan, G. W., & Welge, M. E. (2001). Knowledge management and data mining for marketing. *Decision Support Systems*, *31*(1), 127–137. doi:10.1016/S0167-9236(00)00123-8

Teoh Yi Zhe, I., & Keikhosrokiani, P. (2021). Knowledge workers mental workload prediction using optimised ELANFIS. *Applied Intelligence*, *51*(4), 2406–2430. doi:10.100710489-020-01928-5

Tsai, C. Y., & Chiu, C. C. (2004). A purchase-based market segmentation methodology. *Expert Systems with Applications*, *27*(2), 265–276. doi:10.1016/j.eswa.2004.02.005

Wang, Y., Feng, D., Li, D., Chen, X., Zhao, Y., & Niu, X. (2016). A mobile recommendation system based on logistic regression and Gradient Boosting Decision Trees. *Proceedings of the International Joint Conference on Neural Networks,* 1896–1902. 10.1109/IJCNN.2016.7727431

Wei, J. T., Lin, S. Y., Weng, C. C., & Wu, H. H. (2012). A case study of applying LRFM model in market segmentation of a children's dental clinic. *Expert Systems with Applications*, *39*(5), 5529–5533. doi:10.1016/j.eswa.2011.11.066

Wu, R.-S., & Chou, P.-H. (2011). Customer segmentation of multiple category data in e-commerce using a soft-clustering approach. *Electronic Commerce Research and Applications*, *10*(3), 331–341. doi:10.1016/j.elerap.2010.11.002

Yan, G., Minxi, W., & Xin, L. (2017). Application of an improved Apriori algorithm in a mobile e-commerce recommendation system. *Industrial Management & Data Systems*, *117*(2), 287–303. doi:10.1108/IMDS-03-2016-0094

Zhao, X., & Keikhosrokiani, P. (2022). Sales prediction and product recommendation model through user behavior analytics. *Computers. Materials and Continua*, *70*(2), 3855–3874. doi:10.32604/cmc.2022.019750

Zhou, W., Wen, J., Qu, Q., Zeng, J., & Cheng, T. (2018). Shilling attack detection for recommender systems based on credibility of group users and rating time series. *PLoS One*, *13*(5), 1–17. doi:10.1371/journal.pone.0196533 PMID:29742134

Chapter 7
Consumer Big Data Analytics: A Treasure for Businesses in the Socio-Digital Era

Princi Gupta
JECRC University, India

Risha Khandelwal
JECRC University, India

ABSTRACT

Data is generated from a variety of sources in the digital world, and the rapid adoption of digital technology has resulted in the creation of big data. The accumulation of massive datasets enables evolutionary breakthroughs in a variety of domains. Consumer behavior and analytics is a short, innovative, unique, and approachable literature that introduces new ideas, concepts, and structures to meet the current realities of analytics-driven marketing. This chapter is a groundbreaking and informative volume that connects new possibilities and techniques with existing academic consumer research. This chapter outlines the dimensions of big data and framework of consumer data analysis. This chapter also focuses on the case study of companies using big data.

INTRODUCTION

Data is generated from a variety of sources in the digital world, and the rapid adoption of digital technology has resulted in the creation of big data. The accumulation of massive datasets enables evolutionary breakthroughs in a variety of domains. It refers to a collection of vast, complicated datasets that are difficult to process with typical database administration tools or data processing apps.

In the last two decades, Consumer Marketing has been at the center of a social and economic revolution, and the forces driving this shift, particularly the wealth of data and pervasive digital technology, continue to exert major effect. The capacity of an organization's analytical talents, especially the ability to assess consumers' wants and desires, is critical to gaining a lasting competitive edge. According to research, companies that rely on modern data analysis outperform their competitors in terms of both

DOI: 10.4018/978-1-6684-4168-8.ch007

financial and operational performance. Organizations have been receiving a new stream of data for analysis, known as big data, for several years. Advances in business technology have dramatically improved organizations' ability to capture information on consumer behavior and demand, resulting in new strategic decision-making options. Data-driven tactics advocate the use of a wide range of consumer data to get a comprehensive understanding of customer behavior, motives, and expectations. Businesses now have more options for tailoring product, service, and experience delivery to fit the needs of different (individual) customers. To examine a significant number of data created by various business organizations, big data and business analytics methodologies have recently been developed and used. As a result, every company need more visibility into ever-increasing volumes of transactional data. Real-time data analysis allows businesses to peer into the past and predict the future.

"Data-driven insight is the essential underpinning of many firms, and consumer marketing is becoming increasingly analytics-driven." Consumer Behavior and Analytics is a short, innovative, unique, and approachable literature that introduces new ideas, concepts, and structures to meet the current realities of analytics-driven marketing. This chapter is a ground-breaking and informative volume that connects new possibilities and techniques with existing academic consumer research.

In complex corporate scenarios, data analytics aims to deliver operational insights. The concept of big data has been around for years, and most firms now realize that if they capture all of the data that flows into their operations, they can use analytics to extract tremendous value. Businesses were employing basic analytics (just figures on a spreadsheet that were manually inspected) to identify insights and trends as early as the 1950s, decades before the term "big data" were coined. The new advantages of big data analytics, on the other hand, are speed and efficiency. Whereas a corporation would have gathered data, ran analytics, and unearthed knowledge for future decisions a few years ago, today's organization can identify insights for current decisions. Data analytics has grown at such a rapid rate around the world that the Big Data market revenue is predicted to increase by 50% in the near future. Travel and transportation, financial analysis, retail, research, energy management, and healthcare are all affected.

Figure 1 illustrates how, in this era of Big Data, data on customer behavior and habits may be a valuable source for businesses to develop appropriate marketing strategies. Consequently, data might be considered a buried treasure in today's commercial world.

The main goal of this chapter is to review big data analytics techniques and frameworks which are available to track consumer behavior. This chapter organized outlined as follows: (1) Literature Review, (2) An integrative 7v- framework for big data, (3) Big data analytics: challenges and issues, (4) Tools and Framework of Big Data, (5) Big Data Application in Companies, (6) Findings and Conclusions, and finally (7) Future research Implications.

LITERATURE REVIEW

Consumer Analytics

Big data and business analytics are two business trends that are having a good impact. According to previous studies, the amount of data generated in the modern world is enormous and expanding at an exponential rate.

Figure 1. Consumer behavior analysis: input to business strategy (Zhao et al., 2021)

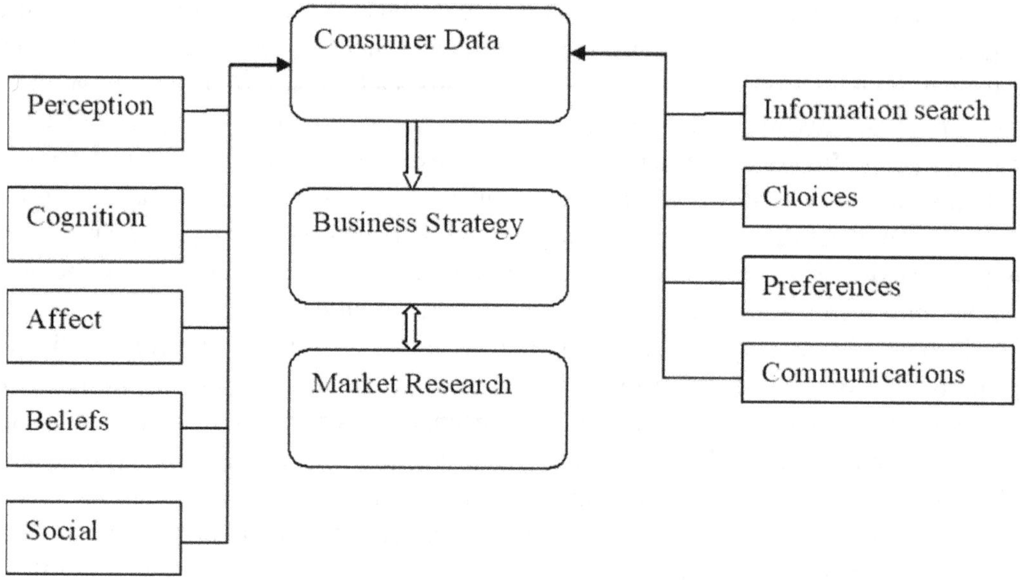

These include the structured and unstructured data that inundates businesses on a daily basis. Text files, web and social media posts, emails, photos, audio, movies, and other unstructured data make up the majority of the world's digital data. The standard relational database management system cannot manage unstructured data (RDBMS). Thus, data growth necessitates a rethinking of data capture, storage, and processing approaches. This is the role that big data has taken on.

Consumer analytics refers to the process of using customer data to gain the level of insight needed to make important business choice. (Surabhi Verma, 2018) define cognitive analytics as "the use of learning algorithms and technologies to multiple sources of information to improve decision making at scale."

According to a Commonwealth of Australia assessment from 2013, almost 90% of today's data was created in the previous two years. According to estimates, data creation will be 44 times higher in 2020 than it was in 2009. According to other estimates, 2.5 quintillion bytes of data are created every day. For the purposes of this study, "high-volume, high-velocity, and/or high-variety information assets that necessitate cost-effective, novel forms of information processing for better insight, decision making, and process optimization" has been used as the definition (Commonwealth of Australia, 2013). Big data has three dimensions, according to this description. However, there are two additional issues to consider: truthfulness and value.

According to (German et al., 2014), there is a strong link between an organization's performance and the use of consumer analytics. (Elgendy & Elragal, 2016) believe that sophisticated analytics can help people make better decisions by revealing insights from data that would otherwise go unnoticed. To assess this, a framework (known as Big-Data, Analytics, and Decisions) was put to the test in a real-world setting; with results demonstrating that incorporating big-data analytics into decision-making processes adds value (Elgendy & Elragal, 2016). As a result, cognitive analytics may play an important role in customer marketing by offering the ability to respond to fast changing consumer expectations that necessitate the prompt supply of appropriate solutions at scale.

Organizational decision-making tools may be created as a result of big-data analytics. “A store that can use big-data properly has the potential ability to raise 60 percent of operating margins by winning market dominance over its rivals and leveraging precise consumer data,” (Ram et al., 2016) wrote while assessing the implications of big-data analytics (Tankard, 2012).

According to (Ram et al., 2016), big-data research tends to focus on new solution approaches and/ or possible solution design. While various studies (Lansley and Longley, 2016) demonstrate how predictive analytics is applied to large data to gather consumer insight to aid decision making (retail and marketing strategy), consumer analytics frameworks have not been provided as a solution artefact for consumer analytics design.

Big data was declared the next frontier for productivity, innovation, and competition in May 2011 (Manyika et al., 2011). From 2016 to 2018, the number of Internet users increased by 7.5 percent to over 3.7 billion individuals (Finger & Genolet, 2016). In 2010, the world generated over 1 zettabyte (ZB) of data, which increased to 7 ZB by 2014 (Gretzel, 2015). The three V’s (Volume, Velocity, and Variety) were used to identify the developing characteristics of big data in 2001 (Laney, 2001). In 2011, IDC used the four V’s (Volume, Variety, Velocity, and Value) to characterize big data (Gretzel, 2015). The sixth characteristic of big data, veracity, was presented in 2012 (Silva, 2019).

AN INTEGRATIVE 7V- FRAMEWORK FOR BIG DATA

Big Data Analytics

The phrase “Big Data” has recently been applied to datasets that have become so vast that working with them using typical database management systems has become difficult. They are data sets that are too large for frequently used software tools and storage systems to gather, store, manage, and process within a reasonable amount of time (Kitchens & Dobolyi, 2018). The scale of big data is constantly growing, with single data sets now ranging from a few dozen terabytes (TB) to many petabytes (PB). As a result, some of the challenges associated with big data include data collection, storage, search, sharing, analytics, and visualization. Today, businesses are sifting through massive amounts of extremely detailed data in order to uncover previously unknown truths (Russom, 2011).

What is “big data” exactly? It’s hardly surprising that the term’s precise meaning is frequently vague, given its extensive use in the media. Big data is defined by the convergence of four dimensions, or the five V’s: volume, variety, velocity, veracity, and value. The 7sVs is a data management trend that was established to help businesses recognize and cope with big data’s development. The volume, velocity, variety, veracity, variability, visualization, and value of data generated and shared by various actors in the digital economy has increased immeasurably, paving the way to an era of Big Data (BD) (Wedel and Kannan, 2016)

Data is produced at an ever-increasing rate. Google receives 3.8 million search inquiries every minute. 156 million emails are sent each day by email users. 243,000 photographs are uploaded to Facebook by users. Data scientists must figure out how to collect, interpret, and use massive volumes of data as they come in. (Mikalef et al., 2019) discuss how numerous resources and contextual factors contribute to big data analytics performance gains (BDA). Organizations, on the other hand, continue to struggle with efficient data analysis and comprehension. This is owing to the characteristics of big data, which are commonly referred to as the 7V, or Volume, Velocity, Variety, Veracity, Variability, Visualization, and

Value (See Figure 2). The Velocity and Unpredictability dimensions become particularly significant in a modern fast-changing economy—the aspects that cause the most challenges in the analysis process are the speed and variability of data input, and hence the temporal dimension of big data. This component is linked to the underlying assumption that time is an indivisible factor influencing the phenomena of large data and the analysis process. The temporal dimension appears in three forms: as the fourth dimension of space-time, as a logical sequence of events (as defined by big data), and as a direct determinant of these events (Soroka, 2017). Because the organization's environment changes, the temporal dimension concerns both the phenomena of data input and the reality reflected in these data. It is given a formal description of time and temporality.

Veracity

Veracity (uncertainty of data) is related to the quality, relevance, predictive value and meaning of data (Chen & Mao, 2014). This dimension describes the biases, noise, and irregularities in the data being generated. Is the data being saved and mined relevant to the problem being investigated? Given the tremendous number of data being generated at an ever-increasing rate and in ever-more-diverse ways, you must clearly manage the uncertainty associated with specific categories of data. Validity and volatility are two additional characteristics that are critical to operationalizing big data, in addition to the 4Vs.

Value

The worth of information to various stakeholders/ decision makers is considered as Value (Clifford, 2008). Value, like big data veracity, refers to data that is correct and accurate for its intended use. If the results are to be used for decision-making, the legitimacy of big data sources and subsequent analysis must be correct.

Value denotes the context and usefulness of data for decision-making, whereas the previous V's were primarily concerned with reflecting big data difficulties. Facebook, Google, and Amazon, for example, have tapped into the potential of big data through analytics in their individual products. Amazon uses enormous datasets of customers and their transactions to make product recommendations, resulting in increased sales and user interaction. Google obtains location data from Android users in order to improve Google Maps' location services. Facebook tracks user behavior in order to deliver personalized ads and friend suggestions. These three organizations have grown to be gigantic by analyzing large amounts of raw data and extracting relevant information to help them make better business decisions. (Court, 2015).

Volume

Volume (scale of data) states the management of the amount of data, usually referred to in terms of terabytes or petabytes of data. It involves management of data storage (Fiaidhi, 2019). Volume refers to the enormous amount of data produced every second and to the extent and scope of a dataset. Because the time and kind of data might influence its definition, defining a universal threshold for large data volume (i.e., what defines a 'huge dataset') is unrealistic (Gandomi, 2015). Big data is currently defined as datasets in the exabyte (EB) or zettabyte (ZB) ranges (wyber, 2015), however datasets in lesser size ranges also face issues. Walmart, for example, collects 2.5 PB per hour from over a million customers (Marr, 2015). Such massive amounts of data might cause scalability and unpredictability issues (e.g., a database tool may not be able to accommodate infinitely large datasets). Many present data analysis techniques are not meant for large-scale databases, and they often fail when scanning and understanding data at scale (Saidulu, 2017).

"This dimension refers to the amount of data, as big data is typically characterized in terms of huge data sets, with petabytes and zettabytes being commonly used". And these enormous volumes of data are generated every day. Previously, this was employee-generated data. Nowadays, big data is generated by machines, networks, and human engagement on systems like social media.

Variety

Variety (different forms of data) is the format of data that can be structured, semi structured and unstructured. Data arrives in a variety of formats. Structured data is information that can be properly structured within a database's columns. Entering, storing, querying, and analyzing this type of data is relatively simple. It's more difficult to sort and extract value from unstructured data.

Velocity

Velocity refers to the frequency of data that is produced, processed, and analyzed (Finger, 2016). "The growing pace at which data floods in from sources such as corporate processes, machines, networks, and human engagement with things like social networking sites, mobile devices, and so on is known as big data velocity". The data flow is vast and never-ending.

Variability

Variability is not the same as variety. The term "variability" refers to data that is always changing. Understanding and interpreting the right meanings of raw data is the main emphasis of variability. For example, a soda shop may offer six different soda mixes, but if you get the same soda blend every day and it tastes different, that is variability. The same is true of data, which can have an impact on the quality of your data if it is constantly changing. The meaning of data is always shifting. Language processing by computers, for example, is extremely challenging due to the fact that words frequently have several meanings. Data scientists must account for this variation by developing clever algorithms that comprehend context and meaning.

Visualization

The term "visualization" relates to the way you can show your data to management for decision-making. We are all aware that data can be presented in a variety of formats, including excel files, word documents, graphical charts, and so on. Data should be easily legible, comprehensible, and accessible regardless of format, which is why data visualization is so crucial. After the data has been processed, you'll need a way to show it in a comprehensible and accessible format, which is where visualization comes in. Finding a way to present this information in a way that makes the findings clear is one of the challenges of Big Data. Visualizations can contain dozens of variables and parameters—a far cry from the x and y variables of your standard bar chart—and finding a way to present this information that makes the findings clear is one of the challenges of Big Data.

Figure 2. Framework for big data (Uddin, 2014)

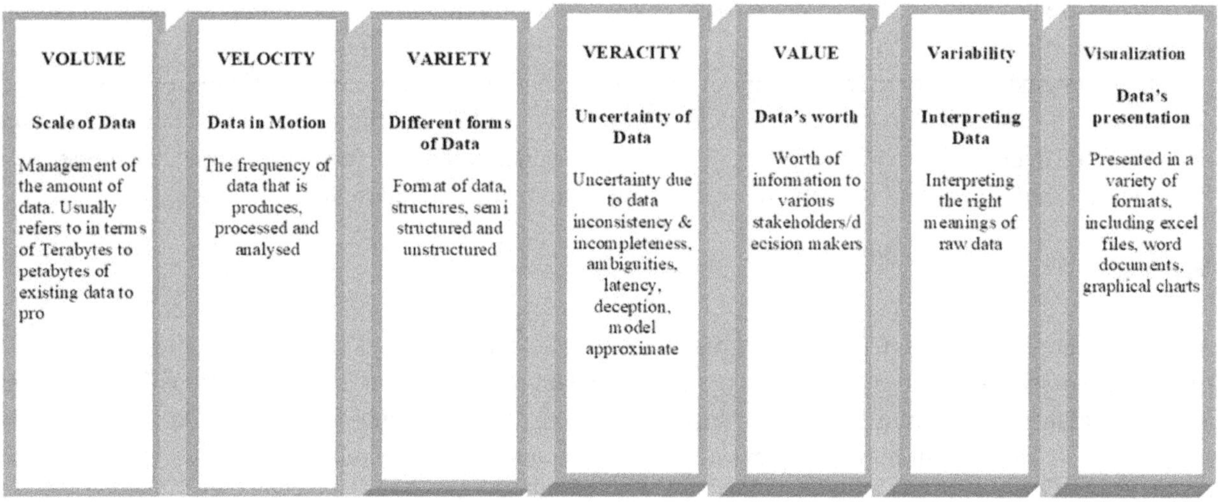

BIG DATA ANALYTICS: CHALLENGES AND ISSUES

The concept of *big* is problematic to pinpoint, not least because a dataset that appears to be massive today will almost surely appear small in the near future (Meng, 2014). One of the most difficult aspects of the big data environment is that it does not provide clear guidance on how to achieve business goals by aligning with current company culture and capabilities (Kiron et al., 2014).In this regard, Barton (2012) stated that the key challenge for managers is to make big data trustworthy and understandable to frontline employees, citing the example of frontline employees who are typically hesitant to use big data because they either do not trust a big data-based model or lack the ability to understand how it works. Managers should provide big data in an intelligible fashion, such as through a dashboard, reports, or a visualization system, in order to obtain more acceptability from employees and other end-users (Bose, 2009).

The term "big data" is vital and interconnected in a world brimming with information, which is especially visible in information societies with access to the Internet. Data is being transferred to the global network not only by people who do so knowingly and manually (e.g., via social networks or e-mails), but also by various sensors and cloud computing. Big data is one of the major pillars of the Web 3.0 sector (Mohammadi, 2018).

As a young notion, big data has had a tumultuous history of attempts to describe it, with (Gandomi and Haider, 2015) making an attempt to organize the definitions. The opinion that big data, which can be considered as a "new era" of the data-driven paradigm, has opened new opportunities for improved decision support is the common axis of all definitions. Large data can also be characterized using the 7V characteristics, however when looking at the temporal elements of big data, the concept of velocity is the most essential (Power, 2015). Big data is not only large and dynamic, but it also needs the analysis and processing of cutting-edge technologies (Zakir et al., 2015). Big data differs from regular "data" notation in that it cannot be analyzed and managed using traditional data mining methods due to its enormous size (Sajana et al., 2016).

The term "big data mining" (BDM) is synonymous with "traditional data mining notation." The only difference between these two notions is in the methodology for gathering data, not in the concept itself. BDM allows for the extraction of relevant information from databases or data streams that are large in terms of the "big data V's," such as volume, velocity, and variety (Jaseena, 2014). The two primary functions of data mining are descriptive (such as grouping, association, and pattern mining) and predictive (such as regression analysis) (such as classification, time series analysis, etc.) These functions (enablers) differ only slightly in terms of temporal reference, i.e., descriptive functions primarily concern the present and established dependencies, whereas predictive functions primarily concern the future and uncertain dependencies. After gathering (large) data, it is important to analyze it in order to extract information. It is critical to apply big data analysis tools in this instance. BDA was developed in response to the necessity to assess large amounts of complicated data collected quickly (Constantiou et al., 2015). As a result, data collecting and processing may happen quickly, which is impossible with current computational approaches. As a big data derivative, big data analytics can be defined using big data "V" characteristics. "Action on insight," as (Akhtar et al., 2019) put it, is the final and most important phase in the BDA process. BDA, as one of the most important aspects for generating relevant insights for decision-making, (Dubey et al., 2019) must be used and implemented in order to extract value from the vast amount of data available (Wedel, 2016). To create value, an organization's ability to handle BDA has lately become mainstream. However, due to a lack of IT infrastructure, data storage facilities, and organizational strategy, the flowering of BDA potential in enterprises can be stifled (Raut et al., 2021).

BDA is used in a wide range of situations. Apart from technological applications, BDA has economic applications (Balasaraswathi et al., 2020), the most important of which is social media analytics (SMA) for revealing client behavior (Sarin et al., 2020). This is due to the sheer volume of data: as of January 2021, Facebook had 2.74 billion users, Instagram had 1.22 billion, and Twitter had 353 million. Given the large number of posts posted by each user, this represents a potential gold mine of information and a large area for research, such as segmentation and prediction. Social media analytics is a branch of big data analytics that is defined as "the analysis of structured and unstructured data from social media channels" (Anshari, 2019). Conducting SMA, including sentiment analysis, is especially beneficial in assessing and comprehending user (or, more broadly, society) behavior in unpredictable situations, such as the present pandemic scenario, as scientific study has shown (Rahmanti, 2021). Social media analytics is widely employed in big data-enabled businesses, which include both corporate and public sector entities. Improved client experience and overall operational efficiency help SMA generate new leads. Big data (together with derivative methodologies such as big data mining or, more broadly, big data analytics) is useful for extracting the hidden value of consumer information. After presenting the historical and theoretical context for the value of customer insights, it is possible to delve deeper into the subject, focusing on the actual application of big data for consumer insights in businesses.

Big Data Analytics Tools

Traditionally, data and business analytics have been carried out with the use of a combination of machine learning and data mining techniques (Hasheem, 2015). These tools make it possible to examine little to huge amounts of data in order to make business decisions. The following are some of the most common tools for data analytics:

1. **Clustering and segmentation:** This technique divides a huge number of things into smaller groups that share some characteristics. Analyzing a group of clients to separate smaller segments for focused marketing is one example.
2. **Classification** is the process of grouping data into specified categories based on features that are either pre-selected by an analyst or discovered by a clustering model. Using the segmentation model to determine which segment a new consumer belongs to is an example.
3. **Regression** is a technique for identifying associations between a dependent variable and one or more independent factors, as well as determining how the dependent variable's values fluctuate in relation to the values of the independent variables. Using mobile money subscription data, usage level, transaction type, transaction value, and geographic area to forecast future mobile money payment penetration is an example.
4. **Association and itemset mining:** In a huge data set, association and itemset mining looks for statistically relevant associations between variables. This could, for example, assist digital banking representatives in directing what services they should provide users of mobile money apps receive specific incentives based on their usage level, transaction value, and transaction volume
5. **Similarity and correlation:** Undirected clustering algorithms are informed by similarity and correlation. The similarity of elements placed in a proposed cluster can be determined using similarity-scoring methods.

However, the massive volume of big data, on the other hand, has rendered classical data analysis inefficient for processing massive volumes of created data in today's cyber-physical and mobile connected world.

CONSUMER ANALYTICS FRAMEWORK

Figure 3 depicts a framework for capturing consumer insights that integrates structured, unstructured, and semi-structured data to provide dynamic and adaptive capabilities, resulting in value creation for marketing innovations that assist achieve long-term competitive advantage. Our proposed approach focuses on including physical capital resources, human capital resources, and organizational capital resources by modifying the resource-based view. It shows how consumer data can be used to assist marketing skills, decisions, and innovations. Table 1 details each component of the suggested strategy. Consumer analytics has transformed the competitive landscape of modern marketing, with businesses using consumer data insights to improve marketing operations and innovations. The impact of Big Data on marketing activities was addressed, and a resource-based theory-based conceptual framework was presented. The study recognizes that the potential to extract hidden consumer insights from large data allows for a new level of consumer awareness. As a result, by enhancing marketing ideas, businesses can obtain a competitive advantage.

Several frameworks for analyzing customer behavior have been introduced. A resource-based framework was described by (Erevelles et al., 2016). Data that is structured, unstructured, or semi-structured for gathering consumer information in order to enable dynamic and personalized marketing. As a result of these adaptive capabilities, marketing value generation is possible. Innovations aid in achieving a long-term competitive edge. As (Balasaraswathi, 2020) contextualized the necessity for corporate resources to establish sustainable competitive advantage, our suggested framework adapts the resource-based paradigm to include physical capital resources, human capital resources, and organizational capital resources. Consumer data is used to support marketing capabilities, decisions, and innovations, as seen in Figure 3. Table 1 details each component of the suggested strategy.

Figure 3: Consumer analytics framework (Camilleri et al., 2017)

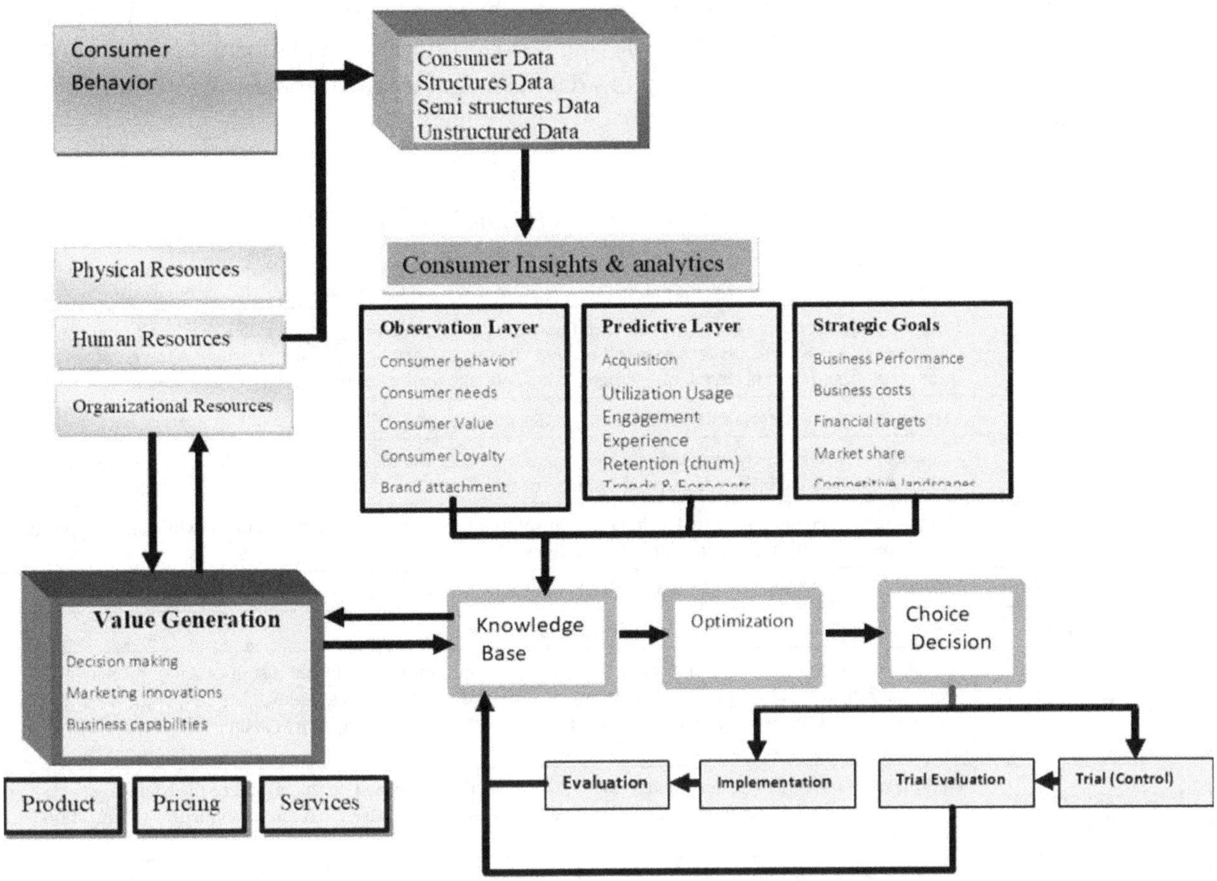

BIG DATA AND BUSINESS ANALYTICS- APPLICATIONS

Big data analytics technology has benefited a wide range of business and industry sectors. These domains generate a large volume of data, which necessitates the use of big data analytics to make informed decisions. Healthcare, telecommunications, network optimization, trip prediction, retail, financial industries, and energy consumption are only a few of the application areas (Wang et al., 2016). The application areas are explained below

1. **Network Optimization:** A mobile network can be designed to provide efficient services using a big data and business analytics approach. Content-centric analysis, traffic analysis, and network signaling are all areas of interest for ensuring effective service delivery and quality of service delivery. For efficient signaling, predict traffic variation, network overload, intelligent network optimization,

autonomous self-configuration of the network, and intelligent transportation development, network operators can implement framework to collect, store, and analyze user or core network data (Lee, 2021).

2. **Travel Estimation:** Researchers have been able to aggregate, store, process, and analyze travel estimation, particularly in route recommendation, location tracking, trip generation, commuter origin and destination information, and transportation management planning in the developing economy, thanks to the large volume of data generated by mobile users during calls, known as call data records (CDRs) (Dobre, 2014). By deploying a smart multimodal platform that uses personal information and global constraints, mobile big data can also improve route suggestion in a complicated setting.

Table 1. Description of consumer analytics components (Camilleri et al., 2017)

Consumer Data	Consumer data (transactional, digital, social, etc.) that is recorded and made available for analysis
Consumer Insights and Analytics	Insights, patterns, and metrics produced from pertinent components of consumer data that can be interpreted. The observation layer recognizes past and present customer behavior and demand, whereas the predictive layer recognizes future behavior and demand. This contains predicted market activity and trends.
Strategic Goals	Metrics that quantify corporate performance, goals, and aims, as well as market and competitor data
Knowledge Base	Considers customer behavior in the past, present, and future, as well as corporate performance, goals, and targets, as well as the influence of previous acts (or decisions).
Optimization	Utilizes the information base to develop optimal solutions that match consumer demand while also supporting the company's goals, aims, and strategic objectives.
Choice Decision	Determines which option is the best (derived at optimization step)
Trial (control)	Deploy the best answers to the tiniest of problems.
Trail Evaluation	Assess the potential value and impact of implementing the solution to a larger customer group by analyzing trial results and quantifying the value and impact provided by optimized solutions. The outcomes of the evaluation are also saved in the knowledge base for future optimization and decision-making possibilities.
Implementation and evaluation	Optimized solutions can be deployed to the customer population based on the results of the trial stage. The results of the implementation are also saved in the knowledge base for future monitoring, optimization, and decision-making.
Value Generation	The knowledge base adds value by recommending optimal solutions to complicated management decision problems for new innovations, in addition to providing the value provided by implemented solutions.
Resources	The quality of organizational resources determines the effectiveness of each framework component, from data gathering and storage to analytics, optimization, and deployment. Management's understanding of and experience with the value provided by the suggested framework guarantees that the organization's resources are maintained and improved. People and technology, as well as the mindset required to accept a data-driven operational paradigm, are all factors in this situation.

In order to make alternative recommendations, the algorithms monitor the situation of the cities in real time and detect congested routes. This process isn't new; it's been used in drone navigation, infectious illness detection, hotspot identification, and emergency situations. To ensure security, datasets are typically anonymized by replacing subscriber phone numbers with computer-generated unique identities. Mobile big data research for travel estimation has proven to be crucial in improving transportation planning.

3. **User behavior modeling:** User behavior modelling aids in the understanding of navigation patterns and the development of user-centric systems. These apps are useful for detecting abnormalities, fraud, and spam in social media, as well as changing social behavior for targeted marketing (Lima, 2016).
4. **Human mobility modeling:** Over time, human beings follow a predictable pattern. As a result, repeating such patterns allows for efficient global movement prediction, which can be used in disease containment, transportation planning, emergency situations, and disease outbreak prevention by leveraging social network platforms, GPS data, call data records, and geo-tagged data through big data analytics methods (Finger, 2016).
5. **Service recommendation**: big data and business analytics approaches have played a critical part in service recommendation, targeted advertising based on user location information, product reviews, and time and product buying behavior. For example, in a recent study by (Salehan and Kim, 2016), Hadoop and Map Reduce were used to evaluate customer reviews in order to determine the product's strengths and drawbacks. This method can be used to figure out what factors influence review readership and how to boost sales.
6. **Energy consumption analysis:** Determining the quantity of energy used in the home is a surefire technique to encourage green energy efficiency and conservation. By equipping electricity supply with sensors, a communication network, and an analytics engine to digitalize, store, and analyze the consumption rate, the study utilizing big data approaches gives usage patterns to boost green energy (Hashem, 2015). Furthermore, this will assist energy corporations in increasing their sales and return on investment.
7. **Educational development:** The educational industry offers a wealth of data for big data analytics. These data can be used to forecast student performance and achievement. Furthermore, by leveraging fields such as natural language processing and text summarization, big data analytics in education play an essential role in course material management, tailored recommendation modules, and the creation of smart education. Furthermore, data created by massive online courses (MOOCs) aids in the identification of challenging topic areas and provides support to students in order to improve teaching and learning (Awan et al, 2021).
8. **Financial Industries:** The financial industry's use of social media and internet-based initiatives has resulted in the collection of a large amount of data. As a result, big data techniques are required to examine these data for effective decision-making. Furthermore, financial statement and data analysis would lead to the discovery and management of anti-money laundering, financial statement fraud, financial spamming, impersonation, identity theft, and other financial fraud incidents (Bhadani, 2016).
9. **Healthcare:** Economic progress, as well as physical and mental wellness, are all dependent on improved health. The healthcare business creates a large amount of data that can be utilized to help doctors and other health practitioners make better decisions. Furthermore, the use of big data in healthcare can aid in the development of real-time disease analysis, thereby increasing the public's quality of life. There has been a lot of study in this area, ranging from fault tolerance systems to assist data collection, integration, and analysis to continuous monitoring for early identification of an environmental situation that could trigger an asthma attack (Villars, 2011). Furthermore, because of their large scale, public health care data necessitates big data analytics techniques to track, monitor, store, and analyze individual moving objects with their level of exposure to harmful environmental factors in order to determine the relationship between the data and environmental

risk. Furthermore, combining call detail records and sensor data to give feedback mechanisms in order to improve the quality of healthcare delivery, big data analytics has played a critical role in anticipating the breakout of diseases such as the Ebola virus (Khatib, 2016).

EXAMPLES OF COMPANIES USING DATA AS A TREASURE

Amazon

Customers' names, addresses, payment histories, and search history are among the data that the online retail juggernaut has access to. While much of this data is utilized in advertising algorithms, Amazon also uses it to improve customer experiences, which many big data users overlook.

If you phone the Amazon help desk with a question, don't be surprised if the person on the other end of the line already knows the bulk of the answers. Without having to repeat your name three times, this allows for a faster, more efficient customer service experience.

American Express

The American Express Company is analyzing and anticipating consumer behavior using big data. By looking at earlier transactions and integrating more than 100 variables, the company uses complex predictive models instead of traditional business intelligence-based hindsight reporting.

This makes it possible to predict client turnover and loyalty with greater accuracy. In fact, American Express claims to be able to predict that 24 percent of accounts in their Australian market will close within four months.

BDO

During audits, BDO, a national accounting and auditing firm, uses big data analytics to uncover risk and fraud.

Finding the source of a discrepancy used to require multiple interviews and hours of manpower; now, by consulting internal data first, the field is greatly restricted, and the procedure is significantly expedited.

BDO Consulting Director Kirstie Tiernan explained that in one situation, they were able to reduce a list of thousands of vendors to a dozen and then evaluate each piece of data individually for inconsistencies. It was quite easy to pinpoint a specific source.

Capital One

One of the most common applications of big data is marketing, and Capital One is on top of the game, using big data management to assure the success of all consumer products.

Capital One finds the best times to provide various offers to customers by analyzing their demographics and spending habits, resulting in higher conversion rates from their communications.

Not only does this improve uptake, but it also makes marketing campaigns significantly more focused and relevant, resulting in better budget allocation.

General Electric (GE)

GE is using data from sensors on gear like gas turbines and jet engines to come up with ways to improve operating procedures and reliability.

The reports are then sent to GE's analytics division, which will develop tools and adjustments to assist the corporation become more efficient.

According to the firm, data may boost US productivity by 1.5 percent, saving enough money to boost average national incomes by as much as 30% over a 20-year period.

Miniclip

Miniclip, a company that creates, publishes, and distributes digital games around the world, uses big data to track and improve user experience. Miniclip prioritizes client retention due to the nature of the firm and industry in order to make games more profitable and, as a result, assist business growth.

The corporation can use big data reporting, analysis, experimentation, and machine learning data products to quantify the successful features of their products and use them in future initiatives, while also eliminating or enhancing the problematic elements.

Netflix

The entertainment streaming service has a wealth of data and analytics that may be used to obtain insight into millions of people's viewing habits around the world.

Netflix uses this data to commission original programming for a global audience and to buy the rights to films and series boxsets that they know will appeal to specific groups.

While Adam Sandler has been unpopular in the United States and the United Kingdom in recent years, Netflix approved four new projects with him in 2015, knowing that his previous work in Latin America had been profitable.

Next Big Sound

Next Big Sound (NBS) has figured out how to anticipate the next big thing in music using data from Spotify streams, iTunes sales, SoundCloud plays, Facebook likes, Wikipedia page views, YouTube clicks, and Twitter mentions.

The company's analytics provide important insight into social media popularity, the influence of TV appearances, and a slew of other data points for the music industry. Thanks to a collaboration between NBS and Spotify, artists can also utilize the data for their own promotion.

Billboard currently produces two charts that are solely based on NBS data, and they've partnered with firms like Pepsi and American Express to help influence billions of dollars spent on music-related marketing and sponsorships.

T-Mobile

Similarly, to American Express, the mobile network is integrating consumer transaction and interaction data to forecast client swings.

T-Mobile USA claims to have reduced customer defections in a quarter by combining internal data on billing and customer relations management with data on social media activity. The data collection technologies have been integrated into the company's IT systems.

Starbucks

Have you ever wondered how Starbucks is able to build three stores on the same block without losing customers?

The coffeehouse behemoth employs big data to forecast the viability of each new location, taking into account factors like geography, traffic, demographics, and consumer behavior.

By conducting this type of analysis prior to opening a store, Starbucks can get a reasonably decent approximation of the success rate and choose locations based on the possibility of revenue growth.

FINDINGS AND CONCLUSION

The chapter is essential for understanding the Consumer Data Analytics – "A Treasure for Businesses in Digital Era". This chapter highlights Consumer Analytics and Dimensions of Big Data analytics. Big data is defined by the convergence 7sVs. The volume, velocity, variety, veracity, variability, visualization, and value of data generated and shared by various actors in the (digital) economy has increased immeasurably, paving the way to an era of BigData.

The chapter further studies the framework of Big Data Analytics and identifies some tools of Data Analytics. This chapter also focuses on the companies using Big Data analytics as a Treasure. This chapter aims at identifying the challenges and issues of Big Data Analytics that appears to be massive today will almost surely appear small in the near future as well as its Applications in Business world.

Due to the problems and opportunities produced by the information revolution, big data analytics (BDA) has emerged as the new frontier of innovation and competition throughout the whole e-commerce industry. Big data analytics (BDA) is increasingly providing value to e-commerce companies by transforming data into insights for sound decision-making and solutions to business problems by leveraging the dynamics of people, processes, and technologies. Some limitations may limit the generalizability of the findings. As a result, the study's findings outline consumer analytics can provide tremendous benefit to businesses, designing and implementing a data-driven operational model comes with a number of hurdles.

Further, lack of business support for analytical resources may stem from a failure to either produce or grow business value. Because the success of a data-driven operational model is determined by the quality of an organization's analytical resources (people and technology), analytical skills to generate value are further limited. As a result, optimising analytical solutions that match customer demand in relation to important business performance measurements is critical. This not only adds or improves business value, but also ensures that the value created is quantified and visible to the rest of the organisation.

FUTURE RESEARCH DIRECTIONS

With the advancement of big data analysis technology in the modern network economy, many network platforms or e-commerce enterprises will collect personalised consumer behaviour information, use big data analysis and processing technology to integrate and extract effective information, and accurately make targeted recommendations to consumers.

The main issue is sifting through a massive volume of data to locate the right information about each consumer; therefore, future research might analyse this massive amount of data which empower customers more than ever before, allowing marketers to build e-commerce relationships built on trust and loyalty. Quantitative and qualitative research may be used in the future to better understand the Consumer Data Analytics. Secondary data can be analysed using a variety of social sciences tests, which can aid in focusing on factors influencing the consumer- perceived value of Big datasuch as data cost, quality, retention, visualization, governance, security, and privacy.

REFERENCES

Akhtar, P., Frynas, J. G., Mellahi, K., & Ullah, S. (2019). Big data-savvy teams' skills, big data-driven actions and business performance. *British Journal of Management, 30*(2), 252-271. doi:10.1111/1467-8551.12333

Awan, U., Shamim, S., Khan, Z., Zia, N. U., Shariq, S. M., & Khan, M. N. (2021). Big data analytics capability and decision-making: The role of data-driven insight on circular economy performance. *Technological Forecasting and Social Change*, *168*, 120766. doi:10.1016/j.techfore.2021.120766

Balasaraswathi, M., Srinivasan, K., Udayakumar, L., Sivasakthiselvan, S., & Sumithra, M. G. (2020). Big data analytic of contexts and cascading tourism for smart city. *Materials Today: Proceedings*. Advance online publication. doi:10.1016/j.matpr.2020.10.132

Barton, A. (2013). Mining big data in real time. *Informatica (Vilnius)*, *37*(1).

Barton, D., & Court, D. (2012). Making advanced analytics work for you. *Harvard Business Review*, *90*(10), 78–83. doi:10.4236/apm.2016.612062 PMID:23074867

Blondel, V. D., Decuyper, A., & Krings, G. (2015). A survey of results on mobile phone datasets analysis. *EPJ Data Science*, *4*(1), 10. https://doi.org/10.1140/epjds/s13688-015-0046-0

Borne, K. (2014). Top 10 big data challenges a serious look at 10 big data v's. *Blog Post, 11*.

Bose, R. (2009). Advanced analytics: Opportunities and challenges. Industrial Management & Data Systems. https://doi.org/10.1108/02635570910930073.

Camilleri, E., & Miah, S. (2017, December). A Consumer Analytics Framework for Enabling Data-Driven Marketing Intervention Methods. In *2017 4th Asia-Pacific World Congress on Computer Science and Engineering (APWC on CSE)* (pp. 8-12). IEEE. doi:10.1109/APWConCSE.2017.00011

Chen, M., Mao, S., & Liu, Y. (2014). Big data: A survey. *Mobile Networks and Applications*, *19*(2), 171–209. https://doi.org/10.1007/s11036-013-0489-0

Constantiou, I. D., & Kallinikos, J. (2015). New games, new rules: Big data and the changing context of strategy. *Journal of Information Technology*, *30*(1), 44–57. https://doi.org/10.1057%2Fjit.2014.17

Court, D. (2015). Getting big impact from big data. *The McKinsey Quarterly*, *1*(1), 52–60.

De Domenico, M., Lima, A., González, M. C., & Arenas, A. (2015). Personalized routing for multitudes in smart cities. *EPJ Data Science*, *4*(1), 1–11. https://doi.org/10.1140/epjds/s13688-015-0038-0

Dobre, C., & Xhafa, F. (2014). Intelligent services for big data science. *Future Generation Computer Systems*, *37*, 267–281. https://doi.org/10.1016/j.future.2013.07.014

Dubey, R., Gunasekaran, A., Childe, S. J., Blome, C., & Papadopoulos, T. (2019). Big data and predictive analytics and manufacturing performance: Integrating institutional theory, resource-based view and big data culture. *British Journal of Management*, *30*(2), 341–361. https://doi.org/10.1111/1467-8551.12355

Elgendy, N., & Elragal, A. (2014). Big Data Analytics: A Literature Review Paper. In P. Perner (Ed.), Lecture Notes in Computer Science: Vol. 8557. Advances in Data Mining. Applications and Theoretical Aspects. ICDM 2014. Springer. https://doi.org/10.1007/978-3-319-08976-8_16.

Elgendy, N., & Elragal, A. (2016). Big data analytics in support of the decision making process. *Procedia Computer Science*, *100*, 1071–1084. https://doi.org/10.1016/j.procs.2016.09.251

Fiaidhi, J., & Mohammed, S. (2019). Thick data: A new qualitative analytics for identifying customer insights. *IT Professional*, *21*(3), 4–13. https://dx.doi.org/10.1109/MITP.2019.2910982

Finger, F., Genolet, T., Mari, L., de Magny, G. C., Manga, N. M., Rinaldo, A., & Bertuzzo, E. (2016). Mobile phone data highlights the role of mass gatherings in the spreading of cholera outbreaks. *Proceedings of the National Academy of Sciences of the United States of America*, *113*(23), 6421–6426. https://doi.org/10.1073/pnas.1522305113

Gandomi, A., & Haider, M. (2015). Beyond the hype: Big data concepts, methods, and analytics. *International Journal of Information Management*, *35*(2), 137–144. https://doi.org/10.1016/j.ijinfomgt.2014.10.007

Garg, P., Gupta, B., Dzever, S., Sivarajah, U., & Kumar, V. (2020). Examining the relationship between social media analytics practices and business performance in the Indian retail and IT industries: The mediation role of customer engagement. *International Journal of Information Management*, *52*, 102069. https://doi.org/10.1016/j.ijinfomgt.2020.102069

Germann, F., Lilien, G. L., Fiedler, L., & Kraus, M. (2014). Do Retailers Benefit from Deploying Customer Analytics? *Journal of Retailing, 90*(4), 587-593. doi:10.1016/j.jretai.2014.08.002

Gretzel, U., Sigala, M., Xiang, Z., & Koo, C. (2015). Smart tourism: Foundations and developments. *Electronic Markets*, *25*(3), 179–188. https://doi.org/10.1007/s12525-015-0196-8

Hariri, R. H., Fredericks, E. M., & Bowers, K. M. (2019). Uncertainty in big data analytics: Survey, opportunities, and challenges. *Journal of Big Data*, *6*(1), 1–16. https://doi.org/10.1186/s40537-019-0206-3

Hariri, R. H., Fredericks, E. M., & Bowers, K. M. (2019). Uncertainty in big data analytics: Survey, opportunities, and challenges. *Journal of Big Data*, *6*, 44. https://doi.org/10.1186/s40537-019-0206-3

Hashem, I. A. T., Yaqoob, I., Anuar, N. B., Mokhtar, S., Gani, A., & Khan, S. U. (2015). The rise of "big data" on cloud computing: Review and open research issues. *Information Systems*, *47*, 98–115. https://doi.org/10.1016/j.is.2014.07.006

Hermon, R., & Williams, P. A. (2014). *Big data in healthcare: What is it used for?* doi:10.4225/75/57982b9431b48

Ittmann, H.W. (2015). *The impact of big data and business analytics on supply chain management.* Academic Press.

Jaseena, K. U., & David, J. M. (2014). Issues, challenges, and solutions: big data mining. *CS & IT-CSCP, 4*(13), 131-140. doi:10.5121/csit.2014.41311

Jukić, N., Sharma, A., Nestorov, S., & Jukić, B. (2015). Augmenting data warehouses with big data. *Information Systems Management, 32*(3), 200–209. https://doi.org/10.1080/10580530.2015.1044338

Kastouni, M. Z., & Lahcen, A. A. (2020). Big data analytics in telecommunications: Governance, architecture and use cases. *Journal of King Saud University-Computer and Information Sciences.* doi:10.1016/j.jksuci.2020.11.024

Khatib, E. J., Barco, R., Muñoz, P., De La Bandera, I., & Serrano, I. (2016). Self-healing in mobile networks with big data. *IEEE Communications Magazine, 54*(1), 114–120. https://doi.org/10.1109/MCOM.2016.7378435

Kiron, D., Prentice, P. K., & Ferguson, R. B. (2014). The analytics mandate. *MIT Sloan Management Review, 55*(4), 1.

Kitchens, B., Dobolyi, D., Li, J., & Abbasi, A. (2018). Advanced customer analytics: Strategic value through integration of relationship-oriented big data. *Journal of Management Information Systems, 35*(2), 540–574. https://dx.doi.org/10.1080/07421222.2018.1451957

Kozak, J., Kania, K., Juszczuk, P., & Mitręga, M. (2021). Swarm intelligence goal-oriented approach to data-driven innovation in customer churn management. *International Journal of Information Management, 60*, 102357. https://doi.org/10.1016/j.ijinfomgt.2021.102357

Laney, D. (2001). 3D data management: Controlling data volume, velocity and variety. *META Group Research Note, 6*(70), 1. doi:10.4236/jcc.2014.26001

Lansley, G., & Longley, P. (2016). Deriving age and gender from forenames for consumer analytics. *Journal of Retailing and Consumer Services, 30*, 271–278. https://doi.org/10.1016/j.jretconser.2016.02.007

Lee, H. J., Lee, M., Lee, H., & Cruz, R. A. (2021). Mining service quality feedback from social media: A computational analytics method. *Government Information Quarterly, 38*(2), 101571. https://doi.org/10.1016/j.giq.2021.101571

Lynch, C. (2008). How do your data grow? *Nature, 455*(7209), 28–29. https://dx.doi.org/10.1038/455028a

Mach-Król, M., & Hadasik, B. (2021). On a Certain Research Gap in Big Data Mining for Customer Insights. *Applied Sciences (Basel, Switzerland), 11*(15), 6993. https://doi.org/10.3390/app11156993

Manyika, J., Chui, M., Brown, B., Bughin, J., Dobbs, R., Roxburgh, C., & Hung Byers, A. (2011). *Big data: The next frontier for innovation, competition, and productivity.* McKinsey Global Institute. doi:10.12691/iteces-4-1-3

Marr, B. (2015). How much data do we create every day? The mind-blowing stats everyone should read. *Forbes*, *21*, 1–5.

Meng, S., Dou, W., Zhang, X., & Chen, J. (2014). KASR: A keyword-aware service recommendation method on mapreduce for big data applications. *IEEE Transactions on Parallel and Distributed Systems*, *25*(12), 3221–3231. https://doi.org/10.1109/TPDS.2013.2297117

Mikalef, P., Boura, M., Lekakos, G., & Krogstie, J. (2019). Big data analytics and firm performance: Findings from a mixed-method approach. *Journal of Business Research*, *98*, 261–276. https://doi.org/10.1016/j.jbusres.2019.01.044

Mikalef, P., van de Wetering, R., & Krogstie, J. (2021). Building dynamic capabilities by leveraging big data analytics: The role of organizational inertia. *Information & Management*, *58*(6), 103412. https://doi.org/10.1016/j.im.2020.103412

Mohammadi, M., Al-Fuqaha, A., Sorour, S., & Guizani, M. (2018). Deep learning for IoT big data and streaming analytics: A survey. *IEEE Communications Surveys and Tutorials*, *20*(4), 2923–2960. https://doi.org/10.48550/arXiv.1712.04301

Nasution, F. B. B. (2018). *Integrated Double Loop Data Driven Model For Public Policymaking*. Academic Press.

Ochoa, S. F., Fortino, G., & Di Fatta, G. (2017). Cyber-physical systems, internet of things and big data. *Future Generation Computer Systems*, *75*, 82–84. https://doi.org/10.1016/j.future.2017.05.040

Olszak, C. M., & Mach-Król, M. (2018). A conceptual framework for assessing an organization's readiness to adopt big data. *Sustainability*, *10*(10), 3734. https://doi.org/10.3390/su10103734

Power, D. J. (2015, May). 'Big data'decision making use cases. In International Conference on Decision Support System Technology (pp. 1–9). Springer. https://doi.org/10.1155/2020/8850096.

Qin, S., Man, J., Wang, X., Li, C., Dong, H., & Ge, X. (2019). Applying big data analytics to monitor tourist flow for the scenic area operation management. *Discrete Dynamics in Nature and Society*. doi:10.1155/2019/8239047

Raghupathi, W., & Raghupathi, V. (2014). Big data analytics in healthcare: Promise and potential. *Health Information Science and Systems*, *2*(1), 1–10. https://dx.doi.org/10.1186%2F2047-2501-2-3

Rahmanti, A. R., Ningrum, D. N. A., Lazuardi, L., Yang, H. C., & Li, Y. C. J. (2021). Social media data analytics for outbreak risk communication: Public attention on the "New Normal" during the COVID-19 pandemic in Indonesia. *Computer Methods and Programs in Biomedicine*, *205*, 106083. https://doi.org/10.1016/j.cmpb.2021.106083

Ram, J., Zhang, C., & Koronios, A. (2016). The implications of big data analytics on business intelligence: A qualitative study in China. *Procedia Computer Science*, *87*, 221–226. https://doi.org/10.1016/j.procs.2016.05.152

Raut, R., Narwane, V., Mangla, S. K., Yadav, V. S., Narkhede, B. E., & Luthra, S. (2021). Unlocking causal relations of barriers to big data analytics in manufacturing firms. *Industrial Management & Data Systems*. doi:10.1108/IMDS-02-2020-0066

Russom, P. (2011). Big data analytics. *TDWI Best Practices Report, 19*(4), 1-34. doi:10.12691/jcsa-3-6-6

Saidulu, D., & Sasikala, R. (2017). Machine learning and statistical approaches for Big Data: Issues, challenges and research directions. *International Journal of Applied Engineering Research, 12*(21), 11691–11699.

Sajana, T., Rani, C. S., & Narayana, K. V. (2016). A survey on clustering techniques for big data mining. *Indian Journal of Science and Technology, 9*(3), 1–12. https://dx.doi.org/10.17485/ijst/2016/v9i3/75971

Salehan, M., & Kim, D. J. (2016). Predicting the performance of online consumer reviews: A sentiment mining approach to big data analytics. *Decision Support Systems, 81*, 30–40. https://doi.org/10.1016/j.dss.2015.10.006

Sarin, P., Kar, A. K., Kewat, K., & Ilavarasan, P. V. (2020). Factors affecting future of work: Insights from Social Media Analytics. *Procedia Computer Science, 167*, 1880–1888. https://dx.doi.org/10.1016/j.procs.2020.03.207

Silva, B. N., Diyan, M., & Han, K. (2019). Big data analytics. In *Deep Learning: Convergence to Big Data Analytics* (pp. 13–30). Springer.

Soroka, A., Liu, Y., Han, L., & Haleem, M. S. (2017). Big data driven customer insights for SMEs in redistributed manufacturing. *Procedia CIRP, 63*, 692–697. https://dx.doi.org/10.1016/j.procir.2017.03.319

Tankard, C. (2012). Big data security. *Network Security, 2012*(7), 5–8. https://doi.org/10.1016/S1353-4858(12)70063-6

Uddin, M. F., & Gupta, N. (2014, April). Seven V's of Big Data understanding Big Data to extract value. In Proceedings of the 2014 zone 1 conference of the American Society for Engineering Education (pp. 1–5). IEEE. https://dx.doi.org/10.1109%2FASEEZone1.2014.6820689.

Verma, S., Bhattacharyya, S. S., & Kumar, S. (2018). An extension of the technology acceptance model in the big data analytics system implementation environment. *Information Processing & Management, 54*(5), 791–806. https://doi.org/10.1016/j.ipm.2018.01.004

Villars, R. L., Olofson, C. W., & Eastwood, M. (2011). *Big data: What it is and why you should care.* White paper, IDC. doi:10.1186/s40537-019-0206-3

Wang, J., Zhang, W., Shi, Y., Duan, S., & Liu, J. (2016). *Industrial big data analytics: challenges, methodologies, and applications*. doi:10.35683/jcm18096.0014

Wedel, M., & Kannan, P. K. (2016). Marketing analytics for data-rich environments. *Journal of Marketing, 80*(6), 97–121. https://doi.org/10.1509%2Fjm.15.0413

Wyber, R., Vaillancourt, S., Perry, W., Mannava, P., Folaranmi, T., & Celi, L. A. (2015). Big data in global health: Improving health in low-and middle-income countries. *Bulletin of the World Health Organization, 93*, 203–208. https://doi.org/10.2471/BLT.14.139022

Yang, T. Y., Brinton, C. G., Joe-Wong, C., & Chiang, M. (2017). Behavior-based grade prediction for MOOCs via time series neural networks. *IEEE Journal of Selected Topics in Signal Processing*, *11*(5), 716–728. https://doi.org/10.1109/JSTSP.2017.2700227

Zakir, J., Seymour, T., & Berg, K. (2015). Big Data Analytics. *Issues in Information Systems, 16*(2). _iis_2015_81-90 doi:10.48009/2

Zhan, X., Ukkusuri, S. V., & Zhu, F. (2014). Inferring urban land use using large-scale social media check-in data. *Networks and Spatial Economics*, *14*(3), 647–667. https://doi.org/10.1007/s11067-014-9264-4

Zhang, G. L., Sun, J., Chitkushev, L., & Brusic, V. (2014). *Big data analytics in immunology: a knowledge-based approach.* BioMed Research International. doi:10.1155/2014/437987

Zhao, J., Xue, F., Khan, S., & Khatib, S. F. (2021). Consumer behaviour analysis for business development. *Aggression and Violent Behavior*, 101591. doi:10.1016/j.avb.2021.101591

ADDITIONAL READING

Anshari, M., Almunawar, M. N., Lim, S. A., & Al-Mudimigh, A. (2019). Customer relationship management and big data enabled: Personalization & customization of services. *Applied Computing and Informatics, 15*(2), 94-101. doi:10.1016/j.aci.2018.05.004

Bhadani, A. K., & Jothimani, D. (2016). Big data: challenges, opportunities, and realities. In *Effective big data management and opportunities for implementation* (pp. 1–24). IGI Global. doi:10.4018/978-1-5225-0182-4.ch001

Biesialska, K., Franch, X., & Muntés-Mulero, V. (2021). Big Data analytics in Agile software development: A systematic mapping study. *Information and Software Technology, 132*, 106448. doi:10.1016/j.infsof.2020.106448

Dong, H., Wu, M., Ding, X., Chu, L., Jia, L., Qin, Y., & Zhou, X. (2015). Traffic zone division based on big data from mobile phone base stations. *Transportation Research Part C: Emerging Technologies, 58*, 278-291. doi:10.1016/j.trc.2015.06.00

Erevelles, S., Fukawa, N., & Swayne, L. (2016). Big Data consumer analytics and the transformation of marketing. *Journal of Business Research, 69*(2), 897-904. doi:10.1016/j.jbusres.2015.07.001

KEY TERMS AND DEFINITIONS

Big Data Analytics: Is the often complex process of examining big data to uncover information such as hidden patterns, correlations, market trends and customer preferences.

Big Data Mining: Is referred to the collective data mining or extraction techniques that are performed on large sets /volume of data or the big data.

Cognitive Analytics: Is a data forward approach that starts and ends with what's contained in information.

Customer Experience (CX): Is the internal and subjective response customers have to any direct and indirect contact with a company.

Data: Is information that has been translated into a form that is efficient for movement or processing.

Relational Database Management System Cannot Manage Unstructured Data (RDBMS): Is a type of database management system that stores data in a row-based table structure which connects related data elements.

Social Media Analytics: Refers to the approach of collecting data from social media sites and blogs.

Section 2

Theories, Conceptual Frameworks, and Modelling to Predict Consumer Behavior Change in the Socio-Digital Era

Chapter 8
Modelling Socio-Digital Customer Relationship Management in the Hospitality Sector During the Pandemic Time

Ali B. Mahmoud
https://orcid.org/0000-0002-3790-1107
St John's University, USA & London South Bank University, UK & Brunel University London, UK

Alexander Berman
St. John's University, USA

Shehnaz Tehseen
https://orcid.org/0000-0002-4039-0256
Sunway University, Malaysia

Dieu Hack-Polay
Crandall University, Canada

ABSTRACT

The chapter builds on previous research and offers an updated theoretical model to determine the relationships among social media technologies, customer experience flow, customer relationship management, brand loyalty, word of mouth, firm performance, and customer engagement across a set of moderators in pandemic time. In line with the literature, customer engagement serves as a mediator that fully translates the effects of social media technology, customer flow experience, and customer relationship management into positive levels of brand loyalty, word of mouth, and firm performance. However, all of the relationships conceptualized in the model are hypothesized to be moderated by COVID-19 developments and perceptions.

DOI: 10.4018/978-1-6684-4168-8.ch008

INTRODUCTION

This chapter focuses on customer relationship management (CRM) in the hospitality sector in the context of a sharp rise in digitization during the COVID-19 pandemic. CRM has become a strategic approach in business that is underlined by relationship marketing theory (RMT). CRM can be defined as the "process of acquiring, retaining, and partnering with selective customers to create superior value for the company and the customer" (Parvatiyar & Sheth, 2001, p. 6). CRM can generate differentiation, address competition, and offer increased customer value (Dewnarain, Ramkissoon, & Mavondo, 2019; Foltean, Trif, & Tuleu, 2019). CRM's technology-driven transformation is called social customer relationship management or SCRM or CRM 2.0 (Sigala, 2018). Accordingly, CRM has been renamed SCRM or CRM 2.0 (Hidayanti, Herman, & Farida, 2018; Sigala, 2018).

The recently coined term SCRM describes the new way of managing as well as developing relationships with customers (Dewnarain et al., 2019; Greenberg, 2010; Wang & Kim, 2017). Greenberg (2010, p. 50) define SCRM as a "business strategy of engaging customers through social media with the goal of building trust and brand loyalty". The rise of social media has unfavourable impacts on the management of relationships with customers and has raised specific speculations regarding the application of theoretical concepts or/and traditional CRM models (Foltean et al., 2019; Harrigan, Soutar, Choudhury, & Lowe, 2015).

Turbulent markets and low brand loyalty are essential factors contributing to implementing CRM as the business strategy by the service-based firms (Rahimi, 2017; Saarijärvi, Karjaluoto, & Kuusela, 2013; Sigala, 2018). Customers are willing to get more value in purchases due to which firms are facing challenges of expanding their customers' base because of the rising acquisition cost of customers, increase in price-sensitive customers, and higher customers' expectations (Harrigan et al., 2015). The exposure of customers to various social media platforms such as Trip Advisor and Facebook has made them more sophisticated in their decision-making.

While the existing literature retraces well social-CRM's evolution and its conceptualization, it fails to provide examples and a framework about the usage of social media for implementing the social-CRM's strategy and meeting new customers' needs (Dewnarain et al., 2019; Marolt, Pucihar, & Zimmermann, 2015). Owing to the limited understanding of the effective use of tools for social CRM (Marolt et al., 2015; Sigala, 2018), the firms may continue facing problems for successful implementation of social CRM (Dewnarain et al., 2019; Jami Pour & Hosseinzadeh, 2021; Torugsa & Yawised, 2019). This also implies in the context of hospitality as well as in tourism, where the CRM strategies and loyalty programmes of several firms are outdated and are not able to exploit new technologies to attract the Millennials (Bowen & Chen McCain, 2015; Sigala, 2018). In the contexts of hospitality and tourism, scholars have emphasized the essential need to study the dimensions of CRM as Web 2.0 technology has increasingly become an influential force for daily business operations (Dewnarain et al., 2019; Medjani & Barnes, 2021). Web 2.0 applications are specialist software that can help individuals create and disseminate online-based data (Natale & Cooke, 2020). Some popular applications of Web 2.0 can be blogs, podcasts and social networks, voice assistants etc. Due to social media's growing place in the marketplace and their effects on key performance indicators (KPIs) such as customer flow experience and brand loyalty, social CRM has become a global trending topic in hospitality-related businesses (Munjal & Bhushan, 2021). The more significant usage of online review sites, including *Trip Advisor* and *Holiday Check*, as well as *social networking* domains has become a common practice among hotels where they invest large amounts of money in improving social interactions (Foltean et al., 2019; Garrido-Moreno, García-Morales, Lockett,

& King, 2018). However, customer engagement (CE) in hospitality contexts has drawn less attention, and future research is essential on CE's antecedents for practitioners' guides (So, Li, & Kim, 2019).

This study aims to reimagine previously hypotheses (Dewnarain et al., 2019) regarding implementing Social Customer Relationship Management (SCRM) effectively and hence achieving customer-based benefits, including brand loyalty, brand word-of-mouth, and organizational performance in pandemic time. More importantly, this study considers the relevance of the COVID-19 developments to the suggested framework, emphasising how pandemic-related experiences and perceptions enhance the benefits of the effectively implemented SCRM. Therefore, the current study makes a significant contribution to the emerging knowledge of SCRM by challenging pre-pandemic theoretical frameworks emphasising the increasing benefits of effective SCRM strategies due to COVID-19-related developments and perceptions in the context of the hotel service industry, which can aid hospitality managers in their decision-making regarding the adoption or implementation of effective post-pandemic SCRM strategy.

Background

Relationship marketing is aligned with the concept of developing the long-term relationship between the firms and their customers, which assist them in creating *sustainable competitive advantage* (SCA) (Chi, 2021; Kang & Lee, 2021). Thus, retaining the current customers and developing strong relationships with them is the most effective method in minimising the marketing cost compared to repeatedly seeking and getting new customers (Gashi & Ahmeti, 2021). In previous research, Frost, Fox and Strauss (2018) and Wang and Kim (2017) state that social media tools help companies create structural and social relationships with customers due to the value co-creation process, which results in increased customers' retention. The current research pays attention to how COVID-19 perception can shape the integration of CRM strategy, social media, and customer flow experience can assist service-based firms, including hotels, in promoting customer engagement strategies, brand loyalty, information co-creation, and firm performance. The factors that act as drivers of CE and relevant benefits like positive word of mouth (WOM) and loyalty are discussed.

STUDY PROPOSITIONS AND THEORETICAL MODEL

Dimensions of CRM and Hotel Performance

The traditional CRM definition is still considered valid. However, owing to the widespread and rapid popularity of social media platforms for both customers and business markets, it is essential to consider further the traditional CRM view (Li, Larimo, & Leonidou, 2021). Reinartz, Krafft and Hoyer (2004, p. 295) define CRM as a procedure that "entails the systematic and proactive management of relationships as they move from the beginning (initiation) to end (termination), with execution across the various customer-facing contact channels". Marketing researchers defined social CRM as "the integration of customer-facing activities, including processes, systems, and technologies, with emergent social media applications to engage customers in collaborative conversations and enhance customer relationships" (Trainor, 2012, p. 319). Not much scholarship has so far explored the association between CRM dimensions and the performance of hotels (Wang & Kim, 2017). Scholars have argued that the concept of relationship relies on the theory of *resource-based view* (RBV), which suggests that any firm can achieve outstanding financial success by effectively managing its internal capabilities and resources compared to its rival firms (Harrigan et al., 2015). Mohammed and Rashid (2012) have proposed four dimensions of CRM, including customer orientation, firm competence, use of technology, and knowledge management, to interpret the conceptual relationships between CRM's dimensions and hotel's performances. These four dimensions are explained below.

Firm Competence

Firm competence is the crucial foundation of a worthwhile CRM project. The effective working environment of any firm supports customer-oriented behaviours to attain a sustainable competitive advantage. Mechinda and Patterson (2011) claim that transformational leadership and well-designed reward systems are evenly required in building customer-focused attitudes and/or behaviours. A firm's employees directly interact with potential consumers. Thus, the service' level delivered by employees is often revealed on social media through customers' ratings, brand loyalty, and positive word-of-mouth. This shows the most significant role played by a leader in attaining the financial performance of the firm through employee engagement.

Customer Orientation

Although better segmentation of customers and customer orientation are essential to attain the firm's objectives, customer orientation is one of the main challenges for service-based firms (Mahmoud, Grigoriou, Fuxman, Reisel, Hack-Polay, & Mohr, 2020; Mahmoud, Reisel, Fuxman, & Hack-Polay, 2021d). Similar to other service-based firms, the hotel sector has an intrinsic characteristic which is service providers' inseparability from the customers (Mahmoud et al., 2021d). Firms' employees have a significant contribution to building and maintaining long-term relationships with potential customers, who are considered as an essential part of the process of service production. Therefore, a *customer-oriented strategy* is perceived to have positive effects on marketing planning as well as the efficient implementation of innovations and marketing actions.

Technology

The CRM strategy's success is based on the integration of modern technology along with the service orientation culture and employees' capability to communicate the procedures of the firm's operations (Saarijärvi et al., 2013). This reflects another vital dimension proposed by Mohammed and Rashid (2012): the *technology-based CRM*. Generally, the new technologies would operate as essential drivers for adaptations in the context of the hotel service industry. The utilisation of technology is essential in developing relationships with customers because it is crucial to attaining accurate information about people in a timely manner (Desmond & Zhaohao, 2021; Saha, Tripathy, Nayak, Bhoi, & Barsocchi, 2021). For example, if a consumer is allergic to nuts and the first individual from room service comes to know about this, then such information can be shared easily to several consumers touchpoints at the hotel through the effective system of CRM (cf Dew, Russell, Allen, & Bej, 2021). Many customer-based strategies may not be successful without the utilisation of most related information technology (Payne & Frow, 2005). Firms can employ new technologies like social media to create knowledge as well as to facilitate the value co-creation process (Ramkissoon & Uysal, 2018; Saarijärvi et al., 2013). With the support of Web 2.0 technology, the new media would bring CRM to an entirely new dimension (Al-Omoush, Simón-Moya, Al-ma'aitah, & Sendra-García, 2021; Saarijärvi et al., 2013).

Knowledge Management

The concept of CRM is incomplete without *knowledge management*. Knowledge is another necessary foundation of CRM (cf Migdadi, 2021); a firm's values depend on producing better customers' experience through data transformation from CRM systems into actual knowledge (Anshari, Almunawar, Lim, & Al-Mudimigh, 2019). In South Asia, for example, very few hotels are converting information related to customers to customer data and into competitive knowledge (e.g. Ramkissoon & Uysal, 2018) since most related hotels miss the opportunity to offer value to the customers in the form of co-creation of services or the development of a new product (Solakis, Peña-Vinces, & Lopez-Bonilla, 2022). Moreover, hotel competitiveness relies on customer relationship's performance (Alnawas & Hemsley-Brown, 2019; Ofori & Appiah-Nimo, 2021; Salem, 2021). It has been observed that the key products in the industry, such as the lodging rooms, are similar in all hotel categories, whereby a hotel can compete effectively by using a one-to-one marketing strategy only. Indeed, firms that are better at converting the customer data into knowledge and then developing personalised relationships with their customers (Lindecrantz, Tjon Pian Gi, & Zerbi, 2020), are more likely to generate brand loyalty and attain and maintain outstanding profitability.

Social Media Technologies

The social-CRM is a new marketing domain, and researchers have initiated emphasising the boundary between social media and CRM (Itani, Krush, Agnihotri, & Trainor, 2020). Social media's powerful technologies to increase CRM by involving customers in brand building and value co-creation are critical challenges for managers of the marketing field (Foltean et al., 2019). For managers to successfully deal with this challenge, understanding social media technologies and the effective utilisation of these technologies in CRM has become a central research topic. Kaplan and Haenlein (2010, p. 60) define social media (SM) as "a group of Internet-based applications that build on the ideological and technological foundations of Web 2.0 and allow the creation and exchange of user-generated content".

Existing studies generally emphasised the advantages and challenges of social media implementation, but employees' roles and characteristics of firms have been often ignored (Colton, 2018; Schultz & Peltier, 2013). Charoensukmongkol and Sasatanun (2017) investigated how social media network integration with CRM can be used to enhance business performance in the context of micro-enterprises in Thailand. These researchers claim that the absence of face-to-face communication can be overcome easily by communicating on social media platforms. This is very relevant to the hotel industry because time zones and geographic locations alienate the transactions that occur between customers and firms.

Social media network' expansion is an excellent contribution towards the rapid-changing technology like Web 2.0 that is also producing a distinctive experience for the user (Dwivedi, Ismagilova, Hughes, Carlson, Filieri, Jacobson, Jain, Karjaluoto, Kefi, Krishen, Kumar, Rahman, Raman, Rauschnabel, Rowley, Salo, Tran, & Wang, 2021). The interaction opportunities of marketers with existing and potential customers on various social media platforms, including Instagram and Facebook, enable them to appeal to and retain customers in the CRM process (Dewnarain et al., 2019; Foltean et al., 2019). Indeed, new technologies and/or social media networks would act as essential drivers for the hotel industry changes after incorporating it into its CRM processes. It has also been pointed out that the relationship between CRM and social media technologies is the topic that is being under-researched in the context of the hospitality sector (Chan, Fong, Law, & Fong, 2018; Ho, Chen, & Shih, 2021; Rosário, 2021). The above findings lead to the development of the following proposition.

Proposition One: The social media technologies' use positively impacts the CRM's processes towards the hotel industry.

Social Media Usage and Customer Engagement

Customer engagement is a relatively new advancement in CRM for a society where customers easily interact with other firms and customers via social media (Lim, Rasul, Kumar, & Ala, 2022). From a strategic standpoint, practitioners defined engagement as user experiences that "allow businesses to build deeper, more meaningful and sustainable interactions between the company and its customers or external stakeholders" (Sashi, 2012, p. 255). Customer engagement depends on creating relationships between customers and a firm and developing new and high-value relationships with customers(Alvarez-Milán, Felix, Rauschnabel, & Hinsch, 2018; Harrigan, Evers, Miles, & Daly, 2018).

Service firms report CE as essential amongst various particular advantages they expect from their existence on social media (Srivastava & Sivaramakrishnan, 2021). Growing attention in CE has imitated the continual Internet's evolution as well as new digital technologies, and tools' emergence has dubbed Web 2.0, mainly social media platforms like video sites like YouTube, microblogging sites like Twitter; blogs and wikis; and social networking sites like LinkedIn, MySpace, and Facebook (Tuten, 2020; Wang & Kim, 2017). The emergence of the concept of CE acknowledges the opportunities which are provided by the interactive aspects of tools and technologies of Web 2.0 in order to transform the relationship between customers and service providers/firms (Harrigan, Evers, Miles, & Daly, 2017; Wang & Kim, 2017).

Social media platforms have enabled a successful process of customer engagement. However, this is sparsely researched in the tourism and hospitality context. Most existing studies have focused only on using social media to achieve short-term sales objectives and have not assessed the influence of social media platforms on achieving brand loyalty (Harrigan et al., 2017; Ong, Lee, & Ramayah, 2018; So, Kim, & King, 2021; van Asperen, de Rooij, & Dijkmans, 2018). Social media serves as a method of reengineering business by allowing two-way communication between firms and consumers. This transformation in the traditional way of conducting the businesses would offer various opportunities and several challenges in the tourism and hospitality sector. More research is required to prepare industry practitioners to face this situation more efficiently. The focus of involving and connecting with customers in developing the value customers with a business will lead to loyalty and more prolonged customers willing to spend more money (van Asperen et al., 2018). A feeling of connectedness among customers towards a firm (e.g. hotel) can be generated through social media (van Asperen et al., 2018). However, only tiny hotel firms have come to know about the CRM's benefits as the enabler of CE while incorporating with networks of social media (Castillo, Benitez, Llorens, & Luo, 2021; Dai & Wang, 2021; Dewnarain et al., 2019; Lee, Hong, Chung, & Back, 2020). Thus, based on the above literature, proposition two is proposed as below:

Proposition Two: Social media activities predict the levels of customer engagement.

CRM and Customer Engagement

Previous literature shows that the term 'engagement' is originated from the literature of psychology (Chen, Han, Bilgihan, & Okumus, 2021). Various scholars have suggested that engagement constitutes a cognitive, behavioural, and affective dimension in the field of marketing (Dessart, Aldás-Manzano, & Veloutsou, 2019; Ferreira, Zambaldi, & Guerra, 2020). Engagement is seen as a two-way interaction between subjects such as tourists, consumers and objects such as hotels brands (Jeong & Hyun, 2019).

Many studies have explored the definitions and developed conceptual frameworks to recognise CE's antecedents and consequences (e.g. Harmeling, Moffett, Arnold, & Carlson, 2017). Gallup (2014) shows that highly engaged customers of any firm contribute 23% more for the share of wallet, income, profitability, and the growth of relationship compared to the hospitality sector's average customer. Moreover, Fully engaged customers bring in 46% more revenue in the hospitality industry (Cognizant, 2018).

Social Customer Relationship Management (SCRM) highlights a firm capability to involve consumers in collaborative interactions as well as to improve close relationships with customers (Wang & Kim, 2017). In the hospitality industry, exploring the concept of CE serves as a challenge because it requires the participation of employees and traditional marketing practices' alterations that focuses more on sales. According to Reinartz and Venkatesan (2008), the progress in the customer relationship is visible through many stages, including acquisition, growth, retention, and finally, win-back. Due to the growth of social media, hotel service providers got an opportunity to track the digital journey of customers as well as monitor the customer experience' evolution with the brand/provider (Homburg, Jozić, & Kuehnl, 2017). There are various kinds of consumers who interact with the brand or provider with the hotel business in their repeated journeys. The interactions which take place between the customers and hotel providers during the journey of purchase, i.e. pre-purchase, during purchase as well as post-purchase (Ramkissoon & Nunkoo, 2010), do produce valuable information at many touchpoints in the firm (Dew et al., 2021).

Various CRM strategies remained unsuccessful in the last decades because consumers' check-outs used to be stored only in a database used for sending out the messages regarding promotions only (e.g. Payne & Frow, 2005). Such experiences' accumulation may indicate a rapport's evolution that the firm shares with its consumers and hotels would be required to review the strategies and resources to stay beside the evolving behaviour of consumers (e.g. Ramkissoon & Mavondo, 2015). Specified the present hype regarding social media's platforms, the primary purpose of this study will be on exploring customer engagement via social media that has enabled activities of CRM in the hotel sector. Based on the above findings, proposition three is forwarded.

Proposition Three: The use of social media enabled CRM activities improves customer engagement.

Customer Flow Experience and Customer Engagement

The flow experience is critical in order to measure the degree and/or pleasure's intensity and the consumers' concentration all through their *online experience* (Kaur & Singh, 2007). As a result, flow is the unconscious experience in which the individual entirely focuses and enjoys the developing activity (Carvalho & Fernandes, 2018). In other words, consumers who experience flow are expected more to assume such experience as compelling and become more involved with brand/firm (Carlson, de Vries, Rahman, & Taylor, 2017; Obadă, 2013; Shim, Forsythe, & Kwon, 2015). Therefore, customer flow experience can be considered customer engagement's antecedent (Brodie, Hollebeek, Jurić, & Ilić, 2011; Carvalho & Fernandes, 2018). Based on the above, Proposition 4 is proposed:

Proposition Four: Customer flow experience on social media platforms positively predicts customer engagement.

Brand Loyalty

Loyal customers give little importance to alternatives and repetitively buy products/services from the same brand/firm (Akbari, Nazarian, Foroudi, Seyyed Amiri, & Ezatabadipoor, 2021; Tanford, 2016; van Asperen et al., 2018; Wu, Ye, Zheng, & Law, 2021). They are likely to generate positive e-WOM and share positive experiences (Harrigan et al., 2017; Mahmoud, Ball, Rubin, Fuxman, Mohr, Hack-Polay, Grigoriou, & Wakibi, 2021a; Mahmoud, Hack-Polay, Grigoriou, Mohr, & Fuxman, 2021b; van Asperen et al., 2018).

Furthermore, CE in the industry of hospitality and tourism has revealed that the social interactions' highest level through various web-based platforms such as Facebook, Twitter, and Instagram can significantly affect brand evaluations, trust, and loyalty (Arghashi, Bozbay, & Karami, 2021; Ibrahim & Aljarah, 2021; Zhong, Shapoval, & Busser, 2021). Since the use of social media has become an essential norm in certain tourism firms such as *Lonely Planet, Expedia, and Travelocity*, other networks of social media, including *Booking.com, Airbnb, and Trip Advisor,* may act as key influencers in the process of decision-making of customers (Leung, Bai, & Stahura, 2013; Siti-Nabiha, Nordin, & Poh, 2021). Although, the growth of social media has resulted in the new customer segment's generation who are generally known as "social customers" or "hybrids" as they are likely to integrate both offline and online channels when making the purchases (Greenberg, 2010). Social media tools allow social interactions that provide a large amount of data to hotels. Online interactions with consumers cause user-created content before consumers arrive at the hotel (Bygstad & Presthus, 2013; Gligorijevic, 2016; Han & Lee, 2021; Santos, 2021; Zhang, Ye, Law, & Li, 2010). Hence, exchanging information between customers and hotel firms may guide to value's co-creation that leads to brand loyalty. Proposition five is stated as below:

Proposition Five: The level of customers' engagement of hotels on social media is positively related to brand loyalty.

Customer Engagement and Word-of-Mouth

Word-of-mouth (WOM) is a well-researched theme in the hospitality sector because of its capability to reduce the perceived risk linked with the purchase of the high engagement and intangible offerings (Dewnarain et al., 2019; Yen & Tang, 2015). Positive WOM communication covers all customers' communications with members of their professional and social networks (Choi & Kandampully, 2019). Positive WOM is generally articulated by talking and/or e-mailing to friends, family members, colleagues, relatives, and nowadays because of the use of platforms of social media (Dewnarain et al., 2019). While replying to the question "where to stay", the customer would turn to a family member, friend, travel agency, tour operator or internet by looking at travel sites or Trip Advisor, and this highlights the significance of WOM during the purchase process. On the one hand, Serra Cantallops and Salvi (2014, p. 41) define WOM as "informal, person to person communication between a perceived non-commercial communicator and a receiver regarding a brand, a product, an organisation or a service". Whereas electronic word of mouth (eWOM) is defined as "online reviews, online recommendations or online opinions, it has gained much attention with the emergence of new technology tools" (Serra Cantallops & Salvi, 2014, p. 45).

Due to the growth of customer opinion sites like Trip Advisor, word of mouth took the form of e-WOM as one-to-many communication occurs at extreme speed in a virtual atmosphere. As traditional WOM was dependent on face-to-face interaction, primarily e-WOM lost its integrity because of its loss of personal touch online. Individuals were unwilling to trust social media content posted by anonymous people (de Matos & Rossi, 2008). Although this hindrance was controlled with the emergence of social media platforms, which encouraged users to generate a profile earlier to communicate with other individuals, face-to-face interaction was restored. E-WOM can take the two forms in the shape of viral advertising that includes online videos which go viral because of its content and also through peer-to-peer's sharing and the second one which is online customer reviews in which consumers share their opinions regarding services and products based on their experience which they observed personally (Belch & Belch, 2021). Word of mouth is considered as one of the most crucial factors in the success of service firms, thereby the motivation of the present research to ascertain drivers of positive WOM behaviour. de Matos and Rossi (2008) suggested that customers who share a psychological connection with a brand/firm show higher commitments and are generally the best brand advocates. Thus, it is required to study whether the customers who are engaged with brands/hotel providers on social media platforms are more likely to suggest its services in the shape of positive word of mouth. This leads towards the development of proposition 6 as follow:

Proposition Six: The level of engagement of the hotel's customers on social media is positively related to word of mouth.

Customer Engagement and Firm Performance

Social media technologies may assist firms in attaining three types of strategic goals: increasing loyalty, creating awareness regarding the brand, and increasing sales (Li et al., 2021). CE extends customers' role by involving them in the process of value-adding as value's co-creators. Due to the higher levels of CE on social media, firms can implement better interactive social media's attributes to generate a good customer experience, better firm's image, and more intentions towards future purchase (Kumar & Pansari, 2016). Practitioners have strived to employ social media to create long-term relational exchanges with higher emotional connections to enhance firms' performances (Li et al., 2021; Sashi, 2012; Wang & Kim, 2017). In conclusion, CE has great strategic importance for leading towards the increased performance of firms. Therefore, CE is also a vital aspect which affects customer brand loyalty and firm's performance. Based on it, proposition seven is proposed:

Proposition Seven: The level of engagement of the hotel's customers on social media is positively related to the firm's performance.

COVID-19 Consequences and Perceptions

COVID-19 virus is among the most significant environmental challenges in modern history (He & Harris, 2020; Mahmoud, Reisel, Hack-Polay, & Fuxman, 2021e). The pandemic caused rapid structural and policy-related changes, with significant consequences across diverse social and economic matters (Bartik, Bertrand, Cullen, Glaeser, Luca, & Stanton, 2020). In response, companies and regulators have implemented a wide range of operating and strategic changes that affect people's job security, career prospects, and consumer behaviour (Di Crosta, Ceccato, Marchetti, La Malva, Maiella, Cannito, Cipi, Mammarella, Palumbo, Verrocchio, Palumbo, & Di Domenico, 2021; Seetharaman, 2020). Specifically, organisations and governments have enacted restrictions to people's mobility, implemented lockdowns, and enforced severe limitations on various types of social gatherings (BBC, 2020). While the challenges of the COVID-19 pandemic have translated into widespread consequences worldwide (Mahmoud, Hack-Polay, Reisel, Fuxman, Grigoriou, Mohr, & Aizouk, 2021c; Sönmez, Apostolopoulos, Lemke, & Hsieh, 2020), related effects have been particularly profound in select customer-facing industries, such as hotels, retail, and airlines (OECD, 2020). Furthermore, while the adaptation of web-based communication technologies, such as Zoom and WebEx, enhanced many companies' ability to maintain operations, these same developments reduced the importance of face-to-face business meetings, the need for business travel, and, therefore, the demand for hotels and air travel services (BBC, 2020). Notably, some of the COVID-19-related changes are expected to become permanent, with long-lasting effects on work-related conditions, societal anxiety, and the structure of personal and commercial interactions (Mahmoud et al., 2021e).

The implications of these developments have been previously considered in the literature, indicating that pandemic-related lockdowns and restrictions to mobility increased consumer reliance on modern technology (Kumar, Gupta, & Srivastava, 2020; Mahmoud et al., 2021a), thus enhancing the significance of technology-based CRM. As noted earlier, the absence of face-to-face communication can be overcome by the effective utilisation of social media platforms (Charoensukmongkol & Sasatanun, 2017). Given the profound effects of the COVID-19 pandemic on the hospitality industry (OECD, 2020), the ability of hotel companies to develop and execute an effective SCRM strategy is particularly pertinent. Such a strategy should be both internal and client-oriented. Expressly, it should incorporate the development of internal reward systems designed to promote customer-focused employee behaviour (Mechinda & Patterson, 2011), as well as the implementation of tailored technology-based CRM tactics, such as interactive customer engagements via multiple social media platforms(Li et al., 2021). The development and implementation of an effective SCRM strategy are essential to hotel companies' ability to evaluate customer preferences, build brand loyalty, and enhance the flow of relevant information among firms, existing consumers, and prospective clients (Harrigan et al., 2017; Ong et al., 2018; So et al., 2021; van Asperen et al., 2018). Accordingly, the development and implementation of such a strategy are essential to hotel companies' efficacy in leveraging key resources and capabilities, mitigating the effects of the pandemic, and, therefore, attaining a sustainable competitive advantage. This leads towards the development of proposition eight as follows:

Proposition Eight: The consequences and perceptions of the COVID-19 pandemic moderate the perceived benefits of effectively-implemented SCRM in the hotel industry. These benefits include (1) higher levels of customer engagement, (2) increase in brand loyalty, (3) enhanced flow of knowledge via word-of-mouth interactions, and (4) improved firm-level performance.

Theoretical Model

Theoretical models are essential for the illustration and integration of synthesised knowledge as well as extant literature (Snyder, 2019). Therefore, conceptual modelling needs to encapsulate generic knowledge derived from different fields and offer support in diverse, multifaceted occasions. The aim of the proposed theoretical model (see Figure 1) is to amalgamate knowledge from various sources as well as to support the informed decision-making process while implementing SCRM within the hotel context. The model further incorporates the moderating effects of the COVID-19 pandemic on the SCRM framework.

The present research suggests a theoretical model (see Figure 1) to mention the relationships between social media technologies, customer relationship management, customer flow experience, brand loyalty, positive word of mouth, customer engagement, and firm's performance. The proposed theoretical model comprises technologies of social media, CRM dimensions, and customer flow experience as three latent variables that represent the drivers of customer engagement. Furthermore, it represents brand loyalty, positive word of mouth and firm performance as engagement's outcomes through social media platforms. Finally, the model illustrates the enhanced value of an effective SCRM strategy in the hospitality industry due to the consequences and perceptions of the COVID-19 pandemic.

Social media technologies facilitate companies to associate and communicate with current as well as potential customers. After following the literature review, it can be suggested that social media's integration with customer relationship management and flow can increase customer engagement, which is vital to promote brand loyalty either in the shape of positive word of mouth or through repeat purchase and also builds firm's performance. Customer engagement guides the value co-creation process, affecting customer relationship outcomes like brand commitment, advocacy, and profitability. The landscape of marketing communication is adapting, and digital customers are presently more empowered. The recommended study model has been adapted for this change in customers' behaviour as well as to attend to consumers' emerging needs.

Figure 1. The framework of social customer relationship management in pandemic time
Note. *Illustrated based on the current study*

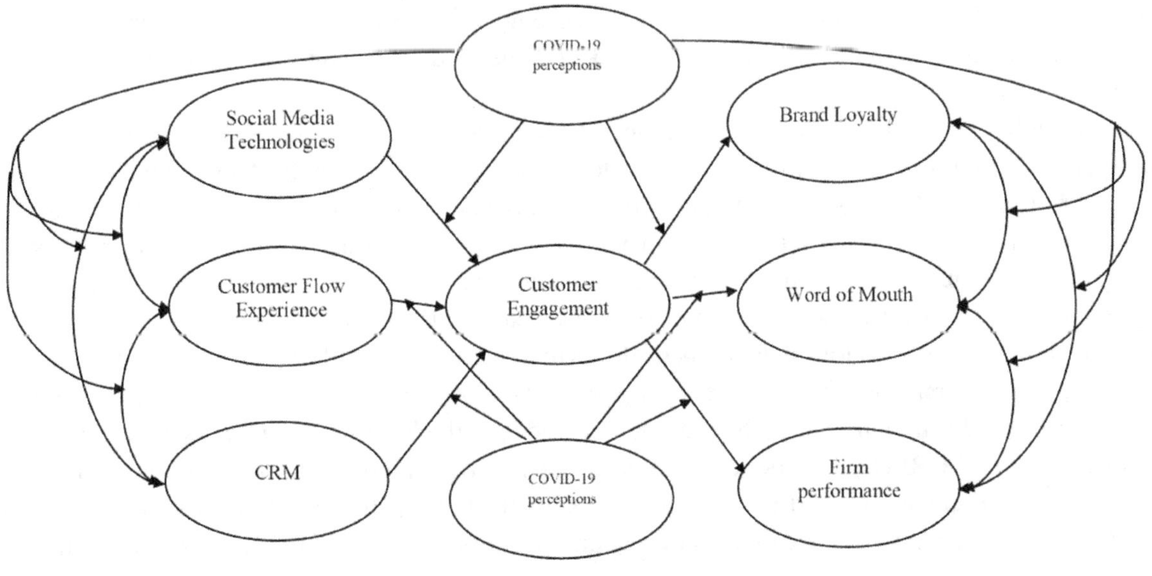

SOLUTIONS AND RECOMMENDATIONS

In tourism and hospitality firms, the use of technology in CRM continues to have the orientation for the short-term in the shape of transactional relationships, particularly when customers are looking for value co-creation and engagement (Harrigan et al., 2017). The literature review offers opportunities by Social-CRM like value co-creation and collaboration, mainly in the context of manufacturing from the firm's perspective (Solakis et al., 2022; Wang & Kim, 2017). Despite the studies' proliferation on social media concerning the hotel industry, researchers argue that some doubts exist about the actual value added by the Web 2.0 technologies to service-based organisations (Garrido-Moreno et al., 2018; Mutimukwe, Kolkowska, & Grönlund, 2020). While the market frequently witnesses an increase in social media platforms like *Facebook, Snapchat,* and *Instagram* that are more picture-based, the social-CRM strategy foundation remains a customer-oriented emphasises. Besides, as this study suggests, employees can also play an essential role in the effective and/or successful Social-CRM strategy implementation. Currently, one of the crucial challenges faced by the hotel sector is the employees' capability to derive meaning from structured as well as unstructured data accessible on social media networking platforms (Chan et al., 2018). Therefore, employees with analytical skills of sophisticated data can develop constructive insights, which are essential for the process of decision making, which is data-driven to attain a higher degree of satisfaction of customers that will be needed in future.

Regarding the outcomes of S-CRM's performance, it is essential to note that most of the time, the hotel firms implement promotional tactics like redeemable points, discounts, and coupons to create the loyalty of customers (Farmania, Elsyah, & Tuori, 2021; Ramkissoon & Mavondo, 2015). Nevertheless, these loyalty programs and usage of sales promotion's strategies do not often provide many benefits in the long run. The customers who wait only for price reductions to save money generally cannot be perceived as loyal because of their high tendency to switch brands. Although engagement's level can promote brand loyalty in the shape of positive WOM, repurchase intentions or willingness to purchase (Mahmoud et al., 2021a; Ong et al., 2018), loyal customers are considered as brand evangelists who are also emotionally associated with the brand and are hence are not price-sensitive (Clement Addo, Fang, Asare, & Kulbo, 2021). Higher levels of customer engagement can generate brand-loyal customers who can pay more owing to the quality received through precedent interactions. Notably, the benefits of a well-designed SCRM strategy are magnified by the ongoing effects of the Covid-19 pandemic, with restrictions to people's mobility, implemented lockdowns, and severe limitations on various types of social gatherings.

Prior studies in S-CRM's field have commonly focused on components like culture, people, top management commitment, technology, and knowledge management as essential factors for CRM's implementation (Rahimi, 2017). Nonetheless, the present study contributes to our knowledge of social-CRM strategy within the hospitality industry in several ways. First, this research adds to relation marketing theory (RMT*)* by investigating the drivers or antecedents and consequences or customer engagement's outcomes on social media networks. Second, the present study identifies CE as a crucial factor of success for the customer as well as for the benefits of the firm that has been rarely mentioned in previous studies. Also, this research contributes value to *engagement theories, marketing communication theory* and *online consumer behaviour*. Third, the present study adds to the hospitality CRM research evolution in the shape of Social-CRM by considerably exploring and involving theories from various other disciplines like information technology and knowledge management. Finally, the study exemplifies an effective SCRM strategy's enhanced value due to consequences and perceptions of the COVID-19 pandemic.

The present study adds to emerging customer engagement and customer engagement behaviour (CEB) management literature by examining types of CEBs (cf Azer & Alexander, 2020). CEB, as conceptualised in this study, also includes advocacy for services firms (e.g., word-of-mouth), which would promote a brand reputation for the firm.

FUTURE RESEARCH DIRECTIONS

The escalating popularity of adopting different social media platforms in CRM in the hospitality sector implies that future research is required to validate the proposed model empirically. Future research is needed to gain astute insights on customers, employees and managers. That would help the hoteliers monitor the inconsistencies between their expectations and the willingness of other stakeholders to support the efforts aimed for improved firm-customer relationships, leading to higher performance outcomes.

This study only takes into account a few essential factors in SCRM, social media and customer engagement. Future scholars could integrate other elements into the framework. The theoretical framework focuses on the antecedents of CE (social media, CRM, and flow experience) and customer outcomes (WOM, brand loyalty and firm performance). Therefore, future research can extend the framework by integrating dependent constructs like customer delight, satisfaction, and commitment. Finally, this study considers only one factor that moderates the relationships conceptualised in our SCRM model: ongoing COVID-19 developments and perceptions. Future researchers can expand this direction of inquiry by considering other potential moderating variables, such as customers' gender or their generational cohort.

This paper provides a framework to deliver valuable theoretical and practical insights for hospitality practitioners and academics. Regardless of this paper's limitations, it has integrated different SCRM and customer engagement themes to develop a conceptual framework based on pre-existing theories. It is widely acknowledged that theoretical framework testing includes adapting existing scales in management and marketing fields quantitative methods for data collection and analysis.

CONCLUSION

The present research adds to the tourism and hospitality practitioners understanding of the multifaceted nature of social-CRM (Dewnarain et al., 2019; Harrigan et al., 2017; Wang & Kim, 2017). This study proposes a theoretical model that combines the indicators of CRM effectiveness in social media, where customer engagement is crucial to attaining financial gains in the shape of customer loyalty and business performance. The model also incorporates the moderating effects of the COVID-19 pandemic on the value of an effectively designed social-CRM strategy. Hospitality and tourism practitioners can assess their online marketing strategy and CRM by reviewing the competitiveness of their firms concerning a variety of factors. Such factors relate to the working environment, customer orientation management process, technology-based CRM, and knowledge management processes and identify early the obstacles to investing resources on new CRM 2.0 technology.

Moreover, customers are no longer service-passive. The present study explores this change in customer behaviour in hospitality settings where social media have provided customers with platforms where they can co-create and communicate their experience through collaboration with service firms. The research identifies CE as an essential factor in the relationship between social media, CRM, firm performance,

WOM and loyalty. The innovative service experience of co-creation may lead to positive WOM, significantly reducing marketing expenditure and enhancing revenue. Furthermore, brand advocacy in the form of e-WOM can bring benefits in the shape of consumer confidence and trust.

Most firms seek loyal consumers emotionally attached to the brand because engaged consumers are likely to be risk-averse and be highly valuable for firm performance for a lifetime. However, a key variable that this conceptual model does not depict is negative WOM. The customer-company relationship does not necessarily create positive relationship outcomes in social media networks. However, hotel brand managers can undoubtedly learn from comments and posts on interactive platforms, whether the reviews are positive or negative. Managers can, consequently, make improvements in their product offerings, processes, and service delivery that can bring and help retain new customers. Finally, this research suggests an integrated theoretical framework that would assist hotel brand managers in making informed decisions regarding adopting a successful social-CRM strategy.

ACKNOWLEDGMENT

This research received no specific grant from any funding agency in the public, commercial, or not-for-profit sectors.

REFERENCES

Akbari, M., Nazarian, A., Foroudi, P., Seyyed Amiri, N., & Ezatabadipoor, E. (2021). How corporate social responsibility contributes to strengthening brand loyalty, hotel positioning and intention to revisit? *Current Issues in Tourism*, *24*(13), 1897–1917. doi:10.1080/13683500.2020.1800601

Al-Omoush, K. S., Simón-Moya, V., Al-ma'aitah, M. A., & Sendra-García, J. (2021). The determinants of social CRM entrepreneurship: An institutional perspective. *Journal of Business Research*, *132*, 21–31. doi:10.1016/j.jbusres.2021.04.017

Alnawas, I., & Hemsley-Brown, J. (2019). Market orientation and hotel performance: Investigating the role of high-order marketing capabilities. *International Journal of Contemporary Hospitality Management*, *31*(4), 1885–1905. doi:10.1108/IJCHM-07-2018-0564

Alvarez-Milán, A., Felix, R., Rauschnabel, P. A., & Hinsch, C. (2018). Strategic customer engagement marketing: A decision making framework. *Journal of Business Research*, *92*, 61–70. doi:10.1016/j.jbusres.2018.07.017

Anshari, M., Almunawar, M. N., Lim, S. A., & Al-Mudimigh, A. (2019). Customer relationship management and big data enabled: Personalization & customization of services. *Applied Computing and Informatics*, *15*(2), 94-101.

Arghashi, V., Bozbay, Z., & Karami, A. (2021). An Integrated Model of Social Media Brand Love: Mediators of Brand Attitude and Consumer Satisfaction. *Journal of Relationship Marketing*, *20*(4), 319–348. doi:10.1080/15332667.2021.1933870

Azer, J., & Alexander, M. (2020). Negative customer engagement behaviour: The interplay of intensity and valence in online networks. *Journal of Marketing Management*, *36*(3-4), 361–383. doi:10.1080/0267257X.2020.1735488

Bartik, A. W., Bertrand, M., Cullen, Z., Glaeser, E. L., Luca, M., & Stanton, C. (2020). The impact of COVID-19 on small business outcomes and expectations. *Proceedings of the National Academy of Sciences of the United States of America*, *117*(30), 17656–17666. doi:10.1073/pnas.2006991117 PMID:32651281

BBC. (2020). *Unemployment during coronavirus: The psychology of job loss*. BBC. Retrieved 08 January from https://www.bbc.com/worklife/article/20200327-unemployment-during-coronavirus-the-psychology-of-job-loss

Belch, G. E., & Belch, M. A. (2021). *Advertising and Promotion. An Integrated Marketing Communications Perspectives*. McGraw-Hill Education. https://books.google.co.uk/books?id=PYpSzQEACAAJ

Bowen, J. T., & Chen McCain, S.-L. (2015). Transitioning loyalty programs. *International Journal of Contemporary Hospitality Management*, *27*(3), 415–430. doi:10.1108/IJCHM-07-2014-0368

Brodie, R. J., Hollebeek, L. D., Jurić, B., & Ilić, A. (2011). Customer Engagement: Conceptual Domain, Fundamental Propositions, and Implications for Research. *Journal of Service Research*, *14*(3), 252–271. doi:10.1177/1094670511411703

Bygstad, B., & Presthus, W. (2013). Social Media as CRM? How two airline companies used Facebook during the "Ash Crisis" in 2010. *Scandinavian Journal of Information Systems*, *25*(1), 3.

Carlson, J., de Vries, N. J., Rahman, M. M., & Taylor, A. (2017). Go with the flow: Engineering flow experiences for customer engagement value creation in branded social media environments. *Journal of Brand Management*, *24*(4), 334–348. doi:10.105741262-017-0054-4

Carvalho, A., & Fernandes, T. (2018). Understanding customer brand engagement with virtual social communities: A comprehensive model of drivers, outcomes and moderators. *Journal of Marketing Theory and Practice*, *26*(1-2), 23–37. doi:10.1080/10696679.2017.1389241

Castillo, A., Benitez, J., Llorens, J., & Luo, X. (2021). Social media-driven customer engagement and movie performance: Theory and empirical evidence. *Decision Support Systems*, *145*, 113516. doi:10.1016/j.dss.2021.113516

Chan, I. C. C., Fong, D. K. C., Law, R., & Fong, L. H. N. (2018). State-of-the-art social customer relationship management. *Asia Pacific Journal of Tourism Research*, *23*(5), 423–436. doi:10.1080/10941665.2018.1466813

Charoensukmongkol, P., & Sasatanun, P. (2017). Social media use for CRM and business performance satisfaction: The moderating roles of social skills and social media sales intensity. *Asia Pacific Management Review, 22*(1), 25-34.

Chen, S., Han, X., Bilgihan, A., & Okumus, F. (2021). Customer engagement research in hospitality and tourism: A systematic review. *Journal of Hospitality Marketing & Management*, *30*(7), 871–904. doi:10.1080/19368623.2021.1903644

Chi, N. T. K. (2021). Innovation capability: The impact of e-CRM and COVID-19 risk perception. *Technology in Society*, *67*, 101725. doi:10.1016/j.techsoc.2021.101725

Choi, H., & Kandampully, J. (2019). The effect of atmosphere on customer engagement in upscale hotels: An application of S-O-R paradigm. *International Journal of Hospitality Management*, *77*, 40–50. doi:10.1016/j.ijhm.2018.06.012

Clement Addo, P., Fang, J., Asare, A. O., & Kulbo, N. B. (2021). Customer engagement and purchase intention in live-streaming digital marketing platforms. *Service Industries Journal*, *41*(11-12), 767–786. doi:10.1080/02642069.2021.1905798

Cognizant. (2018). *How to Deliver Exceptional Customer Engagement*. Cognizant. Retrieved 22 January from https://www.cognizant.com/whitepapers/how-to-deliver-exceptional-customer-engagement-codex2794.pdf

Colton, B. (2018). *Customers are important, but firms ignore employees at their peril*. LSE. Retrieved 22 January from https://blogs.lse.ac.uk/management/2018/05/23/customers-are-important-but-firms-ignore-employees-at-their-peril/

Dai, Y., & Wang, T. (2021). Prediction of customer engagement behaviour response to marketing posts based on machine learning. *Connection Science*, *33*(4), 891–910. doi:10.1080/09540091.2021.1912710

de Matos, C. A., & Rossi, C. A. V. (2008). Word-of-mouth communications in marketing: A meta-analytic review of the antecedents and moderators. *Journal of the Academy of Marketing Science*, *36*(4), 578–596. doi:10.100711747-008-0121-1

Desmond, N., & Zhaohao, S. (2021). Big Data Analytics for Smart Airport Management. In S. Zhaohao (Ed.), *Intelligent Analytics With Advanced Multi-Industry Applications* (pp. 209–231). IGI Global. doi:10.4018/978-1-7998-4963-6.ch010

Dessart, L., Aldás-Manzano, J., & Veloutsou, C. (2019). Unveiling heterogeneous engagement-based loyalty in brand communities. *European Journal of Marketing*, *53*(9), 1854–1881. doi:10.1108/EJM-11-2017-0818

Dew, R., Russell, B., Allen, C., & Bej, G. (2021). *Lean CX: How to Differentiate at Low Cost and Least Risk*. De Gruyter.

Dewnarain, S., Ramkissoon, H., & Mavondo, F. (2019). Social customer relationship management: An integrated conceptual framework. *Journal of Hospitality Marketing & Management*, *28*(2), 172–188. doi:10.1080/19368623.2018.1516588

Di Crosta, A., Ceccato, I., Marchetti, D., La Malva, P., Maiella, R., Cannito, L., Cipi, M., Mammarella, N., Palumbo, R., Verrocchio, M. C., Palumbo, R., & Di Domenico, A. (2021). Psychological factors and consumer behavior during the COVID-19 pandemic. *PLoS One*, *16*(8), e0256095. doi:10.1371/journal.pone.0256095 PMID:34398916

Dwivedi, Y. K., Ismagilova, E., Hughes, D. L., Carlson, J., Filieri, R., Jacobson, J., Jain, V., Karjaluoto, H., Kefi, H., Krishen, A. S., Kumar, V., Rahman, M. M., Raman, R., Rauschnabel, P. A., Rowley, J., Salo, J., Tran, G. A., & Wang, Y. (2021). Setting the future of digital and social media marketing research: Perspectives and research propositions. *International Journal of Information Management*, *59*, 102168. doi:10.1016/j.ijinfomgt.2020.102168

Farmania, A., Elsyah, R. D., & Tuori, M. A. (2021). Transformation of CRM Activities into e-CRM: The Generating e-Loyalty and Open Innovation. *Journal of Open Innovation*, *7*(2), 109. Advance online publication. doi:10.3390/joitmc7020109

Ferreira, M., Zambaldi, F., & Guerra, D. S. (2020). Consumer engagement in social media: Scale comparison analysis. *Journal of Product and Brand Management*, *29*(4), 491–503. doi:10.1108/JPBM-10-2018-2095

Foltean, F. S., Trif, S. M., & Tuleu, D. L. (2019). Customer relationship management capabilities and social media technology use: Consequences on firm performance. *Journal of Business Research*, *104*, 563–575. doi:10.1016/j.jbusres.2018.10.047

Frost, R., Fox, A. K., & Strauss, J. (2018). *E-marketing*. Taylor & Francis. https://books.google.co.uk/books?id=8PErDwAAQBAJ

Gallup. (2014). *Why Customer Engagement Matters So Much Now*. Gallup. Retrieved 22 January from https://news.gallup.com/businessjournal/172637/why-customer-engagement-matters.aspx

Garrido-Moreno, A., García-Morales, V. J., Lockett, N., & King, S. (2018). The missing link: Creating value with Social Media use in hotels. *International Journal of Hospitality Management*, *75*, 94–104. doi:10.1016/j.ijhm.2018.03.008

Gashi, R., & Ahmeti, H. (2021). Impact of Social Media on the Development of New Products, Marketing and Customer Relationship Management in Kosovo. *Emerging Science Journal*, *5*(2), 125–138. doi:10.28991/esj-2021-01263

Gligorijevic, B. (2016). Review platforms in destinations and hospitality. In R. Egger, I. Gula, & D. Walcher (Eds.), *Open tourism* (pp. 215–228). Springer., doi:10.1007/978-3-642-54089-9_15

Greenberg, P. (2010). The impact of CRM 2.0 on customer insight. *Journal of Business and Industrial Marketing*, *25*(6), 410–419. doi:10.1108/08858621011066008

Han, Y., & Lee, H. (2021). Lifestyle Experiences: Exploring Key Attributes of Lifestyle Hotels Using Instagram User-Created Contents in South Korea. *Sustainability*, *13*(5), 2591. Advance online publication. doi:10.3390u13052591

Harmeling, C. M., Moffett, J. W., Arnold, M. J., & Carlson, B. D. (2017). Toward a theory of customer engagement marketing. *Journal of the Academy of Marketing Science*, *45*(3), 312–335. doi:10.100711747-016-0509-2

Harrigan, P., Evers, U., Miles, M., & Daly, T. (2017). Customer engagement with tourism social media brands. *Tourism Management*, *59*, 597–609. doi:10.1016/j.tourman.2016.09.015

Harrigan, P., Evers, U., Miles, M. P., & Daly, T. (2018). Customer engagement and the relationship between involvement, engagement, self-brand connection and brand usage intent. *Journal of Business Research*, *88*, 388–396. doi:10.1016/j.jbusres.2017.11.046

Harrigan, P., Soutar, G., Choudhury, M. M., & Lowe, M. (2015). Modelling CRM in a social media age. *Australasian Marketing Journal*, *23*(1), 27–37. doi:10.1016/j.ausmj.2014.11.001

He, H., & Harris, L. (2020). The impact of Covid-19 pandemic on corporate social responsibility and marketing philosophy. *Journal of Business Research*, *116*, 176–182. doi:10.1016/j.jbusres.2020.05.030 PMID:32457556

Hidayanti, I., Herman, L. E., & Farida, N. (2018). Engaging Customers through Social Media to Improve Industrial Product Development: The Role of Customer Co-Creation Value. *Journal of Relationship Marketing*, *17*(1), 17–28. doi:10.1080/15332667.2018.1440137

Ho, C.-I., Chen, M.-C., & Shih, Y.-W. (2021). Customer engagement behaviours in a social media context revisited: Using both the formative measurement model and text mining techniques. *Journal of Marketing Management*, 1–31. doi:10.1080/0267257X.2021.2003421

Homburg, C., Jozić, D., & Kuehnl, C. (2017). Customer experience management: Toward implementing an evolving marketing concept. *Journal of the Academy of Marketing Science*, *45*(3), 377–401. doi:10.100711747-015-0460-7

Ibrahim, B., & Aljarah, A. (2021). The era of Instagram expansion: Matching social media marketing activities and brand loyalty through customer relationship quality. *Journal of Marketing Communications*, 1–25. doi:10.1080/13527266.2021.1984279

Itani, O. S., Krush, M. T., Agnihotri, R., & Trainor, K. J. (2020). Social media and customer relationship management technologies: Influencing buyer-seller information exchanges. *Industrial Marketing Management*, *90*, 264–275. doi:10.1016/j.indmarman.2020.07.015

Jami Pour, M., & Hosseinzadeh, M. (2021). An integrated framework of change management for social CRM implementation. *Information Systems and e-Business Management*, *19*(1), 43–75. doi:10.100710257-020-00479-z

Jeong, J. Y., & Hyun, S. S. (2019). Roles of passengers' engagement memory and two-way communication in the premium price and information cost perceptions of a luxury cruise. *Tourism Management Perspectives*, *32*, 100559. doi:10.1016/j.tmp.2019.100559

Kang, E., & Lee, H. (2021). Employee Compensation Strategy as Sustainable Competitive Advantage for HR Education Practitioners. *Sustainability*, *13*(3), 1049. Advance online publication. doi:10.3390u13031049

Kaplan, A. M., & Haenlein, M. (2010). Users of the world, unite! The challenges and opportunities of Social Media. *Business Horizons*, *53*(1), 59–68. doi:10.1016/j.bushor.2009.09.003

Kaur, P., & Singh, R. (2007). Uncovering retail shopping motives of Indian youth. *Young Consumers*, *8*(2), 128–138. doi:10.1108/17473610710757491

Kumar, A., Gupta, P. K., & Srivastava, A. (2020). A review of modern technologies for tackling COVID-19 pandemic. *Diabetes & Metabolic Syndrome*, *14*(4), 569–573. doi:10.1016/j.dsx.2020.05.008 PMID:32413821

Kumar, V., & Pansari, A. (2016). Competitive Advantage through Engagement. *JMR, Journal of Marketing Research*, *53*(4), 497–514. doi:10.1509/jmr.15.0044

Lee, M., Hong, J. H., Chung, S., & Back, K.-J. (2020). Exploring the Roles of DMO's Social Media Efforts and Information Richness on Customer Engagement: Empirical Analysis on Facebook Event Pages. *Journal of Travel Research*, *60*(3), 670–686. doi:10.1177/0047287520934874

Leung, X. Y., Bai, B., & Stahura, K. A. (2013). The Marketing Effectiveness of Social Media in the Hotel Industry: A Comparison of Facebook and Twitter. *Journal of Hospitality & Tourism Research (Washington, D.C.)*, *39*(2), 147–169. doi:10.1177/1096348012471381

Li, F., Larimo, J., & Leonidou, L. C. (2021). Social media marketing strategy: Definition, conceptualization, taxonomy, validation, and future agenda. *Journal of the Academy of Marketing Science*, *49*(1), 51–70. doi:10.100711747-020-00733-3

Lim, W. M., Rasul, T., Kumar, S., & Ala, M. (2022). Past, present, and future of customer engagement. *Journal of Business Research*, *140*, 439–458. doi:10.1016/j.jbusres.2021.11.014

Lindecrantz, E., Tjon Pian Gi, M., & Zerbi, S. (2020). *Personalizing the customer experience: Driving differentiation in retail*. McKinsey & Company. Retrieved 22 January from https://www.mckinsey.com/industries/retail/our-insights/personalizing-the-customer-experience-driving-differentiation-in-retail

Mahmoud, A. B., Ball, J., Rubin, D., Fuxman, L., Mohr, I., Hack-Polay, D., Grigoriou, N., & Wakibi, A. (2021a). Pandemic pains to Instagram gains! COVID-19 perceptions effects on behaviours towards fashion brands on Instagram in Sub-Saharan Africa: Tech-native vs non-native generations. *Journal of Marketing Communications*, 1–25. doi:10.1080/13527266.2021.1971282

Mahmoud, A. B., Grigoriou, N., Fuxman, L., Reisel, W. D., Hack-Polay, D., & Mohr, I. (2020). A generational study of employees' customer orientation: A motivational viewpoint in pandemic time. *Journal of Strategic Marketing*, 1–18. doi:10.1080/0965254X.2020.1844785

Mahmoud, A. B., Hack-Polay, D., Grigoriou, N., Mohr, I., & Fuxman, L. (2021b). A generational investigation and sentiment and emotion analyses of female fashion brand users on Instagram in Sub-Saharan Africa. *Journal of Brand Management*, *28*(5), 526–544. doi:10.105741262-021-00244-8

Mahmoud, A. B., Hack-Polay, D., Reisel, W. D., Fuxman, L., Grigoriou, N., Mohr, I., & Aizouk, R. (2021c). Who's more vulnerable? A generational investigation of COVID-19 perceptions' effect on Organisational citizenship Behaviours in the MENA region: Job insecurity, burnout and job satisfaction as mediators. *BMC Public Health*, *21*(1), 1951. doi:10.118612889-021-11976-2 PMID:34706702

Mahmoud, A. B., Reisel, W. D., Fuxman, L., & Hack-Polay, D. (2021d). Locus of control as a moderator of the effects of COVID-19 perceptions on job insecurity, psychosocial, organisational and job outcomes for MENA region hospitality employees. *European Management Review*, 1–20. doi:10.1111/emre.12494

Mahmoud, A. B., Reisel, W. D., Hack-Polay, D., & Fuxman, L. (2021e). No one is safe! But who's more susceptible? Locus of control moderates pandemic perceptions' effects on job insecurity and psychosocial factors amongst MENA hospitality frontliners: A PLS-SEM approach. *BMC Public Health*, *21*(1), 2032. doi:10.118612889-021-12071-2 PMID:34742272

Marolt, M., Pucihar, A., & Zimmermann, H.-D. (2015). Social CRM adoption and its impact on performance outcomes: a literature review. *Organizacija, 48*(4), 260-271. http://organizacija.fov.uni-mb.si/index.php/organizacija/article/view/659

Mechinda, P., & Patterson, P. G. (2011). The impact of service climate and service provider personality on employees' customer-oriented behavior in a high-contact setting. *Journal of Services Marketing*, *25*(2), 101–113. doi:10.1108/08876041111119822

Medjani, F., & Barnes, S. (2021). Social customer relationship management and organizational performance: Testing a conceptual model in the North African context. *Industrial Management & Data Systems*, *121*(7), 1617–1641. doi:10.1108/IMDS-10-2020-0601

Migdadi, M. M. (2021). Knowledge management, customer relationship management and innovation capabilities. *Journal of Business and Industrial Marketing*, *36*(1), 111–124. doi:10.1108/JBIM-12-2019-0504

Mohammed, A. A., & Rashid, B. (2012). Customer Relationship Management (CRM) in Hotel Industry: A framework Proposal on the Relationship among CRM Dimensions, Marketing Capabilities, and Hotel Performance. *International Review of Management and Marketing*, *2*(4), 220–230. https://www.econjournals.com/index.php/irmm/article/view/297

Munjal, S., & Bhushan, S. (2021). *The Indian Hospitality Industry: Dynamics and Future Trends*. Taylor & Francis Group. https://books.google.co.uk/books?id=NI08zgEACAAJ

Mutimukwe, C., Kolkowska, E., & Grönlund, Å. (2020). Information privacy in e-service: Effect of organizational privacy assurances on individual privacy concerns, perceptions, trust and self-disclosure behavior. *Government Information Quarterly*, *37*(1), 101413. doi:10.1016/j.giq.2019.101413

Natale, S., & Cooke, H. (2020). Browsing with Alexa: Interrogating the impact of voice assistants as web interfaces. *Media Culture & Society*, *43*(6), 1000–1016. doi:10.1177/0163443720983295

Obadă, D. R. (2013). Flow Theory and Online Marketing Outcomes: A Critical Literature Review. *Procedia Economics and Finance*, *6*, 550–561. doi:10.1016/S2212-5671(13)00173-1

OECD. (2020). *OECD Policy Responses to Coronavirus (COVID-19): Investment in the MENA region in the time of COVID-19*. Retrieved 18 January from https://www.oecd.org/coronavirus/policy-responses/investment-in-the-mena-region-in-the-time-of-covid-19-da23e4c9/

Ofori, D., & Appiah-Nimo, C. (2021). Relationship Management, Competitive Advantage and Performance of Hotels: A Resource-Based View. *Journal of African Business*, 1–19. doi:10.1080/15228916.2021.1924573

Ong, C. H., Lee, H. W., & Ramayah, T. (2018). Impact of brand experience on loyalty. *Journal of Hospitality Marketing & Management*, *27*(7), 755–774. doi:10.1080/19368623.2018.1445055

Parvatiyar, A., & Sheth, J. N. (2001). Customer relationship management: Emerging practice, process, and discipline. *Journal of Economic & Social Research*, *3*(2).

Payne, A., & Frow, P. (2005). A Strategic Framework for Customer Relationship Management. *Journal of Marketing*, *69*(4), 167–176. doi:10.1509/jmkg.2005.69.4.167

Rahimi, R. (2017). Customer relationship management (people, process and technology) and organisational culture in hotels. *International Journal of Contemporary Hospitality Management*, *29*(5), 1380–1402. doi:10.1108/IJCHM-10-2015-0617

Ramkissoon, H., & Mavondo, F. T. (2015). The satisfaction–place attachment relationship: Potential mediators and moderators. *Journal of Business Research*, *68*(12), 2593–2602. doi:10.1016/j.jbusres.2015.05.002

Ramkissoon, H., & Nunkoo, R. (2010). More than Just Biological Sex Differences: Examining the Structural Relationship Between Gender Identity and Information Search Behavior. *Journal of Hospitality & Tourism Research (Washington, D.C.)*, *36*(2), 191–215. doi:10.1177/1096348010388662

Ramkissoon, H., & Uysal, M. (2018). Authenticity as a value co-creator of tourism experiences. In Creating experience value in tourism (pp. 98-109). doi:10.1079/9781786395030.0098

Reinartz, W., Krafft, M., & Hoyer, W. D. (2004). The Customer Relationship Management Process: Its Measurement and Impact on Performance. *JMR, Journal of Marketing Research*, *41*(3), 293–305. doi:10.1509/jmkr.41.3.293.35991

Reinartz, W. J., & Venkatesan, R. (2008). Decision models for customer relationship management (CRM). In B. Wierenga (Ed.), *Handbook of marketing decision models* (Vol. 121, pp. 291–326). Springer. doi:10.1007/978-0-387-78213-3_9

Rosário, A. (2021). The background of artificial intelligence applied to marketing. *Academy of Strategic Management Journal*, *20*, 1–19.

Saarijärvi, H., Karjaluoto, H., & Kuusela, H. (2013). Extending customer relationship management: From empowering firms to empowering customers. *Journal of Systems and Information Technology*, *15*(2), 140–158. doi:10.1108/13287261311328877

Saha, L., Tripathy, H. K., Nayak, S. R., Bhoi, A. K., & Barsocchi, P. (2021). Amalgamation of Customer Relationship Management and Data Analytics in Different Business Sectors—A Systematic Literature Review. *Sustainability*, *13*(9), 5279. Advance online publication. doi:10.3390u13095279

Salem, S. F. (2021). Do Relationship Marketing Constructs Enhance Consumer Retention? An Empirical Study Within the Hotel Industry. *SAGE Open*, *11*(2). doi:10.1177/21582440211009224

Santos, M. L. B. d. (2021). The "so-called" UGC: An updated definition of user-generated content in the age of social media. *Online Information Review*. doi:10.1108/OIR-06-2020-0258

Sashi, C. M. (2012). Customer engagement, buyer-seller relationships, and social media. *Management Decision*, *50*(2), 253–272. doi:10.1108/00251741211203551

Schultz, D. E., & Peltier, J. (2013). Social media's slippery slope: Challenges, opportunities and future research directions. *Journal of Research in Interactive Marketing*, *7*(2), 86–99. doi:10.1108/JRIM-12-2012-0054

Seetharaman, P. (2020). Business models shifts: Impact of Covid-19. *International Journal of Information Management*, *54*, 102173. doi:10.1016/j.ijinfomgt.2020.102173 PMID:32834338

Serra Cantallops, A., & Salvi, F. (2014). New consumer behavior: A review of research on eWOM and hotels. *International Journal of Hospitality Management*, *36*, 41–51. doi:10.1016/j.ijhm.2013.08.007

Shim, S. I., Forsythe, S., & Kwon, W.-S. (2015). Impact of online flow on brand experience and loyalty. *Journal of Electronic Commerce Research*, *16*(1), 56.

Sigala, M. (2018). Implementing social customer relationship management. *International Journal of Contemporary Hospitality Management*, *30*(7), 2698–2726. doi:10.1108/IJCHM-10-2015-0536

Siti-Nabiha, A. K., Nordin, N., & Poh, B. K. (2021). Social media usage in business decision-making: The case of Malaysian small hospitality organisations. *Asia-Pacific Journal of Business Administration*, *13*(2), 272–289. doi:10.1108/APJBA-08-2020-0276

Snyder, H. (2019). Literature review as a research methodology: An overview and guidelines. *Journal of Business Research*, *104*, 333–339. doi:10.1016/j.jbusres.2019.07.039

So, K. K. F., Kim, H., & King, C. (2021). The thematic evolution of customer engagement research: A comparative systematic review and bibliometric analysis. *International Journal of Contemporary Hospitality Management*, *33*(10), 3585–3609. doi:10.1108/IJCHM-04-2021-0470

So, K. K. F., Li, X., & Kim, H. (2019). A Decade of Customer Engagement Research in Hospitality and Tourism: A Systematic Review and Research Agenda. *Journal of Hospitality & Tourism Research (Washington, D.C.)*, *44*(2), 178–200. doi:10.1177/1096348019895562

Solakis, K., Peña-Vinces, J., & Lopez-Bonilla, J. M. (2022). Value co-creation and perceived value: A customer perspective in the hospitality context. *European Research on Management and Business Economics*, *28*(1), 100175. doi:10.1016/j.iedeen.2021.100175

Sönmez, S., Apostolopoulos, Y., Lemke, M. K., & Hsieh, Y.-C. (2020). Understanding the effects of COVID-19 on the health and safety of immigrant hospitality workers in the United States. *Tourism Management Perspectives*, *35*, 100717. doi:10.1016/j.tmp.2020.100717 PMID:32834958

Srivastava, M., & Sivaramakrishnan, S. (2021). Mapping the themes and intellectual structure of customer engagement: A bibliometric analysis. *Marketing Intelligence & Planning*, *39*(5), 702–727. doi:10.1108/MIP-11-2020-0483

Tanford, S. (2016). Antecedents and Outcomes of Hospitality Loyalty: A Meta-Analysis. *Cornell Hospitality Quarterly*, *57*(2), 122–137. doi:10.1177/1938965516640121

Torugsa, N., & Yawised, K. O. D. W. (2019). Social Customer Relationship Management in Small and Medium Enterprises: Overcoming Barriers to Success. In C. Machado & J. Davim (Eds.), Management Science. Management and Industrial Engineering. Springer. doi:10.1007/978-3-030-13229-3_7

Trainor, K. J. (2012). Relating Social Media Technologies to Performance: A Capabilities-Based Perspective. *Journal of Personal Selling & Sales Management*, *32*(3), 317–331. doi:10.2753/PSS0885-3134320303

Tuten, T. L. (2020). *Social Media Marketing* (4th ed.). SAGE Publications, Limited.

van Asperen, M., de Rooij, P., & Dijkmans, C. (2018). Engagement-Based Loyalty: The Effects of Social Media Engagement on Customer Loyalty in the Travel Industry. *International Journal of Hospitality & Tourism Administration*, *19*(1), 78–94. doi:10.1080/15256480.2017.1305313

Wang, Z., & Kim, H. G. (2017). Can Social Media Marketing Improve Customer Relationship Capabilities and Firm Performance? Dynamic Capability Perspective. *Journal of Interactive Marketing*, *39*, 15–26. doi:10.1016/j.intmar.2017.02.004

Wu, J. S., Ye, S., Zheng, C. J., & Law, R. (2021). Revisiting customer loyalty toward mobile e-commerce in the hospitality industry: Does brand viscosity matter? *International Journal of Contemporary Hospitality Management*, *33*(10), 3514–3534. doi:10.1108/IJCHM-11-2020-1348

Yen, C.-L., & Tang, C.-H. (2015). Hotel attribute performance, eWOM motivations, and media choice. *International Journal of Hospitality Management*, *46*, 79–88. doi:10.1016/j.ijhm.2015.01.003

Zhang, Z., Ye, Q., Law, R., & Li, Y. (2010). The impact of e-word-of-mouth on the online popularity of restaurants: A comparison of consumer reviews and editor reviews. *International Journal of Hospitality Management*, *29*(4), 694–700. doi:10.1016/j.ijhm.2010.02.002

Zhong, Y., Shapoval, V., & Busser, J. (2021). The role of parasocial relationship in social media marketing: Testing a model among baby boomers. *International Journal of Contemporary Hospitality Management*, *33*(5), 1870–1891. doi:10.1108/IJCHM-08-2020-0873

KEY TERMS AND DEFINITIONS

COVID-19 Perception: The perceived probability of discomfort and/or worry, during the COVID-19 pandemic, concerning the pandemic adverse health, economic and social ramifications articulated as disruptions to the people's pre pandemic everyday life – lead to redefining of the everyday life to the "new normal."

Customer Engagement: A user experience that allows businesses to build deeper, more meaningful, and sustainable interactions between the company and its customers or external stakeholders.

Customer Relationship Management: The process of acquiring, retaining, and partnering with selective customers to create superior value for the company and the customer.

Electronic Word of Mouth: Online reviews, online recommendations, or online opinions have gained much attention with the emergence of new technology tools.

Social Customer Relationship Management: A business strategy of engaging customers through social media to build trust and brand loyalty.

Social Media: A group of Internet-based applications that build on the ideological and technological foundations of Web 2.0 and allow the creation and exchange of user-generated content.

Word of Mouth: Informal, person-to-person communication between a perceived non-commercial communicator and a receiver concerning a brand, a product, an organisation, or a service.

Chapter 9
E-Consumer Behavioral Analytics:
Paradigm Shift in Online Purchase Decision Making

Kamaladevi Baskaran
Amity Business School, Amity University, Dubai, UAE

ABSTRACT

During the COVID-19 pandemic, the electronic commerce industry hit a phenomenal change. Many retail locations had to close, and customers were forced to place orders from home. Online retailers had a challenge in the supply of products on time due to unpredictable demand. Goods sold out at an alarming rate, supply diminished, and conveyance periods diminished. Online business stores slowly began to acquire new and expanded interest from the consumers. The purpose of this chapter is to investigate the effect of e-tail factors such as quality of information on the online store, price of product/ service, user-friendly website design, privacy/security control, online customer service, and post purchase delivery service on Malaysian-based consumers purchase decision. This research is based on primary samples collected from 154 Malaysian residents online. The results indicate that there is a significant effect of e-tail factors on Malaysian-based consumers' purchase behavior, which transforms web traffic into actual purchase behavior.

INTRODUCTION

Covid 19 pandemic forced organizations to go online because of the rapid changes in the current business due to recent trends, cutting edge innovation and digitalization. Marketers are brainstorming to frame better strategies to reach their customers. Digital Innovation is truly necessary for powerful customer commitment, loyalty and brand exposure. Online business greatly affects monetary regions like banking, infrastructure and retail trade. It can possibly further to develop transportation, education, information technology and government. Online business has developed and flourished due to technological advance-

DOI: 10.4018/978-1-6684-4168-8.ch009

ments and accessibility of online resources. Electronic Commerce can contribute to the economic, social, technological and financial development of the country.

Today's corporate motto is "survival of the fittest and fastest." The shift of customers from traditional shops to online shopping has forced retail outlets to transform into electronic retail outlets. To compete in highly competitive marketplace, e-tailers need to focus on the e-customer's shopping experience. E-business can be defined as any commercial operation that uses information and communication technology (ICT), to facilitate e-customers' purchasing experiences. Customer Experience Management (CEM) is a term that has emerged in the e-world when organizations can rest comfortably on the cushion known as Customer Relationship Management (CRM). Although they are similar in many ways, the concepts can be difficult to identify.

Professionals, academicians, executives and service researchers often address the topic of customer experience. Research shows that no matter what service or product a customer purchases, they will have an experience. A service is always associated with an experience (Carbone & Haeckel 1994). E-tailers need to understand what the "e-customer experience" means in order to improve their customers' buying experience. CEM is a business strategy that focuses on the company's operations and procedures to meet each client's unique needs. This is a way for e-retailers and customers to trade value in a win/win situation.

Macro elements of the retail environment can have a significant impact on customer experiences and behavior. These macro elements include branding, pricing and advertising as well as how they may influence customer relationships and customer relations. These macro elements enhance the customer experience and result in higher customer satisfaction. This leads to increased online shopping, higher wallet shares and greater revenues.

The relationship between corporate and customer allows the company to learn about the customer by understanding the needs and communicating their opinions. Businesses can effectively manage specific customer profitability by addressing their needs. Customer Experience Management's principle is almost identical. According to this theory, every time a buyer and a company meet, they learn something about the organization. As a result, they may alter their behavior so that it impacts their profitability. Businesses may be able to design more profitable and healthier interactions for their customers by monitoring customer experiences.

CRM collects customer profiles and segments them by category. It also performs predictive analytics to determine the consumer's conceptual structure. CRM helps customers understand their preferences and tendencies, so they can be directed to the most profitable route. CEM analyzes data about online retailers and customer interactions. The feedback will be sent back to CEM in a self-calibrating system, which (theoretically speaking) maximizes every opportunity to influence e–customer behavior. These are interrelated techniques that can be used together, but each one has its own benefits if it is well designed and implemented. Because of its technological superiority, CRM has received the most attention. As CRM becomes more popular, its limitations are more obvious. Customers are asked for access to information and given no indication of what will they receive. It assigns customers a category based on their past actions, but does not advise them how to create a more impressive profile. Customers are motivated to be more valuable to the company without the need for the corporate to charge more (Baskaran, 2020a).

While CRM can measure its successes fairly well, it doesn't deliver much evidence about failures. However, it doesn't provide much insight if clients don't reply in the expected manner. CRM cannot determine if failures are due to erroneous assumptions, improper records, or unsuitable execution. CRM is also unable to tell whether these "failed" interactions have an impact on the consumer relationship. It treats all disasters equally, even though the fabric of the connection could be weakened or compromised by a poorly executed service encounter. CEM's strengths are precisely in the regions where CRM is weak. CEM examines how customer experience affects behavior. CEM aligns the consumer's wishes with the company's ability to fulfill them, resulting in business interactions that are both constructive to the company and consumer (Baskaran, 2020b).

In today's ecommerce digital environment, businesses must concentrate on the e-shopping experience of their customers. To focus on an experience of customer with e-tailing, businesses must first comprehend what "e-tailing" entails. E-commerce refers to the ability of e-customers to purchase goods and services directly from an e-tailer over the internet using a web browser. The terms e-store, internet shop, webshop, webstore, online store, virtual store, and e-shop are all used to describe e-tailing. Customer Experience Management, on the other hand, isn't a outdated concept wrapped in a new package. Customer Experience Management has seen a lot of quick changes in the online platform buying environment in recent years, making it a rapidly-growing field. It also includes a number of important tools and sets. These developments have been assisted by technological improvements, which have expanded the amount of services available to clients and raised consumer expectations. As a result, there are more products and services available than ever before, yet customer happiness is on the decline stage. Customer Experience Management is the strategy to halt this downward trend. It provides effective business solutions that make e-tailer, customer and supplier interactions more profitable for all stakeholders involved.

The e-commerce industry in Malaysia is still in its infancy. As a result, identifying characteristics that may impact online buying behavior is crucial. The necessity to examine the major antecedents of online buying behavior in Malaysia also motivated this study. This is due to the difficulties of internet firms interpreting online customer behavior. While various studies have looked at the factors that influence internet shopping from the viewpoint of developed countries, few have looked at the impact of developing regions like Malaysia. This chapter will build on the existing set of research in Malaysia concerning various aspects of shopping behaviour.

LITERATURE REVIEW

Every sector, including online buying behavior has been transformed by the internet revolution. In today's busy environment, online shopping is the most convenient method to shop. Over the last decade, the customer buying experience has vastly improved. Despite the convenience of internet shopping, many people still prefer to purchase in physical stores. It is developing at an even faster pace due to the increased penetration of the internet and its affordability for internet users. Retailers have been able to develop their online presence in order to reach a larger number of customers through ecommerce portal. Local and global businesses can sell their items over the internet, such as online platforms or mobile applications, through electronic retail. Customers may pick from a wide range of consumer products and services, like needles and helicopter, when they order online. In Malaysia, there are several online shopping sites such as Lazada and Shopee, Mudah.my, Taobao, Carousell.com.my, eBay.com.my and Amazon.com. These websites sell a wide range of products including clothing, electronics, home furnishings and needs, as well as pharmaceuticals.

The relative advantage, according to the current study, comprises convenience, time savings, and financial rewards, each characteristic brings numerous advantages of purchasing online. Malaysians are more inclined to purchase online because of the convenience and time savings. As the popularity of online commerce and internet use develops, complexity becomes smaller concern. The majority of consumers believe that adopting a positive attitude regarding internet buying is significant. They also think about how it will fit into their routines. It's significant to note that, based on Malaysian respondents, it's obvious that, while trust and safety in computer systems are strengthening, and online buying is now a regular practice in Malaysia, risk perceptions continue to influence attitudes about online purchasing. This emphasizes the significance of perceived risk while making an online purchase (Zendehdel, 2015).

In Malaysia, e-commerce is getting increasingly popular. Consumers may now purchase goods online. Malaysia's most popular e-commerce websites are Shopee and Lazada. In 2019, male clients are becoming quite interested in online purchase. Male customers purchase online for electronic devices and accessories for their phones, such as headphones, power banks, speakers, and so on. Blouses, shoes, and purses are among the items purchased by female consumers. Malaysians like to buy Fast Moving Consumer Goods (FMCG) online. Working adults prefer to buy household supplies such as Cereal, detergent powder, and diapers online. Also online shopping for kitchen and home appliances such as plates, cups, and cooking utensils is another option (Vasudevan, 2021).

Many external variables, such as pricing and the environment, are influencing consumer behavior. Ecommerce usage is rapidly expanding and propelling the industry forward. Because of its design flexibility, ecommerce is simple to operate. E-commerce is used by large corporations to market their products. Ecommerce allows large corporations to market their products. For small and medium-sized firms, however, ecommerce is not a choice. They lack the IT capabilities, human resources, security concerns, and organizational limitations required by ecommerce. For large firms, ecommerce trading may be a successful investment. They may earn from their ecommerce business as well. Malaysians are slowly embracing the digital economy. This will ensure that ecommerce continues to expand in the future. Customers will be increasingly open to shopping online for new product categories. Customers will be more delighted with their new product purchases as a result of online shopping (Vasudevan, 2021).

Web based shopping in Malaysia has expanded with reported web-based retail transactions adding up to RM1.8 billion out of 2011 (70 percent more than the earlier year) and anticipated to arrive at RM 22.6 billion by 2020 (Pristiwa, 2017). Malaysia's total number of internet users was 20.6 million in 2015, as indicated by the Malaysian Communication and Multimedia Commission (MCMC). As indicated in the same survey, 44.5 percent of online customers are between the ages of 20 and 29, while 28.2 percent are between the ages of 30 and 39. These figures shed light on the development of online business in Malaysia; especially the web based shopping inclinations for Malaysia's younger age group. The clients who have security and privacy concerns won't wait for long time to receive the product and reluctant to pay extra conveyance costs because of past unpleasant experience in service.

Xingwen's study investigates the influence of online and offline channel interactivity on consumers' Value Co-creation Behavior (VCB), the mediating effect of brand participation, and the moderating effect of Cross-Channel Consistency (CCC) by surveying 387 customers in omnichannel shopping. Brand participation partially moderated the association between VCB and interactivity from omnichannel to offline shopping. When CCC was low, the interaction effect of online channel interactions had a detrimental impact on brand participation, but when it was high, it had a non-significant positive impact. The findings contribute to theoretical understanding of value co-creation and give new perspectives on omni-channel management. (Xingwen & et al., 2022). Digital transformation gained its importance due to competitive business in the market. Disruptive changes are not only happening in corporate level but also in environment level, which is one of the key area for research. This qualitative study divides the literature review in three different dimensions technology, business and society (Kraus, 2021).

E-tail is the most powerful platform in today's e-world. It allows e-tailers to place orders for A-Z items and have them delivered to their customers' homes. The e-tail elements such as Quality of information on the online store, Price of Product/Service, User-friendly Website Design, Privacy/Security control on the web, Online Customer Service and Post Purchase Delivery Service can simply explain the e-customer experience.

QUALITY OF INFORMATION ON ONLINE STORE

Information quality on the online website helps consumers to navigate the relevant, accurate, timely information on e-store. The detailed information about the product gives the overall image of the product's features, consumer feedback, product FAQ's and service information which improves the satisfaction of the consumers in purchasing the product. The consumers who are not satisfied with the information quality will not end up in purchasing online store (Majji, 2021). Al-Tit found that the online store quality dimensions such as accuracy, relevancy and updated information helps to develop consumer loyalty (Al-Tit, 2020). The research gap is to identify the information accuracy of web store, ensure the online store information is up-to-date, order status of online transaction, format of product variety and the language provided in the online store should be understandable. The research questions related to quality of information on online store has been addressed in the survey using Likert five point Scale.

Price of Product/Service

Though e-commerce has been grown exponentially in post Covid era, online transactions are based on product price, delivery cost, discounts and offers. Such target group focuses on volume of sales and reduced cost with updated information (Gupta & et al., 2020). The research gap is to find the convincing answer related to product or service price in web store which includes whether the web store has any hidden fees behind the purchase of product or service and the price of web store is lesser than traditional store (Mohan, 2021). In addition, to ensure online transactions are safer to access using credit card, easiness of online transaction, availability of installment payment transaction and possibility for negotiation of price. These research questions related to Price of Product/Service on online store has been addressed in the questionnaire using Likert Scale.

User Friendly Website Design

Jewellery retailers should focus on online store product variety, worth for money, product packaging, image attribute, transaction safety and product delivery (Moncey, 2020). Website design should highlight security features of online transactions (Haridasan & Fernando, 2018). The research gap related to website design is to ensure the easiness of transactions in the web store, availability of selection of products, comfort level in browsing the products on web store, time consuming or time saving store layout, easiness in search of products and services online. Such research questions related to Website Design has been addressed in the questionnaire.

Privacy/Security Control on Web

Online consumers have concern about the data collected during the time of purchase and unauthorized usage of such personal information. Online retailers should increase their policy towards protection of consumer's confidential information they disclose while doing the online transaction. Privacy concerns are nothing but person's beliefs about the risks and the potentially negative consequences of sharing private information (Gogus & Saygın, 2019). Online consumers look for safety of online transaction in the website of specific web store, security features enables in particular web store, protection of privacy, possibility of leakage of private consumer information and protection of online transaction passwords (Ashok, 2022). Such research gap has been highlighted in the questionnaire for further analysis.

Online Customer Service

Customer Service is much important in online web store such as home delivery, return policy and easy completion of online transactions. Timely delivery of product is primary expectation of online consumers (Cyriac, 2020). Online retailers should provide customers with superior service quality by ensuring timely delivery, transaction accuracy and prompt delivery conditions Such delivery factors have significant impact on consumer satisfaction and further leads to further purchase of online products (Rita & et al., 2019). It is crucial for the online consumers to focus on factors makes appealing online store, values makes priority of web store, supportive customer service in solving consumer problems, after sales service, process for returns and replacements of products, immediately response or action from customer service needs to be analyzed from strategic and operational perspective. All these parameters have been included as research questions which is related to online Customer Service in the questionnaire.

Post Purchase Delivery Service

As indicated by Ariff and et.el., Malaysian internet based purchasers are worried about seven kinds of dangers (financial risk, product performance risk, time or convenience risk, privacy risk, psychological risk, social risk, and delivery risk)) in web based shopping (Ariff, 2014). Importantly, the post purchase delivery service plays a key role in highlighting the status of delivery of product, well informed delivery time of product, prompt delivery of such product, reliability of service delivery and possibility of return of goods via cargo upon damage (Baskaran, 2014 & 2019). Such points play a key role in enhancing smooth delivery options and included in the survey questionnaire to address the research hypothesis.

Mobile Penetration

The growth in the e-commerce sector is partially attributed to high mobile penetration in every country especially smartphone penetration globally. Initially, the country's e-commerce sector lagged behind because of lack of enough traction with regards to the user-base. However, mobile has changed that narrative since more device suppliers have set operations in the country. Telecom operators have also boosted mobile and internet connectivity. As a result, mobile devices have bridged the gap in the e-commerce sector.

E-commerce players are leveraging on mobile penetration to ensure they improve their customers' buying experience. Online store provides the customer with competitive prices and after sales services and support. Several e-commerce players have also invested in development in the country's mobile technologies. At least 40 percent of online shoppers use mobile devices to access e-commerce sites. This makes mobile significant to the country's e-commerce sector. The uptake of videos on tablets and phones has also increased considerably (Cyriac, 2021).

The success of e-commerce industry because of mobile penetration has led to more investment from telecom operators in the region. The investment in 4G and LTE by the telecom operators is aimed at ensuring that the countries in the region have the same access to mobile services. It will also help e-commerce sites compete with other regions in Europe and Asia. Going forward, e-commerce will focus on improving the mobile experience of customers by creating a whole ecosystem that is mobile-based. The main focus will be the personalization of mobile apps and platforms because customers use different mobile devices.

At first glance, ecommerce may appear to be unappealing. Due to the unreliability of digital purchases, many individuals choose to purchase physically. Because internet access was previously confined to laptops and PCs. In many regions, accessibility was limited, making internet alternatives less accessible. In the early 2010s, the smartphone technology was introduced, such technology altered people's perspectives. People's daily life required the use of cellphones. The emergence of Samsung and Apple phones was a tremendous success due to their internet connectivity. Many individuals have upgraded from their old phones to smartphones, which allow them to utilize the internet and their phone at the same time. They can now access the internet from their smartphones without having to rely on computers and laptops (Baskaran, 2020a).

Many individuals may now connect with one another via mobile phones. The introduction of WhatsApp on smartphones gained large number of individuals to access the internet on a regular basis. Because of the rising usage of smartphones, ecommerce has taken on a new dimension. Many businesses have set up websites to offer their products online. As more individuals utilized cellphones and internet access increased, ecommerce sales skyrocketed. Ecommerce has become a necessity in people's life like smartphones. Smart phones have substituted many industries such as food, grocery, fashion, home appliances and technological devices.

Malaysia's digital economy contribute 22.6% to country's GDP and it is expected to create 500, 000 jobs by 2025. Digital technologies are crucial in promoting new job opportunities, supporting country's future economic resilience, allowing students to continue their education, helping business to stay active, supporting job seekers in enhancing their knowing through online courses and bonding the family to stay connected online. Malaysian government aims to convert 80% of public sector services online by 2025 (Vasudevan, 2021). The key challenges for e-tailers in Malaysia is to reach out the audience who have lack of knowledge to shop online. By the end of 2021, 80% of e-commerce companies in Malaysia invest in employing and executing their digital platform.

RESEARCH METHODOLOGY

The purpose of this research is to investigate the effect of six e-tail factors Quality of information on online store, Price of Product/Service, User friendly Website Design, Privacy/Security check on web, Online Customer Service and Post Purchase Delivery Service on Malaysian based Consumer Purchase decision.

Descriptive research design has been applied, as the research is focused to study the characteristics of population. Google Forms was developed as a survey tool to obtain primary data from Malaysian residents. Then, data were imported to SPSS for analytics. 154 samples obtained from online customers who reside in Malaysia. Simple Random Sampling has been applied. The first segment of the survey questionnaire covers the demographic factors, second segment covers the usage of internet, frequency of consumer purchase over internet, enjoyment and safety aspects of online shopping and the last segment focuses on the measurement of e-tail factors using Likert Scale. The following hypothesis have been framed and analysed using Statistical Package for Social Science (SPSS) version 28.

H1: There is no effect of Quality of online store information on Consumer Purchase Decision
H2: There is no effect of Price of Product/Service sold online on Consumer Purchase Decision
H3: There is no effect of Website Design on Consumer Purchase Decision
H4: There is no effect of Privacy/Security on Consumer Purchase Decision
H5: There is no effect of Online Customer Service on Consumer Purchase Decision
H6: There is no effect of Post Purchase Delivery Service on Consumer Purchase Decision
The above hypotheses have been tested using reliability analysis, regression analysis and customer perceived value.

Limitations of the Study:

The surveys targets the consumers who uses the internet. There are online customers who does online purchase through third person could not be reached in this study. The sample size is again a major drawback as only 154 samples have represented the entire Malaysian population. The survey questionnaire is quantitative in nature. The consumers doesn't have option to express their opinions orally.

RESULTS, ANALYSIS, AND DISCUSSION

Table 1 describes the demographic characteristics of 154 samples received from Malaysia. 54% of samples are received from female respondents and 46% are from male. 36% of respondents are from the age group of 20-29 followed by 30% belong to 30-39, 19% are between 40-49, 8% are less than 20 and 7% are above 50 age group. Out of 154 samples, 76% of them are married, 23% of them are single and 1% is either divorced/separated. They are mostly master degree holders (62%), followed by undergraduate (17%), diploma holders (10%), doctorate holders (8%) and 3% completed high school. 37% of respondents are manager/administrator, 15% are Government employees, 14% are student, 13% are teacher/lecturer, 6% are business owner and self-employed each, 4% are trade worker and 3% are home maker. 31% of respondents are earning income level of $30000 - $39999 per annum. 41% of respondents use average internet for the period of 5-7 years, 39% of respondents are using internet for more than 7 years, 20% are using between 3-5 years and no respondents were in the category of 1-3 years and less than one year. 31% of respondents do 5-10 times yearly online purchase, 29% do once yearly, 22% do 2-4 times yearly and 18% do more than 10 times yearly. All the respondents have done online purchase atleast once and no respondents were in the category of never shopped online. 93% of Malaysian shoppers enjoy shopping online and 96% of respondents feels online shopping is safe.

Table 1. Characteristics of Malaysian respondents

Category	Sub-Category	Total Samples (154)	%
Gender	Male	71	46%
	Female	**83**	**54%**
Age	Below 20	12	8%
	20-29	**55**	**36%**
	30-39	46	30%
	40-49	30	19%
	Above 50	11	7%
Marital Status	Single	35	23%
	Married	**117**	**76%**
	Divorced/ Separate	2	1%
Education	High School	5	3%
	Diploma	15	10%
	Undergraduate	26	17%
	Masters	**96**	**62%**
	Doctorate	12	8%
Occupation	Business Owner	9	6%
	Manager/Administrator	**57**	**37%**
	Teacher/Lecturer	21	13%
	Self-employed	9	6%
	Government Employees	26	17%
	Trade Worker	7	4%
	Student	21	14%
	Homemaker	4	3%
Income Per Annum	Not Applicable	29	18%
	< $9999	0	0%
	$10000 - $19999	22	14%
	$20000 - $29999	4	3%
	$30000 - $39999	**48**	**31%**
	$40000 - $49999	11	7%
	$50000 - $59999	18	12%
	$60000 - $69999	4	3%
	> $70000	18	12%
Average Internet Usage Period	< 1 Year	0	0%
	1 - 3 Years	0	0%
	3 - 5 Years	31	20%
	5 - 7 Years	**63**	**41%**
	> 7 Years	60	39%

continues on following page

Table 1. Continued

Category	Sub-Category	Total Samples (154)	%
Frequency of purchase online	Never shopped online	0	0%
	Once Yearly	44	29%
	2 - 4 times yearly	34	22%
	5 - 10 times yearly	**48**	**31%**
	More than 10 times yearly	28	18%
Enjoyment of e-shopping	**Yes**	**142**	**93%**
	No	10	7%
Safety of e-shopping	**Yes**	**148**	**96%**
	No	6	4%

In Malaysia, male are highly satisfied with website design and female are concerned about cost of product or service offered online. The age group of below 20 years purchase online due to website design and age group between 20-29 years hesitate to purchase online due to cost of product. With respect to education, diploma holders' online purchase is due to information quality but the under graduates doesn't checkout the product if the website design is not appealing. Homemakers and students are particular on quality of information provided on e-store but the income group of $20000 - $29999 per annum are concerned about Privacy/Security issued in purchasing online. The consumers who use internet for more than 7 years on average are focused on information quality during purchase but the average internet users of 5-7 years are looking for best price offered. In Malaysia, all the 154 samples have made the online purchase. Also, 92% of Malaysian consumers enjoy shopping online. The findings indicate that there is a significant effect of e-tailing factors on Malaysia based online consumers purchase behavior, which turns web traffic into actual purchasing behavior.

Reliability Analysis

The mean value of e-tail factors ranging from 3.69 to 4.02. Cronbach alpha is a measure, which assess the reliability or internal consistency of the items in the scale. Cronbach alpha value normally ranges between 0 and 1. The rule of thumb is to accept the Cronbach alpha value greater than or equal to 0.7, 0.6-0.7 is acceptable range. Table 2 shows the Cronbach alpha values between 0.541 and 0.706. The Mean value of six e-tail factors Quality of information on online store, Price of Product/Service, user friendly Website Design, Privacy/Security check on web, Online Customer Service and Post Purchase Delivery Service is between 3.69 and 4.02.

Table 3 provides the model summary of regression analysis. R value represents the degree of correlation of 0.404. R2 value indicates how much of the total variation in the dependent variable, Frequency of online purchase, can be explained by independent variables i.e., six e-tail factors include Quality of information on online store, Price of Product/Service, User friendly Website Design, Privacy/Security check on web, Online Customer Service and Post Purchase Delivery Service. In this case, 16.3% of frequency of online purchase can be explained by the given independent variables.

Table 2. Mean, standard deviation and reliability of e-tail factors

E-tail factors	Mean	Std. Deviation	Number of Items	Cronbach's Alpha
Quality of information on online store	3.97	0.57	5	0.637
Price of Product/Service	3.69	0.64	5	0.541
User friendly Website Design	3.96	0.66	5	0.706
Privacy/Security control on web	3.93	0.52	5	0.633
Online Customer Service	3.98	0.54	5	0.669
Post Purchase Delivery Service	4.02	0.53	5	0.670

Table 3. Model summary of regression analysis

Model	R	R Square	Adjusted R Square	Std. Error of the Estimate	Change Statistics		
					R Square Change	F Change	df1
1	.404	.163	.129	1.014	.163	4.786	6

Table 4 indicates the ANOVA value, which predicts the dependent variable, which reports how well the regression equation fits the data. Table 4 also highlights that the regression model predicts the frequency of online purchase behavior significantly well. The level of significance indicates the statistical significance of the regression model. Here, $p < 0.001$, which is less than 0.05 indicates that the regression model is statistically significant and predicts the outcome variable that is a good fit.

Table 4. ANOVA

Model		Sum of Squares	df	Mean Square	F	Sig.
1	Regression	29.515	6	4.919	4.786	<.001
	Residual	151.108	147	1.028		
	Total	180.623	153			

Table 5 highlights the standardized coefficients that provides us with the necessary information to predict dependent variable from independent variable, as well as determine whether independent variable contributes statistically significantly to the model by looking at the level of significance. The model is significant ($F=4.786$, $p<0.001$). The level of significance resulted in Table 5 indicates User friendly Website Design has significant relationship with the frequency of online consumer purchase decision at 0.05 significant level. In contrast, Quality of information on online store, Price of Product/Service, Privacy/Security check on web, Online Customer Service and Post Purchase Delivery Service have no significant relationship with the frequency of online consumer purchase decision at 0.05 significant level.

Table 5. Multiple regression results for e-tail factors affecting online purchase decision

Independent Variable	Standardized Coefficients (Beta)	t	Sig.
(Constant)		1.132	0.259
Quality of information on online store	0.106	0.843	0.401
Price of Product/Service	0.149	1.676	0.096
User friendly Website Design	0.379	3.154	0.002
Privacy/Security control on web	-0.034	-0.318	0.751
Online Customer Service	-0.014	-0.154	0.878
Post Purchase Delivery Service	-0.166	-1.606	0.110
R2	0.163		
Adjusted R2	0.129		
F Value	4.786		<0.001

Table 6 provides the results of testing of hypothesis. H3 indicates that there is not enough evidence to accept that there is no effect of Website Design on Consumer Purchase Decision. H1, H2, H4, H5 and H6 has evidence to accept the null hypothesis i.e., there is no effect of Quality of online store information, Price of Product/Service, Privacy/Security check on web, Online Customer Service and Post Purchase Delivery Service on Consumer Purchase Decision.

Table 6. Hypothesis result

	Hypothesis	Result
H1	There is no effect of Quality of online store information on Consumer Purchase Decision	Accept the null hypothesis
H2	There is no effect of Price of Product/Service sold online on Consumer Purchase Decision	Accept the null hypothesis
H3	There is no effect of Website Design on Consumer Purchase Decision	Reject the null hypothesis
H4	There is no effect of Privacy/Security on Consumer Purchase Decision	Accept the null hypothesis
H5	There is no effect of Online Customer Service on Consumer Purchase Decision	Accept the null hypothesis
H6	There is no effect of Post Purchase Delivery Service on Consumer Purchase Decision	Accept the null hypothesis

Customer Perceived Value

Customer Perceived Value (CPV) measures a customer's current value impression by asking particular survey questions and comparing responses to historic value. The result indicates 0% as worst percentile score, 100% best percentile score and 50% being the historic average.

Figure 1 reveals the customer perceived value of Malaysian respondents. Here, D1 to D24 indicates the e-tail factors. In Malaysia, the highest perceived value given to Website Design (82%), Privacy/Security check on web (78%), Online Customer Service (78%), and Post Purchase Delivery Service (78%), Quality of online store information (77%) and Price of Product/Service (76%).

Figure 1. Customer perceived value - Malaysia

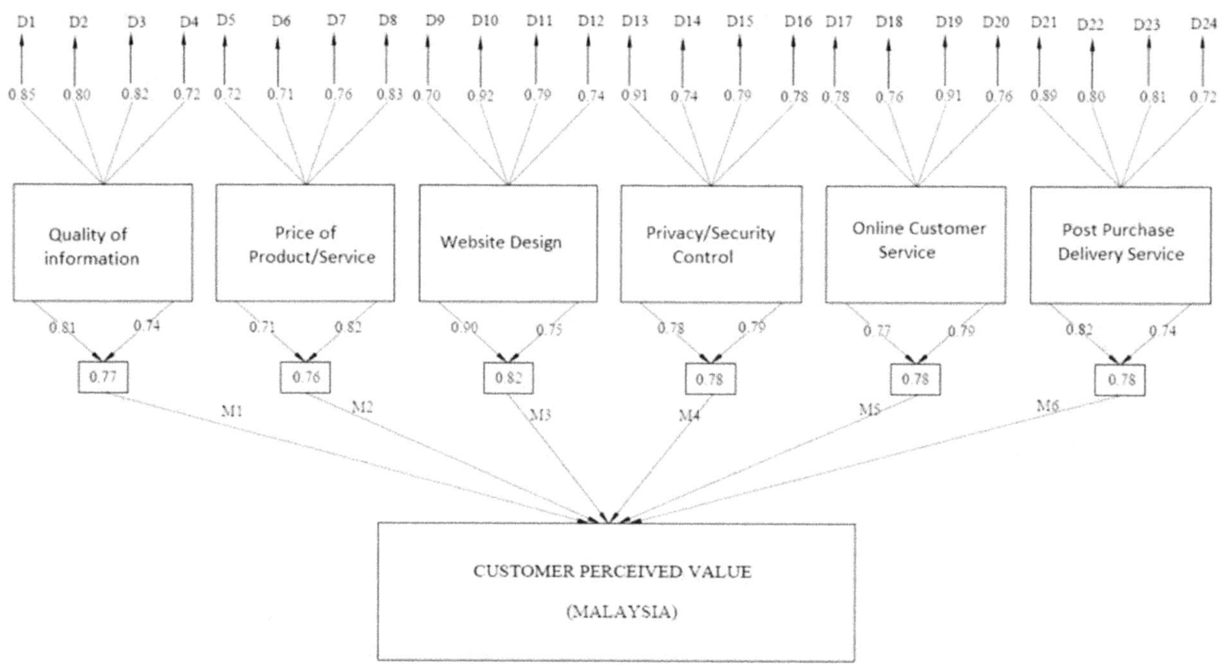

Managerial Implications

The purpose of this research was to gain a better understanding of the factors that affect online buying behavior. Once customers have beyond the initial stage of acceptance and are more comfortable with the benefits of purchasing online, e-commerce may be expected to spread extensively in Malaysia. In order to foster a good attitude toward their websites among their customers, managers should ensure that they have procedures in place to reduce perceived risk. These findings can also benefit brick-and-mortar businesses, since using online platforms will attract more shoppers.

This study's implications are as follows. Retailers should take measures to address the security issue and eliminate any potential risks. Retailers should also develop a method to improve online privacy and security in order to limit the possibility of consumers making purchases without completing safe transactions. The loss of their financial information or credit card numbers should not be their primary concern. Use the SSL protocol for payment to safeguard and prevent them from sharing information.

According to this report, Malaysian online businesses should try to strengthen a trustworthy image by cooperating with trusted partners and delivering adequate transactions. To minimize risk, purchasers should be informed about their rights, be given security approval symbols, money-back guarantee, be informed about high security standards, and have their personal information protected. Because the subjective norm might impact online buying behavior, online businesses should employ word-of-mouth marketing to promote their sites. This is one of the most effective marketing strategies.

Despite the fact that ecommerce is quickly expanding, Malaysian ecommerce transactions face several hurdles. One of the most difficult aspects of ecommerce is delivery. Deliveries must be handled appropriately by ecommerce firms. This is due to the fact that ecommerce's reliability is dependent on it. To mitigate the drawbacks of ecommerce enterprises, they must invest in the delivery process. Building trust and confidence is critical to ensuring that customers continue to purchase online. For entrepreneurs and managers, consumers are the most significant revenue-generating asset. Managers and entrepreneurs must pay particular attention to how the virtual store may be leveraged to help consumers buy more easily and effectively (relative edge). They must also consider consumer work and lifestyle compatibility, as well as high-quality goods and services. Retailers selling high-quality goods and services should prioritize reduced costs. The findings of the study should be utilized to advise Malaysian online vendors who offer products and services over the internet. They must recall the most important strategies and approaches to reach out to potential clients.

The greatest point to focus in online store is the reduced cost. Online retailers should promise financial rewards like discounts and coupons. Online retailers should offer buyer-friendly techniques, such as simple payment alternatives or customized information based on previous buying behavior. Customers who buy products or services online are concerned about the security and privacy of their transactions. As a result, online businesses may reassure their consumers by giving personal information privacy policies and ensuring transaction security by upgrading their technological systems. For retailers, handling the ecommerce website may be critical. They may be unable to access the site, have lengthy delays, lose their orders, discover the erroneous items online, or mistakes when filling out orders. Delivery timeframes, delivery fees, and refund policies may be more important to online vendors.

Consumers may benefit from online retailers that make purchasing easier, quicker and more fun. Due to the absence of personal privacy and online payment, internet purchasing might be less trustworthy than traditional buying. Hacking, privacy, and fraud are all concerns when it comes to online security. Hackers, viruses and other cybercriminals can breach business and personal security systems, raising concerns about online security. Any data security or privacy breaches might result in a loss of confidence and reputation. This might diminish consumer trust, which could be catastrophic for web-based businesses.

Technology and Innovation has progressed significantly over these years to give online customers a superior online shopping experience. Customers have anticipated that internet shopping will surpass traditional store because of the rapid rise in products and services available online. It is high time for e-tailers to strengthen their e-tail factors in order to increase their emerging business volume. The quality of information provided in online store can be improved by providing excellent service and periodical update of information during the pre-sale and post-sale stages. The cost of online shopping product can be decreased by giving reduced prices than in traditional stores. Online Store Design can be made more qualitative by incorporating creativity into the website's usability, design, and content quality. Online Privacy/Security can be improved by incorporating privacy and security features into e-commerce sites. Satisfaction surveys, fast response, and e-loyalty programs are all ways to measure online customer service. When products are delivered fast and product quality exceeds customers' expectations, e-delivery service quality will boost their perceived value.

CONCLUSION

Many factors influence customers' purchase decisions, according to the study. Consumers will buy for products online for a various reasons because it saves time. Consumers think that internet shopping is the most appealing. Other aspects that encourage online purchasing include accessibility, availability of 24/7, huge choice of brands, reasonable cost, different offers for products online and shopping enjoyment. The importance of being flexible and quick to adapt has been highlighted during the COVID-19 outbreak.

Traditional demand triggers won't have as much influence at this time, thus leading indicators will be used to keep track of new behavior signals. It will be required to employ dual strategy. One, evaluate government and media statements subjectively, and two, track customer data statistically. Leading companies also have a defined trigger strategy in place to guarantee that they can react swiftly and decisively.

All ages of consumers have had to adapt quickly their buying habits. In short-term, the retailers should focus on streamlining or creating online offerings. This could be done through an existing website, or via a business-to consumer marketplace. Limit the initial product offering to core products in order to maximize profit and minimize the amount of effort needed to create a product range. Customers will be happy if inventories are managed effectively and shipping times are reduced. As more people are used to shopping online, and more businesses embrace e-commerce, the online competition will only increase. These shifts will make it difficult to determine the best way to manage Omnichannel Strategy. Many businesses sell their products only on their online stores like Kogan or use a mix of brick-and mortar marketplaces and online, as Bosch does.

Direct to Consumer (DTC) e-commerce has changed the way people engage with one another and shop for nearly everything. Even before the epidemic, DTC companies were seen to be the most technologically aware in retail industry. Traditional retailers and branded organizations have learned from DTC brands in order to compete in the e-commerce space. Because of the rise in online sales and shopping, manufacturers and merchants must have ecommerce channels. Ecommerce is a challenging task. It's a path that needs periodical updating, as well as a strong understanding of internet trends, changes, and patterns as well as the constraints of entering into this industry. Furthermore, finding and attracting suitable clients as well as competitors is more challenging online.

Knowing what customers think, perceive, and want allows the e-tailers to better influence them, which is both a challenge and an opportunity. The e-tailer can use this research report to better understand how online customers feel about each e-tail factor and address their concerns. In the next years, customer retention will be more crucial than generating a sale. E-tailers will need to engage their clients on a daily basis in order to build the long-term loyal advocates required to compete in these challenging times. The most crucial thing is to be able to spot strategies to keep profitable clients on board.

During holiday seasons, traditional stores may be shuttered for weekend, leaving online businesses with free flow of revenue at all the times. Customers can benefit even more during festival and weekend deals which promotes online purchasing. The digital transformation towards online shopping has rapid reach due to penetration of smart phones and investment of retailers in multichannel marketing. Digital transformation gathers large amount of data through touch points that is input for predictive analytics to target the right audience at the right platform. Digital transformation is different for each company and same strategy may not be applicable for all corporates.

In the e-business scenario, the retailer should focus on customer experience to survive in the modern world. To improve e-customer experience approach, the retailer should focus on e-tail factors. It includes updated quality of information on online store, comparatively lower price of products or service offered in e-store and website design should be user friendly, easy to access and check out. Higher level of privacy and security level of customer information protection provided on website during the time of purchase. Online Customer Service through phone calls, emails, electronic enquiry system and 24/7 live chat services. Most importantly, customer service after purchase of product or services like solving post purchase complaints, dealing with enquiry related to warranty and guarantee. E-commerce retailers should pay attention to the e-tail factors to compete and succeed with Malaysia based national and international competitors. Consumer Purchase decision towards online products and services are based on e-tail factors. Using advanced business analytics tools, e-tailers can measure the digital performance management of new business systems and promote their e-store in the global scale.

Scope for Future Study

The questionnaire reaches only the customer who uses the internet. The future study could focus on the customers who do online shopping through third parties and the shoppers who don't do the e-shopping. The findings are based on the limited area of scope with only Malaysia. The future research should focus either wider countries in scope or narrow down to each country. The sample size is again a major drawback. Out of multi million users, only 1000 copies of questionnaire sent to the customers. The larger sample with more diversity would have benefited the results, which could be the opportunity for further research. The questionnaire is quantitative in nature. The respondents couldn't have chance to express their opinions orally. The questionnaire used in the future research could possibly include the qualitative options as well.

REFERENCES

Ahmed, A., Moncey, A., Mohan, M., Cyriac, N. T., Ali, S. A., Mariam, S., Lyu, M., & Baskaran, K. (2020). Journey of education technology towards innovation. *2020 Advances in Science and Engineering Technology International Conferences (ASET)*. 10.1109/ASET48392.2020.9118334

Al-Tit, A. A. (2020). E-commerce drivers and barriers and their impact on e-customer loyalty in small and medium-sized enterprises (SMEs). *Verslas: Teorija Ir Praktika*, *21*(1), 146–157. doi:10.3846/btp.2020.11612

Ariff, M. S. M., Sylvester, M., Zakuan, N., Ismail, K., & Ali, K. M. (2014). Consumer perceived risk, attitude and online shopping behavior : Empirical evidence from Malaysia. *Proceedings of the 2014 International Conference on Manufacturing, Optimization, Industrial and Material Engineering*.

Ashok, S., & Baskaran, K. (2022). The prominence of corporate governance in banking sector with reference to UAE. In *Pervasive Computing and Social Networking* (pp. 417–430). Springer Singapore. doi:10.1007/978-981-16-5640-8_33

Baskaran, K. (2019). An Interpretive Study of Customer Experience Management towards Online Shopping in UAE. *International Journal of Mechanical Engineering and Technology*, *10*(02), 1071–1077.

Baskaran, K. (2019b). The impact of digital transformation in Singapore e-tail market. *International Journal of Innovative Technology and Exploring Engineering*, *8*(11), 2320–2324. doi:10.35940/ijitee.I8046.0981119

Baskaran, K., & Rajavelu, S. (2020). Digital innovation in industry 4.0 era – rebooting UAE's retail. *2020 International Conference on Communication and Signal Processing (ICCSP)*. 10.1109/ICCSP48568.2020.9182301

Baskaran, K., & Vanithamani, M. R. (2014). E-Customers Attitude towards E-Store Information and Design Quality in India, Applied Research in Science, Engineering and Management. *Applied Research in Science, Engineering and Management. World Applied Sciences Journal*, 51–56. doi:10.5829/idosi.wasj.2014.31.arsem.555

Carbone, L. P., & Haeckel, S. H. (1994). Engineering Customer Experiences. *Marketing Management*, *3*(3), 8–19.

Cui, X., Xie, Q., Zhu, J., Shareef, M. A., Goraya, M. A. S., & Akram, M. S. (2022). Understanding the omnichannel customer journey: The effect of online and offline channel interactivity on consumer value co-creation behavior. *Journal of Retailing and Consumer Services*, *65*(102869), 102869. doi:10.1016/j.jretconser.2021.102869

Cyriac, N. T., & Baskaran, K. (2020). A study on the effectiveness of non-monetary retention strategies in UAE. *2020 8th International Conference on Reliability, Infocom Technologies and Optimization (Trends and Future Directions) (ICRITO)*. 10.1109/ICRITO48877.2020.9197867

Cyriac, N. T., & Baskaran, K. (2021). Predictive Analytics in a Post Covid-19 World: India's Travel and Tourism Industry. *Proceedings of International Conference on Advances in Technology, Management & Education*. 10.1109/ICATME50232.2021.9732706

Gogus, A., & Saygın, Y. (2019). Privacy perception and information technology utilization of high school students. *Heliyon*, *5*(5), e01614. doi:10.1016/j.heliyon.2019.e01614 PMID:31193323

Gupta, V., Gupta, L., & Dhir, S. (2020). Customer competency for improving firm decision-making performance in e-commerce. *Foresight*, *22*(2), 205–222. doi:10.1108/FS-06-2019-0053

Haridasan, A. C., & Fernando, A. G. (2018). Online or in-store: Unravelling consumer's channel choice motives. *Journal of Research in Interactive Marketing*, *12*(2), 215–230. doi:10.1108/JRIM-07-2017-0060

Kraus, S., Jones, P., Kailer, N., Weinmann, A., Chaparro-Banegas, N., & Roig-Tierno, N. (2021). Digital transformation: An overview of the current state of the art of research. *SAGE Open*, *11*(3). doi:10.1177/21582440211047576

Majji, K. C., & Baskaran, K. (2021). Artificial intelligence analytics—virtual assistant in UAE automotive industry. In *Inventive Systems and Control* (pp. 309–322). Springer Singapore. doi:10.1007/978-981-16-1395-1_24

Mohan, M., & Baskaran, K. (2021). Financial analytics: Investment behavior of middle income group in south India. *2021 11th International Conference on Cloud Computing, Data Science & Engineering (Confluence)*. 10.1109/Confluence51648.2021.9377029

Moncey, A. A., & Baskaran, K. (2020). Digital marketing analytics: Building brand awareness and loyalty in UAE. *2020 IEEE International Conference on Technology Management, Operations and Decisions (ICTMOD)*. 10.1109/ICTMOD49425.2020.9380579

Pristiwa, N., Huang, W. T., & Ayuningtyas, D. (2017). The effect of internet user behavior on effective marketing via online group buying in Taiwan. *Proceedings of AICS Social Sciences*, *7*, 326–333.

Rita, P., Oliveira, T., & Farisa, A. (2019). The impact of e-service quality and customer satisfaction on customer behavior in online shopping. *Heliyon*, *5*(10), e02690. doi:10.1016/j.heliyon.2019.e02690 PMID:31720459

Vasudevan, P., & Arokiasamy, L. (2021). Online shopping among young generation in Malaysia. *Electronic Journal of Business and Management*, *6*(1), 31–38.

Zendehdel, M., Paim, L. H., & Osman, S. B. (2015). Students' online purchasing behavior in Malaysia: Understanding online shopping attitude. *Cogent Business & Management*, *2*(1), 1078428. doi:10.1080/23311975.2015.1078428

Chapter 10
Predicting Consumer Behavior Change Towards Using Online Shopping in Nigeria:
The Impact of the COVID-19 Pandemic

Chiamaka Miriam Ezimmuo
School of Computer Sciences, Universiti Sains Malaysia, Malaysia

Pantea Keikhosrokiani
https://orcid.org/0000-0003-4705-2732
School of Computer Sciences, Universiti Sains Malaysia, Malaysia

ABSTRACT

This study aims to ascertain the factors responsible for the behavior change of consumers in Nigeria towards the use of online shopping as impacted by the COVID-19 pandemic. For this reason, two quantitative studies were conducted to find user behavior towards using online shopping before and during the COVID-19 pandemic. Questionnaire was used as the research instrument and an online survey was conducted in which 82 respondents in Nigeria participated for both studies. Both studies develop hypotheses through the integration of technology acceptance models, unified theory of acceptance and use of technology, and theory of planned behavior. The results of the study before and during COVID-19 pandemic are compared accordingly. Based on the findings of this study, recommendations were proffered in relation to the results of the various hypothesized factors. Lastly, the study gave suggestions for subsequent research.

DOI: 10.4018/978-1-6684-4168-8.ch010

INTRODUCTION

Background

The dynamic nature in the business today has prompted that for business owners to stay in business, they should adjust to the evolving condition particularly in the area of technology to meet the necessities of consumers (Otika et al., 2019). For instance, Wilson and Gilligan (2012) argued that marketing agents should match the abilities of the business with the environmental conditions. In addition, Pride and Ferrell (2016) suggested that businesses ought to be proactive in adjusting their business strategies to align with the changes taking place in environment. However, one of such changes is the fast increase of displacing traditional way of shopping with online shopping. Shopping via online portals has made it convenient for consumers to shop at any time and in any place with just a click on the mouse or via smart phones, reshaping consumer experiences in comparison to traditional shopping. Consumers no longer need to be present at stores to search for items to purchase, or look for space to park their cars, or to queue to pay for their purchased items. Consumers make purchases easily with smart phones, tablets or laptops at any time and in any place, according to personal convenience. Internet has become a vital means for communication and business worldwide. The Internet World Stats (2020) revealed that there are huge number of internet users currently ranging from four billion and above.

The evolution of consumer behavior and shopping experience took a more radical explosive development with the advent of coronavirus (COVID-19) pandemic, resultant isolation and global lockdown. Coronavirus disease (Covid-19) is an emerging disease that has given concerned globally due to the rapid increase in cases since its first discovery in Wuhan, China, in December 2019 (Zu et al., 2020). WHO Emergency Committee declared Covid-19 a pandemic because of rapid increase in cases globally. This disease is not only hard to be controlled by undeveloped country but also for the developed country like the United States, United Kingdom, Italy and other with a high number of positive cases. The pandemic has facilitated a huge shift towards a more digital world and triggered changes in online shopping behaviors that are probably going to have a long effect. From a recent report from Digital Commerce 360, 36% of buyers shop online week by week since the ascent of COVID19, up from 28% pre-pandemic, 29% state that as of now they shop more online than face-to-face while 90% of customers prefer home delivery to a store visit.

The COVID-19 has caused us extraordinary hardships, with thousands of businesses closing its doors. The general people have heeded the government's plea to stay at home. Retail stores in the physical world have been significantly impacted. Advancement of data science and analytical methods provides an opportunity for sellers to track their consumer behaviors and recommend proper product to them. For instance, a research conducted by Zhao and Keikhosrokiani (2022) intends to use historical sales data for analyzing, creating sales forecast, and recommendation models in order to change a traditional offline sales model to a Business-to-Customer (B2C) model and improve the shopping experience. A novel analytical method was proposed for sales prediction and product recommendation by utilizing user behavior analytics. Consumer behavior change is one of the main important criteria which needs to be considered in every kind of business for better decision making and business success (Keikhosrokiani, 2019, 2020a, 2020b; Keikhosrokiani et al., 2013; Keikhosrokiani et al., 2018; Keikhosrokiani, Mustaffa, Zakaria, & Abdullah, 2019).

Nigeria, the focus point of this study is a multinational state located in the west of the African continent and the most populous country in Africa with an estimated 206 million inhabitants as of late 2019.

Nigeria is one of the highest penetrators of internet user in Africa. Despite the high penetration of the internet usage in Nigeria the online shopping is still slow compare to other countries (Otika et al., 2019). However, the movement restrictions during the ongoing Covid-19 pandemic across the nation facilitate a change in attitudes with consumers exploring online shopping out of necessity. According to recent survey, one of the leading online retailers in Nigeria detailed a huge increase in online shopping as demand from consumers grew from four-fold in the first quarter of the year during the Covid-19 lockdown compared to last year. The change in consumer behavior in Nigeria is also leading a reaction from other domestic and global brands, as many sellers and buyers shift their attention from offline to online for strategic partnerships. Given the short-term boon amidst of an absence of choices for consumers during the Covid-19 pandemic, "the main question is whether the consumers behavior has been altered forever and will this trend stick in a post-COVID era''. Hence, this study seeks to access the consumer's behavior change towards online shopping as a resultant effect of the Covid-19 pandemic in Nigeria.

Since the entry of online shopping in Nigeria, Nigerians find it difficult to believe things they cannot see and contact. Trust is diminished in the web-based shopping climate because of absence of physical contact and personal communication between seller, customer, and item (Cho, 2006). Online buyers not just need to confide in online sellers, they additionally need to confide in the Web itself as an exchange medium (McKnight et al., 2002). Product delivery: Attached with online trust is item conveyance. It is the greatest dread of an online customer in Nigeria. Knowing how deceitful a few stages can be, item or administration conveyed may not be what you requested. However, the messenger accomplice might be the issue sometimes.

Credibility is the capacity of the nature of merchandise and ventures showed to be met the manner in which it is shown for example purchasers ought to get the specific quality showed on the web. Numerous association and business arrangement in Nigeria give appealing sites, creating inferior quality item and given bad quality services yet showing excellent products and enterprises in order to draw in more buyers (Bhupal et al., 2020).

These problems and inhibitors are valid and enough to swindle the consumer behavior and shopping habits to the status quo (offline shopping) of a great percentage of Nigerians during the COVID-19 pandemic and following its departure. In addition, possible solutions to these problems are far from reach with limited empirical studies to its effect. It is therefore of paramount importance that the consumers behavior changes towards the use of online shopping be investigated in an attempt to provide answers to its inhibitors and ensure that the country reaps into the numerous benefits online shopping opens to other developed nations.

Therefore, this chapter aims to examine the consumer behavior change towards using online shopping before and during Covid-19 pandemic. For this reason, a framework for consumers behavior changes towards using of online shopping in Nigeria is proposed. The proposed framework assists the researchers to ascertain the impact of COVID-19 pandemic on consumer behavior change towards the use of online shopping in Nigeria. Furthermore, this study utilized Structural Equation Modeling (SEM)-Partial least Square (PLS) to evaluate the COVID-19 pandemic related factors which affect behavior change of consumers towards the use of online shopping in Nigeria. Finally, this chapter proffers recommendations to online shopping ventures to ensure consumers' behavior changes towards the use of online shopping in Nigeria. The flow of this chapter is as follows: The first section introduces the chapters. The second section highlight the important concepts and existing literature. The thirds section focuses on methodology followed by analysis, results, and discussion. Finally, the chapter is wrapped up with concluding remarks and future directions.

LITERATURE REVIEW

Concept of Online Shopping

Online Shopping is a relationship of two words, "Online" and "Shopping". Beginning with what could be viewed as much more straightforward term, shopping is a term in which marketing implies looking at items from a shop and making payments. However, according to (Gabriel et al., 2016; y Monsuwé et al., 2004) online shopping is characterized as "the shopping conduct of buyers in an online store or site utilized for web based buying purposes." Online shopping is the movement or activity of purchasing items or goods over the Internet. It implies going on the internet, arriving on a merchant's site, choosing something, and organizing its conveyance. The consumer either pays for the item online with accredit or check card or upon conveyance. The term does not just incorporate purchasing things on the web yet additionally looking for them on the web. More researcher defined online shopping as a form of electronic commerce, which gives the consumers a privilege to directly purchase goods or services from a seller via the Internet with the use of electronic devices (Nwankwo et al., 2019).

Online shopping utilizes internet browser to straightforwardly permits buyers to purchase products or items from a merchant over the internet. An online shop summons the actual resemblance of buying items at a "bricks and mortar" store; the cycle is called Business-to-Customer (B2C) online shopping. A common online store empowers the client to peruse the company's scope of items and administrations. Online stores enable customers to utilize "search" highlights to discover explicit models, brands or things. Online customers must approach the Internet with a substantial strategy for payment to finish an exchange. The most famous online retailing organizations are Alibaba, Amazon.com, and eBay.

In online shopping, buyers discover a result of interest by visiting the site of the retailer legitimately or via looking among elective sellers utilizing a shopping web crawler. When a specific item has been found on the site of the dealer, most online retailers use shopping basket programming to permit the shopper for organizing and arranging various things and to alter amounts, similar as filling an actual shopping basket or bin in a regular store. A "checkout" measure follows in which payment and conveyance data is gathered, if important (Pappas, 2016).

Concept of Consumer Behavior

Consumer behavior refers to the actions of a consumer in the market environment and the underlying motives for those actions. According to (Kardes et al., 2011), Consumer behavior includes "all exercises concerned with the buying, utilizing and disposal of products and services, not devoid of the buyer's enthusiastic, mental and social responses that precede or follow these activities." The term, consumer can allude to a singular consumer, as organizational consumers, and the more explicitly, "an end client, and not necessarily a buyer, in the trade chain of a good or services." (Business dictionary.com, 2019). In addition, Kardes et al. (2011) states in their study that Consumer behavior is concerned about: (1) purchase activities which concern about the acquisition of items or services; how consumers gain items/services, and all the procedures paving the way to a purchase choice, including information search, products and services assessment and payment strategies, purchase experience inclusive. Analytical methods are very useful to track, classify, and predict purchase activities (Zhao & Keikhosrokiani, 2022). (2) Use or utilization activities which refers to asking the questions, who, where, when, and how the items are utilized and utilization experience inclusive. (3) Disposal activities indicate the way that consumer scar items and their packaging, which may likewise incorporate exchanging activities, for example, eBay and recycled markets. (4) Consumer behavior bothers around understanding how purchasing choices are made also how items or services are cons or experienced. Purchasers are dynamic leaders. They choose what they need to buy, regularly reliant on their discretionary cash flow or financial plan. They may change their inclinations identified with their spending plan and a scope of different variables." (Kardes et al., 2011; Minton & Khale, 2014).

Consumer Behavior and Online Shopping

Consumer behavior has become an imperative study for researchers in electronic commerce, because having an insight of online consumer behavior helps to retain customers (Azam & Qiang, 2014). Earlier, researchers have studied the consumer behavior in several fields such as information systems, management science, marketing, economic, and psychology, etc. (Azam & Qiang, 2014; Hansen, 2008; Keikhosrokiani, 2021; Keikhosrokiani et al., 2013; Khoi et al., 2018; Koufaris, 2002; Pavlou & Fygenson, 2006). Singh et al. (2017) studies consumer purchase behavior for Jordanian e-commerce platform and find out that effort expectancy, expectancy social influence, facilitating conditions, perceived trust are significant factors which affect consumer behavioral change towards using online shopping.

Accordingly, risk as well as trust are among significant components influencing individuals' behavior in online shopping. Consumers weighs the option to make a switch between electronic channels, knowing that they are impacted by the correlation with offline shopping, including development of security, budgetary and execution risk. However, consumers may believe by shopping online that they may be in a position to get more danger than persons shopping in stores. There are three elements that may influence an individuals' purchasing choice, at the top of the list is the fact that individuals cannot inspect whether the item fulfill their necessities and needs prior to acquiring them. Secondly, customers may worry about after-purchase services. Lastly, customers may perhaps be apprehensive that they can't completely comprehend the language utilized in e-commerce. In view of those variables' consumers, perceived risk is an essential reason that influences the online purchasing behavior (Pappas, 2016).

Online Shopping in the Federal Republic of Nigeria

Nigeria having more than one hundred and eighty-six million individuals pride itself as the biggest market in Africa. Obviously, it is Africa's biggest economy and the quickest developing economies on the planet amongst others. Earlier 2016, Nigeria was viewed as Africa's second biggest economy and its Gross DomesticiProducti (GDP) was $263 billion (Ogbuji & Udom, 2018). Report by World Bank and Euromonitor International noted that Nigeria's working class increased by 28% and its GDP which was reliant on buying power has expanded by 21.67% over the most recent four years. Presently, Nigeria is viewed as Africa's biggest economy.

Ecobank is said to be the first to dispatch a universally acknowledged Credit card (Ecobank MasterCard) in the year 2004. Different banks like Zenith, GTB, UBA, and so on trailed subsequently. This gave buyers in Nigeria the medium to purchase for items online from the abroad (Ogbuji & Udom, 2018). The moment of change came with the report of study of Master card Worldwide of June 11, 2012, which demonstrated that approximately 92% of the Nigerians who participated in the study showed an inspirational disposition towards utilization of online shopping. It likewise showed that 52% of Nigerians who had shopped online over the most recent three months preceding the review said they intend to keep on shopping on the web inside the following six months. With this report, this study is enticed to accept an enticingly wonderful establishment was laid for Online shopping in Nigeria (Ogbuji & Udom, 2018).

Online shopping in Nigeria by neighborhood stores may have been birthed with the activity by Fouani Nigeria Ltd, as a merchant of LG Electronic items in 2011. Nevertheless, on July 3, 2012, online store named Jumia was established, at first it went by the name, Kasuwa, a Hausa word synonymous with Market (Ogbuji & Udom, 2018). It later changed its name to Jumia till date. Konga.com, DealDey, and numerous others were additionally established. The online stores such as Jumia.com.ng, DealDey.com, Supermart.ng, Regalbuyer, Konga.com, Kaymu, Kara.com.ng, Mystore.com, Slot.ng, Parktelonline, Gidimall.com, Ojashop.com, OLX.com.ng, Jiji.ng, Gloo.com, Adibba.com, Coliseum/Taafoo.com, Yudah.com.ng, Fouani.com and Buyam.com.ng were recorded as the main 20ionline shops in Nigeria (Ogbuji & Udom, 2018). The online business in Nigeria has been developing quickly, bolstering Africa's development pace of 25.8% against the remainder of the world's development of 15.8%. Nigeria all alone is acknowledged with development pace at 25% yearly (Ogbuji & Udom, 2018).

With an infusion of $10 million market capital into Jumia (at that point Kasuwa), and 5 staff Jumiai (the principal online shop) is today working with more than 500 staff on its finance. Different shops were likewise dispatched and are working, and today the online utilization as per the then Minister of Finace Dr. Omobola Johnson "is worth about $12 billion, with a projection of $154 billion by 2025". There exist additional reports stating that more than 300,000 requests are made day by day, though there are more than 500 visits to each destinations of the online shops every day (Mutum et al., 2013). Jumia has been acknowledge as the main online shop in Nigeria, trailed by Konga and DealDey. Nigeria's online shopping has kept on seeing quick development and new territories are being opened and investigated (Ogbuji & Udom, 2018). Nigeria has put itself as the pioneer in online shopping in Africa with 66% (Ogbuji & Udom, 2018). It was extended that Nigeria's online shopping will hit $13 Billion by 2018.

Consumer Behavior and Online Banking in Nigeria

Technologies have expanded to include all aspects of industry, including financial institutions. For example, by creating a direct channel connecting bank customers to their services (Alsajjan & Dennis, 2010). Banks are using different types of Self-Service Technologies (SST) to increase profit and gain a competitive edge in the sector. The first SST type to be incorporated in banking is the Automated Teller Machine (ATM) and it inspired banks to aim at providing customers with banking requirements in a way that is convenient while at the same time reducing cost (Yadav et al., 2016). Mobile banking took center stage following the ATM Self-Service Technology in the online banking evolution, it availed bank clients the opportunity to utilize their telephones in interacting with the banks by the means of phone call in carrying out their financial transactions (Alalwan et al., 2015). Banks began exploiting the advantages of internet technology, which subsequently resulted in online banking, this enabled customers to remotely access their accounts and carry out their financial needs in an easy way on the World Wide Web (WWW) (Arenas Gaitán et al., 2015; Callaway & Jagani, 2015). Currently, in the evolution of online banking, mobile apps are being developed to further ease the process of carrying out financial activities by customers of various financial institutions. The mobile applications are being download into the customer's mobile devices and can be readily assessed without a prior visitation to an internet browser or the World Wide Web.

The Nigerian banking industry began to witness its revolution in year, 2003; it started with the Central Bank of Nigeria (CBN) introducing guideline of electronic banking. This left only 25 banks standing from a total of 89 which used to exist by the reformation of Nigerian banks. The remaining twenty-five banks, now recapitalized engaged in the utilization of Information Communication Technology for a more effective and efficient banking services delivered to customers (Akanbi et al., 2014). Information Communication Technology have formed the base for financial activities in Nigeria over the past few years. Customers' need and desire for efficient banking services brings a huge spring up in financial institution to embark on a radical transformation to their business, which prompted the adoption of electronic banking. Financial institutions began improving their service delivery platforms with websites, USSD codes and mobile apps, enabling customers to open a new bank account, apply for loans, check their account balances and pay for utilities such as airtime, light bill, satellite subscription and receive payments over the Internet (Oni & Ayo, 2010). Of the various forms of online shopping available to Nigerians, online banking is the most widely used as customers are now able to beat queues at the banks and the stress of making trips to purchase airtime or pay utility bills.

Surprisingly, regardless of the huge transformations witnessed in the Nigerian banking industry, most of the customers still prefer the traditional carrying of cash while avoiding taking advantage of online banking services. Despite online banking gaining prominence in Nigeria, customers' attitudes, behaviors and confidence in the system is yet to be adopted wholly. More than 50% of customers who have attempted the use of online banking services failed to become active users. Research have indicated that a host of limitations have hampered the acceptance of online banking in Nigeria, some of which include; inadequate telecommunications infrastructure, mass illiteracy, lack of security, unreliable electricity supply, lack of trust, fear of internet fraud and limited privacy (Agwu, 2012).

Impact of COVID-19 Pandemic on Consumer Behavior towards Online Shopping

The advent of COVID-19 has facilitated a huge shift towards a more digital world and triggered changes in online shopping behaviors that are probably going to have a long effect. With the lives of consumers overturned by COVID-19 and long-term trends quickened in the space of only weeks, there have been generous and enduring changes in the manner individuals live, work and shop (Sheth, 2020; Zhao & Keikhosrokiani, 2022).

According to a report by Numerator intelligence in the later week of July 2020, 88% of consumers in the United States said that their shopping habits had been affected by Coronavirus, up from 83% toward the finish of June. This ascent in sway goes with an ascent in cases, which was normal as more states opened organizations and diminished COVID-19 safety measures. They recommended that until the nation can restrict the spread of the infection, we will keep on observing raised degrees of consumer sway and repetitive examples of behavior (*COVID-19 Consistently Impacts Shopping Behavior of 9 in 10 Consumers*, 2021).

Aside from the lockup of retail shops, which declined for the 3rd month in a row, every COVID-19 period effect on shopping practices resurfaced in the month of August 2020. Purchasers encountering item deficiencies and those abstaining from eating out both rose almost 10% from late June. Online shopping rose altogether also, with one of two customers picking on the online in lieu of going to a store (*COVID-19 Consistently Impacts Shopping Behavior of 9 in 10 Consumers*, 2021).

Three-fourths of consumers surveyed by Numerator in the United States said they had set an internet-based conveyance (ship-to-home) request as of late, and 50% said they had put in an online request pick-up (click and-collect). 10% of the individuals who set an online ship-to-home request showed that it was their first in their lifetime or first time in the previous six months doing as such; 25% of click and-pick clients said the equivalent. While these numbers certainly will vary week-to-week, the general pattern is obvious: there is an enormous, continued move to online that doesn't have all the earmarks of being halting soon. Retailers must proceed to organize and put resources into these deliveries and click and-collect alternatives. The shopping behavior and habits developed by consumers with the arrival of the COVID-19 pandemic is most likely to remain with consumers following the exit of the coronavirus pandemic. Understanding the COVID-19 Effect on Online Shopping Behavior' opined that "the COVID-19 global pandemic will likely not be one of the defining events of i2020, and that it will leave impacts that last will last long." In a new consumer research, it stated that "habits formed during the COVID-19 crisis will last long after it, forever changing values, attitudes and behavior." (*COVID-19: How consumer behavior will be changed*, 2020). Buyers are as yet deciding to remain at home. Regardless of the easing of the lockdowns, and numerous organizations resuming, home keeps on being the center of all things. What consumers are purchasing and how they are shopping has changed significantly because of the pandemic, and these new behaviors are proceeding. The drastic ascent in the reception of online business and omnichannel services, which has been apparent since the beginning of Accenture's examination, sees no indication of subsiding. The most recent information proposes there will be a gigantic increment of 169% in internet-based shopping from new or low recurrence consumers, post pandemic. More so, by far most of consumers who have expanded their utilization of computerized and omnichannel administrations, for example, home delivery, curbside pickup or shopping by means of online social media hope to support these exercises into the future.

Review of Related Studies

Various related studies are reviewed in Table 1. All of the studies reviewed besides 'Factors Affecting Consumers' Internet Shopping Behavior During the COVID-19 Pandemic: Evidence From Bangladesh' by Neger and Uddin (2020) failed to evaluate factors responsible for the change in consumer behavior towards online shopping as an effect of the COVID-19 pandemic. The study by Neger and Uddin (2020) was very clinical in taking into consideration the diverse factors, which can encourage and inhibit consumer online shopping behavior. However, its respondents were mostly online shoppers in Bangladesh who have always shopped online prior to the advent of the COVID-19 pandemic and not necessarily new users of the online shopping in Bangladesh.

Theories on Technology Acceptance Models (TPB, TAM, and UTAUT)

Theory of Planned Behavior (TPB) was presented by Ice Azjen in 1985 and as of then it was referred to as social cognition model (SCM) (Ajzen, 1985). TPB and Technology Acceptance Model (TAM) can initially be accessed on Theory of Reasoned Action (TRA) which is a model for foreseeing and clarifying human conduct in various spaces (Ajzen & Fishbein, 1975). TPB integrates perceived behavioral control to the model where perceived social control is dictated by presence of opportunities to arrive at preferred results, abilities and assets. It is firmly connected to self-efficacy belief concept (Ajzen, 1991). The idea of self-efficacy is concerned about individuals' confidence in their capacity to deliver impacts. TPB shows attitude (AT), subjective Norm (SN), and perceived behavioral control (PBC) as immediate determinants of aims that will impact behavior. A focal point of the examination lies on the attitude (AT) as well as behavioral intention (BI) in TPB model. AT alludes to "how much the individual has a good or negative assessment of the behavior being referred to" (Ajzen, 1989). While BI alludes to "the subjective probability of one's commitment in any given behavior." The more grounded the behavior, the more certain is the execution of the behavior (Fishbein & Ajzen, 1977).

Table 1. Related studies of impact of COVID-19 Pandemic towards online shopping.

Research Name	Location	Research Objective	Target Population	Research Outcome
Factors Affecting Consumers' Internet Shopping Behavior During the COVID-19 Pandemic: Evidence From Bangladesh (Neger & Uddin, 2020).	Bangladesh.	The aim of the study was to investigate the factors affecting consumers' internet shopping behavior during the coronavirus disease (COVID-19) pandemic in Bangladesh.	230 Bangladeshi online consumers.	All other factors except price factor and security factor had a momentous and positive association with consumers' online shopping behavior during the coronavirus disease (COVID-19) pandemic in Bangladesh.
Buying Behavior Under Coronavirus Disease (COVID-19) Pandemic Situation: A Online Perspective Case in Bangladeshi Shoppers (Alam, 2020).	Bangladesh	To investigate the buying behavior in face of coronavirus disease (COVID-19) pandemic situation in case of online perspective in Bangladeshi shoppers.	One hundred and fifty-five Shoppers	The outputs showed that perceived risk of shoppers has negative impact on shopping decision, and consumer trust has a positive impact on shopping decision.
To buy or not buy food online: The impact of the COVID-19 epidemic on the adoption of ecommerce in China (Gao et al., 2020).	China	To examine the impact of the COVID-19 on consumers' online food purchase behavior in the short-term in China	820 respondents.	The findings indicated that persons in bigger cities are more likely to shop online after COVID-19 epidemic outbreak. The findings also, suggest that persons in large cities are less likely to be affected by the pandemic since the fewer constraints on the logistics system enable them to buy food (and other living items) online.
Examining the Influence of COVID 19 Pandemic in Changing Customers' Orientation towards EShopping (Hashem, 2020).	Jordan	To examine the change in customer behavior during COVID 19 pandemic towards e-shopping.	Five hundred (500) citizens in Jordan	Results of study demonstrated the COVID19 pandemic changed consumers behavior to conduct towards relying more upon internet shopping and e-payment strategies during COVID19 pandemic and the conditions of lockdown and isolation.

The technology acceptance model (TAM) proposed a hypothesis-based framework that models how users come to acknowledge and utilize a technology. The real framework use is the endpoint where individuals utilize the technology. Behavioral Intention is a factor that leads individuals to utilize the technology. The Behavioral Intention (BI) is impacted by the attitude (A) which is the overall impression of the technology. The model proposes that when users are given another technology, various components impact their choice about how and when they will utilize it, strikingly: Perceived Usefulness (PU) was characterized by Davis et al. (1989) as "how much an individual accepts that utilizing a specific system would improve their job efficiency". It implies whether somebody perceives that technology to be valuable for what they need to do. Perceived ease-of-use (PEOU) was characterized this as "how much an individual accepts that utilizing a specific system would be free from exertion" (Davis et al., 1989). If the technology is anything but difficult to utilize, at that point the barriers have been conquered. In the event that it is difficult to utilize, and the interface is confounded, nobody has an uplifting mentality towards it. Outer variables, for example, social impact is a significant factor to decide the attitude. At the point when all constructs of TAM are set up, individuals will have the disposition and expectation to utilize the technology. Notwithstanding, the observation may change contingent upon age and sex since every individual is extraordinary.

Unified theory of acceptance and use of technology (UTAUT) was founded by (Venkatesh et al., 2003) in an attempt to combine old TAM related studies. UTAUT is an integration of TAM, TRA, TPB, TAM-TPB, motivational model, innovation diffusion theory, and social cognitive theory. It is built for use in ICT related research. It aims to clarify user intention to use an information system (IS) and consequent usage behavior. The theory comprises four major constructs: performance expectancy, effort expectancy facilitating condition and social influence. These constructs are immediate deciders of usage behavior (Venkatesh et al., 2003). The focal point of this study is on performance expectancy (PE) as well as effort expectancy (EE) in UTAUT model. PE is "the extent an individual trust that utilizing a system will lead to efficient attainment of goals in job performance"; whereas EE is "how easy a system can be used, a friend user interface." (Keikhosrokiani, 2021; Keikhosrokiani, Mustaffa, Zakaria, & Baharudin, 2019).

RESEARCH METHODOLOGY

This section presents the preliminary study of consumer behavior intention to online shopping in Nigeria before Covid -19 pandemic and the methodology of this current study which contains the research design, the nature of the study, the model of the study, the method of data formation and collection, the questionnaire structure, the population of the study, area of the study and the method of data analysis as the hypothetical statements to be investigated in the study.

Flow of the Research Process

The flow of research process is shown in Figure 1. The first step of the research process of this study is the review of literatures related to the topic of concern, which includes reviews of previous studies, by other researchers as well as theories developed to assess the consumer's behavior change towards the use of online shopping and technology. The second step of the research process identifies the problem of the study that is the problems associated with the change in consumer behavior towards online shopping. Upon those problems the research question and objective of the study are developed. The broad objective and specific objectives of the study are constructed following the problem of the study and is stipulated as the third step of the methodology of the study. Furthermore, the fourth step in the research process presents the analysis of the preliminary study on finding consumers online shopping behavior before the Covid-19 pandemic. The fourth steps also present the method of data analysis as well as the statistical software utilized and finally the findings and results generated. Similarly, to the fourth step, the fifth step presents the analysis of the main study, which intends to determine consumer behavior change towards the use of online shopping during Covid-19 pandemic. The data generated shall be analyzed using Smart PLS statistical software. The obtained result and findings will be presented and summarized. The sixth step compares the findings of the fourth step against that of the fifth step upon which the finalized findings will be made and presented. The penultimate step of the research process interprets the findings of the study based on the comparison of the preliminary study and the main study. Finally, the last step presents a conclusion summed up from the findings and result of the study.

Figure 1. The flow of research process

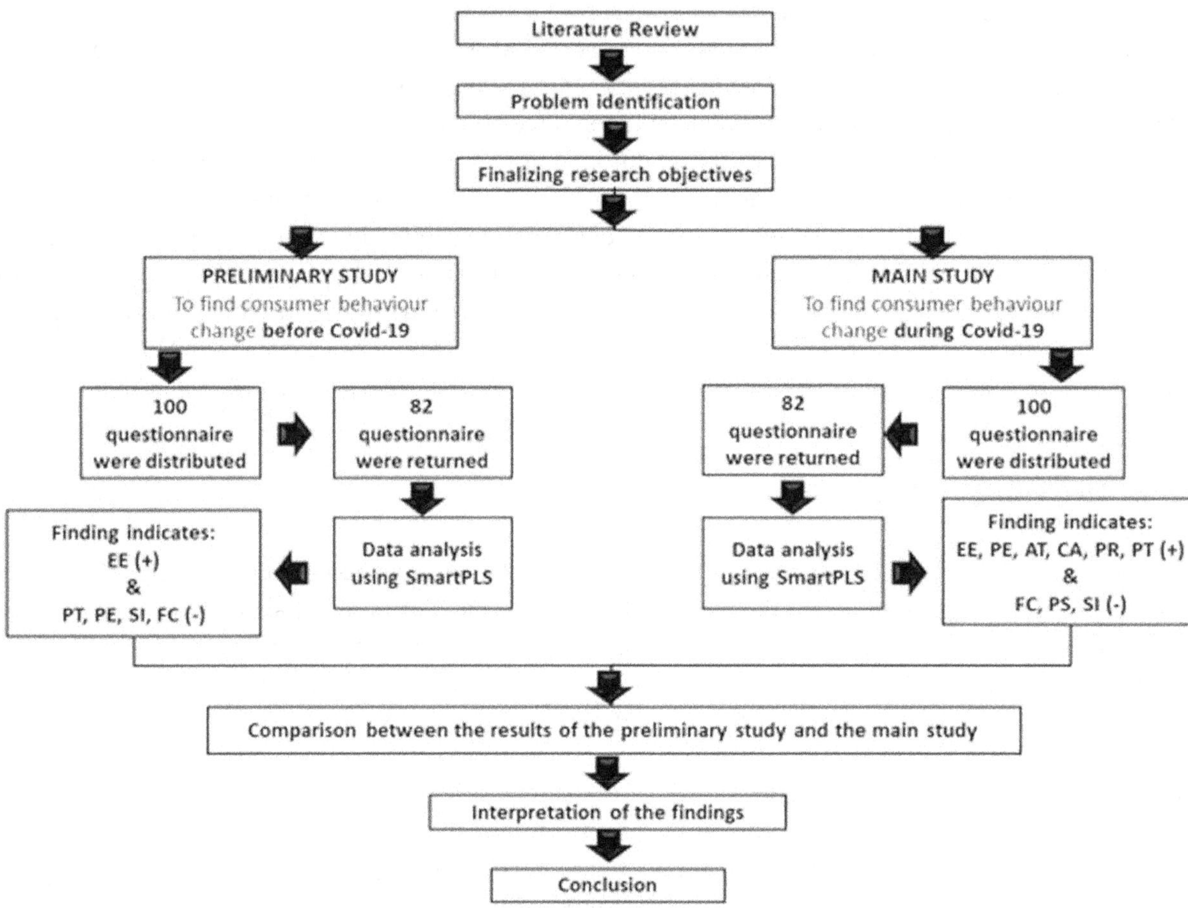

Preliminary Study

The preliminary study of this research was conducted before Covid-19 pandemic to determine "consumer behavior intention towards online shopping" using a quantitative research approach and a means of survey method. The researcher identified the problem of the study based on scholar's literature review with respect to consumer behavioral intention towards using online shopping. The study aimed at identifying the factors that influence behavioral intention to online shopping in Nigeria in order to understand the customers and help online business managements to know the area to work on for expansion of more online buyers in Nigeria. A research model was proposed which was adapted from The Unified Theory of Acceptance and use of Technology Model II (UTAUT II) and integrated with perceived trust because trust is very vital in online environment. As shown in Figure 2, the proposed research model for the preliminary study comprises five independents variable which are Effort Expectancy (EE), Performance Expectancy (PE), Social Influence (SI), Facilitating Condition (FC), and Perceived Trust (PT) and a dependent variable (Behavioral Intention (BI) to online shopping).

Figure 2. The research model for preliminary study

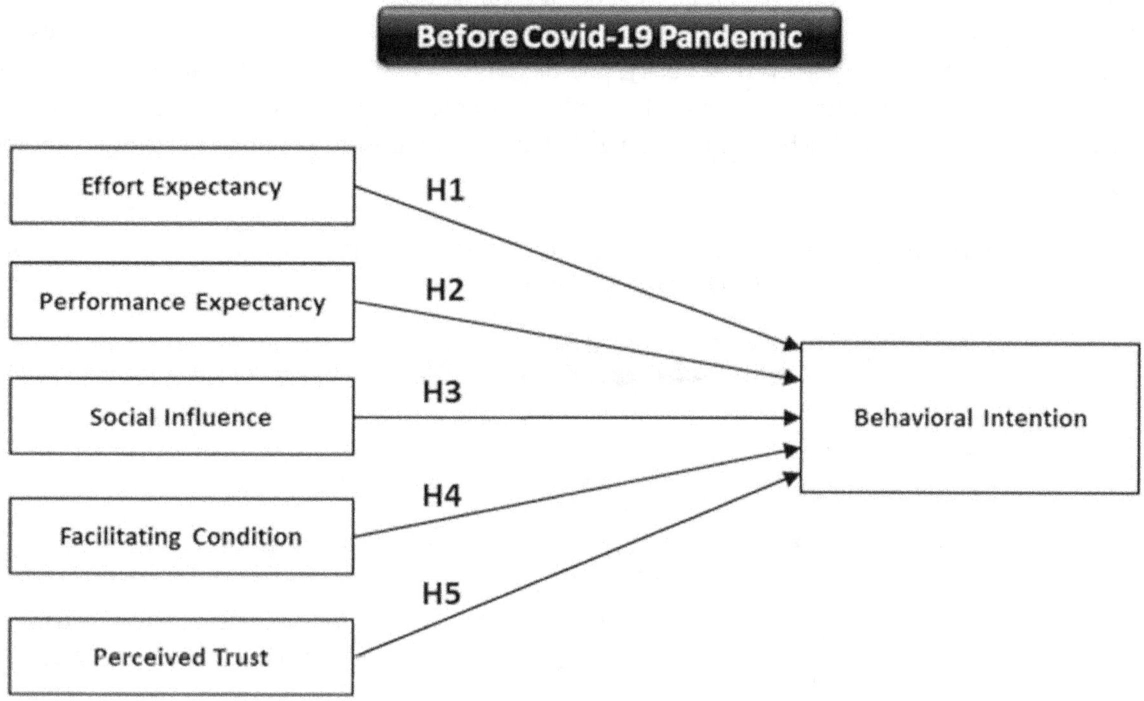

Research Design

The study employs a quantitative method using structured questionnaires, which consists of questions appeals to the objective of this study. Also, the original data from the respondents are collected, analyzed and are used in making a generalized representation of the entire population.

Nigeria was selected as the study location. Nigeria is formally the Federal Republic of Nigeria, is a sovereign nation in West Africa flanking Niger in the north, Chad in the upper east, Cameroon in the east, and Benin in the west. Its southern coast is on the Gulf of Guinea in the Atlantic Ocean. Nigeria is a government republic involving 36 states and the Federal Capital Territory, where the capital, Abuja, is found. Lagos is the most crowded city in the nation and the African mainland, just as one of the biggest metropolitan zones on the planet. Nigeria is Africa's most crowded and is the seventh most crowded nation on the planet, with an expected 206 million occupants starting late 2019. Nigeria has the third-biggest youth populace on the planet, after India and China, with almost a large portion of its populace younger than eighteen.

Proposed Research Model

The proposed research model for the main study is illustrated in Figure 3. The research model consists of ten constructs and nine hypotheses. This study adopts the research model implemented by Keikhosrokiani, Mustaffa, Zakaria and Baharudin (2019) in their study - User Behavioral Intention toward Using Mobile Healthcare System. Mugerwa et al. (2018) utilized the model in their study based on effort expectancy, performance expectancy, social influence and facilitating conditions as predictors of behavioral intentions to use ATMS with Fingerprint Authentication in Ugandan Banks.

This study proposes the integration of TPB, TAM, and UTAUT alongside four added variables: perceived risk, perceived trust, perceived security, and anxiety (COVID-19 anxiety) affecting behavioral change towards the use of online shopping. These other variables have been included because they have strong influences in determining behavioral change in humans towards the adoption of a new technology.

Figure 3. Proposed conceptual framework for predicting the behavior changes towards the use of online shopping in Nigeria as an impact of COVID-19 pandemic.

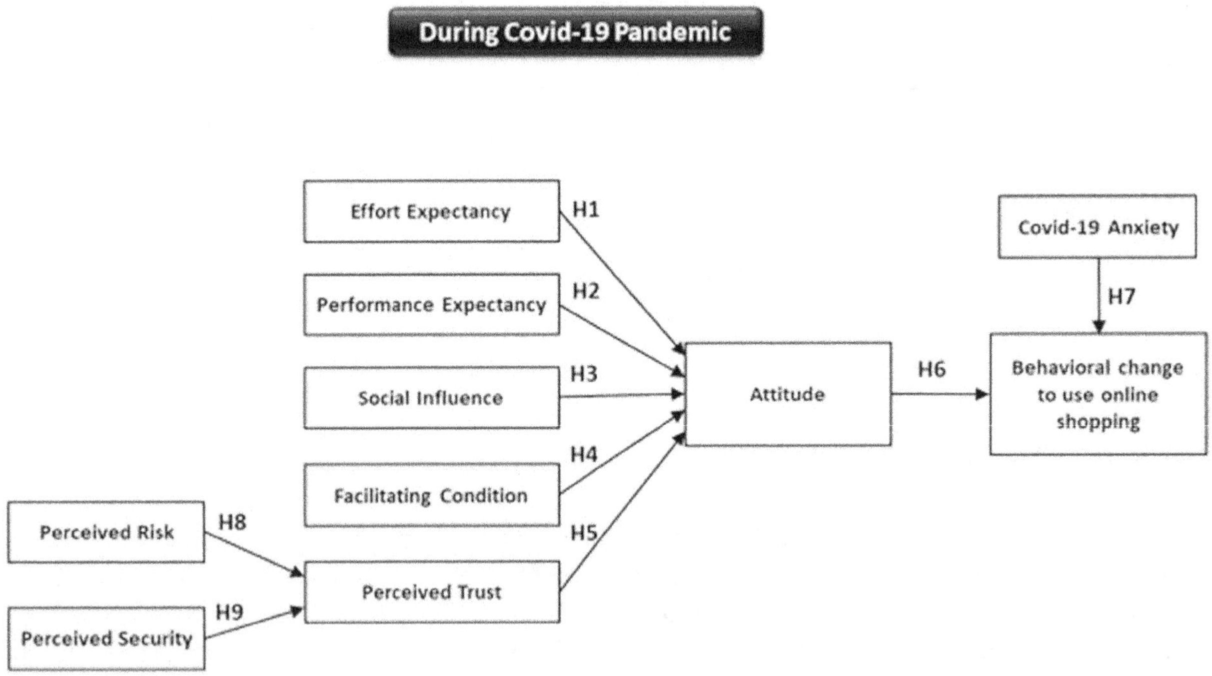

Research Variables

The conceptual model depicts nine independent variables (social influence, facilitating conditions, perceived risk, perceived trust, perceived security, effort expectancy, performance expectancy, and anxiety) which affect dependent variable which is behavioral change towards the use of online shopping. The definitions of the constructs for the proposed conceptual framework are listed in Table 2.

Table 2. Contextual definition of independent variables

No.	Independent Variables	Contextual Definitions
1	Facilitating conditions	Perceived propellers or barriers in the environment that determines a person's view of ease or difficulty of utilizing online shopping.
2	Performance Expectancy	Performance expectancy is a person's belief that the proposed online shopping will aid him or her to deliver duties to the organization efficiently.
3	Effort Expectancy	Effort expectancy is an individuals' belief that the proposed online shopping will be relatively easy for him or her to utilize
4	Social Influence	Social influence is a person's feeling of other people thoughts of him or her when he or she utilizes online shopping.
5	Anxiety	The extent to which a person's fear, hesitation and concern of being embarrassed to use online shopping
6	Attitude towards using online shopping	A someone's positive or negative emotion about using online shopping.
7	Perceived Trust	The height of confidence an individual believes in online shopping to perform satisfy his needs without suffering a loss.
8	Perceived Risk	The doubts a person has when purchasing items online, mostly those that are expensive
9	Perceived Security	The extent a person believes online shopping won.t be risky to conduct customer to customer ecommerce.

Research Model and Hypotheses Development

The research model and hypotheses adopted for this study for the purpose of ascertaining the behavior change towards the use of online shopping is reliant on the integration of the theories of Technology Acceptance Model (TPB, TAM, and UTAUT). Five other relevant and important system variables believed to play a vital role in influencing the behavior change of consumers were included to the proposed research model. Those five system variables include social influence, facilitating conditions, perceived risk, perceived trust, perceived security, effort expectancy, performance expectancy, and anxiety. Technology acceptance models and theories are considered suitable for this study because it have been applied in existing studies to understand and to predict users' behavior related to voting, dieting, family planning, donating blood, choice of transport mode women's occupational orientations, breast cancer test, women's occupational orientations and computer usage (Taherdoost, Masrom, et al., 2009; Taherdoost, Namayandeh, et al., 2009; Taherdoost et al., 2011). TAM ideals with outer variables influencing perceived ease of use and usefulness. Perceived ease of use and usefulness influence attitudes toward usability that shapes intention to use. Perceived usefulness has however direct impact on intention to use. It is also the fact that behavioral intention impacts the actual behavior. This model has been implemented by many researchers and their findings reported, agree to this relationship (Guritno & Siringoringo, 2013).

Dependent Variable

Behavior-Change Towards the Use Online Shopping

The Behavior-change towards the use online shopping means the consumers' willingness to use online shopping with respect to the effort expectancy, performance expectancy, social influence, facilitating conditions, perceived security and perceived trust of online shopping.

Independent Variables

The independent variables in this study are factors that will have either positive or negative impact on the Behavior change towards the use online shopping. These factors include effort expectancy, performance expectancy, social influence, facilitating conditions, anxiety, perceived security, perceived trust and attitude to use.

Effort Expectancy

Venkatesh et al. (2003) define effort expectancy as "the extent of easiness experienced while using any system." which means effort expectancy is the effort needed to use the system, if simple, hard, or complex. Effort expectancy is a very significant factor in influencing attitude to use. However, this could be the reason why most of the Nigerian companies that conduct their business online had fewer commercial activities taking place (Gabriel et al., 2016). Many studies show a positive impact of the effort expectancy on the consumer behavior towards online shopping. Effort expectancy refers to the view of ease in using online shopping in different studies (Dwivedi et al., 2019; Sánchez-Torres et al., 2017; Singh et al., 2017). We therefore hypothesize that:

H1: Effort expectancy of online shopping will have positive influence on behavior change towards the use of online shopping.

Performance Expectancy

Performance expectancy alludes the degree to which a user believes that using the system will help him/her to attain goals in job performance. This factor is synonymous to perceived usefulness from TAM and is accepted to be a fundamental attribute in influencing individual's attitude towards using any system. Several studies revealed the positive impacts of performance expectancy on behavioral change to online shopping (Dwivedi et al., 2019; Kaplan, 2018; Sánchez-Torres et al., 2017; Singh et al., 2017; Venkatesh et al., 2003). We therefore hypothesize that:

H2: Performance expectancy of online shopping will have positive influence on behavior change towards the use of online shopping.

Social Influence

Social influence can be defined as the extent to which a person perceives that important people (such as relatives, peers and subordinate) believe that he or she should use the new system (Venkatesh et al., 2003). According to Pietro et al. (2012), "word of mouth is determined by reference groups, and it includes friends and IT experts, which in turn play a big role in the adoption of communication technologies." Social influence can be either subjective norm, social factors, or image. For this study, subjective norm measured social influence. A person's subjective norm is ascertained by his or her perception that salient social referents think he/she should or should not perform a particular behavior (Fishbein et al., 1980). A person is motivated to comply with the referents even if he/she does not favor the behavior. The referents may be superiors like parents, employers or teachers or peers like friends, workmates or classmates. This study considered that most users tend to have their decision making reliant on others' suggestions, therefore social influence should play more important role. We therefore hypothesize that:

H3: Social influence will have a positive influence on behavior change towards the use of online shopping.

Facilitating Conditions

Facilitating conditions is "the degree to which an individual believes that an organizational and technical infrastructure exists to support use of the system" which is similar to perceived behavioral control of (TPB, DTPB). In online context, it is vital to have an assistance when finding it difficult to purchase through their portals. Facilitating conditions has proven to positively influenced consumer behavior in online context. Sánchez-Torres et al. (2017) used Facilitating conditions to study moderating effect of educational level and socioeconomic status on electronic purchase intention in Columbia and it shows that it positively influenced consumer behavioral change towards online context. Different studies also show a positive impact of facilitating condition towards online context (Kaplan, 2018; Singh et al., 2017; Venkatesh et al., 2003). We therefore hypothesize that:

H4: Facilitating conditions will have positive influence on behavior change towards the use of online shopping.

Perceived Trust

Moorman et al. (1993) defined trust as willingness to rely on an exchange partner in whom one has confidence. Trust is very vital in online business. When user knows that his or data is safe with the shopping portal, the shop can gain more confidence. Trust has a significant impact in e-commerce (Gabriel et al., 2016; Kim et al., 2012). Chiles and McMackin (1996) found that apparent trust could decrease the expense of non-financial exchanges, including the time and exertion needed by clients to pick the correct vender. Seen trust could likewise diminish the degree of danger in online exchanges (Kim et al., 2012). We therefore hypothesize that:

H5: Perceived trust will have positive influence on behavior change towards the use of online shopping.

Attitude Towards the Use of Online Shopping

Attitude is a mental develop, a psychological and passionate substance that inheres in, or describes an individual (Perloff et al., 2016). Attitude is unpredictable and it is a gained state through encounters. It is a person's inclined perspective with respect to a worth and it is encouraged through a responsive articulation towards oneself, an individual, spot, thing, or function (the attitude object) which thusly impacts the person's idea and activity. In this study, attitude to utilize online shopping alludes to somebody's positive or negative feeling about utilizing online shopping. We therefore hypothesize that:

H6: Consumer's attitude towards using online shopping will have positive influence on behavior change towards the use of online shopping

Anxiety (COVID-19 Anxiety)

Anxiety is the extent to which a person's fear, concern and hesitation of being embarrassed to use online shopping prevents him from using online shopping. We therefore hypothesize that:

H7: Anxiety (COVID-19 anxiety) will have positive influence on behavior change towards the use of online shopping

Perceived Risk

The consumer trust on product depicts the level of trust that a person has in another entity to perform expected activities without taking advantage. The perceived trust a consumer has in an entity which is determined by perceived risk and perceived security of using the product. In the case of this study, the perceived trust a consumer has towards the use of online shopping is based on the perceived risk and security of using online shopping. Perceived risk is the vulnerability a purchaser has when purchasing things, generally those that are especially costly, for instance, vehicles, houses, PCs. Each time a shopper thinks about purchasing an item, the individual has certain questions about the item, particularly if the item being referred to is exceptionally valued (Lake, 2019). We therefore hypothesize that:

H8: perceived risk will have positive influence on perceived trust towards the use of online shopping

Perceived Security

Perceived security is the extension individual believes a mobile device will be free of risk to conduct Consumer-to-Consumer (C2C) e-commerce. It is the "customers' perception of the degree of protection against these threats" (Yousafzai et al., 2003). Based on these features, we hypothesize that:

H9: perceived security will have positive influence on perceived trust towards the use of online shopping.

Questionnaire Development

Structured questionnaire is used as the research instrument for data collection in this study. The questionnaire is titled – A study of consumer behavior change towards using online shopping in Nigeria: The impact of the pandemic. The questionnaire is designed in two categories in English Language. The first category includes questions addressing the demographic and internet usage experience of the respondents while, the second category comprise questions that relates to the variables obtained from model of the study. The type of questions in the first category of the questionnaire is selective, while the second category questions require answers structured in a five-point Likert-type scale ranging from one, labeled "strongly disagree" to five, labeled "strongly agree".

Data Collection and Analysis

The questionnaire was distributed online to the respondents in Nigeria through various platforms like, Facebook, WhatsApp, email, telegram and any other social media platform at the disposal of the researcher. This is considered the most reliable form of data collection for the researcher since she is not physically present at area of the study – Nigeria.

The data obtained from respondents of this study in Nigeria is analyzed utilizing Structural Equation Modelling (SEM)- Partial Least Square (PLS) (Hair Jr et al., 2021) using Statistical Package for Social Science (SPSS) and SmartPLS. The statistical software analyzes the data by running test in accordance to determining the right hypothesis for the study.

Study Population and Sample Size

The study population involves male and female dwellers in Nigeria who are internet savvy and are able to access the internet, which according to Dwivedi et al. (2019) is 99.05 million people. However, the focus of this study is on Nigerians who are the main consumers of online shopping. Some statisticians believe that the minimum sample size to arrive at a meaningful result is between 30 and 500 (Shamsuddin et al., 2014). Thus, his research settles for a minimum sample size of 82 Nigerians that shop online.

Questionnaire Construction

Items for the questionnaire are adapted from the previous literatures and are measured based on the five-point Likert scale, ranging from strongly disagree to strongly agree (Table 3).

Table 3. Questionnaire construct and items

Constructs	Items	Source
Effort expectancy (EE)	- I think that buying through online portals is very easy and simple. - I think that buying online allows me to do it my way. - I think that buying online does not require a lot of learning.	(Sánchez-Torres et al., 2017)
Performance expectancy (PE)	- In general, I think online shopping is very useful - In general, I think online shopping gives me advantages over traditional means of purchase (physically in stores) - Overall, I think that buying on the Internet does not take a long time when I perform the operation	(Dwivedi et al., 2019)
Social influence (SI)	- People whose opinions that I value prefer that I buy via online channels. - The important people in my life, such as family and friends, recommend me to purchase online - People who influence my behavior think that I should buy over the internet	(Kaplan, 2018)
Facilitating conditions (FC)	- I have what I need (computer, Internet access, credit card, or other means of payment, etc.) to make an online purchase. - I have the knowledge to perform the entire buying process online (Entering the web, browsing, shopping, and paying online) - I have assistance or support on the websites where I buy,	(Sánchez-Torres et al., 2017)
Perceived trust (PT)	- Online shopping stores have integrity - Online shopping stores are reliable - Online shopping stores are trustworthy	(Escobar-Rodríguez & Bonsón-Fernández, 2017; Lim, 2014)
Perceived risk	- I felt the risk associated with buying from online portals is high. - I'm worried that the account number of my credit card will be at risk when buying in online platforms - I don't think it's safe to buy in online platforms	(Ariff et al., 2014)
Perceived Security (PS)	- I felt secure in providing personal information when purchasing in online portals. - Online portals has adequate security features. - I'm confident that online websites will protect my credit card information.	(Neama et al., 2016)
Attitude (AT)	- I like online shopping. - I think online shopping is interesting. - I think online shopping is pleasant. - I think online services is fun	(Neama et al., 2016)
Covid-19 Anxiety (CA)	- I'm anxious to use online shopping as I am worried about covid-19. - I'm afraid to buy a wrong item online during covid-19. - I'm scared to receive a fake item due to economic crisis during covid-19 lockdown. - I have avoided online shopping during covid-19 pandemic.	
Behavior Change (BC)	- Covid-19 pandemic changed my behavior towards using online shopping. - Covid-19 pandemic lockdown increased my frequency of buying online. - I think online shopping is going to replace my traditional offline shopping after this lockdown. - I think online platforms is playing a vital role during the lockdown period.	(Li et al., 2020)

ANALYSIS AND RESULTS

Introduction

This section presents the data analysis and explains the results and findings. The hypotheses stated in the previous section are tested and their individual validation are stated. The process of Data preparation and the demographics of the respondents are also explained and discussed in this section. The remaining sub-sections shows the analyses of the various questionnaire items using SmartPLS 3.0 Software which explains the measurement model including the convergent and discriminant validity.

Analysis and Result of Preliminary Study (before COVID-19 Pandemic)

Data was collected using Google forms online from 82 Nigerian respondents. Table 4 shows that the preliminary study consists of 55 females (66.3%) and 27 males (33.7%). The majority of the respondents are aged between 31-35 years old (40.2%) while the least are between 41years old and above (7.3%). For the educational level, a total of 35 (42.2%) participants finished graduate's degree, 33 (39.8%) postgraduates' degree, 9 (10.8%) college diploma and 6 (7.2%) high. More so, most of the respondents (68.7%) have experience of using internet between 6 years and above. However, the large number of respondents (51.3%) has online shopping experience of more than 10 times. Lastly approximately 56% of the respondents reported that they have frequently used online shopping for one month and above.

Table 4. Preliminary study demographic data

Item	Option	Frequency	Percent (%)
Gender	Male	27	33.7%
	Female	55	66.3%
Age	16-25	14	17.1%
	26-30	24	29.3%
	31-35	32	40.2%
	36-40	7	8.5%
	41 and above	5	7.3%
Education Level	High School	6	7.2
	College Diploma	9	10.8
	Graduate Degree	35	42.2
	Post Graduate Degree	33	39.8
Level of Internet Experience	Below One Year	6	7.2
	One to Three Years	7	8.4
	Four to Six Years	12	15.7
	Six Years and Above	57	68.7
Frequency of online shopping	One to five times	23	27.2%
	Six to ten times	15	17.3%
	10 times and above	44	53.1%

Measurement Model of Preliminary Study

The measurement model for this study consists of 18 items (indicators) and a total of six (6) constructs. The reflective measurement items were evaluated by assessing the construct validity test that comprises of convergent and discriminant validities after which the hypotheses are tested. The Partial Least Squares (PLS) is considered suitable in this study for analyzing the measurement model.

Convergent Validity of Preliminary Study

The reliability of the individual item was assessed by examining the loading of items on their respective constructs that are illustrated in Table 5. The result indicates that the entire loading of the items revealed values above 0.5 that suggested a proper item reliability (Keikhosrokiani, Mustaffa, Zakaria, & Baharudin, 2019). Furthermore, the reliability of the items was evaluated using Cronbach's alpha and the entire construct revealed a Cronbach alpha value greater than 0.06 which implies a good level of reliability, it also indicates that a significant variance was exchanged between each item and the construct. The findings of the convergent validity in Table 5 further reveals that the composite reliability of the entire constructs is more than 0.6. Finally, the entire AVE values are all above 0.05. This result affirms the AVE variables suitable enough and very much acceptable (Keikhosrokiani, Mustaffa, Zakaria, & Baharudin, 2019).

Table 5. Assessment of convergent validity of preliminary study

Constructs	Items	Item Loading	Composite Reliability	AVE	Cronbach'α
EE	EE1	0.873	0.899	0.747	0.832
	EE2	0.862			
	EE3	0.858			
PE	PE1	0.875	0.914	0.779	0.858
	PE2	0.889			
	PE3	0.883			
SI	SI1	0.871	0.874	0.699	0.786
	SI2	0.811			
	SI3	0.825			
FC	FC1	0.892	0.901	0.753	0.835
	FC2	0.925			
	FC3	0.779			
PT	PT1	0.619	0.805	0.584	0.636
	PT2	0.890			
	PT3	0.759			
BI	BI1	0.814	0.870	0.691	0.777
	BI2	0.868			
	BI3	0.812			

Discriminant Validity of Preliminary Study

As opposed to convergent validity, discriminant validity tests whether concepts or measurements that are not supposed to be related are actually unrelated. Applying Fornell and Larcker Criterion (Ab Hamid et al., 2017), all the diagonal values should be greater than off diagonal values, the diagonal value should be more than the correlations between it and all other constructs. The results in Table 6 meets those conditions and illustrate a high degree of discriminant validity.

Table 6. Assessment of discriminant validity of preliminary study

	BI	EE	FC	PT	PE	SI
BI	**0.831**					
EE	0.775	**0.864**				
FC	0.665	0.665	**0.868**			
PT	0.618	0.568	0.532	**0.764**		
PE	0.721	0.811	0.683	0.686	**0.883**	
SI	0.521	0.475	0.557	0.531	0.619	**0.836**

Note: The bold-italic numbers in the diagonal row are square roots of AVE

Statistical Analysis and Hypothesis Testing of Preliminary Study

In order to examine the causal relationships among the constructs, a structural model was built. In order to evaluate the structural model, two steps are required. The first is to estimate standardized path coefficients and their statistical significance for testing the hypotheses. However, PLS does not support a significance test or confidence interval estimation as it fails to provide for it. Alternatively, Complete Bootstrapping analysis is utilized in estimating the path coefficients, statistical significance, and relevant parameters, such as means, standard errors, item loadings, and item weights.

The second step is obtaining the coefficient of determination (R-Squared) for endogenous variables in a bid to assess the predictive strength of the structural model. The R-squared value for the endogenous variables on behavioral intention to use online shopping before Covid-19 pandemic is 0.753 and it affirms the quality of the model as fit (Figure 4). Figure 4 illustrates the results of the preliminary study hypotheses testing.

The results and implications for the individual hypotheses are shown in Table 7 and explained as follows:

H1: Effort expectancy (EE) (β =2.996, $p < 0.05$) poses significant influence on behavioral intention. The alternative hypothesis is accepted and affirms that effort expectancy positively influences behavioral intention towards online shopping.

H2: Performance Expectancy (PE) (β =1.315, $p > 0.05$) indicates a non-significant influence on behavioral intention. The null hypothesis is therefore accepted which states that performance expectancy does not have a significant influence on behavioral intention towards online shopping.

H3: Social Influence (SI) ($\beta = 0.564$, $p > 0.05$) indicates a non-significant influence on behavioral intention. The null hypothesis is therefore accepted which states that social influence does not have a significant influence on behavioral intention towards online shopping.

H4: Facilitating Conditions (FC) ($\beta = 0.804$, $p > 0.05$) indicates a non-significant influence on behavioral intention. The null hypothesis is therefore accepted which states Facilitating conditions does not have a significant influence on behavioral intention towards online shopping.

H5: Perceived Trust (PT) ($\beta = 1.661$, $p > 0.05$) indicates a non-significant influence on behavioral Intention. The null hypothesis is therefore accepted which states that perceived trust does not have a significant influence on behavioral intention towards online shopping.

H6: The coefficient of determination (R2) is used to determine the joint influence of the entire independent variables (Effort expectancy, performance expectancy, social influence, facilitating condition and perceived trust) on behavioral intention towards online shopping. The coefficient of determination (R^2) examines the combined effect of the independent variables on the dependent variable (Keikhosrokiani, Mustaffa, Zakaria, & Baharudin, 2019). In measuring the coefficient of determination, the guidelines from Chin (1998) are being utilized where 0.19, 0.33 and 0.67 signify weak, moderate and strong effect respectively. Based on the data analysis results, it was seen that the independent variables (Effort expectancy, performance expectancy, social influence, facilitating condition and perceived trust) ($\beta = 0.753$, $p < 0.05$) has a strong significant influence on behavioral intention towards online shopping. The alternative hypothesis is therefore accepted.

*Figure 4. Results of preliminary study structural model. Value on path: standardized coefficients (β), R2: Coefficient of determination, **p<0.01, *p<0.05*

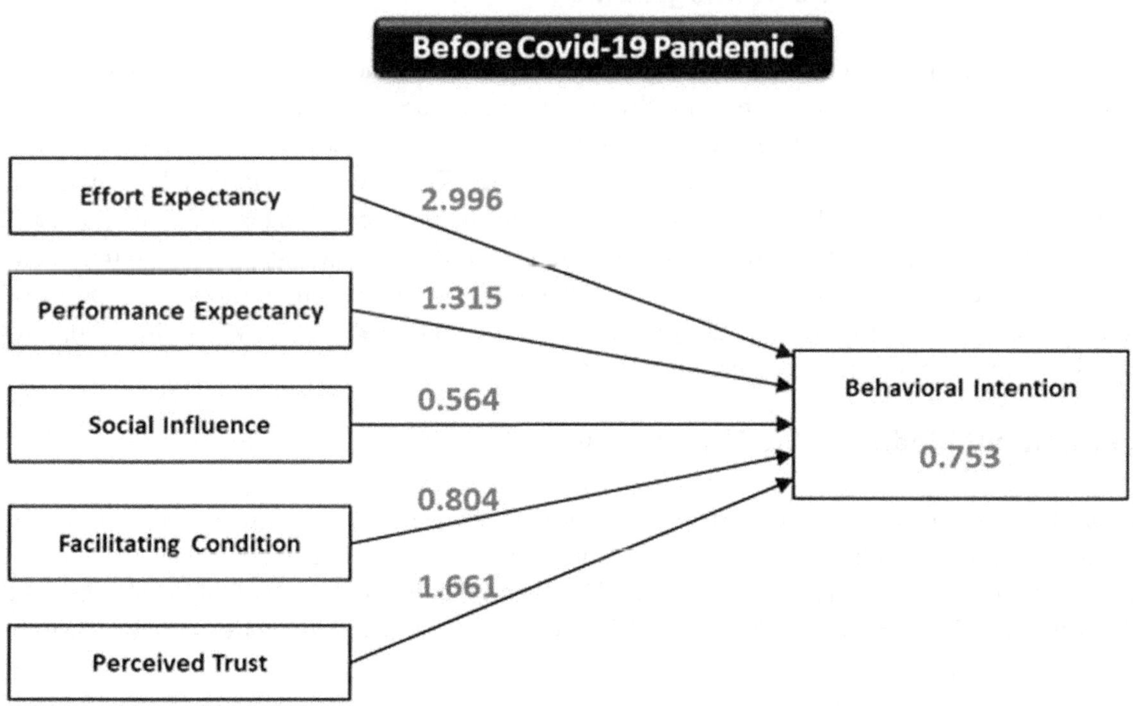

Table 7. Results of preliminary study hypotheses testing

Path	Beta	Standard Error (SE)	T-value	P-value
EE ® BI	2.996	0.132	2.996	0.003
PE ® BI	1.315	1.315	1.315	0.189
SI ® BI	0.564	0.126	0.564	0.573
FC ® BI	0.804	0.116	0.804	0.421
PT ® BI	1.661	0.125	1.668	0.097

Data Preparation and Pre-Processing of the Main Study (during COVID-19 Pandemic)

The questionnaire for the study was developed using google form. A link was generated and distributed to respondents through social media platforms, majorly WhatsApp, Facebook etc. The questionnaire was distributed to a total of 200 respondents in the area of the study, however, only 100 of the questionnaires were properly and accurately filled. The data collection phase of this lasted a period of 14 days.

After data collection, a few misrepresentations and omission were noted in the data, thus, we reduced the number of acceptable questionnaires to 82. The demographic responses as well as that of the other variables were inspected thoroughly in ensuring no errors or missing values occurred. With the completion of the inspection, the data was converted to comma delimited version (CSV) and then analyzed using Smart-PLS software.

Analysis of Respondents' Demographics

This section represents the descriptive analysis of respondents' demographics. In this study, basic descriptive analysis with frequency table is utilized to present a demographic profile of respondents. A total of six (6) questions were utilized in obtaining the demographic details of the respondent. Table 8 illustrates the entire results of the respondents' demographics. The result presents that the majority of the respondents are females (68.3%). Most of the respondents are between the ages of 26 and 30 years and possess a master's degree qualification. A greater number of the respondents have utilized the internet for a period of seven years and above. In addition, the total number of online shopping experience for most of the respondents is more than 12 times. Lastly, the total usage frequency of online shopping for a majority of the respondents is one month and above.

Measurement Model for the Main Study

The measurement model comprises thirty-three (33) items and ten (10) constructs. The reflective measurement items were evaluated by assessing the construct validity test which comprises, the convergent validity using the Average Variance Extracted (AVE); and the discriminant validity using the Fornell-Lacker criterion. The Partial Least Squares (PLS) is considered suitable for analyzing the measurement model in this study.

Table 8. Demographic data of main study

Items	Options	Frequency	Percent (%)
Gender	Male	26	31.7%
	Female	56	68.3%
Age	16-25	15	18.3%
	26-30	48	58.5%
	31-35	15	18.3%
	36-40	4	4.9%
	41 and above	0	0.0%
Education Level	High School	5	6.1%
	College Diploma	22	26.8%
	Master's degree	37	45.1%
	PhD	10	12.2%
	Professional Degree	8	9.8%
Level of Internet Experience	Less than One Year	1	1.2%
	One to Three Years	4	4.9%
	Three to Five Years	7	8.5%
	Five to Seven Years	11	13.4%
	Seven years and above	59	72.0%
Total Number of online shopping Experience	One times only	11	13.4%
	Two to Five times	14	17.1%
	Five to Nine times	10	12.2%
	Nine to Twelve times	2	2.4%
	More than 12 times	45	54.9%
Total Usage frequency of online shopping	Everyday	2	2.4%
	Less than one week	31	37.8%
	Two to Three weeks	18	22.0%
	Three to Four weeks	6	7.3%
	One month and above	25	30.5%

Convergent Validity

Convergent validity refers to the degree to which two measures of constructs that theoretically are related. Convergent validity of a construct is assessed by few criteria including:

1. The entire items loading in a construct must be above 0.5 (Keikhosrokiani, Mustaffa, Zakaria, & Baharudin, 2019) which suggests item reliability while the Cronbach's alpha values must exceed 0.6 for the construct reliability. The items loading values must be greater than 0.5 in order to indicate that a significant variance was exchanged between each item and the construct.
2. Composite reliability (CR) for a construct should exceed 0.6 and Cronbach's alpha coefficient or composite reliability coefficient can be utilized in its interpretation (Bagozzi & Yi, 1988).

3. The third vital factor in assessing the convergent validity is the Average Variance Extracted (AVE). The value of the Average Variance Extracted for a construct should be greater than 0.5 (Bagozzi & Yi, 1988).

The reliability of the individual items was assessed by examining the items loading of the individual items on their respective constructs. As show in Table 9, some of the items loading revealed values above 0.5 while some others indicated values below 0.5, they include SI1(0.439), SI3(0.330), PS1(0.209), PR3(-0.026) CA2(-0.336), CA4(-0.315), BC1(0.031), BC2(0.056), BC4(0.113). It is recommended that these items be removed from the model.

The reliability of the constructs was evaluated using Cronbach's alpha and the entire construct revealed a Cronbach alpha value greater than 0.6 except Social Influence (SI), Facilitating Conditions (FC), Perceived Risk (PR) and Behavior Change (BC), which indicated Cronbach alpha values of 0.482, 0.456, 0.295 and 0.395 respectively. This result implies a not very good level of reliability; it also indicates that a significant variance was exchanged between each item and the construct except for the constructs with Cronbach alpha values less than 0.6.

All of the evaluated constructs had their composite reliability higher than 0.6 except perceived Risk (PR), Perceived Security (PS) and Behavior Change (BC) which had composite reliability values of (0.512), (0.563) and (0.299) respectively (Table 9).

The convergent validity of the constructs was evaluated using the Average Variance Extracted, after removing SI1, SI3, PS1, PR3 CA2, CA4, BC1, BC2 and BC4 from the model. Then the model was recalculated and AVE for Social Influence (SI) changed from 0.414 to 1.000, AVE for perceived Security (PS) changed from 0.347 to 0.804, AVE for Perceived Risk (PR) changed from 0.363 to 0.560, AVE for Covid-19 Anxiety (CA) changed from 0.389 to 0.687 and the AVE for Behavior Change (BC) changed from 0.250 to 1.000. All the constructs in the model were studied and had their AVE higher than 0.5.

Discriminant Validity

As opposed to convergent validity, discriminant validity tests whether concepts or measurements that are not supposed to be related are unrelated. Applying Fornell and Larcker Criterion, all the diagonal values should be greater than off diagonal values, the diagonal value should be more than the correlations between it and all other constructs. The results in Table 10 meets those conditions and illustrates a high degree of discriminant validity.

Statistical Analysis and Hypothesis Testing for the Main Study

In order to examine the causal relationships among the constructs, a structural model was built. Two steps are required to evaluate the structural model. The first step is the estimation of standardized path coefficients and their statistical significance for testing the hypotheses. However, PLS does not support a significance test or confidence interval estimation as it fails to provide for it. Alternatively, Complete Bootstrapping analysis is utilized in estimating the path coefficients, statistical significance, and relevant parameters, such as means, standard errors, item loadings, and item weights. The second step is obtaining the coefficient of determination (R-Squared) for endogenous variables in a bid to assess the predictive strength of the structural model. Figure 5 illustrates the results of hypotheses testing.

Table 9. Assessment of reliability of items, constructs and convergent validity

Constructs	Items	Item Loading	Composite Reliability	AVE	Cronbach'α
EE	EE1	0.746	0.840	0.636	0.717
	EE2	0.848			
	EE3	0.796			
PE	PE1	0.784	0.879	0.708	0.795
	PE2	0.875			
	PE3	0.863			
SI	SI1	0.439	0.632	0.414	0.482
	SI2	0.969			
	SI3	0.330			
FC	FC1	0.608	0.722	0.470	0.456
	FC2	0.822			
	FC3	0.604			
PT	PT1	0.781	0.889	0.728	0.816
	PT2	0.925			
	PT3	0.848			
PR	PR1	0.878	0.512	0.363	0.295
	PR2	0.562			
	PR3	-0.026			
PS	PS1	0.209	0.563	0.347	0.885
	PS2	0.846			
	PS3	0.532			
CA	CA1	-0.902	0.680	0.389	0.642
	CA2	-0.336			
	CA3	-0.728			
	CA4	-0.315			
AT	AT1	0.778	0.927	0.762	0.895
	AT2	0.912			
	AT3	0.909			
	AT4	0.886			
BC	BC1	-0.031	0.299	0.250	0.395
	BC2	0.056			
	BC3	0.993			
	BC4	0.113			

The results and implications for the individual hypotheses are added in Table 11. Based on the path analysis, six hypotheses are significant whereas the other three are non-significant.

Table 10. Assessment of discriminant validity of main study

	AT	BC	CA	EE	FC	PR	PS	PT	SI	PE
AT	**0.873**									
BC	0.558	**1.000**								
CA	0.220	0.319	**0.829**							
EE	0.602	0.627	0.209	**0.798**						
FC	0.331	0.187	0.066	0.191	**0.686**					
PR	-0.023	-0.106	0.248	-0.045	0.049	**0.748**				
PS	0.327	0.450	0.111	0.043	0.157	-0.053	**0.897**			
PT	0.154	-0.023	-0.216	-0.066	0.000	-0.233	-0.106	**0.855**		
SI	0.315	0.075	-0.021	0.229	0.363	0.009	0.176	0.035	**1.000**	
PE	0.597	0.587	0.210	0.653	0.403	0.082	0.608	-0.169	0.329	**0.841**

Note: The bold-italic numbers in the diagonal row are square roots of AVE

Table 11. The results of hypotheses testing for the main study

Path	Beta	Standard Error (SE)	T-value	P-value	Result
EE → AT	0.054	0.014	3.845	0.005	Significant
PE → AT	0.036	0.013	2.743	0.006	Significant
SI → AT	0.086	0.088	0.978	0.329	Non-significant
FC → AT	0.011	0.011	1.009	0.313	Non-significant
PT → AT	0.026	0.009	2.844	0.005	Significant
CA→BC	0.022	0.011	1.978	0.048	Significant
AT→BC	0.057	0.011	5.208	0.000	Significant
PS→PT	0.013	0.019	0.706	0.481	Non-significant
PR→PT	0.027	0.012	2.247	0.025	Significant

The results and implications for the individual hypotheses are as follows:

H1: Effort expectancy (EE) (β =0.054, $p < 0.05$) poses significant influence on attitude towards behavioral change. The alternative hypothesis is accepted and affirms that effort expectancy to use online shopping will have positive influence on behavioral change towards the use online shopping during covid-19 pandemic.

H2: Performance Expectancy (PE) (β =0.036, $p < 0.05$) indicates a significant influence on attitude towards behavioral change. The alternative hypothesis is therefore accepted which states that performance expectancy to use online shopping will have positive influence on behavioral change towards the use of online shopping during covid-19 pandemic.

H3: Social Influence (SI) ($\beta = 0.086$, $p > 0.05$) indicates a non-significant influence on attitude towards behavioral change. The null hypothesis is therefore accepted which states that social influence to use online shopping will not have positive influence on behavioral change towards the use of online shopping during covid-19 pandemic.

H4: Facilitating Conditions (FC) (β = 0.011, p > 0.05) indicates a non-significant influence on attitude towards behavioral change. The null hypothesis is therefore accepted which states that facilitating conditions to use online shopping will not have positive influence on behavioral change towards the use of online shopping during Covid-19 pandemic.

H5: Perceived Trust (PT) (β = 0.026, p < 0.05) indicates a significant influence on attitude towards behavioral change. The alternative hypothesis is therefore accepted which implies that perceived trust to use online shopping will have a positive influence on behavioral change towards the use of online shopping during covid-19 pandemic.

H6: Attitude towards the use of online shopping (AT) (β = 0.057, p < 0.05) indicates a significant influence on behavioral change. The alternative hypothesis is therefore accepted which implies that attitude towards online shopping will have positive influence on behavioral change towards the use of online shopping during covid-19 pandemic.

H7: Covid-19 Anxiety (CA) (β = 0.022, p < 0.05) indicates a significant influence behavioral change. The alternative hypothesis is therefore accepted which implies that Covid-19 Anxiety to use online shopping will have a positive influence on behavioral change towards the use of online shopping during covid-19 pandemic.

H8: Perceived Risk (PR) (β = 0.027, p < 0.05) indicates a significant influence Perceived Trust. The alternative hypothesis is therefore accepted which implies that perceived risk will have positive influence on perceived trust towards the use of online shopping during covid-19 pandemic.

H9: Perceived Security (PS) (β = 0.013, p > 0.05) indicates a non-significant influence of perceived Trust. The null hypothesis is therefore accepted which implies that Perceived risk will not have positive influence on perceived trust towards the use of online shopping during covid-19 pandemic.

*Figure 5. Results of the structural model for the main study. value on path: standardized coefficients (β), R2: Coefficient of determination, **p<0.01, *p<0.05*

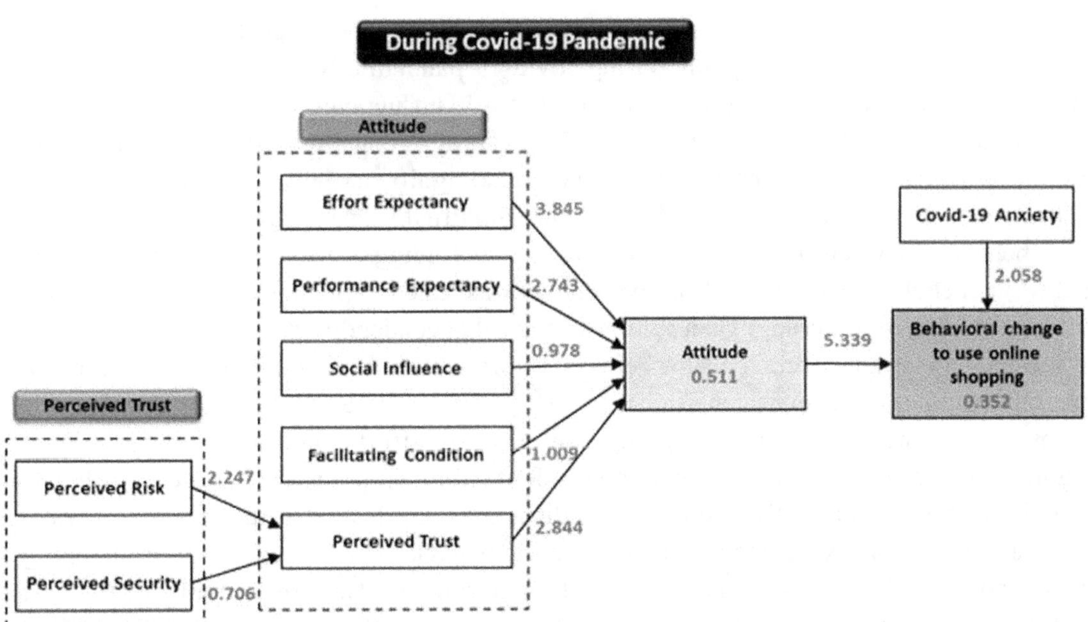

The Coefficient of Determination (R^2)

The coefficient of determination (R^2) is utilized in explaining the joint influence of the independent variables on the dependent variable (Hair Jr et al., 2021; Hair Jr et al., 2014). The predictive strength of the coefficient of determination are measured following the guidelines of (Chin, 1998) where 0.068, 0.35 and 0.51 signify weak, moderate and nearly strong effect respectively. Based on the data analyzed, it was seen that the independent variable (effort expectancy, performance expectancy, social influence, facilitating conditions and perceived trust) explained for 51% (0.511) in attitude towards the use of online shopping by the respondents, which is a moderate effect or nearly strong. Similarly, the independent variables; perceived risk and perceived security explained for 6.7% (0.068) in perceived trust on behavior change to use online shopping, which is a weak effect. In addition, attitude towards the use of online shopping and covid-19 anxiety explained for 35% (0.352) in behavior change, which is a moderate effect. Table 12 summarizes the coefficient of determination of the dependent constructs.

Table 12. R^2 values for the dependent constructs of the main study

	R2	Effect
EE, PE, SI, FC, PT®AT	51% (0.511)	Moderate/nearly strong
PS, PR®PT	6.7% (0.068)	Weak
CA, AT®BC	35% (0.352)	Moderate

DISCUSSION

H1: EE → BC

The first hypothesis tested was to determine the influence of effort expectancy on attitude towards behavior change to use online shopping during covid-19 pandemic Nigeria. Based on the findings of the path analysis, effort expectancy is significant towards influencing behavior change to use online shopping during covid-19 pandemic in Nigeria. This finding is consistent with the study conducted by Hungilo and Setyohadi (2020) where effort expectancy had significance influence on behavioral intention to purchase online. This is also supported in utilizing modified UTAUT to understand students' online shopping behavior in Malaysia (Hassan et al., 2015). This finding is also in line with the findings from Pascual-Miguel et al. (2015) where effort expectancy was tested to predict the influence of gender and product type on online purchasing. Their results revealed that gender differences, not considering product type effect are significant in relationships between effort expectancy and purchase intention. However, in some other studies effort expectancies have revealed no significance in driving behavior change or intentions towards the use of online shopping. For example, effort expectancy was reported to have a non-significant influence on behavior intention to adopt online shopping (Tarhini et al., 2018). Contrary to the study by Tarhini et al. (2018), this study indicated a significance influence of effort expectancy, which means that, effort expectancy contributes to the behavior change to use online shopping during covid-19 pandemic. The results of this study are different from the results by Tarhini et al. (2018) because of the different environmental context or circumstance which is the covid-19 pandemic. This study is concerned with the behavior change to use online shopping during covid-19 pandemic. The findings of effort expectancy can be justified to have a positive influence on behavior change to use online shopping during covid-19. Due to consumers limited movements, choice and means of purchasing items had to settle for the available since the preferred shopping method of most consumers which is the traditional store or market visit wasn't available as a result of the covid-19 lockdown and preventive measures implemented by the government. Consumers have had to settle for online shopping and subsequently acquainting themselves with the utilization methods of online shopping which overtime became a lot easier to use and as such influenced their behavior change to use online shopping.

H2: PE → BC

The second hypothesis was tested to determine if performance expectancy will have a positive influence towards behavior change to use online shopping during covid-19 pandemic in Nigeria. However, based on the path analysis, it was discovered that performance expectancy has positive significant influence towards behavior change to use online shopping during covid-19 pandemic in Nigeria. This is consistent with prior studies where performance expectancy was discovered to have a strong positive influence towards behavioral intention in understanding students' online shopping behavior (Hassan et al., 2015). Tarhini et al. (2018) also revealed that behavioral intention has a positive influence in influencing behavioral intention towards the adoption of online shopping. Performance expectancy which pertains to the "extent of how much people perceive a new technology is useful in their daily life in terms of having more productivity as well as saving their time and effort" indicates positive significant influence towards behavioral change to use online shopping during covid-19 pandemic in Nigeria (Venkatesh et al., 2003). Since consumers as well as sellers were restricted from carrying out physical buying and selling transactions during the covid19 pandemic in Nigeria, online shopping became a lot relevant to consumers as the only possible means to ensure their daily productivity and needs are met while ensuring their safety with very limited effort. As such consumers who have previously relied on stores or market visit for their shopping changed their behavior towards online shopping basically because of the lack of any alternative but also because of online shopping have proven effective in meeting its performance expectancy.

H3: SI → BC

The third hypothesis aimed to determine the influence of social influence towards behavior change to use online shopping during Covid-19 pandemic in Nigeria. Social influence was discovered in this study to have a non-significant influence towards behavior change to use online shopping during Covid-19 in Nigeria. This finding is supported by some previous studies such as the study by Tarhini et al. (2018) which identified social influence to have a non-significant influence towards behavior intention to adopt online shopping. Some other studies revealed opposing findings to this study. For instance, Pascual-Miguel et al. (2015) revealed that social influence is significant in influencing gender and product type on online purchasing. In addition, social influence was found to have strong significant relationship with behavioral intention in understanding students' online shopping behavior (Hassan et al., 2015). The findings of these studies are justified because people tend to conform to others' opinions and behaviors in a trust game and in this case online shopping (Wei et al., 2019). However, based on the field study, social influence which is the "extent to which an individual perceives that important other believe he or she should apply the new system" (Venkatesh et al., 2003) is seen to have a non-significant influence towards behavior change to use online shopping during covid-19 pandemic in Nigeria. This might be due to several reasons. Firstly, some consumers restricted by the lockdown directives had to improvise to sort out ways to get their basic needs and groceries without violating the social distancing. This need prompted their utilization of online shopping regardless of recommendations from friends and families. Secondly, people previously aware of online shopping but reluctant to utilize it but with their backs against the wall by the lockdown directives had to forget their neglect of online shopping and subsequently adopted it. However, 58% of the total respondents are within the ages of 26-30 years, which are referred to as millennials and people of the digital age with 72% of them possessing and internet experience of seven years and more. This can imply that a large percentage of them had prior knowledge of online shopping or frequented it as could be seen in the demographic analysis that 54% of the respondents indicated that they have shopped online 12 times or more.

H4: FC → BC

The fourth hypothesis tested the influence of facilitating conditions towards behavior change to use online shopping during Covid-19 pandemic in Nigeria. Facilitating conditions which is "consumers perceptions of resources and support available to perform a behavior" (Venkatesh et al., 2012) was found to have a non-significant influence towards behavior change to use online shopping. However, a study by Miladinovic and Hong (2016) discovered a contradicting result in their study on factors affecting the behavioral intention to use mobile shopping fashion apps in Sweden. They discovered that facilitating conditions affect users' behavioral intention to use m-shopping fashion apps. This finding by Miladinovic and Hong (2016) was justified to imply that consumers find it important to have necessary support and help while using m-shopping fashion app. However, in this study, the circumstances surrounding the behavior change of consumers to adopt online shopping which is the Covid-19 pandemic increased the urgency and the necessity of purchasing commodities online which left consumers with limited choice of abandoning an online shopping platform because of the unavailability of necessary support. In addition, with the availability of limited or no support consumers were willing to continue shopping online during the covid-19 pandemic in Nigeria.

H5: PT → BC

The fifth hypothesis tested the influence of perceived trust towards behavior change to use online shopping during Covid-19 pandemic in Nigeria. The result indicates that perceived trust has significance in influencing behavior change to use online shopping during covid-19 pandemic. This finding contradicts the results of the study done by Miladinovic and Hong (2016) which was related to finding the factors affecting the behavioral intention to use mobile shopping fashion app in Sweden. In their study, it was discovered that perceived trust had a non-significant influence on behavioral intention to use online shopping. A major reason that perceived trust is seen to have a positive influence on behavioral change could be because the consumers or respondents of this study are conversant with the use of online shopping. Thus, a good relationship has been established as many of the respondents had over seven years and more internet experience. In other words, people in Nigeria are used to shopping online, have experience with online shopping platform, and vendors, which most have been further developed during the Covid-19 pandemic. Therefore, they have overcome the trust concerns regarding relying on online shopping.

Similarly, consumers were practically left with no choice than to trust online shopping platforms and vendors since they have been restricted to their homes by the Covid-19 pandemic prevention directives.

H6: AT → BC

The sixth hypothesis investigated the influence consumers' attitude towards online shopping on behavior change to use online shopping during covid-19 pandemic in Nigeria. The study found that attitude towards online shopping has a positive influence on behavior change to use online shopping during Covid-19 pandemic. This indicates that effort expectancy, performance expectancy, social influence, facilitating conditions and perceived trust all contributes to influence the attitude of consumers towards behavior change to use online shopping during covid-19 pandemic. This is evident in previous study related to consumers attitude towards online shopping in China by Jun and Jaafar (2011), where perceived usability, perceived security, perceived privacy, perceived after-sales services, perceived marketing mix, and perceived reputation were found to significantly influence consumers' attitude to adopt online shopping. Individuals attitude towards any behavioral change is determined by various factors and in this study the attitude of Nigerian consumers towards the use of online shopping during the Covid-19 pandemic required little or no factor to influence them as they were practically forced to adopt online shopping similar to other nations of the world as a result of the global lockdown of physical stores and market.

H7: CA → BC

The seventh hypothesis of this study analyzed the influence of Covid-19 anxiety towards behavior change to use online shopping during Covid-19 in Nigeria. Covid-19 anxiety in this study was discovered to have a positive influence on behavior change to use online shopping. Anxiety is a normal reaction to uncertainty that may harm a person. For example, Covid-19 pandemic prompted people to worry about their own health and the health of their loved ones, both in Nigeria and other countries. People had many concerns around their ability to relate and take part in their community, social invents and other parts of the life. Therefore, in a bid for consumers to avoid too much anxiety leading to panic which can cause harm, they tend to take Covid-19 precautions one of which is online shopping to limits their contacts with other people and reduces their chances of contacting the virus. This finding is in line with a study on the impact of anxiety caused by Covid-19 on consumer behavior conducted by Paksoy et al. (2020). Paksoy et al. (2020) found that deprivation and suffering dimensions of the anxiety caused by Covid-19 have significant effects on the dimensions of consumer behavior.

H8: PR (PT) → BC

The eighth hypothesis of this study analyzed the influence of perceived risk to use online shopping on perceived trust. Perceived risk indicated a positive significant influence on perceived trust to use online shopping during Covid-19 pandemic in Nigeria. The finding of this study corresponds to the results of a study on consumer perceived risk in online shopping environment via Facebook as medium conducted by Panwar (2018). The study utilized universally accepted determinants of consumers' perceived risk and discovered that this multipronged perceived risk has significant impact on the online shopping behavior. Similarly, in a study conducted by (Doolin et al., 2005), both perceived risk and perceived benefits of internet shopping were found to be significantly associated with the amount and frequency of online purchases made. Perceived risk which is the

"Doubt a consumer has when purchasing items, mostly those that are particularly expensive" (Lake, 2019) indicated a positive influence on perceived trust to use online shopping during Covid-19 pandemic in Nigeria. Many reasons can justify this result, one of which is that perceived risk is always associated with expensive items such as cars, houses and computers. However, majorities of the items purchased during the covid-19 pandemic by consumers are basic groceries and food items, which are relatively less expensive than cars, houses and computers. In addition, the consumers aware of the risk of not receiving the actual commodity ordered on the web through online shopping had very limited option or alternatives to online shopping during the covid-19 pandemic in Nigeria mainly because of the lockdown directives implemented by the government to curtail the spread of the virus.

H9: PS (PT) → BC

The last hypothesis of this study investigates the influence of perceived security on perceived trust to use online shopping during Covid-19 pandemic in Nigeria. Perceived security indicated a non-significant influence on perceived trust to use online shopping. The result is not supported by some other studies such as the study by Damghanian et al. (2016) on the "impact of perceived security on Trust, Perceived Risk, and Acceptance of online banking in Iran". In their study, perceived security in internet banking had significant positive impact on the acceptance of online banking. In addition, the effect of perceived trust, perceived security, perceived usefulness and perceived ease of use on consumers' intention to use mobile payment. In their study perceived security was found to have a significant impact on the consumers' intention to use mobile payment. Perceived security which is the "extent an individual feels protected against security threats resulting from the use of online shopping" indicated a non-significant influence on perceived trust to use online shopping during the Covid-19 pandemic in Nigeria. Security have always been an issue in Nigeria mainly because of the series of internet fraud threads, impersonation as well as blackmail which have robbed the country of its security credibility, as such consumers have grown to appreciate the traditional bureaucracy of direct buying as opposed to buying over the internet. Regardless of the need to utilize online shopping during the Covid-19 pandemic, consumers still feel insecure as they might believe that their data (identity and credit card numbers) have been lodged into the web during online shopping can be subject to internet fraud and blackmail at any moment. This tends to affect the perceived trust consumers have in the act of online shopping.

COMPARISON OF CONSUMER'S BEHAVIOR TOWARDS ONLINE SHOPPING BEFORE AND DURING COVID-19 PANDEMIC IN NIGERIA

The preliminary study analyzed "consumer behavior towards intention to use online shopping in Nigeria" before the Covid-19 pandemic. The main objective of the preliminary study was to examine the consumer behavior towards online shopping. Five variables or factors affecting consumers behavioral intention were utilized in developing hypothetical statements to aid in realizing the objectives of the study. The variables include effort expectancy, performance expectancy, social influence, facilitating conditions and perceived trust. The study utilized data generated from online questionnaire distributed to 82 respondents in Nigeria. The findings of the study indicated that effort expectancy has significant positive influence on consumer behavior intention towards online shopping while social influence, perceived trust, performance expectancy and facilitating conditions all indicated non-significant influence in consumers' behavior intention to use online shopping.

This study on the other hand analyzed the "Behavior change towards using online shopping in Nigeria: The impact of Covid-19 pandemic". The major aim of the study was to examine consumer behavior change towards using online shopping during Covid-19 pandemic in Nigeria. As opposed to the preliminary study, seven factors affecting consumers' behavior were utilized in developing hypothetical statements for the study with another two factors affecting perceived risk to use online shopping. The seven main variables or factors utilized in this study include effort expectancy, performance expectancy, social influence, facilitating conditions, perceived trust, attitude towards online shopping and Covid-19 anxiety. The two other variables that influence perceived trust utilized in this study are perceived security and perceived risk. Similar to the preliminary study, this study utilized data generated from online questionnaire distributed to 82 respondents in Nigeria. The findings of the study indicate that effort expectancy, performance expectancy, perceived trust, covid-19 anxiety and attitude towards online shopping all have positive significant influence on behavior change to use online shopping during covid-19 pandemic in Nigeria. However, social influence and facilitating conditions indicated non-significant influence on behavior change to use online shopping during Covid-19 pandemic in Nigeria.

As opposed to this study, the preliminary study utilized only five variables in ascertaining consumers' behavior intention to use online shopping while the main study incorporated two additional variables to the other five variables in the preliminary study in determining the behavior change to use online shopping during Covid-19 pandemic in Nigeria. The notable similarity between both studies, besides the common five variables shared between them, is the number of respondents (82) utilized in both studies. The findings also exhibited some other similarities; effort expectancy indicated positive significant influence on behavior intention and behavior change to use online shopping. In addition, facilitating conditions and social influence both indicated non-significant influence in both studies.

The main study can be considered to elaborate as opposed to the preliminary study because it embodies some other factors that influence consumer behavior other the common five variables shared by both studies. The main study also included perceived risk and perceived security in ascertaining the influence of perceived trust on online shopping. Meanwhile, attitude to use online shopping and Covid-19 anxiety were also included in the main study in determining behavior change to use online shopping in Nigeria.

The preliminary study perceives performance expectancy to have a non-significant influence on behavior intention to use online shopping, while the main study perceives performance expectancy to have significant influence on behavior change to use online shopping during Covid-19 pandemic in Nigeria. This is justified considering the restriction put in place during the Covid-19 pandemic, consumers perceived that online shopping will be useful in their daily life in terms of having more productivity as well as saving their time and effort. This is however not the case before the Covid-19 pandemic as consumers would naturally prefer visiting a store or the market to make purchases as opposed to ordering online. Because they are ignorant of the ways online shopping will increase their daily productivity as well as save their time and effort or they were simply trying to avoid additional costs involved in online shopping such as delivery charges.

Furthermore, the coefficient of determination (R^2) in the preliminary study indicated that the factors explaining the influence of consumer intention to use online shopping explained for 0.753 (75%) effect on behavior intention to use online shopping which indicates a strong effect. However, the coefficient of determination in the main study indicated that the factors influencing behavior change explained for

0.352 (35%) effect on behavior change to use online shopping during Covid-19 in Nigeria, which is a rather weak effect.

Majority of the respondents in the preliminary study are females with a percentage of 66.3% as against male with a percentage of 33.7. The greater number of respondents in the preliminary study are aged between 31-35 year, which make up 40.2% while the least are between 41years and above (7.3%). A greater number of respondents who have attained an educational level of a graduate degree took part in the in answering the questionnaire of the preliminary study. Majority of the respondents in the preliminary study have used the internet for over six years and above. Most respondents have utilized online shopping more than 10 times.

In the main study, the gender of majority of the respondents are females with a percentage of 68.3%. Most of the respondents who took part in the study were aged 26 to 30 with master's degree. The level of internet usage for most of the respondents averaged a period of seven years and above. Majority of the respondents have an online shopping experience of more than 12 times. The total usage of the online shopping for most of the respondents is less than one week.

Both studies share a demographic similarity in the total number of respondents utilized in the study as well as gender. However, the main study included 'the total number of online shopping experience' in determining the demographic factors of the respondents but the preliminary study did not. The main study ensured that it indicates the entire forms of postgraduate educational level, but the preliminary study summed them up as postgraduate degree.

RECOMMENDATIONS

Significant Variables

Recommendations in this section are based on dependent variables in this study which indicated a significant influence on behavioral change towards the use of online shopping.

Effort Expectancy

Effort Expectancy, which is a belief that the use of online shopping will be easy and effortless, indicated a positive influence on behavioral change towards the use of online shopping. This finding is in line with the findings of a study conducted by Keikhosrokiani, Mustaffa, Zakaria and Baharudin (2019) where effort expectancy had a positive influence and reported to be an important antecedent of behavioral intention towards using mobile healthcare system. This study suggests that online shopping platforms makes it relatively easy for customers to assess their platforms with less stress and achieve their goals with less discomfort. There are some recommendations as follows to incorporate effort expectancy with online shopping: (1) make navigation intuitive and easy. Convenient online store navigation enables customers to locate desired products and services quickly and hassle-free, (2) enhance product page, as the first impression is vital for an online store. Customer's initial impression should be captured by showcasing products and services in a unique way, and (3) design a simple user experience checkout process which is essential when consumers make the ultimate final decision to purchase goods or empty their cart.

Performance Expectancy

Performance expectancy is the belief that the utilization of a particular technology will be of advantage or will enhance the performance of the user. It revealed a significant influence on behavioral change towards the use of online shopping. This finding is consistent with the findings of a study conducted by Hassan et al. (2015) where performance expectancy was discovered to have a strong positive influence towards behavioral intention in understanding students' online shopping. In order to ensure a trend of positive influence on behavioral change towards online shopping the business owners should incorporate the following recommendation: (1) online shopping users should be entitled to rewards. These rewards should be related directly to their performance and the sellers must ensure that the rewards provided are deserving rewards and those wanted by the recipients.

Perceived Trust

Perceived trust is the amount of trust that a customer has in online shopping to perform expected activities without taking advantage of the user. In this study, perceived trust indicated a significant influence on behavioral change towards the use of online shopping. Trust is the crux of every business entity and when missing, businesses tend to go under. Therefore, it is vital that every business preserve and sustain the trust of their customers. Online shopping vendors and platforms can ensure this through the following recommendations: (1) render excellent customer service. The level of customer service mainly influences customers' loyalty and retention, (2) publish Customer reviews and testimonials. Customers will always trust consumers as opposed to companies. Thus, it is important to build a trustworthy brand to ensure consumers understand companies always place their business in a positive light, and (3) be limpid. Trust is earned. In order to be on the right books of customers, online shopping platforms need to be deserving of their trust. That implies being honest and transparent about what customers can expect from an online store.

COVID-19 Anxiety

Anxiety is a normal reaction to uncertainty. Things that may harm a person such as the Covid-19 pandemic indicated a significant influence on behavior change towards the use of online shopping. In an attempt for consumers to avoid too much anxiety, they tend to take Covid-19 precautions one of which is online shopping to limit their contacts with other people and reduces their chances of contacting the virus. This finding is in line with the results of a study on the impact of anxiety caused by Covid-19 on consumer behavior (Paksoy et al., 2020). Paksoy et al. (2020) found that deprivation and suffering dimensions of the anxiety caused by Covid-19 have significant effects on the dimensions of consumer behavior. To ensure that consumers stay subscribed to online shopping platforms after the Covid-19 pandemic, there are some recommendations for online shopping vendors and business owners as follows: (1) they must adopt sensitization campaigns channeled towards informing consumers on the need to continue shopping online despite the absence of Covid-19 pandemic, (2) they should adopt more radical digital marketing strategies aimed at fostering a healthy and good relationship with the customers during the Covid-19 pandemic, and (3) campaigns insisting anxiety for open air marketplace should be carried out by online shopping platforms and vendors to encourage consumers to shop online as opposed to visiting the marketplace.

Attitude Towards the Use of Online Shopping

Attitude is a mental develop, a psychological and passionate substance that inheres in, or describes an individual. In this study, attitude to utilize online shopping alludes to somebody's positive or negative feeling about utilizing online shopping and it indicates a significant influence on behavior change towards the use of online shopping. The change in attitude of consumers in Nigeria to utilize and adopt online shopping was led by the Covid-19 pandemic and the resultant lockdown. To ensure that the attitude of consumers towards online shopping doesn't depreciate or switch to a negative following the exit of Covid-19 pandemic, the following recommendations should be adopted by online shopping business owners and platform: (1) implementation of the psychological mechanism of promos (discounts), and (2) the utilization of social media activities and promotion through delivering marvelous and engaging contents.

Perceived Risk

Perceived risk is the vulnerability a purchaser has while purchasing costly items such as vehicles, houses, and PCs. Based on the findings of this study, perceived risk indicated a positive influence on perceived trust towards the use of online shopping. The study suggests that the online shopping stores ensured transparency with their customers during the Covid-19, reduced or eliminated the risk perceived by the consumers. This is a good position for every online shopping platform, and it can be further encouraged by: (1) managing the expectations of online shopping users by clarifying the objectives and eliminating uncertainty and doubt, which helps in mitigating the risk perception of the users, and (2) leveraging quantitative data, online stores owners should combine internal documentation with external sources of validation and share relevant feedbacks and testimonies of other users.

Non-Significant Variables

Recommendations in this section are based on independent variables in this study, which indicated a non-significant influence on behavioral change towards the use of online shopping.

Social Influence

Social influence comprises the manner in which individuals adjust their behavior to meet the demands and styles of a social environment. It exhibited a negative influence on behavioral intentions towards online shopping. The influence on consumer behavior is one of the major determinants of a customer utilizing a product or abandoning it; it is an integral aspect of every online store and should be enhanced through the implementation of the following recommendation: (1) give value; give customers useful, helpful tips that will benefit them. The more value given to customers, the more they will engage and tell others.

Facilitating Conditions

Facilitating condition is the degree to which an individual believes that an organizational and technical infrastructure exists to support the use of the system. Moreover, it is considered as the extent to which he or she has the appropriate knowledge and resources to make use of the system. Facilitating condition in this study indicates a negative influence on behavioral intention towards online shopping. The absence of support for customers on an online store discourages the utilization of an online shopping store. The following recommendations should be adhered to in other to obtain positive influence from facilitating conditions.: (1) to provide systematic pop-up guidelines for customers on the shopping platform for encouraging a smooth purchase process, (2) customer service representative should be available to customers through WhatsApp chat-heads and phone calls, and (3) Frequent Asked Questions (FAQs) should be updated regularly to incorporate new solutions to complaints and questions.

Perceived Security

Perceived security is the extent an individual believes a mobile device, or a system will be free of risk to conduct C2C e-commerce. It is the "customers' perception of the degree of protection against these threats (Yousafzai et al., 2003). Perceived security indicated a non-significant influence on behavior change towards the use of online shopping. To improve the trust in the security system of online store, it is recommended that: (1) online stores implement SSL certificates which is the standard for securing online transaction, (2) implementation of two-factor authentication (2FA) as an extra layer of security on the e-commerce platform to prevent the compromise of consumers' credentials.

CONCLUSION AND FUTURE WORK

With the world advancing in technology, e-commerce is taking a major stand in various economies of the world (not just in Nigeria) and so many small business owners have either capitalized on the numerous benefits or have started considering having an online presence that enables them to sell and showcase their products to a much broader audience. However, a lot of factors influence the decision and willingness of consumers to utilize online shopping in Nigeria, some of these factors are not far from reach and influence on a great extent in the purchasing behaviors of consumers. This study examined the consumer behavioral change towards the use of online shopping in Nigeria before and during the Covid-19 pandemic.

To achieve the objectives of this study, a research model was designed to examine the influence of effort expectancy, performance expectancy, social influence, facilitating conditions, Covid-19 anxiety, attitude and perceived trust on consumers behavioral change towards the use of online shopping. Quantitative analysis was utilized as the research methodology and a survey was conducted on internet savvy Nigerians. The total number of 82 respondents were utilized in obtaining the reliability of the hypotheses using SEM-PLS.

The first objective of the study was actualized by ascertaining from previous studies by other researchers that effort expectancy, performance expectancy, social influence, facilitating conditions, anxiety, attitude and perceived trust, perceived security and perceived risk are factors that influence consumer's behavior change towards online shopping. Social influence, facilitating conditions and perceived security were found to have no significance towards the consumers' behavioral change towards the use of online shopping in Nigeria during the Covid-19 pandemic. This can be likened to the absence of vital information to assist and facilitate the online experience of consumers. The second specific objective of the research aimed at determining the most vital factors that influence consumer behavior change towards the use of online shopping during the Covid-19 pandemic in Nigeria. The results indicates that effort expectancy, performance expectancy, attitude, anxiety and perceived trust, were the variables/

factors to indicate a positive influence on consumer behavior change towards online shopping during Covid-19 pandemic. With the attainment of the final objective of this study, some recommendations were discussed in relation to the findings of the study.

The study contributes to existing literatures on the behavioral factors influencing the decision of consumers to purchase product over the internet before and during Covid-19 pandemic. In addition, this study expands and updates literature on the topic of concern. This study serves as a reference hub for subsequent researchers looking to further investigate this topic in Nigeria. The study is beneficial to e-commerce businesses who are seeking to research on enhancing consumer's behavior intentions.

This work is limited to some part in Lagos State, Nigeria. This is insufficient to arrive at an in-depth knowledge of the factors that influence consumer change towards the use of online shopping in Nigeria. More research studies should be conducted on many more parts of the country in order to understand the factors that influence consumer behavioral change towards online shopping in general.

REFERENCES

Ab Hamid, M. R., Sami, W., & Mohmad Sidek, M. H. (2017). Discriminant Validity Assessment: Use of Fornell & Larcker criterion versus HTMT Criterion. *Journal of Physics: Conference Series*, *890*, 012163. doi:10.1088/1742-6596/890/1/012163

Agwu, M. (2012). A qualitative study of the problems and prospects of online banking in developing economies–case of Nigeria. *Journal of Internet Banking and Commerce*, *17*(3), 1–20. doi:10.2139srn.3112130

Ajzen, I. (1985). From Intentions to Actions: A Theory of Planned Behavior. In J. Kuhl & J. Beckmann (Eds.), *Action Control: From Cognition to Behavior* (pp. 11–39). Springer Berlin Heidelberg. doi:10.1007/978-3-642-69746-3_2

Ajzen, I. (1991). The Theory of Planned Behavior. Decision Processes, 50(2), 179-211. doi:10.1016/0749-5978(91)90020-T

Ajzen, I., & Fishbein, M. (1975). A Bayesian analysis of attribution processes. *Psychological Bulletin*, *82*(2), 261–277. doi:10.1037/h0076477

Akanbi, P. A., Ayodele, T. D., & Adedipe, O. A. (2014). An investigation into some factors influencing the intention to use internet banking among undergraduates in Nigeria. *Research Journal of Finance and Accounting*, *5*(8), 1–9.

Alalwan, A. A., Dwivedi, Y. K., Rana, N. P., Lal, B., & Williams, M. D. (2015). Consumer adoption of Internet banking in Jordan: Examining the role of hedonic motivation, habit, self-efficacy and trust. *Journal of Financial Services Marketing*, *20*(2), 145–157. doi:10.1057/fsm.2015.5

Alam, J. (2020). Buying Behavior Under Coronavirus Disease (COVID-19) Pandemic Situation: A Online Perspective Case in Bangladeshi Shoppers. *The China Business Review*, *19*(3), 82–90. doi:10.1371/journal.pone.0256095

Alsajjan, B., & Dennis, C. (2010). Internet banking acceptance model: Cross-market examination. *Journal of Business Research*, *63*(9-10), 957–963. doi:10.1016/j.jbusres.2008.12.014

Arenas Gaitán, J., Peral Peral, B., & Ramón Jerónimo, M. (2015). Elderly and internet banking: An application of UTAUT2. *Journal of Internet Banking and Commerce*, *20*(1), 1–23. doi:10.1088/1757-899X/58/1/012007

Ariff, M. S. M., Sylvester, M., Zakuan, N., Ismail, K., & Ali, K. M. (2014). Consumer perceived risk, attitude and online shopping behaviour; empirical evidence from Malaysia. *IOP Conference Series. Materials Science and Engineering*.

Azam, A., & Qiang, F. (2014). Online consumer behaviour: Extension of decomposed theory of planned behaviour with consumers' perception of online retailing ethics. *International Journal of Electronic Business*, *11*(3), 199–219. doi:10.1504/IJEB.2014.063017

Bagozzi, R. P., & Yi, Y. (1988). On the evaluation of structural equation models. *Journal of the Academy of Marketing Science*, *16*(1), 74–94. doi:10.1007/BF02723327

Bhupal, D. P., Bhaskar, D., Tathagata, G., Han, T., & Zhang, Y. (2020). Leptonic scalars at the LHC. *Journal of High Energy Physics*, *2020*(7), 1–39. doi:10.48550/arXiv.1910.01132

Callaway, S. K., & Jagani, S. B. (2015). The impact of banks' entrepreneurial orientation on strategic control systems. *American Journal of Business*, *30*(1), 49–71. doi:10.1108/AJB-10-2013-0067

Chiles, T. H., & McMackin, J. F. (1996). Integrating variable risk preferences, trust, and transaction cost economics. *Academy of Management Review*, *21*(1), 73–99. doi:10.2307/258630

Chin, W. W. (1998). The partial least squares approach to structural equation modeling. *Modern Methods for Business Research, 295*(2), 295-336.

Cho, J. (2006). The mechanism of trust and distrust formation and their relational outcomes. *Journal of Retailing*, *82*(1), 25–35. doi:10.1016/j.jretai.2005.11.002

COVID-19 Consistently Impacts Shopping Behavior of 9 in 10 Consumers. (2021). *Numerator Intelligence*. https://www.numerator.com/resources/blog/impact-covid-19-consumer-behavior

COVID-19: How consumer behavior will be changed. (2020). *Accenture*. https://www.accenture.com/us-en/insights/consumer-goods-services/coronavirus-consumer-behavior-research

Damghanian, H., Zarei, A., & Siahsarani Kojuri, M. A. (2016). Impact of Perceived Security on Trust, Perceived Risk, and Acceptance of Online Banking in Iran. *Journal of Internet Commerce*, *15*(3), 214–238. https://doi.org/10.1080/15332861.2016.1191052

Davis, F. D., Bagozzi, R. P., & Warshaw, P. R. (1989). User Acceptance of Computer Technology: A Comparison of Two Theoretical Models. *Management Science*, *35*(8), 982–1003. https://www.jstor.org/stable/2632151

Doolin, B., Dillon, S., Thompson, F., & Corner, J. L. (2005). Perceived risk, the Internet shopping experience and online purchasing behavior: A New Zealand perspective. *Journal of Global Information Management*, *13*(2), 66–88. https://doi.org/10.4018/jgim.2005040104

Dwivedi, Y. K., Rana, N. P., Jeyaraj, A., Clement, M., & Williams, M. D. (2019). Re-examining the unified theory of acceptance and use of technology (UTAUT): Towards a revised theoretical model. *Information Systems Frontiers*, *21*(3), 719–734. https://doi.org/0.1007/s10796-017-9774-y

Escobar-Rodríguez, T., & Bonsón-Fernández, R. (2017). Analysing online purchase intention in Spain: Fashion e-commerce. *Information Systems and e-Business Management*, *15*(3), 599–622. https://doi.org/10.1007/s10257-016-0319-6

Fishbein, M., & Ajzen, I. (1977). Belief, attitude, intention, and behavior: An introduction to theory and research. *Philosophy & Rhetoric*, *10*(2).

Fishbein, M., Jaccard, J., Davidson, A. R., Ajzen, I., & Loken, B. (1980). Predicting and understanding family planning behaviors. In *Understanding attitudes and predicting social behavior*. Prentice Hall.

Gabriel, J., Ogbuigwe, T., & Ahiauzu, L. (2016). Online shopping systems in Nigeria: Evolution, trend and prospects. *Asian Research Journal of Arts & Social Sciences*, *1*(4), 182-276. doi:10.9734/ARJASS/2016/29170

Gao, X., Shi, X., Guo, H., & Liu, Y. (2020). To buy or not buy food online: The impact of the COVID-19 epidemic on the adoption of e-commerce in China. *PLoS One*, *15*(8), e0237900. https://doi.org/10.1371/journal.pone.0237900

Guritno, S., & Siringoringo, H. (2013). Perceived usefulness, ease of use, and attitude towards online shopping usefulness towards online airlines ticket purchase. *Procedia: Social and Behavioral Sciences*, *81*, 212–216. https://doi.org/10.1016/j.sbspro.2013.06.415

Hair, J. F. Jr, Hult, G. T. M., Ringle, C. M., & Sarstedt, M. (2021). *A primer on partial least squares structural equation modeling (PLS-SEM)*. Sage Publications.

Hair, J. F., Jr., Sarstedt, M., Hopkins, L., & Kuppelwieser, G. V. (2014). Partial least squares structural equation modeling (PLS-SEM). *European Business Review*, *26*(2), 106-121. doi:10.1108/EBR-10-2013-0128

Hansen, T. (2008). Consumer values, the theory of planned behaviour and online grocery shopping. *International Journal of Consumer Studies*, *32*(2), 128–137. https://doi.org/10.1111/j.1470-6431.2007.00655.x

Hashem, T. N. (2020). Examining the influence of covid 19 pandemic in changing customers' orientation towards e-shopping. *Modern Applied Science*, *14*(8), 59–76. https://doi.org/10.5539/mas.v14n8p59

Hassan, S., Rashid, R., & Li, F. (2015). Utilising modified UTAUT to understand students' online shopping behaviour: A case of e-retail co-operative website in Malaysia. *Journal of Electronic Commerce in Organizations*, *13*(4), 74–90.

Hungilo, G. G., & Setyohadi, D. B. (2020). Factors influencing acceptance of online shopping in Tanzania using UTAUT2. *Journal of Internet Banking and Commerce*, *25*(1), 1–23. https://doi.org/10.4018/JECO.2015100104

Jun, G., & Jaafar, N. I. (2011). A study on consumers' attitude towards online shopping in China. *International Journal of Business and Social Science*, *2*(22), 122–132.

Kaplan, H. E. (2018). Examination of factors affecting online consumer behavior from the perspective of the unified theory of acceptance and use of technology. *Turkish Studies*, *13*(30), 203–212. https://doi.org/10.7827/TurkishStudies.14647

Kardes, F. R., Cline, T. W., & Cronley, M. L. (2011). *Consumer behavior: Science and practice* (1st ed.). Cengage.

Keikhosrokiani, P. (2019). *Perspectives in the Development of Mobile Medical Information Systems: Life Cycle, Management, Methodological Approach and Application*. Academic Press.

Keikhosrokiani, P. (2020a). Behavioral intention to use of Mobile Medical Information System (mMIS). In P. Keikhosrokiani (Ed.), Perspectives in the Development of Mobile Medical Information Systems (pp. 57–73). Academic Press. https://doi.org/https://doi.org/10.1016/B978-0-12-817657-3.00004-3

Keikhosrokiani, P. (2020b). Success factors of mobile medical information system (mMIS). In P. Keikhosrokiani (Ed.), Perspectives in the Development of Mobile Medical Information Systems (pp. 75–99). Academic Press. https://doi.org/https://doi.org/10.1016/B978-0-12-817657-3.00005-5

Keikhosrokiani, P. (2021). Predicating smartphone users' behaviour towards a location-aware IoMT-based information system: An empirical study. *International Journal of E-Adoption*, *13*(2), 52–77. https://doi.org/10.4018/IJEA.2021070104

Keikhosrokiani, P., Mustaffa, N., Sarwar, M. I., & Zakaria, N. (2013). E-Torch: A Mobile Commerce Location-Based Promotion System. *The International Technology Management Review, 3*(3), 140-159. doi:10.2991/itmr.2013.3.3.1

Keikhosrokiani, P., Mustaffa, N., & Zakaria, N. (2018). Success factors in developing iHeart as a patient-centric healthcare system: A multi-group analysis. *Telematics and Informatics*, *35*(4), 753–775. https://doi.org/10.1016/j.tele.2017.11.006

Keikhosrokiani, P., Mustaffa, N., Zakaria, N., & Abdullah, R. (2019). Assessment of a medical information system: the mediating role of use and user satisfaction on the success of human interaction with the mobile healthcare system (iHeart). *Cognition, Technology & Work*. doi:10.1007/s10111-019-00565-4

Keikhosrokiani, P., Mustaffa, N., Zakaria, N., & Baharudin, A. S. (2019). User behavioral intention toward using mobile healthcare system. In Consumer-driven technologies in healthcare: breakthroughs in research and practice (pp. 429–444). IGI Global. https://doi.org/10.4018/978-1-5225-6198-9.ch022

Khoi, N. H., Tuu, H. H., & Olsen, S. O. (2018). The role of perceived values in explaining Vietnamese consumers' attitude and intention to adopt mobile commerce. *Asia Pacific Journal of Marketing and Logistics*.

Kim, C., Galliers, R. D., Shin, N., Ryoo, J.-H., & Kim, J. (2012). Factors influencing Internet shopping value and customer repurchase intention. *Electronic Commerce Research and Applications*, *11*(4), 374–387. https://doi.org/10.1016/j.elerap.2012.04.002

Koufaris, M. (2002). Applying the technology acceptance model and flow theory to online consumer behavior. *Information Systems Research*, *13*(2), 205–223.

Lake, R. (2019). *Grocery shopping statistics: 23 fun size facts to know*. CreditDonkey. https://www.creditdonkey. com/grocery-shopping-statistics. html

Li, D., Chaudhary, H., & Zhang, Z. (2020). Modeling spatiotemporal pattern of depressive symptoms caused by COVID-19 using social media data mining. *International Journal of Environmental Research and Public Health, 17*(14), 4988. https://www.mdpi.com/1660-4601/17/14/4988

Lim, Y.-J. (2014). Psychometric characteristics of the Korean Mental Health Continuum–Short Form in an adolescent sample. *Journal of Psychoeducational Assessment, 32*(4), 356–364.

McKnight, D. H., Choudhury, V., & Kacmar, C. (2002). The impact of initial consumer trust on intentions to transact with a web site: A trust building model. *The Journal of Strategic Information Systems, 11*(3-4), 297–323.

Miladinovic, J., & Hong, X. (2016). *A Study on factors affecting the behavioral intention to use mobile shopping fashion Apps in Sweden* [Student thesis]. DiVA. http://urn.kb.se/resolve?urn=urn:nbn:se:hj:diva-30245

Minton, E. A., & Khale, L. R. (2014). Belief Systems. *Religion and Behavioral, 5*(1).

Monsuwé, T. P., Dellaert, B. G., & De Ruyter, K. (2004). What drives consumers to shop online? A literature review. *International Journal of Service Industry Management, 15*(1), 102–121. https://doi.org/10.1108/09564230410523358

Moorman, C., Deshpande, R., & Zaltman, G. (1993). Factors affecting trust in market research relationships. *Journal of Marketing, 57*(1), 81–101.

Mugerwa, S., Moya, M. B., & Kituyi, G. M. (2018). Determinants of Behavioral Intention in Adopting Network Monitoring System. *International Journal of Computer Applications Technology and Research, 07*(3), 139–157. https://doi.org/10.7753/IJCATR0703.1006

Mutum, R. D., Balyan, S. C., Kansal, S., Agarwal, P., Kumar, S., Kumar, M., & Raghuvanshi, S. (2013). Evolution of variety-specific regulatory schema for expression of osa-miR408 in indica rice varieties under drought stress. *The FEBS Journal, 280*(7), 1717–1730.

Neama, G., Alaskar, R., & Alkandari, M. (2016). Privacy, security, risk, and trust concerns in e-commerce. *Proceedings of the 17th International Conference on Distributed Computing and Networking*.

Neger, M., & Uddin, B. (2020). Factors affecting consumers' internet shopping behavior during the COVID-19 pandemic: Evidence from Bangladesh. *The China Business Review, 19*(3), 91–104.

Nwankwo, C. A., Kanyangale, M., & Abugu, J. O. (2019). Online shopping industry and its consumers in Nigeria. *Journal of Economics. Management and Trade, 24*(3), 1–12.

Ogbuji, C. N., & Udom, A. O. (2018). A holistic presentation of online shopping in Nigeria. *Researchers World, 9*(3), 22–33.

Oni, A. A., & Ayo, C. K. (2010). An empirical investigation of the level of users' acceptance of e-banking in Nigeria. *Journal of Internet Banking and Commerce, 15*(1), 1–13.

Otika, U., Olise, E., & Oby, O. B. (2019). Risk Perceptions and Online Shopping Intention among Internet Users In Nigeria. *Global Journal of Management and Business Research.*

Paksoy, H. M., Durmaz, Y., Çopuroğlu, F., & Özbezek, B. D. (2020). The Impact of Anxiety Caused by COVID-19 on Consumer Behaviour. *Transnational Marketing Journal*, *8*(2), 243–270.

Panwar, C. (2018). Consumer perceived risk in online shopping environment via Facebook as medium. *IACSIT International Journal of Engineering and Technology*, *7*(4), 2485–2490. https://doi.org/10.14419/ijet.v7i4.11017

Pappas, N. (2016). Marketing strategies, perceived risks, and consumer trust in online buying behaviour. *Journal of Retailing and Consumer Services*, *29*, 92–103.

Pascual-Miguel, F. J., Agudo-Peregrina, Á. F., & Chaparro-Peláez, J. (2015). Influences of gender and product type on online purchasing. *Journal of Business Research*, *68*(7), 1550–1556.

Pavlou, P. A., & Fygenson, M. (2006). Understanding and predicting electronic commerce adoption: An extension of the theory of planned behavior. *Management Information Systems Quarterly*, 115–143.

Perloff, J., DesRoches, C. M., & Buerhaus, P. (2016). Comparing the cost of care provided to Medicare beneficiaries assigned to primary care nurse practitioners and physicians. *Health Services Research*, *51*(4), 1407–1423.

Pride, W. M., & Ferrell, O. C. (2016). *Foundations of marketing*. Cengage Learning.

Sánchez-Torres, J. A., Varon-Sandobal, A., & Sánchez-Alzate, J.-A. (2017). Differences between e-commerce buyers and non-buyers in Colombia: The moderating effect of educational level and socioeconomic status on electronic purchase intention. *Dyna (Bilbao)*, *84*(202), 175–189. https://doi.org/10.15446/dyna.v84n202.65496

Shamsuddin, A., Ruslan, M. M., Halim, A., Zahari, N. F., & Fazi, N. M. (2014). Educators' awareness and acceptance towards Goods and Services Tax (GST) implementation in Malaysia: A study in Bandar Muadzam Shah, Pahang. *International Journal of Business. Economics and Law*, *4*(1), 1–10.

Sheth, J. (2020). Impact of Covid-19 on consumer behavior: Will the old habits return or die? *Journal of Business Research*, *117*, 280–283. https://doi.org/https://doi.org/10.1016/j.jbusres.2020.05.059

Singh, A., Alryalat, M. A. A., Alzubi, J. A., & Sarma, H. (2017). Understanding Jordanian consumers' online purchase intentions: Integrating trust to the UTAUT2 framework. *International Journal of Applied Engineering Research*, *12*(20), 10258–10268.

Taherdoost, H., Masrom, M., & Ismail, Z. (2009). Adoption model to assess the user acceptance of smart card technology. *Journal of US-China Public Administration*, *6*(3), 47–58.

Taherdoost, H., Namayandeh, M., & Masrom, M. (2009). Development a Smart Card Acceptance Model from Ethical Perspective. *International Conference on Frontiers in Education: Computer Science & Computer Engineering*, Las Vegas, NV.

Taherdoost, H., Sahibuddin, S., & Jalaliyoon, N. (2011). Smart card security; Technology and adoption. *International Journal of Security*, *5*(2), 74–84.

Tarhini, A., Alalwan, A. A., Al-Qirim, N., & Algharabat, R. (2018). An analysis of the factors influencing the adoption of online shopping. *International Journal of Technology Diffusion*, *9*(3), 68–87. https://doi.org/10.4018/978-1-7998-8957-1.ch019

Venkatesh, V., Morris, M. G., Davis, G. B., & Davis, F. D. (2003). User Acceptance of Information Technology: Toward a Unified View. *Management Information Systems Quarterly*, *27*(3). https://doi.org/10.2307/30036540

Venkatesh, V., Thong, J. Y., & Xu, X. (2012). Consumer acceptance and use of information technology: Extending the unified theory of acceptance and use of technology. *Management Information Systems Quarterly*, *36*(1), 157–178. https://ssrn.com/abstract=2002388

Wei, Z., Zhao, Z., & Zheng, Y. (2019). Following the majority: Social influence in trusting behavior. *Frontiers in Neuroscience*, *13*, 89. https://doi.org/10.3389/fnins.2019.00089

Wilson, R. M., & Gilligan, C. (2012). *Strategic marketing management*. Routledge.

Yadav, R., Sharma, S. K., & Tarhini, A. (2016). A multi-analytical approach to understand and predict the mobile commerce adoption. *Journal of Enterprise Information Management*, *29*(2), 222–237. https://doi.org/10.1108/JEIM-04-2015-0034

Yousafzai, S. Y., Pallister, J. G., & Foxall, G. R. (2003). A proposed model of e-trust for electronic banking. *Technovation*, *23*(11), 847–860. https://doi.org/10.1016/S0166-4972(03)00130-5

Zhao, X., & Keikhosrokiani, P. (2022). Sales Prediction and Product Recommendation Model Through User Behavior Analytics. *Computers, Materials & Continua, 70*(2), 3855--3874. http://www.techscience.com/cmc/v70n2/44651

Zu, Z. Y., Jiang, M. D., Xu, P. P., Chen, W., Ni, Q. Q., Lu, G. M., & Zhang, L. J. (2020). Coronavirus disease 2019 (COVID-19): A perspective from China. *Radiology*, *296*(2), E15–E25. https://doi.org/10.1148/radiol.2020200490

Chapter 11
Age in the Consumer Behavior Change:
Evidence From Awareness, Perceived Value, and Use of Mobile Banking

Savdeep Vasudeva
https://orcid.org/0000-0002-0098-9635
Department of Business Administration, University of the People, USA

ABSTRACT

This chapter deals with the issue of consumer behavior change by taking the case of a digital service such as m-banking and supports the arguments with suitable data analytics. To fulfill this objective, it utilizes the two indicators of awareness and perceived value as the determinants of consumer behavior. The chapter intends to throw light on the relationship between awareness, perceived value, and usage of m-banking, and also helps to find out how the interaction of age affects this relationship. For this purpose, a sample of 524 m-banking users was utilized from the state of Punjab in India. Further, the generated data is analyzed using linear regression and moderated regression analysis. The findings reveal important implications for the banks and other researchers in terms of awareness and perceived value and also depict how the behavior of consumers can change as per their age in this socio-digital era.

INTRODUCTION

Consumer behavior change in the era of rapid technological developments is an inevitable phenomenon. It is witnessed by both the online and offline modes of business and could be attributed to the dynamic socio-digital scenarios existing in the environment. This continuous change in the behavior of the consumer poses great challenges in front of business organizations and marketing decision-makers. There is an emergent need for some concepts and methodologies that can effectively guide these stakeholders based on data analytics. Recently, the world has seen a sudden change in the behavior of consumers due to the compulsions of the Covid19 pandemic whereas this change could also be considered as part

DOI: 10.4018/978-1-6684-4168-8.ch011

of a regular process of consumer transformation. It may include the change in the consumer behavior because of a gradual maturity along with time and involve the factors such as aging, major life events, and changes in personal priorities. This transition in consumer behavior may be equally evident in both the manufacturing and service sectors. However, the intangible nature of services makes it more challenging to address this behavioral change. So, it becomes crucial to deal with this issue in the case of a service organization.

In this chapter, the issue of natural aging and consumer behavior change is specifically dealt with by taking the case of the two determinants i.e. awareness and perceived value of a digital service represented by mobile banking (also known as m-banking). M-banking service is generally provided by financial institutions such as banks and helps the users to transact using mobile phones or any other handheld devices (George, 2016). The mission of this study is to examine the relationship between awareness, perceived value, and m-banking usage. Further, the moderating role of age in the relationship between perceived value and use of the service is also investigated. In marketing studies, awareness and perceived value are considered as the important indicators of consumer behavior which lead to a more visible output in the form of consumer actions. In this chapter, the above relationship is examined to understand the issue of consumer behavior change with the support of data analytics. As per the nature of this study, the statistical techniques of linear regression and moderated multiple regression analysis using dummy variables are applied to provide some meaningful contribution to this issue. This study addresses the following research questions whether (a) awareness has a significant effect on the perceived value of m-banking (b) perceived value has a significant effect on m-banking usage (c) age moderates the relationship between perceived value and use of m-banking. Hence, this chapter helps to understand the dynamics of consumer behavior based on the above constructs in the case of technology services. Further components including the background, theoretical basis, methodology, analysis, and findings are presented in the subsequent sections.

BACKGROUND

To gain some insights into the nature of the current study, a brief background of the topic including the literature review is presented further.

M-Banking

M-banking is an offshoot of the financial industry that is specifically related to banks (Baabdullah et al., 2019). It is a type of electronic service and is also viewed as one of the latest channels of banking. In a broader sense, it is considered as a facility that helps in transacting through mobile phones or other hand-held devices (Vishnuvardhan, Manjula, & Naik, 2020). M-banking is the positive outcome of the collective development of financial services and m-commerce applications (Chung & Kwon, 2009), and allows the consumers to keep a track of their banking operations through mobile phones (Parvin, 2013). It enables the banks to provide different types of personal banking services to customers primarily through a mobile phone. Some of these services may be balance enquiry, cheque book request, funds transfer, bills payment, movie ticket booking, etc. M-banking could be assessed by the customers through different ways such as SMS banking, WAP-based banking, USSD, mobile web banking, and m-banking apps. Out of these, m-banking apps are primarily promoted by the banks as the most efficient medium of accessing the service.

Awareness

Awareness is considered as an important constituent of consumer behavior where its higher level may lead to effective use of a product or service (Schiffman & Kanuk, 2007, p. 175). Among banks, it is viewed as a prerequisite for understanding the perceived value and use of electronic banking services (Noor, 2011; Amin, Hamid, Lada, & Anis, 2008), and could be observed at the level up to which the banks' customers are familiar with the existence of a service (Tibenderana, Ogao, Ikoja-Odongo, & Wokadala, 2010). In the case of m-banking, awareness could be evident from the knowledge about different types of services being offered to individual customers through mobile phones (Amin et al., 2008). It has been observed in the past that increased efforts from the banks for promoting the awareness could provide more understanding about m-banking service to the customers (Cudjoe, Anim, & Nyanyofio, 2015).

Perceived Value

It is viewed as a key indicator of consumer behavior change. There is a direct relationship between quality of service and perceived value (Zeithaml, 1988). Marketing studies have highlighted the key role of perceived value in examining the usage of various goods and services. Perceived value is also known as customer value (Butz & Goodstein, 1996) or simply value (Zeithaml, 1988). Previous research has highlighted the importance of perceived value in understanding consumer behavior (Xie, Ye, Huang & Ye, 2021) and its utility for evaluating consumer behavior towards different technology-based services (Shaikh & Karjaluoto, 2016; Li & Mao, 2015). Zeithaml (1988) has proposed that perceived value is dependent upon the perception of consumers and is based on the utility of goods or services to the individuals. It means that there could be a difference among the perceived value of individuals even for the same goods or services and this may be true even in the case of different financial services such as m-banking. Measurement of perceived value is of crucial importance as it helps the business organization to gain a competitive advantage (Lee & Overby, 2004). Roy (2016) mentioned that this value could be generated through exchange and experience gained by using different kinds of services.

Perceived Value Scale

The measurement of perceived value could be based on multiple dimensions (Yeh, Wang & Yieh, 2016). In the present work, it is determined by utilizing a four-item scale that includes the constructs such as price paid, overall value, perceived control, and convenience. This is aligned with the measurement of perceived value undertaken in the previous studies by Dodds, Monroe and Grewal (1991), and Sirdeshmukh, Singh and Sabol (2002). Further, the four items of perceived value have been adapted as per the focus of the current study. Brief information about these items is given below:

1. **Price Paid:** It is the cost of m-banking usage and helps in determining whether the service is considered economical.
2. **Perceived Convenience:** It helps to know about the ease that m-banking provides to its users.

3. **Perceived Control:** It is the feeling about control over one's banking operations among the m-banking customers.
4. **Overall Value:** It is the total gain that m-banking customers feel by using the service.

Awareness of M-Banking and Perceived Value

Laforet and Li (2005) in their study conducted in Finland have mentioned that a lower level of awareness could be one of the main hurdles in understanding the merits of m-banking. This means that increase in knowledge could only be possible by providing the users with some tips or assistance on how to avail the service. Chen (2013) carried out a study in Taiwan in which it was proposed that awareness significantly affects m-banking usage. Further, the findings of the study undertaken by Cudjoe, Anim and Nyanyofio (2015) also supported this view. In their study in the UK, Howcroft, Hamilton and Hewer (2002) highlighted that awareness about the service is an important predictor of telephone-based banking. Mutahar et al. (2018) conducted a study on the perceived value of m-banking in Malaysia and found awareness as one of its important determinants. In another work on predicting the intention to use m-banking, Mutahar et al. (2021) have highlighted that awareness considerably influences the mobile banking perceived value. So, this discussion leads to the formation of the following hypothesis:

H_1: Awareness has a significant effect on the perceived value of m-banking.

Perceived Value and M-Banking Usage

Literature provides strong evidence about the association between perceived value and the use of mobile commerce services (Wang, 2008). Perceived value could be considered as an important driver of m-banking usage and also influences its behavioral intentions (Ciunova-Shuleska, Palamidovska-Sterjadovska, & Prodanova, 2022). It is widely recognized as the indicator of perceived benefits of a technology-based service (Komlan, Koffi, & Kingsford, 2016; Kumar & Reinartz, 2016) such as m-banking. A high level of perceived value leads to a greater tendency to adopt the m-banking service (Demirhan, 2020). Karjaluoto, Shaikh, Saarijarvi and Saraniemi (2019) in their study on the relationship between perceived value and use of mobile financial service apps have found a direct relationship between the two where higher perceived value leads to increased service usage. Xiong (2013) in the study on the adoption of m-banking in China has proposed that perceived value considerably affects the actual usage intention. Prodanova, Ciunova-Shuleska and PalamidovskaSterjadovska (2019) have mentioned that perceived value drives the m-banking usage of consumers and even guides their service reuse intention. This relationship leads to the formation of the following hypothesis:

H_2: Perceived value has a significant effect on m-banking usage.

Age and Perceived Value of M-Banking

The perceived value may vary among banking customers based on their demographic background (Alsheikh, & Bojei, 2012). Age is considered as a key moderating variable in consumer behavior research (Thaichon, Lobo, & Quach, 2016) and has an important role to play in the segmentation of consumers (Kim, Cho, & Kim, 2019; Loureiro & Roschk, 2014) as well as among the determinants of consumer behavior (Sindwani, 2017). Variable age significantly affects the satisfaction towards m-banking service (Mkpojiogu, Hashim, & Adamu, 2016). There may be a difference among the old and young consumers in terms of the potential value of a product or service (Thaichon, Lobo, & Quach, 2016; Loureiro & Roschk, 2014; Daughtrey, Vowles, & Black, 2013) such as m-banking. Young age people usually have a higher perceived value for technology-enabled services in comparison to the elderly (Sharma, Chen, & Luk, 2012). Previous studies suggest that demographic differences considerably affect the intention to use m-banking (Abayomi et al., 2019; Alkhaldi & Kharma, 2019; Ntseme, Namatsagang, & Chukwuere, 2016). Abayomi et al. (2019), and Ntseme, Namatsagang and Chukwuere (2016) in their studies on m-banking have found a positive relationship between age and use of the service. Alkhaldi and Kharma (2019) revealed that age plays an important moderating role in the adoption and m-banking usage. On the contrary, Laforet and Li (2005), and Demirhan (2020) in their study highlighted that effect of age on the use of m-banking is insignificant. Thus, this discussion leads to the following hypothesis:

H_3: Age has a significant moderating effect on the relationship between perceived value and m-banking usage.

Further, the research model based on the relationships discussed above is presented in Figure 1. It includes the different hypotheses which need to be tested further to examine the issue of consumer behavior change among the m-banking customers.

Figure 1. Model of hypotheses

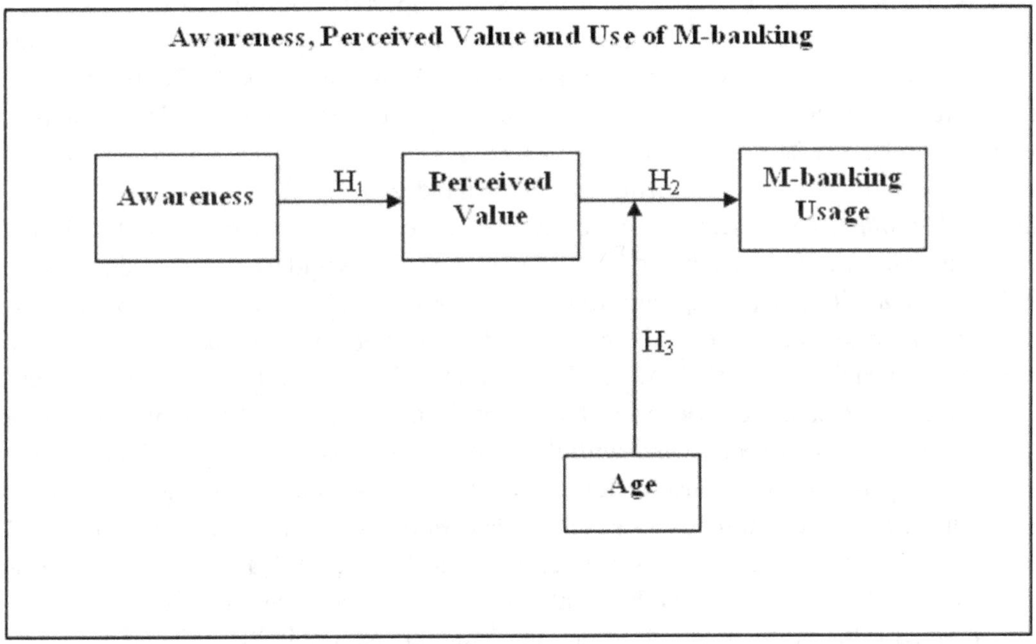

MAIN FOCUS OF THE CHAPTER

Consumer behavior change poses great challenges for the m-banking service providers. The main issues and concerns that may evolve in this context are presented further.

Issues and Problems

In the dynamic business scenario providing service through electronic means creates a lot of challenges for those involved in its delivery that is equally applicable to the banking sector. Most businesses are rapidly adopting different mobile commerce applications and the banks have also responded effectively to this transition. Mobile commerce has influenced business organizations and personal banking through the latest channels of service delivery such as m-banking (Luo, Li, Zhang, & Shim, 2010). There has been greater concern among the banks to find a new channel of electronic service for quite a long and it has resulted in the launch of m-banking. M-banking is considered as most suitable for carrying out personal banking operations that involve individual consumers and has immense scope for the implementation of technology. The individualistic nature of personal banking presents huge prospects for the automation of banking operations through m-banking and demands the greater focus of the banks. M-banking has proved to be vital for improving operational efficiency and is considered a unique way of delivering banking services to consumers via mobile phones or handheld devices. It has transformed the way how banking operations were carried out in the past and is considered a service that is more suitable for retail or personal banking due to its individualistic nature. M-banking is also viewed as an important channel of personal banking for the future (Moser, 2015).

Awareness and perceived value are recognized as the important constituents of consumer behavior where higher awareness may positively influence the perceived value. The creation of value for the customers is one of the foremost objectives of a business (Kumar & Reinartz, 2016) and may also reflect their awareness about its goods or services. Thus, awareness could be regarded as an ascendant of perceived value and may affect customer relationships. It is linked with several business processes and has a key impact on the success of a firm (García-Fernández et al., 2018). Higher perceived value is also considered an important indicator of good service quality (De Leon, Atienza, & Susilo, 2020), and this increases its relevance for consumer studies. Perceived value is widely acknowledged as the driving force for the sustainability of banking operations (Ling, Sook Fern, Kah Boon, Seng Huat, 2016). Maintaining higher perceived value is generally considered a challenge as the banks are unable to control it directly (Medberg & Heinonen, 2014). Also, it has a direct and positive influence on consumer behavior in the case of electronic banking services such as m-banking (Tumewah, 2020). M-banking involves a direct interaction of individual consumers with the bank and influences their perceived value about the service. Customer perceived value also reflects m-banking service quality (Langat, Bonuke, & Kibet, 2021; Hanaysha, 2018) and customer service (Samudro, Sumarwan, Yusuf, & Simanjuntak, 2018), and is even regarded as a key determinant of consumer behavior (Pobee, 2021; Keshavarz & Jamshidi, 2018; Wei, He, & Zhu, 2016). Previous research reveals a dearth of studies in the literature focused on examining the perceived value of the m-banking service (Alsheikh, & Bojei, 2012). There has been a lesser concern to evaluate the perceived value among the m-banking users (Mutahar et al., 2021) and requires some future research focus (Salem & Alanadoly, 2020) to investigate consumer behavior.

Previous research reveals that the demographics of the customer such as age moderates the different determinants of consumer behavior (Cooil, Keiningham, Aksoy, & Hsu, 2007; Schirmer, Ringle, Gudergan, & Feistel, 2018), and this could also be true in case of perceived value. Individuals belonging to different age cohorts may vary in terms of their values, needs, and preferences (Cardoso, Costa, & Novais, 2010; Hervé & Mullet, 2009). Consumers' intention to use a product or service could be significantly moderated by age (Merhi, Hone, Tarhini, & Ameen, 2020). Also, there could be considerable differences among the users of electronic banking in terms of age (Nasuminnisa, Dawood, & Sowmya, 2014). There is a shortage of studies in the m-banking literature dealing with the perceived value and demographics such as age (Demirhan, 2020). So, this shows a gap in the literature and presents an opportunity to understand the issue of awareness, perceived value, and age in this new channel of banking.

The above discussion highlights the key concerns and challenges related to the subject matter of this study. Different banks are trying to stay closer to their target audience and provide them customized services based on perceived value and age in the technology-enabled settings. It is believed that awareness affects the perceived value that may in turn influence the actual usage of m-banking. Further, age may also play an important moderating role in this association. Till now, there has been a lesser concern to understand this relationship. So, the current chapter addresses this issue and helps to examine the dynamics of consumer behavior represented by these constructs that may further affect the overall satisfaction of the banks' services. Very little evidence is available in the previous studies that deal with the effect of change in consumer behavior on this relationship. The literature related to consumer behavior in m-banking shows a shortage of studies in this field. The current work may raise certain issues and concerns which need to be tackled with a greater focus.

Research Methodology

Data collection in the current study has been conducted through a survey-based approach that involved the districts of Ludhiana, Jalandhar, and Amritsar in the state of Punjab in India. These districts were having the highest banking density in the state and were also considered to be the most economically significant. The sampling technique adopted in the survey was convenience sampling and data was collected through personal visits to the branches of the top 10 private and public sector banks in the three districts. The ranking of these banks was done based on the number of m-banking transactions from the last year. During the survey, firstly a total of 600 questionnaires were distributed to the respondents with 200 each in the three districts. But after, 524 usable questionnaires were obtained which kept the response rate to 87.3%. Further, the missing values were dealt with using the best guess approach. It has been observed that this approach could be effectively utilized by filling the missing values in the data set based on the pattern shown by the previous data values (Zikmund, Babin, Carr & Griffin, 2013). Among the 524 respondents, 295 (56.29%) were between 18 to 30 years (YA), 194 (37.02%) were between 31 to 45 years (MA) and 35 (6.67%) were of 46 years and above the age (OA). The collected data is then evaluated through Excel and SPSS.

In the questionnaire, firstly the respondents were asked about their awareness of types of services provided through m-banking that may be enquiry-based as well as transaction-based services. These included funds transfer (within & outside the bank), immediate payment services (IMPS), mobile top-up, DTH top-up, shopping from mobile, paying insurance premium, utility bills payment, paying credit cards bills, railway ticket booking, airline ticket booking, movie ticket booking, donations payment, paying subscriptions (new/renewal), balance enquiry, mini statement, cheque book request, stop cheque request, message to a relationship manager and demat enquiry service. Next, the responses related to m-banking usage were collected based on a frequency scale ranging from very frequent, frequent, occasional, rare, and very rare usage of service. This range was represented by the Likert scale items with values 1 to 5 with 1 denoting the very rare and 5 very frequent use of m-banking. Next, the statements based on a four-item scale were presented to the respondents in the questionnaire. This scale matches with the studies conducted by Dodds, Monroe and Grewal (1991) and Sirdeshmukh, Singh, and Sabol (2002). The statements based on the four parameters of this scale i.e. price paid, overall value, perceived control, and convenience is listed in Table 1 and adjusted as per the nature of the current study.

Table 1. Statements representing perceived value items

Variable	Statements
PV	1. M-banking service makes my banking economical.
	2. M-banking offers me convenience in banking with 24-hour access.
	3. M-banking gives me a feeling of being in control of my banking from a distant location.
	4. M-banking service provides me value for my efforts made in its usage.
	5. I will do more transactions using mobile banking in the coming months

Data Analysis

In this phase, the data generated from the survey is put to test subsequently using the suitable statistical technique that may provide the required data analytics support to judge the dynamics of consumer behavior based on the constructs of this chapter.

Appropriateness of the Statistical Model

In the current study, linear regression and moderated multiple regression analysis using dummy variables are applied to evaluate the relationships mentioned in Figure 1. Moderating analysis helps to identify the strength of the relationship between the predictor and a criterion variable (Loureiro & Roschk, 2014). Further to judge the suitability of this technique, its different assumptions are tested one by one and the values generated are presented in Table 2.

Table 2. Values depicting appropriateness of the regression model

Relationships in the Models	Durbin-Watson	Collinearity Statistics		Residual Means	Outliers
		Tolerance	VIF		Cook's Distance
AW → PV	1.644	1.00	1.000	.000	.002
PV → MBU	1.847	.976 .980	1.025 1.021	.000	.002

Independence of Residuals: Table 2 shows the Durban-Watson values of 1.847 and 1.644 for relationships between awareness and perceived value, and perceived value and m-banking usage. These values are greater than 1 and suggest that there is an absence of autocorrelation in the sample. It is also an indicator of the independence of residuals.

Multicollinearity: Table 2 shows that the values of VIF (variance inflation factor) are all less than 10 which reflects that the predictor variables in the sample are not correlated with each other. This shows that the sample is free from the problem of multicollinearity.

Residual Mean and Outliers: Table 2 shows the residual mean value of .000 for both the relationships and depicts the proper regression fit. In addition, Cook's Distance value of .002 reflects the absence of outliers in the data set. Cook and Stanford (1982) mentioned that the Cook's Distance value of less than 1 indicates the non-existence of possible outliers.

The satisfaction of the above assumptions assures the appropriateness of the regression model for further application.

Effect of Awareness on Perceived Value

In the current study, the summated four-item perceived value score is considered as the criterion variable. Further, the effect of awareness on the perceived value is ascertained using the linear regression model. The summated score of awareness (AW) of different m-banking services is calculated for each respondent and then its effect on perceived value (PV) is determined. The equation representing this relationship is as follows:

$$PV = a+b1(AW) \quad (1)$$

Where, a = intercept

b1 = regression coefficient
AW = predictor variable
PV = criterion variable

The values generated after the application of the regression model based on equation (1) are presented in Table 3.

Table 3. Linear regression results show the effect of awareness on the perceived value

Hypothesis	Model	Adjusted R^2 Value	ANOVA	
			F	Sig.
H_1	Model-1 *Categories .... Coefficient* AW → PV .... .147	.030 *Sig.* .000	17.244	.000

Table 3 shows the adjusted R^2 value of .030 and F value of 17.244. The calculated F value under the ANOVA is found to be statistically significant. Hence, hypothesis H_1 is supported and depicts that awareness about the service positively affects the perceived value of the respondents.

Moderating Effect of Age between Perceived Value and M-Banking Usage

To understand the moderating role of age on the association between perceived value and m-banking usage, firstly the summated score of the four items of perceived value is fitted as the predictor variable and the frequency scale of m-banking usage (MBU) as the criterion variable for the regression models. The two equations represented by model-2 and model-3 showing the direct and interaction effect (_mod) involving these variables are listed below:

Model-2

$$MBU = a + b1(PV) \quad (2)$$

Model-3
YA_mod = PV*(YA)
MA_mod = PV*(MA)

$$MBU = a + b1(PV) + b2(YA\_mod) + b3(MA\_mod) \quad (3)$$

Where, a = intercept

b1, b2, b3 = regression coefficients
PV, YA_mod, MA_mod = predictor variables
MBU = criterion variable

In this case, category '46 years & above' (OA) is the omitted comparison variable

Further, multiple regression analysis has been applied on equations (2) and (3), and the results obtained have been presented in Table 4.

Table 4. Multiple regression results showing the moderation effect of age on the relationship between perceived value and use of m-banking

Hypothesis	Model	Adjusted R^2 Value	Sig. F Change	ANOVA	
				F	Sig.
H_2	Model-2 *Categories .... Coefficient* PV → MBU .... .184	.185 *Sig.* .000	.000	119.931	.000
H_3	Model-3 *Categories .... Coefficient* PV → MBU .... .139 YA_mod → MBU .... .043 MA_mod → MBU .... .038	.214 *Sig.* .000 .000 .000	.000	48.346	.000

Table 4 depicts that in the case of m-banking usage, the value of adjusted R^2 increases from .185 in model-2 to .214 in model-3. The F change value in the table reveals that this change in adjusted R^2 is statistically significant. Both model-2 and model-3 have significant F statistics values of 119.931 and 48.346 respectively. It shows that there is a considerable effect of perceived value on the usage of m-banking and this effect continues to be significant even when this relationship is moderated by the variable age. So, the hypotheses H_2 and H_3 are supported and it is observed that there is a significant effect of perceived value on the use of m-banking and also the age of the respondent effectively moderates the relationship between perceived value and overall service usage.

Next, taking the case of model-3 specifically dealing with the interaction of different categories of variable age with the perceived value, it is observed that all the predictors including the categories young age and middle age have a significant interaction effect on the usage of m-banking. The coefficient value of 0.043 in the case of young age is the highest followed by 0.038 in the case of the middle age group. This shows that there is the greatest interaction effect in the young age followed by the middle age and omitted old age group.

RESULTS DISCUSSION

The data analysis presented in the previous section reveals a direct relationship between awareness, perceived value, and usage of m-banking. Firstly, it showed that the awareness of consumers about the different services offered in m-banking affects their perceived value and that further has a significant effect on the use of the service. Further, it is also found that the age of consumers considerably moderates the relationship between perceived value and m-banking usage. The results have revealed that the perceived value of m-banking is highest in young age people and this value reduces with the increase in age and is least among the elderly. These findings lead to important implications for those involved in understanding the consumer behavior in the case of m-banking service which is discussed further.

IMPLICATIONS

The current chapter shows that awareness of the service has a significant effect on the perceived value of the m-banking customers. It means that people who have more knowledge about the different types of services provided through m-banking tend to possess high value in the service. So, the financial institutions involved in the delivery of m-banking should work on promoting the awareness of service among all sections of society. Hence, the planning of m-banking promotion campaigns focused on increasing the know-how about various m-banking services should be pivotal for the banks to attain their objective of financial inclusion. The study proposed that higher awareness leads to higher perceived value that may further induce more people to utilize the facilities provided by m-banking. It is important to mention here that awareness about the service could be increased by providing different learning materials by the banks such as newsletters or pamphlets to the consumers both in the physical as well as digital forms.

In addition, the significant effect of perceived value on the usage of m-banking reveals that the consumers tend to use the service only if they find any utility from its usage in their day-to-day life. The banks should make continuous efforts in increasing the perceived value of m-banking among the consumers through different means of promotion. It may involve the right kind of advertising and could only be possible by selecting the proper communication channel to reach the customers and making them aware of the benefits of the service. Next, it is observed that the consumers differ in terms of the perceived value of m-banking based on the variable age. This study proposes that the perceived value of the service is highest among young consumers and further reduces with the natural maturity. Elderly people have the lowest perceived value of the service. So, the banks should keep track of this change in consumer behavior based on aging and work on understanding the variations among different age cohorts. They need to address the challenges of behavioral change among the consumers based on their maturity and may effectively deal with them based on the following recommendations:

Understand Cognitive Differences

It is generally observed that young consumers have greater cognitive abilities in terms of the acceptance of new technology and that may be the reason for their higher perceived value of m-banking in the current study. In comparison, the elderly experience decline in physical strength and cognition due to aging. Consequently, a hassle-free user interface of the different m-banking applications should be designed with the ability for increased customization based on the preferences of individual consumers. It may include the setting of the color scheme, font size, and style of text for different apps and websites accessed through mobile phones or any other handheld devices based on the age-based preferences of users. This would help the banks to respond to the distinct needs of the elderly as well as the young age effectively and may contribute towards the increase in the perceived value of m-banking, especially for the higher age groups.

Enable Real-Time Assistance

Banks involved in the delivery of m-banking should arrange for providing service support to consumers in real-time i.e. while performing transactions. This could be possible through appropriate customer support and involvement of humans or artificial intelligence-enabled virtual digital assistants or chatbots. For this purpose, the banks should work on conducting required training sessions for their human resource through effective internal marketing and equip them with the needed skills on how to handle the m-banking users. It may in turn help to boost confidence, particularly among the elderly consumers by clarifying any doubts and concerns in their minds regarding m-banking. This would lead to more trust among the older cohorts such as middle age and old age, and eventually, help to increase their perceived value and m-banking service usage.

Utilize the Power of Social Media

In the present era, the maturity of social media applications has reached newer levels and social media marketing has been recognized as an effective tool for reaching customers. This transformation even can affect the banking sector and target customers. It could be observed that the consumers belonging to different age cohorts including the elderly may also be users of any of the social media applications such as Facebook, Instagram, Twitter, and LinkedIn. So, the banks could effectively utilize the channel of social media to reach their target audience based on their age and other demographics. It could further help them to minimize the gap in digital literacy among the young age and the elderly groups for m-banking and create the right kind of positioning of service in their minds. This may enable the banks to increase the perceived value of m-banking especially among the elderly consumers which may further affect their ability to use the service effectively.

Promote M-Banking as a Ubiquitous Cost-Effective Channel

M-banking has always been acknowledged as the channel which could assist the stakeholders to achieve their goal of financial inclusion in a lesser time frame. The service could be availed anywhere and anytime even in remote and distant locations. Different banks should try to promote m-banking as a cost-effective channel for accessing their services and work on publicizing the availability of this service at a lower cost even without physically visiting their branches. It is observed that in the higher ages consumers have more orientation towards savings due to their family, health, and safety concerns. So, if the banks can position m-banking as an economical mode of service in their minds then this may again help to increase its perceived value among both the young and the elderly population equally.

Address the Security Concerns

Security of the transactions has been considered as a crucial factor for conducting electronic banking operations which includes both internet banking and mobile banking. In a similarity between the two, m-banking also suffers from this limitation during its acceptance among the users. There may be a difference in the reliability of a technology service both among the young age and old consumers. Old-age people mostly have a lower tendency to take the risk and are apprehensive towards the adoption of new technology. This concern needs to be addressed with utmost care in the case of m-banking. The employees of banks should work on clarifying any doubts about the security of transactions for all ages. This would help to minimize the perceived risk of m-banking specifically among the elderly consumers and would in turn increase their perceived value and usage of the service.

FUTURE RESEARCH DIRECTIONS

This chapter deals with the issue of consumer behavior change by taking the case of the awareness and perceived value of m-banking of the respondents belonging to the state of Punjab in India. It also takes into account the interaction of age with the perceived value of service. However, in the future, some research could be conducted based on these constructs in a distinct geographic location with a separate population. This study was focused on one of the first implementations of m-commerce i.e. m-banking. So, there may be a need for some research work that could be undertaken with the same constructs but on its different applications such as mobile ticketing, mobile shopping, or others. Further, it is observed that out of the different indicators the current study has utilized the awareness and perceived value as the construct to understand the issue of consumer behavior change. But in the future, some work may be carried out involving the other constituents of consumer behavior which are not given due attention in this study. Lastly, this study focused on the interaction of only variable age with the perceived value thereby ignoring the interaction of other demographics such as gender, income, occupation, education, etc. So, this also demands some future work involving the interaction of similar variables.

CONCLUSION

The understanding of the issue of consumer behavior change in the case of digital technologies is considered as an area of thrust for the modern days' business. It has also emerged as a field of prime importance to the banking sector. The ability of the banks to respond rapidly to the changing customer demands and market influences is the key to staying competitive within their customer groups. Bank's ability to cater to evolving user requirements would help them to compete and remain up to date with the latest technological infrastructure. This chapter was focused on this theme with an endeavor to address this concern by taking the case of m-banking service and supporting it with suitable data analytics. It utilized awareness and perceived value as the predictors of consumer behavior and provided important suggestions for the banks, researchers, and other service providers to follow. The banks need to understand the role of awareness and perceived value in the usage of the m-banking service. Further, they may create suitable strategies for dealing with the dynamics of perceived value concerning age and address the concerns of customers with utmost care. This would enable them to maintain higher customer retention and achieve healthy relationships with them. Finally, it is concluded that the banks or those involved in the delivery of m-banking should give due attention to the issue of digital consumer behavior and change as highlighted in this chapter.

REFERENCES

Abayomi, O. J., Olabode, A. C., Reyad, M. A. H., Tetteh Teye, E., Haq, M. N., & Mensah, E. T. (2019). Effects of demographic factors on customers' mobile banking services adoption in Nigeria. *International Journal of Business and Social Science*, *10*(1), 63–77. doi:10.30845/ijbss.v10n1p9

Alkhaldi, A. N., & Kharma, Q. M. (2019). Customer's intention to adopt mobile banking services: The moderating influence of demographic factors. *International Journal of Innovation and Technology Management*, *16*(5), 1–26. doi:10.1142/S0219877019500378

Alsheikh, L., & Bojei, J. (2012). Customer's perceived value to use mobile banking services. *Proceedings of the International Conference on Management, Behavioral Sciences and Economics Issues (ICMBSE'2012).*

Amin, H., Hamid, M. R. A., Lada, S., & Anis, Z. (2008). The adoption of mobile banking in Malaysia: The case of Bank Islam Malaysia Berhad (BIMB). *International Journal of Business and Society*, *9*(2), 43–53.

Baabdullah, A. M., Alalwan, A. A., Rana, N. P., Patil, P., & Dwivedi, Y. K. (2019). An integrated model for m-banking adoption in Saudi Arabia. *International Journal of Bank Marketing*, *37*(2), 452–478. doi:10.1108/IJBM-07-2018-0183

Butz, J. H. E. Jr, & Goodstein, L. (1996). Measuring customer value: Gaining the strategic advantage. *Organizational Dynamics*, *24*(3), 63–77. doi:10.1016/S0090-2616(96)90006-6

Cardoso, P., Costa, H., & Novais, L. A. (2010). Fashion consumer profiles in the Portuguese market: Involvement, innovativeness, self-expression and impulsiveness as segmentation criteria. *International Journal of Consumer Studies*, *34*(6), 638–647. doi:10.1111/j.1470-6431.2010.00891.x

Chen, C. (2013). Perceived risk, usage frequency of mobile banking services. *Managing Service Quality*, *23*(5), 410–436. doi:10.1108/MSQ-10-2012-0137

Chung, N., & Kwon, S. J. (2009). The effect of customers' mobile experience and technical support on the intention to use mobile banking. *Cyberpsychology & Behavior*, *12*(5), 539–543. doi:10.1089/cpb.2009.0014 PMID:19772441

Ciunova-Shuleska, A., Palamidovska-Sterjadovska, N., & Prodanova, J. (2022). What drives m-banking clients to continue using m-banking services? *Journal of Business Research*, *139*, 731–739. doi:10.1016/j.jbusres.2021.10.024

Cooil, B., Keiningham, T., Aksoy, L., & Hsu, M. (2007). A longitudinal analysis of customer satisfaction and share of wallet: Investigating the moderating effect of customer characteristics. *Journal of Marketing*, *71*(1), 67–83. doi:10.1509/jmkg.71.1.067

Cook, R. D., & Sanford, W. (1982). *Residuals and influence in regression*. Chapman and Hall.

Cudjoe, A. G., Anim, P. A., & Nyanyofio, J. G. N. T. (2015). Determinants of mobile banking adoption in the Ghanaian banking industry: A case of access bank Ghana limited. *Journal of Computer and Communications*, *3*(2), 1–19. doi:10.4236/jcc.2015.32001

Daughtrey, C. L., Vowles, N. S., & Black, G. S. (2013). The effects of membership and demographics on consumer satisfaction and loyalty in service organizations. *Services Marketing Quarterly*, *34*(4), 292–308. doi:10.1080/15332969.2013.827066

De Leon, M. V., Atienza, R. P., & Susilo, D. (2020). Influence of self-service technology (SST) service quality dimensions as a second-order factor on perceived value and customer satisfaction in a mobile banking application. *Cogent Business & Management*, *7*(1), 1794241. doi:10.1080/23311975.2020.1794241

Demirhan, M. (2020). Demographic characteristics and perceived value differences in mobile banking: An empirical study in Turkey. *Erciyes Üniversitesi Sosyal Bilimler Enstitüsü Dergisi*, *48*, 237–263.

Dodds, W. B., Monroe, K. B., & Grewal, D. (1991). Effects of price, brand, and store information on buyers' product evaluations. *JMR, Journal of Marketing Research*, *28*(3), 307–319. doi:10.2307/3172866

García-Fernández, J., Gálvez-Ruíz, P., Fernández-Gavira, J., Vélez-Colón, L., Pitts, B., & Bernal-García, A. (2018). The effects of service convenience and perceived quality on perceived value, satisfaction and loyalty in low-cost fitness centers. *Sport Management Review*, *21*(3), 250–262. doi:10.1016/j.smr.2017.07.003

George, S. (2016). Mobile banking in the present scenario. *International Journal of Research in Commerce and Management*, *7*(2), 61–64.

Hanaysha, J. R. (2018). Customer retention and the mediating role of perceived value in retail industry. *World Journal of Entrepreneurship, Management and Sustainable Development*, *14*(1), 2–24. doi:10.1108/WJEMSD-06-2017-0035

Hervé, C., & Mullet, E. (2009). Age and factors influencing consumer behaviour. *International Journal of Consumer Studies*, *33*(3), 302–308. doi:10.1111/j.1470-6431.2009.00743.x

Howcroft, B., Hamilton, R., & Hewer, P. (2002). Consumer attitude and the usage and adoption of home-based banking in the United Kingdom. *International Journal of Bank Marketing*, *20*(3), 111–121. doi:10.1108/02652320210424205

Karjaluoto, H., Shaikh, A. A., Saarijärvi, H., & Saraniemi, S. (2019). How perceived value drives the use of mobile financial services apps. *International Journal of Information Management*, *47*, 252–261. doi:10.1016/j.ijinfomgt.2018.08.014

Keshavarz, Y., & Jamshidi, D. (2018). Service quality evaluation and the mediating role of perceived value and customer satisfaction in customer loyalty. *International Journal of Tourism Cities*, *4*(2), 220–244. doi:10.1108/IJTC-09-2017-0044

Kim, W. H., Cho, J., & Kim, K. S. (2019). The relationships of wine promotion, customer satisfaction, and behavioral intention: The moderating roles of customers' gender and age. *Journal of Hospitality and Tourism Management*, *39*, 212–218. doi:10.1016/j.jhtm.2019.03.001

Komlan, G., Koffi, D., & Kingsford, K. M. (2016). MCDM technique to evaluating mobile banking adoption in the Togolese banking industry based on the perceived value: Perceived benefit and perceived sacrifice factors. *International Journal of Data Mining Knowledge Management Process*, *6*(3), 37–56. doi:10.5121/ijdkp.2016.6304

Kumar, V., & Reinartz, W. (2016). Creating enduring customer value. *Journal of Marketing*, *80*(6), 36–68. doi:10.1509/jm.15.0414

Laforet, S., & Li, X. (2005). Consumers' attitudes towards online and mobile banking in China. *International Journal of Bank Marketing*, *23*(5), 362–380. doi:10.1108/02652320510629250

Langat, D. K., Bonuke, R., & Kibet, Y. (2021). Mobile banking service quality and customer retention: A moderated mediation model of customer perceived value and perceived corporate image. *SEISENSE Journal of Management*, *4*(4), 47–61. doi:10.33215jom.v4i4.672

Laukkanen, T., & Kiviniemi, V. (2010). The role of information in mobile banking resistance. *International Journal of Bank Marketing*, *28*(5), 372–388. doi:10.1108/02652321011064890

Lee, E. J., & Overby, J. W. (2004). Creating value for online shoppers: Implications for satisfaction and loyalty. *Journal of Consumer Satisfaction, Dissatisfaction & Complaining Behavior*, *17*(1), 54–67.

Ling, M., Fern, Y. S., Boon, L. K., & Huat, T. S. (2016). Understanding customer satisfaction in internet banking: A case study in Malaca. *Procedia Economics and Finance*, *37*, 80–85. doi:10.1016/S2212-5671(16)30096-X

Loureiro, S. M. C., & Roschk, H. (2014). Differential effects of atmospheric cues on emotions and loyalty intention with respect to age under online/offline environment. *Journal of Retailing and Consumer Services*, *21*(2), 211–219. doi:10.1016/j.jretconser.2013.09.001

Luo, X., Li, H., Zhang, J., & Shim, J. P. (2010). Examining multi-dimensional trust and multi-faceted risk in initial acceptance of emerging technologies: An empirical study of mobile banking services. *Decision Support Systems*, *49*(2), 222–234. doi:10.1016/j.dss.2010.02.008

Medberg, G. & Heinonen, K. (2014). Invisible value formation: a netnography in retail banking, *International Journal of Bank Marketing, 32*(6), 590-607.

Merhi, M., Hone, K., Tarhini, A., & Ameen, N. (2020). An empirical examination of the moderating role of age and gender in consumer mobile banking use: A cross-national, quantitative study. *Journal of Enterprise Information Management, 34*(4), 1144–1168. doi:10.1108/JEIM-03-2020-0092

Mkpojiogu, E. O. C., Hashim, N. L., & Adamu, R. (2016). Observed demographic differentials in user perceived satisfaction on the usability of mobile banking applications. *Proceedings of the Knowledge Management International Conference (Kmice)*, 263-268.

Moser, F. (2015). Mobile banking: A fashionable concept or an institutionalized channel in future retail banking? analyzing patterns in the practical and academic mobile banking literature. *International Journal of Bank Marketing, 33*(2), 162–177. doi:10.1108/IJBM-08-2013-0082

Mutahar, A. M., Aldholay, A., Isaac, O., Jalal, A. N., & Alkibsi, S. (2021). Predicting intention to use mobile banking services among Yemeni Banks' Clients: Is Perceived value important? *Proceedings of the International Conference on Emerging Technologies and Intelligent Systems (ICETIS 2021)*, 498-520.

Mutahar, A. M., Daud, N. M., Ramayah, T., Putit, L., & Isaac, O. (2018). Predicting perceived value in mobile banking: Are awareness and perceived risk important? *Research Journal of Applied Sciences, 13*(2), 112–124.

Nasuminnisa, A., Dawood, D. A. K., & Sowmya, K. R. (2014). Influence of demographic factors on e-banking service quality in banking sector. *Indian Journal of Applied Sciences, 4*(3), 235–237.

Noor, M. M. (2011). Determining critical success factors of mobile banking adoption in Malaysia. *Australian Journal of Basic and Applied Sciences, 5*(9), 252–265.

Ntseme, O. J., Namatsagang, A., & Chukwuere, J. E. (2016). Risks and benefits from using mobile banking in an emerging country. *Risk Governance and Control: Financial Markets & Institutions, 6*(4), 355–363. doi:10.22495/rgcv6i4c2art13

Parvin, A. (2013). Mobile banking operation in Bangladesh: Prediction of future. *Journal of Internet Banking and Commerce, 18*(1), 1–15.

Pobee, F. (2021). Assessing online repurchase intention in a developing country: The role of perceived value. *International Journal of Strategic Decision Sciences, 12*(1), 61–76. doi:10.4018/IJSDS.2021010104

Prodanova, J., Ciunova-Shuleska, A., & Palamidovska-Sterjadovska, N. (2019). Enriching m-banking perceived value to achieve reuse intention. *Marketing Intelligence & Planning, 37*(6), 617–630. doi:10.1108/MIP-11-2018-0508

Salem, S. F., & Alanadoly, A. B. (2021). Personality traits and social media as drivers of word-of-mouth towards sustainable fashion. *Journal of Fashion Marketing and Management, 25*(1), 24–44. doi:10.1108/JFMM-08-2019-0162

Samudro, A., Sumarwan, U., Yusuf, E. Z., & Simanjuntak, M. (2018). Perceived value, social bond and switching cost as antecedents and predictors of customer loyalty in the B2B chemical industry context: A literature review. *International Journal of Marketing Studies, 10*(4), 124–138. doi:10.5539/ijms.v10n4p124

Schiffman, L. G., & Kanuk, L. L. (2007). *Consumer behavior* (9th ed.). Pearson Education.

Schirmer, N., Ringle, C., Gudergan, S., & Feistel, M. (2018). The link between customer satisfaction and loyalty: The moderating role of customer characteristics. *Journal of Strategic Marketing*, *26*(4), 298–317. doi:10.1080/0965254X.2016.1240214

Shaikh, A. A., & Karjaluoto, H. (2016). Mobile banking services continuous usage--case study of Finland. In *Proceedings of the 49th Hawaii International Conference on System Sciences* (pp. 1497-1506). IEEE.

Sharma, P., Chen, I., & Luk, S. (2012). Gender and age as moderators in the service evaluation process. *Journal of Services Marketing*, *26*(2), 102–114. doi:10.1108/08876041211215266

Sindwani, R. (2017). The effect of demographic characteristics on mb-loyalty: A study of mobile banking customers. *International Journal of Applied Marketing & Management*, *2*(1), 9–17.

Sirdeshmukh, D., Singh, J., & Sabol, B. (2002). Consumer trust, value, and loyalty in relational exchanges. *Journal of Marketing*, *66*(1), 15–37. doi:10.1509/jmkg.66.1.15.18449

Thaichon, P., Lobo, A., & Quach, T. N. (2016). The moderating role of age in customer loyalty formation process. *Services Marketing Quarterly*, *37*(1), 52–70. doi:10.1080/15332969.2015.1112184

Tibenderana, P., Ogao, P., Ikoja-Odongo, J., & Wokadala, J. (2010). Measuring levels of end-users' acceptance and use of hybrid library services. *International Journal of Education and Development using ICT, 6*(2), 33-54.

Tumewah, E., Juniarta, Y. K., & Kurniawan, Y. (2020). The effect of m-banking service quality and customer perceived value to satisfaction and loyalty of bank XYZ customers. *International Journal of Management and Humanities*, *4*(6), 132–138. doi:10.35940/ijmh.F0634.024620

Vishnuvardhan, B., Manjula, B., & Naik, R. L. (2020). A study of digital banking: Security issues and challenges. *Advances in Intelligent Systems and Computing*, *1090*, 163–185. doi:10.1007/978-981-15-1480-7_14

Wang, Y. S. (2008). Assessing e-commerce systems success: A respecification and validation of the DeLone and McLean model of IS success. *Information Systems Journal*, *18*(5), 529–557. doi:10.1111/j.1365-2575.2007.00268.x

Wei, X., He, C., & Zhu, B. (2016). Relationship between customer perceived value and loyalty of mobile banking. In *Proceedings of the International Conference on Education, Management, Computer and Society*. Atlantis Press. 10.2991/emcs-16.2016.269

Xiong, S. (2013). Adoption of mobile banking model based on perceived value and trust. *Proceedings of the 6th International Conference on Information Management, Innovation Management and Industrial Engineering*, *1*, 632-635. 10.1109/ICIII.2013.6703015

Yeh, C. H., Wang, Y. S., & Yieh, K. (2016). Predicting smartphone brand loyalty: Consumer value and consumer-brand identification perspectives. *International Journal of Information Management*, *36*(3), 245–257. doi:10.1016/j.ijinfomgt.2015.11.013

Zeithaml, V. A. (1988). Consumer perceptions of price, quality, and value: A means-end model and synthesis of evidence. *Journal of Marketing*, *52*(3), 222. doi:10.1177/002224298805200302

Zikmund, W. G., Babin, B. J., Carr, J. C., & Griffin, M. (2013). *Business research methods*. Cengage Learning.

ADDITIONAL READING

Berraies, S., Ben Yahia, K., & Hannachi, M. (2017). Identifying the effects of perceived values of mobile banking applications on customers: Comparative study between baby boomers, generation X and generation Y. *International Journal of Bank Marketing*, *35*(6), 1018–1038. doi:10.1108/IJBM-09-2016-0137

Clifford, G. (2011). Banking and finance: theory, law and practice. PHI Learning.

Hong, I. B. (2019). Understanding and predicting behavioral intention to adopt mobile banking: The Korean experience. *Journal of Global Information Management*, *27*(3), 182–202. doi:10.4018/JGIM.2019070110

Komulainen, H., & Saraniemi, S. (2019). Customer centricity in mobile banking: A customer experience perspective. *International Journal of Bank Marketing*, *37*(5), 1082–1102. doi:10.1108/IJBM-11-2017-0245

Munoz-Leiva, F., Climent-Climent, S., & Liébana-Cabanillas, F. (2017). Determinants of intention to use the mobile banking apps: An extension of the classic TAM model. *Spanish Journal of Marketing-ESIC*, *21*(1), 25–38. doi:10.1016/j.sjme.2016.12.001

Pham, L., Williamson, S., Mohebbi, C., Nguyen, B., & Nguyen, H. (2019). The mediating role of perceived value in the effect of multi-dimensional risk in mobile banking. *International Journal of Enterprise Information Systems*, *15*(4), 1–25. doi:10.4018/IJEIS.2019100101

Rajaobelina, L., Brun, I., Line, R., & Cloutier-Bilodeau, C. (2021). Not all elderly are the same: Fostering trust through mobile banking service experience. *International Journal of Bank Marketing*, *39*(1), 85–106. doi:10.1108/IJBM-05-2020-0288

Singh, S., & Srivastava, R. K. (2014). Factors influencing the adoption of mobile banking in India. *International Journal of E-Services and Mobile Applications*, *6*(4), 1–15. doi:10.4018/ijesma.2014100101

KEY TERMS AND DEFINITIONS

Dummy Variables: These are a special type of variables with values 0 or 1 and are utilized for examining the effect of categorical variables during regression analysis.

Enquiry-Based Service: A type of m-banking service whose sole objective is to provide information to the customers without the involvement of any financial transaction.

Mobile Shopping: An application of mobile commerce that includes the sale and purchase of goods and services using handheld devices such as mobile phones.

Mobile Ticketing: It provides the ability to purchase tickets for different purposes such as movies, railway journeys, and any event.

Multicollinearity: A situation that shows the higher correlation between variables in the regression analysis.

Outliers: These are the values that are quite distant from others in the regression model and may significantly influence its predictive capability.

Residual Mean: It is widely used as a measure of the accuracy of the fit in the regression model.

Transaction-Based Service: A type of m-banking service based on the purpose and generally involves the transactions such as funds transfer.

Chapter 12
The Impact of Social Media and Digital Marketing on Consumer Behavior

Md. Ashrafuzzaman
Military Institute of Science and Technology, Bangladesh

Md. Sharif Hossain
Military Institute of Science and Technology, Bangladesh

A. S. M. Adib Hasan Rishat
Military Institute of Science and Technology, Bangladesh

Mohammad Tareq Alam
Military Institute of Science and Technology, Bangladesh

ABSTRACT

For the time being, people are becoming habitual on social media and digital marketing. This has changed the behaviour of the consumer and the strategies in which companies run their business. Social-media and digital marketing offer significant opportunities to organizations through lower costs, improved brand awareness, and increased sales. This chapter tries to highlight the impact of social media and digital marketing on consumer behaviour from the collective discussion from several experts and researchers. This chapter offers a significant and timely contribution to both researchers and practitioners in the form of challenges and opportunities where the authors highlight different factors that affect the consumer behaviour as well as strategies adopted by the companies to attract the consumers.

INTRODUCTION

Digital marketing refers to using the internet through social media search engines and other channels by using electronic gadgets like computers, mobile devices, tablets, etc., to reach consumers. Digital marketing promotes products on brands through one or more forms of electronic media. It is distinguished from conventional marketing as it includes channels and methods allowing businesses to analyze marketing campaigns and to understand what is working and what is not working. As this is the world of inventions and technology usage is rising, digital markets are increasing exponentially. Digital market-

DOI: 10.4018/978-1-6684-4168-8.ch012

ing mainly uses the internet. Other channels are being used for digital marketing: electronic billboards, mobile instant text messaging, mobile apps, podcasts, digital television and radio channels, etc. In a nutshell, it can be said that the digital market covers all the digital platforms and modern technologies in interaction. That is why digital marketing is often referred to as electronic commerce, also known as e-commerce representing the economic activity of buying and selling products and services through online platforms. Digital marketing includes a wide range of economic activities such as retail stores, online banking services, transport and hotel booking services, money transfers, online payments, etc. In digital marketing, business activities can occur in all three main transaction categories such as business to business, business to customer, and customer to customer. Consumers are getting attracted to digital marketing day by day as they get a wide range of information about products. Consumers found digital markets the easiest way of completing the purchase of products from anywhere in the world. Digital marketing not only makes way for companies to attract customers for their products, but it also paves the way for companies to expand their sales all over the world.

Several studies have been conducted so far to find out the reasons behind the popularity of digital marketing by finding out its impact on consumers. It has been found that digital marketing helps build customer loyalty and customer satisfaction, which are significantly correlated. In the digital markets, the behavior of the internet users plays a significant role in the purchase of the market, and one of the most significant impacts of digital marketing is that it is successful in satisfying customers' wishes which increases customer satisfaction (Mackinney et al., 2002). Due to the extensive usage of digital marketing, customer loyalty has been implemented, which indicates that customers are loyal to a particular firm or company from where they purchase their necessary products. It is one kind of repetitive purchasing behavior of customers that means that they are choosing a particular company while buying products. The role of digital marketing here to increase customer loyalty is that it helps to provide sufficient information about their products. That's why customers have the privilege of being fully aware of the product fully (Zeithaml, 2000). Loyal customers are considered a blessing to business firms as they work as a catalyst to improve the profit of the company doing business (Anderson & Mittal, 2000).

This study tries to examine the impact of social media and digital marketing on consumer behavior through the collective discussion from different scholars and researchers. The remaining sections of this chapter are organized as follows. Section 2 presents an overview of social media and digital marketing with consumers within the current literature. Section 3 presents multiple experts' discussions about the impact of social media and digital marketing on consumer behavior. Section 4 concludes the discussions with limitations.

Literature Reviews

Electronic Direct Mail

Ray Tomlinson established an electronic Director known as EDM in 1961. There are two types of EDM: direct mail and retention direct mail. Direct mail can be known as an email, which involves sending a promotional message. It might be an announcement of a special offer. In contrast, retention mail is a promotional email designed only to encourage the recipient to take action (buy something or sign-up for something).

Digital Marketing

Digital marketing can be defined as a projection of conventional marketing which uses tools and strategies on the internet. Today, digital marketing has become a phenomenon that combines customization and mass distribution to accomplish marketing goals. Technological convergence and the multiplication of devices have led to how we think about marketing on the internet. They have pushed the boundaries toward a new concept of digital marketing — user-centered, more measurable, ubiquitous, and interactive (Teresa Pineiro-Otero, 2016). Advertising on the Internet can take many forms (e.g., banners, pop-ups and similar ads, e-mail advertising, newspaper, and classified ads, search engine advertisement, advertising in chat rooms, blogs, and social networks). The most common is the use of search engines and banners, and mobile has been popular in recent years (Jun Xu, 2014, E-Resources).

Social Media Marketing

Social media are an excellent opportunity to establish significant relationships and create social interaction defined through dynamic exchanges between their members. Social media is booming regarding the number and variety of platforms and users. Thus, one can find audiovisual platforms such as YouTube, Vimeo, and SoundCloud; image platforms such as Flickr, Picasa, Pinterest, or Instagram; general social networks such as Facebook, Twitter, Google+ or specialized ones such as LinkedIn; news or bookmark aggregators such as Digg or Delicious; blogs; and wikis, etc., a vast digital arena where they become the new Web winners (Georgios Tsimonis Sergios Dimitriadis, 2014). Given these trends and the high potential for marketing use of social media, the critical question for marketing managers became how to take full advantage of social media and find ways in which social media can contribute to marketing objectives and support marketing strategies. Early studies on online communities have tried to explain why firms may be interested in social platforms. (Georgios Tsimonis Sergios Dimitriadis, 2014) proposes two reasons for this interest in online brand communities: word of mouth and market research. Indeed, the emergence of internet-based media has facilitated the development of word of mouth online. WOM occurs on various online channels, such as blogs, forums, virtual communities, and social networks (Georgios Tsimonis Sergios Dimitriadis, 2014). Social media are ideal tools for eWOM, as users freely create and spread brand-related information in their networks composed of their friends (Vollmer and Precourt, 2008). Second, as social media provide new opportunities for consumer interaction, they also open up new possibilities for marketing researchers to get close to the consumers and collect info about their preferences, desires, and needs. Propositions of consequent studies on the motivations, expected benefits, and objectives related to the use of social media can be summarized as follows:

- Brands can effectively develop and enhance relationships with customers. Social media not only intensifies the existing firm-to-customer and customer-to-firm relationships but also creates new variations on conventional options, increasing the ability of firms to interact in firm-customer dialog, strengthening their communications. There are fundamental changes in the ease of contact, volume, speed, and nature of these interactions (Gallaugher and Ransbotham, 2010).
- Firms can reach out to people that otherwise could not be reached (Dong-Hun, 2010; Newman, 2003). Social media transfers content to a more diverse range of people compared to the mass media. They create a "small-world" network (Newman, 2003) where content is easily distributed

to a large number of people, as the network is formed through voluntary connection and requires fewer steps for sharing information

- Social media can establish and raise brand awareness (Newman, 2003). Social media tools allow firms to access millions of people. Since a huge number of people are already visiting social media, a brand's name presence all over those networks can help inform people about it and become familiar with the firm, creating brand awareness (Newman, 2003).

However, because of the constant evolution of social media platforms and the multiple applications that they offer, companies, in fact experiment constantly by testing various ways of using social media and observing their use by competitors. Expected results and benefits are still unclear and need to be further studied. It should be noted here that besides the benefits that social media offer to firms, there are some risks concerning their use. For instance, one of the most frequent unpredictable situations is negative Facebook comments made by users (Dekay, 2012). Recent studies reveal that many companies do not respond to such comments and/or delete them. Moreover, even those firms that respond to negative comments do not adopt explicit strategies that transform these comments into valuable opportunities for communication (Dekay, 2012). Ineffective handling of such situations may lead to negative word of mouth among social media users. As a result, a significant challenge for social media active companies is to develop appropriate response strategies to negative word of mouth (Hennig-Thurau et al., 2010; Roehm and Tybout, 2006); otherwise, social media marketing may have negative impacts on a firm's brand image and sales (Gallaugher and Ransbotham, 2010). The present study focuses on the positive aspect of social media marketing. It aims to examine why companies create brand pages on social media, how they use them, and what benefits they expect from this use. Also, it intends to provide preliminary evidence of what benefits users may get from using such pages, according to managers' opinions.

Consumer Behavior

Consumer behavior is the practice of understanding and analyzing individuals, groups, or organizations and all the activities associated with the purchase, how the customer journey flows, consumer use and disposal of goods and services, and how the consumer's emotions, attitudes, and preferences affect buying behavior. Businesses require Wikipedia Consumer behavior data all around the world. This is because they are always looking for ways to improve their shopping experience and, as a result, their sales figures. They can learn more about market expectations by doing consumer behavior research. It also helps them create enhancements that allow customers to make better purchasing decisions.

Consumer behavior can be classified into five stages as shown in Figure 1:

1. Problem recognition
2. Search of information
3. Evaluation of alternatives,
4. Final decision
5. Post-purchase decisions.

Figure 1. Showing 5 stages of the consumer decision process. (Jansson-Boyd, 2010)

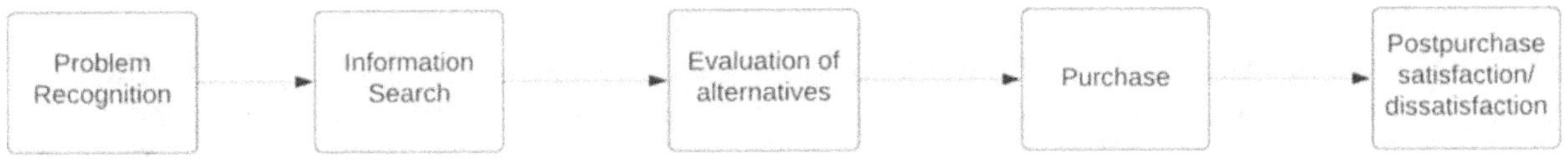

Problem Recognition

Problem recognition takes place whenever a consumer recognizes a significant difference between the desired and the actual state of affairs, which is the insufficient magnitude to arouse and activate the decision process (Solomon, Bamossy and Askegaard, 2002). At the point when an individual is activated remotely, for example, an individual may see a TV notice for a get-away, the upgrade triggers musings or thoughts regarding the chance of making. Once consumers recognize a want, they need to gather information to understand how they can fulfill that want, which leads to step 2.

Search of Information

The last buy choice will not be made without a moment's delay, in any event, when people recognize, perceive their issues, and focus on the accessible items; similarly, when possibilities have a particular enthusiasm for an item or administration, they will in general experience the accompanying strides before completing any activity – recognizing accessible choices, considering data of chose alternatives, and in the end judging which of these choices can no doubt convey the best result. While inquiring about their choices, purchasers again depend on inside and outside elements, just as past associations with an item or brand, both positive and negative. In the search for information, they may pursue alternatives at a physical area or online counsel assets, for example, Google or client audits.

Evaluation of Alternatives

When data has been gathered, the customer utilizes it to assess and survey the elective item decisions to show up at a buy choice. The elective assessment and data search stages, however, introduced independently, are unpredictably interlaced during dynamic, and shoppers frequently move to and fro between the two. Elective assessment includes the determination of decision options and evaluative measures. When decided, the exhibition of the considered decisions is thought about along the notable rules. Lastly, choice standards are applied to limit the choices to make the last determination. This stage prompts the arrangement of convictions, perspectives, and goals, prompting the resulting phase of the procurement. The alternative that is simpler to use or arrange, or what is the preference of the majority or various other reviews and experiences matters in the evaluation.

Final Decision

Purchase choice alludes to the last decision or choice made concerning which item to purchase. The act of purchase is the last major stage, with the consumer deciding on what to buy, where to buy, and how to pay. Purchase is a function of intentions, environmental influences, and individual situations. Some of the influences that can affect the purchase.

Brand Awareness

It can be defined as the level of consumer consciousness of a company's product or service. There are a few keys of consideration in brand awareness: human behavior, advertising management, brand management, and strategy development, which makes consumers able to proceed with purchasing the product or service of the company. Brand awareness can also be best spread through both inbound and outbound marketing efforts. When competition in an industry is high, brand awareness can be one of a business's most significant assets (TrackMaven, Online source).

Consumer Perception towards Brand Awareness

Brand awareness has a neutral effect on consumers. An advertisement's first job is to let people know that your product or service is available to them. People who view advertisements find out about your products similarly to how they find out about current events in the news. At this stage, consumers go from not knowing that your business exists to gaining awareness of your brand in the case of a future purchase (Mike Tortorice, 2017).

Problem Statement

The world has become increasingly comfortable online, living more and more in the digital world. Therefore, agencies need to wake up to the future of digital marketing. Advertising expenses are getting expensive; it suffered where consumers were overwhelmed by the quantity of traditional advertisements (e.g., flyers, brochures, etc.), which makes it difficult to attract their interest. And it also affects consumer behavior toward brand awareness. For example, consumers nowadays spend much time on the internet, such as online shopping, where they not only buy a product but to compare the product or services, compare the price, product features, to get information, etc., towards online marketing rather than being conscious about the brand. Therefore, to ensure a product or service success, awareness level must be managed across the entire product life-cycle - from product launch to market decline.

IMPACT OF DIGITAL MARKETING ON CONSUMER BEHAVIOR

Decision Making Model

The traditional model of the consumer decision-making process "Five-stage model of the consumer buying process" (Figure 1), involves five steps consumers move through when buying a product or service. A marketer has to understand these steps to properly move the consumer to buy the product, communicate effectively to consumers and close the sale. consumer decision-making process.

For example, in their book, Kotler & Keller (2012) describe this model in detail and explain an additional stage of the model – the disposal stage. Also, they discuss Moderating effects on consumer decision-making (like consumer involvement).

Belch G. & Belch M. (2009) went further and discussed relevant internal psychological processes for each stage of the model (Figure 2)

Figure 2. Internal psychological processes

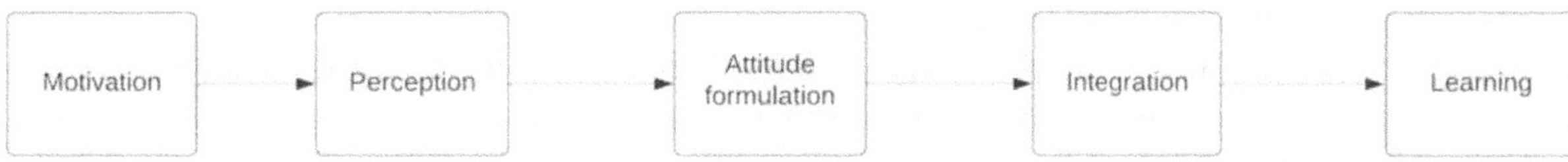

One of the most active academic research spheres in marketing has been behavioral decision theory over the past decades. Behavioral decision theorists have identified many situations in which consumers make irrational choices. All these and other studies emphasize that consumer behavior is precious and the context of decisions is essential. Understanding how these effects manifest in the marketplace can be crucial for marketers. The work of these and other scholars has also challenged predictions from economic theory and assumptions about rationality, leading to the appearance of the field of behavioral economics.

Hereafter, for each stage of the model, the "moments that matter" and factors that influence them will be identified and discussed. Moreover, a self-developed framework about factors and their influences on relevant moments for consumers will be introduced to understand better the process and how and when it is a good time to interrupt it with a promotion. Later on, research by other scholars about factors that affect decision-making will be presented for a broader view of the topic, the consumer decision-making process.

At this stage, for marketers, it is essential to determine when their target demographic develops these needs/wants. Therefore, it would be an ideal time to advertise to them. Marketers may also help recognize the consumer's need/problem or circumstances that trigger a need/want. Moreover, marketers may create the circumstance/need by themselves – to make the consumer feel insecure without this product or create a desired status for customers.

Factors that influence these moments are the existence/creation of desired (preferred) status, availability of information about new status (new products or versions of the products), related/complementary products for this product that may create a need, and motives that drive customers, consumer decision-making process.

After the consumer has developed a need/want, he/she starts an information search about the different alternatives that he/she can purchase to satisfy the need/want. It is the second stage of so-called information search. He/she will look both internally and externally for this information to help him/her make a decision. An internal information search consists of utilizing information from memory, such as past experiences with the product/service. An external information search is asking friends and family about their experiences with acquiring a new product. They can also research public sources, such as reviews, blogs. Another external information source would be marketing-controlled sources, such as banners, television ads, brochures, etc.

The amount of time dedicated to this step usually depends on the consumer's past experience with buying the product, the risk involved, and the level of interest. Once a consumer creates a set of alternative products to choose from, he/she has created an evoked set. This set consists of the most preferred alternatives. Once the evoked set has been decided upon, the consumer will conduct final research to shrink his/her choices further.

The process of looking for information, in this case, is a moment that matters for consumers. Marketers have to catch it and provide a relevant description of the product, promotions, etc. Also, recommendations from friends and family and reviews from other consumers will be taken into account. Moreover, previous experience of using the product or similar one and personal experiments while searching (testing the samples) will influence the process.

At some point, the consumer stops to evaluate the evoked set and switches to the buying process – the fourth stage: purchase. Once a consumer chooses which brand to buy, he/she must still implement the decision and make the actual purchase. Also, initially, consumers may make a purchase intention to buy a particular product but do not close a deal. Additional decisions may be needed – factors that influence when to buy, where to buy, and how much money to spend. Often, there is a time delay between the formation of a purchase decision and the actual purchase, particularly for complex purchases such as automobiles, personal computers, and consumer durables. For nondurable products, which include many low-involvement items such as everyday goods, the time between the decision and the actual purchase may be short. At this point, it is critical to hook the consumer in purchase intention and a delay period.

Consumers evaluate and review the product in the last fifth stage – post-purchase (satisfaction or dissatisfaction). Was the product suitable for the consumer? Did their expectations confirm? Suppose a customer finds that the product has matched or exceeded the promises made and their expectations. In that case, they will potentially become a brand ambassador influencing other potential customers in stage two of their customer journey, increasing the chances of the product being purchased again. The same can be said for negative feedback, which is if emerging at stage two can restrain a potential customer's journey towards your product [2]. The moment that matters in the last stage is to catch the point if the customer is not satisfied.

In Figure 3, the self-developed framework of moments that matter and factors that influence them are presented. One note to this model should be added. Consumers do not always move in the exact order through the process. The second and the third stages could be repeated a couple of times; also, the evaluation stage does not, in all cases, finishes with purchase. It can depend on the type of product, the consumer's buying stage, and even financial status.

Many purchase decisions people make as consumers are based on a habitual or routine choice process. For many low-priced, frequently purchased products, the decision process consists of little more than recognizing the problem, engaging in a quick internal search, and purchasing. The consumer spends little or no effort engaging in external search or alternative evaluation (Belch G. & Belch M., 2009). So not all of the stages apply to repeated products because the person already has preferences and brand loyalty, and it is considered an automatic process. Therefore, marketers of products characterized by a systematic response purchase process need to get and/or keep their brands in the consumer's evoked set and avoid anything that may result in their removal from it. Marketers of these brands want consumers to follow a routine choice process and continue to purchase their products. This means maintaining high levels of brand awareness through reminder advertising, periodic promotions, and prominent shelf positions in stores.

Also, the paper of Hoyer (1984) supports the statements above. It presents a view of decision-making based on the idea that consumers are not willing to engage in a big deal of decision-making when they purchase a product repeatedly, and it is relatively unimportant. Consequently, consumers apply very quick and effortless choice tactics that provide a satisfactory decision.

Marketers of new brands or those with a low market share face a different challenge. They must find ways to disrupt consumers' routine choice process and get them to consider different alternatives. High levels of advertising may be used to encourage trial period or brand switching, along with sales promotion efforts in the form of free samples, special price offers high-value coupons, etc. consumer decision making process

Nonetheless, the traditional model was criticized, and other scholars added relevant focuses and factors. For example, McAlister (1979) challenged the current time assumption that product choices are made separately from each other. The scholar offered a model incorporating dependence among selections of items groups.

Figure 3. Framework of factors and moments that influence decision-making

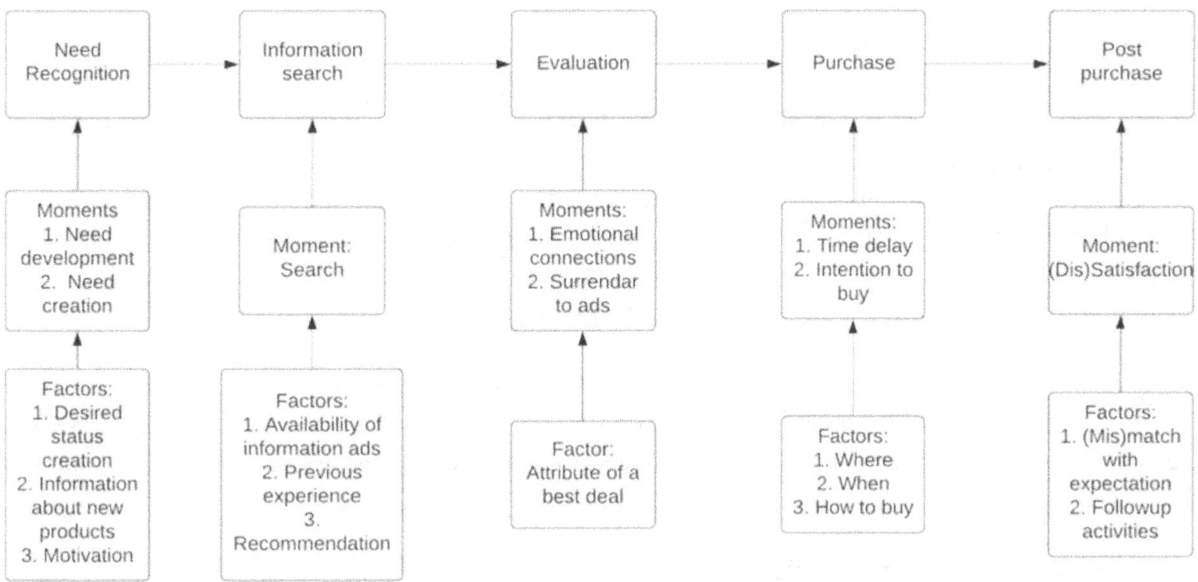

Solomon et al. (2006) criticized the traditional model by saying that it is a rational perspective. However, people may behave irrationally "such a process is not accurately portrayed by many of our purchase decisions." Consumers do not go through this sequence whenever they buy something. The authors talk about purchase momentum (impulses that lead to unplanned purchases at the last moment). Also, the authors argue that consumers possess a repertoire of strategies, and they choose one according to the situation and the level of effort required, so-called constructive processing. Moreover, they discuss behavioral influence perspectives and experimental perspectives.

Dhar, Huber & Khan (2007) also talk about shopping momentum when an initial purchase provides a psychological impulse that enhances the purchase of a second, unrelated product. The authors propose that the most promising theoretical mechanism comes from Gollwitzer's (1990) theory about implementation and deliberation mindsets. Under this theory, shopping momentum occurs because the initial purchase moves the consumer from a deliberative to an implemental mindset, thus driving subsequent purchases. consumer decision making process

Ability to Research and Experiment

Modern-day consumers have become outstanding researchers when making a purchasing decision. They are gaining more insight and awareness as technology empowers them with a critical approach to making decisions online. They are being exposed to a magnitude of content as brands try to market their products on the Internet. This has helped facilitate the purchasing process for consumers, wherein they can now research and compare products online before making a final decision on what to buy. The amount of information available on the Internet has even allowed them to experiment with different brands and conclude. While they have allowed brands to influence their purchasing decisions, the same technology has empowered them considerably. Digital marketing has helped customers make the most of the transparent relationship brands are willing to have with them and provide them with a better understanding of certain services and products.

Accessible Word-of-Mouth

Word-of-mouth is not something new. It is used both by brands and consumers to make business happen. Word-of-mouth is the most significant factor that affects consumers' behavior. Consumers are always looking for what other people say about a brand. This is mainly for a product that they are interested in purchasing. For brands, it means a lot when a consumer shares their experience with their network of people.

With the advent of technology, especially social media, consumers now have the power of projecting their opinion to a large audience. For instance, reviews from bloggers, comments on sponsored posts, and customer reviews left on brand pages have all helped people widen their approach to consumerism.

This has also helped businesses maintain an online presence. Word-of-mouth can significantly affect any brand's sales figure. It would also be safe to say that digital marketing has put consumers in the driving seat.

Inconsistent Customer Loyalty

However, digital marketing has also made it difficult for consumers to stay loyal to a particular brand. Before the digital marketing revolution, consumers were always partial to a brand. They often preferred to stick to familiar products and brands.

This was because they were not exposed to an extensive range of products and services like they are today. Nowadays, customers are looking forward to products that provide better value for the same amount of money.

Not just that, they even consider other factors, like customer support, brand value, discounts, and more. So, as more brands come out with better features and offers, customers now have choices. They show less hesitation when switching from their go-to brands to entirely new ones. When it comes to customer loyalty, we can say that digital marketing did not change consumer behavior. It only highlighted it. This has made brands compete more fiercely, which only helped customers get better services at lower costs.

Boost in Customer Engagement

Customers have always liked to be a part of a more significant thing. They do not let go of an opportunity where they can interact with their favorite brand. There has been a significant increase in customer engagement thanks to the incessant penetration of mobile technology and the internet.

Social media sites are accessible to everyone with an internet connection. Therefore, people actively engage with their brands on social media pages and consumer forums. While customers always have the power of choosing their brand and building its reputation, digital marketing has only amplified its capacity.

Customers can engage with their brands on social media, search engines, and other review websites. They can now instantly share their opinions with their brands. If the brands respond to their feedback quickly, they will ultimately receive even more engagement and witness a growth in sales.

Artificial Intelligence Impacts Consumer Behavior

One should not underestimate the role of artificial intelligence in influencing consumer behavior. It is a powerful medium that enables consumers to make better choices.

The efficiency and feasibility drive digital marketing that technology like artificial intelligence brings to the table.

Artificial intelligence is going to have a significant impact on consumer behavior since brands that make use of artificial intelligence can present their products and services more efficiently than those who do not. Being that consumers are looking for convenience, they generally go forward with such brands.

For example, the AI technology plays a significant role in search engine optimization, and how the Google algorithm works, SEO the user intent on search is taken into consideration for adapting the search results, for example, if you search for SEO in Jordan from UAE market the results will be definitely different than if you are searching for the same query from Jordan! also if you are searching for Arabic SEO services, from KSA the results will differ from UAE.

Moreover, artificial intelligence has helped brands improve customer support and build and maintain solid connections with customers. Such features are going to affect consumer behavior and impact many brands' online success.

Impulsive Buying Behavior

Digital marketing has successfully augmented the impulse buying phenomena. An impulse buying decision is essentially made directly before making the actual purchase. In other words, impulsive buying is a spontaneous decision made in the spur of the moment, when generally, customers usually pre-plan their purchases and pre-choose the products they wish to buy. This common phenomenon is used by digital marketers to steer consumer behavior positively. Through advertising online, brands highlight attractive deals, discounts, and offers those customers are happy to explore. Brands use social media platforms and third-party websites to consistently promote their featured deals, affecting consumer behavior.

Less Patience, High Expectations

With technology, the consumers have become noticeably impatient as their expectations for fast, efficient service have doubled. Exposed to online customer reviews and forums, they receive sentimental, real feedback on products and services. Subpar services and facilities are unacceptable. Consumers expect brands to respond to queries as soon as possible. They express their dismay on public portals when they do not receive what was promised, which negatively impacts a brand's online reputation.

The abundance of information they get through digital marketing seriously affects their purchasing behavior. Services like hassle-free exchanges and next-day delivery are quickly raising consumers' expectations across the globe. Almost every brand is looking to provide standard features and services. However, the brand goes on to provide more value that wins the competition. at Chain Reaction, we work with our clients on clear KPIs, especially for measurable ones such as SEO services in the UAE.

Personalized Shopping Experience

Digital marketing has also accustomed consumers to a personalized shopping experience. Today, they do not want to spend a significant amount of time researching and purchasing their desired products. Brands have realized this change in consumer behavior, and they have geared their online marketing and branding strategies towards providing a personalized experience to all consumers by curating personalized content. This tailors the entire shopping experience to fit the needs of each website visitor.

Factors Affecting Online Consumer Behavior

Understanding the mechanisms of virtual shopping and the behavior of the online consumer is a priority issue for practitioners competing in the fast-expanding virtual marketplace. This topic is also increasingly drawing the attention of researchers. Indicative of this is the fact that more than 120 relevant academic papers were published in 2001 alone Constantinides, Efthymios. (2004). Given the continuous expansion of the Internet in terms of user numbers, transaction volumes, and business penetration, this massive research endeavor is not surprising. More Than 20 percent of Internet users in several countries already buy products and services online Constantinides, Efthymios. (2004). Figure 4 illustrates the factors affecting online consumer behavior.

Web Experience: Definition and Importance

Several academics and practitioners have identified the "online shopping experience" or "virtual experience" as a crucial e-commerce marketing issue. Define the online shopping experience as a process of four stages describing the successive steps of an online transaction. Considering that an online customer is not simply a shopper but also an information technology user, one can argue that the online experience is a more complicated issue than the physical shopping experience: the Web experience can be defined as the consumer's total impression of the online company (Watchfire White paper Series, 2000)resulting from his/her exposure to a combination of virtual marketing tools "...under the marketer's direct control, likely to influence the buying behavior of the online consumer" The Web experience embraces elements like searching, browsing, finding, selecting, comparing and evaluating information as well as interacting and transacting with the online firm. The virtual customer's total impression and actions are influenced by design, events, emotions, atmosphere, and other elements experienced during interaction with a given Web site, elements meant to induce customer goodwill and affect the final outcome of the online interaction. It should be noticed here that the Web experience is important not only for Web sites marketing products or services but also for sites targeting customers interested in informational content (news, weather, sports etc.), sites acting as online intermediaries and generally to all types of Internet ventures competing for the attention of the online public.

Functionality Factors

Factors enhance the online experience by presenting the virtual client with a good functioning, easy to explore, fast, interactive Website. Functionality includes "Usability" and "Interactivity" elements.

Figure 4. Factors affecting online consumer behavior.

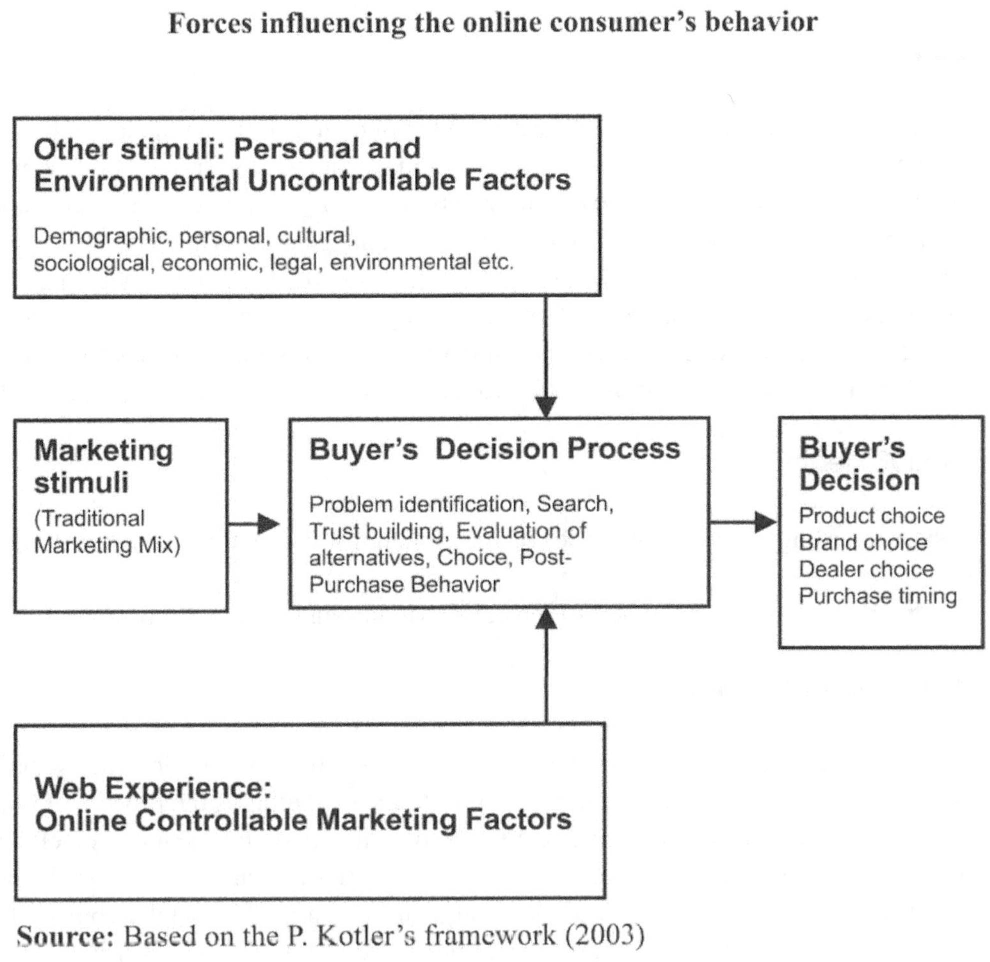

Psychological Factors

Web sites must communicate integrity and credibility to persuade customers to stop, explore them and interact online. Psychological factors play a crucial role in helping online customers unfamiliar with the vendor or unfamiliar with online transactions to overcome fears of fraud and doubts about the trustworthiness of the Web site and vendor.

Content Factors

Factors refer to creative and marketing mix-related elements of the Web site. These factors exercise a direct and crucial influence on the Web experience. They are divided into two sub-categories: "Aesthetics" and "Marketing mix."

The above terms reflect the nature and/or the effect of the Web experience elements on the buying process. As an example, the policies regarding the use of customer data by online vendors and product return policies, factors likely to affect the customer trust, were classified as psychological issues, while design and atmosphere, typical aesthetic elements were considered as elements of the Web site content.

IMPACT OF SOCIAL MEDIA ON CONSUMER BEHAVIOR

Social-Media

Social Media can be defined as a group of Internet-based applications built on the ideological and technological foundations of the Web and allow the creation and exchange of user-generated content. Social media is accessible and enabled by scalable communication techniques. As social media becomes more and more prevalent, connecting people and facilitating the exchange of information, consumer behavior is shifting. Through social media, consumers now can easily watch an exciting advertisement on YouTube while posting their own opinions on Twitter and sharing it with friends on Facebook. Social media differs from paper-based media (e.g., magazines and newspapers) and traditional electronic media such as Radio, and TV in many ways, including quality frequency, interactivity, usability, and performance.

Types of Social-Media

In this discussion regarding different categories of social media, 4 distinct types of social media outlets are focused on:

1) Social networking sites 2) Social news Website 3) Media sharing Sites 4) Blogs

Social-Media and Marketing

According to Weinberg (2009), he refers to social media marketing is leveraging the 'social' through the 'media' to 'market' businesses' constituents. Social Media Marketing is the process of empowering individuals to promote their services or products through different social media channels to attract a larger amount of people that may not have been available via traditional way of advertising. The advertisements via mass media are no longer as efficient as in the past. The social web is a place where people with common interests gather to share ideas, information, thoughts, etc. Through social media, marketers can listen to and respond to communities, feedback and promote their products or services. What makes social media marketing special? Small and medium-sized companies with small budgets can take full advantage of social media marketing when they have insufficient funds to use the traditional way of marketing. Even though social media marketing is an evolving concept, the basic idea of marketing remains the same: target the section of the population, communicate with prospects, build loyalty, and so on.

Social-Media and Consumer

Social media is a means of giving consumers a voice. Companies create brand awareness, engage their existing customers, drive traffic to other marketing properties, and grow channel numbers (Zarrella 2010; Weber 2009; Weinberg 2009; Smith and Zook 2011). Each of the social media platforms plays a role in giving out, receiving, and exchanging information without any boundary limitations, and as mentioned previously that social media enables the two-way flow of information. Since the flow of communication does not merely impact how companies can access their targeted groups but also influences throughout the entire decision process, from interpreting the message, searching for available alternatives, as well as actions carried out the after the purchase; thus, it is important to denote that rejection, misinterpretation, and misunderstanding are the possible pitfalls in the flow of communication (Smith and Zook 2011, 120). Online life presents another element of potential outcomes and difficulties for advertising (PR) and organizations around the globe. It rebrands the idea of the network and reclassifies the manners in which customers and brands impart. Before online networking, purchasers were constrained in how far they could take protests, past reaching client care or telling others in their locale. Web-based social networking changed this. Presently, customers can voice open remarks about organizations in a split second. Online networking, as another segment, has additionally confused the noble purchasing conduct process hypothesis wherein the purchasing perspectives are not affected simply by the traditional channels yet reach out to the online stages. Inclinations and choice checking are incited to rely on the information sources given by parties outside the ability to control online advertisers, for example, peer audits, referrals, websites, interpersonal organizations, and different types of client-produced content. Social media such as Facebook, Twitter, and YouTube are dynamic tools that facilitate online relationships (Golden, 2011). It is a relatively low-cost form of marketing and allows organizations to engage in direct and end-user contact (Kaplan and Haenlein, 2010). Given the choices made available to consumers and the influential role of social media marketing, the brands and consumers have a changing role to play in the organization's strategy in that they now have an economic impact (Lindermann, 2004; Mayfield, 2008). Brands influence customer choice. Customers influence other customers. These chains of events affect repurchases, which further affect future earnings and long-term organizational sustainability (Oliveira and Sullivan, 2003). Peer correspondence through web-based life, another type of buyer socialization, affects dynamic and, in this manner, advertising procedures. The buyer socialization hypothesis predicts that correspondence among buyers influences their psychology, full of feelings and conduct mentalities.

As shown in Figure 5, several factors, internal and external, may lead a firm to get involved with social media. As analyzed above, these external factors are the fast growth and popularity of social media, their viral nature, the competitors' presence on social media, and the low-cost solutions offered by social media platforms. The internal factors include the strategy followed by headquarters as well as the company's strategy, positioning, and targeting, the latter being the general framework into which all marketing activities should fit. For example, if a brand's target group is young people, it is more likely that this brand will have a strong presence on social media. Also, brands which include technological products are more likely to join social media. Given these external and internal factors, a firm decides whether to activate on social media and which social media platforms are more appropriate for its campaign. A Facebook fan page would be more appropriate for a firm that desires full interactive communication with its audience. A Twitter account would more likely be chosen by media firms, such as TV/Radio channels or newspapers, or online news portals, which can spread short informational messages. Brands that have visualized messages such as advertising spots are more likely to prefer a YouTube channel. However, most of the interviewed firms prefer a combination of several social media platforms, utilizing each one according to the needs of their social media strategy. An additional issue especially relevant to companies with a multinational presence is the choice of the appropriate social media platform for each target country.

Theoretical Model of Social Media on Consumer Behavior

Although this is listed at number four on the table, it is probably one of the most used marketing channels in the music industry. As many music labels have been able to create relationships through the use of SM and social networking, as stated, having a visible presence on Twitter and Facebook gives artists a direct link to fans. Also, in a study conducted with MIDEM, we found that our sample of 64 music industry executives collectively spent in the region £1.9m on content marketing. This shows just how important content marketing is for music businesses/labels. Facebook is the top social media outlet to promote your music; this is probably mostly down to the fact that it is the SM site with the most active users (1.65 billion). Also, people love discovering new artists and bands on this site as millions of likes and follows generated by uses each day in the music category alone.

Figure 6 proposes a model for social media impact on consumer behavior. This model supports the view that customers engaged with events services are more likely to communicate through social media, which is why so many events companies are using social media to market all of their events, and why they use their support lines on sites such as Twitter and Facebook messenger. Mangold and Faulds (2009) also believe that customers are much more likely to talk to others about products that support their desired self-image, hence why event companies focus their promotional efforts on people's desired self-image.

Figure 5. Flow chart of social media decision making process.

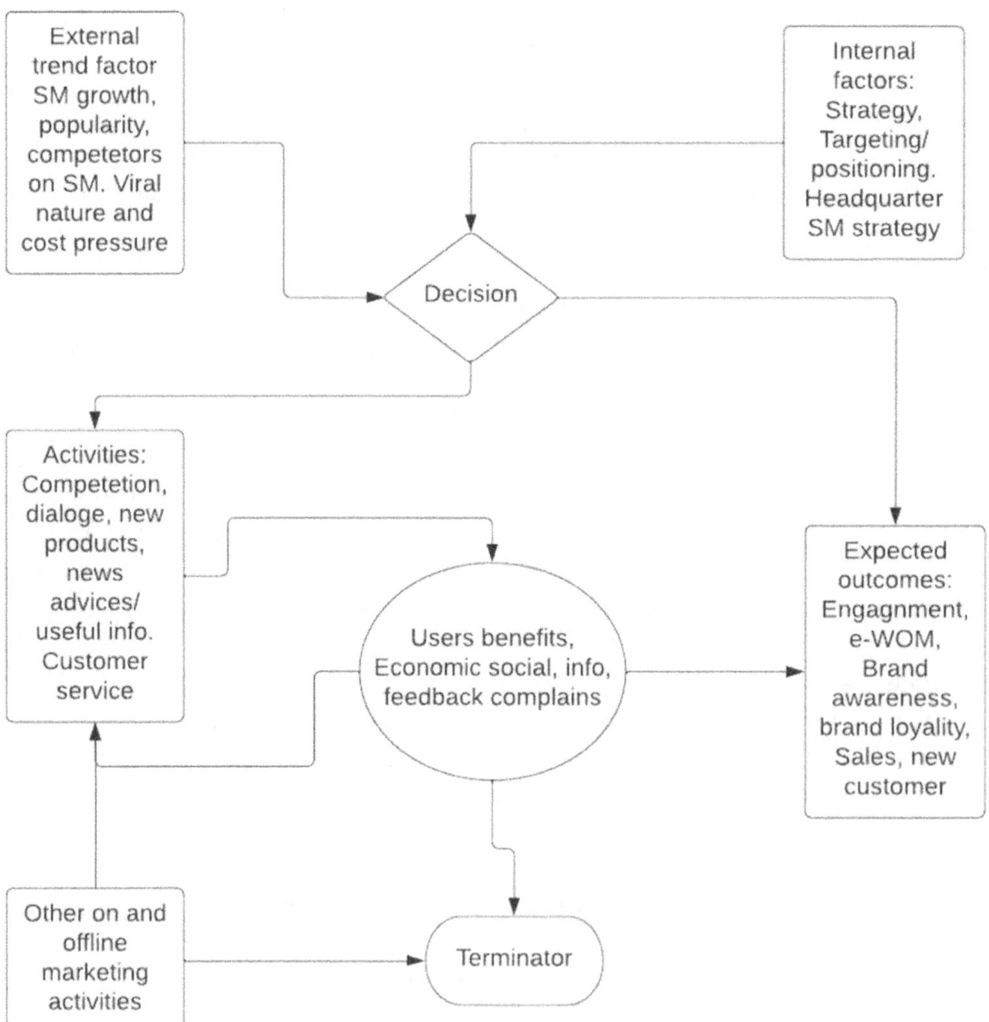

Figure 6. Model of social media impact on consumer behavior.

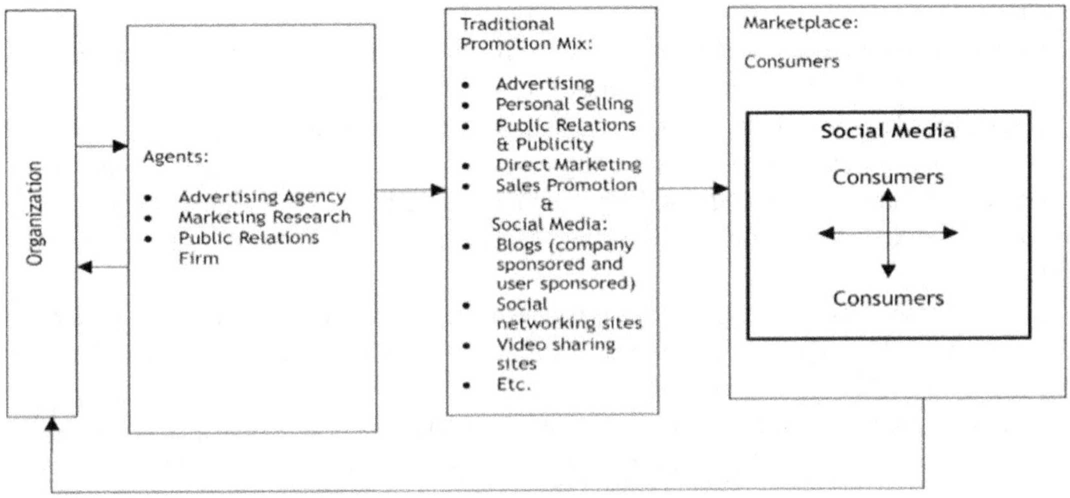

CONCLUSION

As this research is still an on-going development, researchers found that there is a gap and opportunity to explore and further strengthen the needs of identifying consumer behavior towards digital marketing. The research will go further to provide more options for the respondents to react with the visual images, more surveys, interviews and expand the availability of the digital marketing platform. Since smartphones have been increasing day by day, it is an added advantage to both marketer, designer as well as to the consumers in fulfilling their needs and requirements. Social media is taken as the electronic word of mouth by the majority of the respondents. Reviews and preferences by the past consumers on Social-media platforms affect the decision process of potential customers. Social media users found decision-making to be easier and enjoyed the process more, when compared to those who used other information sources. Those who perceived the information on social media to be of higher quality and greater quantity than expectations were more satisfied overall. The results overall show that Social-Media has a strong impact on the consumer decision-making process.

LIMITATIONS

Social media marketing is not a new aspect, and it is constantly changing and evolving. There are many journals/articles on this topic, but very few links social media with changes in consumer behavior. The study is presented in a general manner.

The data sample was relatively small and showed limited generalizability of the study conducted. The sample size should be increased as it would cover more people in society and help create a better and more accurate set of results.

The study can be conducted on a broader scale by collecting data from different parts of the world to understand better the impact social media has on the consumer buying process. As cultures and values change from country to country, consumers' buying behavior may also vary.

A study involving many countries should be conducted on this topic for more accurate and generalized results.

In order to increase the level of focus of the study, objectives have been narrowed down, and the research only contains information on what needs to be studied considering the objectives.

At present, people cannot think about their lives without social media and spend nearly ten to twelve hours every week on social media, either through their smartphones or computers. This has led many companies to think about social media and digital marketing and spend vast amounts of money developing this online marketing. This online marketing system affects consumer behavior positively as well as negatively.

There are adverse outcomes and resulting consequences of the digital and social media marketing that need to be considered by organizations. Aswani et al. (2018) found a negative effect of digital marketing if performed by unskilled service providers.

The emerging trend of targeted personal advertising has led to increased privacy concerns from consumers. Gironda et al., (2018) found that invasiveness, privacy control, perceived usefulness, and consumer innovativeness directly influenced consumer behavior and intention relating to privacy concerns. Companies should be more concerned about consumers' privacy as they develop their advertising strategies and build long-term customer relationships (Mandal, 2019).

Although lots of challenges to its prosperity and the burden of some negative factors, digital marketing via social media platforms is getting popular day by day with customers worldwide. Every day the number of people using this platform has increased, which identifies how this platform has changed the behavior of consumers to be dependent more on technologies for buying their necessary products. Also, it is seen that currently, in the 21st century, the South-East Asian countries are experiencing the fourth industrial revolution, which has increased their reliance on this platform more than any time before. Preferences for digital marketing for shopping and other necessities are growing exponentially, which may also work as a silent catalyst for this region's developing country's rapid economic growth.

REFERENCES

Anderson, E., & Mittal, V. (2000). Strengthening the Satisfaction-Profit Chain. *Journal of Service Research, 3*(2), 107–120. doi:10.1177/109467050032001

Aswani, R., Kar, A. K., Ilavarasan, P. V., & Dwivedi, Y. K. (2018). Search engine marketing is not all gold: Insights from Twitter and SEO Clerks. *International Journal of Information Management, 38*(1), 107–116. doi:10.1016/j.ijinfomgt.2017.07.005

Constantinides, E. (2004). Influencing the online consumer's behavior: The Web experience. *Internet Research, 14*(2), 111–126. doi:10.1108/10662240410530835

Ghazie, D., & Dolah, J. (2018). *How Digital Marketing Affects Consumer Behavior*. doi:10.2991/reka-18.2018.48

Gironda, J. T., & Korgaonkar, P. K. (2018). iSpy? Tailored versus invasive ads and consumers' perceptions of personalized advertising. *Electronic Commerce Research and Applications, 29*, 64–77. doi:10.1016/j.elerap.2018.03.007

Golden, M. (2011). *Social Media Strategies for Professionals and Their Firms: The Guide to Establishing Credibility and Accelerating Relationships*. John Wiley and Sons.

Hennig-Thurau, T., Gwinner, K. P., Walsh, G., & Gremler, D. D. (2004). Electronic word-of-mouth via consumer-opinion platforms: What motivates consumers to articulate themselves on the internet? *Journal of Interactive Marketing*, *18*(1), 38–52. doi:10.1002/dir.10073

Kaplan, A., & Haenlein, M. (2010). Users of the World, Unite! The Challenges and Opportunities of Social-Media. *Business Horizons*, *53*(1), 59–68. doi:10.1016/j.bushor.2009.09.003

Mandal, P. C. (2019). Public policy issues in direct and digital marketing–Concerns and initiatives: Public policy in direct and digital marketing. *International Journal of Public Administration in the Digital Age*, *6*(4), 54–71. doi:10.4018/IJPADA.2019100105

Mayfield, A. (2008). *What is social media?* iCrossing. Retrieved August 25, 2009, from www.icrossing.co.uk/ebook

McKinney, V., Yoon, K., & Zahedi, F. (2002). The Measurement of Web-Customer Satisfaction: An Expectation and Disconfirmation Approach. *Information Systems Research*, *13*(3), 296–315. doi:10.1287/isre.13.3.296.76

Newman, M. (2003). The structure and function of complex networks. *SIAM Review*, *45*(2), 167–256. doi:10.1137/S003614450342480

Piñeiro-Otero. (2016). *Teresa & Martínez-Rolán, Xabier*. Understanding Digital Marketing—Basics and Actions. doi:10.1007/978-3-319-28281-7_2

Smith, P., & Zook, Z. (2011). *Marketing Communications: Integrating Offline and Online with Social Media* (5th ed.). Kogan Page. https://www.webuybooks.co.uk/

Solomon, M., Bamossy, G., Askegaard, S., & Hogg, M. K. (2006). *Consumer Behavior. A European perspective* (3rd ed.). Prentice Hall Financial Times. https://www.research.lancs.ac.uk/portal/en/publications

Solomon, M. R., Bamossy, G., & Askegaard, S. (2002). *Consumer behavior: A European perspective.* London: Financial Times/Prentice Hall. https://books.mec.biz/tmp/books/NXHQRTHBQ2L87NIU6YVN.pdf

Tsimonis & Dimitriadis. (2014). Brand strategies in social media. *Marketing Intelligence & Planning, 32*(3), 328 - 344. doi:10.1108/MIP-04-2013-0056

Weber, M. (2009). *Marketing to the Social Web: How Digital Customer Communities Build Your Business* (2nd ed.). John Willey & Sons Inc. doi:10.1002/9781118258125

Weinberg, T. (2009). *The New Community Rules: Marketing on the Social Web. Publisher*. O'Reilly. doi:10.4148/1051-0834.1141

Xu, J. (2014). Managing Digital Enterprise. *Ten Essential Topics, 55-56*. Advance online publication. doi:10.2991/978-94-6239-094-2

Zarrella, D. (2010). *The Social Media Marketing Book. Publisher*. O'Reilly. http://www.oreilly.de/catalog/9780596806606/index.html

Zeithaml, V. A. (2000). Service quality, profitability, and the economic worth of customers: What we know and what we need to learn. *Journal of the Academy of Marketing Science*, *28*(1), 67–85. doi:10.1177/0092070300281007

Section 3

Case Studies and Reviews on Consumer Behavior Change in the Socio-Digital Era

Chapter 13
Social Media Marketing Strategies in the Lingerie Industry:
The Case of Valentine's Day Campaign in Spain

Ana De Miguel-Pérez
Universidad Pública de Navarra, Spain

Maria Elena Aramendia-Muneta
https://orcid.org/0000-0001-6167-3194
Universidad Pública de Navarra, Spain

ABSTRACT

This chapter presents a qualitative and quantitative analysis on the comparison of social media audience, social posts, and engagement over Instagram, Facebook, and Twitter for the main five lingerie brands in Spain during the week prior to Valentine's Day. The results show that a direct relationship between audience growth and posting frequency could not be confirmed but both factors may affect on engagement and content. Indeed, it was demonstrated that giveaways and influencer collaborations as well as carousel and photos received better feedback on average for Instagram and Facebook and GIFs for Twitter. The most obvious finding to emerge is that Instagram received the title of the "social media queen" in terms of audience and engagement in the lingerie industry. Finally, it was stated that strategies such as adapting content to fit with their followers likes to build a community of engaged and loyal followers is related to social media campaign success.

DOI: 10.4018/978-1-6684-4168-8.ch013

INTRODUCTION

Fashion industry is one of the most effervescent sectors contributing to the European Union (EU) economy (Ananda et al., 2015). Indeed, the EU is one of the biggest importers of fashion lingerie industry, where Spain is both one of the biggest apparels and women's underwear consumers (CBI, 2020). The lingerie market is growing and emerging (Grand View Research, 2019), therefore is an increasing focus of interest for researchers and the fashion industry.

In the meantime, the increasing use of social media has affected the fashion industry (Ananda et al., 2015). Companies are now focusing on strategic planning regarding social media, where it becomes essential to consider the blogs of influence in fashion lingerie, as well as engaging in the management of social networks in Facebook, Twitter and Instagram (Sanchez Torres & Arroyo-Cañada, 2017). All of these media constitute an incredible marketing tool to manage public perception of brands and enable flow of continuous feedback (Aramendia-Muneta, 2017). This feedback is shaped by users' post, which further might be viralized and at the same time, impact brand reputation (Manikonda et al., 2016). Moreover, lingerie generates special attention in social media as it is connected to image body (Filipe et al., 2011) and thus, lingerie brand images might affect potential lingerie consumers projecting beauty canons.

Therefore, the need to propose a study to continue this line of research is presented as there are few studies in the lingerie industry (Filipe et al., 2011; Sanchez Torres & Arroyo-Cañada, 2017) and lingerie industry is a neglected area in fashion research (Hume & Mills, 2013). The aim of this chapter is to determine if posting frequency is somehow linked to engagement and audience growth (Objective 1); describe which type of content receives more interactions (Objective 2); and which social media is more effective and engaging in the lingerie industry (Objective 3). To do this, a comparison of social media strategies carried out by the main successful lingerie brands in Spain in Twitter, Instagram and Facebook during the week prior to Valentine's Day. This period had been selected as marketing expenditures and efforts are large before a specific date (Close & Zinkhan, 2006) and lingerie sales are popular during this period (Criteo, 2017). This chapter is developed as follows: first the theoretical framework (social media and lingerie industry) is developed, and then the methodology, empirical analysis and conclusions are presented.

SOCIAL MEDIA

These days the use of Internet and social media are deep communicator drivers, whose purpose are to socialize (Tham et al., 2013) or to share information (De Valck et al., 2009) and to create community (Brodie et al., 2013). Consequently, companies have evolved and adapted to last technological advances by means of using digital and social media marketing tools such as websites, social media, mobile apps and ads, online video, email, and blogs to engage consumers anywhere via their digital devices.

Social Media Marketing is defined as a form of digital marketing that uses social networking platforms to increase brand and product exposure and to cultivate relationships with consumers (De Vries et al., 2017). It is worthy to mention the role of social media, where consumers are able to socialize, sharing opinions, videos, pictures among others (Kümpel et al., 2015).

For many firms that sell directly to the final consumer (business-to-consumer), being within the social networks is a must. Participation in virtual brand communities offers a positive and significant effect on brand loyalty and a new channel of communication with consumers (Casaló et al., 2013). Most of the large companies are now designing comprehensive social media services to integrate and support other elements of brand marketing content strategy and tactics. Hereafter, to successfully use social media companies must formulate brand-related social sharing through engagement and creating communities (De Valck et al., 2009).

Between the reasons to actively participate in social media, Neti (2011) listed some of the benefits of social media marketing: the size of social media platforms, brand transparency and reach of audience. Indeed, following underneath the advantages are identified as compelling reasons for companies to begin looking at social media as a marketing tool.

Transparency is connected to credibility in consumers. In fact, credibility is built among users, whose trust on the information unveiled in social media (Cheung & Lee, 2006). This credibility helps to improve branding. Thus, social media platforms are the most cost-effective way to increase business visibility (Neti, 2011). Credibility and trust allow the creation of a brand identity based on perception, communication, and image of the brand.

Once the credibility is formulating, social media purposes are to identify market segments. Through social communication channels, companies gather a large range of information about their users and their way of interaction (Arenas-Gaitan et al., 2013). As a result, it is possible to target users based on interests, demographic, geographic or any other factor and therefore to tailor audience strategies.

Social Media in Spain

Turning now to evidence the scale and the scope of Social Media Marketing, a recent report (2020) made by the Interactive Advertising Bureau (IAB) have revealed some interesting figures about the main social networks in Spain where 87% of internet users between 16-65 years old -25.9 million of people- use social networks. Facebook is the most popular social network (94%), followed by Instagram (76%) and Twitter (70%), all of them remaining among the top five social networks in number of users. Moreover, social media users use 4.5 networks on average, practically 1 more than in 2019 (3.7) and Instagram is one of the two most frequently used social networks which has taken over the second position from Facebook in 2020.

The main uses of Social Networks are for entertainment (81%), interaction (77%) and information (66%). The latter includes activities such as contacting a brand's customer service, commenting on current events, following accounts, becoming a fan/following a brand. Another use is following trends or serving as inspiration (30%), which includes becoming a fan following a brand, buying branded products or services, or following accounts. Regarding the 96% of the most followed accounts in Social Network by users are those people in their immediate environment, followed by Influencers (56%) and brands (52%). The intensity of use (minutes dedicated) to Social Networks increases this year in all targets being men and those under 40 are the most intensive in use. Overall, this information indicates that the reach and potential of the social networks is undisputable. To this point, the benefits and the scale of social media in Spain have been analyzed and it was found out that Facebook, Instagram and Twitter were the most popular channels.

LINGERIE INDUSTRY

Lingerie takes part of the fashion industry. The concept was developed during the late 19th century, referring to fashionable undergarment for women. It is a category of women's clothing, which includes undergarments such as brassieres, sleepwear, and lightweight robes. With respect to the lingerie industry, a study made by Statista (2012) shows that the revenue of the lingerie market worldwide in 2012 and 2017 generated an increase from 29.23 billion to 30 billion US$. Besides, according to Grand View Research, 2019, the business of underwear is booming and is expected to growth until 2025.

More specifically, the European Union (EU) has contributed to the significant growth of the global market presenting prominent players and high demand. Western European markets are much larger and better developed than the Central and Eastern European markets. Spain, together with Germany, France, the United Kingdom, the Netherlands and Italy account for 69% of women's underwear imports in the EU and have been growing at an average rate of 3.4% per year in the last five years. In fact, Spanish market is both one of the biggest apparels and women's underwear consumers in Europe and one of the biggest importers of apparel from developing countries (CBI, 2020). Consequently, it encompasses an interesting area to study due to the prominent role the sector is playing in Spain.

Between the factors expected to drive the market over the forecast period, Grand View Research (2019) mentioned: increasing awareness about the best fit, growing millennial population, and rise in spending power among women. Other aspects boosting the women's lingerie market across the world are rapid digitalization and increasing online platforms in present days. Moreover, the growing influence of social media is accelerating the change in consumer preferences toward fashionable apparel products such as lingerie items (ReportLinker, 2020). This idea supports the evidence of the role played by social media in the lingerie sector.

Lingerie in Spain

The lingerie industry in Spain achieved its highest turnover in 2018 since 2015, with revenues exceeding 280 million euros (Statista, 2019a). Companies are focused on introducing innovative lingerie items pursuing fashion and consumer demands. Based on type, the women's lingerie market is segmented into brassiere, panties, shapewear and others. Brassiere held the largest market share in Spain made of materials such as cotton, satin, silk, and nylon.

Regarding the most popular brands of women's lingerie and underwear Statista (2019b) mentioned Primark, Women' secret (from Tendam group), Oysho (from Inditex group) and Intimissimi and Tezenis (from Calzedonia Group) ranked by number of consumers in Spain in 2019. Thus, two out of five brands are from Spain, two from Italy, and one from Ireland respectively.

SOCIAL MEDIA AND COMMERCE

As aforementioned, social media accomplishes a role in the development of commerce into social commerce. Before making a purchase, 59% of users research information on social media with Facebook and Instagram being the main channel (IAB, 2020). In addition, following influencers generates a lot of traction and brands are increasingly collaborating with them for commercial purposes. BrandManic (2018), an influencer-based marketing platform, showed that influencers are positively valued by 79%

of the professionals surveyed and 40% have been collaborating with them for more than 3 years. There is still a great margin for growth because 29% have been programming campaigns with influencers for less than a year. Therefore, the consolidation of the influencers in Spain, and its great growth is explained.

Facebook, Twitter and Instagram are between the preferences by professionals for commercial purposes (91%, 68% and 54%). More specifically the professional objectives of social media addressed to functions such as selling (75%), generate branding (51%) or perform customer service (51%). These may be because they constitute the first point of contact when a potential customer is ready to buy. In fact, Faceebok, Instagram and Twitter were the most popular social media in Spain and also most popular in lingerie industry (Sanchez Torres & Arroyo-Cañada, 2017).

The data emerging from a survey elaborated by IAB (2020) states that brands which have profiles on social networks inspire more trust for 33% of users and the main motivation to have a private conversation with a brand is customer service (75%). Thus, these data show how social media facilitate the social interaction of consumers, leading to increased trust and intention to buy. Indeed, internet users perceive trust trough virtual communities (Sanchez Torres & Arroyo-Cañada, 2017). Social circle snot only formed by family and friends, but experts and strangers affect purchase decision (Petrescu & Korgaonkar, 2011). Consumers are constantly seeking advice and reviews whether to buy offline or online.

The relationship with customers is more direct and closer than ever. Nowadays, increase engagement (customer interaction with the brand) is one of the biggest challenges for organizations seeking effective social media management. Customers engagement through constant online interaction is central as much as attractive visual presentation and copywriting captures the attention (Sheriff et al., 2018). Therefore, through special promotions or key holiday sales companies elaborate social media campaigns to increase sales.

Valentine's Day - Commercial Campaign

Holiday sales remain a great time for brands. Specially, Valentine's Day for the lingerie industry, which has become a worldwide event that is becoming increasingly popular. Underwear is a commonly purchased item and numerous magazines recommend the purchase of lingerie for Valentine's Day this time every year (Cosmopolitan, Vanity Fair and InStyle among others). Indeed, 'lingerie' is ranked number 6 of search terms for products to give as a gift on February 14th (Criteo, 2017). Taking advantage of the day of love, lingerie brands bet every year to promote their products and get sales through original and creative campaigns.

More than 67% of Spaniards will celebrate this day, which translates into a perfect sales occasion. In 2019, they spent on average 71 euros per person, surpassing countries such as Germany, Sweden or Finland. The profile of target customers is between 24 and 44 years old. Regarding the search for products, users start their searches in December, but concentrating 66% of searches the previous days being the busiest (Think with Google, 2020). Lastly, the lingerie sector during the Valentine's Day period generates a lot of interest and the management of social media campaigns during the previous days could represent a growth opportunity for its brands.

METHODOLOGY

This section describes and discusses the methods used in this chapter. Firstly, a comparison of social media activities on Instagram, Facebook and Twitter (top 3 social networks in lingerie industry) from the top 5 Spanish lingerie brands (Women' secret, Oysho, Primark, Tezenis and Intimissimi) in terms of volume of sales will be held. Regarding the period covered, the week prior to Valentine's Day from 8th to 14th February 2021 will be considered. Then, the separate parts are added to describe in greater detail a comparative evaluation of each social media channel which are used for data collection. The data is obtained from a free trial account offered by Rival IQ which is a social media marketing analytics with advanced competitive analysis, search engine optimization, social reporting and content marketing tools.

Before proceeding with the assessment, it will be necessary to recognize the value of doing a comparative analysis between these main competitive brands. Because, tracking the strategies, followed by the competitive brands, allow individuals to understand better the market, how companies invest and behave on social media for commercial purposes, and to identify which are the best practices made by them. Indeed, analytics are greatest with a comparative context aiming to make more effective choices on when, where or what posts makes the best of a social media campaign. Table 1 summarizes the technical details of the research.

Table 1. Technical details of the research.

Objective	Audience and Engagement
Cases	Intimissimi, Oysho, Women'secret, Primark, Tezenis
Reference period	8th-14th February 2021
Sample size	15 profiles
Social media	Instagram, Facebook,Twitter
Methodology	Quantitative and qualitative analysis
Software	Rival IQ

EMPIRICAL ANALYSIS

Regarding the insights, not only it is crucial to know which audience is reached, but also how companies engage social networks users. Due to the engagement rate, the number of users who are currently following, liking, mentioning, or interacting can be measured. Certainly, it can be understood by means of evaluating all the brands and then provide brands how to improve strategies and make smarter decisions through identifying the content or the top social posts. Afterwards, a comparison of the brands' Instagram profiles will be conducted followed by the Facebook and Twitter accounts and a general cross-channel view of the data will be reviewed.

Instagram

Audience

Concerning Instagrammers, a higher number of likes or share of contents apparently shows a priori better success and increase in consumer purchasing intentions (Loureiro & Sarmento, 2019). Undoubtedly, the bigger is the number, the more likely is to attract new audience for increasing the number of likes and share of contents. As a result, the organic growth of a profile will increase. The differences between the five underwear brands in Instagram are highlighted in Figure 1 and Figure 2, providing two types of information for all the companies: the number of followers at the end of the covered period and the weekly net increase in the number of their followers during 8th-14th February respectively.

Figure 1. Instagram followers (in millions)
Source: own elaboration from Rival IQ

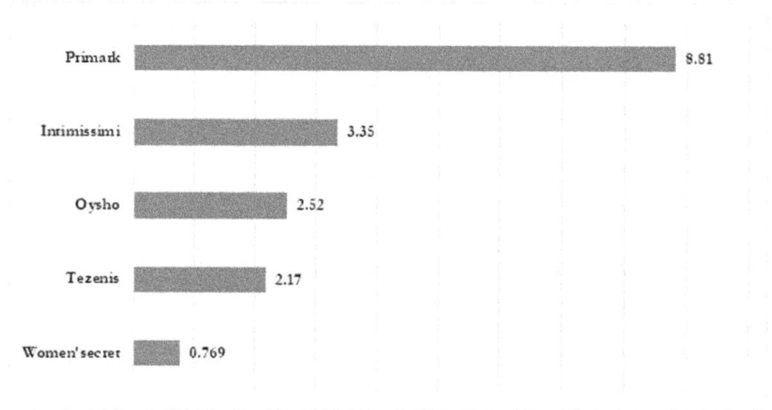

Figure 2. Net increase in followers
Source: own elaboration from Rival IQ

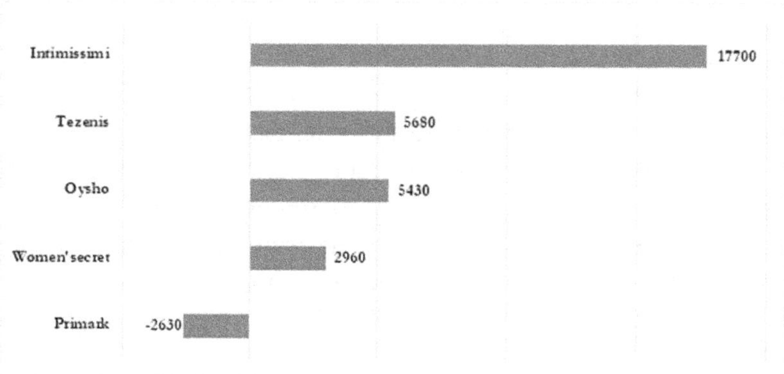

As seen in Figure 1 Primark ranks first out of the five companies for Instagram Followers (F), chased by Intimissimi. Both are above the average number of the landscape (3.52M F). On the other hand, Oysho, Tezenis and Women'secret accounts fewer quantity for the number of followers. Concerning the increase in followers (see Figure 2), Primark is significantly different from the others, being the only one with a negative trend. By contrast, it is striking that the brands with the lowest audience have experienced a fast-growing rate. Manic (2015) suggests that a relationship between high-engagement and visual quality content may have contributed to the increase in fans. For that reason, it will now be considered the content they used.

Instagram Posts and Engagement

A post can be any photo or video published by a user in their Feed or Instagram profile (Latiff &Safiee, 2015), it can likewise add a description, a hashtag, an emoji and even add an access to an URL redirecting to buy a product. The total and the average number of posts -excluding Instagram reels and Instagram video (IGTV)- per brand, their total Engagement and their average Engagement Rate (ER) per post separately, and the average number of likes and comments per post during the selected time period, will be examined as shown in Figure 3, 4 and 5 correspondingly. Regarding these data, it is observed that the Top Posts and the type of media and hashtags have remained as the most popular amongst the available content.

Figure 3. Total and daily average number of Instagram Posts (8th-14th February)
Source: own elaboration from Rival IQ

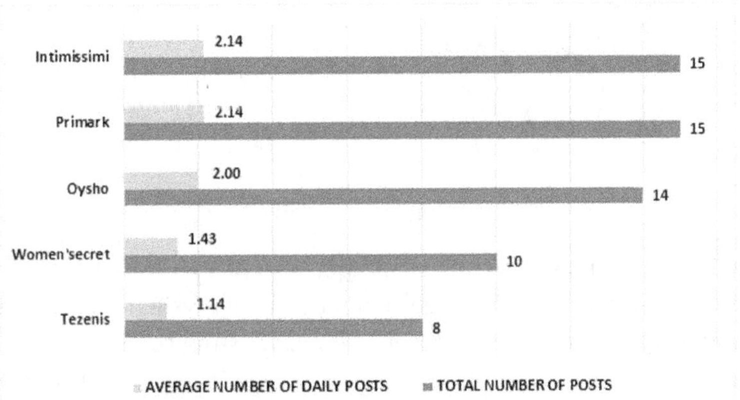

A recent study asserts that the top 25% brands post closer to 7 times per week, or about once a day, which shows the fashion industry are one of the most active industries (Feehan, 2021). It can be seen from the data shown in Figure 3 that the records increase and the average posts in our landscape are 12.4 times per week. Intimissimi, Primark, and Oysho significantly reported a greater number of published posts than the other two: Women'secret and Tezenis lasting below the average. Brands should focus on the importance of frequent updates and incentives for participation (Ashley & Tuten, 2015).

Figure 4. Instagram total engagement
Source: own elaboration from Rival IQ

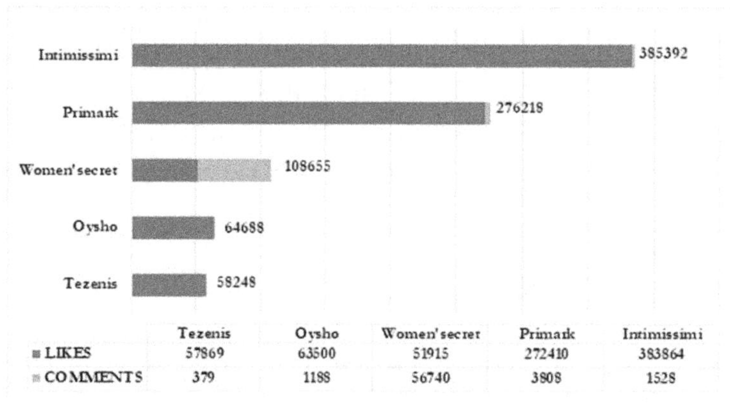

Figure 5. Instagram engagement rate per post
Source: own elaboration from Rival IQ

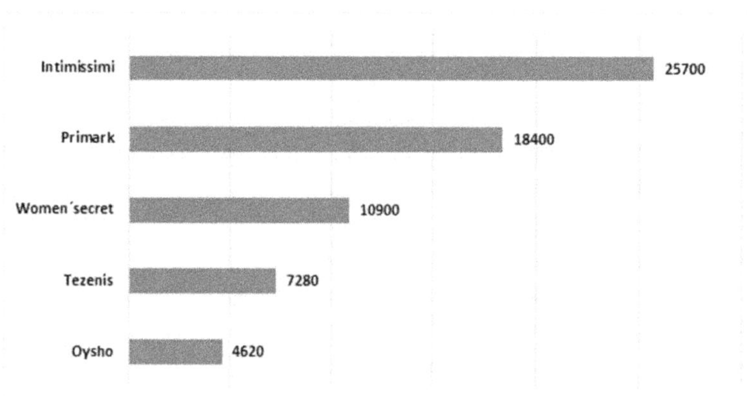

Interestingly, the highest total (see Figure 4) and per post engagement (see Figure 5) is obtained by the most active profiles, but remarkably Women'secret outstand Oysho receiving around 3000 more engagements per post and fifty times more comments. Hence, posting frequency may be somehow related to engagement (Objective 1). However, considering that Oysho's number of posts is higher leads to the idea that posting frequency is not the only factor affecting engagement. Harshtone (2020) explains that the quality, and the relevancy of the content generate more value and engagement. Since quantity does not necessarily reflect quality, content analysis of the posts is required.

The researched brands made use of diverse tools during the campaigns to create innovative and engaging posts which may influence the total interaction registered to each. Similarities between them are the use of original and casual copy writings, visual attracting media and employed hashtags. Relevant hashtags increase chances to be seen through hashtag searches and by hashtag followers. Note that relevant hashtags are better than more hashtags, say #valentinesday in this period results being an appropriate one. In addition, they hired influencers to promote products, which attains a positive effect on the followers' reactions (Belanche et al., 2020) attempting to reach more audience and increase brand awareness. As a result of making usage of these tools, the content become attractive.

Next, having defined the main tools used by the brands, this chapter will now dive into posts with the highest engagement to spot qualitative trends like colors, image patterns, hashtags for content and design ideas. Before proceeding to examine it, it will be of interest to distinguish that the most frequent posts-type included in the landscape are photo by far, followed by carousel and video. Figure 6 shows that carousel and photo generated more engagement than video on Instagram. What follows is the picture of the Top-Performing Posts obtaining the highest ER for every brand, classified per Instagram brand account.

Figure 6. Instagram engagement by type of content as a percentage average of the landscape
Source: own elaboration from Rival IQ

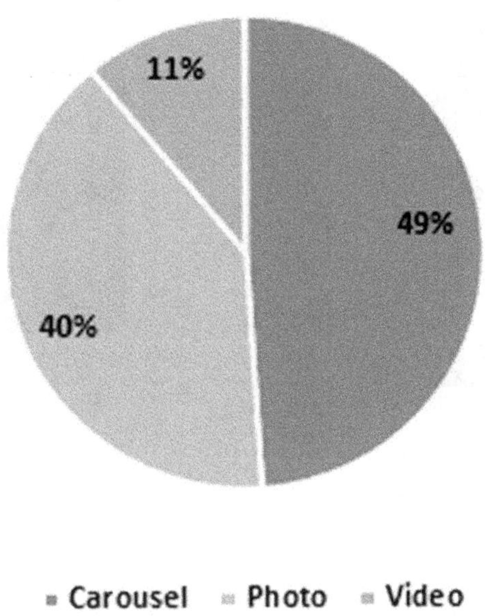

- INTIMISSIMI (@intimissimiofficial)

To begin with, Intimissimi had the second most engaging post in the landscape. Moreover, the relevant posts are 13 out of the top 20 posts. The ones resulting more attractive featured influencers, @ meryturiel and @giuliagaudino (as shown in Figure 7 and Figure 8) who have 879k and 609k followers respectively. The products were tagged with a link that redirects to the specific product page.

They used hashtags such as #intimissimi #madewithlove #italianlingerie. Of the 8 most broadly used hashtags, #intimissimi generated the highest engagement rate by follower. In addition to these influencers, there were other posts where they collaborated with @chiaraferragni (22.6M F), @paolaturani (1.6M F), @littlecrumb (2.8M F), @annacarlaesimona (211k F), @irisashannon (73.8M F), @sylvianovak_ (179k F).

It is interesting to note that Intimissimi has been the brand with the highest content created by influencers and the one with the greatest Total Engagement. This also accords with the earlier observation, which showed the positive effects of hiring influencers (Belanche et al., 2019).

Figure 7. Intimissimi Top 1 Instagram post (photo)
Source: Instagram

Figure 8. Intimissimi Top 2 Instagram (photo)
Source: Instagram

- PRIMARK (@primark)

To continue with, Primark got the third and fourth most engaging posts in the landscape and posted five of the top 20 posts. On average, the top four posts earned three times more engagement than their own other posts at this period, being a night gown set for Valentine´s Day (see Figure 9) and a casual outfit (see Figure 10) the one receiving more interactions.

Influencers like @susana_bicho90 (1M F), @sarafructuoso__ (224k F), @luciaavfdez (144k F) @ romekgelard (29,7k F) appear in their posts. Similarly, they employed hashtags such as #LoveYourself, #ValentinesDay. Despite containing other posts proposing their audience plans to do, suggesting what to eat or to watch on Netflix on Valentine's Day there are none dealing with lingerie, neither they tag their products. Hence, the content they offer is more focused on brand image rather than on concentrating on promoting their products, as Intimissimi did.

Figure 9. Primark Top 1 Instagram post (photo)
Source: Instagram

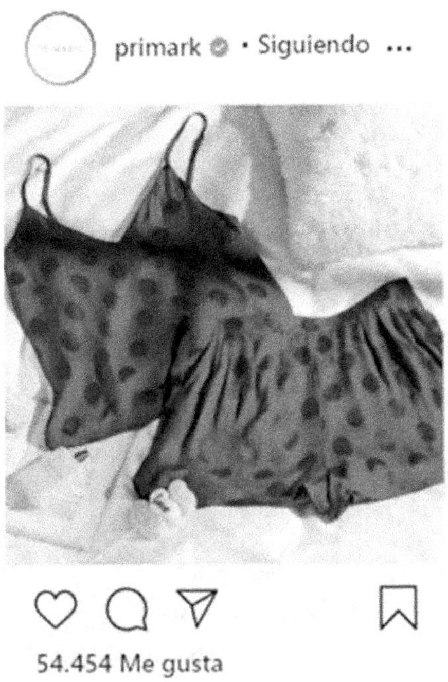

Figure 10. Primark Top 2 Instagram post (photo)
Source: Instagram

- WOMEN'SECRET (@womensecretofficial)

The only giveaway among all the brands has managed to rank Women'secret in the third place in terms of Total Engagement. Definitely, Figure 11 shows the best post scored the highest total engagement in the landscape and in all of the social media with a vast difference over the other posts. Therefore, it could conceivably be hypothesized that giveaways are the best way to interact with the Instagram community. This tactic allowed to reach a much wider audience. Indeed, it is observable in Figure 12 that the type of post is carousel, the most engaging type of post on the landscape average.

Same as the other four companies, they posted photos tagging influencers such as @carlavicob (103k F), @nuriablanco (318k F), @mvillallba (8.93k F), @patzhunter (190k F). However, it has barely used hashtags (3 in total) being #friendshipgoals #Valentine and #SanValentin. Another noteworthy fact is that the products are not tagged in any of the photos although their lingerie campaign collection for Valentine's Day named COMXY, appears in any post.

Figure 11. Women'secret Top 1 Instagram post (photo)
Source: Instagram

Figure 12. Women'secret Top 2 Instagram post (carousel)
Source: Instagram

- OYSHO (@oysho)

On average, the top four posts this period earned three times more engagement than their other posts, being the post where the influencer @elvin (1.1M F) is tagged causing the most of reactions (see Figure 13). Nevertheless, the interactions obtained are below the average per post (shown in Figure 5). It had as well uploaded content with other influencers such as @absmo (57.3k F) and a fact to note is that from all the content uploaded during this week the whole thing is about yoga (for example in Figure 14), and the most repeated hashtags are #oysho #sport, #comfort and #running. In the case of Oysho, products are tagged in the photos. As a result, it can be concluded that despite the large audience, it must have spent more time reinforcing the content to stimulate interactions with their followers and influencers and generate a positive effect on engagement.

- TEZENIS (@tezenisofficial)

Alternatively, Tezenis used #bra in two of their four most engaging posts, among other hashtags. The post that gained the attention was a bodysuit from their Valentine's collection (see Figure 15). Remarkably, all the content is edited with a motif of hearts, pink colors and love, and the products are additionally tagged. The same as the other brands, an influencer is the face of the second most liked post during the period, @maffashion_official (1.4M F), as shown in Figure 16.

Figure 13. Oysho Top 1 Instagram post (photo)
Source: Instagram

Figure 14. Oysho Top 2 Instagram post (photo)
Source: Instagram

Figure 15. Tezenis Top 1 Instagram post (photo).
Source: Instagram

Figure 16. Tezenis Top 2 Instagram post (photo).
Source: Instagram

Because Tezenis received the least total engagement, in reviewing the data provided (see Graphic 6) we found that it is the company receiving the least number of comments. Comments amplify companies' reach by increasing the likelihood of appearing in the Explore feed and Instagram users can also tag their friends in comments. Thus, it is concluded they may had used a strategy which could have helped their content be seen by more people through original copywriting or visual content to generate comments.

Engagement Rate

Regarding the ER by follower, it is calculated after having determined total engagement divided by total followers for each company. In addition, it is another significant aspect to evaluate the performance of their different Instagram accounts. There are several significant differences between the total engagement, previously discussed, and the ER by follower. Undeniably, the reaction totals gave valuable information about how many reactions brands are cooperating with. However, it is equally appreciated to assess how valuable their followers are, because one supporter that engages with social posts is worth more than dozens who do not.

The results provided in Figure 17 reveals the average number of interactions (likes and comments) per posts, per follower on all post published during the selected period expressed as a percentage.

Figure 17. Instagram ER by follower
Source: own elaboration from Rival IQ

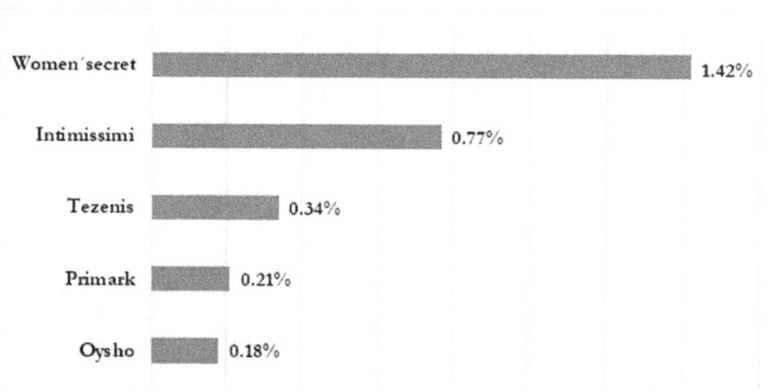

Figure 17 shows that Women'secret saw a higher engagement rate than the rest. Note that Women'secret recorded the lowest number of followers but enjoyed the highest ER by follower. It only garnered about 108,000 total reactions to Intimissimi 380,000, or Primark 276,000, but that number came from just about half of their total reactions as comments reached with the giveaway post (which received the highest engagement between the landscape). The numbers imply that the content on the company's Instagram page is more appealing to followers than that of similar brands.

Intimissimi is found in the second place, which achieved the complicated task of maintaining the interest of the second highest audience in the landscape and presented a balanced ratio between the number of reactions and followers. Similarly, Tezenis obtained a good proportion obtaining the third highest ER by follower. Recall that it was the brand with the second lowest number of followers and total engagement. Moreover, they posted only 8 posts during the week compared to 12.4 of the landscape average. This finding is consistent with that aforementioned of Baer referenced by Harshtone, (2020) meaning that the quality, not the quantity of the content is fundamental.

What is outstanding is the dramatic decline of Primark, which considering it has the wider audience (8 M). However, it has not managed to neither attract nor maintain its audience, presenting a low ER per follower and being the only account that lost followers. Likewise, it occurred with Oysho, the least attractive brand for its supporters. Despite having a huge audience, it did not manage to captivate them. To conclude, it is not vital to own further audience but an effective one. It can be achieved through a firm communication strategy that encourages to interact, like, comment and share their content to make it relevant. As a consequence, Instagram will strive the firms' profile to appear in more searches and their audience will grow.

As a whole, it has been explained that the different brands have experienced a change in the number of audience and interactions. This change may be somehow but not directly linked to frequency posting. Other variables such as content may be generating impact among Instagram users. Indeed, the most engaging posts showed that carousel and photo generated more engagement than video on Instagram. For this reason, this section has reviewed the three key aspects of the campaign carried out for Valentine's Day: the total and increase in audience, the content uploaded, and the engagement received.

Facebook

Audience

Regarding Facebook audience, they are the total number of Page Fans for a company on Facebook. The graphic below summarizes the number of Page Fans at the end of the studied period and the net change increase of them. Just as happened with Instagram, a large number of them indicates that people enjoy firms' content, and they are likely to attract new customers. Additionally, page ratings and reviews are a Facebook tool which helps building trust and gives credibility. When owning a page, it is expected from people to hear about it and visit it. Then, the number of fans jointly with page ratings and reviews help build trust and credibility for a business.

Figure 18. Facebook Page fans at the end of the period (in millions)
Source: own elaboration from Rival IQ

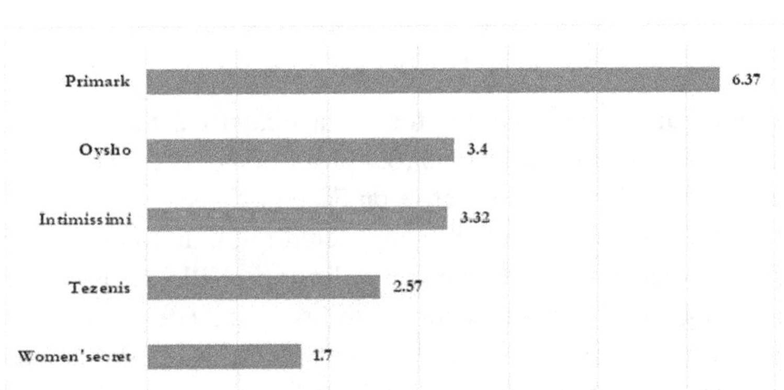

The evidence from Figure 18 showed that Primark conquest in number of fans by a wide margin to the rest brands (6.37 M). It almost doubled Oysho and Intimissimi having around 3.4 M fans and ranked well above Tezenis (2.57M) and Women'secret (1.7M). As it can be seen in Figure 19, the brands who grown the most were Primark and Intimissimi, above the average growth rate of the landscape (3.6k), followed by Oysho. On the other hand, Tezenis' audience growth and size were relatively flat, and out-paced by Women'secret. Hereafter, these differences may be related to the to the activity carried out by the brands during the week.

Facebook POSTS

Regarding Facebook Posts, it can be any comment, picture or other media that is posted on the user's Facebook page or "wall.". In the same way as Instagram, it can likewise add a description, a hashtag, an emoji and even add an access to an URL redirecting to buy a product. The total and the average number of posts per brand, their total engagement and their average Engagement Rate (ER) per post separately, calculated as an average number of likes, comments and shares per post during the selected time period, will be examined. All together are shown in Figure 20, 21 and 22 correspondingly. Afterwards, it will be observed what posts and what type of media and hashtags have remained the most popular amongst the available content.

Figure 19. Fans net increase from 8th Feb-14th Feb 2021
Source: own elaboration from Rival IQ

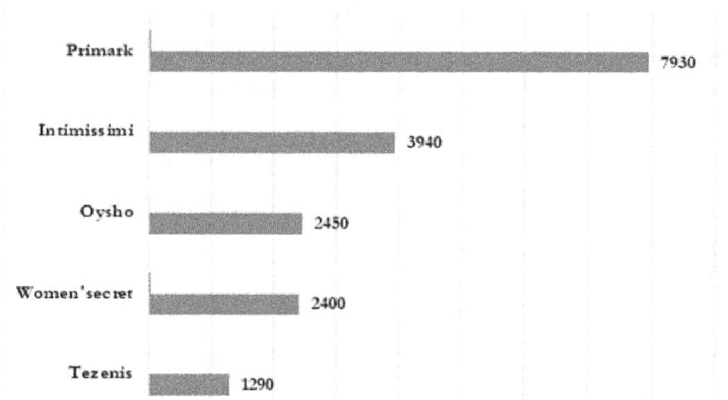

It is observable from Figure 20 a decrease in the average landscape posts from Instagram (recall it was 12.4 posts) to Facebook's landscape average (6.4 posts). Posting frequency and engagement may be linked to audience growth as firms are less active on Facebook because it generated less engagement (4.79 k in average) and less audience growth was registered (3.6k in average) compared to Instagram (Objective 1). In addition, Brands' Key Performance Indicators (KPIs) on Facebook relies on reaching audience instead of focusing on engagement, contrary to Instagram (IAB, 2019). Facebook historically it is detail driven and not only focused on images or video (Jackson, 2019). Women'secret, Tezenis, Intimissimi and Primark reported a fair number of published posts being 9, 8, 8 and 7 posts respectively.

Oysho differs from the rest in a critical aspect: it had no registered activity. Hereafter, the analyzed metrics of Oysho's posts and ER will not be noted.

From Figure 21 and Figure 22, it is highlighted that Intimissimi obtained the highest total engagement by far, almost quintupling Tezenis, the second-ranked in terms of Total Engagement and Engagement per Post numbers, followed by Women'secret and Primark. Largely, the number of reactions outstands shares and comments. Although Primark has uploaded less content than Women'secret, it outperformed it in engagement by generating the highest number of comments across the entire landscape. A reason may be because they asked questions in text copy or due to captivating messaging which are associated with higher conversion lift (Facebook IQ, 2020).

Same as it happened with Instagram, firms' Facebook profiles share a number of key features to achieve campaign success. Similarly, they use of original copy writings expressing themselves in a close manner and use attractive media. However, they shared few influencer posts compared to Instagram and employed less or no hashtags. Regarding the type of content generating more engagement it is found to be carousel and photo, followed by video, similar to Instagram (see Figure 23).

Figure 20. Total and daily average number of Facebook posts (8th-14th February 2021)
Source: own elaboration from Rival IQ

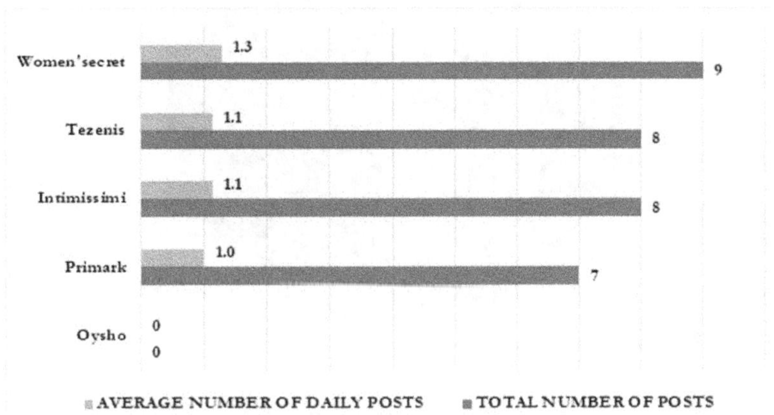

Figure 21. Facebook total engagement
Source: own elaboration from Rival IQ

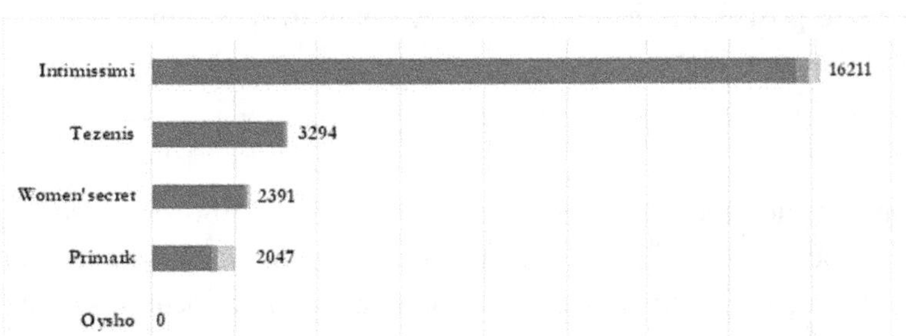

	Oysho	Primark	Women'secret	Tezenis	Intimissimi
REACTIONS	0	1425	2226	3162	15630
SHARES	0	167	83	78	324
COMMENTS	0	455	82	54	257

Figure 22. Facebook engagement rate per post
Source: own elaboration from Rival IQ

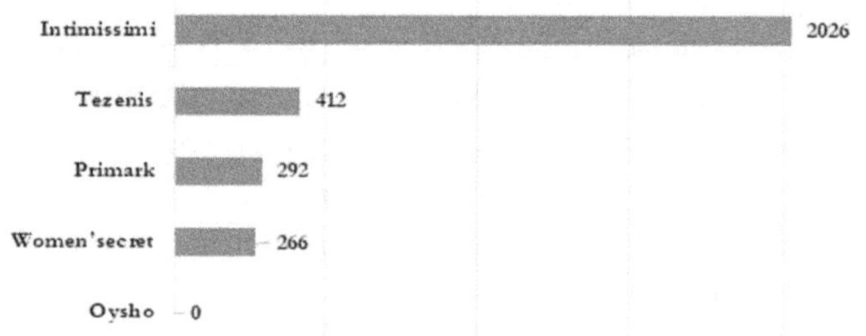

Figure 23. Facebook Engagement by type of content as a percentage average of the landscape.
Source: own elaboration from Rival IQ

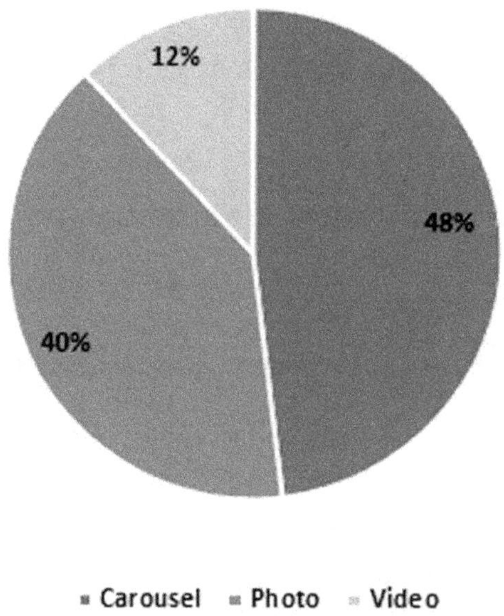

Next, having defined the main features used by the brands and the most engaging type of content, the chapter will now dive into posts with the highest engagement to spot trends like colors, image patterns, hashtags for content and design ideas.

Intimissimi

Five posts of the firm obtained the most engaging numbers in the entire landscape, and it is above the average for weekly Facebook posts. Influencers such as @irisashannon, @chiaraferragni, @giuliagaudino, @paolaturani and @meryturiel, which already were on Instagram appeared in their posts. In fact, with the collaboration of the latter, they achieved the top second performing post. As it can be seen in Figure 24 and Figure 25, in the copyrighting they used terms associated with Valentine's Day such as 'love affair', 'elegance', 'flowers', and added a call to action 'Shop Now' to buy their products. Indeed, it was observed that the photos are more effective than video.

However, it is interesting to note the absence of hashtags. Regarding the images, they all shared the same neutral colors style and showed the Valentine's Day lingerie collection. In this way, the company did branding by achieving Facebook Fans to identify the brand with this simple, elegant and product-focused style.

Figure 24. Intimissimi Top 1 Facebook posts (photo)
Source: Facebook

Figure 25. Intimissimi Top 2 Facebook posts (photo)
Source: Facebook

Tezenis

On the other hand, Tezenis published eight posts this period ahead of the landscape average of about six posts per week. In addition, six of their posts were in the landscape's top 20 and ranked second of 5 companies in total engagement. Despite being the second in total engagement numbers, it is the one that received the fewest comments. Uncreative and unoriginal copywriting may be one of the reasons. Although it used 8/8 of the most engaging hashtags such as #newin or #Valentinesday in two of their four most engaging posts it should review an improvement to generate interaction with their fans through questions or other types of strategies.

The post that gained the attention corresponds to the same post as in Instagram (see Figure 26). Similarly, all the content was edited with a motif of hearts, pink colors and love, and there were a call to action to buy the products (as shown in Figure 26 and Figure 27). Conversely, only one influencer appeared in their posts, @maffashion_official (1.4M F) who also appeared on Instagram. However, it did not manage to be one of the top 2 posts.

Figure 26. Tezenis Top 1 Facebook post (photo)
Source: Facebook

Figure 27. Tezenis Top 2 Facebook post (photo)
Source: Facebook

Women'secret

Women'secret published nine posts this period, ahead of the landscape average of about six posts per week. Three of their posts were in the landscape's top 20. However, it was below average for Facebook total engagement, ranking 3rd of 5 companies. On average, their top four posts this period earned 2 times more engagement than the other posts. Both top performing posts were carousel (see Figure 28 and Figure 29) and stands out for having original copywriting, inviting the fan to interact through questions or with calls to action inviting to discover the collection including links to the website.

Nonetheless, the brand has not used any hashtag, nor it has uploaded the content with influencers. However, it is a notorious fact that it is the one with the fewest fans, but the one that grown the most in ratio. Factors such as original content and copywriting, and high activity may be associated with the growth in fans.

Primark

Primark registered seven posts this period. However, it deleted some of their posts. Thus, it is significant to continue considering the insights generated at the same time of the comparative study with the other brands. The deleting of posts may be linked to engagement problems as it is below average for Facebook total engagement, ranking 4th of 5 companies although it ranked first of five for Facebook Fans.

Surprisingly, Primark has received many more comments than average. Some examples of those current available posts that have generated the most comments are shown in Figure 30 and Figure 31. Indeed, it did promote from Facebook Instagram links to help push traffic to their Instagram account.

Figure 28. Women'secret Top 1 Facebook post (carousel)
Source: Facebook

Figure 29. Women'secret Top 2 Facebook post (carousel)
Source: Facebook

Figure 30. Primark Top 1 Facebook post (photo)
Source: Facebook

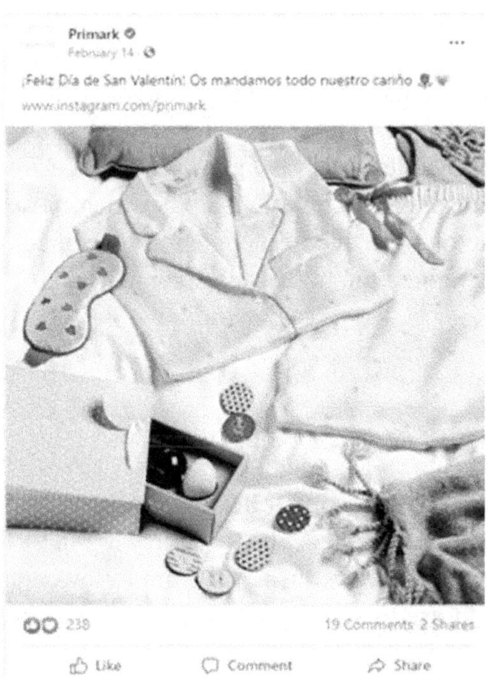

Figure 31. Primark Top 2 Facebook post (photo)
Source: Facebook

Facebook Engagement

Regarding the ER by follower, it is calculated as the total number of interactions (reactions, comments, and shares) of posts during a week prior to Valentine's Day and by follower. In addition, it is worthy to remark the relevancy of this insight (Libai et al., 2010).

Figure 32. Facebook ER by follower
Source: own elaboration from Rival IQ

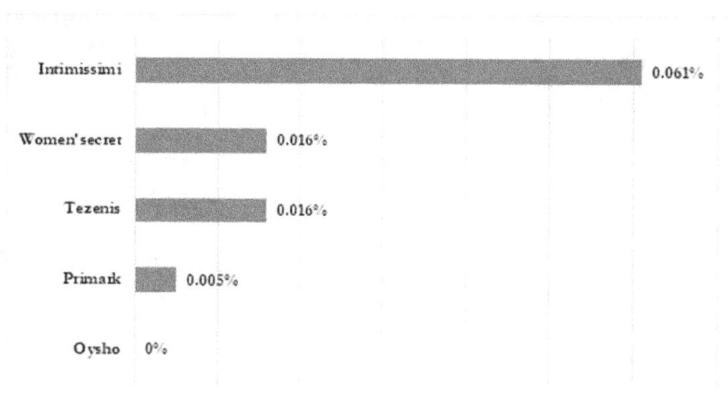

Figure 32 shows that there exists a sizable difference between the two networks (recall Figure 19) for ER by follower. Hence, this data evidence that ER is higher on Instagram than in Facebook.

Firstly, Intimissimi obtained the highest ER by follower. Despite being third-ranked in page fans, its audience has grown at a rapid pace. Its content has been liked by its fans, as they have interacted with it. Coincidentally, it was the brand that shared the most influencer content. Secondly, Women'secret and Tezenis had the same ER (0,016%), but Women'secret audience growth overcome Tezenis. As a consequence, the performance of the latter could be improved. Thirdly, Primark ER is the lowest despite having the largest audience. What is striking, is that its audience has grown considerably. Therefore, the slightest attempt to improve their content could have implied a high rate of audience growth.

To sum up, differences between companies have been commented. Surprisingly, the audience growth, engagement and post frequency were lower compared to Instagram. A relationship between those factors may explain the trends. And similarly, carousel and photos were the most engaging type of content. Indeed, again the brand which upload influencers photos obtained the highest engagement.

Twitter

Audience

Twitter followers are people who receive someone's' Tweets. If someone follows a profile: They will show up in their followers list and see their Tweets in their Home timeline whenever they log in to Twitter. They are prospective customers and are incredibly valuable to every business. More followers mean growing an interested audience with whom engage with and use to amplify a brand message - both on and off Twitter through spread reach, word of mouth, drive web traffic, purchases, leads, downloads, and more (Zhang et al., 2011). Thus, followers allow firms to promote their Twitter accounts within the timeline to attract new followers and grow their audience on Twitter.

The differences between the five underwear brands in terms of Twitter followers are highlighted in Figure 33 and Figure 34 providing two types of information for all the companies: the number of followers at the end of the covered period and the weekly net increase in number of them respectively.

Figure 33. Twitter followers at the end of the studied period.
Source own elaboration from Rival IQ

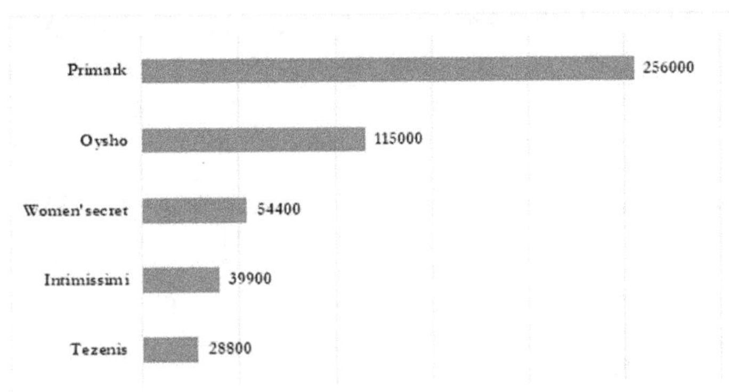

Figure 34. Followers net increase from 8th-14th February 2021
Source: own elaboration from Rival IQ

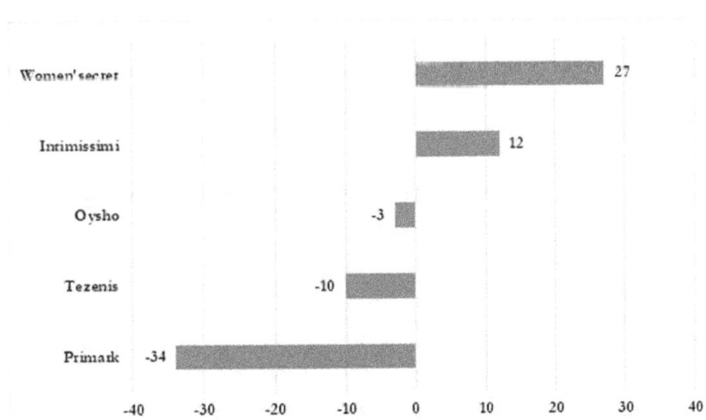

Figure 33 shows that Primark and Oysho are above landscape average (98.8k) for Twitter Followers, ranking the first and second out of 5 companies correspondingly. By contrast, below the average it is found that Women'secret, Intimissimi and Tezenis must put some energy to increase their audience. Similarly, Women'secret and Intimissimi did not see much audience growth this period and Oysho, Tezenis and Primark had even lost followers (see Figure 34). Twitter has the lowest audience of all the compared networks. One of the reasons they did not attract new followers may be the absence of high-engagement content and low activity of brands on this social media. A more detailed account of it is given in the following section.

Tweets and Engagement

Activity is all about how often brands engaged with their followers through tweets, replies, and retweets. The term 'Tweet' is a message posted on Twitter that contains text, photos, GIFs or video. 3 types of tweets were considered: it could be a normal one; a reply: used to respond to someone else's Tweet; or a retweet: which allows to retweet someone else's Tweet and add an own comment. Therefore, the total and the average number of tweets per brand, their total engagement and their average Engagement Rate (ER) per-tweet separately, calculated as an average number of likes, replies and retweets per-post during the selected time period, will be examined. All together are shown in Figure 35, Figure 36 and Figure 37 correspondingly.

Figure 35. Total and daily average number of Tweets (8th-14th February 2021)
Source: own elaboration from Rival IQ

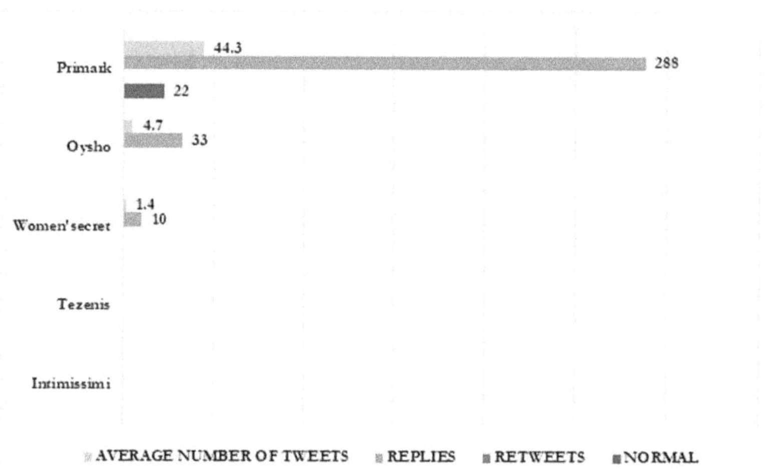

Figure 36. Twitter total engagement.
Source: own elaboration from Rival IQ

	Intimissimi	Oysho	Tezenis	Women'secret	Primark
LIKES	0	0	0	0	1405
RETWEETS	0	0	0	0	58
REPLIES	0	0	0	0	141

Figure 37. Twitter engagement rate per Tweet.
Source: own elaboration from Rival IQ

From Figure 37 the differences between the brands are striking. It can be seen that Primark registered the highest activity by far (310 tweets in total) followed by Oysho (33 tweets). Both registered more daily tweets than daily posts published on any social network (recall Figure 3 and Figure 20). On the other hand, Women'secret posted a similar number in all networks (10 tweets) and surprisingly, Tezenis and Intimissimi did not publish any tweets during the period studied. As it is observable, about 94% tweets are replies, 4% are normal tweets and 0% retweets. Therefore, the landscape average of tweets in the lingerie sector is higher but there are large differences between the brands.

Furthermore, from Figure 38 and Figure 41, it can be seen that social media efforts in Twitter do not pay off for Oysho, -because replies did not receive any engagement- or for Primark, -which received 1604 total engagement-. Indeed, the ratio of Net Followers Increase (recall Figure 36) for both did not relate to the activity carried out by them. Remember that Primark and Oysho lost followers (-32, -4 respectively).

Similarly, to Tezenis, who lost 10 followers but did not publish anything, whereas Women'secret did not obtained any engagement with their replies it is the one that grew the most in followers. Indeed, it is followed by Intimissimi- which did not post any tweet. Therefore, there is no correlation between the total engagement and the increase in followers (Objective 1). But it will be further analyzed the quality of the content that may be related.

There exists content similarities across brands. They limited to 1 or 2 maximum hashtags per tweet, text was short, concise and colloquial and they used images, GIFs or videos. For example, of the 5 most broadly used hashtags, #ootd, #Lockdownlife, #Valentines, #ValentiensDay and #Natioanlpizzaday generated the highest engagement rate by follower. In addition, they retweeted relevant content to maintain a solid presence on Twitter and asked questions to interact with their audience, show brand personality and gather feedback.

Further, the most frequent Posts-Type included in the landscape will be commented. They included photo, status update, link, GIF and video and the most engaging type of content was GIFs (see Graphic 20). What follows is the picture of the Top-Performing Posts obtaining the highest ER in the landscape.

Figure 38. Twitter engagement by type of content as a percentage average of the landscape.
Source: own elaboration from Rival IQ

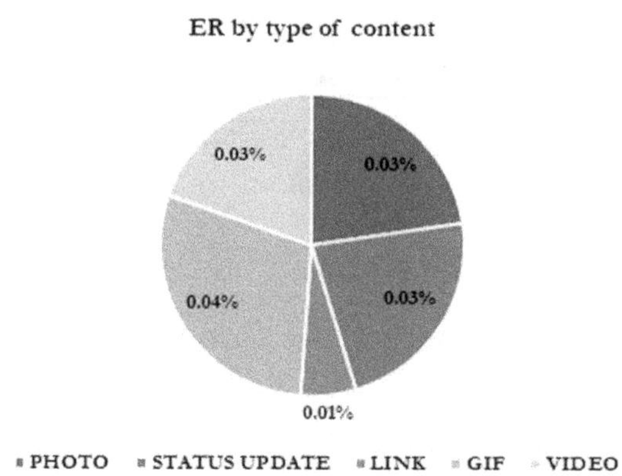

- Primark

The content uploaded by Primark included all the aforementioned hashtags where #ootd generated the highest engagement rate by follower. The topics were mostly related to Valentine's Day. They had also published curated and non-curated URLs such as a link to a romantic playlist on Spotify which results interesting to interact with followers. Moreover, as it can be seen in Figure 39 and Figure 40, the 2 top performing tweets are not related to love. But both included GIFs and an image, the type of content which generated the most engagement on Twitter. In addition, the copywriting was casual, and they asked direct questions to followers.

Figure 39. Primark Top 1 Twitter post (photo).
Source: Twitter

Figure 40. Primark Top 2 Twitter post (GIF).
Source: Twitter

- Oysho

Oysho did not receive any feedback on its responses. All their tweets were responses to customer queries which did not achieved engagement. However, brands need to interact with followers and answers the doubts in order to maintain at least those followers. In addition, social networks are also used to provide customer service and have a direct communication with them (Fogel, 2010).

- Women'secret

Similarly, Women'secret tweets were all replies and did not receive any engagement. The same scenario as that of Oysho applies.

Engagement Rate

Finally, the ER per follower is calculated as the number of engagement actions (likes, retweets and replies) a tweet receives in relation to followers. Shown as a percentage, it gives a great read on the amount of audience engaging in Twitter and helps compare the engagement to competitors regardless of audience size. It can be seen from Figure 41 that Primark ranks 1st of 5 companies for Twitter ER by follower as it is the only brand who received engagement. According to a poll from the Online Advertising Guide (2020), the average Twitter engagement rate is around 0.5%. Brands with excellent Twitter marketing usually achieve an engagement rate of 1-2%, but anything above that is quite rare. Hence, lingerie companies do not stand out or achieve a position of authority on Twitter.

Figure 41. Twitter ER by follower.

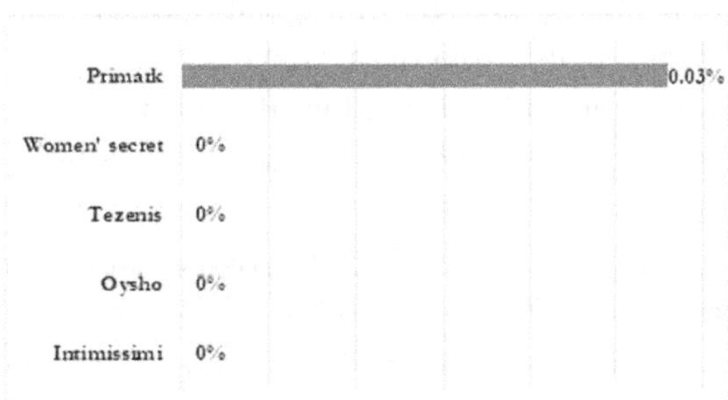

To conclude, Twitter is by far the social media with the least performance for the lingerie industry. The landscape audience decreased during the period studied and it received the fewest engagement, moreover, some of the firms did not publish any tweet. Regarding the most engaging content, GIF received the best feedback from the users. On the other hand, the posting frequency is higher because Twitter is more dynamic, but it did not manage to engage, grow or maintain its audience. Consequently, the relationship between audience growth and posting frequency or engagement in average did not apply for Twitter.

Finally, Table 2 summarizes a cross-channel view of the obtained data from Instagram, Facebook and Twitter. Next, numerous implications and conclusions will be stated.

Table 2. Cross-channel data.

Industry Landscape Average	Instagram	Facebook	Twitter
Audience	3.52M	3.47M	98.8k
Net Increase in Followers	5.82k	3.6k	-1.6k
Post Frequency	12.4	6.4	70.6
Total Engagement	179k	4.79k	321
ER by follower	0.58%	0.02%	0.01%

CONCLUSION

This study has described social media strategies that would help to establish a greater degree of accuracy about which are the most effective content to engage with customers. Throughout investigating the top-5 lingerie brand different social media profiles and certain types of visual media, some conclusions have arisen. Nonetheless, this study was limited by small sample size and in a specific time (Valentine's Day) and in a country.

Firstly, a direct relationship between audience growth and posting frequency could not be confirmed but it may affect (Objective 1). However, Instagram which registered the highest post frequency on average compared to Facebook, was also the one who generated the highest total engagement. Unhopefully, this relationship did not apply to Twitter. It may be hypothesized that several factors such as engagement, content and post frequency are related to the audience growth. On Instagram and Facebook, the brands obtaining the highest engagement rate experienced a high increase in followers respectively. Hence, continuously uploading content and high presence in social media contribute to grow and attract the audience.

Secondly, regarding the most engaging content the 2 top performing posts of the sample size were an Instagram giveaway and an influencer collaboration post. Indeed, it was demonstrated that carousel and photos receive better feedback than video on average for Instagram and Facebook and GIFs for Twitter. Not only photos were welcomed by users, but also visual attracting media including such as GIFs, emojis, linked URLs, and original copywriting which enhances calls to action or interaction with followers and fans (Objective 2).

Thirdly, the next major finding was that the biggest audience in the lingerie industry is found to be divided between Instagram (49.7%) as the leader, followed by Facebook (48.9%) and leaving Twitter aside, which only accounts for 1.39%. The most obvious finding to emerge from this study is that Instagram received the title of the "social media queen" in terms of audience and engagement in the lingerie industry (Objective 3).

Moreover, it was shown that the company with the largest audience is not the one that has grown the most, nor the one that has generated the most engagement. Therefore, the success of a social media campaign is related to strategies such as adapting content to fit with their followers likes to build a community of engaged and loyal followers.

Finally, a further study could assess how far Social Media Advertising can achieve brand recognition and community growth. Indeed, a report made by Instagram for Business (2019) states that every day, 500 million active users make use of Instagram Stories and they are helping businesses make use of story-telling faster and in a more engaging and powerful way. Hence, the analysis of Instagram and Facebook stories would also constitute a fruitful area for further work. Through this research it is intended to open new discussions about the role of visual content on social media in learning about fashion trends and inspire marketing researchers to study the reasons behind these findings.

REFERENCES

Ananda, A. S., Hernandez-García, Á., & Lamberti, L. (2015). Fashion in actions on social media - Spanish SME fashion brands case studies. In *Proceedings of the European Conference on e-Learning* (pp. 488–497). Academic Press.

Aramendia-Muneta, M. E. (2017). Spread the word – the effect of word of mouth in e-marketing. In G. Siegert, M. B. Von Rimscha, & S. Grubenmann (Eds.), *Commercial Communication in the Digital Age* (pp. 227–245). De Gruyter. doi:10.1515/9783110416794-013

Arenas-Gaitan, J., Rondan-Cataluña, F. J., & Ramírez-Correa, P. E. (2013). Social identity, electronic word-of-mouth and referrals in social network services. *Kybernetes*, *42*(8), 1149–1165. doi:10.1108/K-04-2013-0081

Ashley, C., & Tuten, T. (2015). Creative strategies in social media marketing: An exploratory study of branded social content and consumer engagement. *Psychology and Marketing*, *32*(1), 15–27. doi:10.1002/mar.20761

Belanche, D., Cenjor, I., & Pérez-Rueda, A. (2019). Instagram stories versus Facebook wall: an advertising effectiveness analysis Instagram stories versus Facebook wall: un análisis de la efectividad publicitaria. *Spanish Journal of Marketing-ESIC*, *23*(1), 69–94. doi:10.1108/SJME-09-2018-0042

BrandManic. (2018). *Presentamos el estudio sobre marketing de influencers en España, 2018 - BrandManic*. Retrieved February 14, 2021 from https://www.brandmanic.com/estudio-marketing-de-influencers-en-espana-2018/

Brodie, R. J., Ilic, A., Juric, B., & Hollebeek, L. (2013). Consumer engagement in a virtual brand community: An exploratory analysis. *Journal of Business Research*, *66*(1), 105–114. doi:10.1016/j.jbusres.2011.07.029

Casaló, L. V., Flavián, C., & Guinalíu, M. (2013). La construcción de lealtad en comunidades virtuales de marca. *Revista Europea de Dirección y Economía de La Empresa*, *22*(1), 53–60. doi:10.1016/j.redee.2011.10.001

CBI. (2020). *The European market potential for women's underwear*. Retrieved February 14, 2021 from https://www.cbi.eu/market-information/apparel/womens-underwear/market-potential

Cheung, C. M. K., & Lee, M. K. O. (2006). Understanding consumer trust in internet shopping: A multidisciplinary approach. *Journal of the American Society for Information Science and Technology*, *57*(4), 479–492. doi:10.1002/asi.20312

Close, A., & Zinkhan, G. (2006). A holiday loved and loathed: A consumer perspective of Valentine's Day. *Advances in Consumer Research. Association for Consumer Research (U. S.)*, *33*, 356–365.

Criteo. (2017). *Valentine's day gifts hearts, flowers, jewelry, lingerie…and kisses*. Retrieved February 14, 2021 from https://www.criteo.com/wp-content/uploads/2017/02/valentines-day-report-2017.pdf

De Valck, K., Van Bruggen, G. H., & Wierenga, B. (2009). Virtual communities: A marketing perspective. *Decision Support Systems*, *47*(3), 185–203. doi:10.1016/j.dss.2009.02.008

De Vries, L., Gensler, S., & Leeflang, P. S. H. (2012). Popularity of brand posts on brand fan Pages: An investigation of the effects of social media marketing. *Journal of Interactive Marketing*, *26*(2), 83–91. doi:10.1016/j.intmar.2012.01.003

Facebook, I. Q. (2020, July 16). *Text, timing and format tips for effective Facebook creative*. Facebook. Retrieved February 14, 2021 from https://www.facebook.com/business/news/insights/making-creative-impact-on-facebook-platforms-with-text-timing-and-format

Feehan, B. (2021, February 24). How often to post on social media. *Rival IQ*. Retrieved February 14, 2021 from https://www.rivaliq.com/blog/how-often-to-post-social-media/

Filipe, A. B., Montagna, G., & Carvalho, C. (2011). Lingerie product image in Portuguese underwear market: From brand to consumer, a perceived lingerie image. *International Journal of the Image*, *1*(2), 51–68. doi:10.18848/2154-8560/CGP/v01i02/44182

Fogel, S. (2010). Issues in measurement of word of mouth in social media marketing. *International Journal of Integrated Marketing Communications*, *2*(2), 54–60. doi:10.1108/13552550610710153

Grand View Research. (2019, June). *Lingerie market size, share & trends analysis*. Retrieved February 14, 2021 from https://www.grandviewresearch.com/industry-analysis/lingerie-market

Hume, M., & Mills, M. (2013). Uncovering Victoria's Secret: Exploring women's luxury perceptions of intimate apparel and purchasing behaviour. *Journal of Fashion Marketing and Management*, *17*(4), 460–485. doi:10.1108/JFMM-03-2013-0020

IAB. (2019). VII Observatorio de marcas en redes sociales. *IAB Spain*. Retrieved February 14, 2021 from https://iabspain.es/wp-content/uploads/2019/06/observatorio_rrss_2019_vreducidafinal.pdf

IAB. (2020). Estudio de redes sociales 2020. *IAB Spain*. Retrieved February 14, 2021 from https://iabspain.es/estudio/estudio-redes-sociales-2020/

Jackson, D. (2019, June 30). Instagram vs Facebook: Which is best for your brand's strategy? *Sprout Social*. Retrieved February 14, 2021 from https://sproutsocial.com/insights/instagram-vs-facebook/

Kümpel, A. S., Karnowski, V., & Keyling, T. (2015). News sharing in social media: A review of current research on news sharing users, content, and networks. *Social Media + Society*, *1*(2), 1–14. doi:10.1177/2056305115610141

Latiff, Z. A., & Safiee, N. A. S. (2015). New business set up for branding strategies on social media - Instagram. *Procedia Computer Science*, *72*, 13–23. doi:10.1016/j.procs.2015.12.100

Libai, B., Bolton, R., Bügel, M. S., De Ruyter, K., Götz, O., Risselada, H., & Stephen, A. T. (2010). Customer-to-customer interactions: Broadening the scope of word of mouth research. *Journal of Service Research*, *13*(3), 267–282. doi:10.1177/1094670510375600

Loureiro, S. M. C., & Sarmento, E. M. (2019). Exploring the determinants of Instagram as a social network for online consumer-brand relationship. *Journal of Promotion Management*, *25*(3), 354–366. doi:10.1080/10496491.2019.1557814

Manic, M. (2015). Marketing engagement through visual content. *Bulletin of the Transilvania University of Brasov. Series V, Economic Sciences*, *8*(2), 89–94.

Manikonda, L., Venkatesan, R., Kambhampati, S., & Li, B. (2016). *Trending chic: Analyzing the influence of social media on fashion brands*. Retrieved February 14, 2021 from arxiv.org/abs/1512.01174

Neti, S. (2011). Social media and its role in marketing. *International Journal of Enterprise Computing and Business Systems*, *1*(2), 1–15. doi:10.4172/2151-6219.1000203

Online Advertising Guide. (2020, March 20). *Twitter engagement rate*. The Online Advertising Guide. Retrieved February 14, 2021 from https://theonlineadvertisingguide.com/glossary/twitter-engagement-rate/

Petrescu, M., & Korgaonkar, P. (2011). Viral advertising: Definitional review and synthesis. *Journal of Internet Commerce*, *10*(3), 208–226. doi:10.1080/15332861.2011.596007

ReportLinker. (2020, March). *Women's lingerie market to 2027 - Global analysis and forecasts by type; material; distribution channel, and geography*. Retrieved February 14, 2021 from https://www.reportlinker.com/p05882143/Women-s-Lingerie-Market-to-Global-Analysis-and-Forecasts-by-Type-Material-Distribution-Channel-and-Geography.html?utm_source=GNW

Sanchez Torres, J. A., & Arroyo-Cañada, F. J. (2017). Building brand loyalty in e-commerce of fashion lingerie. *Journal of Fashion Marketing and Management*, *21*(1), 103–114. doi:10.1108/JFMM-05-2016-0047

Sheriff, N. M., Zulkifli, A. S., & Othman, W. N. W. (2018). Salient features of customer engagement, visual presentation and copywriting for effective social media marketing: An exploratory perspective. *Journal of Academic UiTM Negeri Sembilan*, *6*(2), 28–37.

Statista. (2012). *Revenue of the global lingerie market in 2012 and 2017*. Statista. Retrieved February 14, 2021 from fhttps://www.statista.com/statistics/418713/revenue-of-the-lingerie-market-worldwide/

Statista. (2019a). *Brands of women's lingerie and underwear ranked by number of consumers in Spain in 2020*. Statista. Retrieved February 14, 2021 from https://www.statista.com/statistics/579362/leading-brands-of-womens-underwear-garment-in-spain/

Statista. (2019b). *Evolución de la facturación del sector de la moda íntima en España de 2015 a 2018*. Statista. Retrieved February 14, 2021 from https://es.statista.com/estadisticas/1171499/facturacion-moda-intima-espana/

Tham, A., Croy, G., & Mair, J. (2013). Social media in destination choice: Distinctive electronic word-of-mouth dimensions. *Journal of Travel & Tourism Marketing*, *30*(1–2), 144–155. doi:10.1080/10548408.2013.751272

Think with Google. (2020, January). *San Valentín 2020: una ocasión para enamorar a tus clientes*. Think with Google. Retrieved February 14, 2021 https://www.thinkwithgoogle.com/intl/es-es/insights/tendencias-de-consumo/san-valentin-2020-que-se-busca-y-se-regala-en-espana/

Zhang, M., Jansen, B. J., & Chowdhury, A. (2011). Business engagement on Twitter: A path analysis. *Electronic Markets*, *21*(3), 161–175. doi:10.100712525-011-0065-z

KEY TERMS AND DEFINITIONS

Audience: People who are interested in content, products, or services.

Community: A group of people which members relate common experiences and interests.

Engagement: The measurement of comments, likes, and shares in social networks.

Facebook: Online social media network platform founded in 2004.

Instagram: Online photo-and video sharing social network platform that was acquired by Facebook in 2012.

Intimissimi: Italian lingerie brand born in 1996 belonging to Calzedonia Group.

Oysho: Spanish lingerie brand born in 2001 belonging to Inditex Group.

Primark: Irish fast-fashion brand born in 1969.

Social Post: Publishing or sharing something on social media.

Tezenis: Italian lingerie belonging to Calzedonia Group.

Twitter: Microblogging online social media network platform founded in 2006.

Women'secret: Spanish lingerie brand born in1993 belonging to Tendam Group.

Chapter 14
Student Learning and Purchasing Behaviour Change During the Coronavirus Pandemic

Kamalendu Pal
https://orcid.org/0000-0001-7158-6481
City, University of London, UK

ABSTRACT

This chapter discusses the challenges for the higher education sector during the coronavirus pandemic. It examines students' changing communication practices and shopping habits during the coronavirus pandemic. The chapter identifies research gaps, highlining the consequential effect on lesser-developed countries, the psychological effect of the transaction, and the vital role of management in handling the coronavirus pandemic. It also presents that the main objective should be to develop more resilient higher education teaching and learning provisions that are responsive and adaptive to future crises. Two case studies describe a group of undergraduate computer science students' views on digital communication channel utilization and shopping behaviour during the coronavirus pandemic. A multiple-choice questions and answers method provided the students' views regarding the relevant research agenda of this chapter. Finally, the students' feedback provides a view of higher education students' communication channel utilization patterns and purchasing behaviours.

INTRODUCTION

Humanity resides on mother earth with ambitious goals to mitigate unprecedented social, economic, and environmental challenges. Education, science, technology, and innovation play a huge role in managing these unthinkable challenges. Education can usher economic change and improve living conditions by increasing productivity, reducing social inequality, and helping to raise living standards. The higher education system is a complex entity that requires many objectivities and levels of analysis to understand

DOI: 10.4018/978-1-6684-4168-8.ch014

its purpose, dynamics, and actors' interactions. In particular, it concerns technological innovations to facilitate courses and improve teaching and learning. Technology provides an essential avenue for enhancing a course delivering a more comprehensive student community. One of the essential constituents of efficient education delivery is the technology and extraordinary change in its breadth, pace, and depth of causal sequence. Accomplishing that breakthrough is the assured path for human society to bring enthusiastic *peace, people*, and *prosperity* standards. Thus, a buoyant education delivery system can accept and convert itself in the face of calamity.

Human society's calamity can take place in different forms and shapes. For example, the international health pandemic (i.e., coronavirus) has casted a bitter light on the susceptibility and challenges humanity faces in recent decades. It has highlighted an analysis of current inequalities and a picture of what steps forward requires taking, primarily among them appreciation the education of billions of students whose daily life and learning has been affected due to academic institutions closures wholly or delivered online teaching to provide moderately the students require.

The epidemic of coronavirus (known as COVID-19) at the end of 2019 forced governments to take invasive measures to prevent the spread of the disease, including closures of educational institutions. The rapid spread of the virus precluded careful, in-depth policy planning. In order to contain the virus, policies were implemented before their positive and negative effects were assessed. Only recently, policymakers have started inquiring into the consequences of various forms of academic institutions (e.g., school, college, university) closures to be better prepared to tackle a similar crisis in the future. While this "unprecedented multidimensional crisis demands coherent policy responses," admittedly, not all countries have developed such comprehensive plans in place (Gouedard et al., 2020).

The coronavirus pandemic has adversely affected higher education daily activities worldwide, with face-to-face teaching and learning practices and student assessment styles being changed or cancelled due to the lockdown imposed by governments. Most educational institutions have also struggled with digital teaching delivery challenges (Talidong & Toquero, 2020). Higher education institutions were asked to formulate crisis management strategies to continue teaching and learning activities. For example, the United Kingdom government requested fellow citizens to minimize social contact as much as possible and went on to advise that "you can still work, but we are asking as many as possible to work from home" (BBC, 2020). Subsequently, face-to-face teaching was stopped for higher education institutions worldwide, with academics and teachers asked to formulate alternative student-support activities as replacements for attendance at lectures, tutorials, laboratory sessions, workshops, and seminars. In addition, the teaching and learning activities were altered due to an overhaul of planned assessment processes. As the coronavirus pandemic threat has developed further, the rapidly changing nature of communication provided to students and educators (e.g., academic, teacher) may have added additional sources of anxiety and pressure. In addition, mental, psychological, and emotional pressures became part of student and educator life. Finally, an early study highlights that the students are now at risk of being left behind the health and wellbeing during a formative stage of learning, the opportunity for appropriate education, personal development, and economic benefits (United Nations, 2020).

The switch to digital learning has had consequences for education's accessibility, quality, and equity. It revealed gaps in the preparedness of both formal and non-formal education providers. Some institutions were unable to adjust well or fast enough, and, as a result, some students were entirely shut out of education. Students from disadvantaged backgrounds were particularly affected, while others, the most privileged and affluent, continued their studies through alternative learning methods, predominantly distance and online learning. However, it soon became apparent that online educational activities were often not inclusive and of lesser quality without uniform access. These shortcomings generated learning gaps, of which the consequences are yet to be assessed.

Countries and education sectors were affected differently due to a variety of factors. Some of the factors are students' age, ability to learn independently, the nature of pedagogies used at each level, and the extent of integrating distance and online learning into usual education provision. In addition, no uniform or consistent formal support was provided to educators and parents; the support that emerged was non-formal, self-organized or unrehearsed training arranged as a bottom-up support network.

To a greater extent, none of the countries was prepared for a swift transition of their higher educational system, eliminating all engagements requiring the personal presence and maintaining the programs. Despite numerous examples of quick inspirational solutions, countries lacked preparedness in terms of digital education infrastructure, service provisions, and digital skills shortage. For example, only fifty-eight per cent of the European Union (EU) citizens in 2019 possessed basic digital skills, ranging from almost eighty per cent in Finland to just over thirty per cent in Italy. Within countries, similar discrepancies exist based on geographical location (i.e., rural areas and regions with lower digital connectivity) (Dutta & Lanvin, 2020). Therefore, the switch to online education and reliance on information and communication technology (ICT) during the current pandemic outbreak exacerbated the existing inequality and digital divide in the world.

Academics and practitioners in international publications have highlighted the current pandemic impact on educational institutions. These research articles address some burning issues (e.g., the impact of technology in changing distance learning practice, post-lockdown analysis of some individual educational institutions). However, the present societal challenges due to the current pandemic problems on higher educational institutions have yet to be determined entirely to understand the initial interventions to transform digital learning to manage the pandemic's effect. Hence, this chapter aims to assess emerging evidence on the impact of the current pandemic on higher educational institutions and analyze the prevalence of digital learning changes in the educational sector. In addition, the World Health Organization (WHO) advocates for rapid reviews to be carried out to understand better the challenges (Roy et al., 2020).

In order to mitigate the above guidance, the following aims have been established for the review process of this chapter: (i) to summarize the impact of the current pandemic as reported from a selection of available studies on educational institutions; (ii) to analyze the measures that were put in place following the COVID-19 lockdown of educational institutions; and (iii) to appraise gaps in knowledge and understanding and revealing possible future research directions regarding the effect of the current pandemic on the educational institutions. Also, this review provides guidelines to educators and institutions regarding the transition from traditional education to an online learning world.

The initial period of the current pandemic has slowed down the economy. The governments of most countries are looking for ways to help fellow citizens (e.g., students), including relaxing the rules of tax payments, paying benefits to support businesses, fact repaying salaries, and helping in rent contributions to solve the disadvantageous impacts on consumer living standards. However, there is no evidence that student communities benefited from any financial benefits from educational institutions.

Students, who include every natural person purchasing goods and services, have changed their shopping behaviour because of the recent pandemic problem. The fact that the condition regarding the current pandemic is uncertain and it is not known how quickly it will pass has drawn students' attention to spending, particularly on healthcare products, safety products (e.g., alcohol-based hand sanitizer, hand gloves, and face masks) and necessities products (e.g., food, house cleaning items).

Retail businesses and other service providers have also had to consider judiciously the current pandemic and offer consumers what they need. In recent months of operation, traders have not had many opportunities to welcome their consumers. After reopening, however, they faced increased costs related to cleanliness and disinfection of their premises. Students are often afraid to visit shops due to the cleanliness and disinfection of their premises. Students are often afraid to visit shops due to possible infection, meaning they buy fast and only purchase necessary products. As a result, many retailers have opened online stores, pushing web-based e-commerce shops to the background. They have also focused on the complexity and variety of products offered, intuitive purchasing, simplifying the shopping process, and shortening the student's purchasing decision-making time.

The remaining structure of this chapter is as follows. The following section presents an overview of the methods used for this research. Next, it provides the descriptive results, the themes identified from academic literature, and a case study to apply an undergraduate software engineering team-based project teaching and learning practice. It also includes significant changes in the shopping patterns of a group of higher education students. Finally, the chapter provides future research directions and concludes with concluding remarks.

BACKGROUND OF THE METHOD ADOPTED FOR THE RESEARCH

Reviewing existing academic literature within a particular area of research is challenging and interdisciplinary. It is ambitious to keep up with the state-of-the-art, be at the forefront of research, and assess the collective evidence in a particular study area. Therefore, the literature review as a research method is more relevant than ever. Traditional literature reviews often lack thoroughness and rigor and are conducted ad hoc rather than a specific methodology. Therefore, there can be questions about the quality and trustworthiness of these types of reviews. The answer to quality and trustworthiness issues is beyond this chapter's scope.

There are diverse ways researchers gather relevant academic literature. In the current work, research articles gathered from standard academic databases (e.g., Science Direct, Emerald, Pro-quest, Wiley online Library, Springer Link, and Taylor & Francis) search. These academic reference databases are valuable sources for researching the phenomena under investigation. Used Google Scholar to double-check the search and find any missing relevant studies during the initial database search (Li et al., 2020).

Using the keyword-based search strategy to retrieve the relevant research articles is one of the most common search strategies (Rodiguez-Hernandez et al., 2020). The keyword search used terms including coronavirus pandemic and education, COVID-19 and teaching, higher education, or university education; these were searched for within the title, abstract, and keyword sections, a technique used in previous research projects (Plockinger et al., 2016). Analyzed the research publications of relevant context for inclusion and exclusion based on the guidance rules as shown in Table 1.

As mentioned earlier in the initial search process, only 126 research articles related to the recent pandemic and general education were selected from the publication. During the selection activity, sixty-two research articles related to non-higher education institutions were rejected, leaving only ninety-four eligible research contributions that presented current pandemic effects in the higher education sector. Some of these research articles were then excluded due to duplication of issues discussed. Also, thirty-seven published research articles were rejected in the selection process since they did not fully match the inclusion and exclusion criteria set out in Table 1. These included research articles, individual or group opinions, editorial that did not offer original data, and studies that presented business cases without sufficient information. Finally, the current research reviewed only the title and abstract section of research articles for the selection process.

Table 1. Exclusion and inclusion guidance rules

Exclusion Rules	Inclusion Rules
Commentaries, editorial comments, news articles, and individual opinions are excluded.	Research articles deal with coronavirus pandemic (i.e., COVID-19).
Publications that discuss general educational settings only; and do not relate to the current pandemic are excluded.	The research discusses the current pandemic impact on how that may have impacted educational institutions.
Presenting relevant issues with another pandemic (e.g., EBOLA virus-related crisis).	

Descriptive Results

This review selected thirty-six research studies that focused on the impact of the coronavirus pandemic on educational institutions. The initial analysis found that most research in the publication searching period was published in the United States of America's educational institutions. The spread of research findings shows that the selected articles were concentrated primarily on specific countries, as shown in Figure 1. Some of these are developing countries with diverse cultural, economic, and social profiles to those of developed nations that seem to deal with pandemic and radical changes in educational institutions more effectively.

The current research collected relevant issues from a sample academic article that reflect the coronavirus pandemic situations for only a few countries, which includes the United States of America, United Kingdom, China, India, Indonesia, Ireland, Italy, Philippines, Australia, Spain, Germany, Kuwait, and other countries (e.g., Brazil, Canada, South Africa). Besides, most of the collected research articles were written and published in the lockdown period; and the presented research primarily used online questionnaires targeted at educational institutions' educators and students.

Figure 1. Geographic coverage of literature

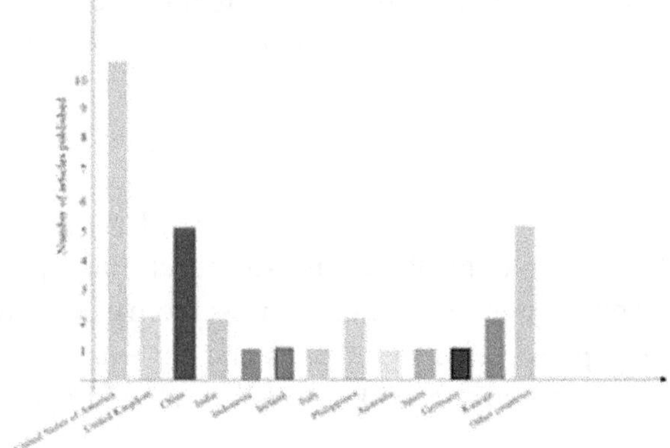

The individual research article analyzed student feedback in the current pandemic, individual subject performance, subject content, academic institutions correspondence, and other official documents. After initial analysis, some of the themes emerged: (i) suggestion to adopt a fully online learning (e-learning) environment, (ii) measures that can support educational institutions' future strategies for teaching and learning activities during and after the pandemic. However, it is problematic to ascertain the generality of these studies used in the review process, as simple textual analysis on its own might not produce generalized views.

Thematic Analysis

At the time of review, different themes started to emerge. It is worth breaking these themes down into the following key areas: digital learning, e-learning challenges, the digital transformation to virtual emergency assessment, the psychological impact of the coronavirus pandemic, and creating collaborative cultures. The thematic analysis will highlight the crucial findings after the initial analysis of collected academic articles below.

Digital Learning

The term digital learning is increasingly used but often fails to provide a clear understanding of what the term means. Moreover, it is sometimes used interchangeably with technology-enhanced learning (TEL) and with e-learning or online learning; however, each of these terms reflects a different stage in the evolution of the discipline. Digital provides many opportunities to engage learners, personalize learning experiences and widen access. It can make it easier for learners and educators to engage with each other actively (e.g., through email, IM (instant messages), video chat, online forums, social media) and with learning materials.

Some researchers expressed that the coronavirus pandemic has forced academic institutions to pursue digital learning (Majanja, 2020). A few researchers highlighted that digital learning has a beneficial influence in combating COVID-19 problems, including educator technical skills enhancement (Abdulrahim & Mabrouk, 2021); teaching and learning delivery systems have been better restructured (Rajhans et al., 2020); and courses have been rapidly transformed (Skulmowski & Rey, 2020). Besides, there has been a rise in multifaceted digital learning techniques (Zainuddin et al., 2020); and it facilitates better feedback to students (Jayathirtha et al., 2020).

However, several educators expressed concerns about the overall efficacy of online teaching techniques, and many doubts are being highlighted regarding the future viability of education institutions if only digital learning infrastructures provide post-pandemic education (Code et al., 2020).

E-Learning Challenges

'E-learning' is a conjugate term that is a hybrid by construction. The two elements have joined together to form a new hybrid term like other conjugate terms. Moreover, this hybrid term consists of two elements: 'e' and ' learning'. The element 'e' of e-learning has a more extended history than many assume, including long-term efforts to capture voice and images and store and then transmit those recordings. With each capture – from records to compact disks (CDs), converted to text chat – there are trade-offs in quality, interactivity, and transferability: trade-offs that mark both the advantages and disadvantages of technological mediation.

Typical of the problems facing researchers in e-learning is the case of electronic interactive whiteboards – touch-sensitive screens, which work in conjunction with a computer and projector – and their efficacy in learning. The detailed discussions about e-learning origin and related issues are beyond the scope of this chapter.

Digital Transformation to Emerging Virtual Assessment

Moving from campus-based face-to-face learning to remote teaching and learning has featured heavily in the academic literature on the coronavirus pandemic and its impact on educational institutions. The findings and recommendations by academics and practitioners who have reported the COVID-19 related issues have tended to concentrate on three areas: methodological, pedagogical, and tactical.

A group of researchers highlighted the importance of methodological approaches, technical difficulties, considering how these may be resolved, and the importance of always having a second strategy ready in case the first strategy fails to deliver the outcome (Dhawan, 2020). An essential technological infrastructure solution to provide a virtual environment is 'cloud technology' (Zhou et al., 2020), and it can act as a part of contingency planning for such factors as traffic overload on online platforms (Dhawan, 2020). Besides, a critical requirement to ensure that academics' ability to change reflects students' needs in online learning behaviour.

The academic articles that focus on pedagogy stress the importance of adopting strategies for designing online courses that make building relationships between students and educators more effectively whilst continuing to meet the goals of the teaching curriculum (Itow, 2020) (Kessler et al., 2020). Besides, the same academics advocate the appropriate uses of pedagogy to prepare teaching materials. Another research suggests a pedagogical approach that may help educators design and provide an e-learning facility where learning takes place in a student-centered self-determined environment (Majanja, 2020). However, few other researchers suggest that educators should be encouraged to use flipped classroom approaches and that higher education institutions should become adept at setting teaching and learning policies about these approaches (Yen, 2020).

Psychological Impact of Coronavirus Pandemic

The sudden closure of academic institutions due to pandemic and the subsequent lockdown has left ordinary students and staff bewildered and dealing with diverse types of problems that can contribute to increased anxiety and stress due to its side effects (e.g., job instability, financial concerns, home-based or hall of residence-based education, loneliness, despair, trauma, and sickness).

Several researchers highlight the mental health-related issues of students and staff. For example, a few published articles commented that the move to online learning had harmed both student and staff mental health-related issues. However, one research finding highlights that those students displayed significant mental health issues when faced with a public health emergency (Cao et al., 2020).

An important finding comes from research of the online migration that followed COVID-19, highlighting the major problem caused to pedagogical roles within the higher education sector, creating problems from an educational perspective and educators' personal lives (Watermeyer et al., 2020). They also report that online learning migration creates extra challenges in academic life, particularly in the academic labour market. In addition, a total change in teaching and learning practice in an online environment and alteration of assessment methods has required rapid and often tricky adaptation.

Creating Collaborative Culture

Changes in teaching and learning service have needed people to communicate and collaborate at various levels of practice in educational institutions. For example, many academic articles discuss that good collaborative culture can often be recognized by traits such as straightforward and flexible structures, prioritizing tasks, challenging work, communication within the professional communities, and relying on goodwill (Talidong & Toquero, 2020) (Regehr & Goel, 2020). Other researchers (Justis et al., 2020) (Krishnamurthy, 2020) suggest that the means of achieving an excellent collaborative culture may be to ensure that an academic institution establishes itself as a community service and does so to find new income streams, respond to cultural shifts, and establish clear opportunities for academics at all levels within the academic institution to collaborate at, and with, higher levels within the industry. Studies provide an essential view about collaboration, suggesting that carefully designed online collaborative learning might be an advantageous method for students to interact with their peers and provide an effective mechanism for them to control their own and others' learning whilst sharpening skills jointly as a community (MacMahon et al., 2020). Some other studies reflect the future of education post-coronavirus pandemic with a view to digital delivery of teaching and learning activities continuing within the educational institutions. A research study suggests that the current situation could drive innovative, new, and elegant technological resources and closer collaboration between academic institutions (Longhurst et al., 2020).

Moreover, a group of researchers recommended that local communities form part of future educational decisions made within the communities in which they reside (Aguliera et al., 2020). Furthermore, a study identifies that academic have a pivotal role in developing sustainable and quality student support. In addition, student support networks are significant in ensuring that online delivery not only works but continues to serve successfully (Raaper & Brown, 2020). Going forward, academic institutions need to ensure that this pivotal contract is maintained through better dialogue and collaboration.

Recommendations from academic literature provide some tactical recommendations (please see Table 2) for handling crucial issues in meeting the current crisis. The different suggestions provided by the researchers usher several themed approaches to online delivery, some of which appear apparent. However, some provide innovative and novel methods that can hugely enhance online teaching services and the students' experience. For example, since the outbreak of the recent pandemic and the subsequent lockdown, such as Microsoft Teams, Google Meets, and Google Classroom, the rise of online teaching platforms has been increasing. So too has the ability of both academic institution educators and students to adapt rapidly to these alternative online support facilities. These platforms' success in supporting everyday life for individuals and families is also true. However, recent research has highlighted the adaptability of the human being to changing circumstances and surroundings. As one study suggests, the educational institution may be about to move into an age of the algorithm as the professor, where educational practitioners and learners collaborate in regular teaching and learning practices (Krishnamurthy, 2020).

It is also apparent that with diminished scopes to spend time together in person come new challenges to remain socially connected. For example, during the first few months of the current coronavirus pandemic, industry reports highlighted that digital media use heavily increased as people spent more time at home due to lockdowns (Kemp, 2020). Such increases were especially prevalent for social media and information technology-based messaging applications, but specifically remarkable was the unprecedented uptake in video conferencing applications. This further bears assessment, given educators' and students' extensive reliance on information and communications technologies (ICTs) for social interaction under such stay-at-home circumstances. The other important aspect of higher education teaching and learning delivery is an appropriate collaborative culture within the digital learning environment. However, there is research gap of students view regarding communication channels used in the current pandemic. The following section describes a students' reflective experience of information technology use in an undergraduate software engineering team project.

BEHAVIOUR CHANGE CASE STUDIES

Case of Collaborative Software Development

Software systems design and development have changed from an individual activity of designing standalone applications to a primarily distributed and collaborative approach that depends on or contributes to large and complicated software ecosystems (Pal, 2020) (Pal, 2019). Thus, software systems designers need to collaborate with, learn from and co-design with many other team members, creating a participatory culture within distributed software development work practice (Pal & Karakostas, 2020).

Promising distributed and collaborative software system design and development needs proper communication mechanisms. Thus, encouraging software developers' collaboration and communication need new technology-supported techniques (e.g., telephone, web-based applications, WhatsApp, email, and Zoom video conferencing system) are adopted. An essential diagrammatic representation of a few of the communication channels is depicted in Figure 2. The affluence and capability of these tools are improving current global software design and development activities. Subsequently, software developers require to learn new skills to use these tools. Moreover, these communication tools permit creativity in work activity, usher engagement, and help software design and development participation. This commitment is also advocated for cultural issues of the global software design team.

Appreciating global software design and development team-based culture is the basis to understanding what goes on in software development teams, coordinating them, and enhancing their work practice (Schein, 1992). Team-based software design and development culture is defined as the shared assumptions, beliefs, and expected behaviours (norms) present in a global team.

Within these new initiatives of software development regular activities, software design includes externalized knowledge (e.g., project-related document exchange, technical guidelines, programming instructions to manage software development) and the tacit knowledge that resides in developers' heads (e.g., design constraints, hardware constraints, operational practices). In reality, communication and software development tools (e.g., Computer-Aided Software Design Environment) provide guidance to generate and share (i.e., externalize) tacit knowledge in a highly collaborative environment.

Knowledge management is a crucial mechanism to foster improvements in software development processes. Organizational culture is an integral factor in knowledge management's success since it influences how software developers learn and share knowledge within a team. A research-based justification is that organizational culture affects how staff learn, acquire, and share knowledge (Knapp & Yu, 1999). Finally, the chapter provides a case study of an undergraduate software development team project to assess KM and organizational culture practices. This case study for software design and development duration was around three months. Twenty-one students expressed their views regarding team project communication channel uses and KM-related issues.

Figure 2. Few communication channels in global software development

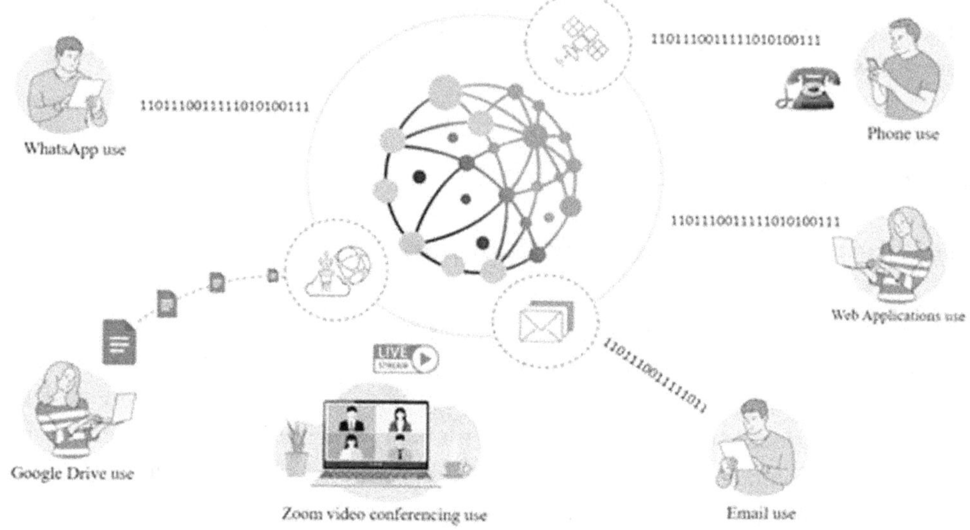

Relevance of Knowledge Management in Software Development

As software development is an abstract engineering discipline, knowledge management is essential. When developing software, a high degree of coordination (Kraut & Streeter, 1995) and management (Sommerville, 2001; Pressman, 2000) become vital tasks. Because the focus is to solve specific problems, software projects' organization often differs enormously from one to the other. A research work (Sveiby, 1997) points out that most companies face similar problems in administrating their intellectual capital. For example, he explains that employees are usually highly educated and qualified professionals whose regular job is using their competence to develop software. Their primary resource is their knowledge; therefore, they are called knowledge workers.

The core activities of software engineering contain the management of documents or competencies and software re-use. With product and project memory, the authors refer to the evolution of software, e.g., with the help of systems for version control, change management or design documentation. Finally, the learning and improvement include a recording of results and experiences. The reason is to learn from that and improve future decisions or activities. The desire to improve in these three areas of concern motivates knowledge management in software development (Pal & Williams, 2021). In order to conduct knowledge management successfully, many different approaches are possible and documented. For example, information systems applied to manage a company's knowledge or support managing a company's knowledge are referred to as knowledge management systems.

COORDINATION AND COMMUNICATION IN SOFTWARE DEVELOPMENT

Coordination between software development team members is one of the most challenging ways to improve software systems design and development. For example, a group of researchers (Kraut & Streeter, 1995) argue that the software design and development industry has been in difficulties mode for its entire existence, and an important reason is a difficulty coordinating work between team members. Academics and practitioners have empirically studied professional software development teams to understand by analyzing software development processes, techniques, CASE tools, and human factors in the coordination process. Inter-team coordination is an essential concern as software development increasingly becomes globally distributed and remains a persistent industry challenge.

Simple coordination can be viewed as decision-making and action-taking *collaboration,* communication, and *cooperation.* These three components of work practices are necessary but insufficient for coordination. Collaboration is an essential part of group work. Communication is necessary because member A needs to communicate with person B, in some form, what needs to be done needed for the group. Cooperation is essential because B requires being willing to do what is required for the group. If any of the three mandatory components are lacking, the outcome will be less than ideal.

Viewing coordination through this framework leads one to ask several research questions:

1. What kinds of behaviours are associated with being helpful or unhelpful to others?
2. How do members of a software team communicate to get work done?
3. How do software teams handle dependencies on a personal level?

This chapter presents a survey-based data analysis to understand inter-team dependencies in software development.

Background of Survey-Based Data Analysis

The experimental work was conducted in an undergraduate team-based student software design and development project. Multiple choice questionaries were used to survey students. The study was based on three individual groups, and each group consisted of pre-assigned team members. The rationale behind students' pre-assignment to teams is to ensure that teams balance talent, skills, and expertise and become aware that one must learn to establish good working relations with "*strangers*" and acquaintances in their future career's friends.

Each team worked independently of others on the same case study. The team members ' joint responsibilities were each team's internal organization, planning the project, defining a management structure, and carrying out the work (technical or organizational). In addition, each team member was expected to adopt two roles in a software development project, associated job titles, and responsibility for those tasks falling within their remit.

Each team member adopts two roles (e.g., project manager, deputy project manager, system analyst, designer, programmer or coding specialist, software tester) described in the policy document. Project manager responsible for team planning, coordination, and risk management. The team manager was the central contact point to the team consultant and the client, and the role must contribute to technical work. The Deputy project manager was second in command and responsible for documentation, reports, and standards, including technical work. A system analyst was responsible for the elicitation of customer requirements; the system designer oversaw the system design process. The programmer was dedicated to implementing the system. The software tester was responsible for writing a test plan, testing the system and its components, and recording the outcomes. Each team member had one primary role and a secondary role, e.g., project manager/systems analyst or designer/programmer. The roles were appropriately spread. Finally, it ensured that essential roles within the team were covered when members were absent.

The survey revealed that the most helpful behaviours between all the teams are related to cooperation and availability. The unhelpful behaviours are related to location (primarily felt by the distributed team members), ownership and awareness, and availability. This research finds that coordination problems in the distributed teams can be considered a superset of collocated teams' problems; distributed development adds additional difficulties caused by location (i.e., time zone), culture, and meetings mode.

Experimental STUDY METHOD

The online survey consisted of one-hour; semi-structured, open-ended multiple-choice questions based on the 'echo' method designed by Bavelas (Bavelas, 1942). The method is used in studies of organizations to examine task interactions in new product development (Duimering et al., 2006) and task structures of a group of professionals (Bjorn et al., 2014).

Student Survey Results

In this step, participating students' opinions were gathered through discussions and questionnaires. The contextual information of communication and collaboration information, channel preference, and the relationship between the knowledge management cycle and organizational culture through the CVF was discussed at length. Then a multiple-choice opinion survey questionnaire was used in the opinion collection process.

In a team-based software design and development practice, groups of people are connected by the similarity of their project activities. Group members do not have to be spatially or socially connected, but they solve similar problems and learn from each other through processes like group discussion or one-to-one subject-specific matter. Members advance through a process called team-based or group-based learning and provide value to the software development community.

For example, a software designer may start acquiring knowledge by reading discussions and reporting bugs (or errors). Over time, the software designer learns from community discussions and collaborations. This way, software designers or developers may start fixing bugs and enhance their skills to the point where they can use the acquired knowledge to help other group members.

Due to the globalization of the software industry, software design and development can take place in a distributed setting, where contributors need not be in the same office or town. These global software developers often communicate on a scale and are mostly interconnected via information and communication technology (ICT) based application tools. These global communication tools can help software project management issues (e.g., sharing technological knowledge, collaboration with project members or clients). In addition, the participating students provided their opinions on the following categories: (i) coordinate with others, (ii) communicate with other members, (iii) learn with other members, (iv) learn by watching, and (v) stay up to date.

Figure 3. Communication channels used by the respondents.

	Face-to-Face	Books	Web Search	Dedicated Websites	Video Conferencing	Private Discussion	Group Discussion	Electronic mail	Telephone Conversation	Online Collaboration
	Analog		Digital							
Communicate with Others	65%				35%	11%	22%	38%	77%	
Coordinate with Others	12%				27%					
Learn	63%				21%					
Find Answers		52%	37%	29%	5%					
Learn with Other Team Members	45%									
Watch Activities				24%	31%					

The student opinion survey also used different communication channels and resources, such as video conferencing, textbook, google search, private discussion, group discussion, and private chat facility, for project collaboration and knowledge management. This section presents more detailed information on why specific channels were considered vital to the team project management. For example, in the student team project context, the current survey on KM practice belongs to more than one quadrant of the SECI model. Figure 3 presents some participating students' opinions in a two-dimensional visual representation.

Most of the team members (65%) expressed their preference for face-to-face communication for software system design. Their primary justification is that they can receive quick feedback from the team members, facilitate talking through complex problems, discuss ideas, and make software design decisions. Thus, the team uses its efforts to make explicit knowledge tacit, supporting the learning process. One example of the internalization practice identified is team members integration, which occurs after a project member learns about the team's software development process. Therefore, knowledge internalization occurs when the team's explicit knowledge (stored on Google Drive) is presented to help project team members to learn it.

The success of a software development team is the ability to coordinate successfully with one another. Private discussion (e.g., Zoom video conferencing, Email, Telephone) is essential for supporting team collaboration through single or multiple channels. Besides, effective teams contain team members who appreciate each other's ideas. If team members are ignored or belittled after providing input, they will probably stop engaging in team activities (e.g., team meetings, discussions). When this disengaging attitude prevails, collaboration is complicated. Also, some team members are not naturally driven to start communication and discussion. Taking the time to assess who is driven to talk things through compared to those who are not allowed a team member ensures everyone is given appropriate airtime.

Electronic mail (or email) is identified as a virtual channel (38%) to support discussion across virtually every platform and among different stakeholders (e.g., client, team member). It is a convenient channel for disseminating information to large groups while keeping conversations private and persistent for later retrieval. This is how one can communicate privately and have proof later.

Team members were introduced with technologies, practices, and tools for software development (e.g., software documentation, technical articles, formal lecture handouts) using different channels (e.g., virtual learning environment – Moodle, Email, Forum, Blogs, and Dedicated websites). Within a team-based software development project, tasks consist of activities that require to be carried out by one or multiple team members. For example, the project manager can allocate a task to multiple team members or leave it unassigned for anyone to carry out the work. Tasks need to have start dates and due dates or be left without dates to be completed anytime. Software project management tools are handy to keep the team members up to date with the progress.

Learning with other team members is an important activity in software development projects. It is part of developing a team, whether a new team leader or an experienced manager. People need training and support throughout their working life, both as individuals and as teams, to develop their skills and work effectively. A substantial number of survey participants (45%) expressed their view positively on team learning.

In addition, team members learn by watching others or finding answers to a problem from books, web searches, or dedicated websites. For example, it can be watching a video on a YouTube channel or watching a recording in a teaching and learning environment (e.g., Moodle). Web search can be a valuable tool for learners, and a bit of instruction in how to search for learning sources will help the learners become critical thinkers and independent learners. More than half of the student participants (52%) in the assessment expressed that they find problem solutions using recommended technical books in software development. At the same time, thirty-seven per cent of the participating students agreed that they get a problem solution by using a web search.

Telephone conversations have the advantage of enabling communication among software development team members and clients of a particular project. For example, many participants (77%) expressed their support favoring telephone conversation.

PANDEMIC EFFECTS ON CONSUMER PURCHASING BEHAVIOUR

The current pandemic has had enormous socioeconomic consequences. A group of researchers (Donthu & Gustafsson, 2020) highlighted the different impacts of coronavirus on regular commercial activists and dramatic changes in business entities' operations and consumers' behaviour. In addition, consumers (e.g., students) are exposed to vast categories of products and services. It creates extra pressure on the consumers' demand and challenges retailers to supply the right products according to customer preferences and requirements (Urbanikova et el., 2020). For example, an unknown panic purchase by consumers appeared and became a phenomenon verified by a group of researchers (Laato et al., 2020). The study of Islam and coresearchers (Islam et al., 2021) examined the panic shopping behaviour of consumers during the current pandemic time. This way, they examined how external stimuli affected consumers' impulsive and obsessive shopping behaviour and produced market analysis results for managers or traders to understand this phenomenon. Another view of pandemic shopping is presented by a group of researchers (Prentice et al., 2020), which followed the method of scarcity, the psychology of the customers, and the consequential effect of panic purchasing habits. Governmental actions, the influence of the media, society, and fear of scarcity have changed consumer behaviour and provoked panic shopping. Their study shows that a smooth supply of products makes sense of security for buyers.

Moreover, a researcher (Naeem, 2021) highlighted the consequential effect of social media on panic shopping during the current pandemic. It also used real-time information about pandemics obtained through social media to provide the information needed for customers to make intelligent decisions, but its disadvantages were also discussed. Researchers claim that this can lead to panic shopping or the accumulation of products in households. This study tries to explain how social media creates and shapes consumer panic. In another research (Ryder et al., 2021) researchers also focused their research on social media, and they explored the digital content implanted during the pandemic and its importance for consumers during the lockdown.

Case of Student Purchasing Behaviour

This section presents a study aimed to examine change in students purchasing behaviour and their psychological attitudes during the lockdown period due to the coronavirus pandemic. The student's behaviours were assessed relating different psychological factors (e.g., anxiety, elevated levels of stress, prominent levels of depressive state increase the need for buying habits, levels of stress can lead students to save money option, or in another way would increase the need to spend money on necessities) by considering their mutual influence. These supporting ideas were developed based on a series of previous consumer behaviour studies (Bentall et al., 2021) (Putrevu et al., 2001) (Shufeldt et al., 1998) (Sudbury & Simcock, 2009).

In this research, a set of questioners were used to get the student's personal view focused on their necessities. They were asked to provide their opinion regarding amounts of health and safety products (e.g., alcohol-based hand sanitizer, gloves, face masks) buying habits in the initial period of total lockdown at the beginning of 2020. Also, the same group were asked to answer the individual impulsive buying habit of necessities of products and willingness to spend more money to buy necessities. The last questionnaire was developed to assess the subjective perception of an individual's economic condition.

Finally, to investigate the psychological underpinning of student behaviour, this research performed a statical analysis to understand the analytical part of the research. Considering "change in general spending", the result showed that, on average, an increase of the general spending level during the first few months of 2020 of coronavirus related lockdown.

Students' behaviour is influenced by a range of criteria, contextual agenda, and subjective issues. Recent years, the COVID-19 problems were incredibly significant for consumer buying behaviours. The increase in COVID-19 cases and its consequences (such as quarantine, isolation, social distancing, and community containment) changed not only the attitude of student toward health continuousness but also their buying behaviour.

Student in lockdown were ordering online more often than normal, for example 45% of student responded for health and safety products purchasing from online sources, and 63% confirmed that they bought substantial number of necessities products. However, a sizable portion (e.g., 35%) of the student were abstained to express their views (Figure 4).

The study was explicitly interested in separating necessity products. It also uses a hypothesis about the role of the identified psychological factors in predicting student behaviour during the coronavirus pandemic. This experimental study was especially interested in separating necessity and non-necessity products.

Figure 4. Student buying behaviour

Students in lockdown environment were using e-commerce retail services more often than normal. They also increased their spending costs (i.e., 59% agree), because more selective, and shifted to local retail outlets. Demand for e-commerce services (e.g., online shopping) has surged. As most students were forced to eat at home (or student accommodation) during the lockdown period, the food and beverage industry saw an increase in online sales.

FUTURE DIRECTIONS FOR RESEARCH

Most of the research included in this analysis has come from the developed or the stronger developing countries, with almost no research published about lesser developed but developing countries or undeveloped countries. Thus far, education is at the heart of all these countries' futures. How those countries have adapted to the coronavirus related crisis and responded to educating citizens is a crucial area of future research that needs to be assessed. It will be alluring to compare the experience of educators, students, and other education business stakeholders in different regions and countries. Given that evidence advocates that people from Black, Asian, and Minority groups (BAME) are more likely to be seriously impacted by coronavirus pandemic, education institutions should concentrate precisely on these groups' impact and contrast the disabled person down the educational activities of BAME staff and students. Other applications may concentrate on, for example, the impact on employment, economic growth, future earning differentials, trade gaps, student recruitment, and digital literacy. The influence of hearing the student voice when decisions are being made in a time of crisis, pandemic, or radical change, may also be a key area to do further investigative research.

However, it would also be interesting to explore the impact of the pandemic on other higher educational institutions and compare the changes in student behaviour and purchasing patterns between different universities. In addition, the use of purposive sampling techniques could be applied to address specific groups of respondents.

CONCLUSION

This chapter reviews the coronavirus pandemic impact on higher educational institutions. It also highlighted that the current pandemic poses extraordinary challenges to global public health, socioeconomic stability, food security, and other social goods. The inequality (e.g., education, healthcare, social well-being) of opportunities, which divide people within and across countries, seem to worsen due to the current pandemic. Public education and public health are very closely interrelated. It is undeniable that education makes a scholarly society. The collective action and collaboration of these common goods (i.e., education, public health) help to defeat future pandemics. It will usher new dawn to build civic trust and understanding, deepen human empathy, create the option of progressing in science and innovation, and appreciate human society's value.

The chapter also presents two case studies to examine changes in student behaviour and their psychological antecedents during the coronavirus pandemic. One of the case studies was specifically interested in student learning related communication and knowledge sharing skills in a group project context. The other case study focused on psychological factors and their influences on students buying behaviour. Furthermore, based on the limited and contrasting literature on consumer (i.e., student) buying behaviour, this research considered the role of individuality traits. Interestingly, it is worth to mention that individuality traits were more relevant in consumer behaviour toward non-necessities than necessities products. Only openness had a role in (negatively) predicting consumer behaviour toward necessities, whereas conscientiousness (negatively) and openness (positively) predicted consumer behaviour towards non-necessities.

Although current literature is still relatively scarce about the coronavirus pandemic's impact on academic institutions, there are significant indications of increased disruption in teaching and learning, particularly in the change from face-to-face teaching to virtual teaching and learning. Many studies have proposed ways to achieve such transitions, such as training in digital literacy, using digital flipped classrooms, encouraging students to use peer to peer learning, and building a collaborative community. Also, the pandemic has pressured educators to go beyond their regular working routine; the reviewed academic articles depict the pandemic's negative psychological impact. Finally, the educators must focus on improving student engagement, whether virtually or onsite, during the pandemic and post-pandemic.

REFERENCES

Abdulrahim, H., & Mabrouk, F. (2020). COVID-19 and the Digital Transformation of Saudi Higher Education. *Asian J. Distance Educ., 15*, 291–306. https://files.eric.ed.gov/fulltext/EJ1289975.pdf

Aguliera, E. & Nightengale-Lee, B (2020). Emergency Remote Teaching across Urban and Rural Contexts: Perspectives on Educational Equity. *Inf. Learn. Sci., 121*, 471–478. doi:10.1108/ILS-04-2020-0100

Baloran, E. T. (2020). Knowledge, Attitudes, Anxiety, and Coping Strategies of Students during COVID-19 Pandemic. *Journal of Loss and Trauma, 2020*(8), 1–8. doi:10.1080/15325024.2020.1769300

Bavelas, A. (1942). A method for investigating individual and group ideology. *Sociometry*, *5*(4), 371–377. doi:10.2307/2785286

BBC. (2020). Coronavirus: Only Go to Your Job If You Cannot Work from Home—Hancock. In *Coronavirus Pandemic*. BBC. https://www.bbc.co.uk/news/uk-52022417

Bentall, R. P., Lloyd, A., Bennett, K., McKay, R., Mason, L., Murphy, J., McBride, O., Hartman, T. K., Gibson-Miller, J., Levita, L., Martinez, A. P., Stocks, T. V. A., Butter, S., Vallières, F., Hyland, P., Karatzias, T., & Shevlin, M. (2021). Pandemic buying: Testing a psychological model of over-purchasing and panic buying using data from the United Kingdom and the Republic of Ireland during the early phase of the COVI-19 pandemic. *PLOS ONE*, *16*(1), e0246339. doi:10.1371/journal.pone.0246339 PMID:33503049

Bjorn, P. M., Esbensen, M., Jensen, E., & Matthiesen, S. (2014). Does distance still matter? Revisiting the CSCW fundamentals on distributed collaboration. *ACM Transactions on Computer-Human Interaction*, *21*(5), 27. doi:10.1145/2670534

Cameron, K. S., & Quinn, R. E. (1999). *Diagnosing and Changing Organizational Culture Based on the Competing Values Framework*. Addison-Wesley Publishing Company, Inc.

Cao, W., Fang, Z., Hou, G., Han, M., Xu, X., Dong, J., & Zheng, J. (2020). The Psychological Impact of the COVID-19 Epidemic on College Students in China. *Psychiatry Research*, *2020*(287), 112934. doi:10.1016/j.psychres.2020.112934 PMID:32229390

Code, J., Ralph, R., & Forde, K. (2020). Pandemic Designs for the Future: Perspectives of Technology Education Teachers during COVID-19. *Inf. Learn. Sci.*, *2020*(121), 419–431. doi:10.1108/ILS-04-2020-0112

Dhawan, S. (2020). Online Learning: A Panacea in the Time of COVID-19 Crisis. *Journal of Educational Technology Systems*, *2020*(49), 5–22. doi:10.1177/0047239520934018

Donthu, N., & Gustafsson, A. (2020). Effects of COVID-19 on business and research. *Journal of Business Research*, *117*, 284–289. doi:10.1016/j.jbusres.2020.06.008 PMID:32536736

Duimering, P. R., Ran, B., Derbentseva, N., & Poile, C. (2006). The effects of ambiguity on project task structure in new product development. *Knowledge and Process Management*, *13*(4), 239–251. doi:10.1002/kpm.260

Dutta, S., & Lanvin, B. (2020). *The Network Readiness Index 2020: Accelerating Digital Transformation in a post-COVID Global Economy, Sumatra Dutta & Bruno Lanvin (Edited)*. Portland Institute.

Gouedard, P., Pont, B., & Viennet, R. (2020). *Education responses to COVID-19: Implementing a way forward*. OECD Education Working Paper No. 224. doi:10.1787/19939019

Islam, T., Pitafi, A. H., Arya, V., Wang, Y., Akhtar, N., Mubarik, S., & Xiaobei, L. (2021). Panic buying in the covid-19 pandemic: A multicounty examination. *Journal of Retailing and Consumer Services*, *59*, 102357. doi:10.1016/j.jretconser.2020.102357

Itow, R. C. (2020). Fostering Valuable Learning Experiences by Transforming Current Teaching Practices: Practical Pedagogical Approaches from Online Practitioners. *Inf. Learn. Sci.*, *2020*(121), 443–452. doi:10.1108/ILS-04-2020-0106

Jayathirtha, G., Fields, D., Kafai, Y. B., & Chipps, J. (2020). Supporting Making Online: The Role of Artifact, Teacher and Peer Interactions in Crafting Electronic Textiles. *Inf. Learn. Sci., 2020*(121), 381–390. doi:10.1108/ILS-04-2020-0111

Justis, N., Litts, B.K., Reina, L., & Rhodes, S. (2020). Cultivating Staff Culture Online: How Edith Bowen Laboratory School Responded to COVID-19. *Inf. Learn. Sci.* doi:10.1108/ILS-04-2020-0136

Kemps, S. (2020). *Report: Most important data on digital audience during coronavirus*. Growth Quarter – The Next Web. https://thenextweb.com/growth-quarters/2020/04/24/report-most-important-data-on-digital-audiences-during-coronavirus/

Kessler, A., Barnes, S., Rajagopal, K., Rankin, J., Pouchak, L., Silis, M., & Esser, W. (2020). Saving a Semester of Learning: MIT's Emergency Transition to Online Instruction. *Inf. Learn. Sci., 2020*(7/8), 587–597. Advance online publication. doi:10.1108/ILS-04-2020-0097

Knapp, E. & Yu, D. (1999). Understanding organizational culture: how culture helps or hinders the flow of knowledge. *Knowledge Management Review*, 16-21.

Kraut, R. E., & Streeter, L. A. (1995). Coordination in Software Development. *Communications of the ACM, 38*(3), 69–81. doi:10.1145/203330.203345

Krishnamurthy, S. (2020). The Future of Business Education: A Commentary in the Shadow of the Covid-19 Pandemic. *Journal of Business Research, 2020*(117), 1–5. doi:10.1016/j.jbusres.2020.05.034 PMID:32501309

Laato, S., Islam, A. N., Farooq, A., & Dhir, A. (2020). Unusual purchasing behavior during the early stage of the COVID-19 pandemic: The stimulus-organism-response approach. *Journal of Retailing and Consumer Services, 57*, 102224. doi:10.1016/j.jretconser.2020.102224

Li, W., Liao, J., Li, Q., Baskota, M., Wang, X., Tang, Y., Zhou, Q., Wang, X., Luo, X., Ma, Y., Fukuoka, T., Ahn, H. S., Lee, M. S., Chen, Y., Luo, Z., & Liu, E. (2020). Public Health Education for Parents during the Outbreak of COVID-19: A Rapid Review. *Annals of Translational Medicine, 2020*(8), 628. doi:10.21037/atm-20-3312 PMID:32566565

Longhurst, G. J., Stone, D. M., Dulohery, K., Scully, D., Campbell, T., & Smith, C. F. (2020). Strength, Weakness, Opportunity, Threat (SWOT) Analysis of the Adaptations to Anatomical Education in the United Kingdom and Republic of Ireland in Response to the Covid-19 Pandemic. *Anatomical Sciences Education, 2020*(13), 301–311. doi:10.1002/ase.1967 PMID:32306550

Majanja, M. K. (2020). The Status of Electronic Teaching within South African LIS Education. *Library Management, 2020*(41), 317–337. doi:10.1108/LM-05-2020-0084

Naeem, M. (2021). Do social media platforms develop consumer panic buying during the fear of Covid-19 pandemic. *Journal of Retailing and Consumer Services, 58*, 102226. doi:10.1016/j.jretconser.2020.102226

Pal, K. (2019). Markov Decision Theory Based Crowdsourcing Software Process Model. In Gupta, V. (ed) Crowdsourcing and Probabilistic Decision-Making in Software Engineering: Emerging Research and Opportunities. doi:10.4018/978-1-5225-9659-2.ch001

Pal, K. (2020). Framework for Reusable Test Case Generation in Software Systems Testing. In Pang, C. Y. (ed) Software Engineering for Agile Application Development. doi:10.4018/978-1-7998-2531-9

Pal, K., & Karakostas, B. (2020). Software Testing Under Agile, Scrum, and DevOps. In Walsh, K. R.; Mahesh, S.; & Cherie, C. (ed) Agile Scrum Implementation and Its Long-Term Impact on Organizations. IGI Global.

Pal, K., & Williams, I. (2021). Software Development Knowledge Management System Using Web Portal. In Gyamfi, A. & Williams, I. (ed) Digital Technology Advancement in Knowledge Management. IGI Global.

Plöckinger, M., Aschauer, E., Hiebl, M. R. W., & Rohatschek, R. (2016). The Influence of Individual Executives on Corporate Financial Reporting: A Review and Outlook from the Perspective of Upper Echelons Theory. *Journal of Accounting Literature*, *2016*(37), 55–75. doi:10.1016/j.acclit.2016.09.002

Prentic, C., Chen, J., & Stantic, B. (2020). Timed intervention in COVID-19 and panic buying. *Journal of Retailing and Consumer Services*, *57*, 102203. doi:10.1016/j.jretconser.2020.102203

Pressman, R. S. (2000). *Software engineering: A Practitioner's Approach (European Adaption)* (5th ed.). McGraw-Hill International.

Putrevu, S., & Lord, K. R. (2001). Search dimensions, patterns and segment profiles of grocery shopping. *Journal of Retailing and Consumer Services*, *8*(3), 127–137. doi:10.1016/S0969-6989(00)00013-8

Raaper, R., & Brown, C. (2020). The Covid-19 Pandemic and the Dissolution of the University Campus: Implications for Student Support Practice. *Journal of Professional Capital and Community*, *2020*(3/4), 343–349. Advance online publication. doi:10.1108/JPCC-06-2020-0032

Rajhans, V., Memon, U., Patil, V., & Goyal, A. (2020). Impact of COVID-19 on Academic Activities and Way Forward in Indian Optometry. *Journal of Optometry*, *2020*(13), 216–226. doi:10.1016/j.optom.2020.06.002 PMID:32703749

Regehr, C., & Goel, V. (2020). Managing COVID-19 in a Large Urban Research-Intensive University. *Journal of Loss and Trauma*, *2020*(6-7), 1–17. doi:10.1080/15325024.2020.1771846

Rodríguez-Hernández, C. F., Cascallar, E., & Kyndt, E. (2020). Socio-Economic Status and Academic Performance in Higher Education: A Systematic Review. *Educational Research Review*, *2020*(29), 100305. doi:10.1016/j.edurev.2019.100305

Roy, D., Tripathy, S., Kar, S. K., Sharma, N., Verma, S. K., & Kaushal, V. (2020). Study of Knowledge, Attitude, Anxiety & Perceived Mental Healthcare Need in Indian Population during COVID-19 Pandemic. *Asian Journal of Psychiatry*, *51*, 102083. Advance online publication. doi:10.1016/j.ajp.2020.102083 PMID:32283510

Rus, I., & Lindvall, M. (2002, June). Knowledge Management in Software Engineering. *IEEE Software*, *19*(3), 26–38. doi:10.1109/MS.2002.1003450

Ryder, B., Zhang, T., & Hua, N. (2021). The Social Media "Magic": Virtually Engaging Visitors during COVID-19 Temporary Closures. *Administrative Sciences*, *11*(2), 53. doi:10.3390/admsci11020053

Schein, E. H. (1992). *Organizational Culture and Leadership* (2nd ed.). Jossey Bass.

Shufeldt, L., Oates, B., & Vaught, B. (1998). Is lifestyle an important factor in the purchase of OTC drugs by the elderly? *Journal of Consumer Marketing*, *15*(2), 111–124. doi:10.1108/07363769810210304

Skulmowski, A., & Rey, G. D. (2020). COVID-19 as an Accelerator for Digitalization at a German University: Establishing Hybrid Campuses in Times of Crisis. *Human Behavior and Emerging Technologies*, *2020*(2), 212–216. doi:10.1002/hbe2.201 PMID:32838228

Sommerville, I. (2001). *Software Engineering* (6th ed.). Addison-Wesley.

Sudbury, L., & Simcock, P. (2009). A multivariate segmentation model of senior consumers. *Journal of Consumer Marketing*, *26*(4), 251–262. doi:10.1108/07363760910965855

Sveiby, K. E. (1997). *The New Organizational Wealth: Managing & Measuring Knowledge-Based Assets*. Berrett-Koehler Publishers, Inc.

Talidong, K. J. B., & Toquero, C. M. D. (2020). Philippine Teachers' Practices to Deal with Anxiety amid COVID-19. *Journal of Loss and Trauma*, *2020*(6-7), 1–7. doi:10.1080/15325024.2020.1759225

United Nations. (2020). Policy Brief: Education during COVID-19 and beyond. United Nations.

Urbanikova, M., Stubnova, M., Papcunova, V., & Hudakova, J. (2020). Analysis of Innovation Activities of Slovak Small and Medium-Sized Family Business. *Administrative Sciences*, *10*(4), 80. doi:10.3390/admsci10040080

Watermeyer, R., Crick, T., Knight, C., & Goodall, J. (2020). COVID-19 and Digital Disruption in UK Universities: Afflictions and Affordances of Emergency Online Migration. *Higher Education*, *2020*(81), 623–641. doi:10.100710734-020-00561-y PMID:32836334

Yen, T. T. F. (2020). The Performance of Online Teaching for Flipped Classroom Based on COVID-19 Aspect. *Asian J. Educ. Soc. Studies*, *2020*(8), 57–64. doi:10.9734/ajess/2020/v8i330229

Zainuddin, Z., Perera, C. J., Haruna, H., & Habiburrahim, H. (2020). Literacy in the New Norm: Stay-Home Game Plan for Parents. *Inf. Learn. Sci.*, *2020*(121), 645–653. doi:10.1108/ILS-04-2020-0069

Zhou, L., Wu, S., Zhou, M., & Li, F. (2020). 'School's Out, But Class' On,' The Largest Online Education in the World Today: Taking China's Practical Exploration During The COVID-19 Epidemic Prevention and Control as an Example. *Best Evid. Chin. Edu.*, *2020*(4), 501–519. doi:10.15354/bece.20.ar023

ADDITIONAL READING

United Nations. (2020). *Policy Brief: The World of Work and Covid-19*. https://un.org/sites/un2.un.org/files/ the_world_of_work_andcovid-19.pdf

United Nations Development. (2021). *Program Responding to the COVID-19 Pandemic: Leaving No Country Behind*. https://www.undp.org/tag/report?type=publications

KEY TERMS AND DEFINITIONS

Build Resilient Education Systems: Strengthening the resilience of education systems enables countries to be responding to the immediate challenges of safely reopening education institutions and positions them to better cope with future crises. In this way, governments could consider the following: (i) focus on equity and inclusion; (ii) reinforce capacities for risk management, and (iii) at all levels of the system; (iv) ensure strong leadership and coordination, and (v) enhance consultation and communication mechanisms.

Coronavirus: The current pandemic (COVID-19) is an infectious disease caused by the SARS-CoV-2 virus.

Education as a Common Good: Education is a fundamental human right that helps understand all other human rights, and it is a global common good.

Protect Education Through Coordinate for Impact: The pandemic has pushed the education work into the center of global recession in living memory, with lasting effects on economies and public finances. Global and country-specific educational authorities need to safe-guard education financing through the following ways: (i) advantage of domestic revenue mobilization, preserve the share of expenditure for education as a top priority, (ii) address inefficiencies in educational spending, (iii) strengthen international coordination to address the debt crisis; and (iv) protect official development assistance for education.

Rebranding Higher Education and Enhance Changes in Teaching and Learning Practices: The huge efforts made within a short time to tackle to the shocks to education systems; and seize the opportunity to find new ways to address the learning crises and bring about a set of solutions previously considered difficult or impossible to implement.

Suppress Transmission of the Virus: The essential step that educational institutions and countries can take to hasten the reopening of institutions is to suppress transmission of the virus to control national or local outbreaks.

Chapter 15
Fashion Resale Behaviours and Technology Disruption:
An In-Depth Review

Iris Mohr
St. John's University, USA

Leonora Fuxman
https://orcid.org/0000-0002-2987-2094
St. John's University, USA

Ali B. Mahmoud
https://orcid.org/0000-0002-3790-1107
St John's University, USA & London South Bank University, UK & Brunel University London, UK

ABSTRACT

This chapter provides an in-depth discussion of the disruptive nature of reselling technologies. The collaborative consumption movement, a popular emerging trend, encourages consumers to live in a more collective, sharing economy. This is where we can discuss the disruptive nature of the reselling technologies, particularly as they impact the fashion industry, prompting an explosion of vintage/second-hand retailing. Secondary market behaviors such as reselling, recycling, gifting, swapping, and reusing are becoming the most significantly growing consumer segments. The notion of a rotating wardrobe has been increasingly frequently accepted. This is especially prominent with younger consumers like Generation Z, who would consider spending more money on sustainably produced and delivered products while showing a strong preference for switching to brands with sustainable initiatives. Mobile apps and personalization have made buying used products as easy as buying new ones.

DOI: 10.4018/978-1-6684-4168-8.ch015

INTRODUCTION

Climate change and growing inequality accompanied the arrival of the twenty-first century, both results of a capitalism paradigm centred on rivalry among economic participants and over-exploitation of human and environmental resources (Juge, Pomiès, & Collin-Lachaud, 2021; Klein, 2019; Latour, 2015; Piketty, 2013). And over the last two decades, increasing consumer awareness of the adverse environmental impacts caused by fashion clothing consumption has given momentum to sustainability-driven initiatives that seek to minimise clothing waste (Peña-Vinces, Solakis, & Guillen, 2020). Consumers are becoming more conscious of the environmental effects of clothing production (Kumar, Prakash, & Kumar, 2021; Lee, 2011; Mohr, Fuxman, & Mahmoud, 2021; Paço, Leal Filho, Ávila, & Dennis, 2020). Thus, it is becoming more critical to understand how people buy clothes that are not new yet ready to wear (Clark, 2008; Cooper, Woodward, Hiller, & Goworek, 2008; Norum & Norton, 2017). Understanding consumer desire for new clothes is critical for fashion brands, educators, and government agencies; nevertheless, the relative scarcity of research about demand, consumption, distribution, and post consumption of used clothing limits the available information about the whole second-hand fashion industry (Norum & Norton, 2017). Used clothing marketplaces are not immune to causing adverse environmental effects (Sandin & Peters, 2018; Valor, Ronda, & Abril, 2022). However, they are widely recognised as a critical strategy for minimising the harmful impacts of textile waste production (Dahlbo, Aalto, Eskelinen, & Salmenperä, 2017; Valor et al., 2022). Whilst, second-hand clothes are not always cheap (Financial Times, 2021), many people purchase used apparel in an effort to live a more sustainable lifestyle (Chi, Ganak, Summers, Adesanya, McCoy, Liu, & Tai, 2021; Kumar & Yadav, 2021). Consumers often purchase used products to replenish their wardrobes with distinctive and affordable pieces (Cervellon, Carey, & Harms, 2012; Guiot & Roux, 2010; Machado, Almeida, Bollick, & Bragagnolo, 2019). They are pressuring clothing firms to increase their commitment to sustainability, which will affect sales growth projections for second-hand apparel products (Mohr et al., 2021; Roy, Silvestre, & Singh, 2020; Todeschini, Cortimiglia, Callegaro-de-Menezes, & Ghezzi, 2017). According to ThredUp's (2021) recent research, the overall resale market for used clothing might reach \$77 billion by 2025, up from \$32 billion in 2020 and \$11 billion in 2012. Younger shoppers — some motivated by environmental concerns, others by a desire to save money — are embracing second-hand fashion at a higher rate than any other demographic (Financial Times, 2021). Second-hand clothing or second-hand clothing marketplaces are promoted in the fashion industry as an effective solution to reduce the environmental repercussions of the business, including textile waste (Armstrong, Niinimäki, Kujala, Karell, & Lang, 2015; Farrant, Olsen, & Wangel, 2010; Fortuna & Diyamandoglu, 2017; Hole & Hole, 2020; Mohr et al., 2021; Sohn, Nielsen, Birkved, Joanes, & Gwozdz, 2021; Valor et al., 2022).

Based on the above, this chapter synthesises the available discourse and literature on reselling technology in the case of fashion, highlighting the following issues. Given that second-hand clothing is relatively inexpensive, do consumers buy more than they need? In other words, is this contributing to a *throwaway* society? On the other hand, are companies responsibly disposing of clothing? Can companies do better in managing second-hand retail? Does second-hand retail lead to fraud or unethical behaviour amongst consumers, businesses, or both?

Background

Fast fashion is an expression that refers to the garment industry's business strategy of reproducing recent catwalk patterns and high-fashion designs, mass manufacturing them inexpensively, and getting them to retail outlets rapidly while demand is strong. Additionally, the phrase fast fashion is used broadly to refer to the items associated with the fast fashion business model. Fast fashion had developed in popularity throughout the late twentieth century as garment production got more affordable where materials such as polyester and nylon, improved supply chain efficiency and new fast response production processes, and more considerable dependence on cheap labour from South, Southeast, and East Asia's textile manufacturing sectors (D'Ambrogio, 2014; Streeter, 2014). Primark, H&M, Shein, and Zara are fast-fashion retailers that have grown to be big multinationals by focusing on a high turnover of affordable seasonal and trendy apparel that attracts fashion-conscious buyers (Monroe, 2021).

The sharing economy represents a system in which assets owned by members of a network may be temporarily accessible by other members, typically via an online platform— in contrast to traditional enterprises, which are owned by a single individual and then rented to the public (Statista, 2022). Therefore, nowadays, there are many options for those who want something but do not want to pay full price. This is done because people have more access to information than they ever did before. For example, more and more people live alone and need fewer things in their homes, so they use collaborative consumption to get what they want without having to buy it new. They either rent or borrow these things instead of buying them. This means less waste is created since fewer items are being made, and fewer items are going into landfills when someone does not need them anymore. One of the most popular collaborative consumption strategies is second-hand clothing- buying clothes second-hand instead of new ones. The production and use of clothing have a negative influence on the environment and waste management (Fletcher, 2012; Lang & Zhang, 2019; Wang, Fu, & Li, 2022). To address these issues, the idea of sustainable consumption was established in order to maximise the use of existing resources and minimise waste (Borusiak, Szymkowiak, Horska, Raszka, & Żelichowska, 2020). As a result of this tendency, sales of used products have increased as well (Ferraro, Sands, & Brace-Govan, 2016; Park & Armstrong, 2020; Wang et al., 2022). The popularity of sharing economy services has grown in recent years. Many anticipate this trend to continue (see Figure 1), with the global sharing economy's total value estimated to reach over 335 billion US dollars by 2025, up from only 15 billion US dollars in 2014 (Statista, 2022). The number one form of this is buying second-hand clothes (Odier, 2021).

Nevertheless, it can be hard to know what customers are actually getting when they buy second-hand and what that means for our planet in the long term. Generally speaking, the concept of "second-hand goods" refers to previously owned and used items (Sihvonen & Turunen, 2016). The financial value of such goods is often lower than that of new products (Cervellon, 2013; Cervellon et al., 2012; Guiot & Roux, 2010; Reis, 2020; Roux, 2006; Sihvonen & Turunen, 2016). Specifically, second-hand can be further defined in three ways as follows.

1. A good being purchased by or otherwise transferred to a second or later end-user.
2. A used product that is no longer in the same condition as when transferred to the current owner. A relatable concept is *vintage*— it refers to a previously owned product (may or may not be used), but is indicative of a specific style of fashion era (Cervellon et al., 2012). Thus, the monetary value of a vintage item is linked to its age, condition, and lack of availability, which is why the price might be considerably higher, as the item can no longer be bought as a brand-new item (Cervellon et al.,

2012; Gerval, 2010; Guiot & Roux, 2010; Medalla, Yamagishi, Tiu, Tanaid, Abellana, Caballes, Jabilles, Himang, Bongo, & Ocampo, 2020; Sihvonen & Turunen, 2016).

3. Second-hand can also be defined as having had a previous owner, whether a consumer or business. In line with this definition, discount retailers such as Nordstrom Rack, Marshall's, TJMax, and so forth can be considered second-hand retailers. Though items sold at these retailers are items with tags and new to the consumer, the items had a prior business owner and, therefore not new to the marketplace; similar to when a seller consigns a clothing item with tags, the merchandise is second-hand, and not new.

Figure 1. Value of the sharing economy worldwide in 2014 and 2025(in billion US dollars)
Source: Statista (2022)

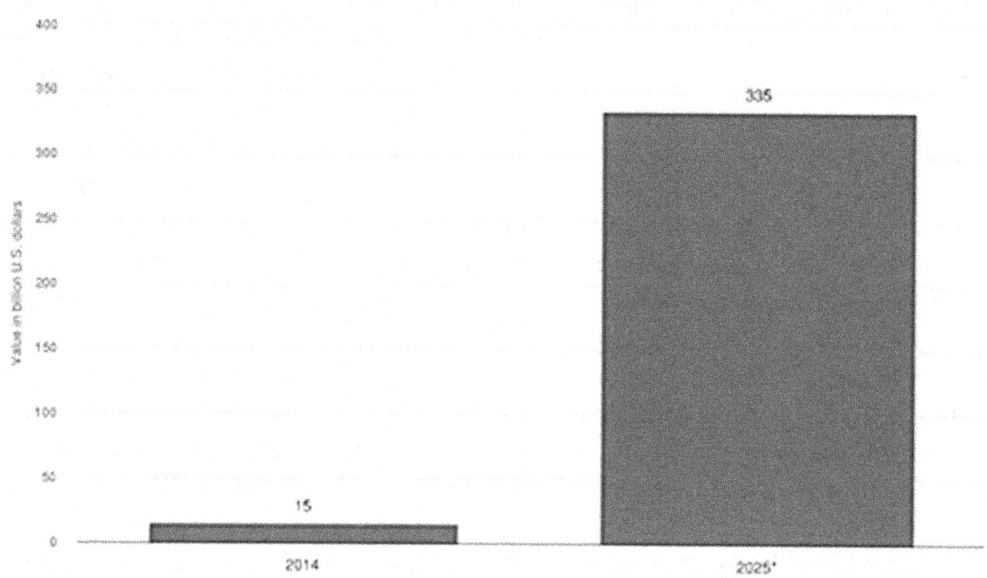

Over 40 years ago, Winakor (1969) observed that clothing acquisition activities include buying used clothes, obtaining hand-me-down clothes, trading clothes, and mending or making over garments (Norum & Norton, 2017; Young Lee, Halter, Johnson, & Ju, 2013). The collection of resource circulation systems lets consumers get and supply valued resources or services, temporarily or permanently, either directly or through a mediator (Ertz, Deschênes, & Sarigöllü, 2021). Collaborative consumption is thus a concept that is diametrically opposed to the concept of conventional consumption (Dreyer, Lüdeke-Freund, Hamann, & Faccer, 2017). Whereas conventional consumption - which underpins traditional marketing philosophy – is a resource distribution system in which consumers have a passive role because they are unable to contribute any resource or service or are not given the opportunity to do so (Ertz, 2020; Ertz, Durif, & Arcand, 2016). Collaborative consumption is becoming a prominent way to get what you need (Cruz, Ganga, & Wahlen, 2018; Nwaorgu, 2018). Unlike past times, when people needed to buy everything for themselves, we now share resources with each other. The easiest way to think of collaborative consumption is through other well-known successful applications of shared consumption, such as Uber in transportation or Airbnb in the hospitality industry (Hamari, Sjöklint, & Ukkonen, 2016; Möhlmann, 2015; Schiel, 2015; Schor & Fitzmaurice, 2015), both of which were major industry disruptors when first arriving on the market, eventually causing their respective industries to fully re-engage the way they interact and serve their consumer. A similar process can also be applied to a variety of other industries, including fashion and, more specifically, second-hand fashion (Choi & He, 2019; Yuan & Shen, 2019).

Fast fashion's market share is predicted to stay relatively stable at around 9% over the next decade, while the second-hand clothing category is expected to increase to 18% by 2030, more than double the rate of fast fashion (TFL, 2021). As a result, an abrupt rise in rental and resale is underway, primarily driven by younger generations, i.e., millennials and Generation Z (Bell, 2022). Therefore, second-hand markets represent an exciting and growing arena for businesses and consumers to buy and sell brands, whether via brick-and-mortar stores or online through websites and/or mobile apps (Sihvonen & Turunen, 2016). Online fashion sales, primarily via mobile apps, have increased and become the norm in recent years in terms of business-to-business (BtoB), business-to-consumers (BtoC), consumer-to-business (CtoB), and consumers-to-consumers (CtoC). The latter is evidenced by the growth in the number of online flea markets, including eBay, Craig list, Facebook, and marketplace apps like PoshMark (Sihvonen & Turunen, 2016). Interestingly, the second-hand market from the perspective of business models and strategic variables that contribute to the success of second-hand businesses has been little researched (Fuxman, Mohr, Mahmoud, & Grigoriou, 2022).

METHODS

This chapter represents a general review paper (e.g. Solakis, Katsoni, Mahmoud, & Grigoriou, 2022). Thus, we went along with Templier and Paré's (2015) multi-step procedure to achieve the objectives of this enquiry. As a first stage, we defined the research objective for this study—we sought to learn more about how second-hand clothing wedded to technology has disrupted the fashion industry and apparel consumption patterns and their ethicality. Second, we sifted through the existing discourse and literature on the global impact of second-hand clothes, the drivers and barriers to second-hand clothing consumption and ultimately, the scene of fashion products resale amidst the disruption that technology has brought into this sector. Third, we called for help from three independent expert peers to ensure our source selection process was free of bias. Finally, we synthesised the fragmented pieces cited in the prior studies that shaped the investigation's discussion and conclusion.

The Global Impact of Second-hand Clothes

Buying second-hand clothing is a worldwide phenomenon. In fact, the percentage of used clothes in people's closets worldwide is predicted to expand over the next several years, rising from 21% in 2020 to roughly 27% in 2023 (Smith, 2022). Notwithstanding the stereotypical patterns associated with second-hand clothing, its use contributes to reducing the clothing industry's environmental and social repercussions (D'Adamo, Lupi, Morone, & Settembre-Blundo, 2022; Peña-Vinces et al., 2020). Additionally, purchasing used clothing provides a number of advantages for customers, including lower pricing (Borg, Mont, & Schoonover, 2020; D'Adamo et al., 2022), which is especially true for luxury brands (D'Adamo et al., 2022). Consumers could become able to spend more money on unique, singular commodities that match their wardrobe by saving money on their overall apparel purchases (D'Adamo et al., 2022; Turunen & Pöyry, 2019). Many people do not want to wear clothes that many other people are also wearing (D'Adamo et al., 2022). Every new fashion trend is made in high-volume, standardised production runs (Backs, Jahnke, Lüpke, Stücken, & Stummer, 2021; Özbölük, 2021). For instance, it has been found (Özbölük, 2021) that luxury originates in the pursuit of uniqueness and autonomy (Dubois & Duquesne, 1993; Hennigs, Wiedmann, Klarmann, Strehlau, Godey, Pederzoli, Neulinger, Dave, Aiello, Donvito, Taro, Táborecká-Petrovičová, Santos, Jung, & Oh, 2012; Potavanich, 2015; Sontag & Lee, 2004). Another customer benefit linked with the used clothing industry is the possibility of discovering one-of-a-kind outfits (D'Adamo et al., 2022; Xiang, 2021). Used clothing has a significant beneficial social and environmental impact. They help the environment by reducing carbon emissions and conserving valuable resources such as water and electricity. Additionally, they keep old garments out of landfills and incinerators (Assoune, 2020). Purchasing used clothing benefits customer finances and the environment. Moreover, the second-hand market extends the life of items, allowing buyers to create their own unique style by blending patterns, forms, and colours from previous collections (D'Adamo et al., 2022). This practice, popularised by celebrities on social media, has recently been labelled as circular fashion (Orminski, Tandoc Jr, & Detenber, 2021). However, it has been argued (e.g. Guo, Choi, & Zhang, 2021) that the second-hand market does not offer the same apparent benefits. In this regard, concerns have been raised regarding a possible link between second-hand clothing *over*-consumption and the throwaway society culture and behaviour. For instance, throughout Covid-19, thrift and charity stores around the United States received an overwhelming amount of donations. Tons of pre-owned clothing continue to end up in landfills or are sold in bulk for extremely low prices elsewhere. These fallacies, Le Zotte explained, are rooted in the long-held belief that clothing donation is a net good for society. We build on current discourse and scholarly work (e.g. Becker, 2018a; Becker, 2018b; Nguyen, 2021; Pucker, 2022) and the work of Becker (2018a) to list a summary of these concerns as follows.

Psychological Factors

- Material possessions evoke a sense of security: if possessing some material belongings provides us with security (a roof over our heads, clothing, and reliable transportation), possessing excess will almost certainly provide us with even more security. However, even when our most basic requirements are met, the actual security that comes with the possession of tangible assets is far less consistent than we imagine and more fleeting.
- Material possessions bring a sense of happiness. While rarely anyone would confess that they seek happiness through worldly possessions, most people do. As a result, we seek larger homes, faster automobiles, more astounding technology, and trendier fashion—all in the hope of increasing our happiness. Regrettably, the satisfaction acquired from the surplus of tangible goods is, at best, transitory.
- Advertising has a greater effect on us than we realise. According to some estimates, we see 5,000 commercials every day. Each advertisement conveys the same message: your life will improve if you purchase what we are offering. We hear this message so frequently and from so many different perspectives that we begin to subconsciously believe it. This is a wake-up call to realise how much we are influenced by others' agendas.
- We hope to impress others. Envy soon becomes a driving factor for economic activity in an affluent society. Although the term "ostentatious consumption" was coined decades ago, it has never been more popular than it is now. Once our fundamental wants are addressed, consumerism must

evolve into something more. It is all too frequently used as a platform to demonstrate our riches, status, and financial success to the world.

- We are envious of others who possess more. Comparing ourselves appears to be a normal state of human beings. We take note of what other people purchase, dress, and drive. Our culture promotes these comparisons. And much too frequently, we purchase items we do not need simply because others in our social circles have done so.
- We are attempting to compensate for our shortcomings. We make the mistake of seeking confidence via the clothing we wear or the automobile we drive. We attempt to compensate for loss, loneliness, or pain by acquiring frivolous stuff. And we strive to alleviate our dissatisfaction with worldly possessions. However, none of these endeavours can ever wholly satisfy our shortcomings. Often, they just prevent us from ever addressing things.
- We are more self-centred than we are willing to accept. While admitting that the human spirit is built toward selfish desires might be challenging, history presents a compelling argument for us. By amassing more goods, we want to expand the size of our own realm. Force, compulsion, dishonesty, and warfare have all been used in the past to achieve this. Our world and our personal lives are still plagued by selfishness.

Exaggerated Benefits of Sustainable Fashion

According to Pucker (2022) few industries are more outspoken about their commitment to sustainability than the fashion industry, where carbon-neutral, organic, or vegan claims are made on everything from swimwear to wedding gowns, whilst yoga mats made from mushrooms (Sergison, 2021), and sneakers manufactured from sugarcane and cork (Bare Fashion, 2019) or coffee grounds (Rens, 2022) adorn shops' shelves.

Despite recent expansion in sustainable fashion, some scholars (e.g. Pucker, 2022) have highlighted that, in practice, only minor carbon emissions have been avoided meaning that the same dynamics that fuelled clothing resale expansion will far outweigh the benefits of bio-based products and new business models. Moreover, other authors (e.g. Hirschlag, 2019) have emphasised that in order to accurately measure all carbon emission reductions from garment reuse, the whole textile sector must adopt a consistent carbon accounting technique.

Gentrification of Thrift Stores

Even though many consumers of second-hand goods are concerned with sustainability, the manufacturing industry is preoccupied with growing markets and profitability (Hansen & Le Zotte, 2019). Some scholars have used the term "retail gentrification" to portray the development of the commercial fabric in some urban areas, which is characterised by the direct and indirect displacement of old retailers by new retail businesses that cater to new and more affluent customers (Guimarães, 2021). Thrift store gentrification describes the phenomenon where wealthy shoppers voluntarily purchase items from second-hand clothing stores such as Goodwill and Goodwill Salvation Army (Cills, 2021). The discourse on thrift store gentrification also touches on the trendy or particularly fine goods purchased from such retailers, thus denying low-income public shops like Goodwill and Salvation Army access to these goods. However, they recognise the increase in sales, meaning that as long as thrifting remains trendy, thrift stores will increase the price point as a way to create additional income (Reid, 2021). When second-hand stores are crowded by an influx of people just getting to know the economy, those who run the stores can charge more, making clothes and other goods out of reach for people in communities who may need them (Maas, 2020).

Therefore, whilst recycling, resale, renting, reuse, and repair are promoted as environmental lifesavers (Pucker, 2022), it is debatable if second-hand fashion is a viable treatment for the clothing industry's ecological and social ramifications and whether it is required to check the implications for manufacturing methods and business models, which would almost surely have to be altered (D'Adamo et al., 2022).

DRIVERS AND BARRIERS TO SECOND-HAND CLOTHING CONSUMPTION

Previously known as a minor type of trade consisting of a few thrift shops, second-hand markets, and antique merchants has evolved into a fundamental trend in Europe and the United States, allowing for resale, recovery, and recycling (Guiot & Roux, 2010; Hansen & Le Zotte, 2019; Lemire, 2012). Second-hand shopping encompasses both the act of not purchasing new — a product dimension— and the practice of frequenting outlets with specific features— a sales dimension (Guiot & Roux, 2010). As such, Guiot and Roux (2010) define *second-hand shopping* as the acquisition of used things using techniques and venues of exchange that are usually distinct from those used to acquire new products. Most of the research on second-hand retailing has focused on the motivational foundations of second-hand fashion since it plays a critical role in modifying consumers' purchasing and disposal habits, thus leading to sustainable consumption (Chan, Choi, & Lok, 2015; Fuxman et al., 2022; Wang et al., 2022).

A recent study by Hur (2020) identifies and characterises two consumer groups: those who are the consumers of second-hand fashion and those who are non-consumers of second-hand clothing, offering insights into the factors that drive each consumer's attitudes and behaviours towards their preferred second-hand clothing consumption strategy. Below we summarise Hur's (2020) findings.

Second-Hand Clothing Consumers (SHC)

Hur (2020) presents four distinctive second-hand clothing consumer groups as below:

1. *Price-conscious:* This consumer group shows the highest association of the SHC product attributes, consequences, and values among SHC consumers. Examples of that are low price, saving money, satisfying a sound financial decision, financial security and a sense of belonging by preserving or enhancing one's public image.
2. *Quality- and style-conscious:* The second-largest consumer segment is the fashion- and quality-conscious segment. This group derives satisfaction from the SHC's quality and style, experimentation with different styles, colours, genres, quality, sizes, originality, social involvement with communities dedicated to second-hand or vintage styled clothes, and self-improvement and self-confidence.
3. *Brand-and self-expressive-conscious:* Consumers who want luxury fashion brands to boost their social image may be separated into two subsegments: those who desire to avoid cheap high-street fast-fashion brands owing to their items' short material lifespan and reusability.
4. *Environmentally and socially conscious groups:* This consumer group bases their decisions on critical views of their purchase's potentially adverse environmental and social consequences (Hur, 2020). Their attitude is reflected in their opposition to the capitalised fast-fashion system and a

desire for more ethical and responsible consumption centred on sustainable products. They are environmentally friendly and contribute to supporting the environment, socially engaging in an active community with a sense of accomplishment through environmental protection and social contribution to the welfare of people and the environment. According to Schwartz's (2012) value theory, this consumer group is motivated by achievement, universalism, and compassion. The members of this group tend to experience a sense of success or enjoyment as a result of their contribution to the local community's wellbeing (Hur, 2020). McNeill and Moore (2015) refer to this consumer category as "sacrifice consumers"; Guiot and Roux (2010) define them as a group of consumers driven by critical motives and exhibiting a high level of environmental concern, aiming to mitigate their social and ecological consequences. Additionally, experiential benefits can be gained through social interaction with a local community organisation (Hur, 2020).

Non-Second-Hand Clothing Consumer

Hur (2020) introduces four major non-second-hand clothing consumer groups classified as follows:

1. *Social acceptance-seeking and status-conscious:* This pertains to a cheap product of lousy quality, poor quality with no style, a sense of inferiority or self-consciousness or anxiety over an unflattering self-portrait, and concerns about social judgment and acceptance.
2. *Quality- and hygiene-conscious:* Worries about product quality and cleanliness are the second prevalent tendency amongst non-SHC consumers. This includes concerns about unclean and low-quality materials, poor quality or uncertainty about product quality/bad smell, feeling dirty or unclean/concerns about hygiene as a result of a lack of transparency, concerns about social image as a result of product quality, and concerns about a sense of belonging in a social group. These perceived unfavourable product characteristics contribute to a lack of confidence in the product and anxiety about one's sense of belonging in a social group.
3. *Style- and self-expression-conscious:* SHC's perceived image as outmoded and giving restricted style alternatives has affected consumers' perceptions of the company, limiting their ability to express themselves and be creative. Tacky clothing or a limited product selection, difficulty finding the right style, size, and colour, feeling uncool, feeling constrained in expressing individuality or creativity, social image concerns about being perceived as unconcerned about appearance, risks to self-confidence and social confidence and expression of self-identity. With fewer product selections, purchasing for SHC requires more work and time.
4. *Time- and professionalism-conscious:* This group is concerned with the image of unknown or low-cost brands, with product information being unknown or not being professionally cleaned, time being wasted trying to find the right products, concerns about social status and self-enhancement, and risks to social status and self-enhancement.

Overall, Hur (2020) concludes that the major drivers of second-hand clothing consumption encompass good value for money, hedonic experiences that come from a unique range of product options (e.g., vintage looks and nostalgia), the general benefits of second-hand clothing, and the environmental and social benefits of ethical consumption. On the other hand, Hur (2020) found that the key barriers to second-hand clothing consumption consist of: the perceived poor material quality, outmoded styles, perceived unclean state and lack of transparency in the product, absence of accessibility of second-hand clothing in both online and offline stores, and worries about personal and social image and acceptance.

CLOTHING RESALE TECHNOLOGICALLY DISRUPTED

A positive trend clearly emerged for the future, and contemporary research (e.g. Fuxman et al., 2022; Gazzola, Pavione, Pezzetti, & Grechi, 2020; Mohr et al., 2021) findings have shown hope for an increase in the ethical approaches to business and the adoption of sustainable strategies and practices in the fashion industry. The transition to buying and selling used clothes is downright easy (notably in the consumer's wallet), especially with the availability of online resale websites and apps where consumers can also make money from their unwanted clothes by reselling them in savings apps (Loanzon, 2021). There are a considerable number of second-hand stores to choose from.

With wardrobe hoarders embarking on a clean purge and a renewed sense of thrift, a new crop of "slow fashion" applications lets consumers experiment with clothing swapping and second-hand purchasing (Quach, 2021). Whereas only a few years ago, purchasing second-hand may entail hours of trawling, technology has made the entire process far more quick and accessible (Bravo, 2020).

Depop, for example, is a CtoC social platform and online marketplace where users can buy and sell used clothing and accessories (Oakes, 2021). Etsy reports that Depop is the 10th most-visited shopping site among U.S. Gen Z consumers (Neate, 2021). Depop now has registered users in nearly 150 countries, and its two million active merchants sold $650 million worth of used clothing and other fashion items last year (Neate, 2021). According to a study (Depop; & Bain & Company, 2020) conducted with Depop users in the United States, the United Kingdom, and Australia, reducing consumption was the leading motivation for users to purchase second-hand items, with 75 per cent of survey respondents citing this. Figure 2 (Sabanoglu, 2021) illustrates those main motivations.

Figure 2. Leading motivations for secondhand item purchases of Depop users in the United States, the United Kingdom, and Australia in 2020
Source: (Sabanoglu, 2021)

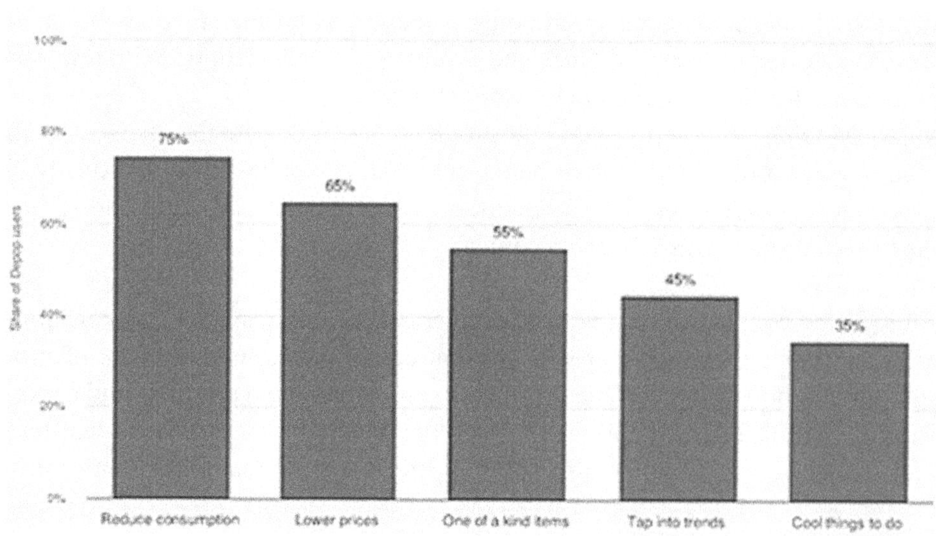

As of March 2021, users in their teens accounted for 34.6 per cent of Depop's active user accounts in the United States, such that, according to this data, users aged 20 to 29 years (Millennials and Generation Z) were the largest user group, accounting for 48.4 per cent of the social shopping app's user base on the Android platform (App Ape, 2021). This concurs with research (Mahmoud, Hack-Polay, Grigoriou, Mohr, & Fuxman, 2021) that examined the use of Instagram across three generations (X, Y and Z) of women in a Sub-Saharan context. They found that Generation Y and Generation Z are more likely to develop positive behavioural intentions towards following fashion brands on Instagram.

Moreover, Depop benefited highly from the e-commerce boom during the COVID-19 pandemic. The number of app users in the United Kingdom (see Figure 3) went from under one million in January 2020 to more than two million as of October 2021 (Pasquali, 2021a).

Figure 4 shows how Depop's app downloads reached their peak in June 2020, amid the coronavirus pandemic, with approximately 275,000 downloads (Pasquali, 2021b). Overall, relevant research (Mahmoud, Ball, Rubin, Fuxman, Mohr, Hack-Polay, Grigoriou, & Wakibi, 2021) suggest that Covid-19 perception positively predicts social media users' enjoyment and usefulness, leading to more satisfaction with fashion brand accounts on digital platforms like Instagram and greater intention to follow and recommend those accounts, especially amongst younger generations who are deemed as *tech-native*, presenting invaluable opportunities of expansion in a post-Covid era for fashion-related social platforms like Depop.

Figure 3. Monthly active users (MAU) of the Depop app in the United Kingdom (UK) from January 2018 to October 2021
Source: (Pasquali, 2021a)

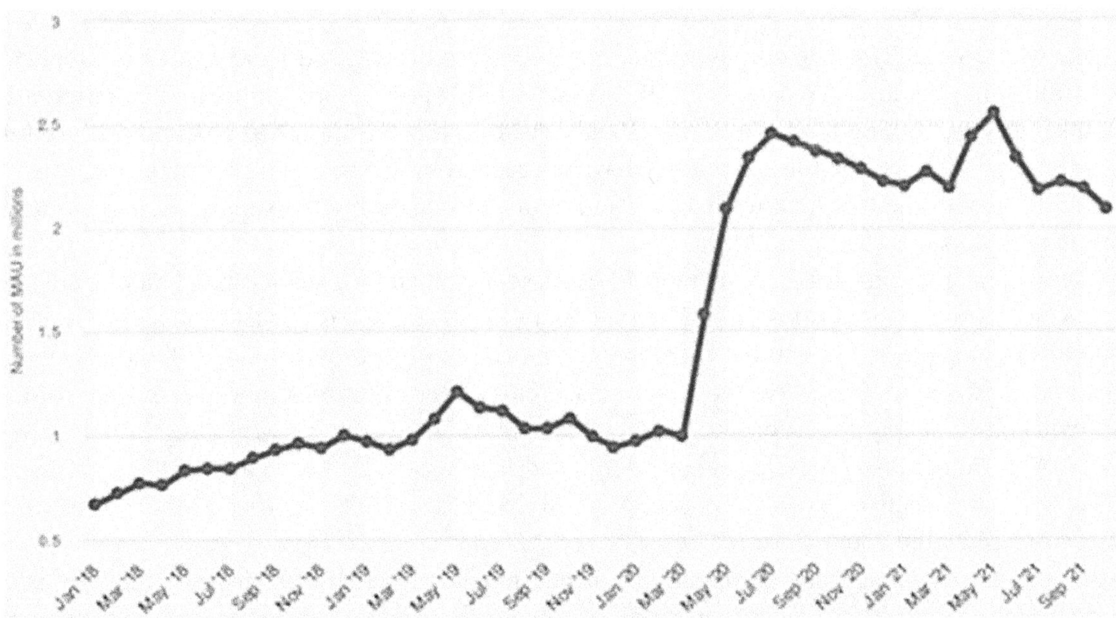

Figure 4. Monthly downloads of the Depop app in the United Kingdom (UK) from January 2018 to October 2021
Source: (Pasquali, 2021b)

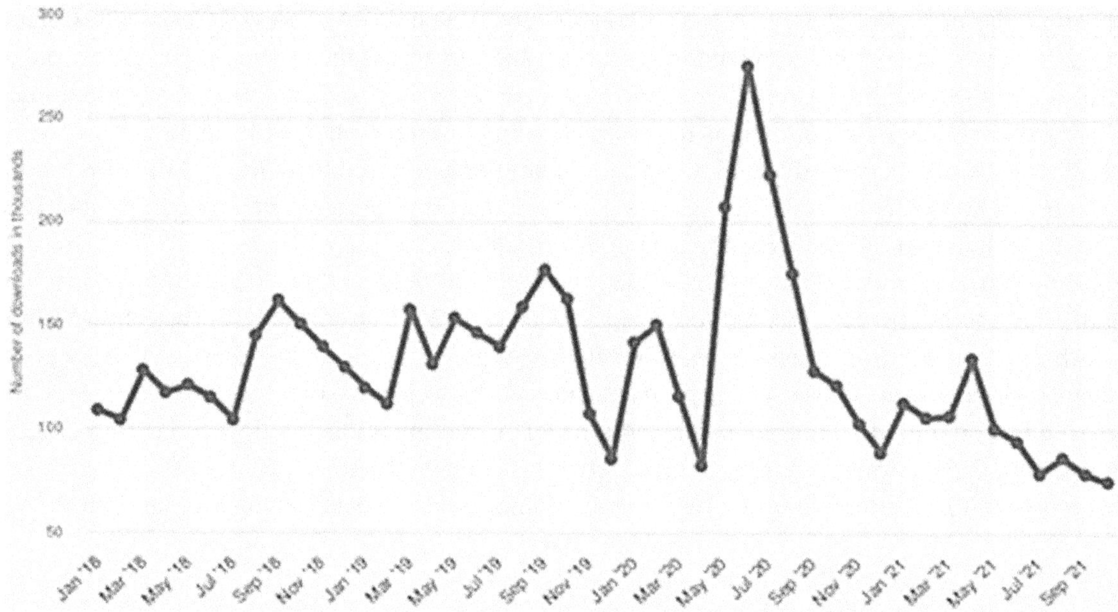

DISCUSSION

In an age where virtually everything is online, it makes sense that second-hand retail has a real chance of revolutionising the industry (Price, 2019). Second-hand is growing much faster than retail fashion, and consumers are turning to resale websites and apps because it is easier to buy and sell used items (Taylor-Singh, 2021). Second-hand retailers have succeeded by focusing on shoppers concerned with sustainability and those that look for hard-to-find items, thus avoiding the supply chain pressures that traditional retailers feel (Doniger, 2021).

Moreover, in an age of inflation, there is an increase in demand for second-hand among consumers since one of its most obvious and well-known benefits is cost savings. Inflation essentially makes a consumer's buying power for clothing decrease, given that it costs more to produce clothes. As the price of materials and textiles increases, the manufacturing of clothes becomes more expensive. Adding to this, Covid caused supply chain constraints, thereby increasing the price of everything from hats to bags to shoes. According to Amed, Balchandani, Berg, Hedrich, Jensen, Le Merle and Rölkens (2022), two-thirds of fashion executives said they expect prices to increase in 2022, with an average price increase of 3% across all clothing and apparel.

Second-hand shopping apps are creating a resale renaissance that is changing what we buy and how we buy it (Price, 2019). Over the past decade, the emergence of peer-to-peer online fashion resale marketplaces has turned the buying and selling of used clothing into a much more traditional business (Bittner & Eisenberg, 2021). Dozens of companies have jumped into the reselling game directly or via partnerships with established companies, from big names like Macy's, Levi Strauss and Lululemon, all of which are in physical stores, to online or app-only sites, including thredUP and Shopify (Akman, 2021).

Peer-to-peer apps have already revolutionized the way we book places to stay, get rides, find dates, and now trade/buy/sell our clothes. According to its CEO Manish Chandra, from clothes swapping parties to online apps, providing a social platform for like-minded individuals is one of the draws of second-hand apps such as Poshmark. Launched ten years ago, with over 80 million users and counting, Poshmark was the first digital marketplace where people from the United States could buy and sell new or used clothing, shoes, and accessories through a smartphone app. According to the site, social engagement rather than online commerce drives 90 per cent of its sales. While the popularity of such peer-to-peer apps is undeniable as more come on the market, misuse and user protection issues have become important as those types of social commerce platforms are vulnerable to unethical and fraudulent user practices. Additional safety features and guarantees are expected to be continuously introduced.

As a pioneer in social commerce, Poshmark recently expanded its services to offer fashion brands direct access to sell on Poshmark via the Brand Closet programme. Thus, brands will have direct access to their consumer, and without the need to maintain an expensive storefront, they will be able to personalise the user experience. Companies that offer more traditional consignment services such as Fashionphile, TheRealReal, and threadUp provide consumers with their own expertise as independent evaluators, thus giving users a piece of mind authenticating fashion items appeal to certain consumer segments. Some of these companies focus on luxury segments of the second-hand market since reselling those items requires extra care and re-authentication to provide consumers with a piece of mind as items are higher priced.

While some companies scale up online via apps or online sales, others expand from online sales to physical stores. TheRealReal, for example, went from an internet consignment site to having 20 brick-and-mortar stores throughout the United States in 10 years. The second-hand retail industry is expanding as it prepares for growth. It has been noted that second-hand retail has grown 21 times faster than the traditional clothing retail market in the past three years alone, thanks to online shopping and mobile apps (Price, 2019), and growing revenue from this hunt has turned the savings into a profitable $28 billion industry that is expected to eclipse fast fashion by 2029 (Sicurella, 2021). Traditional thrift and gift shops (e.g. non-profit organisations such as Goodwill and The Salvation Army) currently account for most second-hand sales in the second-hand market, but independent stores and Depop stores are also set to grow significantly (Nguyen, 2021; ThredUp, 2021).

With their affinity for online resale, Gen Z elevates used clothing to a fashionable level. It was recently discovered that 48 per cent of Millennial customers and 46 per cent of Generation Z customers had used resale or consignment options while shopping (Coppola, 2021). It is estimated that the used clothing market will cover half of the youth in the overall clothing market over the next decade through online reselling, and when it does, every other demographic will catch up with those who already have (Hoffower, 2021). Innovative new business models, such as Thrift+, a digital thrift store, and The Nu Wardrobe, a peer-to-peer garment sharing software, are also emerging to close the gap (MacGilp, 2020). Nuuly Thrift, owned by Urban Outfitters, is amongst the latest entrants to the second-hand industry, recently launched as a smartphone application (Akman, 2021).

Technological innovations are going to continue fuelling the development of second-hand retailing. Peer-to-peer consumer apps are becoming more personalized and integrated with social media and increasingly with a social cause; business-to-business models are being designed to integrate more seamlessly within retailer's mainstream business; innovative AI applications for retail and fashion are being introduced to assist consumers when shopping virtually for second-hand clothing as body scanning and trying on software become more widely available.

Given that the second-hand clothing business is expected to see sales double from $36 billion to $77 billion by 2025 (ThredUp, 2021), the flourishing business raises concerns too. One question is whether second-hand is contributing to a sustainable or throwaway society. In the case of fast fashion, stores like Zara and H&M appeal to consumers' pockets with the production of cheap and disposable clothing, where the environment pays the price. Similarly, second-hand is attractive to consumers in times of inflation, and perhaps given its relatively lower cost, it results in unnecessary purchases. Another question to consider is whether companies are responsibly disposing of clothing. As fashion brands consider the environmental and social impact of the production of clothing, solutions and alternatives to mitigate these problems are taken into account in the production of new goods. However, in the case of second-hand fashion, it becomes questionable of the environmental impact of clothing no longer desirable by consumers, raising concern about the way consumers are disposing of their unwanted items. Further, a question that needs to be raised is whether companies can manage better second-hand retail, clothing that does not sell and whether second-hand retail leads to fraud or unethical behaviour amongst consumers, businesses, or both.

CONCLUSION

This chapter addresses the recent growth of second-hand fashion as a technology-enabled disruptor and provides an in-depth discussion of the nature of reselling technologies. The collaborative consumption movement, a popular emerging trend, encourages consumers to live in a more collective, sharing economy.

Buying second-hand clothing is a worldwide phenomenon. Though previously consisting of thrift shops, second-hand markets, and antique merchants, second-hand has evolved into a fundamental worldwide trend, allowing for resale, recovery, and recycling. Today's consumers also include Generation Z, who are growing up with a concern for the environment and posting opinions and facts on their social media feeds. As Generation Z ages, fashion brands must rethink how they deliver goods to this consumer market whose preference is to spend more money on sustainable products, and brands with green and social initiatives while considering the technology, such as mobile apps, for purchasing second-hand goods.

ACKNOWLEDGMENT

The authors contributed equally to this work.

REFERENCES

Akman, T. (2021). *Used clothing gets hot during the pandemic, driven by young people*. The Philadelphia Inquirer, LLC. Retrieved 19 March from https://www.inquirer.com/business/retail/thrifting-used-clothes-thredup-realreal-macys-nuuly-20210916.html

Amed, I., Balchandani, A., Berg, A., Hedrich, S., Jensen, J. E., Le Merle, L., & Rölkens, F. (2022). *The State of Fashion 2022*. McKinsey & Company. Retrieved 09 April from https://www.mckinsey.com/industries/retail/our-insights/state-of-fashion

App Ape. (2021). *Distribution of Depop monthly active users in the United States as of March 2021, by age group*. Statista. Retrieved 19 March from https://www.statista.com/statistics/1125124/depop-us-users-age/

Armstrong, C. M., Niinimäki, K., Kujala, S., Karell, E., & Lang, C. (2015). Sustainable product-service systems for clothing: Exploring consumer perceptions of consumption alternatives in Finland. *Journal of Cleaner Production*, *97*, 30–39. doi:10.1016/j.jclepro.2014.01.046

Assoune, A. (2020). *Environmental Benefits Of Buying Second Hand Clothing*. Panaprium. Retrieved 13 March from https://www.panaprium.com/blogs/i/environmental-benefits-of-buying-second-hand-clothing

Backs, S., Jahnke, H., Lüpke, L., Stücken, M., & Stummer, C. (2021). Traditional versus fast fashion supply chains in the apparel industry: An agent-based simulation approach. *Annals of Operations Research*, *305*(1), 487–512. doi:10.100710479-020-03703-8

Bare Fashion. (2019). *Cariuma carbon neutral shoes made from sugarcane and cork*. Bare Fashion. Retrieved 14 March from https://barefashion.co.uk/blogs/blog/cariuma-carbon-neutral-shoes-made-from-sugarcane-and-cork

Becker, J. (2018a). *The minimalist home: a room-by-room guide to a decluttered, refocused life*. WaterBrook.

Becker, J. (2018b). *Why We Buy More Than We Need*. Forbes. Retrieved 13 March from https://www.forbes.com/sites/joshuabecker/2018/11/27/why-we-buy-more-than-we-need/

Bell, A. (2022). *Second-hand clothing apps give young shoppers new style twist*. The Financial Times. Retrieved 11 March from https://www.ft.com/content/2a318727-8047-4dca-972e-dba9cfb4229e

Bittner, M., & Eisenberg, D. (2021). *How online marketplaces are making secondhand fashion a first choice*. McKinsey & Company. Retrieved 19 March from https://www.mckinsey.com/industries/technology-media-and-telecommunications/our-insights/how-online-marketplaces-are-making-secondhand-fashion-a-first-choice

Borg, D., Mont, O., & Schoonover, H. (2020). Consumer Acceptance and Value in Use-Oriented Product-Service Systems: Lessons from Swedish Consumer Goods Companies. *Sustainability*, *12*(19), 8079. Advance online publication. doi:10.3390u12198079

Borusiak, B., Szymkowiak, A., Horska, E., Raszka, N., & Żelichowska, E. (2020). Towards Building Sustainable Consumption: A Study of Second-Hand Buying Intentions. *Sustainability*, *12*(3), 875. Advance online publication. doi:10.3390u12030875

Bravo, L. (2020). *How To Break Up With Fast Fashion: A guilt-free guide to changing the way you shop – for good*. Headline. https://books.google.co.uk/books?id=6pypDwAAQBAJ

Cervellon, M.-C. (2013). Conspicuous Conservation: Using Semiotics to Understand Sustainable Luxury. *International Journal of Market Research*, *55*(5), 695–717. doi:10.2501/IJMR-2013-030

Cervellon, M. C., Carey, L., & Harms, T. (2012). Something old, something used. *International Journal of Retail & Distribution Management*, *40*(12), 956–974. doi:10.1108/09590551211274946

Chan, H.-L., Choi, T.-M., & Lok, J. C.-Y. (2015). Mass Market Second-Hand Clothing Retail Operations in Hong Kong: A Case Study. In T.-M. Choi & T. C. E. Cheng (Eds.), *Sustainable Fashion Supply Chain Management* (pp. 155–165)., doi:10.1007/978-3-319-12703-3_8

Chi, T., Ganak, J., Summers, L., Adesanya, O., McCoy, L., Liu, H., & Tai, Y. (2021). Understanding Perceived Value and Purchase Intention toward Eco-Friendly Athleisure Apparel: Insights from U.S. Millennials. *Sustainability*, *13*(14), 7946. Advance online publication. doi:10.3390u13147946

Choi, T.-M., & He, Y. (2019). Peer-to-peer collaborative consumption for fashion products in the sharing economy: Platform operations. *Transportation Research Part E, Logistics and Transportation Review*, *126*, 49–65. doi:10.1016/j.tre.2019.03.016

Cills, H. (2021). *The Complicated Reality of Thrift Store 'Gentrification'*. Jezebel. Retrieved 14 March from https://jezebel.com/the-complicated-reality-of-thrift-store-gentrification-1846113458

Clark, H. (2008). SLOW + FASHION—an Oxymoron—or a Promise for the Future …? *Fashion Theory*, *12*(4), 427–446. doi:10.2752/175174108X346922

Cooper, C. L., Woodward, S., Hiller, A., & Goworek, H. (2008). *Public understanding of sustainable clothing*. A report to the Department for Environment, Food and Rural Affairs.

Coppola, D. (2021). *Most popular sustainable retail models used by consumers in the United States as of December 2019, by generation*. Statista. Retrieved 19 March from https://www.statista.com/statistics/1100335/sustainable-retail-models/

Cruz, I., Ganga, R., & Wahlen, S. (2018). Contemporary collaborative consumption: An introduction. In I. Cruz, R. Ganga, & S. Wahlen (Eds.), *Contemporary Collaborative Consumption: Trust and Reciprocity Revisited* (pp. 1–15). Springer Fachmedien Wiesbaden. doi:10.1007/978-3-658-21346-6_1

D'Adamo, I., Lupi, G., Morone, P., & Settembre-Blundo, D. (2022). Towards the circular economy in the fashion industry: The second-hand market as a best practice of sustainable responsibility for businesses and consumers. *Environmental Science and Pollution Research International*. Advance online publication. doi:10.100711356-022-19255-2 PMID:35171425

D'Ambrogio, E. (2014). *Workers' conditions in the textile and clothing sector*. European Parliament. Retrieved 10 March from https://www.europarl.europa.eu/EPRS/140841REV1-Workers-conditions-in-the-textile-and-clothing-sector-just-an-Asian-affair-FINAL.pdf

Dahlbo, H., Aalto, K., Eskelinen, H., & Salmenperä, H. (2017). Increasing textile circulation—Consequences and requirements. *Sustainable Production and Consumption, 9*, 44-57.

Depop; T., & Bain & Company. (2020). *Report On Gen Z*. Depop x Bain & Company. Retrieved 19 March from https://depopxbainreport.depop.com/report/The-Depop-X-Bain-Company-Report-How-Gen-Zs-Awareness-And-Fluidity-Are-Transforming-Business-As-Usual.pdf

Doniger, A. (2021). *Shoppers are buying from resale retailers more than ever. Here's why*. CNBC. Retrieved 19 March from https://www.cnet.com/home/smart-home/features/rise-of-secondhand-retail-poshmark-thredup-letgo-mercari-ebay-thrift-clothing-selling-apps/

Dreyer, B., Lüdeke-Freund, F., Hamann, R., & Faccer, K. (2017). Upsides and downsides of the sharing economy: Collaborative consumption business models' stakeholder value impacts and their relationship to context. *Technological Forecasting and Social Change*, *125*, 87–104. doi:10.1016/j.techfore.2017.03.036

Dubois, B., & Duquesne, P. (1993). The Market for Luxury Goods: Income versus Culture. *European Journal of Marketing*, *27*(1), 35–44. doi:10.1108/03090569310024530

Ertz, M. (2020). Collaborative consumption, a buzzword that has gone conceptual: Three shades of the sharing economy. *Oikonomics*, *14*(14), 1–14. doi:10.7238/o.n14.2011

Ertz, M., Deschênes, J., & Sarigöllü, E. (2021). From User to Provider: Switching Over in the Collaborative Economy. *Sustainability*, *13*(10), 5662. Advance online publication. doi:10.3390u13105662

Ertz, M., Durif, F., & Arcand, M. (2016). Collaborative consumption: Conceptual snapshot at a buzzword. *Journal of Entrepreneurship Education*, *19*(2), 1–23.

Farrant, L., Olsen, S. I., & Wangel, A. (2010). Environmental benefits from reusing clothes. *The International Journal of Life Cycle Assessment*, *15*(7), 726–736. doi:10.100711367-010-0197-y

Ferraro, C., Sands, S., & Brace-Govan, J. (2016). The role of fashionability in second-hand shopping motivations. *Journal of Retailing and Consumer Services*, *32*, 262–268. doi:10.1016/j.jretconser.2016.07.006

Financial Times. (2021). *Etsy/Depop: hanging on to Gen Z by a thread.* Financial Times. Retrieved 18 February from https://www.ft.com/content/c32f3536-ae6e-4cba-9368-77794723c097

Fletcher, K. (2012). Durability, Fashion, Sustainability: The Processes and Practices of Use. *Fashion Practice*, *4*(2), 221–238. doi:10.2752/175693812X13403765252389

Fortuna, L. M., & Diyamandoglu, V. (2017). Optimization of greenhouse gas emissions in second-hand consumer product recovery through reuse platforms. *Waste Management, 66*, 178-189.

Fuxman, L., Mohr, I., Mahmoud, A. B., & Grigoriou, N. (2022). The new 3Ps of sustainability marketing: The case of fashion. *Sustainable Production and Consumption*, *31*, 384–396. doi:10.1016/j.spc.2022.03.004

Gazzola, P., Pavione, E., Pezzetti, R., & Grechi, D. (2020). Trends in the Fashion Industry. The Perception of Sustainability and Circular Economy: A Gender/Generation Quantitative Approach. *Sustainability*, *12*(7), 2809. Advance online publication. doi:10.3390u12072809

Gerval, O. (2010). *Fashion: Concept to Catwalk.* Firefly Books. https://books.google.co.uk/books?id=P7eaRAAACAAJ

Guimarães, P. P. C. (2021). Unfolding authenticity within retail gentrification in Mouraria, Lisbon. *Journal of Tourism and Cultural Change*, 1–20. doi:10.1080/14766825.2021.1876079

Guiot, D., & Roux, D. (2010). A Second-hand Shoppers' Motivation Scale: Antecedents, Consequences, and Implications for Retailers. *Journal of Retailing*, *86*(4), 355–371. doi:10.1016/j.jretai.2010.08.002

Guo, S., Choi, T. M., & Zhang, J. (2021). Second-Hand-Clothing Imports in Least-Developed-Countries: The Collapse of Local Clothing Manufacturing and Remedial Measures. *IEEE Transactions on Engineering Management*, 1–20. doi:10.1109/TEM.2021.3061528

Hamari, J., Sjöklint, M., & Ukkonen, A. (2016). The sharing economy: Why people participate in collaborative consumption. *Journal of the Association for Information Science and Technology, 67*(9), 2047-2059. doi:10.1002/asi.23552

Hansen, K. T., & Le Zotte, J. (2019). Changing Secondhand Economies. *Business History, 61*(1), 1–16. doi:10.1080/00076791.2018.1543041

Hennigs, N., Wiedmann, K.-P., Klarmann, C., Strehlau, S., Godey, B., Pederzoli, D., Neulinger, A., Dave, K., Aiello, G., Donvito, R., Taro, K., Táborecká-Petrovičová, J., Santos, C. R., Jung, J., & Oh, H. (2012). What is the Value of Luxury? A Cross-Cultural Consumer Perspective. *Psychology & Marketing, 29*(12), 1018-1034. doi:10.1002/mar.20583

Hirschlag, A. (2019). *Can Secondhand Shopping Dent Fast Fashion's Environmental Damage?* Scientific American. Retrieved 14 March from https://www.scientificamerican.com/article/can-secondhand-shopping-dent-fast-fashions-environmental-damage/

Hoffower, H. (2021). *Gen Z's shopping habits are shaping the future of fashion: online thrifting*. Business Insider. Retrieved 19 March from https://www.businessinsider.com/gen-z-driving-online-resale-secondhand-clothes-thrifting-poshmark-depop-2021-4

Hole, G., & Hole, A. S. (2020). Improving recycling of textiles based on lessons from policies for other recyclable materials: A minireview. *Sustainable Production and Consumption, 23*, 42-51.

Hur, E. (2020). Rebirth fashion: Secondhand clothing consumption values and perceived risks. *Journal of Cleaner Production, 273*, 122951. doi:10.1016/j.jclepro.2020.122951

Juge, E., Pomiès, A., & Collin-Lachaud, I. (2021). Digital platforms and speed-based competition: The case of secondhand clothing. *Recherche et Applications en Marketing*. Advance online publication. doi:10.1177/20515707211028551

Klein, N. (2019). *Plan B pour la planète: Le New Deal vert*. Éditions Actes Sud.

Kumar, A., Prakash, G., & Kumar, G. (2021). Does environmentally responsible purchase intention matter for consumers? A predictive sustainable model developed through an empirical study. *Journal of Retailing and Consumer Services, 58*, 102270. doi:10.1016/j.jretconser.2020.102270

Kumar, S., & Yadav, R. (2021). The impact of shopping motivation on sustainable consumption: A study in the context of green apparel. *Journal of Cleaner Production, 295*, 126239. doi:10.1016/j.jclepro.2021.126239

Lang, C., & Zhang, R. (2019). Second-hand clothing acquisition: The motivations and barriers to clothing swaps for Chinese consumers. *Sustainable Production and Consumption, 18*, 156-164.

Latour, B. (2015). *Face à Gaïa: huit conférences sur le nouveau régime climatique*. Empêcheurs de penser rond.

Lee, S. (2011). Consumers' Value, Environmental Consciousness, and Willingness to Pay more toward Green-Apparel Products. *Journal of Global Fashion Marketing, 2*(3), 161–169. doi:10.1080/20932685.2011.10593094

Lemire, B. (2012). The Secondhand Clothing Trade in Europe and Beyond: Stages of Development and Enterprise in a Changing Material World, c. 1600–1850. *Textile (Oxford), 10*(2), 144–163. doi:10.2752/175183512X13315695424392

Loanzon, R. (2021). *How to Sell Clothes Online Like a Pro, from Taking Photos to Shipping*. Brightly. Retrieved 18 March from https://brightly.eco/how-to-sell-your-used-clothing-on-thrifting-apps/

Maas, M. (2020). *A Look Into the Gentrification of Thrifting*. Wit and Delight. Retrieved 14 March from https://witanddelight.com/2020/12/a-look-into-the-gentrification-of-thrifting/

MacGilp, R. (2020). *The Future of Second-Hand Shopping After Coronavirus*. Eco Warrior Princess. Retrieved 19 March from https://ecowarriorprincess.net/2020/05/future-second-hand-shopping-after-coronavirus-pandemic/

Machado, M. A. D., Almeida, S. O., Bollick, L. C., & Bragagnolo, G. (2019). Second-hand fashion market: Consumer role in circular economy. *Journal of Fashion Marketing and Management, 23*(3), 382–395. doi:10.1108/JFMM-07-2018-0099

Mahmoud, A. B., Ball, J., Rubin, D., Fuxman, L., Mohr, I., Hack-Polay, D., Grigoriou, N., & Wakibi, A. (2021). Pandemic pains to Instagram gains! COVID-19 perceptions effects on behaviours towards fashion brands on Instagram in Sub-Saharan Africa: Tech-native vs non-native generations. *Journal of Marketing Communications*, 1–25. doi:10.1080/13527266.2021.1971282

Mahmoud, A. B., Hack-Polay, D., Grigoriou, N., Mohr, I., & Fuxman, L. (2021). A generational investigation and sentiment and emotion analyses of female fashion brand users on Instagram in Sub-Saharan Africa. *Journal of Brand Management, 28*(5), 526–544. doi:10.105741262-021-00244-8

McNeill, L., & Moore, R. (2015). Sustainable fashion consumption and the fast fashion conundrum: fashionable consumers and attitudes to sustainability in clothing choice. *International Journal of Consumer Studies, 39*(3), 212-222. doi:10.1111/ijcs.12169

Medalla, M. E., Yamagishi, K., Tiu, A. M., Tanaid, R. A., Abellana, D. P. M., Caballes, S. A., Jabilles, E. M., Himang, C., Bongo, M., & Ocampo, L. (2020). Modeling the hierarchical structure of second-hand clothing buying behavior antecedents of millennials. *Journal of Modelling in Management, 15*(4), 1679–1708. doi:10.1108/JM2-08-2019-0207

Möhlmann, M. (2015). Collaborative consumption: determinants of satisfaction and the likelihood of using a sharing economy option again. *Journal of Consumer Behaviour, 14*(3), 193-207. doi:10.1002/cb.1512

Mohr, I., Fuxman, L., & Mahmoud, A. B. (2021). A triple-trickle theory for sustainable fashion adoption: The rise of a luxury trend. *Journal of Fashion Marketing and Management*. Advance online publication. doi:10.1108/JFMM-03-2021-0060

Monroe, R. (2021). *Ultra-fast fashion is eating the world*. The Atlantic. Retrieved 10 March from https://www.theatlantic.com/magazine/archive/2021/03/ultra-fast-fashion-is-eating-the-world/617794/

Neate, R. (2021). *Etsy buys secondhand clothing app Depop to tap into gen Z*. The Guardian. Retrieved 19 March from https://www.theguardian.com/fashion/2021/jun/02/etsy-buys-second-hand-clothing-app-depop-to-tap-into-gen-z

Nguyen, T. (2021). *How thrifting became problematic Thrift shopping is popular online, but some are worried about the effects of overconsumption.* Vox. Retrieved 13 March from https://www.vox.com/the-goods/22396051/thrift-store-hauls-ethics-depop

Norum, P., & Norton, M. (2017). Factors affecting consumer acquisition of secondhand clothing in the USA. *Journal of Fashion Marketing and Management, 21*(2), 206–218. doi:10.1108/JFMM-10-2016-0090

Nwaorgu, B. (2018). What is Collaborative Consumption? Platforms and Participation of People in Collaborative Consumption–Impact of the New Technologies. *International Journal of Innovation, Management and Technology, 9*(6), 240–245. doi:10.18178/ijimt.2018.9.6.819

Oakes, C. (2021). *The 6 Best Online Thrift Stores of 2021.* Remake. Retrieved 19 March from https://remake.world/stories/style/the-6-best-online-thrift-stores/

Odier, L. (2021). Is this a new era for old goods? How the second-hand market can promote a circular economy. *The Financial Times.*

Orminski, J., Tandoc, E. C., Jr., & Detenber, B. H. (2021). #sustainablefashion – A Conceptual Framework for Sustainable Fashion Discourse on Twitter. *Environmental Communication, 15*(1), 115-132. doi:10.1080/17524032.2020.1802321

Özbölük, T. (2021). The pursuit of uniqueness and craving for freedom: The meaning of luxury in the age of access. *Leisure Studies, 40*(2), 227–242. doi:10.1080/02614367.2020.1831045

Paço, A., Leal Filho, W., Ávila, L. V., & Dennis, K. (2020). Fostering sustainable consumer behavior regarding clothing: Assessing trends on purchases, recycling and disposal. *Textile Research Journal, 91*(3-4), 373–384. doi:10.1177/0040517520944524

Park, H., & Armstrong, C. (2020). *Secondhand Clothing Sales Are Booming–and May Help Solve the Sustainability Crisis in the Fashion Industry.* The Conversation Newsletter.

Pasquali, M. (2021a). *Monthly active users (MAU) of the Depop app in the United Kingdom (UK) from January 2018 to October 2021.* Statista. Retrieved 19 March from https://www.statista.com/statistics/1122928/depop-monthly-active-users-uk/

Pasquali, M. (2021b). *Monthly downloads of the Depop app in the United Kingdom (UK) from January 2018 to October 2021(in 1,000s).* Statista. Retrieved 19 March from https://www.statista.com/statistics/1119063/depop-monthly-downloads-uk/

Peña-Vinces, J., Solakis, K., & Guillen, J. (2020). Environmental knowledge, the collaborative economy and responsible consumption in the context of second-hand perinatal and infant clothes in Spain. *Resources, Conservation and Recycling, 159*, 104840. doi:10.1016/j.resconrec.2020.104840

Piketty, T. (2013). *Le capital au XXIe siècle.* Média Diffusion.

Potavanich, T. (2015). *The Concept of Luxury from a Consumer Culture Perspective.* Manchester Business School. https://www.research.manchester.ac.uk/portal/files/54586068/FULL_TEXT.PDF

Price, M. (2019). *Fashion disruptors: Welcome to the era of secondhand retail apps*. CNET. Retrieved 19 March from https://www.cnet.com/home/smart-home/features/rise-of-secondhand-retail-poshmark-thredup-letgo-mercari-ebay-thrift-clothing-selling-apps/

Pucker, K. P. (2022). *The Myth of Sustainable Fashion*. Harvard Business Review. Retrieved 2022 from https://hbr.org/2022/01/the-myth-of-sustainable-fashion

Quach, G. (2021). *Reselling, repairing and 'swishing': the rise of sustainable fashion apps*. Guardian. Retrieved 18 March from https://www.theguardian.com/fashion/2021/jan/29/reselling-repairing-and-swishing-the-rise-of-sustainable-fashion-apps

Reid, C. (2021). *The Gentrification of Thrifting: A Guide*. The Bengal. Retrieved 14 March from http://isubengal.com/the-gentrification-of-thrifting-a-guide/

Reis, C. L. d. S. (2020). *Second-hand fashion: the effect of nostalgia on purchase intentions and shopping behaviour*. Academic Press.

Rens. (2022). *Made For You & Our Planet*. Rens US LLC. Retrieved 14 March from https://rensoriginal.co.uk/

Roux, D. (2006). *Am I what I wear? An exploratory study of symbolic meanings associated with secondhand clothing*. ACR North American Advances.

Roy, V., Silvestre, B. S., & Singh, S. (2020). Reactive and proactive pathways to sustainable apparel supply chains: Manufacturer's perspective on stakeholder salience and organizational learning toward responsible management. *International Journal of Production Economics*, *227*, 107672. doi:10.1016/j.ijpe.2020.107672

Sabanoglu, T. (2021). *Leading motivations for secondhand item purchases of Depop users in the United States, the United Kingdom, and Australia in 2020* [Graph]. Statista. Retrieved 19 March from https://www.statista.com/statistics/1276662/depop-users-secondhand-purchase-reasons/

Sandin, G., & Peters, G. M. (2018). Environmental impact of textile reuse and recycling – A review. *Journal of Cleaner Production*, *184*, 353–365. doi:10.1016/j.jclepro.2018.02.266

Schiel, F. (2015). *The Phenomenon of the Sharing Economy in Germany: Consumer Motivations for Participating in Collaborative Consumption Schemes*. Academic Press.

Schor, J. B., & Fitzmaurice, C. J. (2015). Collaborating and connecting: the emergence of the sharing economy. In Handbook of Research on Sustainable Consumption (pp. 410-425). doi:10.4337/9781783471270.00039

Schwartz, S. H. (2012). An Overview of the Schwartz Theory of Basic Values. *Online Readings in Psychology and Culture*, *2*(1), 2307–0919. doi:10.9707/2307-0919.1116

Sergison, D. (2021). *Lululemon to Launch Mushroom-Based Yoga Accessories*. The Business of Fashion. Retrieved 14 March from https://www.businessoffashion.com/news/sustainability/lululemon-to-launch-mushroom-based-yoga-accessories/

Sicurella, S. (2021). *When Second Hand Becomes Vintage: Gen Z Has Made Thrifting A Big Business*. NPR. Retrieved 19 March from https://www.npr.org/1006207991

Sihvonen, J., & Turunen, L. L. M. (2016). As good as new – valuing fashion brands in the online second-hand markets. *Journal of Product and Brand Management*, *25*(3), 285–295. doi:10.1108/JPBM-06-2015-0894

Smith, P. (2022). *Share of secondhand clothing in people's closets in 2020 and 2023*. Statista. Retrieved 10 March from https://www.statista.com/statistics/1235059/share-of-secondhand-clothing-in-peoples-closets-worldwide/

Sohn, J., Nielsen, K. S., Birkved, M., Joanes, T., & Gwozdz, W. (2021). The environmental impacts of clothing: Evidence from United States and three European countries. *Sustainable Production and Consumption, 27*, 2153-2164.

Solakis, K., Katsoni, V., Mahmoud, A. B., & Grigoriou, N. (2022). Factors affecting value co-creation through artificial intelligence in tourism—A general literature review. *Journal of Tourism Futures*. 1-15. doi:1108/JTF-06-2021-0157

Sontag, M. S., & Lee, J. (2004). Proximity of Clothing to Self Scale. *Clothing & Textiles Research Journal*, *22*(4), 161–177. doi:10.1177/0887302X0402200402

Statista. (2022). *Value of the sharing economy worldwide in 2014 and 2025 (in billion U.S. dollars)*. Statista. Retrieved 17 March from https://www.statista.com/statistics/830986/value-of-the-global-sharing-economy/

Streeter, A. (2014). *South-East Asia briefing: A sustainable garment industry in Cambodia?* Reuters Events. Retrieved 10 March from https://www.reutersevents.com/sustainability/supply-chains/south-east-asia-briefing-sustainable-garment-industry-cambodia

Taylor-Singh, H. (2021). *The rise of online thrifting is raising ethical questions*. NOW Magazine.

Templier, M., & Paré, G. (2015). A framework for guiding and evaluating literature reviews. *Communications of the Association for Information Systems*, *37*(1), 6.

TFL. (2021). *Secondhand fashion market is expected to be more than double the size of fast fashion by 2030*. Retrieved 11 March from https://www.thefashionlaw.com/already-displacing-fast-fashion-secondhand-fashion-to-grow-into-a-77-billion-market-by-2026/

ThredUp. (2021). *2021 Resale Report*. ThredUp. Retrieved 18 February from https://www.thredup.com/resale/#size-and-impact

Todeschini, B. V., Cortimiglia, M. N., Callegaro-de-Menezes, D., & Ghezzi, A. (2017). Innovative and sustainable business models in the fashion industry: Entrepreneurial drivers, opportunities, and challenges. *Business Horizons*, *60*(6), 759–770. doi:10.1016/j.bushor.2017.07.003

Turunen, L. L. M., & Pöyry, E. (2019). Shopping with the resale value in mind: A study on second-hand luxury consumers. *International Journal of Consumer Studies, 43*(6), 549-556. doi:10.1111/ijcs.12539

Valor, C., Ronda, L., & Abril, C. (2022). Understanding the expansion of circular markets: Building relational legitimacy to overcome the stigma of second-hand clothing. *Sustainable Production and Consumption, 30*, 77-88.

Wang, B., Fu, Y., & Li, Y. (2022). Young consumers' motivations and barriers to the purchase of second-hand clothes: An empirical study of China. *Waste Management, 143*, 157-167.

Winakor, G. (1969). The process of clothing consumption. *Journal of Home Economics*, *68*(1), 629–634.

Xiang, X. (2021). Factors That Influence Consumers' Behaviors in Fashion Market. *Open Journal of Business and Management, 9*(6), 2772-2779. doi:10.4236/ojbm.2021.96154

Young Lee, J., Halter, H., Johnson, K. K. P., & Ju, H. (2013). Investigating fashion disposition with young consumers. *Young Consumers*, *14*(1), 67–78. doi:10.1108/17473611311305494

Yuan, Q., & Shen, B. (2019). Renting fashion with strategic customers in the sharing economy. *International Journal of Production Economics*, *218*, 185–195. doi:10.1016/j.ijpe.2019.04.034

Chapter 16
From Utilitarian to Hedonic Consumer Behavior:
An Evaluation for the Socio-Digital Age

Mikail Kar
Bursa Uludag University, Turkey

ABSTRACT

How consumers' consumption activities are shaped and what are the motives that push consumers to some behaviors are very important topics in the economics literature. It is widely accepted that consumption is shaped by utilitarian consumption and hedonic consumption motives. It has been observed that the relative utilitarian dimension of consumer activities and consumer behavior has gradually decreased, and the hedonic dimension has gradually increased in the historical process. With the 21st century, it is evaluated that hedonic motives dominate consumption behaviors. This chapter discusses the evolution of consumer behavior from utilitarian consumption to hedonic consumption by considering utilitarian consumption and hedonic consumption approaches and evaluates the latest point of consumer behavior in the socio-digital age that represents the 21st century.

INTRODUCTION

Consumption is defined as the possession, use, or destruction of a good or service in order to satisfy a certain need, and the person who performs this consumption activity is defined as a consumer. The behaviors of consumers at the point of consumption activities are also considered in the literature as consumer behaviors. Since the answer to the question of how consumers' consumption activities are shaped is important for both consumers, companies, and authorities, it has been extensively discussed in the literature. The most important of the main focus points is what is the reason for the purchasing behavior of consumers. At this point, it is argued that there are a number of motives that encourage consumers to buy and consume goods and services, that is, cause consumer behavior to occur. These motives are divided into two as utilitarian motives and hedonic motives. Consumption with utilitarian motives is called utilitarian consumption, consumption with hedonic motives is called hedonic consumption. In

DOI: 10.4018/978-1-6684-4168-8.ch016

the utilitarian consumption approach, consuming for consumers is an activity that is done for necessity or need. Hedonic consumption, on the other hand, focuses on the emotional dimension of consumption and is based on the pleasure to be felt from consumption. In other words, consumers focus on functional, instrumental, and practical benefits in utilitarian consumption in terms of the benefits they obtain after consumption, and on aesthetic, taste, experience, and entertainment benefits in hedonic consumption.

In the ever-changing world, people have undergone great changes and transformations over time, depending on the conditions of each period, and they have changed their activities, habits, and behaviors. Consumption activities and consumer behaviors, which are in the field of interest of many different disciplines, especially economics, sociology, and psychology, are the most important factors that affect and are affected in expressing the change and transformation of societies. In the historical process, while utilitarian approaches were sufficient to explain consumer behavior at the beginning, it was observed that the traditional approach was insufficient as consumers started to consume emotionally in order to meet their psychological, social, and cultural needs over time. At this point, consumption activities and consumer behaviors started to take shape with the hedonic consumption motive. The motive of consumer behavior has evolved over time from utilitarian consumption to hedonic consumption, and after the second half of the 20th century, especially with the 21st century, the utilitarian dimension of the consumption phenomenon has become insignificant compared to the hedonic dimension.

The aim of this study is to discuss the evolution of consumer behavior from utilitarian consumption to hedonic consumption by considering utilitarian and hedonic consumption approaches and to evaluate the final point where consumer behavior comes in the current socio-digital age. The study makes an important contribution to the economics literature in general and to consumer behavior research in particular by addressing different approaches in consumption behaviors and their evolution in the process and making a special evaluation for the socio-digital age. The study is structured in eight sections in line with the above-mentioned aim. After this general introduction, which is the first section, in the second section, consumption, consumer, and consumer behaviors are expressed with the basic framework. In the third section, utilitarian consumption and in the fourth section, hedonic consumption is explained in detail. In the fifth section, utilitarian consumption and hedonic consumption are compared with the literature review. In the sixth section, the historical transformation in the consumption approach is analyzed. In the seventh section, an evaluation has been made for the consumption understanding of the current socio-digital age. In the eighth section, which is the conclusion part, a general summary and evaluation have been made.

CONSUMPTION, CONSUMER AND CONSUMER BEHAVIORS

Consumption is done for the satisfaction of a need, which is the state of feeling that people are deprived of some basic satisfaction. Different levels of definitions have been made regarding the nature of consumption in social sciences. At this point, in terms of economic theory, consumption can be expressed as the sum of goods and services produced to meet or satisfy a need. Considered as a process, consumption is the process of seeking, purchasing, using, or destroying a good or service to satisfy certain needs. The most important element in the definition of consumption is the satisfaction of the "need". Where the definition and scope of needs have changed, so has the definition of consumption. A consumer is a person who has a need to be satisfied, a resource to spend, and a willingness to spend. According to another definition, it is a person who buys and uses goods and services for end-use purposes.

Consumer behavior; is the process of selecting, using, and evaluating goods and services that individuals or households will use to satisfy their needs. In other words, consumer behavior is a person's decisions and related activities in purchasing and using economic goods and services. Consumer behavior includes what, why, when, and where consumers buy, and how the purchased product is used in the process starting from the feeling of need and ending with the experience gained after consumption.

In order to predict and satisfy the needs of consumers in the most accurate way, it is necessary to analyze consumer behavior in detail and accurately. Kotler et al., (2005) classified the characteristics affecting the consumption behavior of consumers under four main headings as cultural, social, personal and psychological factors. As shown in Table 1, the factors affecting consumer decisions are summarized under subheadings. At this point, many features of consumer behavior can be mentioned. It has features such as being a dynamic process, consisting of various activities, being complex and different in terms of timing, carrying different roles, and being affected by environmental factors. However, the primary feature of consumer behavior is that it is a behavior that is motivated to achieve a goal. They are the motives that lead a person to buy a good or service. According to many studies, there are two main motives that affect consumer behavior: utilitarian and hedonic. Consumption with utilitarian motives is called utilitarian consumption, and consumption with hedonic motives is called hedonic consumption (Hirschman & Holbrook, 1982; Solomon, 2006; Arnold & Reynolds, 2003; Babin et al., 1994; Batra & Ahtola, 1990).

Table 1. Characteristics affecting consumer behavior

Cultural Factors	Social Factors	Personal Factors	Psychological Factors
Culture	Membership groups	Age and life-cycle stage	Motivation
Subculture	Family	Occupation	Perception
Social class	Social roles and status	Economic situation	Learning
		Lifestyle	Beliefs and attitudes
		Personality	

Source: Kotler et al., (2005)

UTILITARIAN CONSUMPTION

The concept of utility can be defined in its simplest form as goods, services, and ideas satisfying the concrete needs of people. The idea of utilitarianism is basically the idea that the value of an object or an activity can be determined by its utility. Utilitarianism is a theory that advises people that they should aim for benefit when determining their actions and argues that if an action is taken, it should produce greater benefit than other alternative actions for those who will be affected by the action (West, 2004; Batra & Ahtola, 1990; Lunardo & Mbengue, 2009).

In the literature, utilitarian consumption is considered as a form of consumption in which goods and services are evaluated with their functional characteristics, and the act of consumption is carried out for rational reasons and to meet non-emotional needs. Therefore, the main purpose of the consumer in utilitarian consumption is to evaluate the functional properties of the goods consumed and to meet the real needs in the most appropriate way. Utilitarian consumption refers to a rational and logical information processing and decision-making process. In classical economic theory, the individual is described as "Homo Economicus" and it is thought that human beings should act rationally and pragmatically by nature. In this respect, utilitarian consumption is consistent with classical economic theory (Batra & Ahtola, 1990; Lunardo & Mbengue, 2009; Babin et al., 1994).

When the personalities of consumers and the characteristics of goods and services are evaluated, utilitarian motives are divided into two general utilitarian motives and situational utilitarian motives. General utilitarian motives mean that consumers make utilitarian decisions that are only rational and tailored to their needs, under the influence of their personal characteristics. Situational utilitarian motives, on the other hand, include consumer decisions that vary depending on the good or service and exhibit utilitarian behavior according to the nature of the product or service in question and the purchase situation (Buhrman, 2002; Arnold & Reynolds, 2003; Spangenberg et al., 1997; Hirschman & Holbrook, 1982; Okada, 2005).

According to Babin et al. (1994), utilitarian consumption behavior is driven by a utilitarian purchase value integrated with the search for the best option in terms of price, quality, and time. In this case, the act of consumption depends on the utility value of the consumer, whether the purchased goods or services meet the requirements. In the utilitarian consumption theory, consuming for consumers is an activity done out of necessity or need. For a consumer of this nature, a need arises and the consumer buys the most suitable goods or services for his/her budget by comparing them. The questions "What are the characteristics of the good or service, which needs of the consumer are met with which function in the product, and therefore what benefits do they offer to the consumer?" are the questions whose answers are sought during utilitarian consumption. In the studies of Babin et al. (1994), the utilitarian factors in the evaluation of the goods and services consumed by the consumers are listed as follows; useful-useless, practical-not practical, necessary-unnecessary, functional-not functional, logical-irrational, helpful-not helpful, effective-not effective, impressive-not impressive, useful-harmful, useful-not useful, efficient-unproductive, problem solver - not a problem solver (Lunardo & Mbengue, 2009; Buhrman, 2002; Arnold & Reynolds, 2003; Spangenberg et al., 1997; Okada, 2005).

Utilitarian consumption can be summarized as consuming to achieve a goal. Therefore, utilitarian consumption motivations were discussed within the scope of answers to the question "why are utilitarian attitudes exhibited when a need arises?". At this point, four basic factors are put forward: monetary savings, convenience, success, and efficiency. First of all, the monetary savings obtained in the consumption process are evaluated as a value obtained for utilitarian consumers. Therefore, an increase in utilitarian value occurs when a consumer can find discounted goods or discover that the prices are lower than those in competing stores. Secondly, in utilitarian consumption, the ease of access, ease of search, ease of possession, and ease of operation of a good are very important for the consumer. In utilitarian consumption, this type of convenience saves the effort spent on consumption and increases the utilitarian value. Thirdly, the successful conclusion of the consumption activity ensures the achievement of utilitarian consumption value. Oil, the act of consumption can be perceived as a duty for the utilitarian consumer. If the task is completed effortlessly, success is achieved and the utilitarian value increases accordingly. Fourth, efficiency is an important motivator. The concept of efficiency can be defined as the ratio between the goods, services, etc. obtained and the work spent to obtain it. In utilitarian consumption, it is important for the consumer to save time and resources. The fact that a good to be purchased results in the lowest possible cost and the highest benefit that can be obtained is a factor that increases the utilitarian value (Batra & Ahtola, 1990; Lunardo & Mbengue, 2009; Babin et al., 1994; Buhrman, 2002; Arnold & Reynolds, 2003; Spangenberg et al., 1997; Hirschman & Holbrook, 1982; Okada, 2005).

HEDONIC CONSUMPTION

Hedonic, as a philosophical term, is the feeling of emotional or spiritual joy from something, and in general, it is something that pleases, entertains, and arouses a feeling of contentment in people. Hedonism, on the other hand, is the doctrine advocating behavior that is motivated by the pursuit of pleasure, devotion to sensory pleasures, or psychological desire to seek pleasure and avoid pain. Hedonism asserts that the supreme good is a pleasure as the main purpose of life. According to hedonism, bringing pleasure to the highest level is a goal that all individuals want to achieve. According to this teaching, what gives pleasure is good, what hurts is bad. At this point, it is argued that an important motivation that encourages consumers to consume is hedonic emotions, which are examined in the philosophy of hedonism (Hirschman & Holbrook, 1982; Okado, 2005; Jordan, 2000).

Hedonic consumption can be expressed as the type of consumption realized to provide hedonic satisfaction or to obtain hedonic value. According to Hirschman and Holbrook (1982), hedonic consumption is a type of consumption that appeals to many senses and includes emotions and fantasy. According to Spangenberg et al. (1997), hedonic consumption is a form of consumption that deals with the emotional dimension of consumption and focuses on completing and sustaining emotional pleasure. According to Okado (2005), hedonic consumption is a form of consumption based on the image, fantasy, and emotional stimulation that consumers perceive from the goods. Campbell (1987) mentions that pleasure, motivations, and individuality are very important in hedonistic consumption. In its most general form, hedonic consumption is defined as the feeling, imagination, emotional experiences of the consumer with the goods and consists of multi-sensory, emotional, cognitive, and social dimensions.

When attention is paid to the source of the idea of hedonic consumption, it is noticed that the idea of the limitation and meaninglessness of life is at the forefront. This idea, which can be summarized as "Life is what is lived at the moment and there is no more", brought along the habit of constantly owning and consuming something. Thus, consumption began to be seen as a steady flow of fantasies, emotions, and entertainment. According to the hedonic view of consumption, goods are not defined as objective assets but rather as subjective symbols. What the item represents is more important than what it is, and the focus is not on reality but on the image it carries and creates. Holbrook (1996) emphasized that the aesthetic, immaterial, and subjective dimensions of consumption are related to hedonic consumption, based on the idea that people buy goods not only for their functions but also for the meanings they express.

Although there are many studies on the causes of hedonic consumption, according to one of the most comprehensive studies by Arnold and Reynolds (2003), these reasons are grouped under six main headings: living adventurously (consumption for adventure), relaxing (consumption for cheerfulness), establishing social relationships (consumption for socialization), making others happy (consumption for others), getting ideas (consumption for ideas) and seizing opportunities (consumption for value). Consumption for others, consumption for value, and consumption for ideas are mostly due to motivations for goods. In addition, consumption for socialization, consumption for adventurous, and consumption for cheerfulness are consumption with non-goods motivations. People may not consume for the same reasons of consumption all the time. While the same person sometimes consumes to cheer up or socialize, sometimes consumes for others. In other words, the causes of hedonic consumption can be observed separately in consumption, or several reasons at different levels can occur together (Arnold & Reynolds, 2003).

Adjectives used for goods or services consumed in hedonic consumption can be expressed as follows; exciting-unexciting, delicious-non-tasteful, sensory-non-sensory, fun-not fun, pleasant-unpleasant, funny-non-funny, exciting-non-exciting, happy-unhappy, enjoyable-unpleasurable, cheerful-cheeky, and entertaining-boring (Babin et al., 1994). Hirschman and Holbrook (1982) expressed the emotions that arise as a result of hedonic consumption experience as emotional pleasure, aesthetic pleasure, emotional experiences, pleasure, and entertainment. Jordan (2000) states that pleasure can be experienced in four different ways over goods. These are physio-pleasures arising from the senses, ideo-pleasures arising from interpersonal and group relations, psycho-pleasures arising from emotional and cognitive reactions during the use of goods, and ideo-pleasures arising from the socio meaning of goods and personal values.

Hirschman and Holbrook (1982) evaluated the consumption made with the hedonistic approach in four dimensions. First, emotional desires prevail over utilitarian motives in choosing goods. Second, consumers fill a good with subjective meaning in addition to its tangible qualities. This process is supported by the delivery of advertising content. Third, hedonistic consumption depends on the imaginary idea of reality. Fourth, sensory and emotional stimulation seeking and cognitive information seeking are two independent dimensions. Hirschman (1983), on the other hand, has gathered the aims that lead consumers to hedonic consumption under six main headings; problem projection, role projection, fantasy fulfillment, escapism, novelty, and sensation seeking, and imagery. Arnold and Reynolds (2003) examine the factors that affect the hedonic consumption behavior of consumers in five different categories: flow, store atmosphere, product innovation, and fashion, consumer characteristics, and country culture and economic situation.

LITERATURE REVIEW: COMPARISON OF UTILITARIAN AND HEDONIC CONSUMPTION

When hedonism and utilitarianism are analyzed and thought, although there is an intersection, utilitarian consumption and hedonic consumption emerge as opposite situations. While people who show utilitarian consumption behavior focus on the functional features of the goods in their consumption processes, consumers focus on the dream and fantasy powers created by the goods in hedonistic consumption behavior. For consumers who consume with utilitarian expectations, consumption is a duty, for consumers who consume with hedonic expectations, consumption is an enjoyable activity. From this point of view, while utilitarian consumption gives importance to functionality, continuity, logic, and analysis; hedonic consumption gives importance to interaction, variability, emotion, and uncertainty. In Table 2, utilitarian and hedonic values in goods and services are compared based on the study of Voss et al., (2003).

Lehtonen and Maenpaa (1997) showed their differences by comparing consumption in utilitarian and hedonic understanding in their study. The differences identified in the study of Lehtonen and Maenpaa (1997) are summarized in Table 3.

A study done by Hirschman and Holbrook (1982) is one of the pioneering studies of the study literature. In this study, it was stated that utilitarian and hedonic consumption differs in four dimensions: emotional structure, class of goods, use of goods, and individual differences. In the study, it is emphasized that contrary to the Homoeconomicus approach explained in the utility theory, consumers not only choose a rational behavior that will benefit them but also choose a hedonistic way of consumption that makes them the happiest. In utilitarian consumption, it is stated that the consumer is the one who focuses on the tangible benefits of the good and makes a logical decision. Unlike utilitarian consumption in hedonic consumption, it is stated that it is based on maximizing the pleasure and habits of the consumer. It is stated that hedonic consumers consume for reasons that do not have economic rationales, such as role-playing, entertainment, individual satisfaction, adopting new trends, physical activity, social experience, communication with similar social groups, status, and authority.

Table 2. Utilitarian and hedonic values in goods and services

Utilitarian	Hedonic
Helpful/unhelpful	Not fun/fun
Effective/ineffective	Dull/exciting
Functional/not functional	Not delightful/delightful
Necessary/unnecessary	Not thrilling/thrilling
Practical/impractical	Enjoyable/unenjoyable
Beneficial/harmful	Not happy/happy
Useful/useless	Unpleasant/pleasant
Sensible/not sensible	Not playful/playful
Efficient/inefficient	Cheerful/not cheerful
Unproductice/productive	Amusing/not amusing
Handy/not handy	Not sensuous/sensuous
Problem solving/not problem solving	Not funny/funny

Source: Voss et al., (2003)

Table 3. Consumption in hedonic and utilitarian understanding

Utilitarian Consumption	Hedonic Consumption
A means to an end	An end itself
Always includes purchases	Does not necessarily include purchases
Planned	Impulsive
As efficient as possible	Efficiency not central
Out of necessity	For pleasure
Part of daily routine	Outside of daily routines
Clear beginning and end	No clear beginning or end
Emphasis of rationality	Emphasis of the experience

Source: Lehtonen & Maenpaa (1997)

Batra and Athola (1990) argued in their study that consumers consume by being influenced by two motives, utilitarian and hedonic and that both hedonic and utilitarian attitudes towards a good can be exhibited simultaneously. Crowley et al. (1992) applied the scale developed by Batra and Ahtola (1990) on how consumer behaviors in hedonic and utilitarian dimensions change according to product categories, on twenty-four goods groups. The results obtained are that hedonic and utilitarian dimensions can be seen in almost every category of the goods, but their intensity may vary.

Babin et al. (1994) conducted empirical research to prove the existence of hedonic and utilitarian consumption and interpreted the effects of values such as the amount of money spent and the satisfaction obtained on consumer behavior. According to the study, consumption behavior expectations are twofold: utilitarian and hedonic expectations. According to utilitarian expectations, the person performs his consumption behavior according to the functions of the good. According to hedonic expectations, the person performs his consumption behavior according to such as imagination, fantasy, image, and aesthetics. As a result of this study, it was explained that different hedonic and utilitarian consumption value dimensions could be related to many variables, and they stated that consumers can act both intelligently and emotionally at the same time.

Dhar and Wertenbroch (2000) examined how consumer preferences are shaped between a good with a hedonic dimension and another good with a utilitarian dimension. Goods purchased for pleasure have a different effect on consumers than goods purchased for functional purposes. According to the study, it is said that hedonic motives are more effective in decisions about giving up goods since the salience of hedonic behaviors is directed towards buying the goods. In cases where a decision has to be made about giving up a particular good, it is often emphasized that the goods purchased for pleasure are the first to be given up.

Buhrman (2002) defines hedonic consumers as people who see consumption as a leisure time activity and enjoy it. It has been emphasized that hedonic consumers are more actively involved in seeking information than utilitarian consumers. It has been stated that those who make utilitarian consumption do not like consumption and are neutral towards consumption.

Arnold and Reynolds (2003) study tried to comprehensively illuminate consumers' hedonic consumption motivations. In this study, it was concluded that hedonic consumption has six different dimensions: adventure, social, pleasure, idea, role, and value. according to the results of the research; there is a positive relationship between the pleasure received from consumption and the time spent on consumption. According to the result, hedonic consumers think less while consuming than utilitarian consumers and spend more time performing consumption action.

Bhatnagar and Ghosh (2004) discussed in the study by comparing utilitarian and hedonic consumption. According to the study, utilitarian consumption motifs include convenience, variety, quality of trade research, and reasonable price ratio. On the other hand, hedonic consumption motifs are related to the emotional needs of individuals for pleasurable and interesting consumption experiences.

Okada (2005) states in his study that consumers tend to prefer hedonic when utilitarian and hedonic alternatives are presented separately, but they prefer utilitarian when utilitarian and hedonic alternatives are presented together. He also found that people prefer to spend money and time in different combinations to acquire utilitarian and hedonic goods. They are willing to spend more time on hedonic goods and more money on utilitarian goods.

Carpenter et al. (2005) state that the individual with utilitarian consumption behavior concentrates on the functional concrete features of the goods and services in the consumption process, while the hedonistic consumption trend of the individual concentrates on the dreams and fantasy powers created by the goods and services. Therefore, hedonic consumption is an approach that focuses on personal, subjective, pleasure, and entertainment, while utilitarian consumption is an approach that focuses mainly on the tangible benefits that the good or service will offer to the individual, within the framework of cost-benefit elements. Therefore, compared to utilitarian behavior, hedonistic behavior is the result of a more personal, subjective, enjoyable, and fun-filled adventure.

Solomon (2006) emphasizes that consumptions should not be separated as utilitarian and hedonic. Because every consumption can have hedonic and utilitarian situations. In other words, goods can have both utilitarian and hedonic qualities. Classification of a good as utilitarian or hedonic may vary depending on how the individual perceives this consumption.

To et al. (2007) emphasize that while consumers are experiential and emotional in their evaluation of hedonic consumption, they make concrete and functional evaluations in utilitarian consumption. In hedonic consumption, the consumption process is more important than consumption. While consumption is seen as a fun activity for hedonic consumption, consumption is seen as a duty to be fulfilled in utilitarian consumption.

Geiger (2007), in his study of night consumption, talks about hedonic and utilitarian consumption and says that night consumption has a low hedonic dimension due to low visibility. It is also stated that nighttime consumption is more purposeful, functional and comfortable than spending time with friends or family and satisfying social and psychological needs.

Lim and Ang (2008) presented a comparative cultural analysis on utilitarian and hedonic consumption. It has been stated that characteristics such as the type goods and the need for use cultural indicate appropriateness over the goods in individuals in utilitarian societies that are culturally appropriate for a good. In this study, it is determined that Shanghai consumers are utilitarian rather than hedonic. It is argued that these consumers find utilitarian goods more complex, exciting, useful and they prefer hedonic goods more.

Botti and Ann (2011) argue that consumer goals, goods, and activities can be classified as hedonic and utilitarian by summarizing many interconnected ideas. Hedonic consumption experiences are fun, sensory, and spontaneous. On the contrary, utilitarian consumption is more functional, sensitive, and useful. As a result, utilitarian consumption experiences are easy to defend as useful and necessary. The hedonic experience is an intrinsic motivator. In contrast, utilitarian consumption is an extrinsic motivator.

HISTORICAL TRANSFORMATION IN CONSUMPTION UNDERSTANDING

In the ever-changing world, people have undergone great changes and transformations depending on the conditions of each period, and they have changed their activities, habits, and behaviors. Consumption activities and consumer behavior are the most important factors that show change and transformation. Since the focus of this study is the evolution of consumption from utilitarian consumption to hedonic consumption, in the analysis of the process, attention is paid to the spread of consumption culture in societies from the upper classes to the lower classes over time. This historical process is discussed in many studies subject to various classifications. In this study, a fourfold classification is used as the pre-industrial period covering the 16th and 17th centuries, the industrial period covering the 18th and 19th centuries, the post-industrial period covering the 20th century, and the socio-digital age representing the 21st century. The first three periods are discussed below, and the socio-digital age is evaluated in the next section.

Pre-Industrial Period: The consumption culture dates back to the 16th century, but the consumption of that period only defines the consumption habits of a very limited segment of the upper class, such as aristocrats and nobles. With the 16th century, hedonic consumption began to spread from the nobles to the lower classes. In the 16th and 17th centuries, it entered into a consumption competition with the newly enriched bourgeois section, that is, the "new noble class", and the aristocrats whose wealth dates back to the past, that is, with the "old noble class" ". Thus, the increase in the demand for luxury consumer goods and the spread of consumption and consumption culture to the lower classes started in this period. Beaujot (2011) refers to this period as the gestation period of consumption culture. It can be stated that the change in this period was shaped by the effect of the centralization policies implemented by Elizabeth I. The nobles, brought together by Elizabeth I with various invitations, competed among themselves through the consumption objects they exhibited to make themselves noticed, and pioneered the spread of consumption first in England and then in all of Europe. Consumption competition of old and new nobility began to develop, including local communities. It was also during this period that the first modern fashion bloomed. While the old rich represented themselves with special, rare, and expensive items that they had owned and used for a long time, the new rich represented themselves with the symbols of fashion (the new one), which are consumption objects they acquired with newly earned money. Thus, in this period, hedonic consumption began to spread out of the monopoly of the old nobles. Hedonic consumption has just begun to emerge as an alternative for those who thought that only utilitarian consumption was in question for them until that time (McCracken, 1986; McCracken, 1988; Beaujot, 2011; Bocock, 2008; Davies & Ward, 2001).

Industrial Period: In Western societies, consumption in the modern sense started with the industrial revolution. With the industrialization period covering the 18th and 19th centuries, the use of coal as an energy source and the patenting of the steam engine in 1769 gave unprecedented production power to the production mechanisms. Thus, more manufactured goods, more consumers to buy goods, more sellers to sell, and firms with larger capitals have emerged. The industrial revolution started with the use of inventions and scientific developments in the production process in 18th century Continental Europe and led to an increase in mass production and capital accumulation at the same time. The invention of tools that will make daily life easier and make them available to people has been the most important development that revealed the consumption culture. According to Bocock (2008), consumption increased significantly in this period as individuals became aware of new goods that could decorate their homes and bodies and became more able to buy them. Beaujot (2011) explains the four basic elements that emerged in this period as follows: First, the 18th century was a period of goods innovation in which the number and variety of goods produced in specialized workshops increased. Second, in this period, consumption moved from the aristocratic strata to the middle and laboring ranks of British society. Third, the distribution of consumer goods has begun to shift from simple market stalls to permanent shops. Fourth, the idea of luxury no longer carries a negative connotation such as extremism and immorality, instead, it is perceived as an element symbolizing the increasing poverty of the British people and the wealth of England (Campell, 1987; McCracken, 1986; McCracken, 1988; Beaujot, 2011; Bocock, 2008; Davies & Ward, 2001; Hirschman & Holbrook, 1982; Solomon, 2006).

With the economic development that started with the Industrial Revolution, almost all classes, together with the fashion phenomenon, formed the massification of modern consumption and the beginning of consumer society. The changes in the production and consumption area that emerged in this period indicate that traditional utilitarian consumption styles have begun to move away and hedonic consumption has begun to increase. Magnificent objects such as silk, porcelain, mahogany, candy, and chocolate that were once extremely luxurious began to reach the lower classes. Hats, clothes, shoes, earrings, and hairstyles have been widely used to show fashion trends. However, the 18th and 19th centuries are expressed as a period in which people's sense of identity was not formed by consumption patterns. Because in this period, it is seen that most people's lives are under the influence of their roles in working life.

Therefore, the consumption patterns of the growing working class and middle class in this period have not yet reached a structure similar to the size of an aristocracy or bourgeoisie.

Post-Industrial Period: With the beginning of the 20th century, the production process, which was important until the end of the 19th century, left its place to the consumption process. At the beginning of the 20th century, it is seen that new consumer classes began to emerge. At that time, cities such as Berlin, Paris, London, Glasgow, New York, and Chicago grew by improving their transportation networks until 1914, when the first world war broke out. This shows that modern consumption patterns have emerged and become widespread, to some, as a result of living in cities. The new classes that emerged in the main cities carried out consumption, which played an important role in their lives, in order to create a sense of identity, to differentiate themselves from other individuals, and to be understood and interpreted by other individuals. Therefore, the people of the main city entered into an endless war of being noticed by sharing a set of common cultural symbols with others in order to differentiate themselves. As the middle and lower social status classes and the majority of the working class copied the consumption habits of the higher status classes, the imitated upper classes had to constantly change their consumption patterns in order to differentiate themselves (Bocock, 2008; McCracken, 1988; Beaujot, 2011; Campell, 1987; Davies & Ward, 2001; Hirschman & Holbrook, 1982; Solomon, 2006).

In this period, also known as the automobile age, the model called Fordism plays an important role. The years between 1915 and 1975 can be considered as the Fordist period and the massification of consumption. This period was a period in which durable consumer goods that are easy to reach large masses, as well as heavy capital goods, began to be produced, adding a different dimension to consumption. In the 1950s, television programs and advertisements created the idea that goods were plentiful and easily accessible, and thus consumer goods began to be presented as imaginary objects and relationships that hold daily life together. It is noteworthy that with the 1970s, a new type of consumer, which focused on consumption, developed. Although various economic problems were experienced due to the negativities caused by the oil crises, fashion designers increased in this period, and with the increase in technological opportunities, a period was entered in which the trends were determined by the world of music, television, and sports. Technological developments have caused changes in the production stages, types, and quantities of goods and generally significant in the lives of people. In the period after 1973, service-type businesses such as finance, insurance, and real estate have grown relatively, and cultural production industries such as TV and film industries, folk festivals have flourished. The developments in this post-industrial period have gradually created a system in which utilitarian consumption is tried to be forgotten or trivialized, and hedonic consumption is inculcated (Beaujot, 2011; Bocock, 2008; Davies & Ward, 2001; Solomon, 2006). Towards the end of the 20th century, with the internet starting to enter people's lives, a new era has begun in consumption. This period, which is expressed as the socio-digital age, is examined in detail in the next section.

CONSUMER BEHAVIOR IN THE SOCIO-DIGITAL AGE

At this point, human beings are experiencing the socio-digital age where time and space have lost their content in the known sense. The developments in information and communication technologies have opened the doors of a new world to humankind in the 21st century. Revolutionary changes in digital technologies cause the information to grow exponentially and the speed of change to increase. Smart mobile phones, portable computers, autonomous air, land, and sea vehicles, robots equipped with artificial intelligence that can think and produce, and transportation vehicles, which are the goods of developing technology, cause to reshape the boundaries of individual and social life. This process, which is interpreted by social scientists as an information revolution and affects people's activities and behaviors in social, political, economic, and cultural structuring, has provided the birth of the socio-digital age.

The socio-digital age is also expressed in different studies and approaches by using many different names such as the post-modern era, postindustrial society, post-capitalist society, knowledge society, information society, and network society. Considering the consumption and consumer behaviors in the focus of this study, the basic characteristics of this socio-digital age can be expressed as follows. In this era, e-life models have emerged, the individual has been offered the opportunity to set aside his behavioral determinations and obligations, the concepts of private and public space have become vague, the concept of demassification has emerged, the individual's access to information has diversified regardless of time and space, use of information and communication technologies has provided social benefits in socio-cultural environments, many goods and services have been fused with information and communication technologies, digital bodies, which are extensions of people's physical bodies, can be built through virtual environments, a culture of virtuality has been formed and within the framework of this culture, the lifestyles of societies have been differentiated, human beings have been provided with the possibilities of interactive communication, new media channels have been formed, it has become easier to control and monitor the digitalized masses, artificiality came to the f ore rather than naturalness, virtual environment users have become not only consuming but also producing information, with the new economic system, new generation payment systems and new currencies have emerged, and marketing activities and purchasing processes are shaped according to the needs of the person (Lim & Ang, 2008; Bocock, 2008; Bauman, 2001; Solomon, 2006; Bauman, 2008).

Consumption and consumer behavior come to the fore as the most influential and most affected factors of this socio-digital age. In this age, a large part of life revolves around consumption. Many minds in society have begun to deal with consumption as a channel of desires rather than fulfilling a real need. With the new understanding, the efforts to relieve and reduce the desires that have existed throughout history throughout the past have been replaced by the effort to inflame and multiply. Thus, desires began to find expression in new ways compared to the old ones. The source of this is that hedonic understanding, which has been increasing for centuries, has become the focus. According to Gabriel and Lang (1995), the modern consumer is a hedonist who constantly avoids the realities he encounters, wants to reach his dreams as soon as possible, combines them with his desires, and then gives up on these desires and wishes when he reaches and experiences them. In the Western societies of this age, where excessive consumption is dominant, desires also emerge as a necessity.

Table 4. Traditional hedonism versus modern hedonism

Traditional Hedonism	Modern hedonism
Search for pleasure tied to specific practices	Search for pleasure in any or all experiences
Pleasure tied to sensations	Pleasure tied to emotions
Emotions not under control of subject	Emotions controlled by subject
Pleasure derived from control of objects and events	Pleasure derived from control of the meanings of objects and events

Source: Corrigan (1997)

Hedonic consumption has changed in parallel with the possibilities over time. Corrigan (1997) compares traditional hedonism and modern hedonism in his study. This comparison is given in Table 4.

Desiring and the motivation to be desired, which are revealed in this age with consumer goods and their symbolic meanings, cause the majority of people to seek to add meaning to their lives through consumption. The perception that consumer goods provide symbolic meanings such as happiness, good life, status, respect, etc., causes hedonism to become a dominant culture in a broad sense. With the hasty, shyness, impatience, and novelty-seeking features that appear in people in this age, people quickly adopt new pleasures and turn to a hedonic consumption style by acting with the motivation to deserve these pleasures immediately. The modern hedonist individual receives emotional pleasure from the act of consumption and the dream of consumption and lives his lifestyle and experiences in this focus of pleasure. In this context, it is seen that hedonism has become a culture by spreads throughout society. In other words, the culture of the 21st-century society can be expressed as the hedonistic human culture (Bauman, 2001; Lim & Ang, 2008; Solomon, 2006; Bauman, 2008; Gabriel & Lang, 1995; Baudrillard, 1998).

According to Baudrillard (1998), consumption in this age is a sign system beyond satisfying the needs of individuals through goods and services. Goods have become so abstract that the economy has become a system of signs. What is bought is not just tangible goods with a utilitarian use, but also objects that convey a meaning, which the consumer will use to show who he or she aims to be at that time. Because they are not the goods consumed, but their symbols. Therefore, the act of consumption takes place not for the benefit to be received from the good to be consumed, but for the class position that can be involved by consuming that good. Consumers have the idea that the increase in their reputation around them depends on showing the goods they own. In other words, modern consumers consume for symbolic values rather than meeting their essential needs.

With the increasing prevalence of hedonic consumption, even the developing technology has become hedonized. It has now become the goal of the producer companies that every product developed gives pleasure to the consumer as well as the benefit. In the advertisements of new products, the emphasis on pleasure and entertainment is constantly made. The desire to buy, which is tried to be created in the minds of the consumer with advertisements, the social status or prestige that the consumer will gain if he owns that product, pushes the person to make hedonic consumption. The content of advertisements has a positive effect on the amount of pleasure to be obtained from the good or service to be used. Advertising is basically based on dreams and fantasies, not reality. The reason why it is believable is that the fantasies or dreams it evokes overlap with the fantasies or dreams of the consumer. It is claimed that with the consumption of the goods in the advertisements, life will change completely, and the problem caused by not owning the goods will suddenly disappear (Bocock, 2008; Bauman, 2001; Lim & Ang, 2008; Bauman, 2008; Lim et al., 2012).

With the widespread use of the Internet and the penetration of the Internet into every home, companies directly reach consumers first-hand and consumers can directly contact companies. The electronic consumption process and the experiences they create enrich the consumption experiences of consumers. It is seen that the world of electronic shopping has turned into a world of fantasies with the animations, three-dimensional simulations, and virtual reality goods that shopping sites provide to consumers. With these developments, consumers can realize their fantasies in the imaginary world, even in the virtual environment. Being personal, being free, and having information security also have an effect on the consumption made with hedonic motivations and the widespread use of electronic shopping. Lim et al. (2012) showed in their study that hedonic motivations have a great impact on electronic shopping. According to the study, the graphics, vividness of colors, media quality, and atmosphere used in the creation of online sales websites increase the hedonic expectations of the consumers and cause them to make more hedonic shopping.

Bauman (2008) states that in the 21st-century society, if the dissatisfaction is constantly maintained, it will be successful, and this will be achieved by introducing the goods to the consumers with large advertising campaigns, and then by denigrating and depreciating these goods. According to Bocock (2008), consumption is based on a lack – a never-ending desire for something that is not there. In this case, it will never be possible for modern consumers to reach absolute satisfaction. People living under the influence of the consumerist culture of the socio-digital age, the more they consume, the more they will want to consume, and they will continue to want something that they cannot obtain—that is, the satisfaction of all their desires. According to Bauman (2001), in order to keep the production and consumption wheel operating, the desire to buy is never allowed to fade. The modern consumer has been transformed into a person who can take a negative view of anyone who does not consume more and is not interested in desires. This necessitates hedonic consumption for social acceptance in the socio-digital age.

FUTURE RESEARCH DIRECTIONS

Since consumption activities and consumer behavior are one of the important and constantly changing dynamic topics of the economics literature, this study can be developed and renewed in many different ways and methods. However, as a special suggestion, it is thought that evaluating this change and transformation in the understanding of consumption with a sustainable consumption approach will make significant contributions to the literature. The effect of people's future anxiety on the pleasure obtained from hedonic consumption and its reflection on consumption behavior should be discussed. In addition, how the hedonic consumption approach's dominance affects the acceptances of consumer theory in economic theory should be discussed with advanced microeconomic discussions.

CONCLUSION

The reasons for consumption activities and consumer behaviors are mainly explained in the literature by two motives, utilitarian and hedonic motives. Consumption with utilitarian motives is called utilitarian consumption, and consumption with hedonic motivations is called hedonic consumption. While people who show utilitarian consumption behavior focus on the functional characteristics of the goods in the consumption process, they focus on the dream and fantasy powers created by the goods in hedonic consumption behavior. While utilitarian consumption gives importance to functionality, continuity, logic, and analysis; hedonic consumption gives importance to interaction, variability, emotion, and uncertainty. For consumers who consume with utilitarian expectations, consumption is a duty, for consumers who consume with hedonic expectations, consumption is an enjoyable activity.

In this study, the evolution of consumer behavior from utilitarian consumption to hedonic consumption was discussed by considering utilitarian and hedonic consumption approaches, and consumer behaviors in the socio-digital age, which represents the 21st century, were evaluated. It has been observed that consumption activities and consumer behaviors have changed and transformed in parallel with the change in world conditions. This change and transformation have led to the differentiation of utilitarian and hedonic consumption weights in the historical process due to many reasons. Over time, it is observed that the weight of utilitarian consumption gradually decreases and the weight of hedonic consumption gradually increases. Although the consumption culture dates back to the 16th century, the consumption of that period only defines the consumption habits of a very limited segment of the upper class, such as aristocrats and nobles. With the 16th century, hedonic consumption begins to spread from the nobles down. With this period, hedonic consumption gradually becomes a respectable lifestyle, a means of showing off and competition. Therefore, the 16th and 17th centuries, which represent the pre-industrial period, is the period when the consumption culture gradually broke out of the monopoly of the aristocratic and noble strata in the upper strata and began to spread to the lower strata of the society. In Western societies, consumption in the modern sense started with the industrial revolution. In the 18th and 19th centuries, which express the industrial period, positive meanings were attributed to consumption in order to spread consumption, and the meaning and importance of the consumption phenomenon for the consumer were changed. The changes in the production and consumption areas that emerged in this period indicate that hedonic consumption has started to increase. In the 20th century, which represents the post-industrial period, these developments were followed by the Fordism movement, which opened the doors of consumption by bringing standardization in the mode of production and increasing worker wages. Especially after the Second World War, mass consumption exploded in North America and Europe. In this period, fashion designers increased and with the increase in technological opportunities, trends were determined by the world of music, television, and sports. The post-industrial period is when hedonic consumption surpasses utilitarian consumption.

In the last period, which is called the socio-digital age and refers to the 21st century, it is seen that hedonism is dominant in consumption, and consumption with a utilitarian approach remains relatively small. In this study, although it is called the socio-digital age, this period is also expressed by different names such as post-modern era, post-industrial society, the personal service society, post-capitalist society, knowledge society, information society, and network society in different approaches and studies. The perception that consumers provide symbolic meanings such as happiness, a good life, status, respect, etc., which they try to achieve with these consumer goods, has caused hedonism to become a dominant culture in a broad sense. The hedonist individual of the 21st century takes emotional pleasure from the act of consumption and the dream of consumption and lives his lifestyle in this focus of pleasure. It can be said that the consumer of this age buys goods for symbolic values that reflect their status in society and how they will be recognized and represented by other people. In this context, hedonism has become a culture by spreads throughout society. To put it more clearly, the culture of society has turned into hedonistic consumer culture.

As a result, with the change and transformation in the historical process, consumers have been given behavior that is never possible to reach satisfaction, whose dissatisfaction is constantly ongoing, and therefore, their enthusiasm for consumption is never allowed to fade. Thus, the newer consumers want to consume more and they will continue to want something that they cannot obtain. The basic teaching of this socio-digital age is to teach consumers how and what to need. Thus, utilitarian values are forgotten and hedonic thinking is dominated.

REFERENCES

Arnold, M. J., & Reynolds, K. E. (2003). Hedonic shopping motivations. *Journal of Retailing*, *79*(2), 77–95. doi:10.1016/S0022-4359(03)00007-1

Babin, B. J., Darden, W. R., & Griffin, M. (1994). Work and/or fun: Measuring hedonic and utilitarian shopping value. *The Journal of Consumer Research, 20*(4), 644–657. doi:10.1086/209376

Batra, R., & Ahtola, O. T. (1990). Measuring the hedonic and utilitarian sources of consumer attitude. *Marketing Letters, 2*(2), 159–170. doi:10.1007/BF00436035

Baudrillard, J. (1998). *The consumer society: Myths and structures*. Sage Publications Ltd. doi:10.4135/9781526401502

Bauman, Z. (2001). *The individualized society*. Polity Press. https://www.jstor.org/stable/4194889

Bauman, Z. (2008). *Does ethics have a chance in a world of consumers?* Harvard University Press., doi:10.4159/9780674033948

Beaujot, A. (2011). Consumer revolution in eighteenth-century Britain. In Encyclopedia of Consumer Culture (pp. 310-313). Sage Publications. doi:10.4135/9781412994248.n119

Bhatnagar, A., & Ghosh, S. (2004). A latent class segmentation analysis of EShoppers. *Journal of Business Research, 57*(7), 758–767. doi:10.1016/S0148-2963(02)00357-0

Bocock, R. (2008). *Consumption. Abingdon*. Routledge. doi:10.4324/9780203131091

Botti, S., & Ann, L. (2011). The locus of choice: Personal causality and satisfaction with hedonic and utilitarian decisions. *The Journal of Consumer Research, 37*(6), 1065–1078. doi:10.1086/656570

Buhrman, T. (2002). *Effects of hedonic and utilitarian shopping satisfaction on mall consumption*. University of North Texas. https://digital.library.unt.edu/ark:/67531/metadc3188/manifest/

Campell, C. (1987). *The romantic ethic and the spirit of modern consumerism*. Blackwell Publishers. doi:10.1007/978-3-319-79066-4

Carpenter, J. M., Moore, M., & Fairhurst, A. E. (2005). Consumer shopping value for retail brand. *Journal of Fashion Marketing and Management, 9*(1), 43–53. doi:10.1108/13612020510586398

Corrigan, P. (1997). *The sociology of consumption: An introduction*. SAGE Publications Ltd. doi:10.4135/9781446216903

Crowley, A. E., Spangenberg, R. E., & Hughes, R. K. (1992). Measuring the hedonic and dimensions of attitudes toward product categories. *Marketing Letters, 3*(3), 239–249. doi:10.1007/BF00994132

Davies, B., & Ward, P. (2001). *Managing retail consumption*. John Wiley and Sons Ltd.

Dhar, R., & Wertenbroch, K. (2000). Consumer choice between hedonic and utilitarian goods. *JMR, Journal of Marketing Research, 37*(1), 60–71. doi:10.1509/jmkr.37.1.60.18718

Gabriel, Y., & Lang, T. (1995). *The unmanageable consumer: Contemporary consumption and its fragmentations*. Sage Publications. doi:10.4135/9781446213049.n6

Geiger, S. (2007). Exploring night-time grocery shopping behaviour. *Journal of Retailing and Consumer Services, 14*(1), 24–34. doi:10.1016/j.jretconser.2006.03.001

Hirschman, C. E., & Holbrook, B. M. (1982). Hedonic consumption: Emerging concepts, methods and propositions. *Journal of Marketing*, *46*(3), 92–101. doi:10.1177/002224298204600314

Hirschman, E. C. (1983). Predictors of self-projection, fantasy fulfillment, and escapism. *The Journal of Social Psychology*, *120*(1), 63–76. doi:10.1080/00224545.1983.9712011

Holbrook, M. B. (1996). Romanticism, introspection and the roots of experiential consumption: Morris the epicurean. In Consumption and Marketing Macro Dimensions. South-Western College Pub. doi:10.1080/10253866.1997.9670295

Jordan, P. W. (2000). *Designing pleasurable products: An introduction to the new human factors*. Routledge. doi:10.4324/9780203305683

Kotler, P., Wong, V., Saunders, J., & Armstrong, G. (2005). *Principles of marketing* (4th ed.). Prentice Hall International. https://hdl.handle.net/10520/EJC75657

Lehtonen, T. K., & Maenpaa, P. (1997). Shopping in the East Centre Mall. In S. Experience (Ed.), *Falk & Campbell* (pp. 136–165). SAGE. doi:10.4135/9781446216972.n7

Lim, E., & Ang, S. (2008). Hedonic vs. utilitarian consumption: A cross-cultural perspective based on cultural conditioning. *Journal of Business Research*, *61*(3), 225–232. doi:10.1016/j.jbusres.2007.06.004

Lim, E., Cyr, D., & Tan, C. W. (2012). Untangling utilitarian and hedonic consumption behaviors in online shopping. *PACIS 2012 Proceedings*, 94. https://aisel.aisnet.org/pacis2012/94

Lunardo, R., & Mbengue, A. (2009). Perceived control and shopping behavior: The moderating role of the level of utilitarian motivational orientation. *Journal of Retailing and Consumer Services*, *16*(6), 434–441. doi:10.1016/j.jretconser.2009.06.004

McCracken, G. (1986). The history of consumption: A literature review and consumer guide. *Journal of Consumer Policy*, *10*(1), 139–166. doi:10.1007/BF00411633

McCracken, G. (1988). *Culture and consumption: New aproaches to the symbolic character of consumer goods and activities*. Indiana University Press. doi:10.1086/229266

Okada, E. M. (2005). Justification effects on consumer choice of hedonic and utilitarian goods. *JMR, Journal of Marketing Research*, *42*(1), 43–53. doi:10.1509/jmkr.42.1.43.56889

Solomon, M. (2006). *Consumer behavior: A European perspective*. Prentice Hall Europe. https://lib.ugent.be/catalog/rug01:001018093

Spangenberg, E. R., Voss, K. E., & Crowley, E. (1997). In M. Brucks & D. J. MacInnis (Eds.), *Measuring the hedonic and utilitarian dimensions of attitude: A generally applicable scale. Advances in Consumer Research, 24* (pp. 235–241). Association for Consumer Research. doi:10.1509/jmkr.40.3.310.19238

To, P., Liao, C., & Lin, T. (2007). Shopping motivations on internet: A study based on utilitarian and hedonic value. *Journal of Social. Management Technovation*, *27*(12), 774–787. doi:10.1016/j.technovation.2007.01.001

Voss, K. E., Spangenberg, E. R., & Grohmann, B. (2003). Measuring the hedonic and utilitarian dimensions of consumer attitude. *JMR, Journal of Marketing Research, 40*(3), 310–320. doi:10.1509/jmkr.40.3.310.19238

West, H. R. (2004). *An introduction to Mill's utilitarian ethics*. Cambridge University Press. https://www.cambridge.org/9780521828321

ADDITIONAL READING

Ahtola, O. T. (1985). Hedonic and utilitarian aspects of consumer behavior: An attitudinal perspective. *Advances in Consumer Research. Association for Consumer Research (U. S.), 12*(1), 7–10. https://www.acrwebsite.org/volumes/6348/volumes/v12/NA

Chaudhuri, A., Aboulnasr, K., & Ligas, M. (2010). Emotional responses on initial exposure to a hedonic or utilitarian description of a radical innovation. *Journal of Marketing Theory and Practice, 18*(4), 339–359. doi:10.2753/MTP1069-6679180403

Dhar, R., & Nowlis, S. (2002). The effects of generating options on purchase intent for hedonic and utilitarian products. *Advances in Consumer Research. Association for Consumer Research (U. S.), 29*, 460–462.

Lu, J., Liu, Z., & Fang, Z. (2016). Hedonic products for you, utilitarian products for me. *Judgment and Decision Making, 11*(4), 332–341. https://go.gale.com/ps/i.do?p=AONE&u=anon~593176a4&id=GALE|A461364376&v=2.1&it=r&sid=googleScholar&asid=4fc5f265

Roy, R., & Ng, S. (2012). Regulatory focus and preference reversal between hedonic and utilitarian consumption. *Journal of Consumer Behaviour, 11*(1), 81–88. doi:10.1002/cb.371

Salerno, A., Laran, J., & Janiszewski, C. (2014). Hedonic eating goals and emotion: When sadness decreases the desire to indulge. *The Journal of Consumer Research, 41*(1), 135–151. doi:10.1086/675299

Teller, C., Reutterer, T., & Schnedlitz, P. (2008). Hedonic and utilitarian shopper types in evolved and created retail agglomerations. *International Review of Retail, Distribution and Consumer Research, 18*(3), 283–309. doi:10.1080/09593960802113877

Voss, K., Spangenberg, E., & Grohmann, B. (2003). Measuring the hedonic and utilitarian dimensions of consumer attitude. *JMR, Journal of Marketing Research, 40*(3), 310–320. doi:10.1509/jmkr.40.3.310.19238

Wertenbroch, K. (2002). Hedonic interactions between choice and consumption. *Advances in Consumer Research. Association for Consumer Research (U. S.), 29*(1), 105–107. https://www.acrwebsite.org/search/view-conferenceproceedings.aspx?Id=8570

Xiao, G., & Kim, J. (2009). The investigation of Chinese consumer values, consumption values, life satisfaction, and consumption behaviors. *Psychology and Marketing, 26*(7), 610–624. doi:10.1002/mar.20291

KEY TERMS AND DEFINITIONS

Consumer Behavior: It is the process of selecting, using, and evaluating goods and services that individuals or households will use to satisfy their needs.

Hedonic Consumption: It is a form of consumption that deals with the emotional dimension of consumption and focuses on completing and sustaining emotional pleasure.

Hedonism: It is the doctrine that advocates behavior motivated by the pursuit of pleasure, devotion to sensory pleasures, or psychological desire to seek pleasure and avoid pain.

Industrial Period: The period covering the 18th and 19th centuries and when hedonic consumption emerged as an alternative for the lower classes.

Pleasure: It is something that pleases, entertains, and arouses a sense of satisfaction in people.

Post-Industrial Period: The period of the 20th century when hedonic consumption was made by everyone.

Pre-Industrial Period: The period covering the 16th and 17th centuries and when hedonic consumption began to spread from the upper classes to the lower classes.

Socio-Digital Age: The period that expresses the 21st century and the culture of the society is hedonic consumption culture.

Utilitarian Consumption: It is a form of consumption in which goods and services are evaluated with their functional characteristics, and the act of consumption is carried out for rational reasons and to meet non-emotional needs.

Utilitarianism: It is the idea that the value of a good or an activity can be determined by its utility.

Compilation of References

Ab Hamid, M. R., Sami, W., & Mohmad Sidek, M. H. (2017). Discriminant Validity Assessment: Use of Fornell & Larcker criterion versus HTMT Criterion. *Journal of Physics: Conference Series*, *890*, 012163. doi:10.1088/1742-6596/890/1/012163

Abayomi, O. J., Olabode, A. C., Reyad, M. A. H., Tetteh Teye, E., Haq, M. N., & Mensah, E. T. (2019). Effects of demographic factors on customers' mobile banking services adoption in Nigeria. *International Journal of Business and Social Science*, *10*(1), 63–77. doi:10.30845/ijbss.v10n1p9

Abdelrahman, O., & Keikhosrokiani, P. (2020). Assembly Line Anomaly Detection and Root Cause Analysis Using Machine Learning. *IEEE Access: Practical Innovations, Open Solutions*, *8*, 189661–189672. doi:10.1109/ACCESS.2020.3029826

Abdulrahim, H., & Mabrouk, F. (2020). COVID-19 and the Digital Transformation of Saudi Higher Education. *Asian J. Distance Educ.*, *15*, 291–306. https://files.eric.ed.gov/fulltext/EJ1289975.pdf

Abed, S. S. (2020). Social commerce adoption using TOE framework: An empirical investigation of Saudi Arabian SMEs. *International Journal of Information Management*, *53*, 102118. doi:10.1016/j.ijinfomgt.2020.102118

Abulaish, M. J., Doja, M. N., & Ahmad, T. (2009). Feature and opinion mining for customer review summarization. Lecture Notes in Computer Science, 5909, 219–224. doi:10.1007/978-3-642-11164-8_35

Adekoya, C. O., & Fasae, J. K. (2021). *Social media and the spread of COVID-19 infodemic*. Global Knowledge, Memory and Communication. doi:10.1108/GKMC-11-2020-0165

Adomavicius, G., & Tuzhilin, A. (2005). Toward the next generation of recommender systems: A survey of the state-of-the-art and possible extensions. *Transactions on Knowledge and Data Engineering*, *17*(6), 734–749. doi:10.1109/TKDE.2005.99

Agarwal, R., & Srikant, R. (1994). Fast Algorithms For Mining Association Rules In Datamining. *The Proceeding of the 20th International Conference on Very Large Data Bases*, 487–499.

Agrawal, R., Imielinski, T., & Swami, A. (1993). Mining Association in Large Databases. *Proceedings of the 1993 ACM SIGMOD International Conference on Management of Data - SIGMOD '93*, 207–216. 10.1145/170035.170072

Aguliera, E. & Nightengale-Lee, B (2020). Emergency Remote Teaching across Urban and Rural Contexts: Perspectives on Educational Equity. *Inf. Learn. Sci.*, *121*, 471–478. doi:10.1108/ILS-04-2020-0100

Agwu, M. (2012). A qualitative study of the problems and prospects of online banking in developing economies–case of Nigeria. *Journal of Internet Banking and Commerce*, *17*(3), 1–20. doi:10.2139srn.3112130

Ahani, A., Nilashi, M., Ibrahim, O., Sanzogni, L., & Weaven, S. (2019). Market segmentation and travel choice prediction in Spa hotels through TripAdvisor's online reviews. *International Journal of Hospitality Management, 80*, 52–77. doi:10.1016/j.ijhm.2019.01.003

Ahmed, A., Moncey, A., Mohan, M., Cyriac, N. T., Ali, S. A., Mariam, S., Lyu, M., & Baskaran, K. (2020). Journey of education technology towards innovation. *2020 Advances in Science and Engineering Technology International Conferences (ASET)*. 10.1109/ASET48392.2020.9118334

Ajzen, I. (1991). The Theory of Planned Behavior. Decision Processes, 50(2), 179-211. doi:10.1016/0749-5978(91)90020-T

Ajzen, I. (1985). From Intentions to Actions: A Theory of Planned Behavior. In J. Kuhl & J. Beckmann (Eds.), *Action Control: From Cognition to Behavior* (pp. 11–39). Springer Berlin Heidelberg. doi:10.1007/978-3-642-69746-3_2

Ajzen, I., & Fishbein, M. (1975). A Bayesian analysis of attribution processes. *Psychological Bulletin, 82*(2), 261–277. doi:10.1037/h0076477

Akanbi, P. A., Ayodele, T. D., & Adedipe, O. A. (2014). An investigation into some factors influencing the intention to use internet banking among undergraduates in Nigeria. *Research Journal of Finance and Accounting, 5*(8), 1–9.

Akbari, M., Nazarian, A., Foroudi, P., Seyyed Amiri, N., & Ezatabadipoor, E. (2021). How corporate social responsibility contributes to strengthening brand loyalty, hotel positioning and intention to revisit? *Current Issues in Tourism, 24*(13), 1897–1917. doi:10.1080/13683500.2020.1800601

Akhtar, P., Frynas, J. G., Mellahi, K., & Ullah, S. (2019). Big data-savvy teams' skills, big data-driven actions and business performance. *British Journal of Management, 30*(2), 252-271. doi:10.1111/1467-8551.12333

Akman, T. (2021). *Used clothing gets hot during the pandemic, driven by young people*. The Philadelphia Inquirer, LLC. Retrieved 19 March from https://www.inquirer.com/business/retail/thrifting-used-clothes-thredup-realreal-macys-nuuly-20210916.html

Alalwan, A. A., Dwivedi, Y. K., Rana, N. P., Lal, B., & Williams, M. D. (2015). Consumer adoption of Internet banking in Jordan: Examining the role of hedonic motivation, habit, self-efficacy and trust. *Journal of Financial Services Marketing, 20*(2), 145–157. doi:10.1057/fsm.2015.5

Alcañiz, M., Bigné, E., & Guixeres, J. (2019). Virtual reality in marketing: A Framework, review, and research agenda. *Frontiers in Psychology, 10*, 1530. doi:10.3389/fpsyg.2019.01530 PMID:31333548

Aldayel, M., Ykhlef, M., & Al-Nafjan, A. (2020). Deep learning for EEG-based preference classification in neuromarketing. *Applied Sciences (Basel, Switzerland), 10*(4), 1525. doi:10.3390/app10041525

Alkhaldi, A. N., & Kharma, Q. M. (2019). Customer's intention to adopt mobile banking services: The moderating influence of demographic factors. *International Journal of Innovation and Technology Management, 16*(5), 1–26. doi:10.1142/S0219877019500378

Allegue, S., Abdellatif, T., & Bannour, K. (2020). RFMC: A spending-category segmentation. *Proceedings of the Workshop on Enabling Technologies: Infrastructure for Collaborative Enterprises, WETICE*, 165–170. 10.1109/WETICE49692.2020.00040

Alnawas, I., & Hemsley-Brown, J. (2019). Market orientation and hotel performance: Investigating the role of high-order marketing capabilities. *International Journal of Contemporary Hospitality Management, 31*(4), 1885–1905. doi:10.1108/IJCHM-07-2018-0564

Aloini, D., Dulmin, R., & Mininno, V. (2014). A peer IF-TOPSIS based decision support system for packaging machine selection. *Expert Systems with Applications, 41*(5), 2157–2165. doi:10.1016/j.eswa.2013.09.014

Al-Omoush, K. S., Simón-Moya, V., Al-ma'aitah, M. A., & Sendra-García, J. (2021). The determinants of social CRM entrepreneurship: An institutional perspective. *Journal of Business Research, 132*, 21–31. doi:10.1016/j.jbusres.2021.04.017

Alrababah, S., Gan, K., & Tan, T.-P. (2016). Domain-independent approach for mining opinionated product features using WordNet lexicographer files. *Journal of Information Science*, 1–17. doi:10.1177/0165551510000000

Alrababah, S., Gan, K., & Tan, T.-P. (2017). Comparative Analysis of MCDM Methods for Product Aspect Ranking: TOPSIS and VIKOR. *Proceedings of International Conference on Information and Communication Systems, ICICS 2017*. 10.1109/IACS.2017.7921949

Alsajjan, B., & Dennis, C. (2010). Internet banking acceptance model: Cross-market examination. *Journal of Business Research, 63*(9-10), 957–963. doi:10.1016/j.jbusres.2008.12.014

Alsheikh, L., & Bojei, J. (2012). Customer's perceived value to use mobile banking services. *Proceedings of the International Conference on Management, Behavioral Sciences and Economics Issues (ICMBSE'2012).*

Altarteer, S., & Charissis, V. (2019). Technology acceptance model for 3D virtual reality system in luxury brands online stores. *IEEE Access: Practical Innovations, Open Solutions, 7*, 64053–64062. doi:10.1109/ACCESS.2019.2916353

Al-Tit, A. A. (2020). E-commerce drivers and barriers and their impact on e-customer loyalty in small and medium-sized enterprises (SMEs). *Verslas: Teorija Ir Praktika, 21*(1), 146–157. doi:10.3846/btp.2020.11612

Alvarez-Milán, A., Felix, R., Rauschnabel, P. A., & Hinsch, C. (2018). Strategic customer engagement marketing: A decision making framework. *Journal of Business Research, 92*, 61–70. doi:10.1016/j.jbusres.2018.07.017

Amed, I., Balchandani, A., Berg, A., Hedrich, S., Jensen, J. E., Le Merle, L., & Rölkens, F. (2022). *The State of Fashion 2022*. McKinsey & Company. Retrieved 09 April from https://www.mckinsey.com/industries/retail/our-insights/state-of-fashion

Amin, H., Hamid, M. R. A., Lada, S., & Anis, Z. (2008). The adoption of mobile banking in Malaysia: The case of Bank Islam Malaysia Berhad (BIMB). *International Journal of Business and Society, 9*(2), 43–53.

Ananda, A. S., Hernandez-García, Á., & Lamberti, L. (2015). Fashion in actions on social media - Spanish SME fashion brands case studies. In *Proceedings of the European Conference on e-Learning* (pp. 488–497). Academic Press.

Anastasiadou, E., Chrissos Anestis, M., Karantza, I., & Vlachakis, S. (2020). The coronavirus' effects on consumer behavior and supermarket activities: Insights from Greece and Sweden. *The International Journal of Sociology and Social Policy, 40*(9–10), 893–907. doi:10.1108/IJSSP-07-2020-0275

Andariesta, D. T., & Wasesa, M. (2022). Machine learning models for predicting international tourist arrivals in Indonesia during the COVID-19 pandemic: A multisource Internet data approach. *Journal of Tourism Futures*. doi:10.1108/JTF-10-2021-0239

Anderson, E., & Mittal, V. (2000). Strengthening the Satisfaction-Profit Chain. *Journal of Service Research, 3*(2), 107–120. doi:10.1177/109467050032001

Anshari, M., Almunawar, M. N., Lim, S. A., & Al-Mudimigh, A. (2019). Customer relationship management and big data enabled: Personalization & customization of services. *Applied Computing and Informatics, 15*(2), 94-101.

App Ape. (2021). *Distribution of Depop monthly active users in the United States as of March 2021, by age group*. Statista. Retrieved 19 March from https://www.statista.com/statistics/1125124/depop-us-users-age/

Arafat, S. M. Y., Yuen, K. F., Menon, V., Shoib, S., & Ahmad, A. R. (2021). Panic Buying in Bangladesh: An Exploration of Media Reports. *Frontiers in Psychiatry, 11*, 628393. Advance online publication. doi:10.3389/fpsyt.2020.628393 PMID:33536953

Aramendia-Muneta, M. E. (2017). Spread the word – the effect of word of mouth in e-marketing. In G. Siegert, M. B. Von Rimscha, & S. Grubenmann (Eds.), *Commercial Communication in the Digital Age* (pp. 227–245). De Gruyter. doi:10.1515/9783110416794-013

Arellano, M. (2003). *Panel data econometrics*. Oxford University Press. doi:10.1093/0199245282.001.0001

Arenas Gaitán, J., Peral Peral, B., & Ramón Jerónimo, M. (2015). Elderly and internet banking: An application of UTAUT2. *Journal of Internet Banking and Commerce, 20*(1), 1–23. doi:10.1088/1757-899X/58/1/012007

Arenas-Gaitan, J., Rondan-Cataluña, F. J., & Ramírez-Correa, P. E. (2013). Social identity, electronic word-of-mouth and referrals in social network services. *Kybernetes, 42*(8), 1149–1165. doi:10.1108/K-04-2013-0081

Arghashi, V., Bozbay, Z., & Karami, A. (2021). An Integrated Model of Social Media Brand Love: Mediators of Brand Attitude and Consumer Satisfaction. *Journal of Relationship Marketing, 20*(4), 319–348. doi:10.1080/15332667.2021.1933870

Argyris, Y. A., Wang, Z., Kim, Y., & Yin, Z. (2020). The effects of visual congruence on increasing consumers' brand engagement: An empirical investigation of influencer marketing on Instagram using deep-learning algorithms for automatic image classification. *Computers in Human Behavior, 112*, 106443. doi:10.1016/j.chb.2020.106443

Ariff, M. S. M., Sylvester, M., Zakuan, N., Ismail, K., & Ali, K. M. (2014). Consumer perceived risk, attitude and online shopping behavior : Empirical evidence from Malaysia. *Proceedings of the 2014 International Conference on Manufacturing, Optimization, Industrial and Material Engineering*.

Ariff, M. S. M., Sylvester, M., Zakuan, N., Ismail, K., & Ali, K. M. (2014). Consumer perceived risk, attitude and online shopping behaviour; empirical evidence from Malaysia. *IOP Conference Series. Materials Science and Engineering*.

Armstrong, C. M., Niinimäki, K., Kujala, S., Karell, E., & Lang, C. (2015). Sustainable product-service systems for clothing: Exploring consumer perceptions of consumption alternatives in Finland. *Journal of Cleaner Production, 97*, 30–39. doi:10.1016/j.jclepro.2014.01.046

Arnold, M. J., & Reynolds, K. E. (2003). Hedonic shopping motivations. *Journal of Retailing, 79*(2), 77–95. doi:10.1016/S0022-4359(03)00007-1

Arunachalam, D., & Kumar, N. (2018). Benefit-based consumer segmentation and performance evaluation of clustering approaches: An evidence of data-driven decision-making. *Expert Systems with Applications, 111*, 11–34. doi:10.1016/j.eswa.2018.03.007

Ashley, C., & Tuten, T. (2015). Creative strategies in social media marketing: An exploratory study of branded social content and consumer engagement. *Psychology and Marketing, 32*(1), 15–27. doi:10.1002/mar.20761

Ashok, S., & Baskaran, K. (2022). The prominence of corporate governance in banking sector with reference to UAE. In *Pervasive Computing and Social Networking* (pp. 417–430). Springer Singapore. doi:10.1007/978-981-16-5640-8_33

Aslam, Z., Javaid, N., Ahmad, A., Ahmed, A., & Gulfam, S. M. (2020). A combined deep learning and ensemble learning methodology to avoid electricity theft in smart grids. *Energies, 13*(21), 5599. doi:10.3390/en13215599

Assoune, A. (2020). *Environmental Benefits Of Buying Second Hand Clothing*. Panaprium. Retrieved 13 March from https://www.panaprium.com/blogs/i/environmental-benefits-of-buying-second-hand-clothing

Aswani, R., Kar, A. K., Ilavarasan, P. V., & Dwivedi, Y. K. (2018). Search engine marketing is not all gold: Insights from Twitter and SEO Clerks. *International Journal of Information Management*, *38*(1), 107–116. doi:10.1016/j.ijinfomgt.2017.07.005

Awan, U., Shamim, S., Khan, Z., Zia, N. U., Shariq, S. M., & Khan, M. N. (2021). Big data analytics capability and decision-making: The role of data-driven insight on circular economy performance. *Technological Forecasting and Social Change*, *168*, 120766. doi:10.1016/j.techfore.2021.120766

Aydiner, A. S., Tatoglu, E., Bayraktar, E., Zaim, S., & Delen, D. (2019). Business analytics and firm performance: The mediating role of business process performance. *Journal of Business Research*, *96*, 228–237. doi:10.1016/j.jbusres.2018.11.028

Azam, A., & Qiang, F. (2014). Online consumer behaviour: Extension of decomposed theory of planned behaviour with consumers' perception of online retailing ethics. *International Journal of Electronic Business*, *11*(3), 199–219. doi:10.1504/IJEB.2014.063017

Azer, J., & Alexander, M. (2020). Negative customer engagement behaviour: The interplay of intensity and valence in online networks. *Journal of Marketing Management*, *36*(3-4), 361–383. doi:10.1080/0267257X.2020.1735488

Baabdullah, A. M., Alalwan, A. A., Rana, N. P., Patil, P., & Dwivedi, Y. K. (2019). An integrated model for m-banking adoption in Saudi Arabia. *International Journal of Bank Marketing*, *37*(2), 452–478. doi:10.1108/IJBM-07-2018-0183

Babin, B. J., Darden, W. R., & Griffin, M. (1994). Work and/or fun: Measuring hedonic and utilitarian shopping value. *The Journal of Consumer Research*, *20*(4), 644–657. doi:10.1086/209376

Backs, S., Jahnke, H., Lüpke, L., Stücken, M., & Stummer, C. (2021). Traditional versus fast fashion supply chains in the apparel industry: An agent-based simulation approach. *Annals of Operations Research*, *305*(1), 487–512. doi:10.100710479-020-03703-8

Bagozzi, R. P., & Yi, Y. (1988). On the evaluation of structural equation models. *Journal of the Academy of Marketing Science*, *16*(1), 74–94. doi:10.1007/BF02723327

Bai, C., Dhavale, D., & Sarkis, J. (2014). Integrating Fuzzy C-Means and TOPSIS for performance evaluation: An application and comparative analysis. *Expert Systems with Applications*, *41*(9), 4186–4196. doi:10.1016/j.eswa.2013.12.037

Balahur, A., & Montoyo, A. (2008). A feature dependent method for opinion mining and classification. *Proceedings on the International Conference on Natural Language Processing and Knowledge Engineering,* 1–7. 10.1109/NLPKE.2008.4906796

Balasaraswathi, M., Srinivasan, K., Udayakumar, L., Sivasakthiselvan, S., & Sumithra, M. G. (2020). Big data analytic of contexts and cascading tourism for smart city. *Materials Today: Proceedings*. Advance online publication. doi:10.1016/j.matpr.2020.10.132

Ballantine, P. W., Zafar, S., & Parsons, A. G. (2014). Changes in retail shopping behaviour in the aftermath of an earthquake. *International Review of Retail, Distribution and Consumer Research*, *24*(1), 1–13. doi:10.1080/09593969.2013.821419

Baloran, E. T. (2020). Knowledge, Attitudes, Anxiety, and Coping Strategies of Students during COVID-19 Pandemic. *Journal of Loss and Trauma*, *2020*(8), 1–8. doi:10.1080/15325024.2020.1769300

Bare Fashion. (2019). *Cariuma carbon neutral shoes made from sugarcane and cork.* Bare Fashion. Retrieved 14 March from https://barefashion.co.uk/blogs/blog/cariuma-carbon-neutral-shoes-made-from-sugarcane-and-cork

Barnes, S. J., Diaz, M., & Arnaboldi, M. (2021). Understanding panic buying during COVID-19: A text analytics approach. *Expert Systems with Applications*, *169*, 114360. doi:10.1016/j.eswa.2020.114360

Bartik, A. W., Bertrand, M., Cullen, Z., Glaeser, E. L., Luca, M., & Stanton, C. (2020). The impact of COVID-19 on small business outcomes and expectations. *Proceedings of the National Academy of Sciences of the United States of America, 117*(30), 17656–17666. doi:10.1073/pnas.2006991117 PMID:32651281

Barton, A. (2013). Mining big data in real time. *Informatica (Vilnius), 37*(1).

Barton, D., & Court, D. (2012). Making advanced analytics work for you. *Harvard Business Review, 90*(10), 78–83. doi:10.4236/apm.2016.612062 PMID:23074867

Basalamah, J., Syahnur, M. H., Ashoer, M., & Bahari, A. F. (2020). Consumer behavior in online transportation services: A systematic review of business strategies. *Ilomata International Journal of Management, 1*(3), 134–144. doi:10.52728/ijjm.v1i3.135

Baskaran, K. (2019). An Interpretive Study of Customer Experience Management towards Online Shopping in UAE. *International Journal of Mechanical Engineering and Technology, 10*(02), 1071–1077.

Baskaran, K. (2019b). The impact of digital transformation in Singapore e-tail market. *International Journal of Innovative Technology and Exploring Engineering, 8*(11), 2320–2324. doi:10.35940/ijitee.I8046.0981119

Baskaran, K., & Rajavelu, S. (2020). Digital innovation in industry 4.0 era – rebooting UAE's retail. *2020 International Conference on Communication and Signal Processing (ICCSP).* 10.1109/ICCSP48568.2020.9182301

Baskaran, K., & Vanithamani, M. R. (2014). E-Customers Attitude towards E-Store Information and Design Quality in India, Applied Research in Science, Engineering and Management. *Applied Research in Science, Engineering and Management. World Applied Sciences Journal*, 51–56. doi:10.5829/idosi.wasj.2014.31.arsem.555

Batra, R., & Ahtola, O. T. (1990). Measuring the hedonic and utilitarian sources of consumer attitude. *Marketing Letters, 2*(2), 159–170. doi:10.1007/BF00436035

Baudrillard, J. (1998). *The consumer society: Myths and structures.* Sage Publications Ltd. doi:10.4135/9781526401502

Bauman, Z. (2001). *The individualized society.* Polity Press. https://www.jstor.org/stable/4194889

Bauman, Z. (2008). *Does ethics have a chance in a world of consumers?* Harvard University Press., doi:10.4159/9780674033948

Bavelas, A. (1942). A method for investigating individual and group ideology. *Sociometry, 5*(4), 371–377. doi:10.2307/2785286

BBC. (2020). Coronavirus: Only Go to Your Job If You Cannot Work from Home—Hancock. In *Coronavirus Pandemic.* BBC. https://www.bbc.co.uk/news/uk-52022417

BBC. (2020). *Unemployment during coronavirus: The psychology of job loss.* BBC. Retrieved 08 January from https://www.bbc.com/worklife/article/20200327-unemployment-during-coronavirus-the-psychology-of-job-loss

Beaujot, A. (2011). Consumer revolution in eighteenth-century Britain. In Encyclopedia of Consumer Culture (pp. 310-313). Sage Publications. doi:10.4135/9781412994248.n119

Becker, J. (2018b). *Why We Buy More Than We Need.* Forbes. Retrieved 13 March from https://www.forbes.com/sites/joshuabecker/2018/11/27/why-we-buy-more-than-we-need/

Becker, J. (2018a). *The minimalist home: a room-by-room guide to a decluttered, refocused life.* WaterBrook.

Belanche, D., Cenjor, I., & Pérez-Rueda, A. (2019). Instagram stories versus Facebook wall: an advertising effectiveness analysis Instagram stories versus Facebook wall: un análisis de la efectividad publicitaria. *Spanish Journal of Marketing-ESIC*, *23*(1), 69–94. doi:10.1108/SJME-09-2018-0042

Belch, G. E., & Belch, M. A. (2021). *Advertising and Promotion. An Integrated Marketing Communications Perspectives*. McGraw-Hill Education. https://books.google.co.uk/books?id=PYpSzQEACAAJ

Bell, A. (2022). *Second-hand clothing apps give young shoppers new style twist.* The Financial Times. Retrieved 11 March from https://www.ft.com/content/2a318727-8047-4dca-972e-dba9cfb4229e

Bentall, R. P., Lloyd, A., Bennett, K., McKay, R., Mason, L., Murphy, J., McBride, O., Hartman, T. K., Gibson-Miller, J., Levita, L., Martinez, A. P., Stocks, T. V. A., Butter, S., Vallières, F., Hyland, P., Karatzias, T., & Shevlin, M. (2021). Pandemic buying: Testing a psychological model of over-purchasing and panic buying using data from the United Kingdom and the Republic of Ireland during the early phase of the COVI-19 pandemic. *PLOS ONE*, *16*(1), e0246339. doi:10.1371/journal.pone.0246339 PMID:33503049

Berrar, D. (2019). Cross-Validation. In S. Ranganathan, M. Gribskov, K. Nakai, & C. Schönbach (Eds.), *Encyclopedia of Bioinformatics and Computational Biology* (pp. 542–545). Academic Press. doi:10.1016/B978-0-12-809633-8.20349-X

Bhatnagar, A., & Ghosh, S. (2004). A latent class segmentation analysis of EShoppers. *Journal of Business Research*, *57*(7), 758–767. doi:10.1016/S0148-2963(02)00357-0

Bholowalia, P., & Kumar, A. (2014). EBK-means: A clustering technique based on elbow method and k-means in WSN. *International Journal of Computers and Applications*, *105*(9).

Bhupal, D. P., Bhaskar, D., Tathagata, G., Han, T., & Zhang, Y. (2020). Leptonic scalars at the LHC. *Journal of High Energy Physics*, *2020*(7), 1–39. doi:10.48550/arXiv.1910.01132

Billore, S., & Anisimova, T. (2021). Panic buying research: A systematic literature review and future research agenda. *International Journal of Consumer Studies*, *45*(4), 777–804. doi:10.1111/ijcs.12669

Bittner, M., & Eisenberg, D. (2021). *How online marketplaces are making secondhand fashion a first choice*. McKinsey & Company. Retrieved 19 March from https://www.mckinsey.com/industries/technology-media-and-telecommunications/our-insights/how-online-marketplaces-are-making-secondhand-fashion-a-first-choice

Bjorn, P. M., Esbensen, M., Jensen, E., & Matthiesen, S. (2014). Does distance still matter? Revisiting the CSCW fundamentals on distributed collaboration. *ACM Transactions on Computer-Human Interaction*, *21*(5), 27. doi:10.1145/2670534

Blattberg, R. C., Kim, B.-D., & Neslin, S. A. (2008). *Database Marketing: Analyzing and Managing Customers*. Springer. doi:10.1007/978-0-387-72579-6

Blondel, V. D., Decuyper, A., & Krings, G. (2015). A survey of results on mobile phone datasets analysis. *EPJ Data Science*, *4*(1), 10. https://doi.org/10.1140/epjds/s13688-015-0046-0

Bocock, R. (2008). *Consumption. Abingdon*. Routledge. doi:10.4324/9780203131091

Borg, D., Mont, O., & Schoonover, H. (2020). Consumer Acceptance and Value in Use-Oriented Product-Service Systems: Lessons from Swedish Consumer Goods Companies. *Sustainability*, *12*(19), 8079. Advance online publication. doi:10.3390u12198079

Borne, K. (2014). Top 10 big data challenges a serious look at 10 big data v's. *Blog Post, 11.*

Borusiak, B., Szymkowiak, A., Horska, E., Raszka, N., & Żelichowska, E. (2020). Towards Building Sustainable Consumption: A Study of Second-Hand Buying Intentions. *Sustainability*, *12*(3), 875. Advance online publication. doi:10.3390u12030875

Bose, R. (2009). Advanced analytics: Opportunities and challenges. Industrial Management & Data Systems. https://doi.org/10.1108/02635570910930073.

Botti, S., & Ann, L. (2011). The locus of choice: Personal causality and satisfaction with hedonic and utilitarian decisions. *The Journal of Consumer Research*, *37*(6), 1065–1078. doi:10.1086/656570

Bowen, J. T., & Chen McCain, S.-L. (2015). Transitioning loyalty programs. *International Journal of Contemporary Hospitality Management*, *27*(3), 415–430. doi:10.1108/IJCHM-07-2014-0368

BrandManic. (2018). *Presentamos el estudio sobre marketing de influencers en España, 2018 - BrandManic*. Retrieved February 14, 2021 from https://www.brandmanic.com/estudio-marketing-de-influencers-en-espana-2018/

Bravo, L. (2020). *How To Break Up With Fast Fashion: A guilt-free guide to changing the way you shop – for good.* Headline. https://books.google.co.uk/books?id=6pypDwAAQBAJ

Brida, J. G., Disegna, M., & Osti, L. (2012). Segmenting visitors of cultural events by motivation: A sequential non-linear clustering analysis of Italian Christmas Market visitors. *Expert Systems with Applications*, *39*(13), 11349–11356. doi:10.1016/j.eswa.2012.03.041

Brodie, R. J., Hollebeek, L. D., Jurić, B., & Ilić, A. (2011). Customer Engagement: Conceptual Domain, Fundamental Propositions, and Implications for Research. *Journal of Service Research*, *14*(3), 252–271. doi:10.1177/1094670511411703

Brodie, R. J., Ilic, A., Juric, B., & Hollebeek, L. (2013). Consumer engagement in a virtual brand community: An exploratory analysis. *Journal of Business Research*, *66*(1), 105–114. doi:10.1016/j.jbusres.2011.07.029

Bu, Y., Thaichon, P., & Parkinson, J. (2021). Igniting the Flame with Electronic Word-of-mouth in Digital Marketing. *Developing Digital Marketing*, 181–190. doi:10.1108/978-1-80071-348-220211010

Buhrman, T. (2002). *Effects of hedonic and utilitarian shopping satisfaction on mall consumption.* University of North Texas. https://digital.library.unt.edu/ark:/67531/metadc3188/manifest/

Bult, J., & Wansbeek, T. (1995). Optimal Selection for Direct Mail. *Marketing Science*, *14*(4), 378–394. doi:10.1287/mksc.14.4.378

Butz, J. H. E. Jr, & Goodstein, L. (1996). Measuring customer value: Gaining the strategic advantage. *Organizational Dynamics*, *24*(3), 63–77. doi:10.1016/S0090-2616(96)90006-6

Bygstad, B., & Presthus, W. (2013). Social Media as CRM? How two airline companies used Facebook during the "Ash Crisis" in 2010. *Scandinavian Journal of Information Systems*, *25*(1), 3.

Cahill, D. (2012). Lifestyle market segmentation. The Haworth Press.

Callaway, S. K., & Jagani, S. B. (2015). The impact of banks' entrepreneurial orientation on strategic control systems. *American Journal of Business*, *30*(1), 49–71. doi:10.1108/AJB-10-2013-0067

Cambria, E., Li, Y., Xing, F. Z., Poria, S., & Kwok, K. (2020). SenticNet 6: Ensemble Application of Symbolic and Subsymbolic AI for Sentiment Analysis. *International Conference on Information and Knowledge Management, Proceedings*, 105–114. 10.1145/3340531.3412003

Cameron, K. S., & Quinn, R. E. (1999). *Diagnosing and Changing Organizational Culture Based on the Competing Values Framework*. Addison-Wesley Publishing Company, Inc.

Camilleri, E., & Miah, S. (2017, December). A Consumer Analytics Framework for Enabling Data-Driven Marketing Intervention Methods. In *2017 4th Asia-Pacific World Congress on Computer Science and Engineering (APWC on CSE)* (pp. 8-12). IEEE. doi:10.1109/APWConCSE.2017.00011

Camilleri, M. A. (2020). The use of data-driven technologies for customer-centric marketing. *International Journal of Big Data Management*, *1*(1), 50–63. doi:10.1504/IJBDM.2020.106876

Campell, C. (1987). *The romantic ethic and the spirit of modern consumerism*. Blackwell Publishers. doi:10.1007/978-3-319-79066-4

Cao, W., Fang, Z., Hou, G., Han, M., Xu, X., Dong, J., & Zheng, J. (2020). The Psychological Impact of the COVID-19 Epidemic on College Students in China. *Psychiatry Research*, *2020*(287), 112934. doi:10.1016/j.psychres.2020.112934 PMID:32229390

Carbone, L. P., & Haeckel, S. H. (1994). Engineering Customer Experiences. *Marketing Management*, *3*(3), 8–19.

Cardoso, P., Costa, H., & Novais, L. A. (2010). Fashion consumer profiles in the Portuguese market: Involvement, innovativeness, self-expression and impulsiveness as segmentation criteria. *International Journal of Consumer Studies*, *34*(6), 638–647. doi:10.1111/j.1470-6431.2010.00891.x

Carlson, J., de Vries, N. J., Rahman, M. M., & Taylor, A. (2017). Go with the flow: Engineering flow experiences for customer engagement value creation in branded social media environments. *Journal of Brand Management*, *24*(4), 334–348. doi:10.105741262-017-0054-4

Carpenter, J. M., Moore, M., & Fairhurst, A. E. (2005). Consumer shopping value for retail brand. *Journal of Fashion Marketing and Management*, *9*(1), 43–53. doi:10.1108/13612020510586398

Carvalho, A., & Fernandes, T. (2018). Understanding customer brand engagement with virtual social communities: A comprehensive model of drivers, outcomes and moderators. *Journal of Marketing Theory and Practice*, *26*(1-2), 23–37. doi:10.1080/10696679.2017.1389241

Casaló, L. V., Flavián, C., & Guinalíu, M. (2013). La construcción de lealtad en comunidades virtuales de marca. *Revista Europea de Dirección y Economía de La Empresa*, *22*(1), 53–60. doi:10.1016/j.redee.2011.10.001

Castillo, A., Benitez, J., Llorens, J., & Luo, X. (2021). Social media-driven customer engagement and movie performance: Theory and empirical evidence. *Decision Support Systems*, *145*, 113516. doi:10.1016/j.dss.2021.113516

CBI. (2020). *The European market potential for women's underwear*. Retrieved February 14, 2021 from https://www.cbi.eu/market-information/apparel/womens-underwear/market-potential

Cervellon, M. C., Carey, L., & Harms, T. (2012). Something old, something used. *International Journal of Retail & Distribution Management*, *40*(12), 956–974. doi:10.1108/09590551211274946

Cervellon, M.-C. (2013). Conspicuous Conservation: Using Semiotics to Understand Sustainable Luxury. *International Journal of Market Research*, *55*(5), 695–717. doi:10.2501/IJMR-2013-030

Chakrabarty, S., Chopin, M., & Darrat, A. (1998). Predicting future buyer behavior with consumers' confidence and sentiment indexes. *Marketing Letters*, *9*(4), 349–360. doi:10.1023/A:1008089400754

Chang, C. W., Yeh, S. C., Li, M., & Yao, E. (2019). The introduction of a novel virtual reality training system for gynecology learning and its user experience research. *IEEE Access: Practical Innovations, Open Solutions*, *7*, 43637–43653. doi:10.1109/ACCESS.2019.2905143

Chan, H.-L., Choi, T.-M., & Lok, J. C.-Y. (2015). Mass Market Second-Hand Clothing Retail Operations in Hong Kong: A Case Study. In T.-M. Choi & T. C. E. Cheng (Eds.), *Sustainable Fashion Supply Chain Management* (pp. 155–165)., doi:10.1007/978-3-319-12703-3_8

Chan, I. C. C., Fong, D. K. C., Law, R., & Fong, L. H. N. (2018). State-of-the-art social customer relationship management. *Asia Pacific Journal of Tourism Research*, *23*(5), 423–436. doi:10.1080/10941665.2018.1466813

Charoensukmongkol, P., & Sasatanun, P. (2017). Social media use for CRM and business performance satisfaction: The moderating roles of social skills and social media sales intensity. *Asia Pacific Management Review, 22*(1), 25-34.

Chaturvedi, I., Cambria, E., Welsch, R. E., & Herrera, F. (2018). Distinguishing between facts and opinions for sentiment analysis: Survey and challenges. *Information Fusion*, *44*, 65–77. doi:10.1016/j.inffus.2017.12.006

Chau, A. L., Valle-Cruz, D., & Sandoval-Almazán, R. (2021). Sentiment Analysis in Crisis Situations for Better Connected Government: Case of Mexico Earthquake in 2017. In Web 2.0 and Cloud Technologies for Implementing Connected Government (pp. 162–181). IGI Global. doi:10.4018/978-1-7998-4570-6.ch008

Chen, C.-B., Agrawal, D., & Kumara, S. (2015). *Retail analytics: Market segmentation through transaction data.* Academic Press.

Chenarides, L., Grebitus, C., Lusk, J. L., & Printezis, I. (2021). Food consumption behavior during the COVID-19 pandemic. *Agribusiness*, *37*(1), 44–81. doi:10.1002/agr.21679 PMID:33362340

Chen, C. (2013). Perceived risk, usage frequency of mobile banking services. *Managing Service Quality*, *23*(5), 410–436. doi:10.1108/MSQ-10-2012-0137

Cheng, C.-H., & Chen, Y.-S. (2009). Classifying the segmentation of customer value via RFM model and RS theory. *Expert Systems with Applications*, *36*(3, Part 1), 4176–4184. doi:10.1016/j.eswa.2008.04.003

Chen, M., Mao, S., & Liu, Y. (2014). Big data: A survey. *Mobile Networks and Applications*, *19*(2), 171–209. https://doi.org/10.1007/s11036-013-0489-0

Chen, Q., Zhang, M., & Zhao, X. (2017). Analysing customer behaviour in mobile app usage. *Industrial Management & Data Systems*, *117*(2), 425–438. doi:10.1108/IMDS-04-2016-0141

Chen, S., Han, X., Bilgihan, A., & Okumus, F. (2021). Customer engagement research in hospitality and tourism: A systematic review. *Journal of Hospitality Marketing & Management*, *30*(7), 871–904. doi:10.1080/19368623.2021.1903644

Chen, Z., Mukherjee, A., Hsu, M., & Castellanos, M. (2013). Exploiting Domain Knowledge in Aspect Extraction. In *Proceedings of the 2013 Conference on Empirical Methods in Natural Language Processing* (pp. 1655–1667). Association for Computational Linguistics.

Chen, Z., Mukherjee, A., & Liu, B. (2014). Aspect Extraction with Automated Prior Knowledge Learning. In *Proceedings of the 52nd Annual Meeting of the Association for Computational Linguistics (*Volume 1*: Long Papers)* (pp. 347–358). Association for Computational Linguistics. 10.3115/v1/P14-1033

Cheung, C. M. K., & Lee, M. K. O. (2006). Understanding consumer trust in internet shopping: A multidisciplinary approach. *Journal of the American Society for Information Science and Technology*, *57*(4), 479–492. doi:10.1002/asi.20312

Chiles, T. H., & McMackin, J. F. (1996). Integrating variable risk preferences, trust, and transaction cost economics. *Academy of Management Review*, *21*(1), 73–99. doi:10.2307/258630

Chin, W. W. (1998). The partial least squares approach to structural equation modeling. *Modern Methods for Business Research, 295*(2), 295-336.

Chi, N. T. K. (2021). Innovation capability: The impact of e-CRM and COVID-19 risk perception. *Technology in Society*, *67*, 101725. doi:10.1016/j.techsoc.2021.101725

Ching, F. (2018). *Bird Flu, SARS and Beyond. In 130 Years of Medicine in Hong Kong*. Springer. doi:10.1007/978-981-10-6316-9

Chinwendu, O. D. (2018). An Exploratory Analysis of Market Segmentation and Young Mobile Phone Consumers in Nigeria. *International Journal of Marketing Research Innovation*, *2*(2), 30–37. doi:10.46281/ijmri.v2i2.223

Chi, T., Ganak, J., Summers, L., Adesanya, O., McCoy, L., Liu, H., & Tai, Y. (2021). Understanding Perceived Value and Purchase Intention toward Eco-Friendly Athleisure Apparel: Insights from U.S. Millennials. *Sustainability*, *13*(14), 7946. Advance online publication. doi:10.3390u13147946

Cho, Y. S., Moon, S. C., Noh, S. C., & Ryu, K. H. (2012). Implementation of personalized recommendation system using k-means clustering of item category based on RFM. *2012 IEEE 6th International Conference on Management of Innovation and Technology, ICMIT 2012*, 378–383. 10.1109/ICMIT.2012.6225835

Choi, H., & Kandampully, J. (2019). The effect of atmosphere on customer engagement in upscale hotels: An application of S-O-R paradigm. *International Journal of Hospitality Management*, *77*, 40–50. doi:10.1016/j.ijhm.2018.06.012

Choi, T.-M., & He, Y. (2019). Peer-to-peer collaborative consumption for fashion products in the sharing economy: Platform operations. *Transportation Research Part E, Logistics and Transportation Review*, *126*, 49–65. doi:10.1016/j.tre.2019.03.016

Cho, J. (2006). The mechanism of trust and distrust formation and their relational outcomes. *Journal of Retailing*, *82*(1), 25–35. doi:10.1016/j.jretai.2005.11.002

Chopdar, P. K., Paul, J., & Prodanova, J. (2022). Mobile shoppers' response to Covid-19 phobia, pessimism and smartphone addiction: Does social influence matter? *Technological Forecasting and Social Change*, *174*, 121249. doi:10.1016/j.techfore.2021.121249

Christopher, M., Payne, A., & Ballantyne, D. (2013). *Relationship marketing*. Routledge. doi:10.4324/9780080516042

Chung, N., & Kwon, S. J. (2009). The effect of customers' mobile experience and technical support on the intention to use mobile banking. *Cyberpsychology & Behavior*, *12*(5), 539–543. doi:10.1089/cpb.2009.0014 PMID:19772441

Cills, H. (2021). *The Complicated Reality of Thrift Store 'Gentrification'*. Jezebel. Retrieved 14 March from https://jezebel.com/the-complicated-reality-of-thrift-store-gentrification-1846113458

Ciunova-Shuleska, A., Palamidovska-Sterjadovska, N., & Prodanova, J. (2022). What drives m-banking clients to continue using m-banking services? *Journal of Business Research*, *139*, 731–739. doi:10.1016/j.jbusres.2021.10.024

Clark, H. (2008). SLOW + FASHION—an Oxymoron—or a Promise for the Future ...? *Fashion Theory*, *12*(4), 427–446. doi:10.2752/175174108X346922

Clement Addo, P., Fang, J., Asare, A. O., & Kulbo, N. B. (2021). Customer engagement and purchase intention in live-streaming digital marketing platforms. *Service Industries Journal*, *41*(11-12), 767–786. doi:10.1080/02642069.2021.1905798

Close, A., & Zinkhan, G. (2006). A holiday loved and loathed: A consumer perspective of Valentine's Day. *Advances in Consumer Research. Association for Consumer Research (U. S.)*, *33*, 356–365.

Code, J., Ralph, R., & Forde, K. (2020). Pandemic Designs for the Future: Perspectives of Technology Education Teachers during COVID-19. *Inf. Learn. Sci.*, *2020*(121), 419–431. doi:10.1108/ILS-04-2020-0112

Cognizant. (2018). *How to Deliver Exceptional Customer Engagement*. Cognizant. Retrieved 22 January from https://www.cognizant.com/whitepapers/how-to-deliver-exceptional-customer-engagement-codex2794.pdf

Cohen, S. H., & Ramaswamy, V. (1998). Latent segmentation models. *Marketing Research*, *10*(2), 14.

Colton, B. (2018). *Customers are important, but firms ignore employees at their peril*. LSE. Retrieved 22 January from https://blogs.lse.ac.uk/management/2018/05/23/customers-are-important-but-firms-ignore-employees-at-their-peril/

Constantinides, E. (2004). Influencing the online consumer's behavior: The Web experience. *Internet Research*, *14*(2), 111–126. doi:10.1108/10662240410530835

Constantiou, I. D., & Kallinikos, J. (2015). New games, new rules: Big data and the changing context of strategy. *Journal of Information Technology*, *30*(1), 44–57. https://doi.org/10.1057%2Fjit.2014.17

Cooil, B., Keiningham, T., Aksoy, L., & Hsu, M. (2007). A longitudinal analysis of customer satisfaction and share of wallet: Investigating the moderating effect of customer characteristics. *Journal of Marketing*, *71*(1), 67–83. doi:10.1509/jmkg.71.1.067

Cook, R. D., & Sanford, W. (1982). *Residuals and influence in regression*. Chapman and Hall.

Cooper, C. L., Woodward, S., Hiller, A., & Goworek, H. (2008). *Public understanding of sustainable clothing*. A report to the Department for Environment, Food and Rural Affairs.

Coppola, D. (2021). *Most popular sustainable retail models used by consumers in the United States as of December 2019, by generation*. Statista. Retrieved 19 March from https://www.statista.com/statistics/1100335/sustainable-retail-models/

Corrigan, P. (1997). *The sociology of consumption: An introduction*. SAGE Publications Ltd. doi:10.4135/9781446216903

Côté-Allard, U., Fall, C. L., Drouin, A., Campeau-Lecours, A., Gosselin, C., Glette, K., Laviolette, F., & Gosselin, B. (2019). Deep learning for electromyographic hand gesture signal classification using transfer learning. *IEEE Transactions on Neural Systems and Rehabilitation Engineering*, *27*(4), 760–771. doi:10.1109/TNSRE.2019.2896269 PMID:30714928

Court, D. (2015). Getting big impact from big data. *The McKinsey Quarterly*, *1*(1), 52–60.

COVID-19 Consistently Impacts Shopping Behavior of 9 in 10 Consumers. (2021). *Numerator Intelligence*. https://www.numerator.com/resources/blog/impact-covid-19-consumer-behavior

COVID-19: How consumer behavior will be changed. (2020). *Accenture*. https://www.accenture.com/us-en/insights/consumer-goods-services/coronavirus-consumer-behavior-research

Criteo. (2017). *Valentine's day gifts hearts, flowers, jewelry, lingerie...and kisses*. Retrieved February 14, 2021 from https://www.criteo.com/wp-content/uploads/2017/02/valentines-day-report-2017.pdf

Croft, M. J. (1994). *Market segmentation: A step-by-step guide to profitable new business*. Cengage Learning Emea.

Crowley, A. E., Spangenberg, R. E., & Hughes, R. K. (1992). Measuring the hedonic and dimensions of attitudes toward product categories. *Marketing Letters*, *3*(3), 239–249. doi:10.1007/BF00994132

Cruz, I., Ganga, R., & Wahlen, S. (2018). Contemporary collaborative consumption: An introduction. In I. Cruz, R. Ganga, & S. Wahlen (Eds.), *Contemporary Collaborative Consumption: Trust and Reciprocity Revisited* (pp. 1–15). Springer Fachmedien Wiesbaden. doi:10.1007/978-3-658-21346-6_1

Cudjoe, A. G., Anim, P. A., & Nyanyofio, J. G. N. T. (2015). Determinants of mobile banking adoption in the Ghanaian banking industry: A case of access bank Ghana limited. *Journal of Computer and Communications*, *3*(2), 1–19. doi:10.4236/jcc.2015.32001

Cui, Z. X., Yoo, H. K., Choi, J. Y., & Youn, H. Y. (2011). Multi-criteria group decision making with fuzzy logic and entropy based weighting. *Proceedings of the 5th International Confernece on Ubiquitous Information Management and Communication - ICUIMC '11*, 1. 10.1145/1968613.1968706

Cui, G., Wong, M. L., & Lui, H.-K. (2006). Machine Learning for Direct Marketing Response Models: Bayesian Networks with Evolutionary Programming. *Management Science, 52*(4), 597–612. doi:10.1287/mnsc.1060.0514

Cui, X., Xie, Q., Zhu, J., Shareef, M. A., Goraya, M. A. S., & Akram, M. S. (2022). Understanding the omnichannel customer journey: The effect of online and offline channel interactivity on consumer value co-creation behavior. *Journal of Retailing and Consumer Services, 65*(102869), 102869. doi:10.1016/j.jretconser.2021.102869

Cyriac, N. T., & Baskaran, K. (2020). A study on the effectiveness of non-monetary retention strategies in UAE. *2020 8th International Conference on Reliability, Infocom Technologies and Optimization (Trends and Future Directions) (ICRITO)*. 10.1109/ICRITO48877.2020.9197867

Cyriac, N. T., & Baskaran, K. (2021). Predictive Analytics in a Post Covid-19 World: India's Travel and Tourism Industry. *Proceedings of International Conference on Advances in Technology, Management & Education*. 10.1109/ICATME50232.2021.9732706

D'Adamo, I., Lupi, G., Morone, P., & Settembre-Blundo, D. (2022). Towards the circular economy in the fashion industry: The second-hand market as a best practice of sustainable responsibility for businesses and consumers. *Environmental Science and Pollution Research International*. Advance online publication. doi:10.100711356-022-19255-2 PMID:35171425

D'Ambrogio, E. (2014). *Workers' conditions in the textile and clothing sector*. European Parliament. Retrieved 10 March from https://www.europarl.europa.eu/EPRS/140841REV1-Workers-conditions-in-the-textile-and-clothing-sector-just-an-Asian-affair-FINAL.pdf

Dahlbo, H., Aalto, K., Eskelinen, H., & Salmenperä, H. (2017). Increasing textile circulation—Consequences and requirements. *Sustainable Production and Consumption, 9*, 44-57.

Dai, Y., & Wang, T. (2021). Prediction of customer engagement behaviour response to marketing posts based on machine learning. *Connection Science, 33*(4), 891–910. doi:10.1080/09540091.2021.1912710

Damghanian, H., Zarei, A., & Siahsarani Kojuri, M. A. (2016). Impact of Perceived Security on Trust, Perceived Risk, and Acceptance of Online Banking in Iran. *Journal of Internet Commerce, 15*(3), 214–238. https://doi.org/10.1080/15332861.2016.1191052

Daughtrey, C. L., Vowles, N. S., & Black, G. S. (2013). The effects of membership and demographics on consumer satisfaction and loyalty in service organizations. *Services Marketing Quarterly, 34*(4), 292–308. doi:10.1080/15332969.2013.827066

David, J., Visvalingam, S., & Norberg, M. M. (2021). Why did all the toilet paper disappear? Distinguishing between panic buying and hoarding during COVID-19. *Psychiatry Research, 303*, 114062. doi:10.1016/j.psychres.2021.114062 PMID:34175712

Davies, B., & Ward, P. (2001). *Managing retail consumption*. John Wiley and Sons Ltd.

Davila, T. (2000). An empirical study on the drivers of management control systems' design in new product development. *Accounting, Organizations and Society, 25*(4), 383–409. doi:10.1016/S0361-3682(99)00034-3

Davis, F. D., Bagozzi, R. P., & Warshaw, P. R. (1989). User Acceptance of Computer Technology: A Comparison of Two Theoretical Models. *Management Science, 35*(8), 982–1003. https://www.jstor.org/stable/2632151

Day, G. S. (2012). *The Market Driven Organization: Attracting And Keeping Valuable Customers*. Simon & Schuster UK. https://books.google.co.uk/books?id=8xZiORNX3hIC

De Domenico, M., Lima, A., González, M. C., & Arenas, A. (2015). Personalized routing for multitudes in smart cities. *EPJ Data Science*, *4*(1), 1–11. https://doi.org/10.1140/epjds/s13688-015-0038-0

De Leon, M. V., Atienza, R. P., & Susilo, D. (2020). Influence of self-service technology (SST) service quality dimensions as a second-order factor on perceived value and customer satisfaction in a mobile banking application. *Cogent Business & Management*, *7*(1), 1794241. doi:10.1080/23311975.2020.1794241

de Matos, C. A., & Rossi, C. A. V. (2008). Word-of-mouth communications in marketing: A meta-analytic review of the antecedents and moderators. *Journal of the Academy of Marketing Science*, *36*(4), 578–596. doi:10.100711747-008-0121-1

De Valck, K., Van Bruggen, G. H., & Wierenga, B. (2009). Virtual communities: A marketing perspective. *Decision Support Systems*, *47*(3), 185–203. doi:10.1016/j.dss.2009.02.008

De Vries, L., Gensler, S., & Leeflang, P. S. H. (2012). Popularity of brand posts on brand fan Pages: An investigation of the effects of social media marketing. *Journal of Interactive Marketing*, *26*(2), 83–91. doi:10.1016/j.intmar.2012.01.003

Deepak, R. K. A., & Jeyakumar, S. (2019). *Marketing management*. Educreation Publishing.

Delen, D., & Ram, S. (2018). Research challenges and opportunities in business analytics. *Journal of Business Analytics*, *1*(1), 2–12. doi:10.1080/2573234X.2018.1507324

Demirhan, M. (2020). Demographic characteristics and perceived value differences in mobile banking: An empirical study in Turkey. *Erciyes Üniversitesi Sosyal Bilimler Enstitüsü Dergisi*, *48*, 237–263.

Depop; T., & Bain & Company. (2020). *Report On Gen Z*. Depop x Bain & Company. Retrieved 19 March from https://depopxbainreport.depop.com/report/The-Depop-X-Bain-Company-Report-How-Gen-Zs-Awareness-And-Fluidity-Are-Transforming-Business-As-Usual.pdf

Desmond, N., & Zhaohao, S. (2021). Big Data Analytics for Smart Airport Management. In S. Zhaohao (Ed.), *Intelligent Analytics With Advanced Multi-Industry Applications* (pp. 209–231). IGI Global. doi:10.4018/978-1-7998-4963-6.ch010

Dessart, L., Aldás-Manzano, J., & Veloutsou, C. (2019). Unveiling heterogeneous engagement-based loyalty in brand communities. *European Journal of Marketing*, *53*(9), 1854–1881. doi:10.1108/EJM-11-2017-0818

Dew, R., Russell, B., Allen, C., & Bej, G. (2021). *Lean CX: How to Differentiate at Low Cost and Least Risk*. De Gruyter.

Dewnarain, S., Ramkissoon, H., & Mavondo, F. (2019). Social customer relationship management: An integrated conceptual framework. *Journal of Hospitality Marketing & Management*, *28*(2), 172–188. doi:10.1080/19368623.2018.1516588

Dhar, R., & Wertenbroch, K. (2000). Consumer choice between hedonic and utilitarian goods. *JMR, Journal of Marketing Research*, *37*(1), 60–71. doi:10.1509/jmkr.37.1.60.18718

Dhawan, S. (2020). Online Learning: A Panacea in the Time of COVID-19 Crisis. *Journal of Educational Technology Systems*, *2020*(49), 5–22. doi:10.1177/0047239520934018

Di Crosta, A., Ceccato, I., Marchetti, D., La Malva, P., Maiella, R., Cannito, L., Cipi, M., Mammarella, N., Palumbo, R., Verrocchio, M. C., Palumbo, R., & Di Domenico, A. (2021). Psychological factors and consumer behavior during the COVID-19 pandemic. *PLoS One*, *16*(8), e0256095. doi:10.1371/journal.pone.0256095 PMID:34398916

Dibb, S., & Simkin, L. (2016). Market segmentation and segment strategy. *Marketing theory: A student text, 251279.*

Dobre, C., & Xhafa, F. (2014). Intelligent services for big data science. *Future Generation Computer Systems*, *37*, 267–281. https://doi.org/10.1016/j.future.2013.07.014

Dodds, W. B., Monroe, K. B., & Grewal, D. (1991). Effects of price, brand, and store information on buyers' product evaluations. *JMR, Journal of Marketing Research*, *28*(3), 307–319. doi:10.2307/3172866

Do, H. H., Prasad, P. W. C., Maag, A., & Alsadoon, A. (2019). Deep Learning for Aspect-Based Sentiment Analysis: A Comparative Review. *Expert Systems with Applications*, *118*, 272–299. doi:10.1016/j.eswa.2018.10.003

Dolnicar, S. (2018). Understanding and Satisfying Consumer Needs: Segmentation, Targeting and Positioning. The SAGE Handbook of Tourism Management: Applications of Theories And Concepts to Tourism, 257.

Dolnicar, S., Grün, B., & Leisch, F. (2018a). Market Segmentation. In *Market Segmentation Analysis* (pp. 3–9). Springer. doi:10.1007/978-981-10-8818-6_1

Dolnicar, S., Grün, B., & Leisch, F. (2018b). Step 2: Specifying the Ideal Target Segment. In S. Dolnicar, B. Grün, & F. Leisch (Eds.), *Market Segmentation Analysis* (pp. 31–37). Springer Singapore. doi:10.1007/978-981-10-8818-6_4

Dolnicar, S., Grün, B., & Leisch, F. (2018c). Step 4: Exploring Data. In S. Dolnicar, B. Grün, & F. Leisch (Eds.), *Market Segmentation Analysis: Understanding It, Doing It, and Making It Useful* (pp. 57–73). Springer Singapore. doi:10.1007/978-981-10-8818-6_6

Dolnicar, S., Grün, B., & Leisch, F. (2018d). Step 5: Extracting Segments. In S. Dolnicar, B. Grün, & F. Leisch (Eds.), *Market Segmentation Analysis: Understanding It, Doing It, and Making It Useful* (pp. 75–181). Springer Singapore. doi:10.1007/978-981-10-8818-6_7

Dolnicar, S., Grün, B., & Leisch, F. (2018e). Step 6: Profiling Segments. In S. Dolnicar, B. Grün, & F. Leisch (Eds.), *Market Segmentation Analysis: Understanding It, Doing It, and Making It Useful* (pp. 183–197). Springer Singapore. doi:10.1007/978-981-10-8818-6_8

Dolnicar, S., Grün, B., & Leisch, F. (2018f). Step 10: Evaluation and Monitoring. In S. Dolnicar, B. Grün, & F. Leisch (Eds.), *Market Segmentation Analysis: Understanding It, Doing It, and Making It Useful* (pp. 255–267). Springer Singapore., doi:10.1007/978-981-10-8818-6_12

Doniger, A. (2021). *Shoppers are buying from resale retailers more than ever. Here's why.* CNBC. Retrieved 19 March from https://www.cnet.com/home/smart-home/features/rise-of-secondhand-retail-poshmark-thredup-letgo-mercari-ebay-thrift-clothing-selling-apps/

Donthu, N., & Gustafsson, A. (2020). Effects of COVID-19 on business and research. *Journal of Business Research*, *117*, 284–289. doi:10.1016/j.jbusres.2020.06.008 PMID:32536736

Doolin, B., Dillon, S., Thompson, F., & Corner, J. L. (2005). Perceived risk, the Internet shopping experience and online purchasing behavior: A New Zealand perspective. *Journal of Global Information Management*, *13*(2), 66–88. https://doi.org/10.4018/jgim.2005040104

Dragisa, S., Bojan, D., & Mira, D. (2013). Comparative analysis of some prominent MCDM methods: A case of ranking Serbian banks. *Serbian Journal of Management*, *8*(2), 213–241. doi:10.5937jm8-3774

Dreyer, B., Lüdeke-Freund, F., Hamann, R., & Faccer, K. (2017). Upsides and downsides of the sharing economy: Collaborative consumption business models' stakeholder value impacts and their relationship to context. *Technological Forecasting and Social Change*, *125*, 87–104. doi:10.1016/j.techfore.2017.03.036

Dubey, R., Gunasekaran, A., Childe, S. J., Blome, C., & Papadopoulos, T. (2019). Big data and predictive analytics and manufacturing performance: Integrating institutional theory, resource-based view and big data culture. *British Journal of Management*, *30*(2), 341–361. https://doi.org/10.1111/1467-8551.12355

Dubois, B., & Duquesne, P. (1993). The Market for Luxury Goods: Income versus Culture. *European Journal of Marketing*, *27*(1), 35–44. doi:10.1108/03090569310024530

Duimering, P. R., Ran, B., Derbentseva, N., & Poile, C. (2006). The effects of ambiguity on project task structure in new product development. *Knowledge and Process Management*, *13*(4), 239–251. doi:10.1002/kpm.260

Dursun, A., & Caber, M. (2016). Using data mining techniques for profiling profitable hotel customers: An application of RFM analysis. *Tourism Management Perspectives*, *18*, 153–160. doi:10.1016/j.tmp.2016.03.001

Dutta, S., & Lanvin, B. (2020). *The Network Readiness Index 2020: Accelerating Digital Transformation in a post-COVID Global Economy, Sumatra Dutta & Bruno Lanvin (Edited)*. Portland Institute.

Dwivedi, Y. K., Ismagilova, E., Hughes, D. L., Carlson, J., Filieri, R., Jacobson, J., Jain, V., Karjaluoto, H., Kefi, H., Krishen, A. S., Kumar, V., Rahman, M. M., Raman, R., Rauschnabel, P. A., Rowley, J., Salo, J., Tran, G. A., & Wang, Y. (2021). Setting the future of digital and social media marketing research: Perspectives and research propositions. *International Journal of Information Management*, *59*, 102168. doi:10.1016/j.ijinfomgt.2020.102168

Dwivedi, Y. K., Rana, N. P., Jeyaraj, A., Clement, M., & Williams, M. D. (2019). Re-examining the unified theory of acceptance and use of technology (UTAUT): Towards a revised theoretical model. *Information Systems Frontiers*, *21*(3), 719–734. https://doi.org/0.1007/s10796-017-9774-y

Dzardanova, E., Kasapakis, V., & Gavalas, D. (2018). On the effect of social context in virtual reality: An examination of the determinants of human behavior in shared immersive virtual environments. *IEEE Consumer Electronics Magazine*, *7*(4), 44–52. doi:10.1109/MCE.2018.2816204

Dzyabura, D., & Yoganarasimhan, H. (2018). Machine learning and marketing. In N. Mizik & D. M. Hanssens (Eds.), *Handbook of Marketing Analytics* (pp. 255–279). Edward Elgar Publishing. doi:10.4337/9781784716752.00023

Efron, B. (1992). Bootstrap methods: another look at the jackknife. In *Breakthroughs in statistics* (pp. 569–593). Springer. doi:10.1007/978-1-4612-4380-9_41

Eirinaki, M., Pisal, S., & Singh, J. (2012). Feature-based opinion mining and ranking. *Journal of Computer and System Sciences*, *78*(4), 1175–1184. doi:10.1016/j.jcss.2011.10.007

Elgendy, N., & Elragal, A. (2014). Big Data Analytics: A Literature Review Paper. In P. Perner (Ed.), Lecture Notes in Computer Science: Vol. 8557. Advances in Data Mining. Applications and Theoretical Aspects. ICDM 2014. Springer. https://doi.org/10.1007/978-3-319-08976-8_16.

Elgendy, N., & Elragal, A. (2016). Big data analytics in support of the decision making process. *Procedia Computer Science*, *100*, 1071–1084. https://doi.org/10.1016/j.procs.2016.09.251

Enders, W. (2008). *Applied econometric time series*. John Wiley & Sons.

Ertz, M. (2020). Collaborative consumption, a buzzword that has gone conceptual: Three shades of the sharing economy. *Oikonomics*, *14*(14), 1–14. doi:10.7238/o.n14.2011

Ertz, M., Deschênes, J., & Sarigöllü, E. (2021). From User to Provider: Switching Over in the Collaborative Economy. *Sustainability*, *13*(10), 5662. Advance online publication. doi:10.3390u13105662

Ertz, M., Durif, F., & Arcand, M. (2016). Collaborative consumption: Conceptual snapshot at a buzzword. *Journal of Entrepreneurship Education, 19*(2), 1–23.

Escobar-Rodríguez, T., & Bonsón-Fernández, R. (2017). Analysing online purchase intention in Spain: Fashion e-commerce. *Information Systems and e-Business Management, 15*(3), 599–622. https://doi.org/10.1007/s10257-016-0319-6

Facebook, I. Q. (2020, July 16). *Text, timing and format tips for effective Facebook creative.* Facebook. Retrieved February 14, 2021 from https://www.facebook.com/business/news/insights/making-creative-impact-on-facebook-platforms-with-text-timing-and-format

Farmania, A., Elsyah, R. D., & Tuori, M. A. (2021). Transformation of CRM Activities into e-CRM: The Generating e-Loyalty and Open Innovation. *Journal of Open Innovation, 7*(2), 109. Advance online publication. doi:10.3390/joitmc7020109

Farrant, L., Olsen, S. I., & Wangel, A. (2010). Environmental benefits from reusing clothes. *The International Journal of Life Cycle Assessment, 15*(7), 726–736. doi:10.100711367-010-0197-y

Fatoni, C. S., Utami, E., & Wibowo, F. W. (2018). Online Store Product Recommendation System Uses Apriori Method. *Journal of Physics: Conference Series, 1140*(1), 012034. Advance online publication. doi:10.1088/1742-6596/1140/1/012034

Feehan, B. (2021, February 24). How often to post on social media. *Rival IQ*. Retrieved February 14, 2021 from https://www.rivaliq.com/blog/how-often-to-post-social-media/

Ferraro, C., Sands, S., & Brace-Govan, J. (2016). The role of fashionability in second-hand shopping motivations. *Journal of Retailing and Consumer Services, 32*, 262–268. doi:10.1016/j.jretconser.2016.07.006

Ferreira, M., Zambaldi, F., & Guerra, D. S. (2020). Consumer engagement in social media: Scale comparison analysis. *Journal of Product and Brand Management, 29*(4), 491–503. doi:10.1108/JPBM-10-2018-2095

Fiaidhi, J., & Mohammed, S. (2019). Thick data: A new qualitative analytics for identifying customer insights. *IT Professional, 21*(3), 4–13. https://dx.doi.org/10.1109/MITP.2019.2910982

Figliozzi, M., & Unnikrishnan, A. (2021). Home-deliveries before-during COVID-19 lockdown: Accessibility, environmental justice, equity, and policy implications. *Transportation Research Part D, Transport and Environment, 93*, 102760. doi:10.1016/j.trd.2021.102760 PMID:33649701

Filipe, A. B., Montagna, G., & Carvalho, C. (2011). Lingerie product image in Portuguese underwear market: From brand to consumer, a perceived lingerie image. *International Journal of the Image, 1*(2), 51–68. doi:10.18848/2154-8560/CGP/v01i02/44182

Financial Times. (2021). *Etsy/Depop: hanging on to Gen Z by a thread.* Financial Times. Retrieved 18 February from https://www.ft.com/content/c32f3536-ae6e-4cba-9368-77794723c097

Finger, F., Genolet, T., Mari, L., de Magny, G. C., Manga, N. M., Rinaldo, A., & Bertuzzo, E. (2016). Mobile phone data highlights the role of mass gatherings in the spreading of cholera outbreaks. *Proceedings of the National Academy of Sciences of the United States of America, 113*(23), 6421–6426. https://doi.org/10.1073/pnas.1522305113

Fishbein, M., & Ajzen, I. (1977). Belief, attitude, intention, and behavior: An introduction to theory and research. *Philosophy & Rhetoric, 10*(2).

Fishbein, M., Jaccard, J., Davidson, A. R., Ajzen, I., & Loken, B. (1980). Predicting and understanding family planning behaviors. In *Understanding attitudes and predicting social behavior*. Prentice Hall.

Fletcher, K. (2012). Durability, Fashion, Sustainability: The Processes and Practices of Use. *Fashion Practice*, *4*(2), 221–238. doi:10.2752/175693812X13403765252389

Foedermayr, E. K., & Diamantopoulos, A. (2008). Market Segmentation in Practice: Review of Empirical Studies, Methodological Assessment, and Agenda for Future Research. *Journal of Strategic Marketing*, *16*(3), 223–265. doi:10.1080/09652540802117140

Fogel, S. (2010). Issues in measurement of word of mouth in social media marketing. *International Journal of Integrated Marketing Communications*, *2*(2), 54–60. doi:10.1108/13552550610710153

Foltean, F. S., Trif, S. M., & Tuleu, D. L. (2019). Customer relationship management capabilities and social media technology use: Consequences on firm performance. *Journal of Business Research*, *104*, 563–575. doi:10.1016/j.jbusres.2018.10.047

Fortuna, L. M., & Diyamandoglu, V. (2017). Optimization of greenhouse gas emissions in second-hand consumer product recovery through reuse platforms. *Waste Management, 66*, 178-189.

Friedman, J., Hastie, T., & Tibshirani, R. (2001). *The elements of statistical learning*. Springer.

Frost, R., Fox, A. K., & Strauss, J. (2018). *E-marketing*. Taylor & Francis. https://books.google.co.uk/books?id=8PErDwAAQBAJ

Fuxman, L., Mohr, I., Mahmoud, A. B., & Grigoriou, N. (2022). The new 3Ps of sustainability marketing: The case of fashion. *Sustainable Production and Consumption*, *31*, 384–396. doi:10.1016/j.spc.2022.03.004

Gabriel, J., Ogbuigwe, T., & Ahiauzu, L. (2016). Online shopping systems in Nigeria: Evolution, trend and prospects. *Asian Research Journal of Arts & Social Sciences, 1*(4), 182-276. doi:10.9734/ARJASS/2016/29170

Gabriel, Y., & Lang, T. (1995). *The unmanageable consumer: Contemporary consumption and its fragmentations*. Sage Publications. doi:10.4135/9781446213049.n6

Gallup. (2014). *Why Customer Engagement Matters So Much Now*. Gallup. Retrieved 22 January from https://news.gallup.com/businessjournal/172637/why-customer-engagement-matters.aspx

Gandomi, A., & Haider, M. (2015). Beyond the hype: Big data concepts, methods, and analytics. *International Journal of Information Management*, *35*(2), 137–144. https://doi.org/10.1016/j.ijinfomgt.2014.10.007

Gao, C., & Liu, J. (2015). Uncovering spatiotemporal characteristics of human online behaviors during extreme events. *PLoS One*, *10*(10), 1–14. doi:10.1371/journal.pone.0138673 PMID:26492043

Gao, C., & Liu, J. (2017). Network-Based Modeling for Characterizing Human Collective Behaviors During Extreme Events. *IEEE Transactions on Systems, Man, and Cybernetics. Systems*, *47*(1), 171–183. doi:10.1109/TSMC.2016.2608658

Gao, X., Shi, X., Guo, H., & Liu, Y. (2020). To buy or not buy food online: The impact of the COVID-19 epidemic on the adoption of e-commerce in China. *PLoS One*, *15*(8), e0237900. https://doi.org/10.1371/journal.pone.0237900

García-Fernández, J., Gálvez-Ruíz, P., Fernández-Gavira, J., Vélez-Colón, L., Pitts, B., & Bernal-García, A. (2018). The effects of service convenience and perceived quality on perceived value, satisfaction and loyalty in low-cost fitness centers. *Sport Management Review*, *21*(3), 250–262. doi:10.1016/j.smr.2017.07.003

Garg, P., Gupta, B., Dzever, S., Sivarajah, U., & Kumar, V. (2020). Examining the relationship between social media analytics practices and business performance in the Indian retail and IT industries: The mediation role of customer engagement. *International Journal of Information Management*, *52*, 102069. https://doi.org/10.1016/j.ijinfomgt.2020.102069

Garrido-Moreno, A., García-Morales, V. J., Lockett, N., & King, S. (2018). The missing link: Creating value with Social Media use in hotels. *International Journal of Hospitality Management*, *75*, 94–104. doi:10.1016/j.ijhm.2018.03.008

Gashi, R., & Ahmeti, H. (2021). Impact of Social Media on the Development of New Products, Marketing and Customer Relationship Management in Kosovo. *Emerging Science Journal*, *5*(2), 125–138. doi:10.28991/esj-2021-01263

Gazzola, P., Pavione, E., Pezzetti, R., & Grechi, D. (2020). Trends in the Fashion Industry. The Perception of Sustainability and Circular Economy: A Gender/Generation Quantitative Approach. *Sustainability*, *12*(7), 2809. Advance online publication. doi:10.3390u12072809

Geiger, S. (2007). Exploring night-time grocery shopping behaviour. *Journal of Retailing and Consumer Services*, *14*(1), 24–34. doi:10.1016/j.jretconser.2006.03.001

Gentry, J. (2016). Package 'twitteR.' *Cran*, 1–32. http://lists.hexdump.org/listinfo.cgi/twitter-users-hexdump.org

George, S. (2016). Mobile banking in the present scenario. *International Journal of Research in Commerce and Management*, *7*(2), 61–64.

Germann, F., Lilien, G. L., Fiedler, L., & Kraus, M. (2014). Do Retailers Benefit from Deploying Customer Analytics? *Journal of Retailing, 90*(4), 587-593. doi:10.1016/j.jretai.2014.08.002

Gerval, O. (2010). *Fashion: Concept to Catwalk*. Firefly Books. https://books.google.co.uk/books?id=P7eaRAAACAAJ

Ghazie, D., & Dolah, J. (2018). *How Digital Marketing Affects Consumer Behavior*. doi:10.2991/reka-18.2018.48

Ghorashi, S. H., Ibrahim, R., Noekhah, S., & Dastjerdi, N. S. (2012). A Frequent Pattern Mining Algorithm for Feature Extraction of Customer Reviews. *International Journal of Computer Science Issues*, *9*(4), 29–35.

Gironda, J. T., & Korgaonkar, P. K. (2018). iSpy? Tailored versus invasive ads and consumers' perceptions of personalized advertising. *Electronic Commerce Research and Applications*, *29*, 64–77. doi:10.1016/j.elerap.2018.03.007

Gligorijevic, B. (2016). Review platforms in destinations and hospitality. In R. Egger, I. Gula, & D. Walcher (Eds.), *Open tourism* (pp. 215–228). Springer., doi:10.1007/978-3-642-54089-9_15

Gnanaraj, T. N., Kumar, K. R., & Monica, N. (2014). Survey on mining clusters using new k-mean algorithm from structured and unstructured data. *Int. J. Adv. Comput. Sci. Technol*, *3*(2).

Gogus, A., & Saygın, Y. (2019). Privacy perception and information technology utilization of high school students. *Heliyon*, *5*(5), e01614. doi:10.1016/j.heliyon.2019.e01614 PMID:31193323

Golden, M. (2011). *Social Media Strategies for Professionals and Their Firms: The Guide to Establishing Credibility and Accelerating Relationships*. John Wiley and Sons.

Golestan, S., Mahmoudi-Nejad, A., & Moradi, H. (2018). A framework for easier designs: Augmented intelligence in serious games for Cognitive Development. *IEEE Consumer Electronics Magazine*, *8*(1), 19–24. doi:10.1109/MCE.2018.2867970

Good, M. C., & Hyman, M. R. (2020). Protection motivation theory and brick-and-mortar salespeople. *International Journal of Retail & Distribution Management*, *48*(8), 865–879. doi:10.1108/IJRDM-05-2019-0155

Gouedard, P., Pont, B., & Viennet, R. (2020). *Education responses to COVID-19: Implementing a way forward*. OECD Education Working Paper No. 224. doi:10.1787/19939019

Grand View Research. (2019, June). *Lingerie market size, share & trends analysis*. Retrieved February 14, 2021 from https://www.grandviewresearch.com/industry-analysis/lingerie-market

Greco, F., & Polli, A. (2020). Emotional Text Mining: Customer profiling in brand management. *International Journal of Information Management*, *51*, 101934. doi:10.1016/j.ijinfomgt.2019.04.007

Greenberg, P. (2010). The impact of CRM 2.0 on customer insight. *Journal of Business and Industrial Marketing*, *25*(6), 410–419. doi:10.1108/08858621011066008

Green, P. E., Frank, R. E., & Robinson, P. J. (1967). Cluster Analysis in Test Market Selection. *Management Science*, *13*(8), B387–B400. doi:10.1287/mnsc.13.8.B387

Gretzel, U., Sigala, M., Xiang, Z., & Koo, C. (2015). Smart tourism: Foundations and developments. *Electronic Markets*, *25*(3), 179–188. https://doi.org/10.1007/s12525-015-0196-8

Grewal, D., & Levy, M. (2020). *Loose Leaf for M: Marketing*. McGraw-Hill Education. https://books.google.co.uk/books?id=OIj9yAEACAAJ

Griliches, Z., Heckman, J. J., Intriligator, M. D., Engle, R. F., Leamer, E. E., & McFadden, D. (Eds.). (1983). *Handbook of econometrics*. Elsevier.

Gui, G., Liu, F., Sun, J., Yang, J., Zhou, Z., & Zhao, D. (2019). Flight delay prediction based on aviation big data and machine learning. *IEEE Transactions on Vehicular Technology*, *69*(1), 140–150. doi:10.1109/TVT.2019.2954094

Guimarães, P. P. C. (2021). Unfolding authenticity within retail gentrification in Mouraria, Lisbon. *Journal of Tourism and Cultural Change*, 1–20. doi:10.1080/14766825.2021.1876079

Guiot, D., & Roux, D. (2010). A Second-hand Shoppers' Motivation Scale: Antecedents, Consequences, and Implications for Retailers. *Journal of Retailing*, *86*(4), 355–371. doi:10.1016/j.jretai.2010.08.002

Guo, B., Liu, Y., Ouyang, Y., Zheng, V. W., Zhang, D., & Yu, Z. (2019). Harnessing the power of the general public for crowdsourced business intelligence: A survey. *IEEE Access: Practical Innovations, Open Solutions*, *7*, 26606–26630. doi:10.1109/ACCESS.2019.2901027

Guo, S., Choi, T. M., & Zhang, J. (2021). Second-Hand-Clothing Imports in Least-Developed-Countries: The Collapse of Local Clothing Manufacturing and Remedial Measures. *IEEE Transactions on Engineering Management*, 1–20. doi:10.1109/TEM.2021.3061528

Gupta, V., Gupta, L., & Dhir, S. (2020). Customer competency for improving firm decision-making performance in e-commerce. *Foresight*, *22*(2), 205–222. doi:10.1108/FS-06-2019-0053

Guritno, S., & Siringoringo, H. (2013). Perceived usefulness, ease of use, and attitude towards online shopping usefulness towards online airlines ticket purchase. *Procedia: Social and Behavioral Sciences*, *81*, 212–216. https://doi.org/10.1016/j.sbspro.2013.06.415

Hack-Polay, D., Mahmoud, A. B., Ikafa, I., Rahman, M., Kordowicz, M., & Verde, J. M. (2022). Steering resilience in nursing practice: Examining the impact of digital innovations and enhanced emotional training on nurse competencies. *Technovation*, *102549*. Advance online publication. doi:10.1016/j.technovation.2022.102549

Hair, J. F., Jr., Sarstedt, M., Hopkins, L., & Kuppelwieser, G. V. (2014). Partial least squares structural equation modeling (PLS-SEM). *European Business Review, 26*(2), 106-121. doi:10.1108/EBR-10-2013-0128

Hair, J. F. Jr, Hult, G. T. M., Ringle, C. M., & Sarstedt, M. (2021). *A primer on partial least squares structural equation modeling (PLS-SEM).* Sage Publications.

Hair, J. F. Jr, & Sarstedt, M. (2021). Data, measurement, and causal inferences in machine learning: Opportunities and challenges for marketing. *Journal of Marketing Theory and Practice*, *29*(1), 65–77. doi:10.1080/10696679.2020.1860683

Hajibaba, H., Grün, B., & Dolnicar, S. (2020). Improving the stability of market segmentation analysis. *International Journal of Contemporary Hospitality Management, 32*(4), 1393–1411. doi:10.1108/IJCHM-02-2019-0137

Hall, D. (2016). Exploring wine knowledge, aesthetics and ephemerality: Clustering consumers. *International Journal of Wine Business Research, 28*(2), 134–153. doi:10.1108/IJWBR-09-2015-0044

Hamari, J., Sjöklint, M., & Ukkonen, A. (2016). The sharing economy: Why people participate in collaborative consumption. *Journal of the Association for Information Science and Technology, 67*(9), 2047-2059. doi:10.1002/asi.23552

Hanaysha, J. R. (2018). Customer retention and the mediating role of perceived value in retail industry. *World Journal of Entrepreneurship, Management and Sustainable Development, 14*(1), 2–24. doi:10.1108/WJEMSD-06-2017-0035

Hansen, K. T., & Le Zotte, J. (2019). Changing Secondhand Economies. *Business History, 61*(1), 1–16. doi:10.1080/00076791.2018.1543041

Hansen, T. (2008). Consumer values, the theory of planned behaviour and online grocery shopping. *International Journal of Consumer Studies, 32*(2), 128–137. https://doi.org/10.1111/j.1470-6431.2007.00655.x

Han, Y., & Lee, H. (2021). Lifestyle Experiences: Exploring Key Attributes of Lifestyle Hotels Using Instagram User-Created Contents in South Korea. *Sustainability, 13*(5), 2591. Advance online publication. doi:10.3390u13052591

Haridasan, A. C., & Fernando, A. G. (2018). Online or in-store: Unravelling consumer's channel choice motives. *Journal of Research in Interactive Marketing, 12*(2), 215–230. doi:10.1108/JRIM-07-2017-0060

Hariri, R. H., Fredericks, E. M., & Bowers, K. M. (2019). Uncertainty in big data analytics: Survey, opportunities, and challenges. *Journal of Big Data, 6*(1), 1–16. https://doi.org/10.1186/s40537-019-0206-3

Harmeling, C. M., Moffett, J. W., Arnold, M. J., & Carlson, B. D. (2017). Toward a theory of customer engagement marketing. *Journal of the Academy of Marketing Science, 45*(3), 312–335. doi:10.100711747-016-0509-2

Harrigan, P., Evers, U., Miles, M. P., & Daly, T. (2018). Customer engagement and the relationship between involvement, engagement, self-brand connection and brand usage intent. *Journal of Business Research, 88*, 388–396. doi:10.1016/j.jbusres.2017.11.046

Harrigan, P., Evers, U., Miles, M., & Daly, T. (2017). Customer engagement with tourism social media brands. *Tourism Management, 59*, 597–609. doi:10.1016/j.tourman.2016.09.015

Harrigan, P., Soutar, G., Choudhury, M. M., & Lowe, M. (2015). Modelling CRM in a social media age. *Australasian Marketing Journal, 23*(1), 27 37. doi:10.1016/j.ausmj.2014.11.001

Harrington, P. (2012). *Machine Learning in Action.* Manning Publications Co.

Hashem, I. A. T., Yaqoob, I., Anuar, N. B., Mokhtar, S., Gani, A., & Khan, S. U. (2015). The rise of "big data" on cloud computing: Review and open research issues. *Information Systems, 47*, 98–115. https://doi.org/10.1016/j.is.2014.07.006

Hashem, T. N. (2020). Examining the influence of covid 19 pandemic in changing customers' orientation towards e-shopping. *Modern Applied Science, 14*(8), 59–76. https://doi.org/10.5539/mas.v14n8p59

Hasiloglu, M., & Kaya, O. (2021). An analysis of price, service and commission rate decisions in online sales made through E-commerce platforms. *Computers & Industrial Engineering, 162*, 107688. doi:10.1016/j.cie.2021.107688

Hassan, S., Rashid, R., & Li, F. (2015). Utilising modified UTAUT to understand students' online shopping behaviour: A case of e-retail co-operative website in Malaysia. *Journal of Electronic Commerce in Organizations, 13*(4), 74–90.

He, H., & Harris, L. (2020). The impact of Covid-19 pandemic on corporate social responsibility and marketing philosophy. *Journal of Business Research, 116*, 176–182. doi:10.1016/j.jbusres.2020.05.030 PMID:32457556

Hennig, C., & Liao, T. F. (2013). How to find an appropriate clustering for mixed-type variables with application to socio-economic stratification. *Journal of the Royal Statistical Society: Series C (Applied Statistics), 62*(3), 309-369. doi:10.1111/j.1467-9876.2012.01066.x

Hennigs, N., Wiedmann, K.-P., Klarmann, C., Strehlau, S., Godey, B., Pederzoli, D., Neulinger, A., Dave, K., Aiello, G., Donvito, R., Taro, K., Táborecká-Petrovičová, J., Santos, C. R., Jung, J., & Oh, H. (2012). What is the Value of Luxury? A Cross-Cultural Consumer Perspective. *Psychology & Marketing, 29*(12), 1018-1034. doi:10.1002/mar.20583

Hennig-Thurau, T., Gwinner, K. P., Walsh, G., & Gremler, D. D. (2004). Electronic word-of-mouth via consumer-opinion platforms: What motivates consumers to articulate themselves on the internet? *Journal of Interactive Marketing, 18*(1), 38–52. doi:10.1002/dir.10073

Hermon, R., & Williams, P. A. (2014). *Big data in healthcare: What is it used for?* doi:10.4225/75/57982b9431b48

Hervé, C., & Mullet, E. (2009). Age and factors influencing consumer behaviour. *International Journal of Consumer Studies, 33*(3), 302–308. doi:10.1111/j.1470-6431.2009.00743.x

Hesterberg, T. (2011). Bootstrap. *Wiley Interdisciplinary Reviews: Computational Statistics, 3*(6), 497–526. doi:10.1002/wics.182

Hidayanti, I., Herman, L. E., & Farida, N. (2018). Engaging Customers through Social Media to Improve Industrial Product Development: The Role of Customer Co-Creation Value. *Journal of Relationship Marketing, 17*(1), 17–28. doi:10.1080/15332667.2018.1440137

Hirschlag, A. (2019). *Can Secondhand Shopping Dent Fast Fashion's Environmental Damage?* Scientific American. Retrieved 14 March from https://www.scientificamerican.com/article/can-secondhand-shopping-dent-fast-fashions-environmental-damage/

Hirschman, C. E., & Holbrook, B. M. (1982). Hedonic consumption: Emerging concepts, methods and propositions. *Journal of Marketing, 46*(3), 92–101. doi:10.1177/002224298204600314

Hirschman, E. C. (1983). Predictors of self-projection, fantasy fulfillment, and escapism. *The Journal of Social Psychology, 120*(1), 63–76. doi:10.1080/00224545.1983.9712011

Ho, C.-I., Chen, M.-C., & Shih, Y.-W. (2021). Customer engagement behaviours in a social media context revisited: Using both the formative measurement model and text mining techniques. *Journal of Marketing Management*, 1–31. doi:10.1080/0267257X.2021.2003421

Hoffower, H. (2021). *Gen Z's shopping habits are shaping the future of fashion: online thrifting*. Business Insider. Retrieved 19 March from https://www.businessinsider.com/gen-z-driving-online-resale-secondhand-clothes-thrifting-poshmark-depop-2021-4

Holbrook, M. B. (1996). Romanticism, introspection and the roots of experiential consumption: Morris the epicurean. In Consumption and Marketing Macro Dimensions. South-Western College Pub. doi:10.1080/10253866.1997.9670295

Hole, G., & Hole, A. S. (2020). Improving recycling of textiles based on lessons from policies for other recyclable materials: A minireview. *Sustainable Production and Consumption, 23*, 42-51.

Homburg, C., Jozić, D., & Kuehnl, C. (2017). Customer experience management: Toward implementing an evolving marketing concept. *Journal of the Academy of Marketing Science, 45*(3), 377–401. doi:10.100711747-015-0460-7

Hori, M., & Iwamoto, K. (2014). The Run on Daily Foods and Goods After the 2011 Tohoku Earthquake. *Journal of Political Economy, 40*(1), 69–113. doi:10.2753/JES2329-194X400103

Horowitz, J. L. (2001). The bootstrap. In J. Heckman & E. Leamer (Eds.), *Handbook of Econometrics* (Vol. 5, pp. 3159–3228). Elsevier., doi:10.1016/S1573-4412(01)05005-X

Hosseini, S. M. S., Maleki, A., & Gholamian, M. R. (2010). Cluster analysis using data mining approach to develop CRM methodology to assess the customer loyalty. *Expert Systems with Applications, 37*(7), 5259–5264. doi:10.1016/j.eswa.2009.12.070

Howcroft, B., Hamilton, R., & Hewer, P. (2002). Consumer attitude and the usage and adoption of home-based banking in the United Kingdom. *International Journal of Bank Marketing, 20*(3), 111–121. doi:10.1108/02652320210424205

Hu, M., Li, H., Song, H., Li, X., & Law, R. (2022). Tourism demand forecasting using tourist-generated online review data. *Tourism Management, 90*(104490). Advance online publication. doi:10.1016/j.tourman.2022.104490

Hu, M., & Liu, B. (2004a). Mining and summarizing customer reviews. *Proceedings of the 2004 ACM SIGKDD International Conference on Knowledge Discovery and Data Mining KDD 04, 4*, 168. 10.1145/1014052.1014073

Hume, M., & Mills, M. (2013). Uncovering Victoria's Secret: Exploring women's luxury perceptions of intimate apparel and purchasing behaviour. *Journal of Fashion Marketing and Management, 17*(4), 460–485. doi:10.1108/JFMM-03-2013-0020

Hungilo, G. G., & Setyohadi, D. B. (2020). Factors influencing acceptance of online shopping in Tanzania using UTAUT2. *Journal of Internet Banking and Commerce, 25*(1), 1–23. https://doi.org/10.4018/JECO.2015100104

Hur, E. (2020). Rebirth fashion: Secondhand clothing consumption values and perceived risks. *Journal of Cleaner Production, 273*, 122951. doi:10.1016/j.jclepro.2020.122951

Hyndman, R. J., & Athanasopoulos, G. (2018). *Forecasting: principles and practice*. Otexts.

Hyndman, R. J., & Khandakar, Y. (2008). Automatic time series forecasting: The forecast package for R. *Journal of Statistical Software, 27*(1), 1–22. doi:10.18637/jss.v027.i03 PMID:19777145

IAB. (2019). VII Observatorio de marcas en redes sociales. *IAB Spain*. Retrieved February 14, 2021 from https://iabspain.es/wp-content/uploads/2019/06/observatorio_rrss_2019_vreducidafinal.pdf

IAB. (2020). Estudio de redes sociales 2020. *IAB Spain*. Retrieved February 14, 2021 from https://iabspain.es/estudio/estudio-redes-sociales-2020/

Ibrahim, B., & Aljarah, A. (2021). The era of Instagram expansion: Matching social media marketing activities and brand loyalty through customer relationship quality. *Journal of Marketing Communications*, 1–25. doi:10.1080/13527266.2021.1984279

International Monetary Fund. (1996). *Guide to the Data Dissemination Standards, Module 1: The Special Data Dissemination Standard*. IMF.

Islam, T., Pitafi, A. H., Arya, V., Wang, Y., Akhtar, N., Mubarik, S., & Xiaobei, L. (2021). Panic buying in the COVID-19 pandemic: A multi-country examination. *Journal of Retailing and Consumer Services, 59*, 102357. doi:10.1016/j.jretconser.2020.102357

Itani, O. S., Krush, M. T., Agnihotri, R., & Trainor, K. J. (2020). Social media and customer relationship management technologies: Influencing buyer-seller information exchanges. *Industrial Marketing Management, 90*, 264–275. doi:10.1016/j.indmarman.2020.07.015

Itow, R. C. (2020). Fostering Valuable Learning Experiences by Transforming Current Teaching Practices: Practical Pedagogical Approaches from Online Practitioners. *Inf. Learn. Sci.*, *2020*(121), 443–452. doi:10.1108/ILS-04-2020-0106

Ittmann, H.W. (2015). *The impact of big data and business analytics on supply chain management*. Academic Press.

Ivanov, D. (2020). Predicting the impacts of epidemic outbreaks on global supply chains: A simulation-based analysis on the coronavirus outbreak (COVID-19/SARS-CoV-2) case. *Transportation Research Part E, Logistics and Transportation Review*, *136*, 101922. doi:10.1016/j.tre.2020.101922 PMID:32288597

Jackson, D. (2019, June 30). Instagram vs Facebook: Which is best for your brand's strategy? *Sprout Social*. Retrieved February 14, 2021 from https://sproutsocial.com/insights/instagram-vs-facebook/

Jackson, Wang, & Schultz. (1994). *Strategic database marketing*. Academic Press.

Jain, P. K., Pamula, R., & Srivastava, G. (2021). A systematic literature review on machine learning applications for consumer sentiment analysis using online reviews. *Computer Science Review*, *41*, 100413. doi:10.1016/j.cosrev.2021.100413

James, G., Witten, D., Hastie, T., & Tibshirani, R. (2013). *An introduction to statistical learning*. Springer. doi:10.1007/978-1-4614-7138-7

Jami Pour, M., & Hosseinzadeh, M. (2021). An integrated framework of change management for social CRM implementation. *Information Systems and e-Business Management*, *19*(1), 43–75. doi:10.100710257-020-00479-z

Järvelin, K., & Kekäläinen, J. (2002). Cumulated gain-based evaluation of IR techniques. *ACM Transactions on Information Systems*, *20*(4), 422–446. doi:10.1145/582415.582418

Jaseena, K. U., & David, J. M. (2014). Issues, challenges, and solutions: big data mining. *CS & IT-CSCP*, *4*(13), 131-140. doi:10.5121/csit.2014.41311

Jayathirtha, G., Fields, D., Kafai, Y. B., & Chipps, J. (2020). Supporting Making Online: The Role of Artifact, Teacher and Peer Interactions in Crafting Electronic Textiles. *Inf. Learn. Sci.*, *2020*(121), 381–390. doi:10.1108/ILS-04-2020-0111

Jeong, J. Y., & Hyun, S. S. (2019). Roles of passengers' engagement memory and two-way communication in the premium price and information cost perceptions of a luxury cruise. *Tourism Management Perspectives*, *32*, 100559. doi:10.1016/j.tmp.2019.100559

Jhala, K., Natarajan, B., & Pahwa, A. (2018). Prospect theory-based active consumer behavior under variable electricity pricing. *IEEE Transactions on Smart Grid*, *10*(3), 2809–2819. doi:10.1109/TSG.2018.2810819

Jordan, P. W. (2000). *Designing pleasurable products: An introduction to the new human factors*. Routledge. doi:10.4324/9780203305683

Juge, E., Pomiès, A., & Collin-Lachaud, I. (2021). Digital platforms and speed-based competition: The case of second-hand clothing. *Recherche et Applications en Marketing*. Advance online publication. doi:10.1177/20515707211028551

Jukić, N., Sharma, A., Nestorov, S., & Jukić, B. (2015). Augmenting data warehouses with big data. *Information Systems Management*, *32*(3), 200–209. https://doi.org/10.1080/10580530.2015.1044338

Jun, G., & Jaafar, N. I. (2011). A study on consumers' attitude towards online shopping in China. *International Journal of Business and Social Science*, *2*(22), 122–132.

Justis, N., Litts, B.K., Reina, L., & Rhodes, S. (2020). Cultivating Staff Culture Online: How Edith Bowen Laboratory School Responded to COVID-19. *Inf. Learn. Sci.* doi:10.1108/ILS-04-2020-0136

Kanagaraj, R., Rajkumar, N., & Srinivasan, K. (2021). Multiclass normalized clustering and classification model for electricity consumption data analysis in machine learning techniques. *Journal of Ambient Intelligence and Humanized Computing*, *12*(5), 5093–5103. doi:10.100712652-020-01960-w

Kang, E., & Lee, H. (2021). Employee Compensation Strategy as Sustainable Competitive Advantage for HR Education Practitioners. *Sustainability*, *13*(3), 1049. Advance online publication. doi:10.3390u13031049

Kannan, S., & Bhaskaran, R. (2009). Association Rule Pruning based on Interestingness Measures with Clustering. *International Journal of Computer Science Issues*, *6*(1), 35–43.

Kaplan, A. M., & Haenlein, M. (2010). Users of the world, unite! The challenges and opportunities of Social Media. *Business Horizons*, *53*(1), 59–68. doi:10.1016/j.bushor.2009.09.003

Kaplan, H. E. (2018). Examination of factors affecting online consumer behavior from the perspective of the unified theory of acceptance and use of technology. *Turkish Studies*, *13*(30), 203–212. https://doi.org/10.7827/TurkishStudies.14647

Kardes, F. R., Cline, T. W., & Cronley, M. L. (2011). *Consumer behavior: Science and practice* (1st ed.). Cengage.

Karjaluoto, H., Shaikh, A. A., Saarijärvi, H., & Saraniemi, S. (2019). How perceived value drives the use of mobile financial services apps. *International Journal of Information Management*, *47*, 252–261. doi:10.1016/j.ijinfomgt.2018.08.014

Karlsson, L. (2015). *The impact of checklists on organisational target segment selection*. Academic Press.

Kassas, B., & Nayga, R. M. Jr. (2021). Understanding the importance and timing of panic buying among U.S. Households during the COVID-19 pandemic. *Food Quality and Preference*, *93*, 104240. doi:10.1016/j.foodqual.2021.104240

Kastouni, M. Z., & Lahcen, A. A. (2020). Big data analytics in telecommunications: Governance, architecture and use cases. *Journal of King Saud University-Computer and Information Sciences*. doi:10.1016/j.jksuci.2020.11.024

Kauffmann, E., Peral, J., Gil, D., Ferrández, A., Sellers, R., & Mora, H. (2019). A framework for big data analytics in commercial social networks: A case study on sentiment analysis and fake review detection for marketing decision-making. *Industrial Marketing Management*, *90*, 523–537. doi:10.1016/j.indmarman.2019.08.003

Kaur, P., & Singh, R. (2007). Uncovering retail shopping motives of Indian youth. *Young Consumers*, *8*(2), 128–138. doi:10.1108/17473610710757491

Keane, M., & Neal, T. (2021). Consumer panic in the COVID-19 pandemic. *Journal of Econometrics*, *220*(1), 86–105. doi:10.1016/j.jeconom.2020.07.045 PMID:32863535

Keikhosrokiani, P. (2020a). Behavioral intention to use of Mobile Medical Information System (mMIS). In P. Keikhosrokiani (Ed.), Perspectives in the Development of Mobile Medical Information Systems (pp. 57–73). Academic Press. https://doi.org/https://doi.org/10.1016/B978-0-12-817657-3.00004-3

Keikhosrokiani, P. (2020b). Success factors of mobile medical information system (mMIS). In P. Keikhosrokiani (Ed.), Perspectives in the Development of Mobile Medical Information Systems (pp. 75–99). Academic Press. https://doi.org/https://doi.org/10.1016/B978-0-12-817657-3.00005-5

Keikhosrokiani, P. (2022). *Big Data Analytics for Healthcare: Datasets, Techniques, Life Cycles, Management, and Applications*. Elsevier Science. https://books.google.com.my/books?id=WbJYEAAAQBAJ

Keikhosrokiani, P., Mustaffa, N., Sarwar, M. I., & Zakaria, N. (2013). E-Torch: A Mobile Commerce Location-Based Promotion System. *The International Technology Management Review*, *3*(3), 140-159. doi:10.2991/itmr.2013.3.3.1

Keikhosrokiani, P., Mustaffa, N., Zakaria, N., & Abdullah, R. (2019). Assessment of a medical information system: the mediating role of use and user satisfaction on the success of human interaction with the mobile healthcare system (iHeart). *Cognition, Technology & Work*. doi:10.1007/s10111-019-00565-4

Keikhosrokiani, P., Mustaffa, N., Zakaria, N., & Baharudin, A. S. (2019). User behavioral intention toward using mobile healthcare system. In Consumer-driven technologies in healthcare: breakthroughs in research and practice (pp. 429–444). IGI Global. https://doi.org/10.4018/978-1-5225-6198-9.ch022

Keikhosrokiani, P. (2019). *Perspectives in the Development of Mobile Medical Information Systems: Life Cycle, Management, Methodological Approach and Application*. Academic Press.

Keikhosrokiani, P. (2021). Predicating Smartphone Users' Behaviour Towards a Location-Aware IoMT-Based Information System: An Empirical Study. *International Journal of E-Adoption*, *13*(2), 52–77. doi:10.4018/IJEA.2021070104

Keikhosrokiani, P. (2021). Predicating smartphone users' behaviour towards a location-aware IoMT-based information system: An empirical study. *International Journal of E-Adoption*, *13*(2), 52–77. https://doi.org/10.4018/IJEA.2021070104

Keikhosrokiani, P., & Asl, M. P. (Eds.). (2022). *Handbook of Research on Opinion Mining and Text Analytics on Literary Works and Social Media* (1st ed.). IGI Global. doi:10.4018/978-1-7998-9594-7

Keikhosrokiani, P., Mustaffa, N., & Zakaria, N. (2018). Success factors in developing iHeart as a patient-centric healthcare system: A multi-group analysis. *Telematics and Informatics*, *35*(4), 753–775. https://doi.org/10.1016/j.tele.2017.11.006

Kemp, E., Kennett-hensel, P. A., & Williams, K. H. (2012). *The Calm before the Storm : Examining Emotion Regulation Consumption in the Face of an Impending Disaster*. doi:10.1002/mar

Kemps, S. (2020). *Report: Most important data on digital audience during coronavirus*. Growth Quarter – The Next Web. https://thenextweb.com/growth-quarters/2020/04/24/report-most-important-data-on-digital-audiences-during-coronavirus/

Keshavarz, Y., & Jamshidi, D. (2018). Service quality evaluation and the mediating role of perceived value and customer satisfaction in customer loyalty. *International Journal of Tourism Cities*, *4*(2), 220–244. doi:10.1108/IJTC-09-2017-0044

Kessler, A., Barnes, S., Rajagopal, K., Rankin, J., Pouchak, L., Silis, M., & Esser, W. (2020). Saving a Semester of Learning: MIT's Emergency Transition to Online Instruction. *Inf. Learn. Sci.*, *2020*(7/8), 587–597. Advance online publication. doi:10.1108/ILS-04-2020-0097

Kevin, E. V., Nigel, K. L. P., & Mark, R. B. (2002). Cluster Analysis of Marketing Data Examining On-line Shopping Orientation: A Comparison of K-Means and Rough Clustering Approaches. In A. A. Hussein, S. N. Charles, & S. Ruhul (Eds.), *Heuristic and Optimization for Knowledge Discovery* (pp. 208–225). IGI Global. doi:10.4018/978-1-930708-26-6.ch011

Khatib, E. J., Barco, R., Muñoz, P., De La Bandera, I., & Serrano, I. (2016). Self-healing in mobile networks with big data. *IEEE Communications Magazine*, *54*(1), 114–120. https://doi.org/10.1109/MCOM.2016.7378435

Khoi, N. H., Tuu, H. H., & Olsen, S. O. (2018). The role of perceived values in explaining Vietnamese consumers' attitude and intention to adopt mobile commerce. *Asia Pacific Journal of Marketing and Logistics*.

Kim, C., Galliers, R. D., Shin, N., Ryoo, J.-H., & Kim, J. (2012). Factors influencing Internet shopping value and customer repurchase intention. *Electronic Commerce Research and Applications*, *11*(4), 374–387. https://doi.org/10.1016/j.elerap.2012.04.002

Kim, S.-Y., Jung, T.-S., Suh, E.-H., & Hwang, H.-S. (2006). Customer segmentation and strategy development based on customer lifetime value: A case study. *Expert Systems with Applications*, *31*(1), 101–107. doi:10.1016/j.eswa.2005.09.004

Kim, W. H., Cho, J., & Kim, K. S. (2019). The relationships of wine promotion, customer satisfaction, and behavioral intention: The moderating roles of customers' gender and age. *Journal of Hospitality and Tourism Management, 39*, 212–218. doi:10.1016/j.jhtm.2019.03.001

Kiron, D., Prentice, P. K., & Ferguson, R. B. (2014). The analytics mandate. *MIT Sloan Management Review, 55*(4), 1.

Kitchens, B., Dobolyi, D., Li, J., & Abbasi, A. (2018). Advanced customer analytics: Strategic value through integration of relationship-oriented big data. *Journal of Management Information Systems, 35*(2), 540–574. https://dx.doi.org/10.1080/07421222.2018.1451957

Klein, N. (2019). *Plan B pour la planète: Le New Deal vert*. Éditions Actes Sud.

Knapp, E. & Yu, D. (1999). Understanding organizational culture: how culture helps or hinders the flow of knowledge. *Knowledge Management Review*, 16-21.

Kohli, A., & Gupta, N. (2021). *Big Data Analytics: An Overview*. Academic Press.

Komlan, G., Koffi, D., & Kingsford, K. M. (2016). MCDM technique to evaluating mobile banking adoption in the Togolese banking industry based on the perceived value: Perceived benefit and perceived sacrifice factors. *International Journal of Data Mining Knowledge Management Process, 6*(3), 37–56. doi:10.5121/ijdkp.2016.6304

Kornyshova, E., & Salinesi, C. (2007). MCDM techniques selection approaches: State of the art. *Proceedings of the 2007 IEEE Symposium on Computational Intelligence in Multicriteria Decision Making, MCDM 2007*, 22–29. 10.1109/MCDM.2007.369412

Kotler, P., Keller, K., Brady, M., Goodman, M., & Hansen, T. (2019). *Marketing Management* (4th European Edition). Pearson. https://books.google.co.uk/books?id=_-2hDwAAQBAJ

Kotler, P., Wong, V., Saunders, J., & Armstrong, G. (2005). *Principles of marketing* (4th ed.). Prentice Hall International. https://hdl.handle.net/10520/EJC75657

Koufaris, M. (2002). Applying the technology acceptance model and flow theory to online consumer behavior. *Information Systems Research, 13*(2), 205–223.

Kozak, J., Kania, K., Juszczuk, P., & Mitręga, M. (2021). Swarm intelligence goal-oriented approach to data-driven innovation in customer churn management. *International Journal of Information Management, 60*, 102357. https://doi.org/10.1016/j.ijinfomgt.2021.102357

Kraus, S., Jones, P., Kailer, N., Weinmann, A., Chaparro-Banegas, N., & Roig-Tierno, N. (2021). Digital transformation: An overview of the current state of the art of research. *SAGE Open, 11*(3). doi:10.1177/21582440211047576

Kraut, R. E., & Streeter, L. A. (1995). Coordination in Software Development. *Communications of the ACM, 38*(3), 69–81. doi:10.1145/203330.203345

Krishnamurthy, S. (2020). The Future of Business Education: A Commentary in the Shadow of the Covid-19 Pandemic. *Journal of Business Research, 2020*(117), 1–5. doi:10.1016/j.jbusres.2020.05.034 PMID:32501309

Kumar, A., Gupta, P. K., & Srivastava, A. (2020). A review of modern technologies for tackling COVID-19 pandemic. *Diabetes & Metabolic Syndrome, 14*(4), 569–573. doi:10.1016/j.dsx.2020.05.008 PMID:32413821

Kumar, A., Prakash, G., & Kumar, G. (2021). Does environmentally responsible purchase intention matter for consumers? A predictive sustainable model developed through an empirical study. *Journal of Retailing and Consumer Services, 58*, 102270. doi:10.1016/j.jretconser.2020.102270

Kumar, S., & Yadav, R. (2021). The impact of shopping motivation on sustainable consumption: A study in the context of green apparel. *Journal of Cleaner Production*, *295*, 126239. doi:10.1016/j.jclepro.2021.126239

Kumar, V., & Pansari, A. (2016). Competitive Advantage through Engagement. *JMR, Journal of Marketing Research*, *53*(4), 497–514. doi:10.1509/jmr.15.0044

Kumar, V., & Reinartz, W. (2016). Creating enduring customer value. *Journal of Marketing*, *80*(6), 36–68. doi:10.1509/jm.15.0414

Kümpel, A. S., Karnowski, V., & Keyling, T. (2015). News sharing in social media: A review of current research on news sharing users, content, and networks. *Social Media + Society*, *1*(2), 1–14. doi:10.1177/2056305115610141

Laato, S., Islam, A. N., Farooq, A., & Dhir, A. (2020). Unusual purchasing behavior during the early stage of the COVID-19 pandemic: The stimulus-organism-response approach. *Journal of Retailing and Consumer Services*, *57*, 102224. doi:10.1016/j.jretconser.2020.102224

Laforet, S., & Li, X. (2005). Consumers' attitudes towards online and mobile banking in China. *International Journal of Bank Marketing*, *23*(5), 362–380. doi:10.1108/02652320510629250

Lahath, A., Omar, N. A., Ali, M. H., Tseng, M. L., & Yazid, Z. (2021). Exploring food waste during the COVID-19 pandemic among Malaysian consumers: The effect of social media, neuroticism, and impulse buying on food waste. *Sustainable Production and Consumption*, *28*, 519–531. doi:10.1016/j.spc.2021.06.008 PMID:34722847

Lake, R. (2019). *Grocery shopping statistics: 23 fun size facts to know*. CreditDonkey. https://www. creditdonkey. com/grocery-shopping-statistics. html

Laney, D. (2001). 3D data management: Controlling data volume, velocity and variety. *META Group Research Note*, *6*(70), 1. doi:10.4236/jcc.2014.26001

Lang, C., & Zhang, R. (2019). Second-hand clothing acquisition: The motivations and barriers to clothing swaps for Chinese consumers. *Sustainable Production and Consumption*, *18*, 156-164.

Langat, D. K., Bonuke, R., & Kibet, Y. (2021). Mobile banking service quality and customer retention: A moderated mediation model of customer perceived value and perceived corporate image. *SEISENSE Journal of Management*, *4*(4), 47–61. doi:10.33215jom.v4i4.672

Lansley, G., & Longley, P. (2016). Deriving age and gender from forenames for consumer analytics. *Journal of Retailing and Consumer Services*, *30*, 271–278. https://doi.org/10.1016/j.jretconser.2016.02.007

Larson, L. R. L., & Shin, H. (2018). Fear During Natural Disaster: Its Impact on Perceptions of Shopping Convenience and Shopping Behavior. *Services Marketing Quarterly*, *39*(4), 293–309. doi:10.1080/15332969.2018.1514795

Lasi, H., Fettke, P., Kemper, H.-G., Feld, T., & Hoffmann, M. (2014). Industry 4.0. *Business & Information Systems Engineering*, *6*(4), 239–242. doi:10.100712599-014-0334-4

Latiff, Z. A., & Safiee, N. A. S. (2015). New business set up for branding strategies on social media - Instagram. *Procedia Computer Science*, *72*, 13–23. doi:10.1016/j.procs.2015.12.100

Latour, B. (2015). *Face à Gaïa: huit conférences sur le nouveau régime climatique*. Empêcheurs de penser rond.

Laukkanen, T., & Kiviniemi, V. (2010). The role of information in mobile banking resistance. *International Journal of Bank Marketing*, *28*(5), 372–388. doi:10.1108/02652321011064890

Lee, E. J., & Overby, J. W. (2004). Creating value for online shoppers: Implications for satisfaction and loyalty. *Journal of Consumer Satisfaction, Dissatisfaction & Complaining Behavior*, *17*(1), 54–67.

Lee, H. J., Lee, M., Lee, H., & Cruz, R. A. (2021). Mining service quality feedback from social media: A computational analytics method. *Government Information Quarterly*, *38*(2), 101571. https://doi.org/10.1016/j.giq.2021.101571

Lee, M., Hong, J. H., Chung, S., & Back, K.-J. (2020). Exploring the Roles of DMO's Social Media Efforts and Information Richness on Customer Engagement: Empirical Analysis on Facebook Event Pages. *Journal of Travel Research*, *60*(3), 670–686. doi:10.1177/0047287520934874

Lee, S. (2011). Consumers' Value, Environmental Consciousness, and Willingness to Pay more toward Green-Apparel Products. *Journal of Global Fashion Marketing*, *2*(3), 161–169. doi:10.1080/20932685.2011.10593094

Lehtonen, T. K., & Maenpaa, P. (1997). Shopping in the East Centre Mall. In S. Experience (Ed.), *Falk & Campbell* (pp. 136–165). SAGE. doi:10.4135/9781446216972.n7

Lemire, B. (2012). The Secondhand Clothing Trade in Europe and Beyond: Stages of Development and Enterprise in a Changing Material World, c. 1600–1850. *Textile (Oxford)*, *10*(2), 144–163. doi:10.2752/175183512X13315695424392

Leung, J., Chung, J. Y. C., Tisdale, C., Chiu, V., Lim, C. C. W., & Chan, G. (2021). Anxiety and Panic Buying Behaviour during COVID-19 Pandemic—A Qualitative Analysis of Toilet Paper Hoarding Contents on Twitter. *International Journal of Environmental Research and Public Health*, *18*(3), 1127. Advance online publication. doi:10.3390/ijerph18031127 PMID:33514049

Leung, X. Y., Bai, B., & Stahura, K. A. (2013). The Marketing Effectiveness of Social Media in the Hotel Industry: A Comparison of Facebook and Twitter. *Journal of Hospitality & Tourism Research (Washington, D.C.)*, *39*(2), 147–169. doi:10.1177/1096348012471381

Liao, S. H., Widowati, R., & Hsieh, Y. C. (2021). Investigating online social media users' behaviors for social commerce recommendations. *Technology in Society*, *66*, 101655. doi:10.1016/j.techsoc.2021.101655

Liao, Y., Deschamps, F., Loures, E. F. R., & Ramos, L. F. P. (2017). Past, present and future of Industry 4.0 - a systematic literature review and research agenda proposal. *International Journal of Production Research*, *55*(12), 3609–3629. doi:10.1080/00207543.2017.1308576

Libai, B., Bolton, R., Bügel, M. S., De Ruyter, K., Götz, O., Risselada, H., & Stephen, A. T. (2010). Customer-to-customer interactions: Broadening the scope of word of mouth research. *Journal of Service Research*, *13*(3), 267–282. doi:10.1177/1094670510375600

Li, D., Chaudhary, H., & Zhang, Z. (2020). Modeling spatiotemporal pattern of depressive symptoms caused by COVID-19 using social media data mining. *International Journal of Environmental Research and Public Health*, *17*(14), 4988. https://www.mdpi.com/1660-4601/17/14/4988

Li, F., Larimo, J., & Leonidou, L. C. (2021). Social media marketing strategy: Definition, conceptualization, taxonomy, validation, and future agenda. *Journal of the Academy of Marketing Science*, *49*(1), 51–70. doi:10.100711747-020-00733-3

Li, H., Hu, M., & Li, G. (2020). Forecasting tourism demand with multisource big data. *Annals of Tourism Research*, *83*(102912). Advance online publication. doi:10.1016/j.annals.2020.102912

Lika, B., Kolomvatsos, K., & Hadjiefthymiades, S. (2014). Facing the cold start problem in recommender systems. *Expert Systems with Applications*, *41*(4), 2065–2073. doi:10.1016/j.eswa.2013.09.005

Lim, E., Cyr, D., & Tan, C. W. (2012). Untangling utilitarian and hedonic consumption behaviors in online shopping. *PACIS 2012 Proceedings*, 94. https://aisel.aisnet.org/pacis2012/94

Lim, E., & Ang, S. (2008). Hedonic vs. utilitarian consumption: A cross-cultural perspective based on cultural conditioning. *Journal of Business Research*, *61*(3), 225–232. doi:10.1016/j.jbusres.2007.06.004

Lim, W. M., Rasul, T., Kumar, S., & Ala, M. (2022). Past, present, and future of customer engagement. *Journal of Business Research, 140*, 439–458. doi:10.1016/j.jbusres.2021.11.014

Lim, Y.-J. (2014). Psychometric characteristics of the Korean Mental Health Continuum–Short Form in an adolescent sample. *Journal of Psychoeducational Assessment, 32*(4), 356–364.

Lindecrantz, E., Tjon Pian Gi, M., & Zerbi, S. (2020). *Personalizing the customer experience: Driving differentiation in retail*. McKinsey & Company. Retrieved 22 January from https://www.mckinsey.com/industries/retail/our-insights/personalizing-the-customer-experience-driving-differentiation-in-retail

Ling, M., Fern, Y. S., Boon, L. K., & Huat, T. S. (2016). Understanding customer satisfaction in internet banking: A case study in Malaca. *Procedia Economics and Finance, 37*, 80–85. doi:10.1016/S2212-5671(16)30096-X

Lin, H. C. K., Wang, T. H., Lin, G. C., Cheng, S. C., Chen, H. R., & Huang, Y. M. (2020). Applying sentiment analysis to automatically classify consumer comments concerning marketing 4Cs aspects. *Applied Soft Computing, 97*, 106755. doi:10.1016/j.asoc.2020.106755

Lins, S., & Aquino, S. (2020). Development and initial psychometric properties of a panic buying scale during COVID-19 pandemic. *Heliyon, 6*(9), e04746. doi:10.1016/j.heliyon.2020.e04746 PMID:32895636

Liu, B., & Zhang, L. (2012). A survey of opinion mining and sentiment analysis. In Mining text data (pp. 415–463). Springer. 3 doi:10.1007/978-1-4614-3223-4_13

Liu, B., Hu, M., & Cheng, J. (2005). Opinion Observer: Analyzing and Comparing Opinions. *Proceedings of the 14th International Conference on World Wide Web - WWW '05*, 342. 10.1145/1060745.1060797

Liu, C., Bao, Z., & Zheng, C. (2019). Exploring consumers' purchase intention in social commerce: An empirical study based on trust, argument quality, and social presence. *Asia Pacific Journal of Marketing and Logistics, 31*(2), 378–397. doi:10.1108/APJML-05-2018-0170

Liu, P., Li, M., Dai, D., & Guo, L. (2021). The effects of social commerce environmental characteristics on customers' purchase intentions: The chain mediating effect of customer-to-customer interaction and customer-perceived value. *Electronic Commerce Research and Applications, 48*, 101073. doi:10.1016/j.elerap.2021.101073

Liu, T., Xu, J., Qin, T., Xiong, W., & Li, H. (2007). LETOR: Benchmark Dataset for Research on Learning to Rank for Information Retrieval. *Proceedings of the SIGIR 2007 Workshop Learning to Rank for Information Retrieval, 3*(49), 3–10. 10.1561/1500000016

Li, W., Liao, J., Li, Q., Baskota, M., Wang, X., Tang, Y., Zhou, Q., Wang, X., Luo, X., Ma, Y., Fukuoka, T., Ahn, H. S., Lee, M. S., Chen, Y., Luo, Z., & Liu, E. (2020). Public Health Education for Parents during the Outbreak of COVID-19: A Rapid Review. *Annals of Translational Medicine, 2020*(8), 628. doi:10.21037/atm-20-3312 PMID:32566565

Li, X., Li, H., Pan, B., & Law, R. (2021). Machine learning in internet search query selection for tourism forecasting. *Journal of Travel Research, 60*(6), 1213–1231. doi:10.1177/0047287520934871

Li, X., Zhou, Y., Wong, Y. D., Wang, X., & Yuen, K. F. (2021). What influences panic buying behaviour? A model based on dual-system theory and stimulus-organism-response framework. *International Journal of Disaster Risk Reduction, 64*, 102484. doi:10.1016/j.ijdrr.2021.102484

Li, Y., & Wu, H. (2012). A Clustering Method Based on K-Means Algorithm. *Physics Procedia, 25*, 1104–1109. doi:10.1016/j.phpro.2012.03.206

Loanzon, R. (2021). *How to Sell Clothes Online Like a Pro, from Taking Photos to Shipping*. Brightly. Retrieved 18 March from https://brightly.eco/how-to-sell-your-used-clothing-on-thrifting-apps/

Lombart, C., Millan, E., Normand, J.-M., Verhulst, A., Labbé-Pinlon, B., & Moreau, G. (2020). Effects of physical, non-immersive virtual, and immersive virtual store environments on consumers' perceptions and purchase behavior. *Computers in Human Behavior*, *110*, 106374. doi:10.1016/j.chb.2020.106374

Longhurst, G. J., Stone, D. M., Dulohery, K., Scully, D., Campbell, T., & Smith, C. F. (2020). Strength, Weakness, Opportunity, Threat (SWOT) Analysis of the Adaptations to Anatomical Education in the United Kingdom and Republic of Ireland in Response to the Covid-19 Pandemic. *Anatomical Sciences Education*, *2020*(13), 301–311. doi:10.1002/ase.1967 PMID:32306550

Loureiro, S. M. C., & Roschk, H. (2014). Differential effects of atmospheric cues on emotions and loyalty intention with respect to age under online/offline environment. *Journal of Retailing and Consumer Services*, *21*(2), 211–219. doi:10.1016/j.jretconser.2013.09.001

Loureiro, S. M. C., & Sarmento, E. M. (2019). Exploring the determinants of Instagram as a social network for online consumer-brand relationship. *Journal of Promotion Management*, *25*(3), 354–366. doi:10.1080/10496491.2019.1557814

Loxton, M., Truskett, R., Scarf, B., Sindone, L., Baldry, G., & Zhao, Y. (2020). Consumer Behaviour during Crises: Preliminary Research on How Coronavirus Has Manifested Consumer Panic Buying, Herd Mentality, Changing Discretionary Spending and the Role of the Media in Influencing Behaviour. *Journal of Risk and Financial Management*, *13*(8), 166. Advance online publication. doi:10.3390/jrfm13080166

Lunardo, R., & Mbengue, A. (2009). Perceived control and shopping behavior: The moderating role of the level of utilitarian motivational orientation. *Journal of Retailing and Consumer Services*, *16*(6), 434–441. doi:10.1016/j.jretconser.2009.06.004

Luo, X., Li, H., Zhang, J., & Shim, J. P. (2010). Examining multi-dimensional trust and multi-faceted risk in initial acceptance of emerging technologies: An empirical study of mobile banking services. *Decision Support Systems*, *49*(2), 222–234. doi:10.1016/j.dss.2010.02.008

Lv, Z., Qiao, L., & Singh, A. K. (2020). Advanced machine learning on cognitive computing for human behavior analysis. *IEEE Transactions on Computational Social Systems*, *8*(5), 1194–1202. doi:10.1109/TCSS.2020.3011158

Lynch, C. (2008). How do your data grow? *Nature*, *455*(7209), 28–29. https://dx.doi.org/10.1038/455028a

Maas, M. (2020). *A Look Into the Gentrification of Thrifting*. Wit and Delight. Retrieved 14 March from https://witandelight.com/2020/12/a-look-into-the-gentrification-of-thrifting/

MacGilp, R. (2020). *The Future of Second-Hand Shopping After Coronavirus*. Eco Warrior Princess. Retrieved 19 March from https://ecowarriorprincess.net/2020/05/future-second-hand-shopping-after-coronavirus-pandemic/

Machado, M. A. D., Almeida, S. O., Bollick, L. C., & Bragagnolo, G. (2019). Second-hand fashion market: Consumer role in circular economy. *Journal of Fashion Marketing and Management*, *23*(3), 382–395. doi:10.1108/JFMM-07-2018-0099

Mach-Król, M., & Hadasik, B. (2021). On a Certain Research Gap in Big Data Mining for Customer Insights. *Applied Sciences (Basel, Switzerland)*, *11*(15), 6993. https://doi.org/10.3390/app11156993

Mahmoud, A. B. (2021). Like a Cog in a Machine. In C. Machado & J. P. Davim (Eds.), *Advances in Intelligent, Flexible, and Lean Management and Engineering* (pp. 1–20). IGI Global. doi:10.4018/978-1-7998-5768-6.ch001

Mahmoud, A. B., Ball, J., Rubin, D., Fuxman, L., Mohr, I., Hack-Polay, D., Grigoriou, N., & Wakibi, A. (2021a). Pandemic pains to Instagram gains! COVID-19 perceptions effects on behaviours towards fashion brands on Instagram in Sub-Saharan Africa: Tech-native vs non-native generations. *Journal of Marketing Communications*, 1–25. doi:10.1080/13527266.2021.1971282

Mahmoud, A. B., Grigoriou, N., Fuxman, L., Reisel, W. D., Hack-Polay, D., & Mohr, I. (2020). A generational study of employees' customer orientation: A motivational viewpoint in pandemic time. *Journal of Strategic Marketing*, 1–18. doi:10.1080/0965254X.2020.1844785

Mahmoud, A. B., Hack-Polay, D., Grigoriou, N., Mohr, I., & Fuxman, L. (2021b). A generational investigation and sentiment and emotion analyses of female fashion brand users on Instagram in Sub-Saharan Africa. *Journal of Brand Management*, *28*(5), 526–544. doi:10.105741262-021-00244-8

Mahmoud, A. B., Hack-Polay, D., Reisel, W. D., Fuxman, L., Grigoriou, N., Mohr, I., & Aizouk, R. (2021c). Who's more vulnerable? A generational investigation of COVID-19 perceptions' effect on Organisational citizenship Behaviours in the MENA region: Job insecurity, burnout and job satisfaction as mediators. *BMC Public Health*, *21*(1), 1951. doi:10.118612889-021-11976-2 PMID:34706702

Mahmoud, A. B., Reisel, W. D., Fuxman, L., & Hack-Polay, D. (2021d). Locus of control as a moderator of the effects of COVID-19 perceptions on job insecurity, psychosocial, organisational and job outcomes for MENA region hospitality employees. *European Management Review*, 1–20. doi:10.1111/emre.12494

Mahmoud, A. B., Reisel, W. D., Hack-Polay, D., & Fuxman, L. (2021e). No one is safe! But who's more susceptible? Locus of control moderates pandemic perceptions' effects on job insecurity and psychosocial factors amongst MENA hospitality frontliners: A PLS-SEM approach. *BMC Public Health*, *21*(1), 2032. doi:10.118612889-021-12071-2 PMID:34742272

Mahmoud, A. B., Tehseen, S., & Fuxman, L. (2020). The Dark Side of Artificial Intelligence in Retail Innovation. In E. Pantano (Ed.), *Retail Futures* (1st ed., pp. 165–180). Emerald Publishing Limited. doi:10.1108/978-1-83867-663-620201019

Majanja, M. K. (2020). The Status of Electronic Teaching within South African LIS Education. *Library Management*, *2020*(41), 317–337. doi:10.1108/LM-05-2020-0084

Majji, K. C., & Baskaran, K. (2021). Artificial intelligence analytics—virtual assistant in UAE automotive industry. In *Inventive Systems and Control* (pp. 309–322). Springer Singapore. doi:10.1007/978-981-16-1395-1_24

Ma, L., & Sun, B. (2020). Machine learning and AI in marketing – Connecting computing power to human insights. *International Journal of Research in Marketing*, *37*(3), 481–504. doi:10.1016/j.ijresmar.2020.04.005

Malhotra, S. (2022). Embrace the Data Analytics Chase: A Journey from Basics to Business. In K. Chaudhary & M. Alam (Eds.), *Big Data Analytics* (pp. 1–17). CRC Press. doi:10.1201/9781003175711-1

Mandal, P. C. (2019). Public policy issues in direct and digital marketing–Concerns and initiatives: Public policy in direct and digital marketing. *International Journal of Public Administration in the Digital Age*, *6*(4), 54–71. doi:10.4018/IJPADA.2019100105

Manic, M. (2015). Marketing engagement through visual content. *Bulletin of the Transilvania University of Brasov. Series V, Economic Sciences*, *8*(2), 89–94.

Manikonda, L., Venkatesan, R., Kambhampati, S., & Li, B. (2016). *Trending chic: Analyzing the influence of social media on fashion brands*. Retrieved February 14, 2021 from arxiv.org/abs/1512.01174

Manyika, J., Chui, M., Brown, B., Bughin, J., Dobbs, R., Roxburgh, C., & Hung Byers, A. (2011). *Big data: The next frontier for innovation, competition, and productivity*. McKinsey Global Institute. doi:10.12691/iteces-4-1-3

Mao, F. (2020). *Coronavirus panic: why are people stockpiling toilet paper?* BBC News. https://www.bbc.co.uk/news/world-australia-51731422

Marcus, C. (1998). A practical yet meaningful approach to customer segmentation. *Journal of Consumer Marketing*, *15*(5), 494–504. doi:10.1108/07363769810235974

Marolt, M., Pucihar, A., & Zimmermann, H.-D. (2015). Social CRM adoption and its impact on performance outcomes: a literature review. *Organizacija, 48*(4), 260-271. http://organizacija.fov.uni-mb.si/index.php/organizacija/article/view/659

Marr, B. (2015). How much data do we create every day? The mind-blowing stats everyone should read. *Forbes*, *21*, 1–5.

Mayfield, A. (2008). *What is social media?* iCrossing. Retrieved August 25, 2009, from www.icrossing.co.uk/ebook

McCracken, G. (1986). The history of consumption: A literature review and consumer guide. *Journal of Consumer Policy*, *10*(1), 139–166. doi:10.1007/BF00411633

McCracken, G. (1988). *Culture and consumption: New aproaches to the symbolic character of consumer goods and activities*. Indiana University Press. doi:10.1086/229266

Mccullock, S. P., & Perrault, E. K. (2020). Exploring the Effects of Source Credibility and Message Framing on STI Screening Intentions: An Application of Prospect and Protection Motivation Theory. *Journal of Health Communication*, *25*(1), 1–11. doi:10.1080/10810730.2019.1692262 PMID:31724913

McCurley Hortman, S., Allaway, A. W., Barry Mason, J., & Rasp, J. (1990). Multi-segment analysis of supermarket patronage. *Journal of Business Research*, *21*(3), 209–223. doi:10.1016/0148-2963(90)90029-D

McDonald, M., Christopher, M., & Bass, M. (2003). Market segmentation. In M. McDonald, M. Christopher, & M. Bass (Eds.), *Marketing: a complete guide* (pp. 41–65). Macmillan Education UK. doi:10.1007/978-1-4039-3741-4_3

McKinney, V., Yoon, K., & Zahedi, F. (2002). The Measurement of Web-Customer Satisfaction: An Expectation and Disconfirmation Approach. *Information Systems Research*, *13*(3), 296–315. doi:10.1287/isre.13.3.296.76

McKinsey. (2014). *Big Data, Analytics, and the Future of Marketing & Sales*. Createspace Independent Pub. https://books.google.co.uk/books?id=u-XRoQEACAAJ

McKnight, D. H., Choudhury, V., & Kacmar, C. (2002). The impact of initial consumer trust on intentions to transact with a web site: A trust building model. *The Journal of Strategic Information Systems*, *11*(3-4), 297–323.

McNeill, L., & Moore, R. (2015). Sustainable fashion consumption and the fast fashion conundrum: fashionable consumers and attitudes to sustainability in clothing choice. *International Journal of Consumer Studies, 39*(3), 212-222. doi:10.1111/ijcs.12169

Mechinda, P., & Patterson, P. G. (2011). The impact of service climate and service provider personality on employees' customer-oriented behavior in a high-contact setting. *Journal of Services Marketing*, *25*(2), 101–113. doi:10.1108/08876041111119822

Medalla, M. E., Yamagishi, K., Tiu, A. M., Tanaid, R. A., Abellana, D. P. M., Caballes, S. A., Jabilles, E. M., Himang, C., Bongo, M., & Ocampo, L. (2020). Modeling the hierarchical structure of secondhand clothing buying behavior antecedents of millennials. *Journal of Modelling in Management*, *15*(4), 1679–1708. doi:10.1108/JM2-08-2019-0207

Medberg, G. & Heinonen, K. (2014). Invisible value formation: a netnography in retail banking, *International Journal of Bank Marketing, 32*(6), 590-607.

Medjani, F., & Barnes, S. (2021). Social customer relationship management and organizational performance: Testing a conceptual model in the North African context. *Industrial Management & Data Systems*, *121*(7), 1617–1641. doi:10.1108/IMDS-10-2020-0601

Meng, S., Dou, W., Zhang, X., & Chen, J. (2014). KASR: A keyword-aware service recommendation method on mapreduce for big data applications. *IEEE Transactions on Parallel and Distributed Systems*, *25*(12), 3221–3231. https://doi.org/10.1109/TPDS.2013.2297117

Merhi, M., Hone, K., Tarhini, A., & Ameen, N. (2020). An empirical examination of the moderating role of age and gender in consumer mobile banking use: A cross-national, quantitative study. *Journal of Enterprise Information Management*, *34*(4), 1144–1168. doi:10.1108/JEIM-03-2020-0092

Migdadi, M. M. (2021). Knowledge management, customer relationship management and innovation capabilities. *Journal of Business and Industrial Marketing*, *36*(1), 111–124. doi:10.1108/JBIM-12-2019-0504

Mikalef, P., Boura, M., Lekakos, G., & Krogstie, J. (2019). Big data analytics and firm performance: Findings from a mixed-method approach. *Journal of Business Research*, *98*, 261–276. https://doi.org/10.1016/j.jbusres.2019.01.044

Mikalef, P., van de Wetering, R., & Krogstie, J. (2021). Building dynamic capabilities by leveraging big data analytics: The role of organizational inertia. *Information & Management*, *58*(6), 103412. https://doi.org/10.1016/j.im.2020.103412

Miladinovic, J., & Hong, X. (2016). *A Study on factors affecting the behavioral intention to use mobile shopping fashion Apps in Sweden* [Student thesis]. DiVA. http://urn.kb.se/resolve?urn=urn:nbn:se:hj:diva-30245

Milne, S., Sheeran, P., & Orbell, S. (2000). Prediction and intervention in health-related behavior: A meta-analytic review of protection motivation theory. *Journal of Applied Social Psychology*, *30*(1), 106–143. doi:10.1111/j.1559-1816.2000.tb02308.x

Minton, E. A., & Khale, L. R. (2014). Belief Systems. *Religion and Behavioral, 5*(1).

Mkpojiogu, E. O. C., Hashim, N. L., & Adamu, R. (2016). Observed demographic differentials in user perceived satisfaction on the usability of mobile banking applications. *Proceedings of the Knowledge Management International Conference (Kmice)*, 263-268.

Mohammadi, M., Al-Fuqaha, A., Sorour, S., & Guizani, M. (2018). Deep learning for IoT big data and streaming analytics: A survey. *IEEE Communications Surveys and Tutorials*, *20*(4), 2923–2960. https://doi.org/10.48550/arXiv.1712.04301

Mohammed, A. A., & Rashid, B. (2012). Customer Relationship Management (CRM) in Hotel Industry: A framework Proposal on the Relationship among CRM Dimensions, Marketing Capabilities, and Hotel Performance. *International Review of Management and Marketing*, *2*(4), 220–230. https://www.econjournals.com/index.php/irmm/article/view/297

Mohan, M., & Baskaran, K. (2021). Financial analytics: Investment behavior of middle income group in south India. *2021 11th International Conference on Cloud Computing, Data Science & Engineering (Confluence).* 10.1109/Confluence51648.2021.9377029

Möhlmann, M. (2015). Collaborative consumption: determinants of satisfaction and the likelihood of using a sharing economy option again. *Journal of Consumer Behaviour, 14*(3), 193-207. doi:10.1002/cb.1512

Mohr, I., Fuxman, L., & Mahmoud, A. B. (2021). A triple-trickle theory for sustainable fashion adoption: The rise of a luxury trend. *Journal of Fashion Marketing and Management*. Advance online publication. doi:10.1108/JFMM-03-2021-0060

Molinillo, S., Aguilar-Illescas, R., Anaya-Sánchez, R., & Liébana-Cabanillas, F. (2021). Social commerce website design, perceived value and loyalty behavior intentions: The moderating roles of gender, age and frequency of use. *Journal of Retailing and Consumer Services*, *63*, 102404. Advance online publication. doi:10.1016/j.jretconser.2020.102404

Moncey, A. A., & Baskaran, K. (2020). Digital marketing analytics: Building brand awareness and loyalty in UAE. *2020 IEEE International Conference on Technology Management, Operations and Decisions (ICTMOD).* 10.1109/ICTMOD49425.2020.9380579

Monroe, R. (2021). *Ultra-fast fashion is eating the world.* The Atlantic. Retrieved 10 March from https://www.theatlantic.com/magazine/archive/2021/03/ultra-fast-fashion-is-eating-the-world/617794/

Monsuwé, T. P., Dellaert, B. G., & De Ruyter, K. (2004). What drives consumers to shop online? A literature review. *International Journal of Service Industry Management*, *15*(1), 102–121. https://doi.org/10.1108/09564230410523358

Moorman, C., Deshpande, R., & Zaltman, G. (1993). Factors affecting trust in market research relationships. *Journal of Marketing*, *57*(1), 81–101.

Moser, F. (2015). Mobile banking: A fashionable concept or an institutionalized channel in future retail banking? analyzing patterns in the practical and academic mobile banking literature. *International Journal of Bank Marketing*, *33*(2), 162–177. doi:10.1108/IJBM-08-2013-0082

Mugerwa, S., Moya, M. B., & Kituyi, G. M. (2018). Determinants of Behavioral Intention in Adopting Network Monitoring System. *International Journal of Computer Applications Technology and Research*, *07*(3), 139–157. https://doi.org/10.7753/IJCATR0703.1006

Munjal, S., & Bhushan, S. (2021). *The Indian Hospitality Industry: Dynamics and Future Trends*. Taylor & Francis Group. https://books.google.co.uk/books?id=NI08zgEACAAJ

Mutahar, A. M., Aldholay, A., Isaac, O., Jalal, A. N., & Alkibsi, S. (2021). Predicting intention to use mobile banking services among Yemeni Banks' Clients: Is Perceived value important? *Proceedings of the International Conference on Emerging Technologies and Intelligent Systems (ICETIS 2021)*, 498-520.

Mutahar, A. M., Daud, N. M., Ramayah, T., Putit, L., & Isaac, O. (2018). Predicting perceived value in mobile banking: Are awareness and perceived risk important? *Research Journal of Applied Sciences*, *13*(2), 112–124.

Mutimukwe, C., Kolkowska, E., & Grönlund, Å. (2020). Information privacy in e-service: Effect of organizational privacy assurances on individual privacy concerns, perceptions, trust and self-disclosure behavior. *Government Information Quarterly*, *37*(1), 101413. doi:10.1016/j.giq.2019.101413

Mutum, R. D., Balyan, S. C., Kansal, S., Agarwal, P., Kumar, S., Kumar, M., & Raghuvanshi, S. (2013). Evolution of variety-specific regulatory schema for expression of osa-miR408 in indica rice varieties under drought stress. *The FEBS Journal*, *280*(7), 1717–1730.

Naeem, M. (2021). Do social media platforms develop consumer panic buying during the fear of Covid-19 pandemic. *Journal of Retailing and Consumer Services*, *58*, 102226. doi:10.1016/j.jretconser.2020.102226

Naeem, M., Jamal, T., Diaz-Martinez, J., Butt, S. A., Montesano, N., Tariq, M. I., De-la-Hoz-Franco, E., & De-La-Hoz-Valdiris, E. (2022). Trends and future perspective challenges in big data. In *Advances in Intelligent Data Analysis and Applications* (pp. 309–325). Springer. doi:10.1007/978-981-16-5036-9_30

Naeem, M., & Ozuem, W. (2021). Understanding misinformation and rumors that generated panic buying as a social practice during COVID-19 pandemic: Evidence from Twitter, YouTube and focus group interviews. *Information Technology & People*. Advance online publication. doi:10.1108/ITP-01-2021-0061

Narasimham, N. V., & Gupta, M. K. (2016). Segmenting Consumers in Food and Grocery Retail. *Indian Journal of Marketing*, *46*(4), 24–38. doi:10.17010/ijom/2016/v46/i4/90527

Nasir, V. A., Keserel, A. C., Surgit, O. E., & Nalbant, M. (2021). Segmenting consumers based on social media advertising perceptions: How does purchase intention differ across segments? *Telematics and Informatics*, *64*, 101687. doi:10.1016/j.tele.2021.101687

Nasuminnisa, A., Dawood, D. A. K., & Sowmya, K. R. (2014). Influence of demographic factors on e-banking service quality in banking sector. *Indian Journal of Applied Sciences*, *4*(3), 235–237.

Nasution, F. B. B. (2018). *Integrated Double Loop Data Driven Model For Public Policymaking*. Academic Press.

Natale, S., & Cooke, H. (2020). Browsing with Alexa: Interrogating the impact of voice assistants as web interfaces. *Media Culture & Society*, *43*(6), 1000–1016. doi:10.1177/0163443720983295

Neama, G., Alaskar, R., & Alkandari, M. (2016). Privacy, security, risk, and trust concerns in e-commerce. *Proceedings of the 17th International Conference on Distributed Computing and Networking*.

Neate, R. (2021). *Etsy buys secondhand clothing app Depop to tap into gen Z.* The Guardian. Retrieved 19 March from https://www.theguardian.com/fashion/2021/jun/02/etsy-buys-second-hand-clothing-app-depop-to-tap-into-gen-z

Neger, M., & Uddin, B. (2020). Factors affecting consumers' internet shopping behavior during the COVID-19 pandemic: Evidence from Bangladesh. *The China Business Review*, *19*(3), 91–104.

Neti, S. (2011). Social media and its role in marketing. *International Journal of Enterprise Computing and Business Systems*, *1*(2), 1–15. doi:10.4172/2151-6219.1000203

Newman, M. (2003). The structure and function of complex networks. *SIAM Review*, *45*(2), 167–256. doi:10.1137/S003614450342480

Ngai, E. W. T., Xiu, L., & Chau, D. C. K. (2009). Application of data mining techniques in customer relationship management: A literature review and classification. *Expert Systems with Applications*, *36*(2), 2592–2602. doi:10.1016/j.eswa.2008.02.021

Nguyen, T. (2021). *How thrifting became problematic Thrift shopping is popular online, but some are worried about the effects of overconsumption.* Vox. Retrieved 13 March from https://www.vox.com/the-goods/22396051/thrift-store-hauls-ethics-depop

Noor, M. M. (2011). Determining critical success factors of mobile banking adoption in Malaysia. *Australian Journal of Basic and Applied Sciences*, *5*(9), 252–265.

Norum, P., & Norton, M. (2017). Factors affecting consumer acquisition of secondhand clothing in the USA. *Journal of Fashion Marketing and Management*, *21*(2), 206–218. doi:10.1108/JFMM-10-2016-0090

Novielli, N., Calefato, F., & Lanubile, F. (2015). The Challenges of Sentiment Detection in the Social Programmer Ecosystem. In *Proceedings of the 7th International Workshop on Social Software Engineering (SSE 2015)*. Association for Computing Machinery. 10.1145/2804381.2804387

Ntseme, O. J., Namatsagang, A., & Chukwuere, J. E. (2016). Risks and benefits from using mobile banking in an emerging country. *Risk Governance and Control: Financial Markets & Institutions*, *6*(4), 355–363. doi:10.22495/rgcv6i4c2art13

Nwankwo, C. A., Kanyangale, M., & Abugu, J. O. (2019). Online shopping industry and its consumers in Nigeria. *Journal of Economics. Management and Trade*, *24*(3), 1–12.

Nwaorgu, B. (2018). What is Collaborative Consumption? Platforms and Participation of People in Collaborative Consumption–Impact of the New Technologies. *International Journal of Innovation, Management and Technology*, *9*(6), 240–245. doi:10.18178/ijimt.2018.9.6.819

Oakes, C. (2021). *The 6 Best Online Thrift Stores of 2021.* Remake. Retrieved 19 March from https://remake.world/stories/style/the-6-best-online-thrift-stores/

Obadă, D. R. (2013). Flow Theory and Online Marketing Outcomes: A Critical Literature Review. *Procedia Economics and Finance*, *6*, 550–561. doi:10.1016/S2212-5671(13)00173-1

Ochoa, S. F., Fortino, G., & Di Fatta, G. (2017). Cyber-physical systems, internet of things and big data. *Future Generation Computer Systems*, *75*, 82–84. https://doi.org/10.1016/j.future.2017.05.040

Odier, L. (2021). Is this a new era for old goods? How the second-hand market can promote a circular economy. *The Financial Times*.

OECD. (2020). *OECD Policy Responses to Coronavirus (COVID-19): Investment in the MENA region in the time of COVID-19*. Retrieved 18 January from https://www.oecd.org/coronavirus/policy-responses/investment-in-the-mena-region-in-the-time-of-covid-19-da23e4c9/

Ofori, D., & Appiah-Nimo, C. (2021). Relationship Management, Competitive Advantage and Performance of Hotels: A Resource-Based View. *Journal of African Business*, 1–19. doi:10.1080/15228916.2021.1924573

Ogbuji, C. N., & Udom, A. O. (2018). A holistic presentation of online shopping in Nigeria. *Researchers World*, *9*(3), 22–33.

Okada, E. M. (2005). Justification effects on consumer choice of hedonic and utilitarian goods. *JMR, Journal of Marketing Research*, *42*(1), 43–53. doi:10.1509/jmkr.42.1.43.56889

Olson, D. L. (2004). Comparison of weights in TOPSIS models. *Mathematical and Computer Modelling*, *40*(7–8), 721–727. doi:10.1016/j.mcm.2004.10.003

Olszak, C. M., & Mach-Król, M. (2018). A conceptual framework for assessing an organization's readiness to adopt big data. *Sustainability*, *10*(10), 3734. https://doi.org/10.3390/su10103734

Ong, C. H., Lee, H. W., & Ramayah, T. (2018). Impact of brand experience on loyalty. *Journal of Hospitality Marketing & Management*, *27*(7), 755–774. doi:10.1080/19368623.2018.1445055

Oni, A. A., & Ayo, C. K. (2010). An empirical investigation of the level of users' acceptance of e-banking in Nigeria. *Journal of Internet Banking and Commerce*, *15*(1), 1–13.

Online Advertising Guide. (2020, March 20). *Twitter engagement rate*. The Online Advertising Guide. Retrieved February 14, 2021 from https://theonlineadvertisingguide.com/glossary/twitter-engagement-rate/

Orminski, J., Tandoc, E. C., Jr., & Detenber, B. H. (2021). #sustainablefashion – A Conceptual Framework for Sustainable Fashion Discourse on Twitter. *Environmental Communication, 15*(1), 115-132. doi:10.1080/17524032.2020.1802321

Otika, U., Olise, E., & Oby, O. B. (2019). Risk Perceptions and Online Shopping Intention among Internet Users In Nigeria. *Global Journal of Management and Business Research.*

Özbölük, T. (2021). The pursuit of uniqueness and craving for freedom: The meaning of luxury in the age of access. *Leisure Studies*, *40*(2), 227–242. doi:10.1080/02614367.2020.1831045

Paço, A., Leal Filho, W., Ávila, L. V., & Dennis, K. (2020). Fostering sustainable consumer behavior regarding clothing: Assessing trends on purchases, recycling and disposal. *Textile Research Journal*, *91*(3-4), 373–384. doi:10.1177/0040517520944524

Paksoy, H. M., Durmaz, Y., Çopuroğlu, F., & Özbezek, B. D. (2020). The Impact of Anxiety Caused by COVID-19 on Consumer Behaviour. *Transnational Marketing Journal*, *8*(2), 243–270.

Pal, K. (2019). Markov Decision Theory Based Crowdsourcing Software Process Model. In Gupta, V. (ed) Crowdsourcing and Probabilistic Decision-Making in Software Engineering: Emerging Research and Opportunities. doi:10.4018/978-1-5225-9659-2.ch001

Pal, K. (2020). Framework for Reusable Test Case Generation in Software Systems Testing. In Pang, C. Y. (ed) Software Engineering for Agile Application Development. doi:10.4018/978-1-7998-2531-9

Pal, K., & Karakostas, B. (2020). Software Testing Under Agile, Scrum, and DevOps. In Walsh, K. R.; Mahesh, S.; & Cherie, C. (ed) Agile Scrum Implementation and Its Long-Term Impact on Organizations. IGI Global.

Pal, K., & Williams, I. (2021). Software Development Knowledge Management System Using Web Portal. In Gyamfi, A. & Williams, I. (ed) Digital Technology Advancement in Knowledge Management. IGI Global.

Panwar, C. (2018). Consumer perceived risk in online shopping environment via Facebook as medium. *IACSIT International Journal of Engineering and Technology*, *7*(4), 2485–2490. https://doi.org/10.14419/ijet.v7i4.11017

Paolanti, M., Romeo, L., Martini, M., Mancini, A., Frontoni, E., & Zingaretti, P. (2019). Robotic retail surveying by deep learning visual and textual data. *Robotics and Autonomous Systems*, *118*, 179–188. doi:10.1016/j.robot.2019.01.021

Pappas, N. (2016). Marketing strategies, perceived risks, and consumer trust in online buying behaviour. *Journal of Retailing and Consumer Services*, *29*, 92–103.

Park, H., & Armstrong, C. (2020). *Secondhand Clothing Sales Are Booming–and May Help Solve the Sustainability Crisis in the Fashion Industry*. The Conversation Newsletter.

Park, M., Im, H., & Kim, D. Y. (2018). Feasibility and user experience of virtual reality fashion stores. *Fashion and Textiles*, *5*(1), 1–17. doi:10.118640691-018-0149-x

Parvatiyar, A., & Sheth, J. N. (2001). Customer relationship management: Emerging practice, process, and discipline. *Journal of Economic & Social Research*, *3*(2).

Parvin, A. (2013). Mobile banking operation in Bangladesh: Prediction of future. *Journal of Internet Banking and Commerce*, *18*(1), 1–15.

Pascual-Miguel, F. J., Agudo-Peregrina, Á. F., & Chaparro-Peláez, J. (2015). Influences of gender and product type on online purchasing. *Journal of Business Research*, *68*(7), 1550–1556.

Pasquali, M. (2021a). *Monthly active users (MAU) of the Depop app in the United Kingdom (UK) from January 2018 to October 2021*. Statista. Retrieved 19 March from https://www.statista.com/statistics/1122928/depop-monthly-active-users-uk/

Pasquali, M. (2021b). *Monthly downloads of the Depop app in the United Kingdom (UK) from January 2018 to October 2021(in 1,000s)*. Statista. Retrieved 19 March from https://www.statista.com/statistics/1119063/depop-monthly-downloads-uk/

Pavlou, P. A., & Fygenson, M. (2006). Understanding and predicting electronic commerce adoption: An extension of the theory of planned behavior. *Management Information Systems Quarterly*, 115–143.

Payne, A., & Frow, P. (2005). A Strategic Framework for Customer Relationship Management. *Journal of Marketing*, *69*(4), 167–176. doi:10.1509/jmkg.2005.69.4.167

Peña-Vinces, J., Solakis, K., & Guillen, J. (2020). Environmental knowledge, the collaborative economy and responsible consumption in the context of second-hand perinatal and infant clothes in Spain. *Resources, Conservation and Recycling*, *159*, 104840. doi:10.1016/j.resconrec.2020.104840

Perloff, J., DesRoches, C. M., & Buerhaus, P. (2016). Comparing the cost of care provided to Medicare beneficiaries assigned to primary care nurse practitioners and physicians. *Health Services Research*, *51*(4), 1407–1423.

Petrescu, M., & Korgaonkar, P. (2011). Viral advertising: Definitional review and synthesis. *Journal of Internet Commerce*, *10*(3), 208–226. doi:10.1080/15332861.2011.596007

Pham, D. H., Le, A. C., & Le, T. K. C. (2015). A least square based model for rating aspects and identifying important aspects on review text data. *Proceedings of 2015 2nd National Foundation for Science and Technology Development Conference on Information and Computer Science*, 265–270. 10.1109/NICS.2015.7302204

Piketty, T. (2013). *Le capital au XXIe siècle*. Média Diffusion.

Piñeiro-Otero. (2016). *Teresa & Martínez-Rolán, Xabier*. Understanding Digital Marketing—Basics and Actions. doi:10.1007/978-3-319-28281-7_2

Ping, P., Qin, W., Xu, Y., Miyajima, C., & Takeda, K. (2019). Impact of driver behavior on fuel consumption: Classification, evaluation and prediction using machine learning. *IEEE Access: Practical Innovations, Open Solutions*, *7*, 78515–78532. doi:10.1109/ACCESS.2019.2920489

Pisal, S., Singh, J., & Eirinaki, M. (2011). AskUs: An Opinion Search Engine. *2011 IEEE 11th International Conference on Data Mining Workshops*, 1243–1246. 10.1109/ICDMW.2011.24

Pizzi, G., Scarpi, D., Pichierri, M., & Vannucci, V. (2019). Virtual reality, real reactions?: Comparing consumers' perceptions and shopping orientation across physical and virtual-reality retail stores. *Computers in Human Behavior*, *96*, 1–12. doi:10.1016/j.chb.2019.02.008

Plöckinger, M., Aschauer, E., Hiebl, M. R. W., & Rohatschek, R. (2016). The Influence of Individual Executives on Corporate Financial Reporting: A Review and Outlook from the Perspective of Upper Echelons Theory. *Journal of Accounting Literature*, *2016*(37), 55–75. doi:10.1016/j.acclit.2016.09.002

Pobee, F. (2021). Assessing online repurchase intention in a developing country: The role of perceived value. *International Journal of Strategic Decision Sciences*, *12*(1), 61–76. doi:10.4018/IJSDS.2021010104

Pontiki, M., & Pavlopoulos, J. (2014). SemEval-2014 Task 4: Aspect Based Sentiment Analysis. *Proceedings of the 8th International Workshop on Semantic Evaluation,* 27–35. 10.15520/ajcsit.v4i8.9

Potavanich, T. (2015). *The Concept of Luxury from a Consumer Culture Perspective*. Manchester Business School. https://www.research.manchester.ac.uk/portal/files/54586068/FULL_TEXT.PDF

Power, D. J. (2015, May). 'Big data'decision making use cases. In International Conference on Decision Support System Technology (pp. 1–9). Springer. https://doi.org/10.1155/2020/8850096.

PRB. (2021). *International Data*. Population Reference Bureau. Retrieved 2022 from https://www.prb.org/international/indicator/hh-size-av/map/country/

Prentice, C., Chen, J., & Stantic, B. (2020). Timed intervention in COVID-19 and panic buying. *Journal of Retailing and Consumer Services*, *57*, 102203. doi:10.1016/j.jretconser.2020.102203

Pressman, R. S. (2000). *Software engineering: A Practitioner's Approach (European Adaption)* (5th ed.). McGraw-Hill International.

Price, M. (2019). *Fashion disruptors: Welcome to the era of secondhand retail apps*. CNET. Retrieved 19 March from https://www.cnet.com/home/smart-home/features/rise-of-secondhand-retail-poshmark-thredup-letgo-mercari-ebay-thrift-clothing-selling-apps/

Pride, W. M., & Ferrell, O. C. (2016). *Foundations of marketing*. Cengage Learning.

Pristiwa, N., Huang, W. T., & Ayuningtyas, D. (2017). The effect of internet user behavior on effective marketing via online group buying in Taiwan. *Proceedings of AICS Social Sciences*, *7*, 326–333.

Proctor, T. (2021). *Absolute Essentials of Strategic Marketing*. Routledge.

Prodanova, J., Ciunova-Shuleska, A., & Palamidovska-Sterjadovska, N. (2019). Enriching m-banking perceived value to achieve reuse intention. *Marketing Intelligence & Planning*, *37*(6), 617–630. doi:10.1108/MIP-11-2018-0508

Pucker, K. P. (2022). *The Myth of Sustainable Fashion*. Harvard Business Review. Retrieved 2022 from https://hbr.org/2022/01/the-myth-of-sustainable-fashion

Putrevu, S., & Lord, K. R. (2001). Search dimensions, patterns and segment profiles of grocery shopping. *Journal of Retailing and Consumer Services*, *8*(3), 127–137. doi:10.1016/S0969-6989(00)00013-8

Qalati, S. A., Yuan, L. W., Khan, M. A. S., & Anwar, F. (2021). A mediated model on the adoption of social media and SMEs' performance in developing countries. *Technology in Society*, *64*, 101513. doi:10.1016/j.techsoc.2020.101513

Qin, S., Man, J., Wang, X., Li, C., Dong, H., & Ge, X. (2019). Applying big data analytics to monitor tourist flow for the scenic area operation management. *Discrete Dynamics in Nature and Society*. doi:10.1155/2019/8239047

Qiu, Y., Chen, P., Lin, Z., Yang, Y., Zeng, L., & Fan, Y. (2020). Clustering Analysis for Silent Telecom Customers Based on K-means++. *Proceedings of 2020 IEEE 4th Information Technology, Networking, Electronic and Automation Control Conference, ITNEC 2020, Itnec*, 1023–1027. 10.1109/ITNEC48623.2020.9084976

Quach, G. (2021). *Reselling, repairing and 'swishing': the rise of sustainable fashion apps*. Guardian. Retrieved 18 March from https://www.theguardian.com/fashion/2021/jan/29/reselling-repairing-and-swishing-the-rise-of-sustainable-fashion-apps

Quan, C., & Ren, F. (2014). Unsupervised product feature extraction for feature-oriented opinion determination. *Information Sciences*, *272*, 16–28. doi:10.1016/j.ins.2014.02.063

Raaper, R., & Brown, C. (2020). The Covid-19 Pandemic and the Dissolution of the University Campus: Implications for Student Support Practice. *Journal of Professional Capital and Community*, *2020*(3/4), 343–349. Advance online publication. doi:10.1108/JPCC-06-2020-0032

Raghupathi, W., & Raghupathi, V. (2014). Big data analytics in healthcare: Promise and potential. *Health Information Science and Systems*, *2*(1), 1–10. https://dx.doi.org/10.1186%2F2047-2501-2-3

Rahimi, R. (2017). Customer relationship management (people, process and technology) and organisational culture in hotels. *International Journal of Contemporary Hospitality Management*, *29*(5), 1380–1402. doi:10.1108/IJCHM-10-2015-0617

Rahmanti, A. R., Ningrum, D. N. A., Lazuardi, L., Yang, H. C., & Li, Y. C. J. (2021). Social media data analytics for outbreak risk communication: Public attention on the "New Normal" during the COVID-19 pandemic in Indonesia. *Computer Methods and Programs in Biomedicine*, *205*, 106083. https://doi.org/10.1016/j.cmpb.2021.106083

Raiter, O. (2021). Segmentation of Bank Consumers for Artificial Intelligence Marketing. *International Journal of Contemporary Financial Issues*, *1*(1), 39–54.

Rajhans, V., Memon, U., Patil, V., & Goyal, A. (2020). Impact of COVID-19 on Academic Activities and Way Forward in Indian Optometry. *Journal of Optometry*, *2020*(13), 216–226. doi:10.1016/j.optom.2020.06.002 PMID:32703749

Ram, J., Zhang, C., & Koronios, A. (2016). The implications of big data analytics on business intelligence: A qualitative study in China. *Procedia Computer Science*, *87*, 221–226. https://doi.org/10.1016/j.procs.2016.05.152

Ramkissoon, H., & Uysal, M. (2018). Authenticity as a value co-creator of tourism experiences. In Creating experience value in tourism (pp. 98-109). doi:10.1079/9781786395030.0098

Ramkissoon, H., & Mavondo, F. T. (2015). The satisfaction–place attachment relationship: Potential mediators and moderators. *Journal of Business Research*, *68*(12), 2593–2602. doi:10.1016/j.jbusres.2015.05.002

Ramkissoon, H., & Nunkoo, R. (2010). More than Just Biological Sex Differences: Examining the Structural Relationship Between Gender Identity and Information Search Behavior. *Journal of Hospitality & Tourism Research (Washington, D.C.), 36*(2), 191–215. doi:10.1177/1096348010388662

Rana, T. A., & Cheah, Y.-N. (2016). Aspect extraction in sentiment analysis: Comparative analysis and survey. *Artificial Intelligence Review, 46*(4), 459–483. Advance online publication. doi:10.100710462-016-9472-z

Rathnayaka, S. D., Selvanathan, E. A., & Selvanathan, S. (2022). Modelling the consumption patterns in the Asian countries. *Economic Analysis and Policy, 74*, 277–296. doi:10.1016/j.eap.2022.02.004

Raut, R., Narwane, V., Mangla, S. K., Yadav, V. S., Narkhede, B. E., & Luthra, S. (2021). Unlocking causal relations of barriers to big data analytics in manufacturing firms. *Industrial Management & Data Systems*. doi:10.1108/IMDS-02-2020-0066

Refaeilzadeh, P., Tang, L., & Liu, H. (2009). Cross-validation. Encyclopedia of Database Systems, 5, 532-538. doi:10.1007/978-0-387-39940-9_565

Regehr, C., & Goel, V. (2020). Managing COVID-19 in a Large Urban Research-Intensive University. *Journal of Loss and Trauma, 2020*(6-7), 1–17. doi:10.1080/15325024.2020.1771846

Reid, C. (2021). *The Gentrification of Thrifting: A Guide*. The Bengal. Retrieved 14 March from http://isubengal.com/the-gentrification-of-thrifting-a-guide/

Reinartz, W. J., & Venkatesan, R. (2008). Decision models for customer relationship management (CRM). In B. Wierenga (Ed.), *Handbook of marketing decision models* (Vol. 121, pp. 291–326). Springer. doi:10.1007/978-0-387-78213-3_9

Reinartz, W., Krafft, M., & Hoyer, W. D. (2004). The Customer Relationship Management Process: Its Measurement and Impact on Performance. *JMR, Journal of Marketing Research, 41*(3), 293–305. doi:10.1509/jmkr.41.3.293.35991

Reis, C. L. d. S. (2020). *Second-hand fashion: the effect of nostalgia on purchase intentions and shopping behaviour*. Academic Press.

Rens. (2022). *Made For You & Our Planet*. Rens US LLC. Retrieved 14 March from https://rensoriginal.co.uk/

ReportLinker. (2020, March). *Women's lingerie market to 2027 - Global analysis and forecasts by type; material; distribution channel, and geography*. Retrieved February 14, 2021 from https://www.reportlinker.com/p05882143/Women-s-Lingerie-Market-to-Global-Analysis-and-Forecasts-by-Type-Material-Distribution-Channel-and-Geography.html?utm source=GNW

Rita, P., Oliveira, T., & Farisa, A. (2019). The impact of e-service quality and customer satisfaction on customer behavior in online shopping. *Heliyon, 5*(10), e02690. doi:10.1016/j.heliyon.2019.e02690 PMID:31720459

Rodríguez-Hernández, C. F., Cascallar, E., & Kyndt, E. (2020). Socio-Economic Status and Academic Performance in Higher Education: A Systematic Review. *Educational Research Review, 2020*(29), 100305. doi:10.1016/j.edurev.2019.100305

Rogers, R. W. (1975). A Protection Motivation Theory of Fear Appeals and Attitude Change1. *The Journal of Psychology, 91*(1), 93–114. doi:10.1080/00223980.1975.9915803 PMID:28136248

Rosário, A. (2021). The background of artificial intelligence applied to marketing. *Academy of Strategic Management Journal, 20*, 1–19.

Rousseeuw, P. J. (1987). Silhouettes: A graphical aid to the interpretation and validation of cluster analysis. *Journal of Computational and Applied Mathematics, 20*, 53–65. doi:10.1016/0377-0427(87)90125-7

Roux, D. (2006). *Am I what I wear? An exploratory study of symbolic meanings associated with secondhand clothing.* ACR North American Advances.

Roy, B., & Słowiński, R. (2013). Questions guiding the choice of a multicriteria decision aiding method. *EURO Journal on Decision Processes, 1*(1-2), 69–97. doi:10.100740070-013-0004-7

Roy, D., Tripathy, S., Kar, S. K., Sharma, N., Verma, S. K., & Kaushal, V. (2020). Study of Knowledge, Attitude, Anxiety & Perceived Mental Healthcare Need in Indian Population during COVID-19 Pandemic. *Asian Journal of Psychiatry, 51*, 102083. Advance online publication. doi:10.1016/j.ajp.2020.102083 PMID:32283510

Roy, V., Silvestre, B. S., & Singh, S. (2020). Reactive and proactive pathways to sustainable apparel supply chains: Manufacturer's perspective on stakeholder salience and organizational learning toward responsible management. *International Journal of Production Economics, 227*, 107672. doi:10.1016/j.ijpe.2020.107672

Rufai, S. R., & Bunce, C. (2020). World leaders' usage of Twitter in response to the COVID-19 pandemic: A content analysis. *Journal of Public Health, 42*(3), 510–516. doi:10.1093/pubmed/fdaa049 PMID:32309854

Rus, I., & Lindvall, M. (2002, June). Knowledge Management in Software Engineering. *IEEE Software, 19*(3), 26–38. doi:10.1109/MS.2002.1003450

Russom, P. (2011). Big data analytics. *TDWI Best Practices Report, 19*(4), 1-34. doi:10.12691/jcsa-3-6-6

Ryder, B., Zhang, T., & Hua, N. (2021). The Social Media "Magic": Virtually Engaging Visitors during COVID-19 Temporary Closures. *Administrative Sciences, 11*(2), 53. doi:10.3390/admsci11020053

Saarijärvi, H., Karjaluoto, H., & Kuusela, H. (2013). Extending customer relationship management: From empowering firms to empowering customers. *Journal of Systems and Information Technology, 15*(2), 140–158. doi:10.1108/13287261311328877

Sabanoglu, T. (2021). *Leading motivations for secondhand item purchases of Depop users in the United States, the United Kingdom, and Australia in 2020* [Graph]. Statista. Retrieved 19 March from https://www.statista.com/statistics/1276662/depop-users-secondhand-purchase-reasons/

Saha, L., Tripathy, H. K., Nayak, S. R., Bhoi, A. K., & Barsocchi, P. (2021). Amalgamation of Customer Relationship Management and Data Analytics in Different Business Sectors—A Systematic Literature Review. *Sustainability, 13*(9), 5279. Advance online publication. doi:10.3390u13095279

Saidulu, D., & Sasikala, R. (2017). Machine learning and statistical approaches for Big Data: Issues, challenges and research directions. *International Journal of Applied Engineering Research, 12*(21), 11691–11699.

Sajana, T., Rani, C. M. S., & Narayana, K. V. (2016). A survey on clustering techniques for big data mining. *Indian Journal of Science and Technology, 9*(3), 1–12. doi:10.17485/ijst/2016/v9i3/75971

Salehan, M., & Kim, D. J. (2016). Predicting the performance of online consumer reviews: A sentiment mining approach to big data analytics. *Decision Support Systems, 81*, 30–40. https://doi.org/10.1016/j.dss.2015.10.006

Salem, S. F. (2021). Do Relationship Marketing Constructs Enhance Consumer Retention? An Empirical Study Within the Hotel Industry. *SAGE Open, 11*(2). doi:10.1177/21582440211009224

Salem, S. F., & Alanadoly, A. B. (2021). Personality traits and social media as drivers of word-of-mouth towards sustainable fashion. *Journal of Fashion Marketing and Management, 25*(1), 24–44. doi:10.1108/JFMM-08-2019-0162

Samudro, A., Sumarwan, U., Yusuf, E. Z., & Simanjuntak, M. (2018). Perceived value, social bond and switching cost as antecedents and predictors of customer loyalty in the B2B chemical industry context: A literature review. *International Journal of Marketing Studies, 10*(4), 124–138. doi:10.5539/ijms.v10n4p124

Sánchez García, J., & Cruz Rambaud, S. (2020). A GARCH approach to model short-term interest rates: Evidence from Spanish economy. *International Journal of Finance & Economics*. Advance online publication. doi:10.1002/ijfe.2234

Sanchez Torres, J. A., & Arroyo-Cañada, F. J. (2017). Building brand loyalty in e-commerce of fashion lingerie. *Journal of Fashion Marketing and Management*, *21*(1), 103–114. doi:10.1108/JFMM-05-2016-0047

Sánchez-Torres, J. A., Varon-Sandobal, A., & Sánchez-Alzate, J.-A. (2017). Differences between e-commerce buyers and non-buyers in Colombia: The moderating effect of educational level and socioeconomic status on electronic purchase intention. *Dyna (Bilbao)*, *84*(202), 175–189. https://doi.org/10.15446/dyna.v84n202.65496

Sandin, G., & Peters, G. M. (2018). Environmental impact of textile reuse and recycling – A review. *Journal of Cleaner Production*, *184*, 353–365. doi:10.1016/j.jclepro.2018.02.266

Sann, R., & Lai, P. C. (2020). Understanding homophily of service failure within the hotel guest cycle: Applying NLP-aspect-based sentiment analysis to the hospitality industry. *International Journal of Hospitality Management*, *91*, 102678. doi:10.1016/j.ijhm.2020.102678

Santos, M. L. B. d. (2021). The "so-called" UGC: An updated definition of user-generated content in the age of social media. *Online Information Review*. doi:10.1108/OIR-06-2020-0258

Sarin, P., Kar, A. K., Kewat, K., & Ilavarasan, P. V. (2020). Factors affecting future of work: Insights from Social Media Analytics. *Procedia Computer Science*, *167*, 1880–1888. https://dx.doi.org/10.1016/j.procs.2020.03.207

Sarwar, B., Karypis, G., Konstan, J., & Riedl, J. (2000). Analysis of recommendation algorithms for e-commerce. *Proceedings of the 2nd ACM Conference on Electronic Commerce*, 158–167. 10.1145/352871.352887

Sashi, C. M. (2012). Customer engagement, buyer-seller relationships, and social media. *Management Decision*, *50*(2), 253–272. doi:10.1108/00251741211203551

Schein, E. H. (1992). *Organizational Culture and Leadership* (2nd ed.). Jossey Bass.

Schein, K., & Rauschnabel, P. (2021). Augmented reality in manufacturing: Exploring workers' perceptions of barriers. *IEEE Transactions on Engineering Management*, 1–14. doi:10.1109/TEM.2021.3093833

Schiel, F. (2015). *The Phenomenon of the Sharing Economy in Germany: Consumer Motivations for Participating in Collaborative Consumption Schemes*. Academic Press.

Schiffman, L. G., & Kanuk, L. L. (2007). *Consumer behavior* (9th ed.). Pearson Education.

Schilling, M. A., & Hill, C. W. L. (1998). Managing the new product development process: Strategic imperatives. *The Academy of Management Perspectives*, *12*(3), 67–81. doi:10.5465/ame.1998.1109051

Schirmer, N., Ringle, C., Gudergan, S., & Feistel, M. (2018). The link between customer satisfaction and loyalty: The moderating role of customer characteristics. *Journal of Strategic Marketing*, *26*(4), 298–317. doi:10.1080/0965254X.2016.1240214

Schlager, T., & Christen, M. (2022). Market Segmentation. In C. Homburg, M. Klarmann, & A. Vomberg (Eds.), Handbook of Market Research (pp. 939-967). Springer International Publishing. doi:10.1007/978-3-319-57413-4_29

Schnack, A., Wright, M. J., & Holdershaw, J. L. (2021). Does the locomotion technique matter in an immersive virtual store environment? – Comparing motion-tracked walking and instant teleportation. *Journal of Retailing and Consumer Services*, *58*, 102266. doi:10.1016/j.jretconser.2020.102266

Schor, J. B., & Fitzmaurice, C. J. (2015). Collaborating and connecting: the emergence of the sharing economy. In Handbook of Research on Sustainable Consumption (pp. 410-425). doi:10.4337/9781783471270.00039

Schultz, D. E., & Peltier, J. (2013). Social media's slippery slope: Challenges, opportunities and future research directions. *Journal of Research in Interactive Marketing*, *7*(2), 86–99. doi:10.1108/JRIM-12-2012-0054

Schwartz, S. H. (2012). An Overview of the Schwartz Theory of Basic Values. *Online Readings in Psychology and Culture*, *2*(1), 2307–0919. doi:10.9707/2307-0919.1116

Seetharaman, P. (2020). Business models shifts: Impact of Covid-19. *International Journal of Information Management*, *54*, 102173. doi:10.1016/j.ijinfomgt.2020.102173 PMID:32834338

Sergison, D. (2021). *Lululemon to Launch Mushroom-Based Yoga Accessories*. The Business of Fashion. Retrieved 14 March from https://www.businessoffashion.com/news/sustainability/lululemon-to-launch-mushroom-based-yoga-accessories/

Serra Cantallops, A., & Salvi, F. (2014). New consumer behavior: A review of research on eWOM and hotels. *International Journal of Hospitality Management*, *36*, 41–51. doi:10.1016/j.ijhm.2013.08.007

Serrano-Malebrán, J., & Arenas-Gaitán, J. (2021). When does personalization work on social media? a posteriori segmentation of consumers. *Multimedia Tools and Applications*, *80*(30), 36509–36528. doi:10.100711042-021-11303-2

Shabani, N., Munir, A., & Hassan, A. (2018). E-marketing via augmented reality: A case study in the tourism and hospitality industry. *IEEE Potentials*, *38*(1), 43–47. doi:10.1109/MPOT.2018.2850598

Shahi, G. K., Dirkson, A., & Majchrzak, T. A. (2021). An exploratory study of COVID-19 misinformation on Twitter. *Online Social Networks and Media*, *22*, 100104. doi:10.1016/j.osnem.2020.100104 PMID:33623836

Shaikh, A. A., & Karjaluoto, H. (2016). Mobile banking services continuous usage--case study of Finland. In *Proceedings of the 49th Hawaii International Conference on System Sciences* (pp. 1497-1506). IEEE.

Shamim, A., Balakrishnan, V., Tahir, M., & Shiraz, M. (2014). Critical Product Features' Identification Using an Opinion Analyzer. *TheScientificWorldJournal*, *2014*, 1–9. doi:10.1155/2014/340583 PMID:25506612

Shamsuddin, A., Ruslan, M. M., Halim, A., Zahari, N. F., & Fazi, N. M. (2014). Educators' awareness and acceptance towards Goods and Services Tax (GST) implementation in Malaysia: A study in Bandar Muadzam Shah, Pahang. *International Journal of Business. Economics and Law*, *4*(1), 1–10.

Sharma, P., Chen, I., & Luk, S. (2012). Gender and age as moderators in the service evaluation process. *Journal of Services Marketing*, *26*(2), 102–114. doi:10.1108/08876041211215266

Shaw, M. J., Subramaniam, C., Tan, G. W., & Welge, M. E. (2001). Knowledge management and data mining for marketing. *Decision Support Systems*, *31*(1), 127–137. doi:10.1016/S0167-9236(00)00123-8

Sheriff, N. M., Zulkifli, A. S., & Othman, W. N. W. (2018). Salient features of customer engagement, visual presentation and copywriting for effective social media marketing: An exploratory perspective. *Journal of Academic UiTM Negeri Sembilan*, *6*(2), 28–37.

Sheth, J. (2020). Impact of Covid-19 on consumer behavior: Will the old habits return or die? *Journal of Business Research*, *117*, 280–283. https://doi.org/https://doi.org/10.1016/j.jbusres.2020.05.059

Shih, H.-S., Shyur, H.-J., & Lee, E. S. (2007). An extension of TOPSIS for group decision making. *Mathematical and Computer Modelling*, *45*(7–8), 801–813. doi:10.1016/j.mcm.2006.03.023

Shim, S. I., Forsythe, S., & Kwon, W.-S. (2015). Impact of online flow on brand experience and loyalty. *Journal of Electronic Commerce Research*, *16*(1), 56.

Shindler, M., Wong, A., & Meyerson, A. (2011). *Fast and Accurate k-means For Large Datasets*. Academic Press.

Shufeldt, L., Oates, B., & Vaught, B. (1998). Is lifestyle an important factor in the purchase of OTC drugs by the elderly? *Journal of Consumer Marketing*, *15*(2), 111–124. doi:10.1108/07363769810210304

Sicurella, S. (2021). *When Second Hand Becomes Vintage: Gen Z Has Made Thrifting A Big Business*. NPR. Retrieved 19 March from https://www.npr.org/1006207991

Sigala, M. (2018). Implementing social customer relationship management. *International Journal of Contemporary Hospitality Management*, *30*(7), 2698–2726. doi:10.1108/IJCHM-10-2015-0536

Sihvonen, J., & Turunen, L. L. M. (2016). As good as new – valuing fashion brands in the online second-hand markets. *Journal of Product and Brand Management*, *25*(3), 285–295. doi:10.1108/JPBM-06-2015-0894

Silva, B. N., Diyan, M., & Han, K. (2019). Big data analytics. In *Deep Learning: Convergence to Big Data Analytics* (pp. 13–30). Springer.

Sindwani, R. (2017). The effect of demographic characteristics on mb-loyalty: A study of mobile banking customers. *International Journal of Applied Marketing & Management*, *2*(1), 9–17.

Singh, A., Alryalat, M. A. A., Alzubi, J. A., & Sarma, H. (2017). Understanding Jordanian consumers' online purchase intentions: Integrating trust to the UTAUT2 framework. *International Journal of Applied Engineering Research*, *12*(20), 10258–10268.

Sirdeshmukh, D., Singh, J., & Sabol, B. (2002). Consumer trust, value, and loyalty in relational exchanges. *Journal of Marketing*, *66*(1), 15–37. doi:10.1509/jmkg.66.1.15.18449

Siti-Nabiha, A. K., Nordin, N., & Poh, B. K. (2021). Social media usage in business decision-making: The case of Malaysian small hospitality organisations. *Asia-Pacific Journal of Business Administration*, *13*(2), 272–289. doi:10.1108/APJBA-08-2020-0276

Skulmowski, A., & Rey, G. D. (2020). COVID-19 as an Accelerator for Digitalization at a German University: Establishing Hybrid Campuses in Times of Crisis. *Human Behavior and Emerging Technologies*, *2020*(2), 212–216. doi:10.1002/hbe2.201 PMID:32838228

Smith, P. (2022). *Share of secondhand clothing in people's closets in 2020 and 2023*. Statista. Retrieved 10 March from https://www.statista.com/statistics/1235059/share-of-secondhand-clothing-in-peoples-closets-worldwide/

Smith, P., & Zook, Z. (2011). *Marketing Communications: Integrating Offline and Online with Social Media* (5th ed.). Kogan Page. https://www.wcbuybooks.co.uk/

Sneath, J. Z., Lacey, R., & Kennett-Hensel, P. A. (2009). Coping with a natural disaster : Losses, emotions, and impulsive and compulsive buying. *Marketing Letters*, *20*(1), 45–60. doi:10.100711002-008-9049-y

Snyder, B., & Barzilay, R. (2005). Multiple Aspect Ranking using the Good Grief Algorithm. *Human Language Technologies 2007: The Conference of the North American Chapter of the Association for Computational Linguistics; Proceedings of the Main Conference*, 300–307.

Snyder, H. (2019). Literature review as a research methodology: An overview and guidelines. *Journal of Business Research*, *104*, 333–339. doi:10.1016/j.jbusres.2019.07.039

Sobitha Ahila, S., & Shunmuganathan, K. L. (2015). Multi agent-based aspect ranking review summarization for customer guidance. *Journal of Engineering and Applied Sciences (Asian Research Publishing Network)*, *10*(9), 4090–4096.

Sohn, J., Nielsen, K. S., Birkved, M., Joanes, T., & Gwozdz, W. (2021). The environmental impacts of clothing: Evidence from United States and three European countries. *Sustainable Production and Consumption*, *27*, 2153-2164.

Sohn, J. W., & Kim, J. K. (2020). Factors that influence purchase intentions in social commerce. *Technology in Society, 63*, 101365. doi:10.1016/j.techsoc.2020.101365

So, K. K. F., Kim, H., & King, C. (2021). The thematic evolution of customer engagement research: A comparative systematic review and bibliometric analysis. *International Journal of Contemporary Hospitality Management, 33*(10), 3585–3609. doi:10.1108/IJCHM-04-2021-0470

So, K. K. F., Li, X., & Kim, H. (2019). A Decade of Customer Engagement Research in Hospitality and Tourism: A Systematic Review and Research Agenda. *Journal of Hospitality & Tourism Research (Washington, D.C.), 44*(2), 178–200. doi:10.1177/1096348019895562

Solakis, K., Katsoni, V., Mahmoud, A. B., & Grigoriou, N. (2022). Factors affecting value co-creation through artificial intelligence in tourism—A general literature review. *Journal of Tourism Futures*. 1-15. doi:1108/JTF-06-2021-0157

Solakis, K., Peña-Vinces, J., & Lopez-Bonilla, J. M. (2022). Value co-creation and perceived value: A customer perspective in the hospitality context. *European Research on Management and Business Economics, 28*(1), 100175. doi:10.1016/j.iedeen.2021.100175

Solomon, M. (2006). *Consumer behavior: A European perspective*. Prentice Hall Europe. https://lib.ugent.be/catalog/rug01:001018093

Solomon, M. R., Bamossy, G., & Askegaard, S. (2002). *Consumer behavior: A European perspective*. London: Financial Times/Prentice Hall. https://books.mec.biz/tmp/books/NXHQRTHBQ2L87NIU6YVN.pdf

Solomon, M., Bamossy, G., Askegaard, S., & Hogg, M. K. (2006). *Consumer Behavior. A European perspective* (3rd ed.). Prentice Hall Financial Times. https://www.research.lancs.ac.uk/portal/en/publications

Sommerville, I. (2001). *Software Engineering* (6th ed.). Addison-Wesley.

Sönmez, S., Apostolopoulos, Y., Lemke, M. K., & Hsieh, Y.-C. (2020). Understanding the effects of COVID-19 on the health and safety of immigrant hospitality workers in the United States. *Tourism Management Perspectives, 35*, 100717. doi:10.1016/j.tmp.2020.100717 PMID:32834958

Sontag, M. S., & Lee, J. (2004). Proximity of Clothing to Self Scale. *Clothing & Textiles Research Journal, 22*(4), 161–177. doi:10.1177/0887302X0402200402

Soroka, A., Liu, Y., Han, L., & Haleem, M. S. (2017). Big data driven customer insights for SMEs in redistributed manufacturing. *Procedia CIRP, 63*, 692–697. https://dx.doi.org/10.1016/j.procir.2017.03.319

Spangenberg, E. R., Voss, K. E., & Crowley, E. (1997). In M. Brucks & D. J. MacInnis (Eds.), *Measuring the hedonic and utilitarian dimensions of attitude: A generally applicable scale. Advances in Consumer Research, 24* (pp. 235–241). Association for Consumer Research. doi:10.1509/jmkr.40.3.310.19238

Srivastava, M., & Sivaramakrishnan, S. (2021). Mapping the themes and intellectual structure of customer engagement: A bibliometric analysis. *Marketing Intelligence & Planning, 39*(5), 702–727. doi:10.1108/MIP-11-2020-0483

Statista. (2012). *Revenue of the global lingerie market in 2012 and 2017*. Statista. Retrieved February 14, 2021 from fhttps://www.statista.com/statistics/418713/revenue-of-the-lingerie-market-worldwide/

Statista. (2019a). *Brands of women's lingerie and underwear ranked by number of consumers in Spain in 2020*. Statista. Retrieved February 14, 2021 from https://www.statista.com/statistics/579362/leading-brands-of-womens-underwear-garment-in-spain/

Statista. (2019b). *Evolución de la facturación del sector de la moda íntima en España de 2015 a 2018.* Statista. Retrieved February 14, 2021 from https://es.statista.com/estadisticas/1171499/facturacion-moda-intima-espana/

Statista. (2022). *Value of the sharing economy worldwide in 2014 and 2025 (in billion U.S. dollars).* Statista. Retrieved 17 March from https://www.statista.com/statistics/830986/value-of-the-global-sharing-economy/

Streeter, A. (2014). *South-East Asia briefing: A sustainable garment industry in Cambodia?* Reuters Events. Retrieved 10 March from https://www.reutersevents.com/sustainability/supply-chains/south-east-asia-briefing-sustainable-garment-industry-cambodia

Struhl, S. (2017). *Artificial intelligence marketing and predicting consumer choice: an overview of tools and techniques.* Kogan Page.

Su, X. (2010). Intertemporal pricing and consumer stockpiling. *Operations Research, 58*(4-part-2), 1133–1147. doi:10.1287/opre.1090.0797

Sudbury, L., & Simcock, P. (2009). A multivariate segmentation model of senior consumers. *Journal of Consumer Marketing, 26*(4), 251–262. doi:10.1108/07363760910965855

Sveiby, K. E. (1997). *The New Organizational Wealth: Managing & Measuring Knowledge-Based Assets.* Berrett-Koehler Publishers, Inc.

Taherdoost, H., Masrom, M., & Ismail, Z. (2009). Adoption model to assess the user acceptance of smart card technology. *Journal of US-China Public Administration, 6*(3), 47–58.

Taherdoost, H., Namayandeh, M., & Masrom, M. (2009). Development a Smart Card Acceptance Model from Ethical Perspective. *International Conference on Frontiers in Education: Computer Science & Computer Engineering*, Las Vegas, NV.

Taherdoost, H., Sahibuddin, S., & Jalaliyoon, N. (2011). Smart card security; Technology and adoption. *International Journal of Security, 5*(2), 74–84.

Talidong, K. J. B., & Toquero, C. M. D. (2020). Philippine Teachers' Practices to Deal with Anxiety amid COVID-19. *Journal of Loss and Trauma, 2020*(6-7), 1–7. doi:10.1080/15325024.2020.1759225

Tanford, S. (2016). Antecedents and Outcomes of Hospitality Loyalty: A Meta-Analysis. *Cornell Hospitality Quarterly, 57*(2), 122–137. doi:10.1177/1938965516640121

Tan, K. L., Sia, J. K. M., & Tang, D. K. H. (2021). To verify or not to verify: Using partial least squares to predict effect of online news on panic buying during pandemic. *Asia Pacific Journal of Marketing and Logistics.* Advance online publication. doi:10.1108/APJML-02-2021-0125

Tankard, C. (2012). Big data security. *Network Security, 2012*(7), 5–8. https://doi.org/10.1016/S1353-4858(12)70063-6

Tarhini, A., Alalwan, A. A., Al-Qirim, N., & Algharabat, R. (2018). An analysis of the factors influencing the adoption of online shopping. *International Journal of Technology Diffusion, 9*(3), 68–87. https://doi.org/10.4018/978-1-7998-8957-1.ch019

Taylor, S. (2021). Understanding and managing pandemic-related panic buying. *Journal of Anxiety Disorders, 78*, 102364. doi:10.1016/j.janxdis.2021.102364 PMID:33517219

Taylor-Singh, H. (2021). *The rise of online thrifting is raising ethical questions.* NOW Magazine.

Templier, M., & Paré, G. (2015). A framework for guiding and evaluating literature reviews. *Communications of the Association for Information Systems, 37*(1), 6.

Teoh Yi Zhe, I., & Keikhosrokiani, P. (2021). Knowledge workers mental workload prediction using optimised ELANFIS. *Applied Intelligence, 51*(4), 2406–2430. doi:10.100710489-020-01928-5

TFL. (2021). *Secondhand fashion market is expected to be more than double the size of fast fashion by 2030.* Retrieved 11 March from https://www.thefashionlaw.com/already-displacing-fast-fashion-secondhand-fashion-to-grow-into-a-77-billion-market-by-2026/

Thaichon, P., Lobo, A., & Quach, T. N. (2016). The moderating role of age in customer loyalty formation process. *Services Marketing Quarterly, 37*(1), 52–70. doi:10.1080/15332969.2015.1112184

Tham, A., Croy, G., & Mair, J. (2013). Social media in destination choice: Distinctive electronic word-of-mouth dimensions. *Journal of Travel & Tourism Marketing, 30*(1–2), 144–155. doi:10.1080/10548408.2013.751272

Think with Google. (2020, January). *San Valentín 2020: una ocasión para enamorar a tus clientes.* Think with Google. Retrieved February 14, 2021 https://www.thinkwithgoogle.com/intl/es-es/insights/tendencias-de-consumo/san-valentin-2020-que-se-busca-y-se-regala-en-espana/

Thorndike, R. L. (1953). Who belongs in the family? *Psychometrika, 18*(4), 267–276. doi:10.1007/BF02289263

ThredUp. (2021). *2021 Resale Report.* ThredUp. Retrieved 18 February from https://www.thredup.com/resale/#size-and-impact

Tian, F., Yang, Y., Mao, Z., & Tang, W. (2021). Forecasting daily attraction demand using big data from search engines and social media. *International Journal of Contemporary Hospitality Management, 33*(6), 1950–1976. doi:10.1108/IJCHM-06-2020-0631

Tibenderana, P., Ogao, P., Ikoja-Odongo, J., & Wokadala, J. (2010). Measuring levels of end-users' acceptance and use of hybrid library services. *International Journal of Education and Development using ICT, 6*(2), 33-54.

Tibshirani, R., Walther, G., & Hastie, T. (2001). Estimating the number of clusters in a data set via the gap statistic. *Journal of the Royal Statistical Society: Series B (Statistical Methodology), 63*(2), 411-423. doi:10.1111/1467-9868.00293

Todeschini, B. V., Cortimiglia, M. N., Callegaro-de-Menezes, D., & Ghezzi, A. (2017). Innovative and sustainable business models in the fashion industry: Entrepreneurial drivers, opportunities, and challenges. *Business Horizons, 60*(6), 759–770. doi:10.1016/j.bushor.2017.07.003

To, P., Liao, C., & Lin, T. (2007). Shopping motivations on ınternet: A study based on utilitarian and hedonic value. *Journal of Social. Management Technovation, 27*(12), 774–787. doi:10.1016/j.technovation.2007.01.001

Torugsa, N., & Yawised, K. O. D. W. (2019). Social Customer Relationship Management in Small and Medium Enterprises: Overcoming Barriers to Success. In C. Machado & J. Davim (Eds.), Management Science. Management and Industrial Engineering. Springer. doi:10.1007/978-3-030-13229-3_7

Trainor, K. J. (2012). Relating Social Media Technologies to Performance: A Capabilities-Based Perspective. *Journal of Personal Selling & Sales Management, 32*(3), 317–331. doi:10.2753/PSS0885-3134320303

Tsai, C. Y., & Chiu, C. C. (2004). A purchase-based market segmentation methodology. *Expert Systems with Applications, 27*(2), 265–276. doi:10.1016/j.eswa.2004.02.005

Tsimonis & Dimitriadis. (2014). Brand strategies in social media. *Marketing Intelligence & Planning, 32*(3), 328 - 344. doi:10.1108/MIP-04-2013-0056

Tumewah, E., Juniarta, Y. K., & Kurniawan, Y. (2020). The effect of m-banking service quality and customer perceived value to satisfaction and loyalty of bank XYZ customers. *International Journal of Management and Humanities*, *4*(6), 132–138. doi:10.35940/ijmh.F0634.024620

Tuncer, I. (2021). The relationship between IT affordance, flow experience, trust, and social commerce intention: An exploration using the S-O-R paradigm. *Technology in Society*, *65*, 101567. doi:10.1016/j.techsoc.2021.101567

Turunen, L. L. M., & Pöyry, E. (2019). Shopping with the resale value in mind: A study on second-hand luxury consumers. *International Journal of Consumer Studies, 43*(6), 549-556. doi:10.1111/ijcs.12539

Tuten, T. L. (2020). *Social Media Marketing* (4th ed.). SAGE Publications, Limited.

Uddin, M. F., & Gupta, N. (2014, April). Seven V's of Big Data understanding Big Data to extract value. In Proceedings of the 2014 zone 1 conference of the American Society for Engineering Education (pp. 1–5). IEEE. https://dx.doi.org/10.1109%2FASEEZone1.2014.6820689.

United Nations. (2020). Policy Brief: Education during COVID-19 and beyond. United Nations.

Urbanikova, M., Stubnova, M., Papcunova, V., & Hudakova, J. (2020). Analysis of Innovation Activities of Slovak Small and Medium-Sized Family Business. *Administrative Sciences*, *10*(4), 80. doi:10.3390/admsci10040080

Valanarasu, J. M. J., Sindagi, V. A., Hacihaliloglu, I., & Patel, V. M. (2020). KiU-Net: Towards Accurate Segmentation of Biomedical Images Using Over-Complete Representations. Medical Image Computing and Computer Assisted Intervention, MICCAI 2020.

Valle-Cruz, D., Fernandez-Cortez, V., López-Chau, A., & Sandoval-Almazán, R. (2021). Does Twitter Affect Stock Market Decisions? Financial Sentiment Analysis During Pandemics: A Comparative Study of the H1N1 and the COVID-19 Periods. *Cognitive Computation, 14*(1), 372-387. doi:10.1007/s12559-021-09819-8

Valor, C., Ronda, L., & Abril, C. (2022). Understanding the expansion of circular markets: Building relational legitimacy to overcome the stigma of second-hand clothing. *Sustainable Production and Consumption, 30*, 77-88.

van Asperen, M., de Rooij, P., & Dijkmans, C. (2018). Engagement-Based Loyalty: The Effects of Social Media Engagement on Customer Loyalty in the Travel Industry. *International Journal of Hospitality & Tourism Administration*, *19*(1), 78–94. doi:10.1080/15256480.2017.1305313

van der Aalst, W. (2016). *Process Mining*. Springer. doi:10.1007/978-3-662-49851-4

Vasudevan, P., & Arokiasamy, L. (2021). Online shopping among young generation in Malaysia. *Electronic Journal of Business and Management*, *6*(1), 31–38.

Velasquez, M., & Hester, P. T. (2013). An Analysis of Multi-Criteria Decision-Making Methods. *International Journal of Operations Research*, *10*(2), 56–66.

Venkatesh, V., Morris, M. G., Davis, G. B., & Davis, F. D. (2003). User Acceptance of Information Technology: Toward a Unified View. *Management Information Systems Quarterly*, *27*(3). https://doi.org/10.2307/30036540

Venkatesh, V., Thong, J. Y., & Xu, X. (2012). Consumer acceptance and use of information technology: Extending the unified theory of acceptance and use of technology. *Management Information Systems Quarterly*, *36*(1), 157–178. https://ssrn.com/abstract=2002388

Venter, P., Wright, A., & Dibb, S. (2015). Performing market segmentation: A performative perspective. *Journal of Marketing Management*, *31*(1-2), 62–83. doi:10.1080/0267257X.2014.980437

Verma, S., Bhattacharyya, S. S., & Kumar, S. (2018). An extension of the technology acceptance model in the big data analytics system implementation environment. *Information Processing & Management, 54*(5), 791–806. https://doi.org/10.1016/j.ipm.2018.01.004

Villars, R. L., Olofson, C. W., & Eastwood, M. (2011). *Big data: What it is and why you should care.* White paper, IDC. doi:10.1186/s40537-019-0206-3

Vishnuvardhan, B., Manjula, B., & Naik, R. L. (2020). A study of digital banking: Security issues and challenges. *Advances in Intelligent Systems and Computing, 1090*, 163–185. doi:10.1007/978-981-15-1480-7_14

Wang, B., Fu, Y., & Li, Y. (2022). Young consumers' motivations and barriers to the purchase of second-hand clothes: An empirical study of China. *Waste Management, 143*, 157-167.

Wang, H., Lu, Y., & Zhai, C. (2010). Latent aspect rating analysis on review text data. *Proceedings of the 16th ACM SIGKDD International Conference on Knowledge Discovery and Data Mining - KDD '10*, 783. 10.1145/1835804.1835903

Wang, J. H., & Lee, C. C. (2011). Unsupervised opinion phrase extraction and rating in Chinese blog posts. *Proceedings - 2011 IEEE International Conference on Privacy, Security, Risk and Trust and IEEE International Conference on Social Computing, PASSAT/SocialCom 2011*, 820–823. 10.1109/INFCOM.2011.5935305

Wang, J., Zhang, W., Shi, Y., Duan, S., & Liu, J. (2016). *Industrial big data analytics: challenges, methodologies, and applications.* doi:10.35683/jcm18096.0014

Wang, C., Han, D., Liu, Q., & Luo, S. (2018). A deep learning approach for credit scoring of peer-to-peer lending using attention mechanism LSTM. *IEEE Access: Practical Innovations, Open Solutions, 7*, 2161–2168. doi:10.1109/ACCESS.2018.2887138

Wang, D., Zhu, S., & Li, T. (2013). SumView: A Web-based engine for summarizing product reviews and customer opinions. *Expert Systems with Applications, 40*(1), 27–33. doi:10.1016/j.eswa.2012.05.070

Wang, K., Zhang, T., Xue, T., Lu, Y., & Na, S.-G. (2020). E-commerce personalized recommendation analysis by deeply-learned clustering. *Journal of Visual Communication and Image Representation, 71*, 102735. doi:10.1016/j.jvcir.2019.102735

Wang, X., Wong, Y. D., Qi, G., & Yuen, K. F. (2021). Contactless channel for shopping and delivery in the context of social distancing in response to COVID-19 pandemic. *Electronic Commerce Research and Applications, 48*, 101075. doi:10.1016/j.elerap.2021.101075

Wang, Y. S. (2008). Assessing e-commerce systems success: A respecification and validation of the DeLone and McLean model of IS success. *Information Systems Journal, 18*(5), 529–557. doi:10.1111/j.1365-2575.2007.00268.x

Wang, Y., Bennani, I. L., Liu, X., Sun, M., & Zhou, Y. (2021). Electricity consumer characteristics identification: A federated learning approach. *IEEE Transactions on Smart Grid, 12*(4), 3637–3647. doi:10.1109/TSG.2021.3066577

Wang, Y., Chen, Q., Gan, D., Yang, J., Kirschen, D. S., & Kang, C. (2018). Deep learning-based socio-demographic information identification from Smart Meter Data. *IEEE Transactions on Smart Grid, 10*(3), 2593–2602. doi:10.1109/TSG.2018.2805723

Wang, Y., Feng, D., Li, D., Chen, X., Zhao, Y., & Niu, X. (2016). A mobile recommendation system based on logistic regression and Gradient Boosting Decision Trees. *Proceedings of the International Joint Conference on Neural Networks*, 1896–1902. 10.1109/IJCNN.2016.7727431

Wang, Z., & Kim, H. G. (2017). Can Social Media Marketing Improve Customer Relationship Capabilities and Firm Performance? Dynamic Capability Perspective. *Journal of Interactive Marketing, 39*, 15–26. doi:10.1016/j.intmar.2017.02.004

Wang, Z., Liu, X., & Zhang, S. (2019). A New Decision Method for Public Opinion Crisis with the Intervention of Risk Perception of the Public. *Complexity*, *9527218*, 1–14. Advance online publication. doi:10.1155/2019/9527218

Ward, J. H. Jr. (1963). Hierarchical Grouping to Optimize an Objective Function. *Journal of the American Statistical Association*, *58*(301), 236–244. doi:10.1080/01621459.1963.10500845

Watermeyer, R., Crick, T., Knight, C., & Goodall, J. (2020). COVID-19 and Digital Disruption in UK Universities: Afflictions and Affordances of Emergency Online Migration. *Higher Education*, *2020*(81), 623–641. doi:10.100710734-020-00561-y PMID:32836334

Weber, M. (2009). *Marketing to the Social Web: How Digital Customer Communities Build Your Business* (2nd ed.). John Willey & Sons Inc. doi:10.1002/9781118258125

Wedel, M., Bigné, E., & Zhang, J. (2020). Virtual and augmented reality: Advancing research in consumer marketing. *International Journal of Research in Marketing*, *37*(3), 443–465. doi:10.1016/j.ijresmar.2020.04.004

Wedel, M., & Kannan, P. K. (2016). Marketing analytics for data-rich environments. *Journal of Marketing*, *80*(6), 97–121. https://doi.org/10.1509%2Fjm.15.0413

Wehrens, R., Putter, H., & Buydens, L. M. (2000). The bootstrap: A tutorial. *Chemometrics and Intelligent Laboratory Systems*, *54*(1), 35–52. doi:10.1016/S0169-7439(00)00102-7

Wei, X., He, C., & Zhu, B. (2016). Relationship between customer perceived value and loyalty of mobile banking. In *Proceedings of the International Conference on Education, Management, Computer and Society*. Atlantis Press. 10.2991/emcs-16.2016.269

Wei, J. T., Lin, S. Y., Weng, C. C., & Wu, H. H. (2012). A case study of applying LRFM model in market segmentation of a children's dental clinic. *Expert Systems with Applications*, *39*(5), 5529–5533. doi:10.1016/j.eswa.2011.11.066

Weinberg, T. (2009). *The New Community Rules: Marketing on the Social Web. Publisher*. O'Reilly. doi:10.4148/1051-0834.1141

Weinstein, A. (2013). *Handbook of market segmentation: Strategic targeting for business and technology firms*. Routledge. doi:10.4324/9780203862483

Wei, Z., Zhao, Z., & Zheng, Y. (2019). Following the majority: Social influence in trusting behavior. *Frontiers in Neuroscience*, *13*, 89. https://doi.org/10.3389/fnins.2019.00089

West, H. R. (2004). *An introduction to Mill's utilitarian ethics*. Cambridge University Press. https://www.cambridge.org/9780521828321

Wheelen, T. L., Hunger, J. D., Hoffman, A. N., & Bamford, C. E. (2017). *Strategic management and business policy* (Vol. 55). Pearson.

Wilson, T., Wiebe, J., & Hoffmann, P. (2005). Recognizing contextual polarity in phrase-level sentiment analysis. *Proceedings of the Conference on Human Language Technology and Empirical Methods in Natural Language Processing - HLT '05*, 347–354. 10.3115/1220575.1220619

Wilson, J. M., Fast, S. M., Gonza, M. C., & Markuzon, N. (2015). Modelling the propagation of social response during a disease outbreak. *Journal of the Royal Society, Interface*, *12*(104), 20141105. doi:10.1098/rsif.2014.1105 PMID:25589575

Wilson, R. M., & Gilligan, C. (2012). *Strategic marketing management*. Routledge.

Winakor, G. (1969). The process of clothing consumption. *Journal of Home Economics*, *68*(1), 629–634.

Wooldridge, J. M. (2010). *Econometric analysis of cross section and panel data*. MIT Press.

Wu, G., Deng, X., & Liu, B. (2022). Managing urban citizens' panic levels and preventive behaviours during COVID-19 with pandemic information released by social media. *Cities (London, England)*, *120*, 103490. doi:10.1016/j.cities.2021.103490 PMID:34642529

Wu, J. S., Ye, S., Zheng, C. J., & Law, R. (2021). Revisiting customer loyalty toward mobile e-commerce in the hospitality industry: Does brand viscosity matter? *International Journal of Contemporary Hospitality Management*, *33*(10), 3514–3534. doi:10.1108/IJCHM-11-2020-1348

Wu, J., Lu, F., Zhang, J., Yang, J., & Xing, L. (2019). Choice of distribution channels for experience products using virtual reality. *IEEE Access: Practical Innovations, Open Solutions*, *7*, 85319–85326. doi:10.1109/ACCESS.2019.2920308

Wu, R.-S., & Chou, P.-H. (2011). Customer segmentation of multiple category data in e-commerce using a soft-clustering approach. *Electronic Commerce Research and Applications*, *10*(3), 331–341. doi:10.1016/j.elerap.2010.11.002

Wyber, R., Vaillancourt, S., Perry, W., Mannava, P., Folaranmi, T., & Celi, L. A. (2015). Big data in global health: Improving health in low-and middle-income countries. *Bulletin of the World Health Organization*, *93*, 203–208. https://doi.org/10.2471/BLT.14.139022

Xiang, X. (2021). Factors That Influence Consumers' Behaviors in Fashion Market. *Open Journal of Business and Management*, *9*(6), 2772-2779. doi:10.4236/ojbm.2021.96154

Xiao, Y., & Yu, J. (2007). *Gap statistic and K-means algorithm. Chinese Academic Conference on Classification Technology and Application*, Zhengzhou, China.

Xiong, S. (2013). Adoption of mobile banking model based on perceived value and trust. *Proceedings of the 6th International Conference on Information Management, Innovation Management and Industrial Engineering*, *1*, 632-635. 10.1109/ICIII.2013.6703015

Xu, J. (2014). Managing Digital Enterprise. *Ten Essential Topics*, *55-56*. Advance online publication. doi:10.2991/978-94-6239-094-2

Xu, Y., Du, B., Zhang, L., Cerra, D., Pato, M., Carmona, E., Prasad, S., Yokoya, N., Hansch, R., & Le Saux, B. (2019). Advanced multi-sensor optical remote sensing for urban land use and land cover classification: Outcome of the 2018 IEEE GRSS data fusion contest. *IEEE Journal of Selected Topics in Applied Earth Observations and Remote Sensing*, *12*(6), 1709–1724. doi:10.1109/JSTARS.2019.2911113

Yadav, R., Sharma, S. K., & Tarhini, A. (2016). A multi-analytical approach to understand and predict the mobile commerce adoption. *Journal of Enterprise Information Management*, *29*(2), 222–237. https://doi.org/10.1108/JEIM-04-2015-0034

Yang, J., Lee, J.-Y., Choi, M., & Joo, Y. (2020). A New Approach to Determine the Optimal Number of Clusters Based on the Gap Statistic. Machine Learning for Networking.

Yan, G., Minxi, W., & Xin, L. (2017). Application of an improved Apriori algorithm in a mobile e-commerce recommendation system. *Industrial Management & Data Systems*, *117*(2), 287–303. doi:10.1108/IMDS-03-2016-0094

Yang, D., Gao, X., Kong, L., Pang, Y., & Zhou, B. (2020). An event-driven convolutional neural architecture for non-intrusive load monitoring of residential appliance. *IEEE Transactions on Consumer Electronics*, *66*(2), 173–182. doi:10.1109/TCE.2020.2977964

Yang, T. Y., Brinton, C. G., Joe-Wong, C., & Chiang, M. (2017). Behavior-based grade prediction for MOOCs via time series neural networks. *IEEE Journal of Selected Topics in Signal Processing*, *11*(5), 716–728. https://doi.org/10.1109/JSTSP.2017.2700227

Yan, Z., Xing, M., Zhang, D., & Ma, B. (2015). EXPRS: An Extended PageRank Method for Product Feature Extraction from Online Consumer Reviews. *Information & Management, 52*(7), 850–858. doi:10.1016/j.im.2015.02.002

Yan, Z., Xing, M., Zhang, D., Ma, B., & Wang, T. (2014). A Context-Dependent Sentiment Analysis of Online Product Reviews based on Dependency Relationships. *Proceedings of International Conference on Information Systems*, 1–14.

Yeh, C. H., Wang, Y. S., & Yieh, K. (2016). Predicting smartphone brand loyalty: Consumer value and consumer-brand identification perspectives. *International Journal of Information Management, 36*(3), 245–257. doi:10.1016/j.ijinfomgt.2015.11.013

Yen, C.-L., & Tang, C.-H. (2015). Hotel attribute performance, eWOM motivations, and media choice. *International Journal of Hospitality Management, 46*, 79–88. doi:10.1016/j.ijhm.2015.01.003

Yen, T. T. F. (2020). The Performance of Online Teaching for Flipped Classroom Based on COVID-19 Aspect. *Asian J. Educ. Soc. Studies, 2020*(8), 57–64. doi:10.9734/ajess/2020/v8i330229

Yin, J., & Fernandez, V. (2020). *A systematic review on business analytics.* doi:10.3926/jiem.3030

Yolcu, G., Oztel, I., Kazan, S., Oz, C., & Bunyak, F. (2020). Deep learning-based face analysis system for monitoring customer interest. *Journal of Ambient Intelligence and Humanized Computing, 11*(1), 237–248. doi:10.100712652-019-01310-5

Yoon, J., Narasimhan, R., & Kim, M. K. (2018). Retailer's sourcing strategy under consumer stockpiling in anticipation of supply disruptions. *International Journal of Production Research, 56*(10), 3615–3635. doi:10.1080/00207543.2017.1401748

Young Lee, J., Halter, H., Johnson, K. K. P., & Ju, H. (2013). Investigating fashion disposition with young consumers. *Young Consumers, 14*(1), 67–78. doi:10.1108/17473611311305494

Yousafzai, S. Y., Pallister, J. G., & Foxall, G. R. (2003). A proposed model of e-trust for electronic banking. *Technovation, 23*(11), 847–860. https://doi.org/10.1016/S0166-4972(03)00130-5

Yu, J., Zha, Z.-J., Wang, M., & Chua, T.-S. (2011). Aspect Ranking: Identifying Important Product Aspects from Online Consumer Reviews. *Computational Linguistics*, 1496–1505. https://dl.acm.org/doi/10.5555/2002472.2002654

Yuan, C., & Yang, H. (2019). Research on K-Value Selection Method of K-Means Clustering Algorithm. *J, 2*(2), 226-235. doi:10.3390/j2020016

Yuan, Q., & Shen, B. (2019). Renting fashion with strategic customers in the sharing economy. *International Journal of Production Economics, 218*, 185–195. doi:10.1016/j.ijpe.2019.04.034

Yuen, K. F., Tan, L. S., Wong, Y. D., & Wang, X. (2022). Social determinants of panic buying behaviour amidst COVID-19 pandemic: The role of perceived scarcity and anticipated regret. *Journal of Retailing and Consumer Services, 66*, 102948. doi:10.1016/j.jretconser.2022.102948

Yukseltan, E., Yucekaya, A., Bilge, A. H., & Aktunc, E. A. (2021). Forecasting models for daily natural gas consumption considering periodic variations and demand segregation. *Socio-Economic Planning Sciences, 74*(100937). Advance online publication. doi:10.1016/j.seps.2020.100937

Zainuddin, Z., Perera, C. J., Haruna, H., & Habiburrahim, H. (2020). Literacy in the New Norm: Stay-Home Game Plan for Parents. *Inf. Learn. Sci., 2020*(121), 645–653. doi:10.1108/ILS-04-2020-0069

Zakir, J., Seymour, T., & Berg, K. (2015). Big Data Analytics. *Issues in Information Systems, 16*(2). _iis_2015_81-90 doi:10.48009/2

Zarrella, D. (2010). *The Social Media Marketing Book. Publisher*. O'Reilly. http://www.oreilly.de/catalog/9780596806606/index.html

Zavadskas, E. K., & Turskis, Z. (2011). Multiple criteria decision making (MCDM) methods in economics: An overview. *Technological and Economic Development of Economy*, *17*(2), 397–427. doi:10.3846/20294913.2011.593291

Zeeshan, A., Jun, L., & Zahida, L. (2020). Discovering Knowledge by Comparing Silhouettes Using K-Means Clustering for Customer Segmentation. *International Journal of Knowledge Management*, *16*(3), 70–88. doi:10.4018/IJKM.2020070105

Zeithaml, V. A. (1988). Consumer perceptions of price, quality, and value: A means-end model and synthesis of evidence. *Journal of Marketing*, *52*(3), 222. doi:10.1177/002224298805200302

Zeithaml, V. A. (2000). Service quality, profitability, and the economic worth of customers: What we know and what we need to learn. *Journal of the Academy of Marketing Science*, *28*(1), 67–85. doi:10.1177/0092070300281007

Zendehdel, M., Paim, L. H., & Osman, S. B. (2015). Students' online purchasing behavior in Malaysia: Understanding online shopping attitude. *Cogent Business & Management*, *2*(1), 1078428. doi:10.1080/23311975.2015.1078428

Zhang, G. L., Sun, J., Chitkushev, L., & Brusic, V. (2014). *Big data analytics in immunology: a knowledge-based approach.* BioMed Research International. doi:10.1155/2014/437987

Zhang, S., & Chiu, J. L. (2021). The impact of epidemic outbreak on Chinese consumers spending behavior. *New Normal and New Rules in International Trade, Economics and Marketing*, 349-363.

Zhang, M., Jansen, B. J., & Chowdhury, A. (2011). Business engagement on Twitter: A path analysis. *Electronic Markets*, *21*(3), 161–175. doi:10.100712525-011-0065-z

Zhang, S., & Zhong, H. (2019). Mining users' trust from e-commerce reviews based on sentiment similarity analysis. *IEEE Access: Practical Innovations, Open Solutions*, *7*, 13523–13535. doi:10.1109/ACCESS.2019.2893601

Zhang, Z., Ye, Q., Law, R., & Li, Y. (2010). The impact of e-word-of-mouth on the online popularity of restaurants: A comparison of consumer reviews and editor reviews. *International Journal of Hospitality Management*, *29*(4), 694–700. doi:10.1016/j.ijhm.2010.02.002

Zhan, X., Ukkusuri, S. V., & Zhu, F. (2014). Inferring urban land use using large-scale social media check-in data. *Networks and Spatial Economics*, *14*(3), 647–667. https://doi.org/10.1007/s11067-014-9264-4

Zhao, J., Xue, F., Khan, S., & Khatib, S. F. (2021). Consumer behaviour analysis for business development. *Aggression and Violent Behavior*, 101591. doi:10.1016/j.avb.2021.101591

Zhao, X., & Keikhosrokiani, P. (2022). Sales Prediction and Product Recommendation Model Through User Behavior Analytics. *Computers, Materials & Continua, 70*(2), 3855--3874. http://www.techscience.com/cmc/v70n2/44651

Zhao, X., & Keikhosrokiani, P. (2022). Sales prediction and product recommendation model through user behavior analytics. *Computers. Materials and Continua*, *70*(2), 3855–3874. doi:10.32604/cmc.2022.019750

Zha, Z., Yu, J., & Tang, J. (2014). Product aspect ranking and its applications. *IEEE Transactions on Knowledge and Data Engineering*, *26*(5), 1211–1224. doi:10.1109/TKDE.2013.136

Zheng, R., Shou, B., & Yang, J. (2021). Supply disruption management under consumer panic buying and social learning effects. *Omega*, *101*, 102238. doi:10.1016/j.omega.2020.102238

Zhong, Y., Shapoval, V., & Busser, J. (2021). The role of parasocial relationship in social media marketing: Testing a model among baby boomers. *International Journal of Contemporary Hospitality Management*, *33*(5), 1870–1891. doi:10.1108/IJCHM-08-2020-0873

Zhou, K., Taigang, L., & Lifeng, Z. (2015). Industry 4.0: Towards future industrial opportunities and challenges. *2015 12th International Conference on Fuzzy Systems and Knowledge Discovery (FSKD)*.

Zhou, L., Wu, S., Zhou, M., & Li, F. (2020). 'School's Out, But Class' On,' The Largest Online Education in the World Today: Taking China's Practical Exploration During The COVID-19 Epidemic Prevention and Control as an Example. *Best Evid. Chin. Edu.*, *2020*(4), 501–519. doi:10.15354/bece.20.ar023

Zhou, Q., Xu, Z., & Yen, N. Y. (2019). User sentiment analysis based on social network information and its application in consumer reconstruction intention. *Computers in Human Behavior*, *100*, 177–183. doi:10.1016/j.chb.2018.07.006

Zhou, W., Wen, J., Qu, Q., Zeng, J., & Cheng, T. (2018). Shilling attack detection for recommender systems based on credibility of group users and rating time series. *PLoS One*, *13*(5), 1–17. doi:10.1371/journal.pone.0196533 PMID:29742134

Zikmund, W. G., Babin, B. J., Carr, J. C., & Griffin, M. (2013). *Business research methods*. Cengage Learning.

Zu, Z. Y., Jiang, M. D., Xu, P. P., Chen, W., Ni, Q. Q., Lu, G. M., & Zhang, L. J. (2020). Coronavirus disease 2019 (COVID-19): A perspective from China. *Radiology*, *296*(2), E15–E25. https://doi.org/10.1148/radiol.2020200490

About the Contributors

Pantea Keikhosrokiani received the Bachelor of Science degree in electrical and electronics engineering, the master's degree in information technology from the School of Computer Sciences, Universiti Sains Malaysia (USM), Malaysia, and the Ph.D. degree in service system engineering, information system. She was a Teaching Fellow with the National Advanced IPv6 Centre of Excellence (Nav6), USM, where she is currently a Senior Lecturer with the School of Computer Sciences. Her recent book was published entitled Perspectives in the Development of Mobile Medical Information Systems: Life Cycle, Management, Methodological Approach and Application, in 2019. Her articles was published in distinguished edited books and journals, including Telematics and Informatics (Elsevier), Cognition, Technology, and Work (Springer), Taylors and Francis, and IGI Global. She was indexed by ISI, Scopus, and PubMed. Her research and teaching interests include information systems development, database systems, health and medical informatics, business informatics, location-based mobile applications, big data, and technopreneurship.

* * *

Mansurali A. is a well-rounded academician in the field of business management, with special focus on marketing, analytics and applied research. With innovative and engaging pedagogy, he engages and trains students to understand the current developments in the fields has several academic contributions in the form of publications to his credit. He is proficient in R, Python, Tableau, Power BI and machine learning algorithms. His competence in analytics and research has earned him key roles in sponsored research project. He has spent 8 years of teaching management graduates marketing, analytics related courses and researching the same

Mohammed N. Al-Kabi is an Assistant Professor in the Information Technology Department at Al-Buraimi University College, Buraimi, Sultanate of Oman, and an external Reviewer within the Oman Academic Accreditation Authority (OAAA). Dr. AL-Kabi's research interests include Data Science, Big Data, Sentiment Analysis, and Opinion Mining, Data Mining, Social media, and Natural Language Processing, Information Retrieval, and Web search engines. He is the author of 105 peer-reviewed published articles on these topics and his studies gain 2239 citations with h-Index of 27. His teaching interests focus on Data Science, Information Retrieval, Big Data, Web Programming, Data Mining, DBMS (MYSQL & ORACLE). Furthermore, AL-Kabi has an interest in the quality of higher education and university rankings and published many articles in this field. Before joining Al-Buraimi University College, he worked for 16 years in IT faculty at Yarmouk and Zarqa Universities in Jordan. He also worked as a part-time lecturer at Jordan University of Science and Technology (JUST), Princess Sumaya University for Technology (PSUT) and Sunderland University. Mohammed N. Al-Kaabi obtained his Ph.D. degree in Mathematics from the University of Lodz/Poland (2001), his master's degree in Computer Science from the University of Baghdad/Iraq (1989), and his bachelor degree in statistics from the University of Baghdad/Iraq (1981).

Saif Addeen Ahmad Alrababah is an Assistant Professor in Information Technology Department at Al al-bayt University , Mafraq , Jordan, and a Director of Elearning center since 2020 . Dr. Alrababah 's research interests include Data Science, Big Data, Sentiment Analysis, and Opinion Mining, Data Mining, Social media, and Natural Language Processing, Information Retrieval, and MCDM. He is the author many peer-reviewed published articles on these topics. His teaching interests focus on Data Science, Information Retrieval, Big Data, Web Programming, Data Mining, DBMS (MYSQL & ORACLE). Furthermore, Saif Addeen Ahmad Alrababah obtained his Ph.D. degree in Computer Sciences from the University Science Malaysia USM/Malaysia (2018), his master's degree in Information Computer Systems from the Yarmouk University /Jordan (2006), and his bachelor degree in Computer Sciences from the Yarmouk University/Jordan (2003).

Maria Elena Aramendia-Muneta, PhD, is Associate professor in the Business Administration Department of Universidad Pública de Navarra. She has been a guest lecturer in different universities of Italy, Slovenia, Belgium, France, Latvia and Lithuania among others. Her primary research fields are digital marketing, digital business and history of Marketing. She has published in journals such as Telematics and Informatics, Journal of Promotion Management, Journal of Historical Research in Marketing, Journal of Gender Studies.

Md. Ashrafuzzaman, Ph.D, was born in Dec 1980. His B.Sc and M.Sc degree was in Biotechnology and Genetic Engineering, at Khulna University, Bangladesh and awarded his Ph.D in Drug Development and Biomaterials from Korea Institute of Science and Technology (KIST) South Korea. He had served as the Founder Head of the Biomedical Engineering department of Military Institute of Science and Technology (MIST) from 25-11-2014 to 12-04-2016 and now serving as associate professor and guiding the postgraduate and graduate students with active supervision and mentorship. He has published many research articles and book chapters in different international journals and patented his research works. He is the chairman and member several National Committees and Country Collaborator of CED, IFMBE for the successive development of Biomedical Engineering in Bangladesh.

Kamaladevi B. has over 18 years of international work experience in Industry, Applied Research & Academics. She is currently Programme Leader for MBA in Amity Business School, Dubai, UAE. She holds an Executive Education in Business Analytics from Wharton School at the University of Pennsylvania, USA. She is a certified Trainer to teach Innovation and Entrepreneurship from Stanford University Program Ambassadors. Dr. Kamaladevi has vast skill & experience in creating, producing & executing large scale corporate & academic events. She has managed more than 120 large scale International professional events including business conferences & corporate incentive programs globally. Dr. Kamaladevi completed her Ph.D in Management at Bharathiar University, India and her graduate studies M.Phil & MBA at Dravidian University and Bharathidasan University respectively from India. Dr. Kamaladevi's research interests lie in the area of Business Analytics, Entrepreneurship, Business Research Methods and ecommerce ranging from theory to design to implementation. She has collaborated actively with researchers in several other disciplines of management & engineering in the areas of search engine optimization & digital transformational technologies in addressing real world problems at the process to root cause analysis level for the success of online stores. In her areas of research, Dr. Kamaladevi has written three management books as single author. She also presented and published in more than 35 peer-reviewed international conferences and journal research articles. She has served as a Keynote Speaker at various international conferences and Forums held in France, Spain, Thailand, UAE, India & Malaysia. Dr. Kamaladevi also has substantial influence in professional, community, and outreach activities that is demonstrated by the various roles she has undertaken.

Alexander Berman is an Assistant Professor in the department of Management at St. John's University. He holds a BS from Cornell University, a MBA from Boston University, and a Ph.D. from Temple University. Prior to joining academia, Alexander spend over 10 years in the financial services industry, working as a member of portfolio management teams at Goldman Sachs and at Barings. Alexander is also a founder of BAIS Enterprise, a Registered Investment Advisory firm in New York. Alexander studies entrepreneurship and innovation with a focus on context-specific processes. His research examines the roles of government policy and technological innovation in the formation and sustainability of firms. He also evaluates how linguistic, cultural, cognitive, and geographic contexts relate to consumer behavior, innovation processes, and entrepreneurial outcomes.

Rigoberto R. G. C. Contreras is a professor of the Faculty of Accounting and Administration of the Autonomous University of the State of Mexico. His lines of research are related to the Management of Intangibles and Knowledge Economy in Organizations. Doctor in Administrative Economic Sciences, Master in Administration with a specialty in Organizational Management and Bachelor of Administration from the Autonomous University of the State of Mexico. He carried out a research stay at the Personality Psychology Laboratory, National University of Córdoba, Argentina. He received the award for best presentation of the Chapter: Knowledge Management by the Academy of Administrative Sciences. He has publications in various national and international magazines and publishers. He is currently a member of the Mexican National System of Researchers.

Ana de Miguel Pérez received her Bachelor in International Business Administration and Management in the Universidad Pública de Navarra, Spain. While gaining further qualifications, she works as a Technology Consultant Analyst at Accenture. She is widely interested in issues of digital marketing, communication, business processes and management. Her research is mainly focused on Fashion and Social Media.

Miriam Ezimmuo Chiamaka has recently finished her master's degree in informatics from School of Computer Sciences, Universiti Sains Malaysia.

Leonora Fuxman is a professor in Management department at the Peter J. Tobin College of Business at St. John's University in New York. She earned her Ph.D. in Operations Management and an MA degree in Decision Sciences from the Wharton School, University of Pennsylvania. Dr. Fuxman is a well published researcher with numerous publications in eminent publications including Production and Operations Management Journal, Journal of Business Ethics, Journal of Applied Business Research, International Journal of Commerce and Management among others. Dr. Fuxman research interests have evolved over two and half decades of academic and professional work. Her research interest span areas of production and operations management, service sciences, leadership, international management and more recently she is engaged in research related to sustainability, including fashion industry, as well as developing sustainable strategies across multitude of industries to promote effective consumer education strategies supporting sustainable practices and contributing to circular economy. Her research on the topic sustainability marketing in fashion industry appeared in the journal of Sustainable Production and Consumption, while her work on fashion adoption theories has been published in the Journal of Fashion Marketing and Management, with additional research about fashion industry and consumer's social media interactions with fashion brands appearing in the Journal of Brand Management and Journal of Marketing Communications among others. Covid-19 pandemic has expanded the scope of Dr. Fuxman research towards pursuing knowledge to help better understand the devastating impact of the pandemic-related industry-wide shutdowns on the employee morale and performance, especially in service sector where the necessity to interact with the customer, often in-person, makes employees particularly vulnerable to the pandemic related risks. Investigating organizational citizenship behaviors in the context of the Covid pandemic, understanding the complex dynamics of motivational factors, including job satisfaction, presence of job stressors such as job insecurities, burnouts, and other stress related factors are also subject of Dr. Fuxman recent research pursuits. She is particularly interested in studying generational variations affecting employee responses to stressors situations in the context of work motivation strategies. Understanding work motivation through different generational cohorts especially during unprecedented times our world is challenged with at this time due to global pandemic is the goal. Dr. Fuxman' scholarly work in this area has been published in European Management Review, The International Journal of Human Resource Management, Journal of Strategic Marketing, Scandinavian Journal of Psychology, International Journal of Manpower, International Sociology, and Nonprofit Management and Leadership among others.

Keng Hoon Gan is a senior lecturer in School of Computer Sciences, Universiti Sains Malaysia. She received her Ph. D. degree from Universiti of Malaya (UM) in 2013. She is currently the Cluster Head of Data to Knowledge cluster at the School of Computer Sciences. She was the Program Manager of Research Ecosystem and Innovation at the School of Computer Sciences from 2019-2021. Her domains of specialization include information retrieval, structured retrieval, structured document representation and query optimization. She has initiated a research platform SIIR (Semantics in Information Retrieval @ ir.cs.usm.my) which is a research initiative related to semantically enhanced information retrieval, and its related applications.

Nicholas Grigoriou, PhD, is an experienced lecturer in marketing at Monash University Faculty of Business and Economics, Clayton, VIC, Australia, with a demonstrated history of working in the higher education industry. He is skilled in intercultural communication, analytical skills, research design, lecturing and instructional design. His research interests are focused on marketing and international business.

Princi Gupta is working as Assistant Professor in JECRC University, Jaipur. She has Ph.D in Marketing and area of specialisation are Marketing and international business. she also holds Diploma in German Language, Business Communication & Behavioural Science. To her credit there are research paper publication in various National, International, UGC, Scopus Indexed journals.

Dieu Hack-Polay is a professor of management at Crandall University, Canada. His research interest covers sociology, human resource management, management and migration, areas in which he has published extensively. Dieu Hack-Polay is also a part time faculty at the University of Lincoln, and University of Wales Trinity St David (London), UK, where he supervises a number of doctoral students.

Lv Haibin (Senior Member, IEEE) received the Ph.D. degree from the First Institute of Oceanography, State Oceanic Administration, in 1990. He is currently a Professor with the North China Sea Offshore Engineering Survey Institute, Ministry of Natural Resources North Sea Bureau, Qingdao,China. He has 30 years research and practical experience in geoinformatics, image processing, marine surveying and mapping, and evaluation and assessment of the marine environment. He has completed dozens of consulting and research projects in related fields. He has published more than 80 high quality articles, including five IEEE Transactions on Industrial Informatics (IEEE TII) articles. He has won the Chinese National Oceanic Science and Technology Progress Award for two times. He is a Reviewer of IEEE TII, IEEE Internet of Things Journal, IEEE Access, MTAP, Plos One, and Scientific Reports. He is a member of the Editorial Board of Plos One and IET Image Processing. He is a Leading Guest Editor of IEEE Transactions on Intelligent Transportation Systems.

Md Sharif Hosssin is serving as a lecturer in Science and Humanities department in Military Institute of Science and Technology, Dhaka, Bangladesh. He has completed his graduation, post graduation and PhD in Economics from Aligarh Muslim University, India. He has attended several national and international seminars, conferences and workshops. He has also published several articles in different international journals.

P. Mary Jeyanthi is a fantastic storyteller and cross-organization conversationalist joined with an immensely creative and voracious learner. With 15+ years of experience in Data Science professionals in the Banking Sector with extensive skills and experience in Business Intelligence with Metaheuristics algorithm and Passion in mentoring to enrich the environment with knowledge and Self-discipline. Being an Entrepreneur, intensive knowledge in the research field. She had one decade of industry experience in HDFC Bank Ltd, Business Intelligence Unit, Chennai, Tamil Nadu. She had a hand full of expertise in Business Intelligence and forecasting analytics. She had done her research in "A New Implementation of Mathematical Models with metaheuristic Algorithms for Business Intelligence". Business Intelligence & Analytics initiatives on High Net Worth (HNW) Portfolio and She will be responsible for the creation and execution of strategies. Besides that, she had published many research papers in various national and international reputed journals. Conducted several workshops on Research Methodology and Business Intelligence. The latest edited book, "Decision Intelligence Analytics and the Implementation of Strategic Business Management" is published in Springer. This is the first book in India in the context of Decision Intelligence Analytics.

Mikail Kar is working as an academic at Bursa Uludag University, Department of Economics. He completed his undergraduate degree at Istanbul Marmara University, his master's degree at the State University of New York, and his PhD degree at Bursa Uludag University. He mainly works on economic theory, market analysis, methodological issues, economic policy, industrial economics. He has many book chapters and articles published in distinguished international publishing houses and journals in these fields of study. He is still continuing his academic studies at Bursa Uludag University and giving lectures in the field of economic theory.

Zuoyong Li received the B.S. and M.S. degrees in computer science and technology from Fuzhou University, Fuzhou, China, in 2002 and 2006, respectively, and the Ph.D. degree from the School of Computer Science and Technology, Nanjing University of Science and Technology (NUST), Nanjing, China, in 2010. He is currently a Professor with the College of Computer and Control Engineering, Minjiang University, Fuzhou. He has published more than 70 articles in international/national journals. His current research interests are image processing, pattern recognition, machine learning, and deep learning.

Zhihan Lv (SM'19) has contributed 300 papers including more than 50 papers on IEEE/ACM Transactions. He is Editor-in-Chief of Internet of Things and Cyber-Physical Systems(KeAi), an Associate Editor of 18 journals including IEEE Transactions on Intelligent Transportation System, IEEE Transactions on Network and Service Management, IEEE Technology Policy and Ethics Newsletter, and Leading Guest Editors for 40 special issues including 9 IEEE. He is Co-Chair or TPC of 50 conferences including ACM MM 2021, ACM IUI 2015-2022. He has reviewed 400 papers. He has received more than 20 awards from China, Europe, IEEE. He has received 1.5 million US dollars funding as PI. He has been involved in many European and Chinese projects supported with funding of 25 million US dollars. He has given more than 80 invited talks for universities and companies in Europe and China. He has given 15 keynote speech for international conferences.

Ali B. Mahmoud, PhD is a Visiting Professor in the Peter J. Tobin College of Business at St. John's University in New York City and a Lecturer (Assistant Professor) in Brunel Business School at Brunel University London, alongside Arden University and Bath Spa University's partnership with Global Banking School in Birmingham. Moreover, he is a candidate for the Higher Doctorate from the London Doctoral Academy at London South Bank University in London. Dr Mahmoud's current research interests include topics related to consumer behaviour, entrepreneurial marketing, familial marketing, work psychology, wartime perceptions effects, and research in higher education. He has published over 60 publications, including books, book chapters and journal articles featured in international journals like European Management Review, Technovation, Personnel Review, Journal of Brand Management, Journal of Strategic Marketing, Scandinavian Journal of Psychology, Higher Education Quarterly, Journal of Hospitality and Tourism Management and many others. He has presented his work at leading conferences like the Academy of Marketing Science (AMS), the British Academy of Management (BAM) and the British Educational Research Association (BERA). Dr Mahmoud admires cats, especially his cat, whose name is Gago.

Iris Mohr, Chair of Marketing, earned a Ph.D. in Business Administration in Marketing/Strategy from City University of New York. She also holds an MBA from City University of New York, a Master's in Communications from Hebrew University in Israel, a professional degree in Screenwriting from University of California in Los Angeles, and a New York Film Academy certificate in Documentary Filmmaking. Her articles appeared in publications such as: Journal of Internet Commerce, Harvard Press, Interfaces, Human Resource Management, Quality Management Journal, Industrial Marketing Management, Journal of Marketing Theory and Practice, European Journal of Marketing, Business Horizon, Journal of Product Innovation Management, Society, International Journal of Manpower, International

Sociology, Marketing Management as well as in other professional publications. Currently, she is pursuing research and writing articles that relate to fashion and sustainability. She also provided interviews with various media outlets relating to her expertise in retailing, fashion, and sustainability. Dr. Mohr is a member of the following organizations: Association of Consumer Research, American Marketing Association, and Fashion Group International.

J. Patricia Muñoz-Chávez, Ph.D., is Associate Professor at the Technological University of the Metropolitan Area of the Valley of Mexico. Her research interests are related to Organizations, Higher Education, and Organizational Behavior. She holds a Ph.D. in Strategic Planning and Technology Management (Popular Autonomous University of the State of Puebla.), a Master's Degree in Management, and a Bachelor's Degree in Accountant (Autonomous University of the State of Hidalgo). She did a research stay at the University of Malaga, Spain. She has publications in several national and international journals and publishers. She is currently a member of the Mexican National System of Researchers.

Kamalendu Pal is with the Department of Computer Science, School of Mathematics, Computer Science and Engineering, City University of London. Kamalendu received his BSc (Hons) degree in Physics from Calcutta University, India, Postgraduate Diploma in Computer Science from Pune, India, MSc degree in Software Systems Technology from the University of Sheffield, Postgraduate Diploma in Artificial Intelligence from Kingston University, MPhil degree in Computer Science from University College London, and MBA degree from the University of Hull, United Kingdom. He has published more than seventy research papers (including book chapters) in the scientific community with research articles in the ACM SIGMIS Database, Expert Systems with Applications, Decision Support Systems, and conferences. His research interests include knowledge-based systems, decision support systems, blockchain technology, software engineering, and service-oriented computing. He is on the editorial board in an international computer science journal. Also, He is a member of the British Computer Society, the Institution of Engineering and Technology, and the IEEE Computer Society.

A. S. M. Abid Hasan Rishat completed his graduation and post-graduation from Shahjalal University of Science and Technology from department of Economics with distinction. His thesis tile "Impact of weather on household welfare" is on review in journal of Asian Studies. He also worked as a research intern at center for policy dialogue under the supervision of Dr. Debapriya Bhattacharja. Currently he is working as a lecturer in Military Institute of Science and Technology at science and humanities department.

Javier Sánchez García is a researcher of the University of Almería (Spain) specialized in time series econometrics, macroeconomics and monetary economics and financial stability. He has published in academic journals such as Mathematics (Q1 JCR) and the International Journal of Finance and Economics (Q2 JCR). His work is oriented towards VAR models in high dimensional settings, machine learning in time series econometrics and financial networks and econometrics, among other topics.

Tien-Ping Tan received his PhD in 2008 from Université Joseph Fourier, France. He is currently a senior lecturer in School of Computer Sciences, Universiti Sains Malaysia. Dr. Tan's research interests are automatic speech recognition, machine translation, and natural language processing.

Shehnaz Tehseen (PhD in Management) is working as a full-time senior lecturer and Programme Leader of BSc (Honours) in International Business Programme in Department of Management, Sunway University Business School, Sunway University, Malaysia. Her research interests lie in the areas of entrepreneurship, ethnic entrepreneurship, SMEs, cultural orientations, innovation, entrepreneurial competencies, retail sector, human resource management, strategic management, marketing, tourism, and organizational behaviour. She is an active researcher with more than 40 publications. She is also an editorial team member of some international journals including Journal of Management Sciences, Durreesamin Journal, and Journal of Global Business Insights.

David Valle-Cruz (Ph.D.) is an Assistant Professor at the Universidad Autónoma del Estado de México and is a member of the Mexican National System of Researchers. David is a Computer Engineer and a Computer Scientist; he holds a Ph.D. in Economics and Management. He has been a visiting researcher at the Center for Technology in Government (CTG), SUNY Albany, NY, and at the Computer Science and Multi-Agent Systems Laboratory of CINVESTAV, Guadalajara, Mexico. His articles have been published in leading journals, including Government Information Quarterly, Cognitive Computation, First Monday, Information Polity, and the International Journal of Public Sector Management (among others). His research interests are related to Applied Artificial Intelligence, Social Media, and Emerging Technologies in the Public Sector.

Savdeep Vasudeva is presently working in the Department of Business Administration of the University of the People, Pasadena, USA. He holds a PhD in Management and his area of research interest includes consumer behaviour, e-services, strategic marketing, and understanding behavioural issues in the case of technology-based services. He has published different research papers and book chapters with reputed international publishers related to these fields. His work experience is comprised of more than 20 years that further includes a combination of 14 years of teaching and 6 years of industrial experience.

Chew XinYing is a Senior Lecturer in the School of Computer Sciences, Universiti Sains Malaysia. She holds a PhD. in statistical quality control from University Sains Malaysia. She is a certified trainer with Human Resources Development Fund (HRDF). She is also the trainer for MDEC-Intel AI Academy Program and SAP Next-Gen Program. She is the Adjunct Research Fellow of Swinburne University of Technology, Sarawak Campus. She is also the Professional Technologist with the Malaysia Board of Technologist (MBOT). Prior to her academic career, she worked in the Advanced Analytics research team of a renown U.S. multinational company. Her areas of research are in advanced analytics and statistical quality / process control.

Xian Zhao received the Bachelor of Engineering degree in Metallurgical Engineering from the School of Material Science and Engineering, Jiangsu University (JUS), China, in 2018, and the Master of Science degree in Data Science and Analytics from the School of Computer Science, Universiti Sains Malaysia (USM), Malaysia, in 2021. Currently he is a PhD student in School of Computer Science, USM. His research interests include financial transaction, business informatics, customer service, and health and medical informatics.

Index

S

T

U

W

www.ingramcontent.com/pod-product-compliance
Lightning Source LLC
LaVergne TN
LVHW060354300926
849162LV00006B/1262
* 9 7 8 1 6 6 8 4 4 1 6 8 8 *